AREA HANDBOOK
for
ECUADOR

Co-Authors

Edwin E. Erickson

Helen A. Barth
Frederic H. Chaffee
Gabriel De Cicco
John H. Dombrowski
Susan G. Fortenbaugh
Thomas D. Roberts

Research and writing were completed on December 31, 1965

Published 1966

Library of Congress Catalog Card Number: 67–61681

For sale by the Superintendent of Documents, U.S. Government Printing Office
Washington, D.C. 20402—Price $3.00

FOREWORD

This volume is one of a series of handbooks prepared by Foreign Area Studies (FAS) of The American University, designed to be useful to military and other personnel who need a convenient compilation of basic facts about the social, economic, political and military institutions and practices of various countries. The emphasis is on objective description of the nation's present society and the kinds of possible or probable change that might be expected in the future. The handbook seeks to present as full and as balanced an integrated exposition as limitations on space and research time permit. It was compiled from information available in openly published material. Extensive bibliographies are provided to permit recourse to other published sources for more detailed information. There has been no attempt to express any specific point of view or make policy recommendations. The contents of the handbook represent the work of the authors and FAS and do not represent the official view of the United States Government.

An effort has been made to make the handbook as comprehensive as possible. It can be expected, however, that the material, interpretations and conclusions are subject to modification in the light of new information and developments. Such corrections, additions and suggestions for factual, interpretive or other change as readers may have will be welcomed for use in future revisions. Comments may be addressed to:

The Director
Foreign Area Studies
The American University
5010 Wisconsin Avenue, N.W.
Washington, D.C.   20016

PREFACE

On March 29, 1966, after completion of this handbook, the military junta of government, which had ruled Ecuador since July 1963, resigned under the pressure of mounting popular violence and protest, turning over the reins of government to a provisional regime headed by a civilian, Clemente Yerovi Indaburu. This governmental crisis, the third in 4 years, was another milestone in a long and almost unrelieved history of political turmoil and disorder marked by the alternation of military and civilian regimes and by recurrent violence.

At the roots of this continuing disorder is a complex pattern of political cleavage, engendered by a profound and durable contest of sectionalist interests between the country's two principal cities, Quito and Guayaquil; by the diverse cultural, racial and linguistic backgrounds of the people; and by a rigid social system which concentrates effective power in a very small upper class. Repeatedly, the conflicting claims of regionalist and economic interest groups have proven stronger than the claims of national unity, at times paralyzing the policy initiatives of governments and at times provoking open rebellion. At the lower levels of society the great mass of Ecuadorians have had historically little basis for developing a strong and lasting identification with any government, for they have seen almost no concrete implementation of their needs and wishes in policy. Thus, the splintering of effective political power and a traditional and growing popular discontent combine to produce an atmosphere of turmoil and instability.

Nevertheless, social changes that have taken place in the past few years seem clearly to have created the basis for a more effective national integration. Perhaps the most important of these changes is a rising level of political consciousness on the part of the traditionally apathetic lower class. Responding to this new popular voice, recent governments and political leaders have paid a growing attention to reform and economic development, and this attention has resulted in many concrete achievements. Although the broadening political participation has itself been a component in the recent turmoil, it has also introduced a new and potent force for the development of a truly unified national purpose. In some measure, too, it has substituted issues of broader national import for those arising from the clash of small interest groups.

The challenges and opportunities apparent in Ecuador are common to many other Latin American countries in greater or lesser degree. Consequently, the course of this one country toward a more integrated and effective nationhood could have important implications for similar developments elsewhere in the hemisphere.

This handbook attempts to bring together in unified, but not exhaustive, fashion the social, economic and political elements of the contemporary society. It is intended to provide a meaningful context for the interpretation of current events rather than a detailed account of the events themselves.

As few reliable published sources about Ecuador exist in the United States, three of the authors have relied heavily on data and impressions gathered personally in Ecuador. Among the many people who have contributed their time and experience, special thanks are due to Charles H. Pratt, José A. Baquero and Rafael A. Becerra, Jr., all of whom have extensive and detailed personal knowledge of Ecuadorian life. Responsibility for fact and interpretation must, however, rest with the authors. In the writing of the economic section invaluable assistance and cooperation was rendered by members of the Inter-American Development Bank and officials of the Organization of American States, the Office of International Regional Economics of the United States Department of Commerce and the Department of Economic Research of the Central Bank of Ecuador.

English usage in this handbook follows *Webster's New International Dictionary of the English Language* (3d ed., unabridged). Spanish usage is based on Velazquez, *A New Pronouncing Dictionary of the Spanish and English Languages* (New York: Appleton-Century-Crofts, 1960). For words and phrases drawn from the Indian languages usage follows that of Ecuadorian authors.

ECUADOR

TABLE OF CONTENTS

Rank, Pay and Promotions—Uniforms—Awards and
Decorations—Military Justice

LIST OF ILLUSTRATIONS

LIST OF TABLES

Table   Page
1 Annual Average Temperature and Rainfall in Ecuador   18
2 Population Distribution in Ecuador, by Geographic Region and
   Province, 1962   62
3 Ecuadorian Labor Force, by Field of Activity, 1950 and 1962   64
4 Economically Active Population of Ecuador, Urban and Rural,
   by Field of Activity, Region and Sex, 1962   65
5 Monthly Salaries in Ecuador of Persons Covered by Social Security
   or Government Pensions, 1962 and 1963   70
6 Origin of National Income of Ecuador, 1963 and 1964   329
7 Planned Allocation of Total Investment According to the 10-Year
   Development Plan of Ecuador, 1964–73   330
8 Distribution of Land in Ecuador, 1963   342
9 Size, Number and Area of Agricultural Properties in the Sierran
   and Coastal Regions of Ecuador, 1954   343
10 Principal Crops of the Sierran and Coastal Regions of Ecuador,
   1963   347
11 Daily Production of Crude Petroleum in Ecuador, by Company,
   1963   380
12 Production and Consumption of Petroleum and Petroleum
   Derivatives in Ecuador, 1953–56 and 1959–61   381
13 Major Manufactured Products of Ecuador, 1961 and 1962   387
14 Estimated Consolidated Expenditures of the Ecuadorian Central
   Government, by Function or Agency, 1963   442
15 Exports of Ecuador, by Economic Group, 1960–64   457
16 Imports of Ecuador, by Economic Group, 1960–63   461
17 Direction of Ecuador's Trade, in Percent, 1960–64   463
18 Foreign Investment in Ecuador, by Economic Sector, 1959–63   470
19 Foreign Investment in Ecuador, by Country of Origin, 1958   472
20 Criminal Cases Initiated in Ecuadorian Courts, by Province, 1958   479
21 Ranks in the Ecuadorian Armed Forces   518

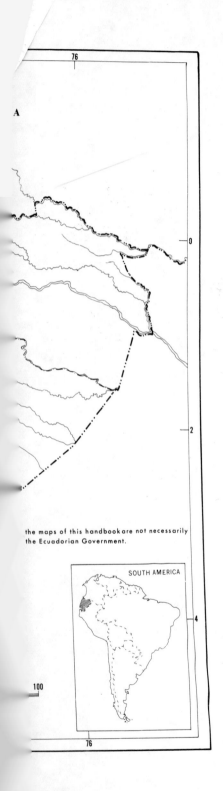

76

A

0

2

the maps of this handbook are not necessarily
the Ecuadorian Government.

SOUTH AMERICA

4

100

76

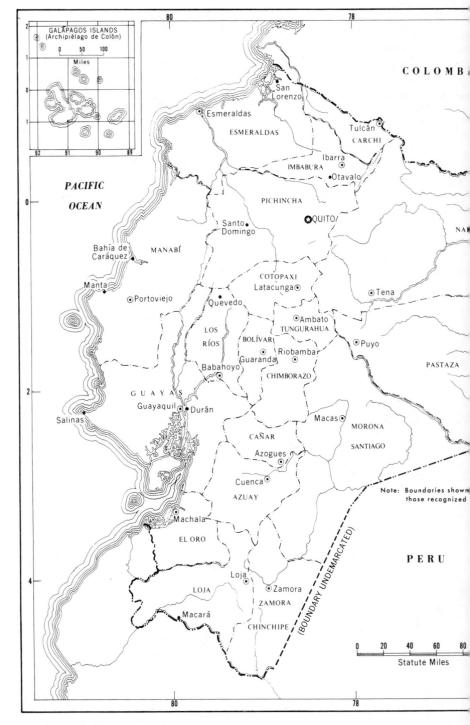

Figure 1. Ecuador.

SECTION I. SOCIAL

CHAPTER 1

GENERAL CHARACTER OF THE SOCIETY

Lying athwart the equator and along the Pacific Coast of South America, the Republic of Ecuador shares land boundaries only with Peru and Colombia. Like its neighbors, it emerged as a nation-state after the wars of independence of the early nineteenth century brought to an end Spain's American empire.

The Ecuadorian people, in 1962 numbering about 4.6 million, trace their descent chiefly from the Spaniards, who imposed their rule on the area in the sixteenth century, and from the native Indian peoples. A smaller component was created by the introduction of Negro slaves during the colonial period.

These diverse groups have lived together in the same territory, under a common rule, for more than four centuries, and to a considerable degree they have admixed. Nevertheless, they have never come to form a single people with a shared language and way of life. The Spanish language, Hispanic cultural traditions and Roman Catholic Christianity set the dominant tone of national life, but large numbers of Ecuadorians continue to speak one of the native languages (chiefly Quechua—see Glossary), in some cases to the total exclusion of Spanish; order their lives in accordance with the Indian traditions; and practice a Catholicism strongly tinged with native folk belief. A rigidly stratified social system, imposed during the Spanish conquest to separate the Spaniards from the subjugated Indians and the Negro slaves, continues to raise barriers of wealth, privilege and prestige among the diverse components, even though intermarriage and the abolition of forced servitude have, to some extent, blurred the ethnic lines.

An area estimated provisionally at slightly more than 100,000 square miles places the country among the smallest in South America, but geographically it is among the most variegated in the world. About one-fourth of the national territory consists of

1

a broad, tropical coastal plain, much of it covered with fertile, well-watered alluvial soils. Another quarter lies within the rugged Andes mountain system, the continental backbone, which in Ecuador consists of two parallel ranges of high volcanic peaks —many of them capped by eternal snows—flanking a series of intermontane basins. About one-half lies in the sparsely populated and largely uncharted tropical forests of the Amazon basin.

Even within the major geographic regions there is a great diversity of climate, topography and vegetation. In its northern half the Coast is covered by dense rain forests of the system which runs in an unbroken band northward through Colombia and into Central America. To the south the landscape changes gradually to semiarid scrub, grading near the Peruvian border into the great coastal desert which extends the length of Peru and well into Chile. The Andean belt (Sierra) presents even greater variations. The basins, most of them containing productive farmlands, range in altitude from less than 6,000 feet to more than 10,000 feet above sea level, and in climate from subtropical through temperate to cold.

Ecuador's natural resources point it toward a predominantly agrarian economy. Unlike neighboring Peru, it is not known to have a rich, easily exploited mineral endowment. Given the existence of large areas of farmland and the variety of climates and soils, however, the country enjoys possibilities of almost limitless agricultural diversification. Virtually any tropical or temperate crop can be grown somewhere in its territory. In consequence, there is a marked regional variation in production. Since colonial times the Sierra has been chiefly a producer of grains, root crops and livestock for internal consumption. The Coast, which became a significant contributor to the economy only in the mid-nineteenth century, has specialized heavily in the cultivation of tropical produce—notably cacao, coffee and, most recently, bananas—for export.

Large areas of forest lands on both sides of the Andes and rich offshore fisheries, having been only incipiently exploited, constitute an almost untapped wealth potential. Manufacturing industry, of recent development, is concentrated chiefly in processed foodstuffs, clothing and other consumer goods.

Until recently communications between regions were poorly developed. As late as 1900 the trip between the national capital, Quito, in the Sierra, and the principal seaport, Guayaquil, entailed a 2-week journey on muleback across formidable mountain barriers and through thick forests. In the past half-century much has been done to link all populated parts of the country with an effective transport network. Railroads connect Quito to Guayaquil and to San Lorenzo on the northern Coast. High-

2

ways, most of them built since the 1950's, run from the Sierra to many points on the Coast and to a few points in the Oriente (Eastern Lowlands).

The great bulk of the population is settled in the western half of the country—about evenly distributed between the Sierra and the Coast. The Oriente remains very thinly settled, for the most part by a dispersed, seminomadic, aboriginal population practicing shifting agriculture and hunting. Only a few Spanish-speaking Ecuadorians, most of them settled near the new roads, share the vast wilderness with the Indians. Consequently, the Oriente scarcely contributes to the national economy.

The native population which was submitted to Spanish rule after 1532 consisted of many linguistically and culturally diverse peoples. In the Andean corridor the population consisted of settled village-dwelling agricultural peoples who, though they spoke several different languages, were much alike culturally. On the Coast and in the Oriente were many small, semisedentary tribes. In addition, there were several groups along the seacoast who had achieved a fairly high level of technical competence and social complexity.

About 50 years before the arrival of the Spaniards the Sierra groups had been incorporated in the Inca Empire, the great aboriginal state which encompassed much of South America. By 1532 the Inca had gone far toward imposing on the whole area their own language, Quechua, as a lingua franca, and an orderly system of tribute and labor conscription. When the Spaniards replaced the Inca as masters of the Ecuadorian Sierra, most of the native population submitted passively, paying tribute and providing labor, much as they had before the conquest.

The new territory was incorporated to the Viceroyalty of Peru as an administrative subdivision called an *audiencia* (see Glossary). The seat of the new political unit was established at what had been the Inca center of Quito.

Although it remained subordinate to the Viceroyalty of Peru, and later to that of New Granada, with its capital at Santa Fe de Bogotá, the Audiencia of Quito was sufficiently distant from both Lima and Bogotá to develop a considerable autonomy. As the colony attracted an increasing flow of settlers from the mother country, it became a center of Spanish culture in its own right. Its cities, churches and universities compared favorably with those in most other parts of the Hispanic world. These traditions of autonomy later provided the basis for independent nationhood.

Like the Inca before them, the Spaniards settled almost exclusively in the temperate basins of the Sierra, where there was a stable and docile population to provide them with labor. Only at Guayaquil and a few other points did they settle in the western lowlands, and at the end of the colonial period, the coastal region held less than 10 percent of the population.

Except for converting the native peoples to Christianity and, because they found lingua franca a convenient medium, completing the substitution of Quechua for the local tongues, the Spaniards did little to change the old ways of life. If the political apparatus and temple cults of the Inca Empire had vanished, the substratum of everyday Indian life remained essentially the same. Even as they began to practice Catholic Christianity, they incorporated in it so many of the pre-existing belief forms that they created what amounted to a new folk religion. Although the Spaniards adopted a few elements of the native culture in their new environment, they were careful to preserve the core of their own way of life. Thus, despite the existence of a large non-Spanish population, the Ecuadorian territory became a part of the Hispanic world.

Founded in conquest, the colonial society was consolidated in a pattern of rigid stratification and hereditary privilege. At the apex of the social structure was a small elite, composed of the descendants of the conquerors, which controlled the local government, owned most of the wealth and constituted the only educated class. Far below this group was a large Spanish-speaking lower class consisting of *mestizos* (see Glossary) and Indians who had abandoned the native communities for the cities and towns. Members of this lower class worked as domestics, artisans, petty merchants and minor functionaries and overseers mediating between the white masters and the native peoples. At the bottom of the structure were the Indians, subjects of the Hispanic-based society, but scarcely figuring in its life except as a source of tribute and enforced labor, both extracted from them by various schemes adapted from the Inca past. The Indians were eventually joined at the lower level of society by a small population of Negro slaves brought over to work in the few lowland areas settled by the colonists.

Like most other parts of Spanish America, the Audiencia of Quito saw the development of a strong separatist fervor toward the end of the eighteenth century and the beginning of the nineteenth. Liberation from Spanish rule was won in 1822, in the Battle of Pichincha, by an armed force under the command of Antonio José de Sucre, chief lieutenant of the great Venezuelan, Simón Bolívar. For 8 years thereafter the ex-colony formed a federated part of the Republic of Gran Colombia, together with present-day Colombia and Venezuela. Then, following the example of Venezuela, what had been the Audiencia of Quito declared its independence as the Republic of Ecuador.

Independence brought with it a republican constitution and a formal commitment to a democratic political order. The tributes and enforced labor schemes of colonial days were legally abolished, and slavery also was soon outlawed. Men of humble background rose, through military service and through the capture of political power in the postwar turmoil, to form a new and distinctly *mestizo* element of the ruling elite.

Although the colonial trappings had disappeared, functionally little had changed in the society. The stable, democratic republican government failed to materialize, partly because *caudillos* (see Glossary) and their followers continued to compete with each other for the exercise of power. Further and more fundamentally, the old rigidities of the social structure proved to be durable. Regardless of who occupied the seat of government, the balance of economic power continued to reside in the predominantly white elite. The Indians remained a subject labor force, having exchanged their position as tributaries for one of entailed tenant laborers on white-owned agricultural estates. The *mestizo* lower class, poor and unlettered, had few means of gaining power and influence.

At another level the values and attitudes of the elite remained little changed from those of the colonial past. Although the framers of various constitutions experimented with anticlericism, the influence of the Church remained as strong as it had been under Spanish rule. The principle of hereditary privilege, denied constitutional support, continued to enjoy tacit acceptance from the majority, even at the more humble levels. Separated from the outside world not only by the ocean but also by the Andean wall, the elite remained well insulated from outside influences.

By the middle of the nineteenth century, however, a new element was introduced to national life as a populous and economically important regional society developed on the Coast. The growth of export markets for tropical agricultural produce attracted an influx of settlement, especially to the fertile Guayas Lowlands, and rapidly shifted the balance of economic dominance from Quito to the port city of Guayaquil. With few roots in the colonial past, the society of the Coast was less tradition-bound than that of the Sierra, and its structure, though marked by great disparities in wealth and privilege, was somewhat more flexible.

Increasingly, the new elite of coastal planters, bankers and merchants began to challenge the political dominance of the Sierra aristocracy. The resulting sectionalist contention was to become a permanent factor in political life and, either directly or indirectly, the cause of several armed conflicts.

The contest of sectionalist interests was underscored by the contrast in attitude and value between the traditionalist, intensely

Catholic Sierra landowners and the less conservative, often anti-clerical coastal plutocracy. Ideological dispute often served as the symbolic banner in regionalist contention. Although there were exceptions on both sides, attitudes toward Church-state relationship—the issue that set the tone of politics in the late nineteenth century—were clearly divided along regional lines. The two great political parties in the country's history, Conservative and Liberal, contended with each other under the twin banners of regionalism and opinion on the Church-state issue.

Out of this dual cleavage also emerged two of the country's greatest historic figures—Gabriel García Moreno, the Sierra Conservative, and Eloy Alfaro, the coastal Liberal. These two men, while transcending the narrower focus of sectionalism to provide a leadership truly national in scope, nonetheless epitomized its ideological terms.

García Moreno, a dominant figure in the 1860's and 1870's, sought to give the country a physical unity by beginning the construction of a railroad between Guayaquil and Quito; he also sought to give it cultural unity by expanding the educational system. Alfaro, whose period of dominance spanned the turn of the century, seeking the same ends, completed García Moreno's railroad and also acted to expand the educational system. The common search for national unity and modernization was, however, tempered by the attachment of the two men to diametrically opposed points of view on the role of the Church in society. García Moreno's new Ecuador was to be as exclusively Catholic as the *audiencia* had been; Alfaro's was to be a completely secular one. Both men died the victims of political violence, and whatever the other motivations might have been, opposition to their respective views on Church and state was an ingredient in their downfalls.

Although the regionalist cleavage remains a durable feature of national life, the Church-state issue moved toward resolution in the early decades of the present century, largely through a series of compromises. By mid-century, new issues had emerged, borne on a wave of social change, reflected in a steady expansion of the base of political participation.

Except when issues flared into armed conflict, in which members of the lower class sometimes participated as soldiers, political activity in the nineteenth and early twentieth centuries was limited largely to a small, wealthy minority. The competing regional interests had been those chiefly of concern to the rich. The Church-state debate was spearheaded almost exclusively by small groups of upper-class intellectuals. The great mass of the people, illiterate and far removed from sources of power and influence, did not vote or otherwise articulate their demands of society. Perhaps most fundamentally, neither Conservatives nor Liberals questioned the economic and social forms that divided wealth and privilege so inequitably throughout the country.

In the past few decades this pattern has been changing. A continuing, if seldom spectacular, economic growth has brought into existence a small middle class which, as an articulate and educated segment of society not bound to the interests of the elite, has added a new political voice. Economic growth has also contributed to the creation of an organized labor movement which, though limited in size and effect, has introduced a degree of political consciousness to the hitherto apathetic urban working class. New communications and transport facilities have brought the rural population into contact with the influences and goods of urban society and, to some degree, of the world beyond Ecuador. Efforts at expanding educational opportunity have borne fruit in a growing literacy rate. In general, larger numbers of people are becoming increasingly aware of the national society within which they live, and they are beginning to aspire to a greater material well-being within it. Even the Sierra Indians, for many of whom the concept of an Ecuadorian nation has never been more than a vague abstraction, are being drawn into the pattern of change.

At higher levels of society there has been a growing concern with the development of a more vigorous and diversified economy. There has also been an emerging conviction that this development, as well as the future stability of the society, depends on the institution of fundamental reforms. This conviction has begun to diffuse widely not only among political thinkers but also within the Catholic Church and the armed forces, crucial elements in national life.

That the nation has entered a period of intensifying change is apparent at many different levels. In each national election since 1940, the register of voters has grown measurably. Increasingly, politicians must, for the sake of this expanding electorate, address themselves to questions of reform. The twin aims of economic development and reform have preoccupied every recent government and have resulted in the establishment of an economic planning and coordination system; in the development of programs for the social and economic integration of the Indians to national life; and, most recently, in the 1965 Agrarian Reform Law.

These processes have encountered serious impediments and have brought new problems in their wake. Although for virtually all segments reform and development stand as the keynote of political discourse, the practical means for their implementation—the redistribution of land and the restructuring of the taxation system, for example—often arouse the opposition of powerful interest groups. Moreover, at the local levels in many areas, there is a strong undercurrent of conservatism which is expressed in attempts to frustrate the efforts of the national government to introduce change.

Another difficulty arises from the lack of stable, broad-based parties to articulate popular wishes, to compose the competing claims of economic and social groups and to maintain lines of communication between electors and governments. The two traditional parties, joined by several new ones, continue to be viable organizations, principally to channel patronage and, to some extent, to provide podiums for the espousal of programs and ideas. Never having fully shed the image of exclusiveness and devotion to elite interests, they have not yet succeeded in capturing the trust and loyalty of the expanding electorate. Consequently, neither major party has elected a president on its own ticket since 1940. All successful candidates were carried to victory with the support of coalitions formed for the specific purpose.

The tone of electoral politics has become overwhelmingly personalist. Candidates must, above all, create a symbolic bond of personal trust with the voters, and their platforms and pledges almost inevitably take on overtones of crusading as they are seen as personal vows. Once a man is elected on the basis of personal appeal, he finds himself faced with a serious problem when he attempts to fulfill his pledges without the support of a stable party system. On the one hand, he lacks clear channels of communication to the small, but powerful interest groups whose opposition could seriously impair the implementation of his platform. On the other hand, he lacks a stable base of popular support not bound specifically to his appeals and promises as a candidate.

This note of personalism and social discord has been sounded most clearly in the career of José María Velasco Ibarra, four times president and three times deposed between 1933 and 1961. Carried to office every time by a strong popular acclaim evoked by his oratory, Velasco Ibarra fell victim to his inability, once in office, to unite the masses and the various special interest groups behind his programs.

The result has been a continuing pattern of governmental instability in which the opposition of interest groups to reform measures and popular impatience with the slow pace of change and reform have created serious tension. On occasion, this tension has led to such disorder that the military establishment, by long tradition the self-appointed guardian of internal peace, has overturned the legally elected government.

The latest instance of such action on the part of the armed forces occurred in July 1963, when the commanders of the navy, army and air force and the director of the national War College (Academia de Guerra) deposed President Carlos Julio Arosemena Monroy and took possession of power. The new government called itself the Junta Militar de Gobierno (Board of Military Government) and ruled in the name of the armed forces. In November 1965 the air force commander, Colonel Guillermo Freile Posso, was removed from the governing board by the other three members for pursuing personal political ambitions. As of the end of 1965 the government was ruled by the remaining triumvirate, composed of Rear Admiral Ramón Castro Jijón (president of the board) and Generals Marcos Gándara Enríquez and Luis Cabrera Sevilla.

Notwithstanding discord and instability, there are many points of optimism. It seems clear that, whatever the opposition of interest groups, the largest segments of society are committed to a course of modernization and reform. This commitment is bearing visible fruit in a population that is both healthier and better educated than it was a generation ago. Furthermore, the construction of roads and other facilities is bringing large areas of fertile, hitherto unused land into the national economy and thus opening new possibilities to masses of peasants crowded into the limited cultivable areas of the Sierra basins.

Since it emerged as an independent republic, Ecuador has maintained basically cordial bonds with its northern neighbor, Colombia. With Peru, however, relations have been more or less consistently tense, as a result of territorial disputes. These disputes, concerning principally lands in the jungled Amazonian lowlands which were never clearly demarcated by Spanish colonial authorities, have given rise to periodic armed conflict, most recently in 1941. The issue remains a live one, both in domestic politics and before the United Nations and other international bodies. With other Latin American nations, relations have been cordial though seldom close, given a lack of common boundaries and a rather small volume of trade.

Relations with the United States have most often been friendly, although disagreements have arisen, chiefly over the United States' occasional role as mediator in the Peruvian border question. Toward the nations of Western Europe, and especially toward those of Latin language and culture, attitudes and policies have generally reflected cordiality and the warmth of cultural kinship. In 1965, Ecuador had no diplomatic ties in any part of the Communist world, including Cuba, with which it broke relations in 1962.

CHAPTER 2

PHYSICAL ENVIRONMENT

With an area determined provisionally to be 106,508 square miles (including the Galápagos Islands), Ecuador is the tenth largest country in Latin America. It is bounded on the north by Colombia, on the south and east by Peru and on the west by the Pacific Ocean. The vague delineation of the boundary with Peru continues to be a source of friction between the two countries (see fig. 1).

The dominant physical feature is the lofty Andean range, which traverses the country from north to south and which contains many snow-covered peaks, including a number of active volcanoes. Most of the country is heavily forested, although deserts occur along the southern coast and in the Sierra (Andean Highlands). There are large grassy areas, called *páramos*, between the tree line and the snowline. The three principal agricultural areas, from which forests have been cleared and which produce a wide variety of grains, fruits and vegetables, are the highland intermont basins, the Guayas River basin and the rather limited coastal plain fronting the Bay of Caráquez.

For a small country, Ecuador has a wide diversity of both landscape and climate. The great variations in altitude, together with a location at the contact point between the warm Equatorial Current and the cold Peru, or Humboldt, Current, make for a temperature range from tropical to frigid and for a rainfall pattern from extremely heavy to sparse.

Through the centuries people have settled in the healthful and productive intermont basins; only after medical science had eliminated most of the endemic diseases of the Coast did large numbers of people settle there. Railroads and highways have provided easy contact between the intermont basins, but they still have not provided direct contact between many areas of the Coast and the Sierra, and they provide almost no access to the Oriente (Eastern Lowlands). Many of the larger settlements on the Coast depend on waterborne transport. Most of the small settlements dispersed through the sparsely populated Oriente are accessible only by pack trails or, in some cases, by light aircraft.

GEOGRAPHIC REGIONS

The three distinct physical regions are the Coastal Lowlands, the Sierra and the Oriente, consisting of the eastern slopes of the Andes and the lowlands of the upper Amazon basin. The Oriente includes about half of the total area and the Sierra and the Coast, about one-quarter each.

The Coastal Lowlands

The Coastal Lowlands, generally defined as including the western slopes of the Andes up to 1,600 feet, encompass about 27,000 square miles. About half the region is composed of the Guayas lowlands. Most of the remaining area consists of a low coastal range (see fig. 2).

The Guayas lowlands—economically the most important region —constitute perhaps the most fertile, rainy tropical lowland in the Western Hemisphere. This lowland, formed between the Andes on the east and the coastal range on the west, also extends as a narrow strip along the Gulf of Guayaquil to the Peruvian border, where it is only about 12 miles wide. It was formed by alluvium (more than 30 feet thick in places) washed down from the Andes by the Guayas River, its tributaries and several short rivers. In the upper reaches the soil is always well watered and, even during the rainy season, is well drained. On the other hand, many parts of the lower basin are under water during much of the rainy season. The Guayas basin is the largest river basin on the Pacific Coast of Latin America, and Guayaquil is the best natural harbor there.

Most of the Coastal Lowlands west and north of the Guayas basin consists of the coastal range, in most places a low plateau which is higher in the north than in the south but seldom more than 2,000 feet above sea level and which frequently juts into the sea. There are also three small coastal plains in this area.

Proceeding south on the Coast, in a few hundred miles the vegetation changes from the tropical rain forest of southern Colombia to desert. The dense tropical rain forest extends south to Cape Pasado, where it gives way to less dense woodlands and finally to desert scrub at the Santa Elena Peninsula. Inland, a narrow band of rain forest grows on the western slopes of the Andes to near the border with Peru, where desert growth extends well up into the piedmont. Mangrove swamps ring the shores of the extreme northern coast and of the Gulf of Guayaquil and line the mouths of the rivers (see fig. 3).

The fertile soil of the Coast produces a great variety of plant-life. The forests are particularly varied in species, many of them with great commercial value. Innumerable varieties of

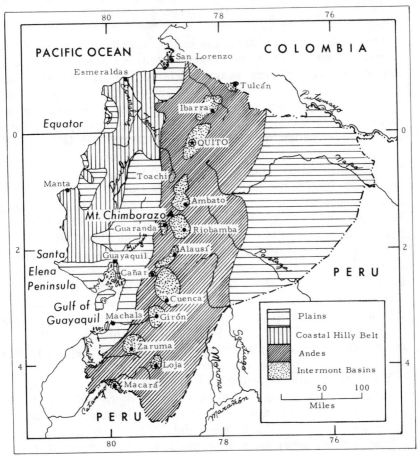

Source: Adapted from Preston E. James, Latin America, p. 145.

Figure 2. Topography of Ecuador.

woods useful for building are found, along with a wide variety
of palms, including the tagua palm, from which vegetable ivory
is obtained; the toquilla palm, from which fibers are used to make
the so-called Panama hat; and the royal palm, from which oil is
derived.   In addition, there is bamboo of many types, mangrove
for piles and posts and, perhaps most important, the lightweight
balsa, from which over 90 percent of the world's supply is furnished.   The country is one of the world's leading producers of
bananas, is a major producer of cacao and produces important
amounts of rice, cotton and coffee, all of which come from the
Coastal Lowlands (see ch. 19, Agriculture).

The Andes, which extend the entire length of western South America, form a narrow and rugged system in Ecuador. Although a vestige of an eastern range exists in the Oriente, the high Sierra is considered to be made up of two parallel cordilleras, both of volcanic origin, which in a much earlier era were connected by an arch of crystalline rock, which has long since collapsed to form an intermont valley, nowhere more than 50 miles wide.

This valley, separating the western and central cordilleras, through the centuries has been divided into a number of separate basins by lava flows from the many volcanoes. The resultant high transverse spurs, usually called *nudos*, initially isolated completely many of the high-altitude basins until water from the heavy rain and melting snow from the peaks above was able to cut through the porous lava to drain either to the Pacific Ocean or to the east through the Amazon basin to the distant Atlantic Ocean. In the part of the Sierra south of the *nudo* of Azuay the rivers have cut deep canyons into the basin, removing much of the volcanic soil from the basin floor. All of the active volcanoes are north of the Azuay *nudo*, indicating that this area is of much more recent formation; here the canyons are less deep, and more soil remains on the floors of the basins.

The volcanic soil is fertile, but in some places it is so porous that it does not retain enough moisture; where the soil is less porous, higher yields can be attained. In the few places where natural vegetation has not been eliminated by centuries of agriculture, forests cover the mountainside to about 10,000 feet. In the nineteenth century, to replace the trees eliminated by agriculture, fast-growing eucalyptus trees were introduced and are now a source of local lumber and firewood. Above 10,000 feet, tall grasses predominate until the snowline, which lies at about 16,000 feet, is reached.

A typical intermont basin can be separated into four altitude zones according to their climates. Above 10,000 feet are the *páramos,* which are used mainly for pasturage. The ground cover consists chiefly of tall grasses, along with some hardy bushes, and there is some cultivation, particularly of potatoes. The *páramos* are always cold, often cloud-covered and receive about 40 inches of rain a year.

The *altiplano,* generally defined as extending from 8,000 feet to the altitude of the *páramos,* is a zone of mixed agriculture and pasturage, where grains of many types are cultivated. The average temperature is low, and the average annual rainfall varies from 30 to 50 inches. Irrigation water is fairly abundant. In the temperate valleys, which constitute the upper stream basins at altitudes between 6,000 and 8,000 feet, agriculture is more important than grazing. All temperate crops can be grown; even though the average rainfall is often no more than 20 inches, the ancient irrigation ditches distribute an adequate flow of water.

The subtropical valleys which lie between 3,000 and 6,000 feet have been formed by streams which have cut deeply into the volcanic soil before cascading out of the Andes. They have an average temperature between 62° F. and 72° F. Although the average annual rainfall is only between 25 and 32 inches, water draining from the mountainsides is abundant. In addition to grains and potatoes, sugarcane, citrus fruit, grapes and many types of vegetables can be grown.

There are 11 more or less distinct intermont basins between the cordilleras. From north to south they are Tulcán, Ibarra, Quito, Ambato, Riobamba, Alausí, Cañar, Cuenca, Jubones, Loja and Macará. In addition, there are three lateral basins west of the main western range of the Andes—Toachi, Guaranda and Zaruma. The basins vary greatly in size and altitude; some discharge into the Atlantic by means of the Amazon system and others into the Pacific by various short river systems.

Tulcán is the second highest basin; most of it is actually located in neighboring Colombia through which it drains into the Pacific. Tulcán, the highest city in the country at 9,800 feet, sits in the frigid basin very close to the Colombian border. Although the soil is fertile, the altitude restricts plantlife, and only potatoes and hardy grains, including barley and some varieties of wheat, grow there.

Separated from the Tulcán basin by the *nudo* of Boliche is the Ibarra basin, which is much lower. The city of Ibarra is only 7,300 feet above sea level. All cereals and some types of subtropical plants grow in profusion; lower in the deep-cut valleys, sugarcane and cotton grow.

The most important basin is Quito, in which the capital city is located at 9,350 feet above sea level. This basin, which drains into the Pacific through a deep gorge at the northern end, gradually rises to the south to a high and relatively level *altiplano*, where grains of all sorts are cultivated. The entire basin is rimmed with snowcapped volcanoes. In a small lateral basin to the west are the headwaters of the Toachi River which, together with the drainage from the basin of Quito, form the Esmeraldas River.

The cities of Ambato and Latacunga are located in the Ambato basin. Separated from it by the lower slopes of the active volcano Chimborazo is the Riobamba basin. Both are large basins, lying between 8,000 and about 9,500 feet in altitude, joined by the narrow valley through which the Pastaza River drains eastward to the Amazon. The soil, of recent volcanic origin, is so porous that many deep gorges have been cut, so that only parts of the basins can be farmed satisfactorily.

The drainage from the small basin of Alausí debouches to the west along with the waters from the nearby lateral basin of Guaranda, where grains of all kinds are grown. The railroad from Guayaquil to Quito uses the Alausí basin and drainage system to climb into the mountains.

The small and very high basin of Cañar marks the southernmost end of the active volcanic region. This basin, which drains to the west, is rimmed almost entirely by the *nudo* of Azuay and its rugged continuation. The town of Cañar, which is always cold, has an elevation of 10,400 feet above sea level. Despite its high altitude, the basin produces grain and corn.

The large basin of Cuenca is made up of much older volcanic ash. Despite the shallowness of the soil there is a rich agrarian economy. In the deep valleys, draining to the east, sugarcane is grown. The city of Cuenca, at an altitude of 8,300 feet, is the third largest in the country.

The large Jubones River basin, containing the town of Girón, drains to the west. In its deep-cut valleys tropical plants grow and sugarcane is cultivated. South of it are three separate basins, the very small one of Loja, which drains into the Amazon system; the small lateral basin of Zaruma, which drains to the west; and the low basin formed by the headwaters of the Túmbez River, which drains south through Peru into the Pacific Ocean. All are low basins with deeply cut valleys, where tropical plants as well as grains can be grown. The southern, or Macará, basin is formed by the Catamayo River, a tributary of which marks the border with Peru.

The Oriente

Approximately half of the area of the country lies in the undeveloped and mostly unexplored eastern part, known as the Oriente, which drains into the Amazon. Most of the area is jungle covered, and only on the eastern slopes of the Andes do mountain rain forests exist. Descent from the flanks of the Andes is steep, but with a fairly constant gradient; the rivers have already cut deeply into the floors of the intermont basin and so do not have a precipitous fall as they flow through the jungle at about a 1,600-foot altitude. The entire area has heavy rainfall, and much of the land is believed to be fertile, but inaccessibility has thus far prevented its development. Except for a few

16

zones of recent settlement, the population consists mainly of different groups of semisedentary Indians (see ch. 5, Ethnic Groups and Languages).

The Galapagos Islands

Centered about 750 miles due west of Ecuador and part of the national territory is a group of islands of volcanic origin known as the Galápagos Islands, or the Archipiélago de Colón (Columbus Archipelago). With a total area of 3,029 square miles, they consist of many islands, of which 12 are sizable, and extend about 200 miles from east to west. They are well known as the site of the studies made there by Charles Darwin in the nineteenth century. Although there are many good fishing grounds around the islands, few people live there, chiefly because fresh water is extremely scarce. During World War II the United States built, on one of the smaller islands, an airbase that is now maintained by the Ecuadorean Government.

CLIMATE

Although the greater part of the country is hot and humid, as would be expected from its position astride the equator, in the Sierra, where altitude is a major factor, temperatures are never high; they vary for the most part from temperate to cold. Nowhere do marked seasonal variations exist in average daily temperature, but the differences between daytime temperature and nighttime temperature in the Sierra may be as much as 40° F. (see table 1).

The rainfall of the coastal region is very heavy in the north and very light in the south. Cape Pasado constitutes an abrupt dividing point. In the Sierra the average rainfall is almost everywhere quite moderate. In the Oriente it is heavy throughout the year. The actual rainfall may vary considerably between proximate localities because of local conditions caused by mountain shadowing from prevailing winds.

At sea level the average annual temperature is about 79° F., and it decreases at the rate of 1° F. per every 360 feet increase in elevation, allowing for small local variations due to prevailing winds. Thus, there is approximately 25° F. difference in the annual average temperature between Guayaquil and Quito.

Much rain is brought to the coastal region, particularly to the western slopes of the Andes, by the warm Equatorial Current, which flows south along the Coast, carrying with it moisture-laden airmasses. Off the Santa Elena Peninsula this current comes into conflict with the cold north-flowing Peru Current, and both flows turn out to sea.

The penetration of the southerly winds of the Peru Current

17

Table 1. Annual Average Temperature and Rainfall in Ecuador

Region	Altitude (in feet)	Temperature (in degrees F.)	Rainfall (in inches)
Coast			
Esmeraldas	5	77	71
Ancón	17	74	14
Machala	17	76	25
Guayaquil	20	77	45
Bucay*	980	76	131
Sierra			
Tulcán	9,800	52	30
Ibarra	7,300	62	25
Quito	9,250	55	54
Latacunga	9,200	55	27
Ambato	8,350	58	19
Riobamba	9,150	55	11
Palmira	10,600	52	16
Alausí	7,800	59	16
Cuenca	8,300	57	37
Loja	7,400	61	30
Oriente			
Tena	1,700	74	153
Macas	3,500	71	85
Galápagos Islands	n. a.	73	17

n. a.—not available.
*50 miles east of Guayaquil.

Source: Adapted from Francisco Téran, Geografía del Ecuador; and Edwin N. Ferdon, Jr., Studies in Ecuadorian Geography.

brings a dry season; when the northerly winds of the Equatorial Current predominate, there are heavy rains. The rainy season at Guayaquil lasts from December through April. The offshore penetration of the Equatorial Current, which ushers in the rainy season, is known as El Niño (The Child), because of its appearance at Christmas time. Every 6 or 7 years El Niño encroaches strongly onto the Peru Current, resulting in heavy rains which have been very destructive in northern Peru and at times have had noticeable impact in Ecuador. In 1925, 41 inches of rain fell in a few months at Ancón on the desert-like Santa Elena Peninsula; thereafter, the average yearly rainfall was only 4 inches until 1932, when 30 inches fell, followed by only 8 inches until 1939, when 46 inches fell.

Although the prevailing winds on the Coast throughout most of the year are from south to north, winds from the north have a more noticeable effect. There are almost no storms except for moderate local disturbances. Calms exist for long periods of time. Although it is cloudy much of the year, fogs are infrequent, except on the coastal hills, where a fine morning mist known as the *garúa* brings some moisture during the dry season. Rainfall in the Sierra and the Oriente is the result of easterly winds blowing across the Amazon basin. There, warm moisture-laden clouds drench the eastern slopes of the Andes and carry over a considerable amount of rain to the Sierra. In July and August there are usually only occasional rains, but in some years more of the moisture clears the eastern slopes, and rain in the Sierra is heavier and more frequent than usual.

The Galápagos, washed by the Peru Current, are cool for their latitude, averaging about 73° F.; the temperature during the warmest month, March, averages 78° F. and during the coolest month, September, averages 70° F. An absolute high of 92° F. was registered in March 1952, and an absolute low of 60° F. was registered in October 1950. The rainfall is sparse, with an annual average of 17 inches, recorded between 1951 and 1964; it varied drastically during this period, from a high of 56 inches in 1953 to a low of 1.45 inches in 1950.

ANIMAL LIFE

The wide diversity of topography and climate provides for the existence of a wide range of animal life, especially when including the almost prehistoric fauna from the Galápagos Islands, where large tortoises are found which no longer exist elsewhere. In the jungles of the northern coast and of the Oriente wildlife is especially abundant. The puma and the condor are among the different animals found in the Sierra. Many centuries of intensive agriculture have greatly reduced the numbers, if not also the varieties, of animals found there. One of the few surviving members of the Western Hemisphere branch of the camel family, the domesticated llama, is seen as far north as Riobamba. Other domesticated animals common in temperate climates, such as cows, horses, donkeys, hogs, sheep and goats, are found in profusion in the Sierra.

Offshore, the confluence of the Peru and Equatorial Currents provides a large variety of fish valuable in commerce.

MINERALS

Although the location of the country between Peru and Colombia, both mineral rich, would suggest the existence of extensive mineral deposits, few have yet been found, and, of the known deposits, few are large enough to justify commercial exploitation. Nevertheless, because a considerable variety of minerals have been found in widely separated parts of the country, it seems probable that further exploration will locate appreciable deposits.

Coal is known to exist in considerable quantity in Loja, Azuay and Cañar Provinces; iron in Guayas and Manabí; copper in Pichincha and Cotopaxi; manganese in El Oro; magnesium in Chimborazo; silver in Azuay; and platinum in Esmeraldas and the Oriente.

At present some gold is panned from streams in Esmeraldas and in the Oriente, and some is mined in El Oro, where small quantities of silver, copper, lead, zinc and cadmium are obtained as byproducts. On the Santa Elena Peninsula important petroleum wells operate and supply most of the needs of the country (see ch. 20, Industry).

TRANSPORTATION

In almost all parts of the country the terrain is so rugged that the building of railroads and roads is a very difficult task. The chief railroad, opened between Quito and Guayaquil in 1908, climbs 10,626 feet in 50 miles. The Pan American highway, which crosses a pass 12,200 feet in altitude, was completed only in December 1962. There is no coastal highway, and few roads connect the Coast with the Sierra. To the Oriente there are only three short access roads terminating in the upper reaches. Airlines serve the important towns, and even some villages in the Oriente are served by light planes. Coastal shipping is important, and the modern harbor of Guayaquil can dock large transoceanic ships. Inland shipping is used extensively on the waterways of the Guayas basin and to a lesser extent in Esmeraldas Province. Navigation on the rivers of the Oriente is limited to small boats and canoes because the boundary fixed with Peru was set at the head of navigation (see ch. 22, Domestic Trade).

Railroads

The railroads have played an important role in the country. Before the railroad was opened between Guayaquil and Quito, the arduous journey between the two cities took 12 days. By train the 288 miles can be covered in 12 hours. In all there are 727 miles of railroad. In recent years a 232-mile line connecting Quito to the northern banana port of San Lorenzo was completed. In 1965 the spur leading south from the Guayaquil-Quito line at Sibambe was completed to service the 81 miles to Cuenca; it had long ended at Azogues, 9 miles from the southern terminus. In addition to these lines there are two short lines, totaling 62 miles, in El Oro Province and one of 64 miles in Manabí Province.

All railroads are single-track meter gauge except for two of the short lines, which are of narrow gauge. All are government owned and carry both passengers and freight. Recent competition from the highways and the difficulties of maintenance have decreased the importance of rail transportation.

Roads

In 1963 there were reported to be 2,630 miles of major roads. In addition, there is at least an equal mileage which can be traveled by automobile, at least during the dry season. Many all-weather roads are subject to frequent blockage by landslides. The Pan American highway, which extends 721 miles from Tulcán to Macará, is paved near Quito and is an all-weather road for its entire extent. The bridge over the Macará River into Peru was almost complete in November 1965.

The chief Guayaquil-to-Quito route follows the Daule River north to Quevedo, from which it turns eastward to climb the mountains and join the Pan American highway at Latacunga. A road also runs westward from Quevedo to the Pacific at Manta and one northward to Santo Domingo de los Colorados. Two other important roads connect Guayaquil to the Sierra and the Pan American highway. In the north a highway joins Quito with the port of Esmeraldas on the Pacific. In the extreme southwest passable roads connect Machala to Cuenca, to Loja in the Sierra and to Tumbes in Peru. A short road joins Quito to Papallacta at the foot of the eastern cordillera in the Oriente. A road runs from Ambato via Baños to Puyo and north to Tena (a spur from this route connects Baños to Riobamba). A newly constructed road in the south joins Loja to Zamora, and a road is being built from Paute to Macas.

Airlines

A number of international airlines serve Quito and Guayaquil, including the Ecuadorian Aviation Company (CEA). In addition, eight small domestic airlines serve about 45 airfields. In the Oriente even many small villages are regularly served by light planes; in many cases this is their only mechanical connection with the rest of the country. About half the domestic air trade is performed by Aerovías Ecuatorianos, the air transport service of the air force, which, in addition to performing the air transport service for the military forces, competes for commercial business.

NATIONAL BOUNDARIES

Bounded on the west by the Pacific Ocean, the country has land boundaries only with two countries—Colombia on the north and Peru on the east and south. Since boundary claims have been based on the extent of the Audiencia of Quito, as created,

21

but never fully delineated, on November 29, 1563, there has been a record of friction with these two countries over boundaries (see ch. 3, Historical Setting).

At the time of the breakup of Gran Colombia in 1830, Colombia used a Colombian law of June 25, 1824, as the basis of the delineation of territory. This delineation was long contested by Ecuador but finally was accepted as a basis for defining the boundary with Colombia, and the controversy no longer exists.

However, delineation by the law of 1824 has also been used by Ecuador as the basis for its recurring claims for territory which has long been incorporated into Peru, as well as for disputed territory in the Amazon basin. In 1941 a border war flared with Peru. Each country accused the other of initiating hostilities, but the far more powerful force of Peru prevailed. El Oro Province was occupied by Peruvian forces until after the Rio Protocol of 1942 awarded most of the disputed territory to Peru. This award preserved the status quo boundary in the south, but in the Amazon basin Peru was awarded all of the disputed territory up to the heads of navigation on the various tributaries of the Amazon. This award continues to be vehemently disputed by Ecuador (see ch. 15, Foreign Relations; ch. 27, The Armed Forces).

Despite the mutual acceptance of the border with Colombia the physical nature of the boundary remains a possible source of friction. The agreed boundary places in Ecuador the town of Tulcán and its immediate vicinity even though most of the surrounding basin lies in Colombia.

The boundary with Peru in the south is well defined by physical features, but that in the Oriente is poorly defined. The dissatisfaction with the 1942 Rio de Janeiro Protocol and the ill-defined border have resulted in a number of border incidents in the Oriente (see ch. 15, Foreign Relations).

ADMINISTRATIVE DIVISIONS

For administrative purposes the country is divided into 19 provinces, each subdivided into a number of cantons, which in turn are divided into parishes. The Galápagos Islands are administered as a separate entity under the minister of defense. In many cases the provincial boundaries do not correspond with the chief geographical features. For example, Pichincha Province, where Quito is located, contains more territory in the littoral than in the Sierra, and Cañar Province is cut in half by a high cross range which makes internal provincial travel difficult.

CHAPTER 3

HISTORICAL SETTING

Ecuador's geographic location has had a continuing influence on its historical role and development. Most often the country has found itself between stronger nations to the north and south. As a result, it has served variously as a passageway or barrier between centers, as a northernmost or southernmost outpost of larger political entities or as an object of the designs of stronger nations.

Until the establishment of the Republic of Ecuador in 1830, Ecuador occupied a dependent position—at first, within the Spanish Empire and, later, in the Gran Colombian Republic. Nonetheless, the distance from power centers made possible a de facto autonomy which encouraged the development of proindependence sentiment. Since the establishment of the republic the maintaining of independence despite the peaceful or belligerent encroachments of neighbors has involved a continuing effort.

Internally, events have taken place within a framework of social and political regionalism. Natural barriers, only recently bridged by railroads and roads, long made communications between the two principal regions, the Coast and the Sierra, difficult (see ch. 2, Physical Environment). Sharp geographic contrasts between the two regions have resulted in the development of different social and economic systems and, consequently, differing interests. Before the coming of the Spaniards in the sixteenth century, the inhabitants of these two regions lived in mutual isolation.

Later, two important population centers emerged—Guayaquil on the Coast, as the economic capital, and Quito in the Sierra, as the political capital—and the two cities became the centers of conflict between coastal and Sierran interests. Rivalry was most strongly expressed in the struggle for political dominance, and as the opposing forces—organized into parties as the Liberals and Conservatives—were persistent and fairly evenly matched, instability, violence and often arbitrary rule were common. The country's two greatest leaders after independence, one from the

Liberal camp on the Coast and the other from the Conservative camp in the Sierra, were assassinated.

These rivalries, though at the heart of national history, have been almost exclusively an expression of the controlling white minority. It is this group which has shaped the historical development since the Spanish conquest. The large Indian population, found primarily in the Sierra, has remained largely outside the stream of national events. Indeed, for the population as a whole, the events have functioned in varying degree as a changing overlay to a fairly rigid social and economic system which has begun to change only in the present century. The great bulk of the native population has passed from the authority of one dominant minority to another since the days of the Inca Empire. Similarly, the elite has been variously Indian, Spanish and *criollo* (Hispanic American) but, in aims and position, fairly alike.

BEFORE THE CONQUEST

Pre-Hispanic Ecuador was populated by a mosaic of linguistically and culturally diverse tribes. Reflecting sharp contrasts in physical environment, cultural differences were most marked between the tribes of the Sierra and those of the lowlands to the east and west, but even within regions there was diversity. Shortly before the arrival of the Spaniards, all of the Sierra and a portion of the coastal lowlands had been incorporated into the Inca Empire, the great Indian state which spread from a center in southern Peru to dominate all of Andean South America. By virtue of this conquest from the south, a unified political rule was imposed on the area, and a measure of linguistic uniformity was established through the introduction of the Inca language, Quechua. Nevertheless, the old tribal differences had by no means been obliterated when the Spaniards arrived in a second wave of conquest.

Oral traditions (the indigenous peoples did not develop a system of writing) and the observations of early Spanish settlers indicate that the Sierra was dominated by five principal tribal groups. In the north, in what are now Imbabura and Pichincha Provinces, the dominant group was known as the Cara. To the south, in a part of present-day Pichincha Province and in present-day Cotopaxi and Tungurahua Provinces, the dominant group was the Panzaleo (or Quito) tribe. What are now Chimborazo and Bolívar Provinces were occupied by the Puruhá. South of the Puruhá, in present-day Cañar, Azuay and Loja Provinces, were the Cañari and Palta.

The highland tribes spoke languages of diverse affiliation, all of which were supplanted by Quechua, although traces of these languages survive in place names, and they remain a focus of interest to Ecuadorian scholars. The native tongues of the Panzaleo, Puruhá and Cañari have never been definitely classified. The Cara language was clearly affiliated with that of the Chibchan groups found predominantly in Colombia. That of the Plata was either very closely related to, or identical with, the language of the Jívaro of the eastern jungles. Other evidence, mainly from oral traditions, suggests that the Plata migrated to the Sierra from the Oriente only shortly before the appearance of the Inca.

In spite of the differences in cultural detail among the various Sierra tribes, there was considerable uniformity in basic patterns. All of them subsisted by sedentary agriculture. The principal food crops—corn and potatoes, for example—and agricultural techniques were shared by all of the groups and were identical with those known throughout the Andes, from Colombia to Chile. Other elements of material culture, such as house forms and clothing design, were also broadly shared and similar to those found elsewhere in the Andes, especially in Colombia.

All of the highland tribes were organized politically as loose confederations which had little power; they became effective only in times of intertribal war, when broad coordination was necessary. Most evidence indicates that the only large-scale political state, with a powerful and well-defined central authority, in pre-Hispanic Ecuador was that imposed by the Inca. One colonial Spanish historian, the Jesuit priest Juan de Velasco, writing in the eighteenth century, asserted that the Cara and Panzaleo had been welded into a powerful, unified kingdom with its capital in Quito, but most scholars find little basis for this theory, in archaeological and historical evidence.

The Oriente was peopled in pre-Hispanic times, as in the present day, by many small groups subsisting from hunting, gathering and slash-and-burn agriculture. In the western lowlands were the Colorado and Cayapa, both of which have survived, and several tribes which became extinct during colonial times (see ch. 5, Ethnic Groups and Languages). Best known of the extinct tribes, both in archaeology and in the accounts of the Spanish conquerors, were the Esmeralda of the northern Coast; the Manta, who inhabited the Coast near the bay of the same name; and the Huancavilca, who occupied much of what is today Guayas Province. The Manta were well known along much of the South American coast as seagoing traders, carrying tons of goods on large balsa-wood rafts.

The Inca Empire, which, for the first time, introduced large-scale political organization to Ecuadorian territory, was a complex, intricately organized and autocratic state. Its ruler, believed to be a descendant of the Sun God and therefore divine, held absolute and ultimate authority. In matters of control and routine administration, however, his power was exercised by a large, pyramidally organized officialdom. At the national level the most important officials were nobles, most of them close kinsmen of the emperor, who served as military, administrative and religious leaders. At the local level there was a hierarchy of lower officials exercising leadership in the same fields over smaller population units.

In spite of the absolutist and centralized nature of imperial organization, many concessions were made to local custom and tradition. Where possible, the traditional rulers in newly conquered territories were confirmed in their positions and incorporated in the imperial hierarchy. Although certain features of Inca religion—notably the worship of the Sun God and his imperial descendants—were imposed, conquered peoples were permitted to retain their own gods and cults. Often, therefore, the imperial and local priesthoods functioned side by side.

Inca political rule was backed up by a powerful military force which maintained permanent garrisons throughout the land. Using the vast and ever-increasing pool of manpower that came under their domain, the Inca built a system of roads to every corner of their empire and thereby facilitated the quick movement of troops on threat of rebellion. When the imperial rule was accepted peacefully and loyally, it was quite benign. Many forms of tribute and enforced labor were imposed on the population, but in return the Inca government, with its vast food resources, offered an almost perfect assurance against famines resulting from local crop failures. When faced with rebellion, however, the Inca rulers responded with harshness, sometimes slaughtering entire provinces. Even the suspicion of revolt was met by the forcible resettlement of untrusted, newly conquered peoples among peoples of proven loyalty, often thousands of miles from their original homelands.

The vanguard of Inca conquest appeared in southern Ecuador some time before 1480. After a series of battles, especially fierce in Cañari territory, the Inca armies arrived in the vicinity of Quito, where the powerful conquering force was halted by determined local resistance. After several years of delay the campaign was continued, this time to meet with success, and the Inca armies, under Emperor Huayna Capac, drove through northern Ecuador and into southern Colombia. This final stage of conquest and its consolidation took place after Columbus had made his first landfall in the New World. Few years remained, therefore, for the full implantation of Inca rule. The rapidity and effectiveness with which that rule was established is demonstrated in the fact that when the Spaniards arrived, Quechua had achieved the status of lingua franca throughout highland Ecuador.

Until his death, probably in 1526, Huayna Capac spent most of his time in Quito, which had become a major administrative and military outpost. There he took as concubine the daughter of a prominent local chieftain. The son of this liaison, Atahualpa, enjoyed the special favor of the Emperor. According to most oral accounts, Huayna Capac ratified this favor by declaring, in defiance of tradition, that the empire be split; the northern portion was to pass on his death to Atahualpa and the southern portion to his legitimate heir, Huáscar, who was born and raised in the imperial capital, Cuzco, in present-day Peru.

On the death of the Emperor, war broke out between the two heirs and their followers. Atahualpa, generally described as the more capable and popular of the two, led his troops south and defeated Huáscar's forces in a battle at Cajamarca, in what is now Peru. Huáscar was taken prisoner and later assassinated. A force sent on to Cuzco in 1530 completed the campaign and reunited the empire under Atahualpa. Pride in Quito-born Atahualpa's military success resulted in his designation by later generations as the "first Ecuadorian." The fruits of victory were not long to be enjoyed, however, for during the civil war the Spaniards had been laying the groundwork for their invasion and conquest.

THE COLONIAL PERIOD

Discovery and Conquest

Only 20 years after Columbus' initial voyage of discovery, tales of a fabulously wealthy kingdom to the south had begun to filter into the Spanish settlements of the Caribbean. During the next few years several expeditions were launched from Panama, at that time the westernmost point of Spanish settlement. The first of these, led by Vasco Nuñez de Balboa, resulted in the discovery of the Pacific Ocean, and subsequent ones went as far south as the coast of present-day Colombia. Success, which was not easily won, was reserved for the venture of three partners, Francisco Pizzaro, Diego de Almagro and Father Fernando de Luque. It was during the search for Piru, as the Inca nation came to be called, that the territory now known as Ecuador was discovered.

The three partners, who had been in the Caribbean area for some time, began their preparations in 1522. Launched in 1524 with the permission of the Governor of Panama, the first voyage was unsuccessful, reaching only the coast of Colombia. A second expedition was outfitted and set sail in two ships in 1526. After arrival at the terminal point of the previous voyage, the expedition split up. Almagro returned to Panama for more men and supplies; Pizarro went ashore; and a third group, under the navigator Bartolomé Ruiz, continued south by sea. Traveling along the coast, Ruiz and his men disembarked briefly at the Bay of Esmeraldas in Ecuador, where they received gold and emeralds from the inhabitants. Encouraged, they continued south and eventually captured an Inca vessel. After taking some of the sailors and a few articles of gold on board the party headed north to rejoin Pizarro.

Ruiz' favorable reports led Pizarro to travel south to the Bay of Esmeraldas. At first the Spaniards were well received by the Indians, but abuse created ill-feeling which resulted in fierce fighting. Forced to retire to the Isla de Gallos, Pizarro realized that gaining control of the area would be difficult with the resources at hand. Nevertheless, when a ship was sent out by the Governor of Panama to rescue the band, Pizarro used it instead to travel further south, this time reaching the coast of Peru. After confirming the tales of riches, he returned to Panama in 1529.

On arriving in Panama and discovering that the Peruvian venture no longer had the support of the Governor, Pizzaro then traveled to Spain to present the project directly to King Charles V. Pleased by the discoveries of great mineral wealth in Mexico a few years earlier, the King was favorably disposed toward Pizarro and his project, which also offered the prospect of new lands for Christianization, a mission strongly felt by the Spanish monarchs. An agreement was made similar to those contracted in the past between the Crown and private citizens. By its terms, Pizarro was authorized to outfit an expedition at its own expense and claim whatever territories he might discover and conquer for Spain. In return he was to receive a large salary, drawn from the fruits of conquest, and the titles of governor, captain general and *adelantado* (Crown agent) for life. His partner Almagro was to receive a governorship and a salary equal to half of Pizarro's.

In January 1531, Pizarro set sail from Panama with 180 men and several missionaries to launch the conquest. The immediate objective was Peru; Ecuador was the focus of a subsequent and secondary campaign. The entrance into Peru, however, was from the north, along the Ecuadorian coast. Heading straight for the Bay of Esmeraldas, the expedition split into a land force and sea force upon arrival. The land force, under Pizarro, began the arduous march toward Peru but was halted en route for several months by bad weather and ill health. At this point the ships were sent back to Panama for badly needed supplies and reinforcements. Pizarro personally requested the aid of an old friend and colleague, Sebastián de Benalcázar, then in Nicaragua.

Benalcázar, who joined Pizarro when the expedition reached Manabí, was eventually to lead the conquest of Quito. From Manibí the Spaniards continued south by land to Guayas and Puna and then, with reinforcements, by ship to Túmbez, an Inca stronghold in northern Peru. After conquering Túmbez in the spring of 1532, Pizarro established the first Spanish settlement, San Miguel. Benalcázar was left in charge of San Miguel while Pizarro, with most of the men, set out for Cajamarca, where Atahualpa was residing.

Pizarro rapidly gained control of Peru. Upon arriving in Cajamarca in the fall of 1532, he invited Atahualpa to meet in the main square of the city. Aware of Atahualpa's superior forces, which numbered 30,000, and at a great disadvantage with only 167 men, Pizarro adopted a strategy of surprise attack. When Atahualpa and his entourage entered the deserted square, he was set upon by Pizarro and his men, who had been concealed. The Inca army, defenseless before European firearms and horses, quickly succumbed, and the ruler was taken prisoner. By holding captive the absolute ruler, Pizarro held authority over the entire nation. Some months later, despite Atahualpa's value as a hostage and despite the payment of a large ransom which was to gain his release, he was executed by the Spaniards for alleged crimes of treason and immorality. A successor selected by Pizarro soon died, and the Spaniards were faced with the rising discontent of the Inca nobility. Consequently, they set out to establish effective military control.

At roughly the same time, news reached San Miguel of a prospective expedition to Quito, led by Pedro de Alvarado, who had been with Cortez in Mexico and later had become the governor of Guatemala. This knowledge, combined with interest in San Miguel in exploring the northern territory, reputedly the location of great treasure, prompted Benalcázar to organize an expedition early in 1534.

Through informants, Benalcázar's departure became known to Rumiñahui, the Inca general in command of Indian forces in Quito. One of Atahualpa's leading officers, Rumiñahui had participated in the march on Cuzco during the Indian civil war and then had joined his ruler in Cajamarca. After Atahualpa's capture he had been sent to Quito to obtain part of the required ransom but, suspicious of the Spaniards, had not delivered it personally, choosing instead to remain in Quito to consolidate the northern forces. A detachment was sent south to halt the Spanish advance, but this defense proved unsuccessful.

A further advantage came to Benalcázar in the form of unsolicited aid from the Cañari tribe, which bitterly resented Inca domination. The addition of thousands of Cañari warriors to the Spanish expedition made the opposing forces roughly equal in the first principal encounter, in the environs of Liripampa (modern name, Riobamba). A volcanic eruption, which frightened the Indians, proved the decisive factor for Spanish victory. The expedition then swept forward along the western cordillera, reaching Quito in mid-1534. The city had been thoroughly destroyed by Rumiñahui and the remnants of his army, which had retreated to the north.

The Indian campaign had to be abandoned temporarily in the interests of settling the question of Alvarado's invasion into Pizarro's territory. Upon learning of Benalcázar's unauthorized departure from San Miguel and of Alvarado's arrival, Pizarro commissioned his partner Almagro to seek an explanation from the former and to end the ambitions of the latter. Benalcázar was summoned to the area of Liripampa, by Almagro, where, after the required explanation was given, the two hastily proclaimed the establishment of a city in order to establish firm claim to the area.

When Alvarado arrived a few days later, with his forces seriously depleted by the hard march through the coastal jungle and up the Andes, he was easily persuaded to abandon his venture in exchange for 100,000 pesos. Almagro and Alvarado then went to Cajamarca to make the necessary arrangements with Pizarro while Benalcázar returned to Quito. The proclaimed city was moved to this site, and Benalcázar became Pizarro's lieutenant governor. A simple form of municipal government was duly installed, and the residents, 250 in all, were inscribed.

Benalcázar proved to be an able administrator. Of immediate importance was the termination of Indian guerrilla warfare in the surrounding area; the capture of Rumiñahui, who was still at large in the north; and the discovery of the treasure Rumiñahui was believed to have taken from Quito. During the next few months the Spaniards relentlessly pursued the Indian guerrillas, despoiling much of the countryside. Rumiñahui was finally located in a mountain retreat, captured and brought to Quito. His refusal to specify the whereabouts of the treasure brought about his execution in January 1535.

Benalcázar's next project was the establishment of a port which, after the construction of a road, would link Quito to the coast. The new city, Guayaquil, was soon destroyed by neighboring Indian tribes. Reestablished, it was again destroyed and was founded for the third time in 1537. By then Benalcázar, tired of his role as administrator for Pizarro, set out with a few followers and 500 Indians for further exploration and conquest in the north, seeking to obtain an independent governorship from the Crown. For 15 years he ruled the territory of Popayán, in present-day

Colombia; he died in 1551 on his way to Spain to vindicate himself of a murder charge.

Benalcázar's successors in Quito were interested principally in exploring the lands to the east, which were reputed to be rich in gold and spices. The first expedition, led by Diaz de Pineda in 1538, was soon halted by hostile Indians, but the second, under the leadership of Francisco Pizarro's brother, Gonzalo, brought remarkable results. Departing in 1541, Gonzalo Pizarro found his supplies exhausted and his men gravely diminished in number within a few months. As a navigable point on the Napo River had been reached, he decided to have a boat constructed and search for a friendly Indian tribe which would provide food.

Francisco de Orellana, who was placed in command of the small expeditionary force, set out down the Napo but, intrigued by Indian accounts of a great waterway, continued on instead of returning for Pizarro's forces. The river, which he called the Amazon after a tribe of female warriors who, according to local tradition, lived in the area, took him to the Atlantic. Traveling first to the Antilles and then to Spain, he received a governorship from the Crown over the new territory, but died on the return trip, ironically at the river's mouth.

Meanwhile, Gonzalo Pizarro had tired of waiting and returned to Quito in June 1542. During his absence his brother Francisco was assassinated, and the authority of the Pizarros in the former Inca Empire was terminated.

The Rebellion of the Conquistadors

After the initial discoveries the Crown became increasingly concerned with the establishment of royal authority in the new colonies. Government by the conquistadors, who were originally contracted by the Crown but often acted more in their own self-interest, was not sufficient. The leaders of the Peruvian conquest, moreover, had been particularly independent in the exercise of their rule.

Although conditions in Quito had been relatively peaceful after the downfall of Rumiñahui and his forces, those in the territory under the direct authority of Francisco Pizarro had been chaotic. Indian guerrilla activity was the source of constant annoyance. More crucial, however, was the bitterness and rivalry between the original partners, Pizarro and Almagro, over territorial rights, honors and authority. The personal conflict eventually led to a full-scale battle, resulting in the defeat of the Almagrista faction and the capture, trial and execution of Almagro. Pizarro's triumph was short lived, for a few years later, in 1541, he was assassinated in Lima by Almagro's followers, under the leadership of Almagro's son.

Distance prevented full and immediate knowledge of these events in Spain, but news of the general disorder prevalent in Peru had filtered back to the peninsula. To remedy this situation, the Crown appointed an agent, Cristóbal Vaca de Castro, as administrator of the colony. En route, Vaca de Castro stopped in Quito to initiate an assessment of conditions and to enlist the aid of loyal supporters of the Crown. It was shortly after his arrival that Gonzalo Pizarro returned from his eastern expedition. The general support for Vaca de Castro which Pizarro encountered in Quito left him little choice but to accede to royal authority and retire to the estates assigned him in the territory of Upper Peru, now Bolivia.

Proceeding to Lima with supporters from Quito, Vaca de Castro quickly established his authority and expanded his forces. Confrontation with the Almagristas, centered in Cuzco, came in 1542 in the environs of Ayacucho. After their defeat, the younger Almagro was tried and executed.

The civil order established under Vaca de Castro was almost immediately disrupted. In 1542 the Spanish Crown promulgated the so-called New Laws in a further attempt to impose its authority, not only in the Viceroyalty of Peru, but throughout America. Considerable influence had been exerted on the Crown by powerful elements at court opposed to the harsh treatment of the Indian population. In addition, the Crown was generally displeased by the ambitions of the conquistadors. As a result, administrative machinery was outlined; numerous restrictions were placed on the use and treatment of the Indians; and in Peru all those who had participated in any way in the Almagro-Pizarro conflict lost title to the lands acquired in the conquest. As this included practically all the Spaniards in Peru, opposition was overwhelming.

On the arrival in 1544 of a viceroy, Blasco Núñez de Vela, to head the newly established local administrative system, opposition intensified. A proud, tactless individual, set on implementing the New Laws to the letter, the Viceroy quickly antagonized his own subordinates as well as the resident Spaniards. Charges were brought against him, and arrangements were made for his conduct to Spain. Before they were carried out, however, the Viceroy was able to make his way secretly to Quito.

The Viceroy's reception there was cool, as the local residents were in agreement with the Spanish settlers to the south. After the Viceroy's departure from Lima the Spaniards called upon Gonzalo Pizarro to abandon his retirement and assume the governorship of Peru. Intimidated, the Viceroy's subordinates had quickly joined in accepting Gonzalo. When the news reached Quito, popular support for Gonzalo was immediate. The Viceroy, however, sought and won the assistance of Benalcázar, governor of Popayán, who felt no loyalty to the Pizarros. In addition, he persuaded the local government of Quito to vote him aid and subsidies. About a year after Gonzalo's assumption of the governorship, the opposing forces met near Quito. In the battle which ensued, the Viceroy was killed, and his forces defeated. Remaining in Quito for some time, Gonzalo assured his position there by filling the positions of municipal government with stanch supporters.

Once again, the Crown was not fully informed, but there was knowledge of a generally unsatisfactory state of affairs. Adopting a new technique, the Crown authorized a royal emissary, the priest Pedro de la Gasca, to grant amnesty to the rebels and announce the repeal of the unpopular New Laws. A man of great tact, de la Gasca began his campaign to win over the Peruvians from Panama by correspondence. As many of the Spaniards in Peru had grown tired of the disorder and personal jealousies of the local leadership, de la Gasca's entreaties were well received. In Quito, opposition to Gonzalo Pizarro had arisen and resulted in open revolt. Similar reactions had taken place in Guayaquil. En route to Lima, de la Gasca received the pronouncements of these two cities in favor of the Crown. In addition, volunteers were waiting in Trujillo, on the Peruvian coast, to help him establish his authority. Amnesty was offered to Pizarro, but it was refused. After defeat by de la Gasca's army in 1548, Gonzalo Pizarro was tried and hanged for treason.

Although a spirit of rebellion and discontent continued in much of Peru for a number of years, conditions in Quito were reasonably tranquil after 1548. Energies were turned to activities of a constructive nature. During the rest of the sixteenth century, settlement of the Andean valleys was consolidated, and attempts continued to explore and settle the Amazon area. Crown rule was firmly implanted. Life during the greater part of the next two centuries was uneventful, ruffled only by occasional earthquakes in the Sierra, fires, epidemics and the incursion of pirates on the Coast.

The Colonial System

Legally, the conquered lands of America were the personal patrimony of the king. Policy was based on the Crown's obligation to Christianize the new territories and on the privilege of acquiring material wealth from them. To fulfill this policy, institutions were newly created or adapted from Spanish and local models, which together provided a comprehensive framework for a flexible, but firm, centralized colonial rule. As conceived, the system was quite logical. In practice, it often suffered modification or abuse resulting from local circumstances and distance from royal authority.

Administration was accomplished through a hierarchy of Spanish and American officials and entities. At the apex was the monarch, who, in theory, had absolute control over all matters. Most of the routine administration, however, rested with the Council of the Indies. The Council's energies were devoted chiefly to the formulation of legislation on a multitude of issues. The laws produced from 1524, the year of the Council's creation, to 1680, the publication date of the first compendium, filled nine volumes. In addition, there was a specialized agency, the Casa de Contratación, with its seat in Seville. All matters affecting the colonial economy on both sides of the Atlantic were supervised and regulated by this body, which enjoyed a considerable degree of autonomy.

In the colonies, highest authority was vested in viceroys, who were appointed by the monarch, usually from the elevated ranks of the nobility, and who acted as his personal representatives. Throughout most of the colonial period there were only two viceroyalties. The Viceroyalty of New Spain encompassed Mexico, southwestern United States, most of Central America, the West Indies and the Philippines; that of Peru included Panama and all of Spanish South America except Venezuela.

Beneath the viceroys were the *audiencias,* royally appointed legislative, judicial and advisory bodies which administered the divisions (also called *audiencias*) of the viceroyalty. Most of the nations of contemporary South America were formed from the *audiencias* of the colonial period. The Audiencia of Quito, as Ecuador was known before the War of Independence, was established by royal decree in 1563, largely as a result of a petition submitted to the monarch by the local citizens. Dissatisfaction with the administrative delays caused by dependence on distant Lima, responsible for Ecuadorian affairs after the fall of the Pizarros, had given rise to the desire for the relative independence and the right to deal directly with the Council of the Indies, which *audiencia* status tacitly accorded. As roughly defined by the decree, the territory of the Audiencia of Quito extended from the Pacific Ocean inland to the largely unexplored Amazonian areas known as Quijos and Canela. The southern boundary ran from the Pacific port of Paita, in present-day Peru, some 350 miles to the inland city of Moyobamba, also in Peru. A 100-mile-wide arm of land in present-day Colombia, reaching as far as the port of Buenaventura and the city of Buga, was the only delineation of the Audiencia's northern extension.

Within the Audiencia were a number of subdivisions which had been established before 1563 and were subsequently expanded in number. Largest in size were the four *gobernaciones* (roughly, provinces) of Quito, Yahuarsongo, Quijos and Tacamez, each of which was administered by a governor. Somewhat smaller units, the *corregimientos* were originally set up only in Indian areas, but after 1551 covered Spanish settlements as well. Authority rested with *corregidores* and lieutenant *corregidores*. Several *corregimientos*—Loja, Guayaquil, Riobamba and Cuenca, for example—became extremely important and were eventually raised to *gobernaciones*. At the lowest level were the municipalities, governed by *cabildos* (see Glossary).

Most in touch with local affairs, the *cabildos* often enjoyed great power and influence. Among the functions performed by them were the administration and distribution of land, the maintenance of public order, the regulation of labor, the establishment of prices and wages and, at first instance, the administration of justice. Of all the colonial officials, only the aldermen of the *cabildos* were selected locally by the outgoing membership. Other appointments were made directly by the king or his chief representative, the viceroy.

The economic life of the Audiencia revolved around agriculture. Although there was some gold and silver, deposits were not nearly so rich as those found elsewhere in the hemisphere and were, at any rate, soon exhausted. The original land grants to the conquistadors and their offspring were relatively small, but in time wealthier citizens and the religious orders amassed huge holdings and crowded out the less fortunate. Crop cultivation and care of livestock rested on Indian labor in the highlands and Negro slave labor on the Coast. Through the introduction of such crops as oats, barley, wheat and sugarcane and such animals as pigs, sheep and cattle, indigenous agrarian patterns were modified greatly. Certain local products—cacao, tobacco and corn—however, became extremely popular with the Spaniards and were actively cultivated.

Trade was conducted under Spanish monopoly, in accordance with the concepts prevailing at that time. All articles going to or from European nations, for instance, had to be bought and sold through authorized Spanish merchants, after passing through Spanish customshouses in Seville or Cádiz, the only ports through which trade with America was permitted. Similarly, Spanish ships were allowed to visit only a restricted number of port cities in the Caribbean, which served as centers for the collection of colonial revenues as well as for commerce. Goods were then transported by land or sea to the rest of the hemisphere. In most instances direct trade between colonies was also prohibited, but Guayaquil was exempted from this restriction in compensation for the damages suffered through fires and invasions by

pirates. As a result, the city became an important port and also
the shipbuilding center for the west coast.

The Audiencia's trade beyond its borders was limited. In an
age when rudimentary economic development and long sea voy-
ages limited exchange to such articles as precious metals and
spices, the Audiencia had few commercially valuable commodities.
Among them were cured skins, textiles and preservable plant
products, such as tobacco. Imports were necessarily limited to
essentials, which included wines, oils, iron tools, fine clothing and
Negro slaves.

Spanish influence was visible in the society and culture of the
Audiencia. Although the Audiencia differed in appearance and
background from Spain, given its large number of Indians and
Negro slaves, the rigidity and hierarchical character of Spanish
society were successfully transplanted to the new environment.
Two classes existed—one extremely small, the other extremely
large—and a wide gulf lay in between. The upper class consisted of the high Spanish officials and the somewhat less presti-
gious permanent residents of Spanish descent who possessed
great wealth in land. Education, high social position, leisure and
luxury were reserved to this group.

The lower class was composed of more varied elements. In
order of social standing, these were the poor Spaniards, the *mestizos*, the Indians and the Negro slaves. Finding manual labor
distasteful, the poor Spaniards usually occupied the lower positions of Spanish officialdom, engaged in commerce or joined the
lower ranks of the clergy. Intermarriage with Indian women
occurred early, since Spanish women did not migrate in significant numbers until after the civil system had been firmly imposed.
Although *mestizos* born of legitimate unions between Spanish
conquistadors and Indian noblewomen often became part of the
upper class, the great majority were confined to the lower class,
serving as artisans and *mayordomos* (foremen over Indian labor).

In the highlands the native population became the domestic
servants and manual laborers of upper-class society. Elements
of the Indian nobility were excepted. Accorded the same rights
and privileges as upper-class Spaniards, they soon lost their distinctive identity by intermarriage with the Spaniards. The scarcity of Indians on the coast and the influence of ecclesiastical
elements in Spain seeking to protect the native population
prompted the importation of slaves to work the coastal plantations soon after the conquest.

Many aspects of Spanish culture were introduced by individuals, but the chief cultural agent was the Roman Catholic Church.
The Church's own power, the protection of the Spanish monarchs

and the acquisition of wealth permitted broad and varied activities. One of the most important was education. Religious orders, which had begun to arrive in the 1530's, immediately established schools. Initially, they were small and confined their teaching to rudiments. By 1552, however, a secondary school had been founded, and by 1586, a university. Churchmen were also central to the artistic and intellectual life of the colony (see ch. 10, Artistic and Intellectual Expression). Particular attention was paid to the Indians. Through intensive missionary effort, the Church brought the Indians in heavily populated parts of the Audiencia at least superficially into the faith and, at the same time, taught them many European techniques of farming and artisanry.

Incorporation of the Indians into the society was also encouraged by the Crown through civil institutions. Of these, the *encomienda* and the *reducción* were the most significant. Under the *encomienda* system, Spaniards were charged with the supervision of the moral and civic education of a group of Indians in exchange for a tribute collected from the fruits of Indian labor on the land. Neither the land nor the Indians were owned by the Spaniards, in theory, but as practiced, the *encomienda* system became a form of great exploitation. The *reducciónes* (closely settled, planned villages) were designed to bring the Indian population, which lived in scattered communities or had fled from the conquistadors to remote areas, closer to the seats of civil and religious authority. Most often under the authority of a cleric, the *reducción*, like the *encomienda*, frequently became a source of personal profit.

The Eighteenth Century: Unrest and Rebellion

Beginning in the early eighteenth century the Spanish monarchy fell into a state of increasing decadence, which was reflected in the colonial order. Economic and military exhaustion caused by the succession of European embroilments were certainly instrumental, but a most important factor, too, was the substitution of the French Bourbon line for the older Hapsburg rulers. Under the Bourbons the American empire suffered administrative fragmentation which underscored the regional sentiments and differences that where inevitable in an area so large and varied. Temporarily in 1722 and then permanently in 1739, a third viceroyalty was created—that of New Granada, which had its capital at Santa Fe de Bogotá. The Audiencia of Quito was transferred from the Viceroyalty of Peru to this new administrative unit. In the process the Audiencia's southern border was set slightly to the north of that indicated in the 1563 decree, and the eastern border was more specifically delineated, approximating the present-day Peruvian-Brazilian boundary. A fourth viceroyalty was created with its seat in Buenos Aires some years later.

The firm grip which had been maintained on colonial economic life was relaxed. In the area of trade this relaxation of control was an especially important development. Gradually, it became possible for non-Spanish ships to maintain direct trade with the overseas empire. Concerted effort by the French Government and natural sympathies on the part of the new Spanish royal family brought a particularly favored commercial position to France. Under these conditions the material reliance on Spain diminished. The removal of certain restrictions, moreover, encouraged abuse of those that remained in force.

Foreign influences of a more general sort were also felt, especially during the latter part of the century. Visitors from other European countries, many of whom came on scientific expeditions, were an important source. As individuals of some distinction, they were generally lodged in the homes of the local aristocracy, which thus became informed on developments in Europe. Travel and education abroad also became increasingly common among well-to-do *criollos*. In addition, the restrictions on printed matter entering the American territories, imposed and maintained by the Inquisition early in the colonial period, were reduced.

Through these channels a small group of *criollos* became familiar with the new currents in European philosophical and political thought, most of them sharply contradicting the guiding principles of the colonial system. Honored today as the precursor of independence, Eugenio de Santa Cruz y Espejo was the most outstanding and influential of the Quito intellectual group of the period. Though of mixed parentage, Espejo was able to obtain a university education, which led him to the professions of physician, satirical writer and director of the public library. Gradually, he developed a system of political thinking which advocated complete emancipation from Spain, local autonomy, republicanism and democracy, and Americanization of the predominantly Spanish clergy.

These ideals were communicated verbally to his many friends and associates, principally between 1792 and 1795. The establishment of a group called the Patriotic Society in 1794, composed of members of the *criollo* aristocracy, provided a particularly effective forum for the discussion of ideas and the recent revolutionary developments in France. Such activity and belief did not go unnoticed by the authorities of the Audiencia, however, and as a result Espejo was arrested and confined to prison, where he died in 1795.

New influence and ideas gave impetus and direction to latent social discontent. Among the upper class, feelings of resentment toward Spaniards from the peninsula were strong. Although many of them were equal or superior to the Spaniards in education and wealth, the *criollos* were denied high-level administrative positions. Economic ambitions and ventures were also frequently frustrated by rules and ordinances. Within elements of the lower class, too, restlessness was apparent. In 1765 a popular rebellion took place in Quito after the establishment of a state monopoly on liquor and of a customshouse for foodstuffs. The deeper cause, however, was the weight of the general system of taxes and duties imposed on the populace. Between 1770 and 1800 there were also a number of Indian revolts which resulted in considerable loss of life and property.

THE INDEPENDENCE ERA

The movement for independence in the Audiencia of Quito was not an isolated phenomenon but, rather, part of a continental pattern. Individuals and events in the Audiencia of Quito inevitably became linked with those in contiguous areas. Indeed, cooperation was an important element of success and encouraged the desire in some quarters for continuing association after independence. An additional factor, of no less consequence, was the accumulation of Spain's military and political problems in Europe.

In essence, the movement belonged to elements of upper-class *criollo* society. Theoretical democratic idealism played some part in motivating *criollo* rebellion, but probably more influential was vested self-interest. The *criollo*, lay or religious, did not object so much to the qualities of the Spanish system as to his own inferior position within it. Uneducated and politically inexperienced, the urbane masses supported independence on the basis of emotional anti-Spanish sentiments derived initially from vague social and economic discontent and, later, from abuse by Spanish military forces. Generally, the Indian was a passive figure.

The Struggle

The struggle for independence took place in two phases, separated by a period of 10 years. The first was precipitated by the Napoleonic invasion of Spain in 1808. Charles IV had abdicated in favor of his son Ferdinand VII, who was placed in confinement by Napoleon. Revolting against the assumption of authority by the French, the Spanish people formed a central junta to govern during the legitimate king's absence. News of these developments reached the Audiencia rapidly. Seeing an opportunity to gain a measure of autonomy, a group of the deceased Espejo's aristocratic associates secretly formed their own junta in December 1808, similar to the one in Spain, allegedly to protect the interests of Ferdinand VII.

Discovery of the junta by the Audiencia resulted in the imprisonment of the conspirators for a few weeks. After their release they continued their efforts, this time assuring the support of the Spanish garrison. In August 1809 the president of the Audiencia was informed by the junta that his functions had ceased. The appearance of the garrison in the streets left him no choice but to accede to the junta's pronouncement. An open assembly of the *cabildo* of Quito, held shortly thereafter, confirmed the action of the previous days and affirmed support of the Catholic religion and the rights of Ferdinand VII. All official positions were immediately filled with *criollos*. Within 80 days, however, the junta collapsed, and Spanish authority was reinstated from outside.

The junta had lacked a leader and support from the general public of the city as well as from the influential *gobernaciones* of Cuenca, Guayaquil and Popayán. Consequently, no resistance could be raised to the forces mobilizing on the northern and southern borders of the Audiencia under the orders of the viceroys of Peru and New Granada. Authority was peacefully handed over to the president of the Audiencia, who gave the assurance that no reprisals would be made.

Such was not the case, however. An intensive campaign was launched almost immediately to ferret out all participants, during the course of which many innocent citizens were jailed. The resulting alarm was aggravated by the viceregal troops stationed in the environs of Quito to reinforce the president of the Audiencia and his council. Abuse and theft by the restless soldiers turned the public to the side of the revolutionaries.

In August 1810 the population released its frustrations in street riots which led to the storming of the jails. After 2 days of fighting, the civil and military authorities called a meeting of the citizens of the city. It was agreed that the troops would be withdrawn, the events of 1809 would be forgotten, the recently arrived representative from the Spanish central junta, Carlos Montúfar, would be recognized and a governing junta would be established. Composed of *criollos*, including the Bishop of Quito and Carlos Montúfar, who was the son of one of the leading revolutionary aristocrats, the junta was to be under the leadership of the president of the Audiencia.

The new junta, which soon made the president a mere figurehead, was somewhat more durable than its predecessor. An important factor was the militant support of the people. Support was also forthcoming from the central junta in Spain, but not from the Viceroy of Peru or from the rest of the Audiencia.

After a little more than a year in control the junta attempted to initiate a formal structure of government. A congress called in December 1811 declared complete independence and the establishment of the State of Quito, which included all units of the Audiencia, liberated or not.

After 2 months of deliberation a constitution was drafted and approved. The Constitution of February 1812 was a hybrid document which reflected the difference of opinion that had crystallized among the revolutionary leaders. On the one hand, it provided for limited individual liberties and institutions customarily associated with a democratic republican form of government similar to that of the United States, but on the other, it stated recognition of Ferdinand VII whenever he should resume authority over Spain, as long as recognition was not prejudicial to the Constitution. Of the two groups, constitutional monarchists and republicans, the former, under Carlos Montúfar, was the larger.

Moved by the continuing opposition of the rest of the Audiencia and of the Viceroy of Peru, the junta elected to launch a military offensive. Montúfar took command of the campaigns against Cuenca and Guayaquil, which had been isolated from Quito by the Viceroy. Advances were also made in the north, as far as Popayán. These were fairly successful, but the main force of Montúfar was forced to retreat to Quito because of bad weather and low troop morale.

Sent by the viceroy, General Toribio Montes, with a well-staffed and well-equipped army, had landed on the coast and was advancing along the highlands toward Quito. As the rebel troops were poorly equipped and the leadership was sorely divided, the city was particularly vulnerable. When Montes' troops reached Quito, they found it deserted, the population having been led to Ibarra by the Bishop. Here the final battle took place in December 1812. A rapid trial of those leaders who had not been killed in the conflicts produced numerous sentences of exile. Thus, Spanish authorities were left without organized opposition and retained control for the next 10 years.

In the latter part of 1820 the second phase of the independence movement was launched in Guayaquil. A declaration of independence by young citizens and elements of the local troops was rapidly followed by the formation of a military junta to repress opposition in the city and carry the revolution to other parts of the Audiencia. An open meeting of the *cabildo* of Guayaquil concurred with these activities and sent reports of recent events to the *cabildos* of Quito and Cuenca. In addition, communiques were sent to the principal military leaders of the movement in other parts of the continent—the Venezuelan Simón Bolívar in the north and the Argentine José de San Martín in the south.

Before the end of the year two military campaigns had been launched and ended in failure.

Encouragement soon came in the form of offers of aid by both Bolívar and San Martín. The two leaders, however, expected the inclusion of Guayaquil in their respective spheres of interest, Colombia and Peru. During the early months of 1821 contingents of revolutionary troops came from Colombia, the last group under the command of Bolívar's leading lieutenant, Antonio José de Sucre. A second attempt was made at this time to obtain a commitment from Guayaquil, but the response was ambiguous. Led by Sucre, the revolutionary troops of Colombia and Guayaquil fought a victorious battle with the advancing royalist forces soon thereafter. Sucre then launched an assault on the interior. In the remaining months of 1821, Sucre's army suffered defeat after defeat. When reinforcements sent by San Martín arrived early in 1822, fortunes rose. A series of easily won victories along the highlands brought the revolutionary army to the outskirts of Quito, where the decisive Battle of Pichincha took place on mountain slopes thousands of feet above the city. A capitulation was subsequently signed by the president of the Audiencia.

Two months later, the Liberator, Simón Bolívar, arrived in Quito and was given a tumultuous hero's welcome. A statesman and thinker as well as a military leader, Bolívar had envisioned the formation of several great nations from the former colonies. In the area of his own activities, northern South America, Bolívar wished to create one country from the former Viceroyalty of New Granada. In Quito acceptance of this proposal was easily obtained. Bolívar then went to Guayaquil to attempt to gain the same sort of affirmation.

In Guayaquil a meeting took place between Bolívar and San Martín, who very much wanted Guayaquil to become part of Peru and who was seeking the Venezuelan's aid in the Peruvian liberation. It is not known exactly what took place between the two leaders, but San Martín's subsequent rapid departure without Bolívar's promise of aid suggests that the latter was the more forceful. In the city itself opinion was divided between three possibilities: union with Bolívar's Republic of Gran Colombia; union with Peru; or complete autonomy. As no decision could be made and anarchy reigned, Bolívar temporarily assumed military and civil authority. A congress called in July 1822 finally voted for the incorporation of Guayaquil into Gran Colombia and swore allegiance to the Colombian Constitution of Cúcuta.

The Gran Colombian Experiment

From 1822 to 1830 the Audiencia of Quito remained in the Gran Colombian union, which was formed from the Viceroyalty of New Granada. The new republic was organized as a federation of three districts, corresponding roughly to the present-day republics of Colombia, Ecuador and Venezuela. With the exception of the land north of Pasto, which was included in the Colombian district, and some territory in the southeastern Amazonian region, assigned to Peru by royal degree in 1802, the limits of the Southern District (now Ecuador) were approximately those of the later colonial period. Each district was subdivided into departments, which, in the Southern District, were Quito, Guayaquil and Cuenca. The seat of national government was in Bogotá. Executive authority was held by the president, Bolívar, and the intendants of each district, his chief lieutenants. In the Southern District the intendancy was first occupied by the popular Sucre, then by another of Bolívar's Venezuelan comrades, Juan José Flores.

From the beginning the life of the republic was fraught with threats to unity. Disruptive military operations, which resulted in a drain on resources and civil morale, were a constant theme. Until 1825 the war for the liberation of Peru, supported by Gran Colombia and led by Bolívar after San Martín's resignation in 1822, was being conducted. As the closest of the three districts to the battlefields, Ecuador suffered the greatest strain. The exhaustion of 2 years of fighting was aggravated by the new role of military camp and supply station. From Guayaquil alone, 300,000 pesos were collected for the first expedition. By 1826, Ecuador had contributed a total of 1,669,000 pesos, which was more than the combined contributions of the other two districts.

After the war was won the flood of soldiers returning to Colombia and Venezuela created further demands on the economic resources and patience of the population. Then in 1828, the former partners, Gran Colombia and Peru, entered into armed conflict over border questions. Ecuador again felt the immediate effects most strongly. The sea campaign resulted in the bombardment and destruction by fire of much of the city of Guayaquil. On land, fighting took place along the cordillera, eventually ending in the Battle of Tarqui in February 1829 between the forces of José de la Mar, dictator of Peru, and Juan José Flores, aided by Sucre. Despite defeat, de la Mar refused to relinquish Guayaquil, and hostilities did not cease until the summer of 1829, after a 5-month campaign organized by Bolívar.

Harmony was also broken by the jealousies and rivalries of local groups and Bolívar's lieutenants. Before the end of the war in Peru a minor rebellion, put down by Flores, had taken place in the northern part of the district. Although great loyalty and admiration were felt for Bolívar, resentment existed in many quarters. A number of incidents and conflicts had arisen between Colombian and local authorities. As a result, the *cabildo* of Quito secretly supported an abortive military plot to break away from Gran Colombia in 1827.

In 1830 a constitutional congress was called in Bogotá in an effort to combat the growing separatist tendencies throughout the republic. Before the congress could be convened, however, Venezuela held its own congress and formally withdrew from the Gran Colombian federation. In the face of this action, representatives of the city of Quito met and elected to follow the Venezuelan example. A declaration was drawn up which extended thanks to Bolívar and placed civil and military authority in the hands of Juan José Flores. Later in the same year a constituent assembly drew up a constitution in the name of the "State of Ecuador."

REPUBLICAN ECUADOR

The Conservative Era

Abolition of the political ties with Spain was not accompanied by a corresponding disappearance of Spanish social, political and economic traditions. The chaos and disorder brought by the war, political instability and unbridled personal ambitions encouraged the development of authoritarian rule by a few dynamic individuals. As these individuals, either through conviction or through self-interest, were conservative in outlook, the *criollo* elite was able to assume the role in national life formerly held by the Spaniards. Authoritarianism and the periods of instability that existed between regimes were not favorable for change or opposition generated by groups from below. For these, existence continued much as it had before independence.

During the first 15 years after independence the country was dominated by Juan José Flores, whose only program, according to some historians, was to stay in power. The constitutional convention convened after the break with Gran Colombia had produced a constitution which provided for a democratic, republican government divided into three branches—legislative, executive and judicial. Elected by Congress for a 4-year term, the president was to be an Ecuadorian citizen. Through a clause that conferred citizenship on all those who had fought for independence, the Venezuelan-born Flores was eligible and was easily elected by the convention.

An uneducated soldier who had come up through the ranks, Flores was nevertheless a personable and astute politician whose position was enhanced by connections through marriage with one of the country's socially prominent families. In his first administration, Flores' attention was directed principally toward the maintenance of order. Abuse and disorder caused by unruly soldiers were checked. Political opposition, either from monarchists or liberals, was suppressed. A minority group of young intellectuals and older elements from the independence period, which resented Flores' ties with Venezuela, the military and Gran Colombia, became the object of particularly harsh reprisals.

Other problems of the young nation were largely ignored. Economic conditions were especially bad. The war effort had all but exhausted resources. Maintenance of the armed forces absorbed a great part of the budget. In addition, as a participant in the Gran Colombian federation, Ecuador shared responsibility for the war debt. No Ecuadorian delegates were sent to the conference held in Bogotá to divide the burden between the three republics, and Ecuador consequently was allotted a relatively large percentage. The origins of the contemporary national debt are found in this early obligation.

Dissatisfaction prompted an anti-Flores group to sponsor the candidacy of Vicente Rocafuerte, a former independence leader from the coast, for the 1834 election. Anticipating the move, the astute and flexible Flores staged a coup d'etat, brought Rocafuerte into power and had himself named commander of the armed forces. An attempt by Congress to reverse these actions was put down by government troops led by Flores. A constitutional convention called in the following year produced a new charter and confirmed Rocafuerte's presidency. As president, Rocafuerte was able to provide for a few social advances, such as public education, but the real power lay with Flores. Acting under Flores' influence and the personal conviction that the population was not yet ready for complete political freedom, Rocafuerte continued the practice of sharp reprisals against political opposition.

The 1835 Constitution, like its predecessor, specified a 4-year presidential term and prohibited immediate re-election. Thus, in 1839, Flores was able to return to the presidency and exercise direct control. The prospect of leaving office again in 1843 prompted him to call a new constitutional convention. In line with his wishes the convention drew up a constitution which doubled the presidential term of office and gave the president virtually complete control.

Flores was re-elected. Intense opposition was immediately forthcoming from groups outside the Flores camp who called the new document the "Constitution of Slavery." In Quito the principal center of opposition was the Sociedad Filotécnica (Philotechnical Society), composed of university students under the leadership of Gabriel García Moreno. Throughout the country and from abroad, manifestos against Flores and his constitution appeared. In 1845 a popular insurrection, which produced bloody street fighting, erupted in Guayaquil. The *cabildo* and general public, refusing to recognize the Flores government, established a provisional three-man civilian junta. After this action uprisings took place throughout the country. Always flexible, Flores offered to turn the government over to the rebels in exchange for retention of his rank of general, a general's salary and 20,000 pesos for 2 years' residence in Europe. The offer was accepted.

Called somewhat inaccurately the Liberals, the opposition had based its position on nationalism, civilian rule and anti-Flores sentiments. Of these, two were achieved with the ouster of Flores and his numerous "foreign" officials. The cry of civilian rule rang hollow, however, as the next 15 years were dominated by the national military. The chief figure was General José María Urbína, an army officer who had been a protege of Flores during the Gran Colombian period. As a provincial governor during the third Flores administration, he had gone over to the rebels when the probable course of events had become apparent.

In 1849, after the incomplete presidential term of Vicente Ramón Roca, one of the members of the Guayaquil junta, Urbína, began to exert his influence, leading a revolt against Roca's successor on the grounds that his election had been illegal. Urbína then successfully imposed a man he knew to be inadequate as supreme chief of the nation (Jefe Supremo) and shortly thereafter, as president. A coup d'etat, instigated by Urbína, overthrew the new president in 1851. On this occasion, Urbína's justification was the president's alleged failure to confront the threat to nationalism posed by Juan José Flores' rumored attempts to gain Spanish or French support for a return to power. Following the procedure that had become a tradition, Urbína convened a constitutional convention, which promulgated a new constitution and elected him president.

Urbína's anti-Flores sentiments led to numerous political deportations, imprisonments and confiscations. Also politically expedient were a number of superficial liberal gestures. By decree the Negro slaves were freed, and most went into the army, forming a kind of presidential guard. As Urbína firmly believed in the armed forces as the principal base of power, soldiers were well treated. Open advocacy of the establishment of public elementary schools won popularity among the lower classes, although lack of funds prevented any real implementation. In addition, the best school organizers, the Jesuits, were expelled from the country in an effort to contain the traditionally strong influence of the Church. Although such action spurred criticism, Urbína was able to manage the succession of an easily manipulated as-

46

sociate, General Francisco Robles, when his own term of office expired in 1856.

During the next 4 years of indirect rule by Urbína, opposition intensified. Conflicts with Peru brought matters to a climax. In 1858 a Peruvian squadron entered the Bay of Guayaquil to enforce certain territorial claims. A blockade was maintained for several months. Hindered by division in the army and the ill will of the Congress, the government was able to take little action. Agitation for the overthrow of the government, led by Gabriel García Moreno, who had previously opposed Flores, became widespread. In the spring of 1859 a popular assembly met in Quito and declared its nonrecognition of the government. A three-man provisional junta, which included García Moreno, was instituted.

Developments during the months that followed were confusing and somewhat surprising. In the fighting that broke out all over the country, the rebels were at a grave disadvantage. Military strength lay with the government generals. In spite of his earlier criticism of government behavior before the Peruvian aggression, García Moreno, as director of rebel military operations, went to Peru in search of assistance and arrangements. His efforts produced no results, for a few months later it was learned that a secret agreement had been made between the Peruvians and the commander of the Ecuadorian government troops in which Ecuador conceded all territory west of the Andes. Enraged, García Moreno sought help from Spain and France. During this process, the nature of recent Ecuadorian events came to the attention of Flores, still in Europe. Although Flores was previously a hated opponent, García Moreno called on him to return to Ecuador to lead the rebel forces. With an able and experienced military officer in command, the rebels soon gained control of Guayaquil and eventually the entire country. In January 1861 a constitutional assembly was called by Flores to present a new constitution and elect Gabriel García Moreno president.

García Moreno retained power, either directly or indirectly, for the next 15 years. One of Ecuador's two greatest despots, he is also considered the first of the country's two greatest presidents. Although born in Guayaquil, center of Liberal activity, García Moreno was educated in Quito and became associated with the Conservative cause. Strict religious training, natural inclination and poverty bred an austerity in living habits which contrasted with an emotional extravagance of fanaticism and deep-rooted hatreds. Travels and studies in the late 1840's in Europe, then undergoing a conservative revolution, only served to confirm his positions on politics and religion. Turning away from the military, which, as a staunch proponent of civilian rule, he detested, he became the first to build political power on the strength of the landed aristocracy and the Church.

During his period of influence, García Moreno attempted to carry out a plan which included initial phases of pacification and unification of the nation, material progress and moral reconstruction and a final phase of consolidation. To achieve the first objectives, he ignored the relatively liberal Constitution of 1861 which had provided, among other things, for decentralization of government and the guarantee of many individual rights. Political opposition was implacably repressed, at times with death sentences. In 1865 an organized uprising by Generals Urbína and Robles in the Gulf of Guayaquil was met by government forces under the leadership of García Moreno himself. All those captured and anyone suspected of having had any connection with the plot were shot. Verbal and written opposition was likewise suppressed.

Upon the expiration of his term in 1865, García Moreno turned the reins of government over to a friend, Jerónimo Carrión. Proving inept, Carrión was forced to resign after 3 years in office; his term was completed by another member of the García Moreno camp, Javier Espinosa. Espinosa's relaxation of restrictions permitted the opposition to initiate a campaign in the coming elections. Fearing that the opposition candidate would win in 1869, García Moreno staged a coup with the help of certain military elements. Almost immediately, a constitutional assembly was called which elected García Moreno to a second term and promulgated a new constitution, the eighth in the country's short history, called by its opponents the "Black Charter."

As the assembly had been composed of García Moreno's sympathizers, the Constitution was a reflection of his ideas. Curiously, it bore a strong resemblance to the authoritarian Flores document of 1843, which had been so vehemently opposed by García Moreno. Great power was concentrated in the hands of the president. García Moreno's religious zeal was reflected in the constitutional requirement making citizenship dependent on, among other things, adherence to the Catholic faith.

During his second term, García Moreno turned his tremendous energies and organizational talents to constructive measures. The improvement of internal communications, long a key factor in regionalism, received considerable attention. Principal highways and railroads, including those linking Guayaquil and Quito, were planned. Public education was another area of importance. Under public authorities it had not been well developed, and this situation, combined with García Moreno's personal convictions, inspired the decision to place the schools, from the elementary to the university level, in the hands of the Church. Church-state relations were especially close at this time as a concordat had finally been signed between the government and the Vatican, bringing an end to the undefined position the Church had occupied since independence (see ch. 11, Religion). In addition, the country was formally dedicated to the Sacred Heart of Jesus.

Attempts were also made during these years to promote growth in agriculture, through the introduction of new crops, and in industry. Foreign trade began to develop, principally in tropical and subtropical agricultural products, which stimulated activity greatly in the port of Guayaquil.

Despite the many beneficial accomplishments of the regime, opposition mounted. The growth of Church influence was especially opposed by the Liberals. In general, García Moreno's tactics and authoritarianism created many personal enemies. Toward the end of the constitutional period a conspiracy to overthrow the President was planned by university students and those influenced by Juan Montalvo, an exiled journalist who wrote stern criticisms from abroad. Before the plot could be carried out, however, García Moreno was attacked on the steps of the Palace of Government by an angry citizen and hacked to death with a machete.

Under García Moreno, conservatism and the Conservative Party reached their height. No dynamic personality emerged from the Conservative ranks to fill the void, and popular support was on the wane. For the next 20 years, consequently, the country passed through a period of political transition, no less turbulent than previous ones had been. The power struggle between the still dominant Conservatives and the increasingly strong Liberal opposition resulted in a compromise of "progressive conservatism" in most cases.

The candidate chosen to succeed García Moreno came from the more moderate elements of the Conservative Party. Although a generally popular choice, he was too mild an individual to confront the controversy which developed over the Liberals' campaign to abrogate the "Black Charter," still in force. Within months an uprising took place which brought a new figure to power, General Ignacio de Veintimilla.

Between 1876 and 1878, Veintimilla was occupied with suppressing popular uprisings and rewarding the followers of General Urbina, who had provided his chief support. As in the past, the assembly was called after order was finally established; it elected Veintimilla president and promulgated a new constitution. Under the influence of Veintimilla, a self-styled radical, the Constitution produced was generally liberal in tone but, like most of its predecessors, it was disregarded in practice. Political exiles and executions, for example, were numerous. With the general public, however, Veintimilla achieved great popularity, chiefly through frequent public spectacles and social functions which were rowdy in nature. In addition, prosperity was general during his years in office, as foreign markets had continued to grow.

As was the case for earlier presidents, an opposition developed inclined to achieve Veintimilla's ouster by forceful means. Somewhat ironically, the opposition united in a movement for the restoration of legality, liberty and order. After the termination of hostilities a junta was formed which convened a constitutional assembly. In 1833, uprisings took place that led to 6 months of civil war. A constitution similar to the 1878 document was written, and a president was elected. As the Liberals had been divided, the more extreme Conservatives had imposed their candidate. Disgruntled, the Liberals decided to alter matters by force and plunged the country again into armed conflict. The government forces won, and a number of the rebel leaders were subsequently shot.

From 1883 until 1895 leadership was exercised by a succession of three presidents who came into office by constitutional means. Conservative intellectuals of progressive inclinations, they governed under the principles of Catholic loyalty, political tolerance and sound laws. During these administrations progress was made in public works and education, and intellectual life flourished (see ch. 10, Artistic and Intellectual Expression). One of these presidents was Antonio Flores Jijón, son of General Juan José Flores. Generally, government programs, though solid, were unexciting and inspired little public enthusiasm. Beneath the calm surface, moreover, the Liberals and the more militant elements of the Conservative Party continued their traditional enmity.

In 1895 an opportunity was seized to bring the submerged power struggle into the open. The government was accused of involvement in illegal dealings with Chile, and a call arose for its overthrow. Under much pressure the government resigned. After tremendous political infighting, an arch-Conservative was chosen as interim president. Reacting as they had after the overthrow of Veintimilla, the Liberals refused to accept the unfavorable turn of events. A proclamation was issued in Guayaquil refusing recognition of the new government. Supreme command of the nation was assigned to Eloy Alfaro, who had led the Liberal forces in the clashes after the overthrow of Veintimilla. Returning from exile in Nicaragua, Alfaro organized a revolutionary army that, after months of fighting, defeated the government troops and entered Quito.

The Liberal Reign and Its Aftermath

The assumption of power by the Liberals in 1895 represented the triumph of a movement that had been building gradually since the days of García Moreno. With the exception of a few brief periods, the Liberals remained in power until 1944. During the early Liberal years a number of developments took place to bring a more modern semblance to the country. The reconstruction and sanitation of Guayaquil, long plagued by fires and disease, and favorable world markets encouraged the rise of that city as a commercial center. This, in turn, stimulated the development of a middle class and an organized labor movement. Progress was also made in communications and the establishment of public services. The religious issue, which had inspired dramatic and emotional debate, was resolved by a process of secularization designed to contain Church influence in civil affairs.

The first 20 years under Liberal influence were dominated by the *caudillos*. Chief among them was Eloy Alfaro, considered the second of the country's two greatest presidents. After the victory over the government troops, Alfaro assumed dictatorial powers. Disorder, caused principally by his own restless, machete-wielding soldiers, was rife. By 1896 conditions were calm enough to permit the convocation of a constitutional assembly. Although Alfaro was elected president, he was unable to obtain the kind of constitution he desired. Similar to previous ones, the new constitution, for instance, did not contain a freedom of religion clause, which had been one of Alfaro's principal aims.

Following the course of many of his predecessors, the President chose to disregard the document. Alfaro also continued the tradition of firm suppression of the opposition. Alfaro's administration was not without its constructive aspects, however. Of the greatest consequence was the inauguration of construction of a railroad to link the cities of Guayaquil and Quito, despite the difficulties imposed by arduous terrain and exceedingly high cost.

Alfaro was succeeded by a military colleague, General Léonidas Plaza Gutiérrez. By this time, internal conditions were somewhat more favorable. While the need to keep the troops in check continued, the political opposition had about exhausted its energies. Thus, Plaza was able to establish a truly civil government, despite his own military background. Similarly, a series of laws on civil marriage, divorce and freedom of religion were passed with little resistance. Perhaps as a result of Plaza's success as an administrator and his growing number of followers, rivalry arose between the party's two principal leaders. Consequently, when Plaza's term expired and the man of his choice was elected,

Alfaro responded with a coup d'etat which brought him once again to power.

Alfaro's initial activities were a replica of those of his first administration—dictatorship, followed by election to the presidency by a constitutional assembly. The new constitution, however, was more clearly in line with Alfaro's ideas. The state religion was eliminated; religious personnel were prohibited from holding political office; and free, secular education was affirmed. This constitution, called the "atheist constitution" by Conservatives, brought a resurgence of opposition. The creation of a band of strong men to forcibly persuade opposition senators or deputies to support the administration only aggravated matters. Demonstrations and conspiracies were put down mercilessly. In addition, Alfaro was confronted by dissident elements in his own party. Despite the distraction of these difficulties, Alfaro was able to bring to completion his major project, the Guayaquil-Quito railroad.

At this point, outside events put a temporary end to internal political turmoil. An old issue—the border dispute with Peru—had arisen again. A peaceful settlement had been attempted through arbitration by the King of Spain, but the Spanish decision proved unacceptable to both sides, and troops were mobilizing. In a surge of patriotism before the threat of war with Peru, the entire country rushed to support the President. Armed conflict was avoided, however, through the good offices of Argentina, Brazil and the United States. Subsequently, internal conditions assumed their former turbulent character, and within months of the expiration date of his term of office, Alfaro was overthrown by a military uprising.

Soon thereafter, the rivalry between Alfaro and Plaza came into full play. The death of Alfaro's successor provided an opportune moment for a new coup d'etat. The garrison of Guayaquil issued a proclamation stating refusal to recognize the interim government and called Alfaro from Panama, where he had gone in exile. On his return, a bloody civil war took place between his forces, drawn from the coastal element, and those of the government, under General Plaza. Alfaro and his troops suffered defeat, and many, including Alfaro himself, were captured and taken to Quito on the recently completed railroad. Before any measures could be taken, Alfaro was murdered by an angry mob in Quito.

In 1912, Plaza once again assumed the presidency with the support of powerful factions within the party and the recently reconstituted army. With the exception of a pocket of rebellion in Esmeraldas, where the Negro population for 4 years sought vengeance for Alfaro, order prevailed throughout the country. Plaza was able to continue the progressive kind of administration characteristic of his first term. In particular, there were advances in public education, with the promulgation of new laws, the establishment of teaching missions from Germany and the creation of public libraries. At the same time, work began on several new railroad lines.

The administration's chief difficulties were financial. The civil wars and extensive public works projects had put a tremendous burden on government resources. As a result, the government had found it necessary to borrow heavily from private banks, especially the Commercial and Agricultural Bank of Guayaquil. When war broke out in Europe in 1914, the financial situation became worse. Fearing that a flight of gold reserves to the belligerent nations would take place and believing that the war would be short in duration, the government passed a law which postponed the exchange of currency issued by the banks for gold. Moreover, the banks regularly, and with impunity, exceeded their legitimate issues. Consequently, the banks were able to issue great quantities of paper currency to the government, achieving considerable political influence in the process.

As the Commercial and Agricultural Bank was the largest creditor, it assumed a force in national politics similar to that which the Church and the military had once enjoyed. Presidential candidates were named and elected on the advice of the Bank's directors, who belonged to the wealthy coastal element. Long jealous of the role of Quito in national affairs, Guayaquil had finally come into its own.

In spite of bank control and a ruinous financial situation, the period from 1914 to 1925 was one of political calm. Administrations changed hands peacefully. The political parties abandoned the wornout issue of religion and turned to newer, more pressing social and economic questions. In its first assembly, which took place in 1923, the Liberal Party, for instance, outlined a program advocating the promulgation of labor laws, legislation to protect the rights of women and children, agrarian reform to improve the situation of the rural peasant, and medical help for the poor, indigent and infirm. In addition, the Liberal Party condemned militarism, dictatorship and the influence of the banks. The Conservative Party also assumed a new position, espousing the principles of social, economic and political progress. The shift from traditional concerns was reflected, moreover, in the development of a new political movement, socialism.

By 1925 the government owed the equivalent of US$18 million to the Commercial and Agricultural Bank and smaller but substantial amounts to a number of other banks. Inflation and the high cost of living had provoked serious unrest, most dramatically expressed in a popular uprising in Guayaquil a few years before. In the middle of the year dissatisfaction with existing conditions was manifested in a military pronouncement which declared the termination of the civil government's authority. Throughout the country the action prompted no resistance from the general public. Initially, a provisional junta composed of seven prominent officers and civilians held authority, but government was soon turned over to a junta that was entirely civil in composition. Unfortunately, the junta proved incapable of controlling the wave of political ambitions and infighting that quickly followed. The announcement of a plan to establish a central bank also brought opposition from the private banking interests, which had not lost all their influence.

Isidro Ayora, named provisional president by the junta, quickly stepped into the power void and assumed dictatorial powers. An energetic individual, Ayora immediately set out to consolidate his own position and attack the more pressing national problems. To accomplish the first measure, he dissolved the military juntas that had been directing local government throughout the country. Political enemies were jailed or exiled; the banks closed; and the newspapers which had supported them shut down.

Adjustment of the financial situation, the most immediate nonpolitical problem, was placed in the hands of a specially contracted mission from Princeton University, under the direction of Professor Kemmerer. Acting on the measures suggested by the mission, which included legislation on banking, currency and public finance, devaluation of the currency, collection of debts and the creation of administrative agencies, the government found itself in a good financial position. Programs were subsequently launched in highway construction, sanitation and public health.

In 1928, after 3 years in power, Ayora decided that the country was ready to return to constitutional forms. Early in the following year, Ayora was elected president, and a new constitution was passed. As president, Ayora was not to remain in power long, however. Despite his solid administrative activity in public education and in treaty arrangements to settle the Peruvian border question, political opposition was strong. Through measures included in the new constitution, moreover, the opposition was able to act, as well as to campaign verbally. Congress had the power to voice a vote of confidence or no confidence of the president and his Cabinet. To these political weaknesses were added the negative effects of the depression. In 1931 the contract of a large foreign loan provoked a military uprising and street riots in Quito. As a result, Ayora was forced to resign, and the presidency passed to his constitutional successor, the minister of government.

The 1930's proved to be one of the most troubled and unstable decades of the country's history. Political conditions were especially chaotic. The polarization between the Liberal and Conservative Parties gave way as groups, factions and new parties, some oriented toward the extreme Left, proliferated. During the decade the presidency was held by a total of 14 individuals. On some occasions the presidents were forced to resign by a vote of no confidence. On others, governments were turned out by a show of military force. A semblance of constitutionality was preserved through the practice of selecting interim presidents in accordance with the line of succession prescribed by the Constitution. Although elections, when held, were relatively free, factionalism prevented any of the candidates from winning support broad enough to create stable governments.

In this atmosphere concrete achievement was all but impossible. Attempts were made to develop programs in public works, education and social welfare during the administrations of José María Velasco Ibarra (September 1934–August 1935) and Federico Páez (September 1935–October 1937), resulting in part from the influence of the leftist element, but they could not be completed. Constant change in government, with the attendant growth of bureaucracy, revision of budgets and duplication had a disastrous effect on the economy, already undermined by the depression. Toward the end of the period the situation worsened as disease ravaged one of the country's principal export crops, cacao.

After the elections of 1939, which brought Carlos Arroyo del Río to the presidency, conditions appeared to improve. An attempted military uprising, provoked by José María Velasco Ibarra, who believed himself the true victor in the elections, collapsed before it really got under way. The chaotic economy, moreover, was being brought under some control. Foreign loans and favorable revisions in the reciprocal trade agreements with the United States served as a complement to positive local measures. Outside events, however, were destined to create new disorders.

In 1935, Colombia had ceded to Peru territory which Ecuador claimed, and there were repeated allegations of intrusions on Ecuadorian soil by Peruvian forces. By 1940 the intrusions had begun to cause alarm. Late in the year, Peruvian troops began massing on the border. Sole reliance on diplomatic discussions, at the urging of other nations in the hemisphere, and the political need for keeping troops in the capital left Arroyo del Río unprepared for the Peruvian invasion launched in the summer of 1941. An armistice signed 1 month later was violated by Peru, causing the United States and Mexico to call for mediation by all the countries of Latin America in the interests of establishing hemispheric peace, especially necessary because of the onset of World

War II. The issue was brought up at the Rio de Janeiro foreign ministers' meeting of January 1942 and settled, in the Ecuadorian view, in favor of Peru.

Popular reaction to the defeat in Ecuador was strong. A goodwill tour by Arroyo del Río to a number of the countries of the hemisphere, designed to develop chances for a more favorable solution to the Peruvian question, only produced increased resentment at home. By the time of the 1944 elections emotions were running high, and the government candidate enjoyed little popular support. Arroyo del Río's refusal to permit the popular Velasco Ibarra, in exile in Chile since his unsuccessful attempt at overthrow, to return for the campaign increased public ill will. Traveling to neighboring Colombia, Velasco Ibarra helped to fan popular discontent. In Ecuador his illegal candidacy was supported by the Ecuadorian Democratic Alliance (Alianza Democrática Ecuatoriana—ADE), a coalition of leftist elements.

In May 1944, only days before the scheduled elections, an uprising broke out in Guayaquil which pitted the general public and the military against Arroyo del Río's police. Similar outbreaks occurred in the highlands in Riobamba. Arroyo del Río resigned, and power was turned over by the military to the ADE. After a triumphal entry from Colombia, Velasco Ibarra was decreed president, for a 4-year term.

Shortly thereafter, a constituent assembly was elected in which representatives of the ADE were dominant. Initially, relations between the President, who declared himself a leftist, and the assembly were harmonious. On the one hand, a campaign was launched against Arroyo del Río and his supporters, who constituted the only significant opposition. On the other hand, declarations were made in favor of a drastic social and political transformation of the country.

Under deliberation by the assembly, the new constitution was to be liberal and progressive. Within months, however, all unity was lost. Reversing his initial position, Velasco Ibarra became increasingly hostile toward the assembly and toward the legislation and the constitution it was formulating. When the constitution was finally completed early in 1945, the President disavowed it and dissolved the assembly. During the next year he ruled in an authoritarian manner without the assistance of either an assembly or a congress. Plans and projects, most of which were never realized, proliferated while the government bureaucracy grew rapidly. Extensive government spending and waste and the growth of foreign debts led to severe inflation and, eventually, to the devaluation of the currency. The political opposition, which by this time included the leftists as well as the Arroyo del Río supporters, was generally suppressed. Leftist government officials withdrew from their positions or were forced to resign. Early in 1946, Velasco Ibarra formally suspended the 1945 Constitution, which brought the strong criticism of the leftists, who had authored it. At the suggestion of the Conservatives a new assembly was called to formulate a more suitable document. All other parties and political groups, however, refused to participate, and as a result the Constitution of 1946 was considerably more moderate than its predecessor. Reluctantly, the assembly gave its support to the President.

By 1947, Velasco Ibarra had lost virtually all political and popular support. In August of that year he was removed from office and exiled by his minister of defense, Colonel Carlos Mancheno, who subsequently assumed the presidency. Challenged by both political and military elements, Mancheno was replaced shortly thereafter by Velasco Ibarra's former vice president. Elections were soon held to establish an interim government to complete Velasco Ibarra's term, which expired in 1948.

The disorders of these years gave way to a period of relative stability which lasted from 1948 to 1960. The elections of 1948 brought Galo Plaza Lasso, the candidate of an independent citizens' group, to the presidency. A moderate, Plaza Lasso was dedicated to democratic rule in accordance with the Constitution. During his administration the financial situation was brought rency remained firm. Considerable interest was displayed in improving the standard of living, and, to this end, numerous studies and plans were made with the help of foreign experts. Lack of funds, frequent changes in the government bureaucracy and time, however, prevented the implementation of most. Firmly committed to the peaceful, lawful transfer of presidential power, Galo Plaza worked hard and successfully to insure free and orderly elections when his term came to an end in 1952.

After a heated campaign against one Conservative and two Liberal candidates, José María Velasco Ibarra won an unprecedented third presidential term. As in the past, his chief support came from the lower classes, impressed by his great personal appeal and ardent expression of concern with their interests and problems. Once in office, Velasco Ibarra also won the support of the army through a series of favorable measures. Those he saw as his enemies—the university students, organized labor and the press—were subject at times to heavyhanded treatment, in disregard of the Constitution. As before, he launched an ambitious program of projects and public works, paying little attention to public resources. Although his administration was not generally effective, inflation and general economic instability—hallmarks of earlier Velasco Ibarra governments—were avoided, largely through controls imposed by the Central Bank of Ecuador (Banco Central del Ecuador) and the Monetary Board.

After 8 years of government by political independents the parties entered the 1956 elections with great energy and interest. Chiefly as a result of the split in Liberal forces, Camilo Ponce Enríquez, the candidate backed by the Conservative Party, won the election. The 4 years under Ponce Enríquez were marked by relative calm. To allay the fears of progressive elements, he included members of various political groups in his Cabinet. Although Ponce Enríquez did little to develop the programs of social and economic improvement he had supported in his campaign speeches, the opposition, with the exception of former president Velasco Ibarra, was rather mild in its criticism. In its view, heavy spending and indecisiveness were the chief shortcomings of the administration. With the expiration of Ponce Enríquez's term in 1960, events returned to more traditional patterns (see ch. 14, Political Dynamics).

CHAPTER 4

POPULATION AND LABOR FORCE

Preliminary and uncorrected information from the country's second population census, taken on November 25, 1962, showed a total population of 4,581,476 and a national density of 43 persons per square mile. A comparison of the 1950 census results with those of 1962 (neither including an estimate of the number of jungle Indians) shows an increase rate of 3.2 percent per year, a very rapid growth.

Figures on the ethnic breakdown of the population are of questionable accuracy, particularly because no ethnic breakdown was included in either the 1950 or the 1962 census. Some authorities place great emphasis on racial background and others on language, way of life and social position. Accurate statistics in either case are difficult to obtain, and estimates can therefore be made only at a low level of refinement. By using results from various local and specialized surveys, however, it can be estimated that, in racial terms, between one-third and one-half of the population is Indian, 10 percent white, 10 percent Negro or mulatto and the remainder *mestizo*. The vast majority of the Indians live in the Sierra; the whites live in the provincial capitals; and almost all of the Negroes and mulattoes are found on the Coast.

Since colonial days there has been little immigration, and the government has made no effort to encourage it. During World War II about 2,500 persons immigrated from Europe each year, but this figure dropped to 500 soon thereafter.

In 1962 the economically active population was almost 1.5 million; of these 17.8 percent were women. Of this labor force, 56.5 percent were engaged in agricultural pursuits. Only 14.1 percent were engaged in manufacturing of any kind, and 80 percent of these worked in small establishments employing four or fewer persons. Unemployment and underemployment were serious problems.

The Constitution and the implementing Labor Code are considered to be liberal in terms of worker rights and benefits, but their provisions have had only limited enforcement. Except for the top 1 percent of workers, wages and salaries were extremely low. Tenant laborers on the *haciendas* of the Sierra, for example, received less than the equivalent of S/925 (in 1965, S/18.5 equaled US$1) per year.

POPULATION DISTRIBUTION

The great bulk of the population is concentrated in the Guayas Valley on the Coast and in the many small intermont basins of the Sierra, plateaus between the two ranges of the Andes. The density in Guayas Province, the highest on the Coast, is 120 persons per square mile; that in Tungurahua Province, the highest in the Sierra, is 152 persons per square mile (see fig. 4).

The population is overwhelmingly rural, and the suitability of land for subsistence agriculture has been the principal factor determining population distribution. The 1962 census showed a rural population of 64.7 percent, compared with 76.3 percent in 1956, then the highest in Latin America. In spite of the decrease, the society continues to be primarily rural and agrarian.

The distribution of population between the Sierra and the lowlands for a long time was determined chiefly by the prevalence of tropical diseases in the latter areas. It was only after malaria and other tropical diseases had been brought under control that there was a large-scale movement into the lowlands. In 1780, 91.2 percent of the people lived in the Sierra; by 1941, 60.4 percent of the people still lived there, and almost all of the remainder lived in the coastal region; but by 1962 only 51.5 percent lived in the Sierra, 46.5 percent on the Coast and about 2 percent in the Oriente.

Most of the Sierra is mountainous and unsuitable for agriculture. Even in the intermont valleys the amount of arable land is small, and the number of persons per unit of productive land is extremely high.

The population density on the Coast varies greatly from the high of 120 persons per square mile to 20 persons per square mile in the northern tropical province of Esmeraldas. Most of the northern part of the coastal lowlands and western piedmont is sparsely populated and offers much virgin land which can be put under cultivation.

Successive governments have shown an increasing awareness of the uneven distribution of the population on the scarce agricultural lands of the Sierra. To relieve pressures on the land, projects have been undertaken to build access roads and to open new lands to colonization. The major efforts have been directed toward the forested lands west of the Andes, but several access roads are being built into the Oriente as well. Until July 11, 1964, when the country's first land reform law was enacted, little attempt had been made to alleviate the concentration of population created by restricted ownership and inefficient land use (see ch. 19, Agriculture).

The two large cities—Guayaquil, the principal port, and Quito, the capital city, in the Sierra—included 18.9 percent of the total population in 1962. In addition to these cities, only two others, Cuenca and Ambato, have populations of more than 50,000. Only 19 cities or towns have populations above 10,000, and these comprise 29.2 percent of the population. Because the 1962 census defined the category "urban" to include all persons living in the corporate limits of both provincial and cantonal capitals, the official urban population, given as 35.3 percent, is high, for many persons living in most towns are engaged exclusively in agricultural pursuits (see table 2).

AGE AND SEX DISTRIBUTION

The 1950 census showed that the majority of the population (61.4 percent) were under 25 years of age. A sampling of the 1962 census results confirms that this condition still exists. Accordingly, the population of working age is increasing rapidly.

The 1962 census records an almost equal number of men and women in the total population. The men predominate on the Coast and in the Oriente, whereas there is a slight predominance of women in the Sierra.

In 1963 the estimated birth rate was 44.2 per thousand and the death rate 13.5, indicating the rate of annual population increase to be 30.7 per thousand, which is closely in accord with the figure derived from a comparison of the census of 1950 with that of 1962. It seems highly probable, however, that the reported birth and death rates are considerably lower than the actual rates. Even though the prompt registration of births and deaths is required by law, the isolation of much of the population, together with a traditional mistrust by the Indians, has often resulted in noncompliance.

SETTLEMENT PATTERNS

The nature of settlements and habitations varies greatly according to climate. In the Sierra there are few isolated houses, except on the large *haciendas*. Most highland peasants live in hamlets, villages or towns and go out into the countryside to cultivate their farms. The villages often consist of a row of adobe or lava rock houses on each side of a stream, road or trail. Fronting the road serving the area, there usually is a small plaza faced by a chapel and a few shops. In the towns, which are more regularly laid out, the plaza, on which face the church, the administrative buildings and some stores, is the center.

Table 2. *Population Distribution in Ecuador by Geographic Region and Province, 1962*

Region or province	Population	Capital city	Population
Sierra	2,362,678		
Azuay	275,758	Cuenca	60,817
Bolívar	137,998	Guaranda	9,597
Cañar	112,618	Azogues	8,217
Carchi	93,824	Tulcán	16,535
Chimborazo	279,607	Riobamba	41,689
Cotopaxi	193,929	Latacunga	14,936
Imbabura	174,141	Ibarra	25,806
Loja	285,351	Loja	26,657
Pichincha	587,602	Quito*	355,183
Tungurahua	221,850	Ambato	53,745
Coast	2,138,347		
El Oro	162,595	Machala	30,136
Esmeraldas	124,742	Esmeraldas	33,439
Guayas	986,556	Guayaquil	510,785
Los Ríos	249,651	Babahoyo	16,369
Manabí	614,803	Portoviejo	32,435
Oriente	78,039		
Morona Santiago	28,040	Macas	1,357
Napo	24,487	Tena	1,008
Pastaza	13,840	Puyo	2,353
Zamora Chinchipe	11,672	Zamora	1,068
Galapágos Islands	2,412		
Total Ecuador	4,581,476		

*National capital also.

Source: Adapted from Ecuador, Ministerio de Económia Dirección General de Estadística, *II Censo de Población y I de Vivienda*, July 1963.

Quito, the capital, presents remarkable contrast between the old and the new. In parts, there are narrow, winding streets lined with houses constructed in colonial times from volcanic stone. In other parts of the city, especially to the north, streets are wide, and the predominant architectural styles are modern. The economic and administrative part of the city remains centered on the old Spanish plaza, with its cathedral and other buildings built in colonial times. Small parks and plazas dot the city.

On the coastal lowlands most of the villages are built along or near streams, since these usually are the main arteries of communication. In some areas, particularly in Esmeraldas, settlements are small, containing as few as three or four houses. More typically, however, villages are larger. In many areas, houses are built on stilts. The towns and small cities of the region are distributed along the highways, which serve as main streets. These towns and cities are usually laid out in rectangular form, and the streets are lined with buildings often substantially built of wood or concrete.

Guayaquil, the largest city, the major seaport and the commercial center of the country, is located on the Guayas River 35 miles above its mouth at Guayaquil Bay. It is dotted with many parks and plazas and built around streets made wide as protection against the periodic fires that historically have been the scourge of the city. The overall architectural tone is modern, especially as concrete buildings have replaced the older wooden ones. In recent years there has been a considerable growth of manufacturing industry. A growing influx of rural migrants has given rise to a large slum area on the outskirts of the city.

In the Oriente settlement is confined almost entirely to riverbanks because of the lack of roads. The few towns are generally built along, or at the termini of, roads descending from the Andes and have the primitive character of frontier towns. The few jungle Indians, who alone inhabit the remainder of the area, live in semipermanent settlements.

MIGRATION

An analysis of the regional population changes occurring between 1950 and 1962 indicated that, in comparison with the countrywide population increase of only 43.5 percent, an 85-percent increase was experienced by the two major cities. In addition, there was an extensive migration from the Sierra to the Coast. During the same period the Sierra's population increased by only 27 percent; if that of Quito is excluded, by only 22 percent. The coastal population increased by 63.5 percent; if Guayaquil is excluded, by 55.5 percent.

The increases in each of the provinces of the Coast, excluding the city of Guayaquil, were relatively consistent and indicated a general movement to all parts of the coastal lowlands. The small increase in each of the provinces in the Sierra outside of the city of Quito, were approximately equal throughout the area, except in the province of Loja, which was well above the average. This last increase reflected the extension of the Pan-American highway from the city of Loja to the Peruvian border, which thus opened up much of this formerly isolated province to trade with the rest of the country.

The population of the Oriente more than doubled between 1950 and 1962, increasing by 46,000 persons. Even though the number is small in comparison to the total population, the movement indicates a willingness to pioneer the frontier. These colonists came almost entirely from the overpopulated Sierra.

Settlements in the underdeveloped coastal province of Esmeraldas and in the large lower slopes and lowlands have been established on virgin lands. Colonists in this zone have come almost equally from the Sierra and from other parts of the Coast.

DISTRIBUTION OF THE LABOR FORCE

According to the 1962 census, the economically active population, defined as gainfully employed persons 12 years old and over, was 1,483,735—32.4 percent of the total population and 53 percent of the population 12 years old and over. In 1950 the comparable percentages were 37.6 percent and 58.4 percent, respectively. Thus, there was a marked decline in the economically active sector of the population, and, correspondingly, the proportion of dependent persons grew. The dependent category, by census definition, includes unpaid women and adolescents engaged in household chores, students, institutionalized persons and the unemployed.

The economically active population was 34.5 percent urban and 65.5 percent rural, which percentages were closely in accord with the overall urban-rural distributions. The distribution of employment by economic sector indicates the predominately agricultural nature of the country. According to the 1962 census, 56.5 percent of the economically active population were involved in agriculture or fishing. Even this high percentage does not give a true picture of the number of persons actually working on farms because it does not include the many women and children who live on farms and work in the fields (see table 3).

Comparative statistics from the 1950 and 1962 censuses indicate

Table 3. Ecuadorian Labor Force, by Field of Activity, 1950 and 1962

Activity	1950		1962		Annual rate of change
	Number of workers*	Percent	Number of workers*	Percent	
Agriculture and fishing	641	53.2	839	56.5	2.3
Commerce	75	6.2	92	6.2	
Construction	27	2.2	48	3.2	4.9
Finance	5	0.4	8	0.6	4.0
Manufacturing	233	19.4	209	14.1	—0.9
Mines and quarries	5	0.4	3	0.2	—4.2
Services and public administration	191	15.9	240	16.2	1.9
Transportation	27	2.2	42	2.8	3.8
Utilities	1	0.1	3	0.2	9.6
Total	1,205	100.0	1,484	100.0	1.8

*In thousands.

Source: Adapted from Banco Central del Ecuador, *Memoria del Gerente General: Correspondiente al Ejercicio de 1963*, p. 67.

Table 4. Economically Active Population of Ecuador, Urban and Rural, by Field of Activity, Region and Sex, 1962

Activity	Urban			Rural			Total urban and rural
	Men	Women	Total	Men	Women	Total	
SIERRA							
Agriculture and fishing	16,967	1,933	18,900	390,833	45,700	436,533	455,433
Mines and quarries	634	33	667	533	100	633	1,300
Manufacturing	52,833	19,667	72,500	33,000	33,067	66,067	138,567
Construction	13,766	367	14,133	10,967	133	11,100	25,233
Utilities	1,067	133	1,200	233	......	233	1,433
Commerce	15,967	9,767	25,734	6,466	2,500	8,966	34,700
Transportation and communications	13,533	600	14,133	5,267	67	5,334	19,467
Services and public administration	37,600	44,433	82,033	10,667	12,000	22,667	104,700
Not specified	12,466	3,434	15,900	2,734	333	3,067	18,967
Total Sierra	164,833	80,367	245,200	460,700	93,900	554,600	799,800
COAST							
Agriculture and fishing	34,033	800	34,833	316,367	14,933	331,300	366,133
Mines and quarries	700	......	700	1,300	67	1,367	2,067
Manufacturing	42,600	8,900	51,500	12,066	5,800	17,866	69,366

Table 4—Continued.

Construction	16,599	134	16,733	4,434	66	4,500	21,233
Utilities	1,067		1,067	167		167	1,234
Commerce	37,600	7,600	45,200	9,967	1,533	11,500	56,700
Transportation and communications	17,767	433	18,200	4,100	100	4,200	22,400
Services and public administration	36,167	33,300	69,467	9,200	9,567	18,767	88,234
Not specified	22,467	3,833	26,300	4,699	534	5,233	31,533
Total Coast	209,000	55,000	264,000	362,300	32,600	394,900	658,900

ORIENTE

Agriculture and fishing	1,267	33	1,300	15,867	634	16,501	17,801
Mines and quarries				33		33	33
Manufacturing	434	366	800	266	300	566	1,366
Construction	433	67	500	533		533	1,033
Utilities	33		33				33
Commerce	167	67	234	67	33	100	334
Transportation and communications	100		100	100		100	200
Services and public administration	1,266	234	1,500	1,534	1,033	2,567	4,067
Not specified	33		33	134		134	167
Total Oriente	3,733	767	4,500	18,534	2,000	20,534	25,034
Grand total	377,566	136,134	513,700	841,534	128,500	970,034	1,483,734

Source: Adapted from Banco Central del Ecuador, *Memoria del Gerente General: Correspondiente al Ejercicio de 1963*, p. 68.

not only a large increase in the total number of persons engaged in agricultural pursuits but also an increase in percentage from 53.2 to 56.5. Some of this increase is accounted for by expanded activity in fishing and banana culture and by the new lands opened up in the lowlands. Most of it, however, has resulted from a high rate of natural increase in rural areas and a lack of alternate opportunities. The population living on the already intensively farmed land in the Sierra is growing very rapidly.

Women constituted 17.8 percent of the economically active labor force in 1962. The majority of them were employed in services, which included public administration, where they equaled men in numbers employed. In agriculture the census showed only 10 percent of those registered to be women, and in the coastal region the number was less than 5 percent. In manufacturing in rural areas of the Sierra the number of women equaled that of men, reflecting the prevalence of small handicraft industries there. The only other sector engaging large numbers of women was commerce (23 percent) (see table 4).

The few sizable manufacturing establishments in the country are concentrated largely in Guayaquil and Quito, where establishments having 5 or more employees account for about 4 out of 5 persons working in manufacturing. Scattered throughout the country near the final markets are many small establishments engaged in food processing and in the storage of perishable goods. Also included under manufacturing are the many small handicraft establishments found in most provinces. The chief concentrations are found in Cañar and Azuay Provinces, the center of Panama hat fabrication, and in Imbabura Province, where the well-known Otavalo handloomed textiles are made.

Provisional data from the 1962 census indicated that 41.2 percent of the economically active population were self-employed; 2.4 percent were employers; 46.2 percent were paid employees; 7.5 percent were unpaid family workers; and 2.7 percent were unclassified.

A 1961 estimate showed that in agriculture 45 percent were self-employed; 42 percent, paid employees; and 13 percent, unpaid family workers. In manufacturing the corresponding figures were 32 percent, 63 percent and 5 percent, and in commerce 51 percent, 48 percent and 1 percent, respectively.

Comparison between the 1950 and 1962 industrial distribution of labor indicates a considerable decrease in total employment in manufacturing, which seems to reflect the decrease in the small handicraft industries. The most notable gains in employment occurred in construction and in the services and public administration field.

Except for artisans there are few skilled workers in the country.

The nature of both agriculture and manufacturing, consisting almost entirely of small enterprises, creates little demand for or development of technical skills. The preference for white-collar employment and the limited educational attainment of the people as a whole also inhibit the training of technicians. Technical training schools provide chiefly secretarial or accounting courses. There are, however, five technical schools, operating with the support of the United States Agency for International Development (AID), that provide training in such subjects as carpentry, drafting, printing, ironwork, auto repair, electricity and radio.

GOVERNMENT AND LABOR POLICIES

The Constitution of 1946 includes several articles setting forth labor policies. Article 42 provides that 2 of the 12 functional senators elected to the upper legislative chamber represent labor. Article 170 states that work is compulsory for all, and Article 174 obliges the state to provide for full employment. Article 185 lists the fundamental rules which govern labor laws in the country. These rules require equal pay for equal work, regardless of sex, race, nationality or religion. Also provided are a minimum wage; an 8-hour day; a 44-hour week, with extra pay for night work and overtime; and a paid annual vacation. Special work rules apply to mothers, and employment of minors under 14 years of age is prohibited. In addition, there is a provision calling for profit sharing by employees. Other rules legalize the right to unionize, to strike and to lockout, and they provide for arbitration tribunals for labor disputes (see ch. 13, Constitution and Government; ch. 21, Labor Relations and Organization).

Specific provisions to implement the general rules in article 185 of the Constitution are included in the Labor Code of 1938, amended by seven legislative decrees (the most recent issued on November 16, 1964).

The military government has been active in the formulation of labor policy. Early in its tenure it issued a communique to the military and civilian authorities calling for more sympathetic attitudes toward the problems of labor. In another early action it established a commission to amend the Labor Code—for the first time since 1950. After the revision had been promulgated, a group of textile workers urged the military government to stay in power until the vital needs of the workers were met.

Income and Wages

Cash incomes are extremely low. In 1957 the average annual per capita income for the lower-paid 75 percent of the economically active population was S/1,615. For the next higher 24 percent, consisting of salaried white-collar workers, small merchants and medium-scale farmers, it was S/3,133. The top 1 percent received annually S/33,156 per capita—over 20 times more than that received by all the other groups.

The Labor Code specifies factors which must be considered in arriving at a minimum wage, which may vary between provinces. Minimums are worked out between employers and employees in a particular industry or occupation with the help of government minimum wage commissioners. A number of these commissioners have been established in many different occupations, and in 1960 a minimum daily wage was established for agricultural workers in the Sierra. Indicative of these minimums was one established in 1953 for tanners of S/750 per month for a master, S/660 for assistants and S/600 for helpers. Another typical minimum was established in 1955 for shoemakers—S/540 per month for masters and S/360 for helpers. The 1960 minimum wage set for Sierra farmhands was S/90 per month for tenant farmers (huasipungueros; see Glossary) and S/180 per month for daylaborers. These minimum wages have not changed through the years; fortunately, the rise in cost of living has been small.

Actual wages paid are often above legal hourly minimums, particularly when a person works for a full week. Persons working a 5-day week in industry are frequently paid for 6 days of work, and those working a 5½-day week, for a 7-day week. For agricultural work the wages paid in the Oriente are about double those paid in the Sierra and in the coastal region. In the case of seasonal work, the hourly wages in the Oriente are much higher than those paid in the nearby Sierra. In spite of the low minimums prescribed for the Sierra, many of the workers there do not receive regular payment on completion of the work, but are paid only after the crop is sold. United States firms maintain a high wage level.

Even in nonagricultural pursuits there is a considerable variation of pay in the different parts of the country. This can be appreciated by considering the monthly salaries of persons covered by the social security system or by the governmental pension systems, although this sample, comprising only 12.7 percent of employed persons, may not be wholly representative (see table 5).

According to the Labor Code, the standard working day in industry is 8 hours, and the work week 44 hours. All overtime work must be agreed to in writing between labor and management and must be recompensed at a rate of pay and a half during week days and at double the hourly rate after midnight or after noon on Saturday. The Labor Code also requires that an annual 15-day vacation with full pay be provided and requires paid days off for 11 designated national holidays. In accord with the profit-sharing provision of the Constitution, the code requires that in

Table 5. *Monthly Salaries in Ecuador of Persons Covered by Social Security or Government Pensions, 1962 and 1963*

Region	1962		1963	
	Number of persons covered	Average salary[1]	Number of persons covered	Average salary[1]
Sierra	92,245	872	97,837	[2]987
Coast	83,270	1,077	84,846	1,106
Oriente	1,783	800	1,989	816

[1]In sucres; for value of the sucre, see Glossary.
[2]Increase caused chiefly by an increase in government salaries.

Source: Adapted from Banco Central del Ecuador, *Memoria del Gerente General: Correspondiente al Ejercicio de 1963*, p. 73.

industry all employers, except in the artisan trades, apportion 7 percent of the annual net profits among employees.

Health and Safety

The Labor Code requires that employers provide clean, well-ventilated and well-lighted workplaces. Smoking is forbidden in all factory work areas. Many of the larger establishments not only conform to these rudimentary requirements but also provide lavatories, first-aid equipment and periodic medical examinations for their employees. Many smaller concerns ignore the rules, but all are legally liable to compensate for injuries or occupational diseases.

Expectant mothers must be given 3 weeks' leave with pay both before and after childbirth. Sick leave at half pay, up to 2 months per year, when supported by medical certificates, must be paid.

Unemployment and Job Security

In an editorial appearing in *El Telégrafo* of Guayaquil on August 23, 1964, entitled "Unemployment, a Grave Problem," it was pointed out that, although available data were of doubtful accuracy, the chronic unemployment rate was serious and much in excess of the theoretically acceptable rate of 3 percent. The best estimates by labor experts have indicated that, in 1960, 9 percent of the available labor force was unemployed and seeking work. This rate has gradually increased as the large young population reaches working age and as movement from the countryside to the cities continues.

Underemployment is at least as grave a problem. Although the percentage of farmers owning their own land is large by standards of neighboring countries, their holdings, particularly in the Sierra, are generally so small that the average family has more able-bodied workers than are necessary. This condition results in a great waste of manpower and spurs migration to the already overcrowded cities. The proliferation of petty vendors everywhere in the cities amply testifies to the high rate of urban unemployment.

The law provides for a higher level of job security. Legally, an employee may be discharged without severance pay only for proven incompetence or dishonesty. On the other hand, given the widespread unemployment and underemployment, employers can retain employees with few pay raises. Because most establishments are very small, the chances for advancement in pay and job status are also very restricted.

CHAPTER 5

ETHNIC GROUPS AND LANGUAGES

The people derive largely from two basic physical stocks: South American Indian and white (chiefly Mediterranean, originating in Spain). Although elements of both stocks exist relatively unmixed, almost 500 years of intimate contact between the two have resulted in physical admixture displayed by most of the population in some degree. Still a third physical element, African Negro, was introduced by the Spaniards shortly after their conquest of the New World. This group has mixed to a considerable extent with both whites and Indians.

When first intermingling in the New World, none of the major stocks was physically homogeneous. Spaniards, Indians and Negroes all showed broad variations from previous racial crossings in their native lands. The relatively recent assimilation of persons of European and Middle and Far Eastern extraction has added new ingredients to the already heterogeneous physical composition of the country.

Frequent contact among these various peoples has blurred racial lines to a great extent and has impeded investigation of racial past. Estimates of the proportions of the various racial elements of the population are often widely disparate and inconclusive. Figures for whites range between 10 and 15 percent; those for *mestizos* (see Glossary) vary between 22 and 50 percent; for Indians, between 39 and 60 percent; and for the relatively small Negro and mulatto segment, between 3 and 10 percent.

For census purposes the government avoids the category of "race" and lists instead the number of Indian-language speakers. Although this listing has tacit racial implications, it is neither explicit nor accurate, for it fails to account for distinctions between Negroes and whites, both of which groups are Spanish-speaking. There are, in addition, many Indians for whom Spanish is the first if not the exclusive language.

In any event, the correlation of race and socially defined ethnic identity is tenuous at best. It holds true among Negroes, who are felt to constitute an ethnic group almost wholly on racial criteria. Their culture, including language and religion is predominantly Hispanic with Indian overtones, and little remains of their ancestral African culture. The other principal "racial" terms in common use—white, *mestizo* and Indian—have ceased to reflect principally biological heritage and have also come to have social and cultural meaning (see ch. 6, Social Structure).

From the point of view of culture, persons socially classified as "whites" do constitute a single group. The differences among the various segments of the white population are relatively minor and reflect primarily regional and class variations. Whites, in general, share a similar Hispanic cultural tradition and a common participation in the national society.

Within the group socially defined as "white," however, there is a wide range of racial background—from persons of pure European extraction to those of largely Indian or, very rarely, Negro background. The apparent inconsistency in usage is generally recognized, and such terms as *mestizo* or, more popularly, *cholo*, are sometimes used to describe "whites" of visibly mixed background. Language, way of life and position in the social structure tend to override the biological criteria. An overwhelming majority of *cholos* share the same Hispanic culture as other "whites," speak Spanish exclusively and differentiate themselves sharply from the Indians. The term *cholo* is therefore used primarily in reference to individuals of obvious Indian ancestry, rather than to any other group.

The term "Indian," applied generically, masks a broad spectrum of cultural variation and social identity. One authority, the anthropologist Alfredo Costales Samaniego, counts no fewer than 698 separate Indian groups, many markedly different from one another. Unlike the Hispanic segments—the whites and, to a lesser extent, the Negroes—the mass of the Indians do not acknowledge a broad ethnic unity. Loyalty and identity are focused on a tribal, communal or regional group.

Government-sponsored research, which recognizes the variety of Indian groups, demonstrates perhaps, a greater sophistication regarding cultural distinctiveness than is the case in many other Latin American countries. Nevertheless, the government has grouped the Indians together for the purpose of legislation and government aid, and its failure to account for differences has often thwarted attempts to implement social and economic reforms. Most programs aimed at effecting change are directed at the Indians more as a depressed social segment than as a distinct people with divergent languages and ways of life.

Broadly conceived, the most pronounced division of Indian cultures is that which exists between Sierra inhabitants and those of the lowlands, both on the Coast and in the Oriente. The highland Indians have had continuous contact with Hispanic society and have assumed many Hispanic cultural elements as their own. This Hispanic assimilation, coupled with the cultural variety exhibited by the numerous Sierra groups, often invalidates some of the more common stereotypes made by the casual observer. It is often asserted, for example, that Indians do not wear shoes, sleep in beds or eat butter. Yet exceptions to these rules are numerous, and the rules are often equally applicable to poor rural whites in certain regions.

In the Oriente the cultural contrast between whites and Indians is much more pronounced, for the indigenous inhabitants have been less directly affected by the dominant Hispanic society. In the relatively isolated environment of the coastal lowlands the few remaining Indians resemble closely the peoples of the Oriente in their material way of life.

SIERRA INDIANS

The Ecuadorian Sierra, traversing the country from north to south, is a belt, about 60 miles at its widest point, formed by two parallel ranges enclosing a series of intermontane basins. The basins are separated from one another by transverse ridges or hills. Within these basins relatively advanced cultures developed in pre-Colombian times. The Monjashuaico ruins in the province of Cuenca are possibly the earliest remains in highland Ecuador of the first farmers, dated at around 1000 B. C. Throughout most of the Sierra cultural influences from Colombia and possibly from Central America are more in evidence than those of Peruvian origin, before the Inca period. The Ecuadorian peoples did not develop the high level of technical competence and political organization characteristic of their neighbors to the south.

The Ecuadorian Andes provided the native peoples with fertile valleys in which to pursue agriculture. Each valley was a relatively well-defined and protectable area which, at the same time, was not isolated from contacts with other highland valleys and the lowlands. Developing as similar, but separate societies, the various groups remained independent of each other until the Incas began their conquest, shortly after the middle of the fifteenth century.

Although the Incas ruled the region, setting up a second capital of their empire at Quito (the population center of the Quitu tribe), they never succeeded completely in dominating the various tribes and destroying all vestiges of their cultural uniqueness. Time was against their enterprise of conquest, for first a civil war between two imperial factions and then the arrival of the Spaniards diverted them from their aim. When the Spaniards moved north from Peru into Ecuador, they found several willing allies—the Cañaris of the southern Sierra being perhaps the most significant—who sought the overthrow of the Incas (see ch. 3, Historical Setting).

What the Incas had failed to do, the Spaniards did more or less accomplish—imposing a social and cultural homogeneity on the various highland Indian groups. Even the Quechua language, which the Incas had introduced, did not come into universal use until the Spanish missionaries adopted it as their lingua franca. From the beginning the Spaniards began to implant a new culture among the Indians, the most notable features of which were the Roman Catholic religion, a distinct local political organization and European crops, animals, tools and methods of cultivation. The Indians had little choice but to accept most of these innovations, but at the same time they adapted them to their own culture.

The most effective cultural homogenizer of the hitherto diverse Indian groups was their common status of subjugation to the white overlords. The only possible defense against total domination by the Spaniards was withdrawal, but this was for most impossible. The *encomienda* (see Glossary) of the conquerors and, after independence, the *hacienda* system served to subordinate the native to the demands of the whites. He could withdraw from the dominant society no further than his own hut.

For centuries the Sierra Indians have been dealt with as a single pool of subject labor and usually treated with uniform contempt. In the twentieth century, Ecuadorian writers have referred to them as a "natural resource." Pursuing similar occupations, constituting a single socioeconomic class and subject to the same influences, most now share a generally uniform way of life. Once-distinct tribes, such as the Quitus, Paltas, Cañaris and Panzaleos, are remembered only in an occasional place name.

From this common social experience the highland Indians developed a uniform attitude toward whites and, to a considerable extent, a uniform system of values. They did not, however, become a cohesive group with a common ethnic identity, because of the many social and economic factors, such as the lack of easy communication and the necessity of protecting their own small community interests against outside threats. In fact, the number of distinct groups has probably increased since pre-Hispanic times.

Minor cultural differences continue to distinguish the various Sierra Indian groups from one another. There are differences in dress design, art styles, house types, methods of technology, religious ritual and belief and in magic and curing practices (see ch. 11, Religion). Also present, but less obvious to the casual observer, are distinctions in certain attitudes and values.

One of the most distinctive highland Indian groups is the

Otavaleños of Imbabura Province, known throughout the country as weavers and vendors of fine woolens. Success in commercial weaving has done much to raise their level of living. Many Otavaleños enjoy greater material comfort than neighboring whites of the lower class. As a possible result of this fact, they display less humility and greater independence than is normally characteristic of the Sierra Indians.

The attitudes and values of the Salasacas of Tungurahua and the Saraguros of Loja also differ markedly from those of the great bulk of Sierra Indians. The 2,000 or more Salasacas are all freeholding peasants; none of them are *huasipungeros* (see Glossary). Not beholden to white landlords for their subsistence, they display a great deal of pride and independence. A similar situation prevails among the Saraguros, who enjoy the additional advantage of greater geographical isolation. The only Indians residing in the province, they have used the rugged but fertile terrain to their advantage and have maintained a large measure of independence while simultaneously accepting certain material benefits from the Hispanic culture.

Most Sierra Indians are rural based; only about 2 percent dwell in settlements of more than 2,500 persons. In some provinces, such as Chimborazo and Imbabura, they constitute over 50 percent of the rural population.

Dedicated primarily to subsistence agriculture, the Indians rely principally on vegetable products for their diet. Grain is the staple—barley and, to a lesser extent, corn, quinoa and wheat. These, along with such vegetables as potatoes, cabbage and squash, are used to create innumerable varieties of soup, which is the most common culinary method in the Sierra. Beans are the principal protein source, but on special occasions a guinea pig may be roasted or fried. Although most families keep chickens, eggs are seldom consumed; more commonly, eggs are used as currency in the market. Among the more affluent Otavaleños, a variety of canned goods may be included in the larder.

Manzanilla and various other herb teas are drunk as hot beverages, and *aguardiente* (a raw distilled liquor made of sugarcane extract) is the most frequently consumed alcoholic drink. The more traditional *chicha* (a fermented corn beer made from yucca) is still consumed in many regions. At the weekly market many Indians now purchase bottled beer and soft drinks.

No description of an Indian settlement would be consistently applicable throughout the Sierra. Differences may be the result of custom, or they may arise because of geographic or economic circumstances. The few Indians living in the larger urban or commercial centers dominated by whites generally live in the poorer communities on the fringes of such centers.

In rural areas communities may be either dispersed or nucleated. Among the Salasaca, for example, the family occupies a hut or a small cluster of dwellings surrounded by its farmlands and widely separated from neighbors. There is no real village, but the numerous inhabitants of a neighborhood recognize a social and political unity focused on a small cluster of publicly maintained buildings—the church, the meeting hall, the school, etc.

In the nucleated villages that are found in other parts of the Sierra the orientation is also toward a cluster of public buildings. Around these, however, the houses of the inhabitants are grouped more closely. Any commercial establishments, stores or bars are generally located in the vicinity. The larger houses, inhabited by the more affluent members of the community, are often found close to this focal point. Settlement patterns are irregular; individual houses or small clusters of dwellings are usually oriented according to the owner's preference or in conformity with the irregular terrain. Among the commercially active Otavaleños some of the larger villages have such urban trappings as electricity and water piped to individual homes or at least to several centrally located spigots.

Domestic dwellings in any given village are usually more or less similar, but a variety of forms and shapes are found throughout the highlands. Materials used in construction include adobe, mud, stone, twigs and branches, grass and, very rarely, lumber. The orientation toward the public buildings lends a semblance of pattern to an otherwise irregular settlement. The tendency is toward small clusters of huts inhabited by an extended family. At times the farmlands that are worked are some distance from the village. In some parts of Chimborazo Province, Indians live in semisubterranean dwellings or small manmade caves dug into a hillside. Adobe-walled, tiled-roofed houses are preferred throughout the highlands, and whitewashing is an indication of higher status. For many, however, the dwelling is a simple wattle-and-daub hut with a thatched roof.

Few houses have window openings; the doorway and cracks in the walls and roof provide light and ventilation. Some huts have only a single room, but those who can afford it have a separate section for sleeping and for storing goods. Many huts have porches, where family activity is focused. Much of the cooking is done there, and among the Otavaleños, the loom is kept there. Children generally play on the hard-packed dirt patio in front of the house, where an adobe oven and a chicken run or a pigsty may be located (see ch. 8, Living Conditions).

The amount of furniture is generally small, consisting of wooden stools, platforms of wood on which storage chests or baskets for grain are kept and wooden hooks on the wall for hanging assorted items. Beds are usually lacking, and some observers cite poverty as the reason for this. In fact, however, most Indians are accustomed to sleeping upon mats or blankets on the floor and those who acquire beds often do so only for reasons of prestige.

Most persons are at least loosely tied to the cash economy, and many domestic skills such as pottery making and weaving are giving way to the purchase of manufactured goods. Aluminum pots and pans are seen around the fireplace, along with wooden spoons and earthen waterjugs. Clothing is usually made from factory manufactured goods, but back-strap looms and, among the Otavaleños, full looms made by white craftsmen are found in many homes. Sewing machines are becoming increasingly more common, and transistor radios are widely distributed.

The basic costume, for both sexes, is fairly standard, but many details of dress vary from group to group. Nowhere in the highlands has aboriginal dress survived. The Indian costume is, rather, an adaptation of colonial Spanish styles. For men white, grey or dark *calzones* (shin-length trousers) and a long-sleeved shirt or blouse and a cloth or rope belt constitute the usual costume. Exceptions include the dark knee-length shorts worn by the Saraguros. Modern *mestizo* clothing, consisting of manufactured cotton pants and shirts, sweaters and jackets, is worn by many. Woolen ponchos are worn practically everywhere, but color and design may vary from group to group. Headgear also varies widely, as does hair style, which ranges from the moderately short cut of the Saraguro to the long single braid of the Otavaleño.

Women's clothing is even more distinctive; though the long, wraparound skirt is fairly basic, each local group or village differs according to preferred color, with additional differences between ordinary household dress and market or festival clothing. Blouses, whether handmade or purchased in the market, are usually embroidered to suit the tastes of the individual and the custom of the group. Most women wear blankets draped around the shoulders. Often the manner in which the shawl is fastened— along with the hair style—is indicative of a woman's marital status. The headpiece may be a distinctively draped cloth, usually topped by a felt hat. Footwear is generally worn by men and more rarely by women. It most often consists of sandals made from old rubber tires.

Except among the Otavaleño there are very few full-time non-agricultural specialists. An occasional individual may enter into such commercial activities as storekeeper or middleman, buying surplus agricultural products, but such a move is usually a part of the transformation from Indian to *mestizo* status. Some Indians are learning trades and finding work as carpenters, masons or truckdrivers, but they are still few in number, for the social, cultural and economic problems to be faced in abandoning agriculture are great.

Even the Otavaleños, for whom weaving is a principal source of income, continue to farm. For many, weaving is carried on only during the dry season, and sales are limited to weekend market days. Some of the young Otavaleño men turn to full-time weaving and selling, but usually after a few years they return to the dual activity of farming and weaving. Nevertheless, the Otavaleños are a rare example of native nonagricultural enterprise.

Weaving is not unique to the Otavaleños, for many groups weave for domestic use, selling occasional surpluses in the market. Such activities provide only a small amount of extra cash, however, for these groups rely almost exclusively on agriculture for their subsistence.

Most Indians not living on the *haciendas* consider themselves owners of their own land, although legally perfect titles are rare, and many have no written titles at all. In areas where villages hold lands in common, lands are apportioned to the members of the community, and each family produces for its own consumption. Such lands can be passed on in inheritance, but they cannot be sold. If a family dies out or moves, the land reverts to the village and is given to another family. Communal landholding is not so common as once thought, and where it exists, an individual's portion may be insufficient for his needs. As is the case for many small landowners, such persons may supplement their income by working as wage laborers.

Huasipungueros, settled on the *haciendas,* usually live in small clusters of huts which constitute communities, often of related persons. In exchange for a house site, a small portion of land for his own use and a small cash remuneration, a *huasipunguero* must labor several days per week for the owner. The average pay of the *huasipunguero* is S/3 (in 1965, S/18.5 equaled US$1—see Glossary) per day in areas where social legislation is customarily observed. Thus, in these areas, if the land apportioned to a *huasipunguero* family is fertile, this wage—amounting to about S/800 per year—may be sufficient. Usually, however, the *huasipunguero* receives the least desirable territory, land which is stony, dry, hilly, overworked and, therefore, unprofitable.

The *huasipunguero* may also be expected to use his own animals in his employer's work and members of his family to serve as unpaid domestic help in the owner's house; these requirements are expressly prohibited by law, however. The *huasipunguero* is permitted to graze his animals on *hacienda* lands, but he is generally cautious about letting them multiply, for owners have been known to confiscate such "surplus," on the grounds that the land is being overgrazed. Although the economic status of a private landowner may be no higher than that of a *huasipunguero* or wage laborer, a great deal of prestige attaches to ownership, and most Indians therefore strive to own their own land. Most Otavaleños, for example, do not put their earnings from weaving into more looms and greater production, but use them to purchase land. So strong is the value placed on land that the desire for ownership exists independently of the desire to elevate the level of living. Where Indians have taken advantage of government-sponsored agricultural colonies, they are apparently satisfied with mere subsistence agriculture and seldom produce to the limit of the land's capacity.

Although the agricultural calendar differs slightly according to region, beans, quinoa, peas, squash and melons are generally planted along with corn in early fall. Barley and wheat are planted at different times of the year. Barley is more than merely a staple crop, it is a way of life for some Sierra Indians. An Indian from a barley-growing area plants it even when it is uneconomical, and his reaction to a fertile, productive farm on which other cash crops are grown is sympathy for the owner, who is apparently unable to grow barley.

Methods of agriculture are inefficient by modern standards. Oxen and wooden plows are often used on level ground, and hoes and digging sticks are used on steeper slopes. The digging stick most characteristic of the Sierra is a large ovoid paddle to which a metal point is attached. Irrigation is rare, except on the lands of the whites, and fertilizer is either unknown or inefficiently used (see ch. 19, Agriculture).

Central to the social organization of the Sierra Indians is the nuclear family, comprising a father, mother and their unmarried children, who share a common dwelling and produce as a unit. When the nuclear family is unable to maintain independence and self-sufficiency, it looks to closely related kinsmen. The small clusters of homes characteristic of settlement patterns both in nucleated and extended communities are usually occupied by extended family groups. Although much has been written about the propensity of the Indians for extending mutual aid, detailed investigations show that such aid is extended almost exclusively to kinsmen and that reciprocity is expected, whether the activity be house construction, harvesting or aid in preparing for a ceremony or feast.

On the community level social interaction is not so much on an individual as a familial basis; a person is integrated into the community as a member of his family. Interaction may be superficial and casual, as among widely dispersed neighbors, or frequent and more intense in compact villages. Relations are seldom intimate, however, except among related persons. There exists among some groups a type of formalized friendship established between unrelated persons of the same sex, but an individual seldom has more than one of these in a lifetime.

Since 1937, when the Law of Communes was promulgated, formal government of Indian communities has been invested in the *cabildo*. This elected body consists of a president, vice president, secretary, treasurer and four other members. The traditional system, in which appointed local officials were appointed by and responsible to the *teniente político* (political lieutenant), a white person residing in the parish seat, continues to operate simultaneously (see ch. 13, Constitution and Government).

The *cabildo* is ineffective partly because the office was established in accordance with Western ideals which often have little relevance for the Indian. Universal suffrage, elected officials and town meetings are often foreign to Indian tradition. Elected though it might be, the *cabildo* is seldom representative. In many villages it has been implemented because the Indians have developed a habit of acceding to white demands. They see it as a foreign organization, however, and lack confidence in it. Consequently, rather than elect officers to be effective leaders in internal affairs, Indian villagers commonly choose men who, they feel, will be acceptable to the dominant white society.

More central to real and effective civic authority is an informal system in which leadership is invested in persons of prestige. Requisites for leadership include knowledge of and involvement in community affairs, but the community must be certain that the individual's actions will be directed toward the benefit and defense of the community and not used for personal gain. Leaders are not expected to govern, but are merely to ascertain the wishes of the majority and speak for it. The dominant, forceful personality is abhorred; a leader must display, instead, a reluctant willingness to accept responsibilities. Many of the qualities of leadership within the Indian system of values are the antithesis of those required of the public officeseeker.

A number of outside agencies also exert influence on the Indian community. These include the Church or, more specifically, the local priest, a number of reform groups and the International Labor Organization's Andean Mission. The last-mentioned organization has become increasingly active, and its requests are often seen as demands of the dominant society which must be at least superficially complied with (see ch. 8, Living Conditions).

In their association with whites outside the community the Indians assume a passive, submissive role. This holds true even among the relatively independent Otavaleños, Saraguros and Sala-sacas. A habit of deference is instilled from childhood, and Indians speaking with whites almost instinctively remove their hats, lower their eyes and speak in soft tones. In the friendly environs of his own village, however, the Indian is often disdainful of the whites, making them objects of ridicule and the butts of jokes.

Religion plays an important part in the life of the community. Nominally Catholic, most Indians accept the faith insofar as they understand it. For the most part, however, their religion is characterized by doctrinal ignorance. Native beliefs are often blended with Christianity, as saints assume the attributes of indigenous spirits. Priests seldom live in Indian villages, and they visit only on important feast days. The authority of the priest is generally accepted, however, as much because of his role as representative of the dominant society as for any recognition of his religious office (see ch. 11, Religion).

Most religious activity centers on the *fiesta* calendar; a town may hold between 6 and 12 celebrations a year, but only 1 or 2 are of major importance. Each *fiesta* has a *prioste* (sponsor), who assumes most of the financial burden for food, drink, fireworks, church decorations and cost of the mass and who is nominated by the community or by the priest. Although costs tend to run as high as S/1,000 for the most important *fiestas* of the year, few *priostes* refuse to serve. There is much community pressure to accept, and the expense is often outweighed by the attendant prestige. As an added incentive the *prioste* can use the occasion to poke fun at whites, for the traditional ritual he performs is often little more than a caricature of those Hispanic traits which the Indian finds most ludicrous or offensive.

Religion plays an important role in the life cycle of the individual. The most meaningful events among the Sierra Indians are associated with important religious ritual. Baptism is the occasion for introducing a newborn member to the community, and both the spiritual element and the celebration itself, with its dancing and drinking, are considered important. Furthermore, the selection of godparents is important for the ceremonial kinship ties then established (see ch. 7, Family).

First Holy Communion and Confirmation, normally important in Catholic life, are of lesser consequence to the Indians, although they often undergo the ceremony. Marriage, on the other hand, serves as a rite of passage in which the two main participants undergo an important change of status within the community. Marriage signifies maturity and demonstrates the individual's willingness to accept responsibility. The status achieved cannot be attained by single persons, nor can it be lost by the man concerned should the marriage dissolve. Women, however, fall into disgrace if they are abandoned, whatever the reason. As a result, therefore, few Indian men undergo a second ceremony; usually they merely seek another partner after the loss of a mate.

Death also involves religious ritual, and if the services of a priest are not available, usually individuals in the village act as part-time prayer specialists. Native custom demands that a feast be held as part of the funerary ritual.

The life of the average Indian revolves largely around his family. Women give birth in their own home, usually with a number of midwives in attendance. Almost from birth the baby is carried about in his mother's shawl. The infant receives a great deal of attention for the first 2 years and is the object of the entire family's affection.

During early childhood the individual spends his time at play, usually in the company of brothers and sisters or cousins. Gradually, he begins his informal training in the adult activities which he is expected eventually to perform. Boys receive training in agricultural work by accompanying their fathers to the fields from about the age of 6. Girls begin even earlier to learn domestic duties. Although the span between childhood and adulthood is a short one, the transition is an easy one.

Unmarried children continue to reside in their parental household, producing and consuming as part of the unit. Whereas the selection of a mate is usually left to the individual, help is sought from the family in making marriage arrangements and later in establishing an independent household. Ties with the family of origin remain close for life, and among most Indian groups all children receive at least some portion of the inheritance at the death of the parents.

Life for the average highland Indian is difficult, and the family serves as the only reliable defense against the frustrations and hardships that are his usual lot. He relies on their care when ill and seeks their aid when destitute. The Indian faces life less as an individual than as a member of a family, and in its absence he has little hope for survival. As a result most of his efforts are directed toward assuring the continued existence of this primary group (see ch. 7, Family).

THE COAST

Of the once-numerous tribes the only remaining Indian groups in the western lowlands are the Cayapas and the Colorados. The total number of Indians residing in the area has been augmented recently by a few Yumbos who migrated to the region from the Oriente and by Coayqueres who wandered south from neighboring Colombia.

All that remains of the Malablas, Wassu, Manteños and other groups of the indigenous coastal population are the now-acculturated fishermen and plantation workers who make up the bulk of the rural population. These persons, called *montuvios*, have completely lost their Indian identity, and, except for regional distinctiveness, there is little to distinguish them from white rural inhabitants throughout Ecuador.

A number of the Negroes who occupy the region pursue a life similar to that of the *montuvios*. Some are subsistence fishermen in coastal villages or migratory plantation workers; a number have found employment in the larger cities and ports; but most are occupied in agriculture, some as sharecroppers and some as independent squatters or smallholders. In general, their economy is seldom beyond subsistence level. The areas they occupy are usually devoid of Indians, but the Negroes are at the same general low social level.

Colorados and Cayapas

The Colorados and Cayapas speak mutually unintelligible languages of the Chibchan family. They know of each others' existence and have occasional contact, but no permanent ties. Both tribes are small in numbers, but whereas the Colorados are losing their cultural distinctiveness through frequent contact with highland Ecuadorians, the greater isolation of the Cayapa has permitted them to preserve a more traditional way of life.

Agriculture, supported by hunting and fishing, forms the base of their subsistence. Plantains, sweet manioc, yams, peppers, sugarcane and various fruits are the principal crops. The Cayapas also encourage the growth of wild food plants by weeding and care. Although they keep such domestic animals as pigs and chickens, the Cayapas are less reliant on them than are the Colorados.

Neither group lives in villages, although at dispersed locations a church with its small cluster of houses can be found. The houses are occupied on those infrequent occasions when a Catholic priest visits to celebrate mass; the rest of the year the Indians are dispersed throughout the jungle.

Cayapa and Colorado dwellings are roughly similar, except that those of the Cayapas are elevated on 6- to 12-foot poles. Unwalled structures with large palm thatch roofs supported by posts, the dwellings are usually divided into two parts—one for cooking, the other for sleeping. Hammocks and small handmade wooden seats usually constitute the total inventory of furniture.

The Cayapas continue to manufacture much of what they use: woven cotton cloth, pottery, wooden household items, tools for fishing and agriculture, and canoes. The Colorados are becoming increasingly dependent on factory manufactured articles.

The Colorados are so named for the red body paint which they use. Women confine painting to the face. Their hair is worn long and uncovered. Their costume consists of a knee-length, wrap-around skirt and a shawl thrown over the shoulder and tied at the neck. The men wear a similar skirt and a cloth draped over one shoulder. Their hair, cut at ear length, is parted in the middle, banged and plastered with red dye. Silver bracelets usually adorn their arms. Cayapa men wear a garment somewhat similar to a bathing suit and short-sleeved shirts of colored prints. The skirts of the women are longer than those used by the Colorado, and the upper portion of the body is left bare.

New roads and increased colonization into the Santo Domingo area inhabited by the Colorado have placed them on the fringes of the national economic system. They are efficient farmers, and many of their products, especially bananas, now reach the national market. Some depend almost completely on cash income and even hire labor. For added income members of the tribe who attend the weekly Santo Domingo market permit tourists to take their pictures for a fee. The Cayapas have not yet become involved in the national economy beyond the sale to traders of rubber and nuts extracted from the forest. Recently they have also been selling some of their domestic manufactures, such as mats and basketry.

The political organization that once existed among the Colorado and still prevails among the Cayapa divides the tribe into three units, each with a chief or governor and subordinate officials. These offices are inherited but must be validated by the Catholic priest. Under this system, imposed during colonial times, the chief actually enjoys far more prestige than power.

The basic social unit remains the household. Husband, wife and dependent children cooperate in production and share in consumption. Division of labor is not rigid, and both men and women work at agriculture. Hunting and fishing, however, are the province of men, whereas women are concerned with domestic duties.

When help outside of the household is needed, it is sought from the extended family, which inhabits the small cluster of dwellings making up a settlement. All the men in the settlement work at clearing new land for agriculture and reciprocate in constructing houses. The effective kinship circle is small, seldom containing more than a dozen persons.

Christianity has been long established among both groups, and the religion of the Colorado and Cayapa Indians displays a syncretism of native and European spiritual elements. While similar in form to the spiritual tradition of modern highland Indians, the content differs somewhat. The patron saint of the village, for example—important among the Quechua-speaking highland Indians—is of little consequence in the western lowlands. On the other hand, the traditional Christian *fiestas* of Easter and Christmas have greater significance. On the whole, most religious practice and ritual, while containing elements of Christianity, are left in the hands of the chief, shaman or family head.

Negroes

Introduced into Ecuador soon after the conquest, the Negroes have remained concentrated primarily on the Coast and in the Chota River valley of Esmeraldas Province. The number of Negroes in Ecuador was extremely small until 1573, when Philip II of Spain forbade the transport of Indian laborers from one environmental extreme to another. After that time, Negroes were especially valued for work on the coastal sugar plantations. A few of the slaves had come directly from Africa, but most were descendants of Bantu speakers who had already been introduced to European culture in the West Indies and purchased in the slave markets of the Antilles.

Negroes have never constituted a large proportion of the population, and, given constant contact with whites and Indians, the percentage of racially pure Negroes is small. Dispersed throughout Ecuador, their density on the Coast has always been greater than in the Highlands. In 1781, Quito and Guayaquil each had slightly over 2,000, but this number constituted only .06 percent of the population of Quito whereas it constituted .6 percent of Guayaquil's population. The number of Negroes increased to 7,831 by the time slavery was abolished in 1856. Their current numbers are estimated at about 30,000.

In slave times procreation among Negroes was not encouraged as it was more economical to import slaves than to raise them. Mingling between the sexes was therefore restrained, and records of 1825 list only 1,800 of the almost 7,000 Negroes as married. After Simón Bolívar recommended their liberation in 1825 there was a marked increase in their population.

Despite centuries of enslavement—as contrasted with the "freedom" enjoyed by the Indian—the Negroes hold a slightly higher position than that of the indigenous population. They occupy one of the lower rungs of the social scale, and their relationship with whites is never in doubt; for example, some workers, upon entering a *hacienda,* still ask the benediction of the master. Nevertheless, the Negro is characteristically less subservient than his Indian counterpart. There are few elements in Negro culture in Ecuador that can be classified, with any certainty, as purely African. For the most part their material existence is similar to that of their *mestizo* neighbors.

Agricultural products make up a large part of their staple diet. Yucca, sweet potato, beans, plantains, sugarcane, tomatoes, mangoes and avocados are important items. Most families keep pigs; fish is a major staple along the Coast, but goats, which provide both meat and milk, abound in the Chota region.

There is a strong preference for nucleated villages. Settlements lack any significant pattern, and there are seldom any planned streets or paths. Some houses are round and have conical roofs; others are rectangular and gabled. Most are constructed of interwoven saplings filled in with mud and have roofs of thatch. In the Chota area one corner of the rectangle may be open, creating a low, walled porch. Often, dwellings contain two rooms, one for sleeping and the other for cooking and other domestic activities. The few whitewashed homes indicate the higher status of their occupants.

Negroes practice few native handicrafts. The rather distinctive short-necked spherical pottery jar found in most Negro homes in the Chota are made by Indian potters. Gourds, grown and used for kitchenware, are usually undecorated. On the Coast the Negroes engaged in fishing activities are skillful at the manufacture and repair of nets. Agricultural implements, including Indian-style digging sticks, also are made by Negroes.

Some women's clothing is made at home of manufactured goods, and in general there is little difference between Negro clothing and that of other rural dwellers. Grey or brown cotton trousers and a white shirt buttoned to the neck is the common garb of most men. This may be topped by a grey or blue jacket. Shoes are worn primarily on market day. Women wear either a dress or a blouse and skirt which falls just below the knee. Colors range from black to bright flowered prints. Their shawls and scarves are often made by Indians. Women customarily carry loads on their heads rather than on their backs as do the Indians.

Except for a few full-time fishermen, agriculture is the basis of Negro economic life. The few who own their own lands have small parcels, and they are no better off economically than those who work for others on either a cash or share basis. Although racial barriers do not prevent the Negro from engaging in other than agricultural activities, social circumstances generally prevent him from doing so. The Negro and the Indian provide most of the manual labor. Negroes, however, are more tied to the cash economy than are the Indians, in spite of the extensive bartering within Negro communities.

Most Negro communities are satellites to white-dominated centers or form a part of the administrative structure of plantations. As such, their local government is generally informal, and leadership is based more upon individual prestige than vested in elected officials. Village festivals, while not as highly structured as those of Indian communities, foster some degree of solidarity among the inhabitants. The family is by far the most important social unit. Most intense is the cooperation of the joint family, that is, cooperation between a father and his sons. When a father aids a newly married son to erect a separate residence, it is usually close to his own. The tendency to marry women of neighboring villages creates loose social ties among several communities in a region.

All are nominally Catholic. The Church plays a considerable role in the life of the women, but men have little to do with the institution, though many manifest, less formally, strong religious or spiritual sentiments. The pride often displayed by Indians in the local religious edifice is seldom found in the Negro community. Most churches in their regions are the remains of those built centuries before by the Jesuits.

Most *fiestas* and, therefore, a large part of the recreational pattern, center about religious holidays. The feast of the patron saint is not as important as among Indians, and Holy Week, though celebrated, is of minor importance. Christmas, which is often of minor significance among Indians and *mestizos*, is the main festive occasion.

Unique to the Christmas festivities is the *bomba*, a dance form considered by some authorities to be of African origin. The dancing involves rhythmic body movement, and an African-style goatskin drum provides the accompaniment. Music is also a major part of other festive occasions, and the guitar is universally evident. The Negroes also have a rich folk-tale tradition which is an important recreational element.

The Negro life cycle conforms to rural lower-class patterns. Birth, marriage and death rituals are rooted in Ecuadorian peasant Catholicism. Baptism is important in establishing *compadre* relations, and, while church marriage is held to be ideal, many couples establish a consensual union without benefit of either civil or religious authority. Formal education is either nonexistent or minimal; children are trained, through imitation and practice, to fulfill adult roles.

THE ORIENTE

In the hope of carving himself out a domain equal to that of his brother Francisco in Peru, Gonzalo Pizarro explored the Ecuadorian Oriente as early as 1539. In 1560 several small towns were established in the territory of the Quijo, Cofan, Canelo and Jívaro tribes.

Although missionary activities began early, they made little impression until about the middle of the seventeenth century. The vigorous policies of the Jesuits were highly successful for over 100 years, and the Indians were greatly influenced by them.

The introduction of numerous items, such as new types of tools, plants and dress, indirectly affected many other aspects of their culture. Metal tools facilitated canoe making, which, in turn, allowed for easier transportation and intertribal communication.

More efficient agricultural tools and techniques and the introduction of new crops lessened the Indian's dependence on hunting and collecting. These and other changes subsequently affected the social and political organizations of the tribes. Those tribes not directly influenced felt the subsidiary effects of the conquest through the dislocation of tribes to the east by white settlers and explorers.

Until the nineteenth century most of the whites who inhabited this area were missionaries or traders who purchased the raw materials collected by the Indians in the forest. Settlers began entering the area from the highlands, a movement which has received greater impetus in recent years through the construction of new penetration roads. The government is becoming increasingly interested in the possibilities of the eastern tropical lowlands both for its economic potential and as a means of relieving the population pressure of the densely inhabited highlands.

The government has taken little official action on behalf of the lowland Indians. What little work has been done among the indigenous population is left to the religious missionaries who often serve as the only source of education, medical, social and economic aid.

The remaining tribes—Yumbos, Záparos, Jívaros, Aucas and others—are facing destruction of their cultures and rapid assimilation. Those who wish to escape the full impact of white civilization have moved deeper into the jungle. Yumbos who claim land along newly constructed roads, for example, willingly sell out to highland colonizers and pursue their subsistence activities in more isolated areas.

Yumbos

"Yumbo" is a term applied to the 30,000 to 50,000 Quechua-speaking Indians of the Oriente. Unlike the Aucas and Jívaros, both distinct tribes with origins far back in prehistory, the Yumbo group was formed by the acculturation and detribalization of members of many different tribes—Quijos, Canelos and Baezas, among others—after the Spanish conquest. Subject to the pressures and influences of Quechua-speaking white missionaries and traders, the various elements of the Yumbos adopted that language and lost their original tribal identities.

The Yumbos have been a constant object of acculturating forces, first by Spanish religious missionaries and more recently by colonists from the Sierra. Only the relative isolation of the territory they inhabit—an isolation fast disappearing as roads are built—has enabled them to retain their Indian identity. Most women remain monolingual in Quechua, but most men have learned at least rudimentary Spanish.

Dietary staples include yucca, plantains, papaya and pineapples. Some domestic animals, especially chickens, are kept. Fish from the numerous streams and wild boar supplement the vegetable diet. Those living close to transportation and markets occasionally buy rice and beans, but salt is the most regular cash-bought item. The principal alcoholic beverage is *chicha*, made from yucca.

Many Yumbos reside in the larger settlements of the region, such as Napo, Tena, Puyo, Archidona and Baeza. Most, however, live in small communities consisting of a cluster of huts occupied by closely related persons. Villages are moved frequently as the land surrounding them loses its fertility. Dwellings are built from readily accessible materials, such as bamboo for the walls and grass for the thatched roofs. Many of the structures have two sections: one, built directly on the ground, serves for cooking and storage; the other, a platform raised about 2 feet above ground, serves as a large family bed. Men often build a shelter deeper into the surrounding forest which provides refuge while hunting.

The native technology consists of a few objects directly applicable to domestic and subsistence activities: pottery, wooden utensils, digging sticks, stone hoes, fishing nets and fishweirs and the blowgun for hunting small game. Some groups make and use canoes. Although houses are not built with permanence in mind, most of the men are skillful builders.

Dress may differ from village to village, but, in general, the Yumbos use factory-manufactured cloth in making their clothing. Weaving is still practiced on a small scale for domestic use. Yumbos living in the larger towns and their environs have assumed a dress hardly distinguishable from that of the whites; most, however, do not wear shoes or sandals.

Subsistence is focused on horticulture, in which the slash-and-burn method is practiced. Yucca and a variety of fruits, including plantains, are commonly grown. Along new roads of penetration, the Yumbos, like the white colonists, grow the *naranjilla*, a fruit valued for its juice. This crop is sold to truckers who transport it to more central markets in Ecuador.

For the small amount of cash needed to buy desired manufactured goods, such as rifles, cooking utensils and cloth, men may work on one of the coffee plantations in the region or help clear the land of a white colonist. Many pan for gold in the jungle. Not infrequently, young women seek employment as domestics. In general, however, few are engaged in full-time nonagricultural pursuits. Specialization, even within the family, is not particularly rigid. The men hunt and fish in company with the male children and clear the land for agriculture. The women help in planting and harvesting and, with the children, in caring for domestic animals.

The simple, kin-based community structure promotes interdependence and fosters strong emotional attachments. The male head of the family is simultaneously the leader of the community. Social ties with neighboring communities are created through marriage. In settlements dominated by whites the Yumbos take a passive role in social and political affairs.

Most Yumbos are considered to be Roman Catholic, and those living in close proximity to towns or Catholic mission centers consider themselves as such. Actually, they know little of Catholic doctrine, though many readily accept the authority of the priest and attend services when they are available. The Yumbos hold a variety of animistic beliefs, generally oriented toward their environment, but apparently they lack a highly structured indigenous religion and have no native priestly specialists.

Social harmony and the avoidance of conflict are high in the Yumbo scale of values. The division of labor, while fluid, is accepted, and authority, vested in the family head, is usually mild. A negative value is placed on discord and disputes. A high value is accorded to hospitality; in fact, many girls have been unsuccessful as domestics because they give away their employers' food to friends who request it. To refuse such a request would imply that the individual was *mitza* (miserly), a grievous sin to the Yumbos.

Constantly on the fringe of highland life the Yumbos are aware of the cultural changes that have taken place through the centuries. They have accepted many aspects of the alien culture which they feel will improve their traditional life while rejecting those which they feel might change it drastically.

Aware that they are culturally distinct from the highland Quechua-speaking groups and feeling superior to other forest inhabitants, the Yumbos still recognize an affinity with other Indians. In their relations with whites, they are usually passive and submissive but aloof.

The Indians have some oral tradition which finds expression in creating and reciting poetry, but they have little music or dance. Much of their recreational activity centers around drinking and conversation. Formal drinking parties (*chumas*) are sometimes held between two families. For the most part, however, important life rituals provide the basis for social interaction.

Ceremonies at birth, puberty, marriage and death are not highly elaborate. Girls' puberty rites, still practiced by some, are marked by a period of confinement. Among the less isolated groups such rites are those connected with Catholic doctrine.

An economic asset, children are much desired. Formal education is still rare, and imitation of adult activities is considered both educational and recreational. Promiscuity among youths is not common, but little value is placed on premarital chastity. Residence after marriage is usually patrilocal, but the bridegroom may live and work for his bride's father for some time before the couple takes up final residence with or near his father. Death practices take a variety of forms, such as cremation, burial and simple disposal in the woods or rivers.

Jivaros

The Jívaros are probably the best-known, in North America, of the primitive South American tribes. Occupying Morona Santiago, Zamora and Pastaza near the Peruvian border, the Jívaros have rejected intrusions by Inca, Spaniards and Ecuadorians. Some 75 Jívaro groups now make up a total population estimated at around 13,000. The warlike tendencies for which they, along with the Ancon, are known were probably once shared by most of the now-extinct tribes in the region.

The area lacks modern means of communication with the rest of the country. Contact with missionaries was made early in the conquest period, but since then it has remained superficial. The Jívaros retain their own language and what little bilingualism exists is largely in Quechua, learned through contact with neighboring Oriente tribes.

Jívaro subsistence is focused largely on agriculture. Corn, manioc, a variety of fruits, tobacco and cotton are grown. Unlike some forest groups, the Jívaros keep such domestic animals as guinea pigs, chickens and, occasionally, cattle, The blowgun, spear and rifle are used for hunting, but numerous methods utilizing traps, deadfalls and pits are known. The region abounds in small game, but food taboos often prevent some groups from taking advantage of many animals. Fish is another major food source, as are wild nuts and fruits. Fermented yucca provides the principal alcoholic beverage.

The community usually consists of a single large house occupied by an extended family unit, generally numbering from 80 to a few hundred people. Elliptical in shape, the house has a thatched roof and sapling walls, built to withstand attacks. The males occupy one end of the house; women and small children, the other. Low platforms are used for sleeping, and storage platforms, stools and storage hooks make up most of the rest of the furniture.

The arts of spinning and weaving, the province of men, have long been practiced by the Jívaros. The women make ceramics, some of which are of excellent quality. Basketweaving is also highly developed. A variety of weapons for hunting and warfare are produced, including lances, shields, spears, spear throwers, blowguns, fishing nets and fishhooks.

Craftsmen displaying special skills may be asked to produce objects for others, but there are no full-time specialists. The Jívaros are indifferent to large placer gold deposits in their region.

Villages are separated by 1 or 2 days' walking distance. Although neighboring communities may unite temporarily for warfare, each community is politically independent. Houses are abandoned and new ones constructed in a different location about every 6 years, as a result of exhaustion of the surrounding agricultural soil.

Village leadership is usually vested in the head of family. This person may be simultaneously the shaman or religious authority. His mantle of leadership is loosely worn, however, for agreement is generally reached through discussion and by consensus, except in time of crisis.

The Jívaros have not been converted to Christianity, and their religious system displays practically none of the syncretism found among other indigenous groups. While they are said to recognize a supreme god, he is considered to be remote and to take little interest in human affairs. Their religion focuses instead on a supernatural essence embodied in such deities as the rain god and earth mother, who imbue objects and spirits with power. Gods and spirits are feared and placated through ritual, but there are no organized cults dedicated to their worship. Rather, each person or family performs the necessary ritual for agriculture, hunting and the like.

The principal role of the shaman is to cure sickness—caused by evil spirits—and to augur the fortunes of war or some other important activity. His occult powers may be used for harm as well as good, but while he is sometimes feared, he is not the object of intense respect or prestige.

Most Jívaros are indifferent to other cultures and ways of life. As encroachments into their territory continue and intensify, they will undoubtedly have to make the adjustments they have thus far avoided.

Plastic arts among the Jívaros are generally functional. Carved spear handles and mythological painting on pottery as well as dyeing of fabrics are illustrative of their artistic expression. Shrunken human heads, typical of, but not confined to, the Jívaros, are seldom produced, the decline in output being at least partly the result of stringent government restrictions against their purchase. Originally they were of magical significance, but the ready market for these trophies encouraged their production for other than ceremonial purposes. As in the past, the Jívaros continue to practice this art with animal heads.

During birth the Jívaro mother is isolated so as not to contaminate others. Both she and the father observe certain restrictions afterward in order not to harm the child.

Some reporters assert that puberty ceremonies are observed for both boys and girls, but few details of their nature are given. Others deny the existence of puberty rites. Marriage either by purchase or by bride service (in which the man works for his prospective bride's father for a time) appears to be most prevalent, and, at least in the past, polygyny was apparently common. Cross-cousin marriage is often preferred. Upon the death of her husband, a wife is obliged to marry his brother.

Deceased persons are placed in a hollow log coffin and left in a specially built hut. The dead are then left with a supply of food and water which is supposed to last 2 years. Under the influence of Christian missionaries earth burials are becoming more common.

INTEGRATION OF INDIANS IN THE NATIONAL SOCIETY

The Constitution, promulgated in 1946, calls for measures to promote the moral, economic and social improvement of the Indians and for their incorporation into national life. Sentiments regarding the integration and assimilation of the indigenous population into the mainstream of society appeared in the Constitution of 1830, when the new nation established a policy of Indian education. Until 1906, however, there was no legislation aimed specifically toward the Indian. The Constitution of 1906 called for an end to certain abuses regarding Indian day laborers, and by 1918, President Alfredo Baquerizo Moreno declared that efforts in that direction had been successful.

In 1937 the Law of Communities established the legal status of Indian communities, providing for a new system of local governments. In 1958 the Ministry of Labor and Social Welfare, under whose authority most Indian problems fell, created in Quito the Indian Affairs Board, whose duties were to compile statistics concerning the Indian communities, to supervise the enforcement of protective legislation and to suggest new measures of protection. A similar body was established in Guayaquil a short time later. Ecuador is also a charter member of the National Indigenous Institutes founded at the Interamerican Convention in 1948. The Andean Mission, originally begun in 1954 under the auspices of the International Labor Organization and the United Nations, but now in the hands of the government of Ecuador, is the principal organization concerned with the Indians of the highlands.

In addition a number of agencies, such as UNICEF, CARE, Papal Volunteers for Latin America, the Peace Corps and AID (see Glossary) have served to promote the integration and assimilation of the Indian. Most of the efforts of these groups, coordinated by the Andean Mission, have been oriented toward the lower social strata in general rather than specifically toward the Indian. While the emphasis on the lower class limits the projects largely to work among Indians, the nature of the programs make them better understood in the context of social class rather than ethnic group.

For example, the campaign against illiteracy, fostered by the Ecuadorian Literacy League and the National Union of Journalists (Unión Nacional de Periodistas—UNP), set up 1,100 literacy centers throughout the country. A little more than half of the 150,000 persons who participated in the program were Indians, but the program was not aimed specifically at them. Legislation related to *huasipungueros*, often thought of in terms of the indigenous population, is also effective in the provinces of Carchi, Esmeraldas, Guayas, and Manabí, where the Indian population is negligible. Even the Misión Andina, which works extensively in Indian communities, seldom mentions Indians explicitly but refers to *campesinos* or rural agriculturalists.

The well-intentioned Law of Communities begins with the assumption that communal lands are much more extensive among the Indians than they are in fact. Actually, 19.4 percent of the agricultural population works on communal lands, and some of these are included among the 67.2 percent who are private landowners.

The *minga* (community labor) system is an effective method of accomplishing various public projects such as school construction, roadbuilding and irrigation. The Indians, however, often see it not as a voluntary contribution, but rather as a traditional duty, even though for centuries it has been abused by landowners. Roads from which principally the whites benefit, for example, are

96

often built or repaired by Indians working in *mingas* called by local officials.

Many plans by outside agencies suffer from the fact that they are based on European rather than Indian values. That they have sometimes seemed successful stems from the Indians' superficial acquiescence to the demands of their social superiors. The most idealistically conceived suggestions are seen as demands when made by members of the dominant class. This in part accounts for the general ineffectiveness of the *cabildo* (community council) system of government. The community establishes the *cabildo* as a legal requirement, and it functions in the face of the white society. As an imposed innovation, however, it seldom has the confidence of the community.

Attempts to destroy the *prioste* system (whereby prominent members of the community, in turn, sponsor expensive feasts for the entire community) and to eliminate the costly village religious *fiestas* meet with resistance for similar reasons. Outsiders see the system almost exclusively in terms of economic values, whereas the Indians consider its social aspects as well. The village *fiesta* provides much-needed entertainment in an otherwise monotonous existence. It is also an institutionalized means for shedding inhibitions and displaying hostilities which traditional behavior patterns prohibit under normal circumstances. If these *fiestas* were not financed by an individual, it is doubtful that they would be held at all. Most important to the individual, who acts as *prioste,* this is one of the few methods by which he can gain status and prestige in a society which frowns upon assertive dominating personalities and gives scant recognition to the accumulation of wealth.

The acquisition of material goods, in fact, is often seen as a result of good fortune rather than of individual endeavor. The individual is therefore obliged to demonstrate his appreciation to the spirits which have looked favorably upon him by sacrificing his wealth for the benefit of the community. Failure to do so might, according to Indian concepts, bring supernatural punishments upon the entire village. Evidently, the village religious *fiesta* is more complex than a simple economic explanation might suggest. In the present cultural context abolition could create serious problems.

Change in itself holds no value for the average Indian, and change toward the general Hispanic social system, which many have grown to fear and distrust, is often overtly avoided. This attitude does not preclude the possibility of change, however, but merely colors the conception of it. Education, for example, is not perceived as a means of opening wider vistas or directly improving the status of the individual. It is, rather, valued for its direct bearing on already existent and familiar patterns. More concretely, an Otavaleño does not see in the study of arithmetic a potential career as an engineer, accountant or financier, but rather a means of carrying out more efficiently the business of weaving.

In the face of myriad difficulties the successes and accomplishments of the many programs aimed at developing a national consciousness and increasing the social and economic status of the Indians are noteworthy. Many schools are constructed every year and the percentage of illiteracy is constantly on the decline; irrigation projects and the introduction of new and more productive crops have increased the farm yield; a number of marketing and buying cooperatives have resulted in economic benefits; headway is being made in promoting better health and sanitation facilities; and transportation facilities are continually being improved with the construction of new roads. In short, the forces of acculturation among the Indians are constantly at work.

MINORITY ETHNIC GROUPS

Economic resources that might have encouraged immigration from abroad—petroleum, mineral wealth, vast grazing lands, easily accessible plantation areas and regions suitable for European-style agriculture—are scarce or lacking in Ecuador. With a surplus of common labor to handle existent needs, the government has had little reason to seek workers from abroad. In consequence, persons of foreign extraction account for a very small percentage of the total population.

In 1962 there were about 600 foreign citizens residing permanently in the country, over half of whom are either German or English. No figures are available as to the number of naturalized citizens, but if statistics regarding the number of persons whose native language is other than Spanish or any of the aboriginal Indian languages is indicative, there are only about 20,000. This would not account for persons from Spain or the Latin American republics, but there is nothing to indicate that immigration from either of these sources has been particularly heavy.

Several foreign ethnic groups, though small in numbers, have made a definite impact on Ecuadorian life. One of the most significant of these is the Lebanese. Often referred to as Arabs (*árabes*) or Turks (*turcos*), they are concentrated particularly in the port city of Guayaquil. They have established themselves as merchants and exert considerable influence in this capacity.

Despite their wealth, they do not constitute a socially prominent segment of the population. They are considered members of the middle class, and some have married Ecuadorians of similar social status. Most, however, marry persons of Lebanese extraction and, for the most part, retain their ethnic identity. This characteristic, as well as their affluence, has sometimes made them a target for prejudicial remarks and actions.

If the Lebanese have failed to assimilate Ecuadorian culture, they have at least accomplished a fair degree of sociopolitical integration. The political party currently most prominent in Guayaquil is considerably influenced and in part led by persons of Lebanese descent, which, in view of their relatively small numbers, demonstrates support from outside their own group. Unfavorable remarks directed toward Lebanese from the Quito-based political elite must be interpreted not only in terms of ethnic prejudice but should be seen as part of a Quito-Guayaquil political discord which has long existed.

The Chinese also are centered principally on the Coast, although some are found throughout the country. Most are small shopkeepers or wholesalers. Those who are middlemen deal primarily in agricultural produce, which they acquire either through barter or purchase in their stores. Their focal point seems to be in the town of Quevedo. Excellent merchants and persons of frugal habits, most Chinese have attained at least economic security. Social interrelationships with the cultural majority, however, are generally at the lower- or lower middle-class level.

If the average Ecuadorian is convinced of the accuracy of his stereotypes and judges a people collectively by them, his close personal relations are seldom affected by them. In keeping with his own ideals and behavior, face-to-face relationships are based on individual identity, trust and confidence.

It would not be at all improbable, for example, to hear an Ecuadorian speak of the Germans, Americans or some other nationality group in the most disparaging terms, and then find that he numbers persons from such groups among his closest and most intimate friends.

Not included among ethnic minorities are a number of persons who, although descended from a non-Hispanic European group, do not identify with it. There are, for example, prominent families with English, Irish, German and French surnames, who think of themselves first as Ecuadorians. They feel no special affinity with recently arrived persons of similar ethnic extraction and often do not associate with them.

LANGUAGES

The official language of Ecuador, spoken by the great majority of the population, is Spanish. Many who list Spanish as their first language are bilingual and speak Quechua as well. There is also a significant minority which speaks Quechua either exclusively or at least with greater frequency and fluency than Spanish.

As it is spoken in Ecuador, Spanish is mutually intelligible with that spoken in Spain and its former colonies. The general grammatical structure is the same, and the differences that occur are primarily in vocabulary and pronunciation. The few changes in grammar, such as changing a word which normally receives a masculine ending to the feminine gender, are easily understood by anyone fluent in the language.

Changes in vocabulary might be less readily understood, for most are the result of incorporating Indian (primarily Quechua) words into the language. While most Ecuadorians are familiar with such words—at least as used regionally—they are most frequent in the speech of the less educated and of rural persons in general.

There are three distinct regional dialects of Ecuadorian Spanish: coastal, Sierra and Amazonian. The coastal can be further subdivided into that spoken by the Negro population (extending into the Chota River valley of the highlands) and the dialect used by the rest of the coastal population. In the Sierra there is a difference between northern and southern subdialects. The line between these two is drawn approximately at the border between Cañar and Chimborazo Provinces. There is a formidable geographical barrier here, created by several high Andean peaks. In pre-Hispanic times this barrier separated the Quitu, Cara and Puruhá Indians from the Cañari and Palta, and the current differences in pronunciation may stem from differences in the two aboriginal languages, although at present all Sierra Indians speak Quechua.

The dialectical differences within Ecuador tend to follow a pattern that is not exclusively Ecuadorian, but is found elsewhere in the Spanish-speaking world. The Sierra dialect, used around Quito and in Cuenca, an old university city, is considered the "better" Spanish, as are most dialects spoken in the highlands of South America. It is relatively closer to Castilian Spanish than the other dialects.

As spoken in the Oriente provinces, Spanish shares dialectical similarities with neighboring areas of Peru and Colombia. The coastal dialect is part of a speech pattern characteristic of a vast maritime zone, including such regions as Vera Cruz on the Gulf of Mexico, in Panama and on the coasts of Venezuela and Colombia. It is, in fact, closely related to the Spanish of Andalusia in southern Spain. The Negro subdialect, on the other hand, is shared with persons of that racial origin found in the Antilles and South America's northern Atlantic and Pacific coasts.

Of the numerous Indian languages once spoken in the highlands, only Quechua has survived. Knowledge of the others comes from documents written by early Spanish chroniclers. A number of place names and the surnames of a few individuals are all that remain of these languages.

Although it was the Inca who first brought Quechua to Ecuador, the language became even more widespread after the Spanish conquest, as the conquerors used it as a lingua franca. As it is spoken in the highlands, the language is fairly uniform, with only minor dialectical differences. In the lowlands, as among the Yumbos, there are not only sound changes but grammatical differences caused by the tendency to drop suffixes.

Quechua became a literate language when it assumed the Spanish orthography soon after the conquest of Ecuador. Sermons were given in it; dictionaries were compiled; and books were written. It is still occasionally written for use in religious instruction or for propaganda purposes, and it is still taught for those who work closely with the Indians, such as religious missionaries, social workers and scholars engaged in Indian research.

In the western lowlands only Cayapa and Colorado remain, and these are fast disappearing. While the Indians of the Amazon provinces are also being introduced to Spanish, there is no immediate prospect of the aboriginal languages dying out. Apart from the Quechua spoken by the Yumbos, Jívaro is the most widespread language in the tropical forest. Záparo, Tetete, Cofan, Aushiri and Siona are also in use.

Among the European languages taught in school, English has surpassed French and German as the most popular. Those who can afford to do so in many cases send their children abroad for at least a year or so in order to increase their fluency in a foreign language.

CHAPTER 6

SOCIAL STRUCTURE

The outlines of present-day Ecuadorian society reflect patterns that were set down during the colonial period. Although change has been continuous, it has occurred at a slow rate. Political upheavals, often marked by considerable violence, have provided a means for the social mobility of ambitious individuals (political and military leaders, for example), but they have never resulted in radical changes in structure. Numerous efforts aimed at social reform in the past decade have not significantly altered the conservative attitudes held by a majority of the people.

Probably the most striking feature of the social structure is the deep regionalist cleavage—reflected in social attitudes, in political alignments and in economic interests—dividing the Sierra and the Coast. Centered on Quito, the society of the Sierra represents the most conservative element in national life. From earliest colonial days the region developed economically around a static agrarian system. Quito, Riobamba, Cuenca and other highland cities were founded early in colonial times and attracted large numbers of Spanish colonists, many from wealthy and well-established families. Such cities early became centers of Spanish culture in their own right. Consequently, it is in the Sierra that the forms and attitudes of colonial Hispanic society have been preserved most strongly.

By contrast, the Coast, centered on Guayaquil, remained a marginal element in colonial society. The region, being hot and rather unhealthful before the institution of modern medical and sanitary controls and lacking a large and docile labor force, attracted the adventurer and entrepreneur much more than the settled aristocrat landholder and administrator. After independence, as the country established growing contacts with world markets, especially as an exporter of cacao and other tropical agricultural products, the society of the Coast grew in size, power and complexity. Having developed later than the society of the Sierra and being more directly under the influence of the outside world, the society of the Coast has been much less tradition bound (see ch. 3, Historical Setting; ch. 5, Ethnic Groups and Languages).

Since the founding of the Ecuadorian Republic, Quito has remained the cultural and ecclesiastical center of the country and has retained the balance of political power through most of the period. Weighing against this traditional preeminence has been the massive and growing economic power of Guayaquil. Thus, Sierra and Coast have faced each other as coequal, competing factions, with sharply contrasting traditions and attitudes, visible at all levels of wealth and power.

The society was shaped in a tradition of rigid stratification and hereditary privilege, and these patterns have persisted through history, with relative minor changes. Since the establishment of colonial rule power and wealth have been concentrated overwhelmingly in the hands of a very small group of Spanish-speaking families, many of them descended from the conquistadors. Dominating the major productive resources and controlling labor and trade, this small upper class has usually maintained control over the political processes as well. Political control has often been indirect—exercised through politicians who are not, themselves, members of the elite—and has sometimes been shared with military leaders; it has, nevertheless, always protected upper-class privileges and wealth (see ch. 14, Political Dynamics).

The upper class has remained small, although it has assimilated new members as ambitious individuals have achieved power and wealth in times of economic expansion. It is by no means a unified group, for the cleavages of regionalism are perhaps deepest at the upper levels of society. In effect, the country has two elites—one dominating the Sierra and centered in Quito, the other dominating the Coast and centered in Guayaquil. Between these two elites there has been considerable conflict which has not been effectively bridged by kinship ties for there has been relatively little intermarriage.

The Sierra elite has, by long tradition, based its wealth and power on ownership of land and control of agrarian labor in a poorly coordinated and underproductive agricultural economy. The older and far more conservative segment of the upper class, the Sierra elite has also long considered itself the repository and protector of the cultural heritage. The coastal elite, largely a product of the growth of external commerce after independence, is based economically on the cultivation of export crops and on large-scale trade. At the apex of the relatively flexible society of the Coast, its members have usually been more receptive to social and political changes which do not threaten their vested interests.

The broad base of the society is formed by a vast lower

stratum, chiefly Indian and *mestizo* in racial background, but with a fairly large Negro component as well. The lower stratum is poor and politically powerless but contains great variations in traditions, language and degree of participation in national life.

Both on the Coast and in the Sierra, the masses of Spanish-speaking *mestizos* form a lower class of small farmers, urban workers and petty merchants. Although they are poor and often unlettered, they are generally deemed to form part of the functioning, Hispanic-oriented nation; they are considered citizens rather than mere subjects. For the most part the Negro peasants and laborers occupy a similar position in the national society (see ch. 5, Ethnic Groups and Languages).

The Quechua-speaking Indians, who form the backbone of the Sierra agrarian population, are not only poor and of low social status, but their own rigorous ethnic caste system tends to keep them from full membership in the national society. The Spanish-speaking lower-class groups, identifying with the institutions of the nation, have some active participation in national life, but the Indians have remained at the margin, either as subsistence farmers or as entailed tenant laborers (*huasipungueros*) on the estates of the Sierra elite. They mistrust the Spanish-speaking Ecuadorians and tend to minimize contacts with them. On the other hand, literacy and contact with urban society have resulted in a measure of discontent, especially among younger Indians, with the traditional poverty and subservience.

Traditionally, the society has provided few routes of status advancement. The relatively static, predominantly agrarian economy has offered almost no opportunity for the achievement of wealth by poor but ambitious men, except in limited degree on the Coast. The tradition of rigid class distinctions is supported by a strong social conservatism, especially in the Sierra. Thus, the rare self-made man, no matter how rich or well-connected politically, usually finds it extremely difficult to achieve a social status commensurate with his wealth and power.

The rather static quality of social life and attitudes have been especially apparent in the small size, weakness and poor definition of the middle class. Except in the larger cities, where the concentration of industry and large-scale commerce have permitted the growth of a salaried and professional group, there is little place in the economy for a middle class. The wealthy, leisured class of landowners has provided many of the professionals—chiefly lawyers and physicians—who form the middle classes of many other Latin American nations. Until recently, access to educational facilities was sharply limited, except for the children of the elite. Thus, upward social mobility through occupational advancement has not been possible for many Ecuadorians.

Mirroring the lack of opportunity for mobility, the traditional view of the society conceives it as divided simply between the "decent people" (*gente decente*) and the "populace" (*pueblo*). The concept of a middle class is fairly recent in origin and has entered into popular usage only in the cities.

In the past two decades there have been signs of accelerating change in this long-static social pattern. Improvements in interregional transport facilities, a degree of expansion and diversification in the economy and the slow spread of literacy into rural areas have had a measurable impact on the attitudes of the traditionally passive lower class. The proportion of voters in national elections has grown rapidly, as the poorer and weaker segments of society have come to perceive the possibility of improving their lot through political action. Labor unions, though less powerful than in many other Latin American countries, have to some extent crystallized and expressed the aspirations of the working class. These pressures of change have become apparent, although much more slowly, even among the Indians.

Some members of the upper class have begun to perceive the need for at least moderate reform in the rigid social and economic system, partly as a response to the growing lower-class discontent and partly as a result of the recognition that economic growth and political stability depend on a prosperous educated citizenry. This recognition is by no means generally shared, but it has represented a growing voice in political discourse, both in the writing of intellectuals and on the candidate's podium (see ch. 14, Political Dynamics; ch. 17, Attitudes and Reactions).

Furthermore, the expansion and diversification of the economy, a concomitant growth in demand for skilled workers and the broader availability of schooling have opened new alternatives to the masses of subsistence farmers and menial laborers. This changing pattern of economic roles will undoubtedly lead to a loosening of the rigid social lines, although the process may well be a slow one.

THE ELITE

The elite, small in size, commands the major portion of the nation's power and wealth and, by long tradition, stands as the primary guardian and perpetuator of the Hispanic-based national culture. The elite assumes its social superiority by right of birth, and its exclusiveness is maintained through intermarriage. The closely knit ties of kinship, coupled with the desire to protect heredity privilege, has fostered among them a highly developed class consciousness.

Although a closed segment of society, the elite is not static in membership. Whereas some members trace their genealogies back to the colonial aristocracy, others are descended from persons of humble origin who rose to prominence through the exercise of political power. Foreign surnames—especially German, English and Irish—can also be found among the elite, indicating that immigrants who have made their fortunes in Ecuador have entered this select social circle.

Although the upper stratum displays a highly developed class with respect to the rest of society, in itself it is by no means a unified group. The principal dividing force is the intense regionalism prevailing between the Coast and the Sierra.

Regionalist antagonisms within the elite have usually been expressed in the social and political terms traditional to the society as a whole. The coastal elite has maintained an attitude of strong anticlericism, blaming the Church for many of the ills that befall the country. The elite of the "very Catholic" (*muy Católico*) Sierra contends that life on the Coast is morally degenerate.

Perhaps more fundamental, however, are economic differences. Elite fortunes in both regions are primarily agrarian based, but those on the Coast are founded on plantation agriculture for export markets and in commerce in imported goods, whereas those in the Sierra rest on *haciendas* producing for local markets. The coastal merchants and planters seek to expand foreign trade to broaden the home market for imported goods. The poorly paid tenant labor force of the Sierra is looked upon by coastal elements as a large potential consumer market for cheap imported products. As a consequence, the lowering of tariff restrictions and the passing of more liberal social legislation are major goals.

In trying to promote these aims coastal interests run at cross-purposes with those of the Sierra. Agricultural production from the highlands goes almost entirely to the domestic market. Since most of the tenant laborers produce their own food it is felt that increased wages would only add to expenses without expanding the market for meat and vegetable products. Dependent as they are on a system of cheap labor and inexpensive production methods, the landed aristocracy and the few industrialists of the Sierra violently oppose social legislation and the lowering of protective tariffs. These basic conflicts have set the undertone for much of the historical political strife.

Given a shared pride of ancestry and a recognition of the principles of social status, it is conceivable that the elites of both regions could integrate if, as elsewhere in Latin America, there were a single focus of national life. Cosmopolitan centers, such as Lima, Buenos Aires and many others, attract the wealthy and powerful from all parts of their nations. In the social clubs and schools catering to this class, attachments are formed that eventually lead to close friendships and marriages and serve to unite the interests of the leading families. Neither Quito nor Guayaquil can adequately fulfill such a role, however. Both offer effectively the same limited facilities, and elite members either focus on one or the other regional center or travel abroad for their education and pleasure.

Except for the regional distinctions, basic attitudes and behavior are more or less consistent throughout the elite class. Despite the agrarian base for their wealth, elite members are urbanites whose plantations or *haciendas* serve only as an occasional weekend retreat or vacation residence. Management of their holdings is usually given over to a paid administrator, while the absentee owners pursue their social life—and sometimes practice a profession—in the city.

Gente (lit., people), as persons of high status are known, are easily recognizable by such external characteristics as dress, speech, physical appearance (especially their white complexions) and education. The ambitious social climber would have a difficult time passing himself off in this group, for even were he able to assume the trappings of the elite, he would be hard pressed to create a suitable genealogy. Pride of ancestry is great, and persons not only know their own genealogy, but usually know much about the kinship ties of others in their class. When introduced, strangers casually, but meaningfully, seek out information about each other's family backgrounds in order to determine their social position.

Although the elite is far above the rest of the society, there are differences in socioeconomic status among its members. On the one hand are persons whose prestige and power is wide ranging. Concentrated in the regional capitals of Quito or Guayaquil, they exert influence either through family ties or, more rarely, through dominance over politics.

On the other hand, many families, though generally conceded elite social status, are wealthy only in relation to other Ecuadorians. Concentrated in the provincial capitals, this lower elite is wholly dependent on an agrarian economy. Few of its members can afford to reorganize their holdings into more efficient operations. Lacking capital, they have not—as have the upper elite—begun to invest in commerce and industry. They are opposed to any social change. Often insecure in their positions, they take a more direct part in politics and military affairs as a means of insuring their status. Though their political dominance seldom stretches beyond provincial boundaries, their power in local affairs may outweigh that of the central government.

It is through this lower level that persons of the middle class are occasionally assimilated into the elite. Nevertheless, the pride of ancestry and feeling of exclusiveness remains characteristic of the entire elite. Often related by ties of kinship, the upper and lower elite tend to overlap, constituting a single, closed society.

THE MIDDLE CLASS

Constituting but a small portion of the total population, the middle class is concentrated in the cities and larger towns. Primarily a white-collar class, it includes small businessmen, professionals, managerial and clerical personnel, and middle-grade bureaucrats, army officers and clerics.

Drawn from extremely diverse social origins, the middle class displays a broad ethnic and racial variation. The largest portion, descending from persons who have advanced from the lower class, display *mestizo* physical characteristics. Some, however, are white in appearance and are members of once-wealthy families. It is becoming increasingly common for the sons of prominent, but impoverished, provincial elites to seek new opportunities in the regional capitals, taking their place within the middle class. In addition, the group includes a small number of foreign immigrants.

Middle-class status rests on a complex of social and economic criteria. One of the prerequisites is the acquiring of at least a secondary education. This in itself sets the group apart from the masses, many of whom are illiterate or have only an incomplete primary education. Education is seen as an absolute necessity, and private schools are preferred over public. Residence in a desirable neighborhood is considered important and is often procured at the sacrifice of household furnishings or even proper diet. The level of material well-being varies greatly according to circumstance, but middle-class persons strive to maintain at least the external signs of their status, appearing in public stylishly dressed and well groomed.

Encompassing a wide range of occupational roles, wealth and social origin, the middle class is not a tightly integrated group with well-defined class goals. There is a dividing line, evident in life styles and in patterns of associations, between the lower middle class, which includes clerical workers, schoolteachers and minor functionaries, and the upper middle class, which includes professionals, executives and successful businessmen.

Bridging the gap between the elite and the lower class, the middle class is sharply divided from both. Even wealthy members of the middle class cannot easily integrate into the elite without the requisite ties of kinship. The best most can hope for is to see their heirs assimilated through marriage. The dividing line between the lower and middle classes is based not so much on family origin as on manual labor, for no matter how highly skilled or well paid, those who perform physical labor are excluded from the middle class.

Containing a broad variety of social elements, the middle class remains a poorly defined segment of the population lacking a highly developed group consciousness. With values and aspirations modeled after those of the elite, they tend to see themselves at the margin of upper society. The strong negative value placed on physical labor and the great emphasis on leisure and entertainment, however, is often at cross-purposes with their equally strong desires for material enrichment. In order to maintain a front of prosperity, they expend much time and energy at their jobs and professions, sacrificing those material comforts which are least visible to the public.

The middle class has demonstrated more vitality and mobility than any other segment of the social structure. Nevertheless, it remains relatively static. Few avenues for advancement have been opened up to the lower class, partly because educational facilities are still limited. An expansion of industry or a marked trend toward urbanization might create a need for more managerial and clerical talent as well as for an increased number of administrators and professionals. So far, however, the country remains largely agricultural and rural.

THE LOWER CLASS

Urban Workers

The lower class is predominantly rural. The society is so largely agrarian based that less than one-fifth of the nation's population reside in centers of more than 20,000. The shantytowns characteristic of Lima or Rio de Janeiro are virtually absent in Quito and Guayaquil, where the slums give at least an appearance of stability not found in the exploding metropolises of other South American nations.

In the relative absence of industry the urban centers offer little economic alternative to even the harsh living conditions of the Sierra *haciendas*. Some form of temporary employment can often be found in the vital seaport of Guayaquil, and the rural workers float in and out of this port city, working for a short time and enjoying the life and movement of the urban center. There is a shortage of labor on the coastal plantations, however, and they eventually return for the banana-picking season.

The lower class of the large cities is composed of factory and construction workers, tradesmen, domestics, manual laborers and petty merchants. Together with the irregularly employed rural migrants, they embrace a wide range of income and interests. They share in common the Spanish language and a national identity, but there is little other basis for the integration of all these elements into a cohesive group with well-defined aims.

Labor unions, which have provided a focus for group consciousness in other nations, have failed to develop in the absence of a large industrial lower class. Outside agencies which have attemped to promote civic associations for local initiative projects or to demand better education and welfare facilities have met with little enthusiasm. Beyond the neighborhood-oriented social and athletic clubs, the urban working class has little experience in cooperation.

Nevertheless, the urban lower class constitutes a well-defined social element. Excluded from the middle class by a sharp line of occupation and schooling and feeling superior to his rural counterpart, the poor urbanite acknowledges his status as a member of the working class.

Hampered by the lack of education and by ingrained conservative attitudes, the urban lower class has scarcely begun to articulate its aspirations for more material benefits and a greater voice in national affairs. It has been sought out, however, by political and labor groups willing to provide it with leadership (see ch. 14, Political Dynamics).

Whereas all potential spokesmen for the urban working class stress the need for economic reform, some are strongly political in approach, contending that economic reform can only be accomplished through political control. The activities of these various groups have undoubtedly been responsible for some improvement in health and welfare facilities. Of greater import, however, they have demonstrated the potential power of the lower class. General strikes, usually a failure in the past, are beginning to have greater impact. The unrest displayed by the urban lower class is said to have played a large part in the overthrow of the government of Velasco Ibarra. More recently, civil disturbances and strikes are credited by some observers for the conciliatory attitude taken by the ruling military government toward demands for social and economic reforms.

Mestizo Peasants and Rural Laborers

Between the *mestizo* peasant of the Coast (*montuvio*) and his counterpart in the Sierra (often called *chagra*) there are sharp contrasts in way of life. Paradoxically, the racial component of the *montuvio* is at least as Indian, and sometimes more so, than that of the *chagra*. Yet his language and culture are more Hispanic. Descended from the once numerous Indians who inhabited the coastal regions, the *montuvio* also shows Spanish and Negro physical strains.

The coastal Indian abandoned his native culture early in the distinction between himself and the Indian in order to dissociate himself from the lesser role of Indian in the society. To this end, he usually calls himself "white" (*blanco*). He also buys, often at financial sacrifice, such symbols of difference as shoes, manufactured clothing, tiled roofs and beds.

Many own some land, but given the generally poor quality of the soil, most are forced to supplement their incomes through wage labor. A number of rural *mestizos* work as sharecroppers, and a few are engaged as *huasipungueros* on the *haciendas*. Although a petty merchant or truckdriver is sometimes found in peasant settlements, there are few full-time nonagricultural specialists in the rural Sierra. Few of the *haciendas* have been mechanized, and nothing similar to the rural proletariat of the coastal plantations is found in the Sierra.

Aside from the obvious material differences between poor *mestizos* and their Indian neighbors, the value orientations of the rural non-Indian lower class class are unmistakenly Hispanic. This is given strong evidence in their ballads and folklore, which dwell on romance and valor, themes foreign to Indian traditions. Though dwelling in comparative isolation, poor *mestizos* nevertheless strongly identify with the national society. This identity is given voice in their drive toward urbanization, which they see as typifying the Hispanic way of life. Seeking for their own settlements such urban trappings as movie houses, electric lights and piped water systems, they deny that the Indians could ever desire such amenities.

Larger, more arable landholdings have been a primary aspiration of the impoverished Sierra *mestizo* peasant. Yet, the value placed on landownership is often independent of broader economic considerations. This has been demonstrated in several government-sponsored colonization projects, where the purchase of large, fertile tracts of land has been facilitated. Instead of taking full advantage of the opportunities which such land offers, many of the peasants forego the planting of crops and continue subsistence farming in much the same manner as in the past. Furthermore, they tend to ignore the encouragement and incentive toward technical improvement offered by the government.

Negro Peasants

The dense rural Negro populations of Esmeraldas Province and adjacent portions of Carchi and Imbabura form in many ways a distinct social element. Marked off in racial origin from the predominantly Indian and Spanish peasantry elsewhere in the country, the Negro peasants also display a few cultural distinctive traits, especially in *fiesta* patterns (see ch. 5, Ethnic Groups and Languages).

colonial period, adopting the language, religion, dress and other elements of Spanish life. His low social position prevented him from assuming all of the behavioral characteristics and values of of the dominant group, however. He was spared the relegation to lower-caste status largely because Negro slaves, more pliable and suitable to plantation agriculture, were introduced into Ecuador.

The *montuvio* remains fiercely independent. His independence manifests itself especially in his reluctance to remain settled for long in one place. Taking advantage of the shortage of plantation workers, he moves frequently from job to job. His rural residence is often interrupted by periods spent in Guayaquil or one of the other port towns. Unlike the Sierran peasants who go to the city in search of work, the *montuvio* is not lost or disoriented away from his rural environment. Familiar with the city, he establishes friendships and personal relations with both men and women who are more permanent urban dwellers of his class. He can usually find employment on the docks or as an unskilled factory worker. Nevertheless, given the economic dominance of agriculture, his ties remain primarily rural.

Not all of the coastal rural population is quite so unstable, and there are small landholding peasants and various forms of tenancy rooting the peasants to their place of origin. The numerous fishing villages located along the coast are relatively permanent settlements. Moreover, many of the plantations are large, mechanized operations, many of whose workers are engaged in tasks not specifically agricultural. Such workers form a rural proletariat in many ways indistinguishable from their urban counterparts.

By and large, the rural society of the Coast is more mobile and open than that of the Sierra. The shortage of agricultural labor, the greater concentration of industry in the cities and the constant movement of goods through the ports have created more economic alternatives and more opportunity for social and economic advancement. The greater dependency on cash wages has lessened somewhat the drive of the coastal rural worker for landownership.

In the Sierra there are about 750,000 non-Indian lower-class peasants. Derived from various mixtures of Indian, Spanish and, in lesser degree, Negro strains, in many cases these rural inhabitants are separated from the Indians more by ancestry than by culture. Their Spanish language is strongly flavored with Quechua and other Indian-language words; their dress is a combination of Hispanic and aboriginal; and their customs and curing practices are derived largely from native tradition.

Whenever possible, the *mestizo* peasant strives to stress the

Nevertheless, given the lack of a strong racist sentiment, the barriers to integration are by no means insurmountable, and instances of intermarriage between coastal Negroes and *montuvios* occur with some frequency. If the Negro peasants are poor and politically powerless, so are a majority of their *mestizo* compatriots. If they have been marginal to the national culture and economy, this has been more the result of geographic isolation and a poorly developed agrarian economy than of any explicit racial prejudice (see ch. 5, Ethnic Groups and Languages).

THE SIERRA INDIANS

The traditional Sierra *hacienda* requires a large, cheap labor force, and by social tradition dating from the conquest, this need has been filled by the Indians. The social structure, within which the Indians occupy an underprivileged position, has offered them few alternatives to subsistence farming on isolated marginal lands or, as tenants, on white-owned *haciendas*.

Many of the Indians' disadvantages are shared in equal measure by members of the *mestizo* lower class, but age-old ethnic prejudices against the Indians tend to form what amounts to a caste barrier. In most areas the *mestizos*, identified as members of the "white" segment, can aspire to improvement in their social and economic position, but in most areas such social mobility is denied to the Indians by prevailing attitudes. The *mestizo* peasant, no matter how rustic and poor, has some claim to being part of the Hispanic-based nation, whereas the Indian, even if prosperous and formally schooled, is seen as properly confined to his caste as long as he maintains any of the visible manifestations of his ethnic origins.

The strength and persistence of these ethnic attitudes is perhaps most graphically apparent in the case of the Otavaleños, many of whom have achieved levels of prosperity and formal education considerably above the average of the rural whites. In the local society of Otavalo the traditional patterns of deference and subordination remain an ingrained part of the way of life. To some extent the persistence of the ethnic caste system in Otavalo rests on the attitudes of the Indians, themselves, most of whom steadfastly refuse to abandon their native dress, the use of Quechua and other hallmarks of their ancestral identity (see ch. 5, Ethnic Groups and Languages).

In most parts of the Sierra the white-owned *haciendas* occupy the best and most accessible lands, and in many areas these large holdings have expanded at the expense of neighboring peasant communities. For those Indians whose lands were taken over by the *haciendas*, there was no alternative but to become *huasipungueros*. Those whose lands were never so absorbed (generally called "free Indians") were often crowded onto plots so small, isolated and unproductive that they could eke out an existence only by supplementing their poor yields with wages as part-time laborers on the *haciendas*.

In most parts of the Sierra the *hacienda* community traditionally has been isolated from the political functioning of the nation. Typically, it is ruled on behalf of an absentee owner by a hired administrator, usually a local "white," who enjoys broad powers, sometimes including the right to administer corporal punishment to the *huasipungueros*. These powers are, by long usage, subject to little interference by the civil authorities. Local administrative, judicial and police officials are usually reluctant to exercise their powers within *haciendas* in their jurisdictions, except on request of their owners.

In view of the poor quality of the typical tenant plot and the low wages, few *huasipungueros* can avoid falling into the debt of their landlords. Such indebtedness, which can be paid off only slowly, has traditionally been deemed sufficient cause to hold a *huasipunguero* in the service of his landlord. This principle of debt bondage is expressly outlawed in recent statutes, but still is enforced in some areas.

Living under a regime which is, in considerable measure, divorced from the national government, with little to buy and sell, and perceiving no economic alternatives, the *huasipungueros* have few bases of common participation with those outside their *haciendas*—even with Indians on neighboring estates or in nearby free communities. Moreover, the hostility of the social environment has bred a mistrust into most Indians, a mistrust directed almost as readily at Indians of other communities as at the whites and *mestizos*.

In most parts of the Sierra the "free" Indians live separated from their white and *mestizo* neighbors. Parish seats and other sizable villages are, as a rule, occupied only by Spanish speakers, whereas the Indians are settled, typically, in small hamlets called *anejos* (annexes) in the surrounding countryside. In addition, a fairly large segment of the "free" Indian population is settled in remote and inaccessible areas, usually in the mountains ringing the intermont basins.

The Indian hamlets located close to centers of white and *mestizo* population are usually under the control of local civil and ecclesiastical authorities. Such control has been exercised in part through a series of hamlet officials who, whether appointed by the Spanish-speaking authorities or elected by their neighbors, have little independent power. Most commonly these Indian officials transmit the orders of the political lieutenant (*teniente político*—the chief civil officer of the parish) and the parish priest to their hamlets; organize compulsory public works parties (*mingas*), usually on the orders of higher authority; and mediate minor disputes.

In many other ways the Indians of the *anejos* have a dependent, and usually disadvantageous, relationship with their Spanish-speaking neighbors. In most parts of the rural Sierra trading is a monopoly of the *mestizos*. Indian hamlets offer few facilities for trade above the level of informal and occasional barter. To sell produce or to buy manufactured goods, the Indians must journey either to a market town or to a nearby parish center, where there are normally a few general stores. Indian farmers commonly sustain long-term trading and debt relationships with the village storekeepers, mortgaging portions of their future harvests, usually at very low price equivalents, against current cash purchases.

Although many Indian hamlets have their own chapels in which mass is celebrated occasionally, for the most religious observances the residents must journey to the parish seat. In many areas, too, the dependence is reinforced by the fact that the priest, and sometimes the parish civil officials, intervene actively in the selection of sponsors for the religious *fiestas* that are so important a part of the annual cycle (see ch. 5, Ethnic Groups and Languages; ch. 10, Religion).

By contrast with the *anejos* the communities located in the more distant and isolated zones enjoy considerable freedom from the control of Spanish-speaking officialdom. Government officials, census takers and others representing the white authority are often greeted with showers of stones, and, according to several reports, even a priest has to be escorted by local Indians into and out of certain communities.

In the broader context, however, even this fiercely maintained independence has its well-defined limits. Freedom from the direct control of the Spanish-speakers is made possible only by physical isolation and a measure of economic self-sufficiency. As soon as an Indian enters the parish seat or other center of white population—for trading or for any other purpose—he becomes subject to the rules of the ethnic caste's system. Because of the low productiveness of land in the higher zones, Indians of the independent communities often find it necessary to seek temporary employment in Spanish-speaking areas.

Living either in isolation from the dominant Hispanic society, or in subservience to it, the Indians have tended, where possible, to withdraw from any unnecessary contact with the world outside their communities. For most, trust and loyalty are narrowly focused on kinsmen and community, and even Indians from outside those circles are often mistrusted. It is extremely difficult to mobilize the Indians on grounds of ethnic unity, if any is perceived by them. The narrowness of the base of trust and participation is demonstrated perhaps most clearly in the absence of widespread Indian revolt. There have been occasional uprisings, especially on the *haciendas,* but they have almost never spread beyond the bounds of the communities in which they began.

In recent years some trends toward change have become apparent, largely reflecting changes that have taken place in the national society as a whole. The construction of new roads has resulted in growing contact between many of the most isolated areas of the Sierra and the larger urban centers. Moreover, for several decades there has been a growing concern with extending educational facilities to serve the entire population.

Further pressures for change have been generated by the ambitious rural development programs of the government, several international agencies and the Catholic Church (see ch. 8, Living Conditions). Indian communities have been encouraged, under these programs, to establish village councils independent of the white-dominated parish government, and considerable stress has been placed on technical improvement in agriculture and in training the Indians in occupations traditionally closed to them.

Nevertheless, the pace of change is extremely slow. Perhaps the most important block is the continuing underdevelopment of the national economy. An Indian who would abandon his heritage of subsistence farming would find few alternative ways of life open to him. Furthermore, the local political and economic power structures, long dependent on a docile Indian population, have often raised violent opposition to any attempt at abolishing the old social forms. Finally, most Indian communities exhibit a strong cultural conservatism, in part the result of centuries of mistreatment and a reaction of mistrust and in part the result of a reluctance to abandon ways that have proved satisfactory for generations. It appears likely that, given continuing change in the national society, the rural social structure will inevitably undergo modification, but that the pace will continue to be slow.

CHAPTER 7

FAMILY

A majority of Ecuadorians find their most effective source of material and emotional security in bonds of family and kinship loyalty. Although there are broad regional, class and ethnic variations in specific aspects of kinship and family life, social values drawn from both the Spanish and Sierra Indian traditions emphasize duty and affection among kinsmen. No other institution of national life has shown the endurance and stability characteristic of the family and the broader kin grouping. Ancestry plays a large part in the assignment of prestige and other marks of high social status. Trust and responsibility in business and politics are channeled along lines of kinship, and, in general, a man without broad and intimate kin ties is looked upon as defenseless (see ch. 6, Social Structure; ch. 12, Social Values).

Kinship cohesion and family stability are generally strongest at the upper levels of society, where the importance of ancestry in determining social status and the concentration of wealth in such hereditary assets as land have combined to give rise to large, overlapping kin groups. Most upper-class families maintain close and enduring bonds with even distant kin in all parts of the country, standing ready to offer them economic and political support, where necessary, and expecting the same in return. Obligations to kinsmen through marriage are scarcely less compelling than those to blood relatives, and marriage plays an important part in cementing alliances among powerful and wealthy families. At least partly as a corollary of this importance, upper-class families place great stress on stability of marriage and tend to intervene actively in the mate choices of their members.

Although the stress on kinship loyalties is common to the entire society, in practice the circle of effectively cooperating kinsmen is much smaller for most lower-class families and for many middle-class families. Less prosperous families usually lack both the resources and the motivations to maintain ties with distant and broadly dispersed kin.

Regional variations are especially apparent in lower-class patterns of marriage and domestic life. On the Coast common-law unions occur with greater frequency than do formal marriages among the lower class of both rural and urban areas. Moreover, family units tend to be unstable, as there is a high incidence of paternal desertion. In the Sierra, by contrast, formal marriages predominate strongly over common-law unions, especially in rural areas, and conjugal ties, however based, are in most cases quite durable. This divergence in patterns seems generally to reflect the greater conservatism and stability of Sierra society and especially the greater influence of the Catholic Church in the Sierra (see ch. 11, Religion).

In many respects, both the values and the practice of family life among the Quechua-speaking Indians are distinct from those of the Hispanic segment. Nevertheless, a long history of influence and domination by representatives of Spanish culture and the Catholic Church have brought about considerable modification. The degree of acculturation has been such that, in many parts of the rural Sierra, Indian family and kinship life is little different from that of poorer *mestizo* peasants (see ch. 5, Ethnic Groups and Languages).

MARRIAGE

Under law only a civil marriage, performed as a rule by a *teniente político* (political lieutenant who is the administrative head of a parish) or *jefe político* (political chief who is the administrative head of a canton), has legal effect in establishing the legitimacy of offspring and regulating inheritance. Nonetheless, social custom—especially in the tradition-bound Sierra—requires both ecclesiastical and civil sanction, and a majority of marriages are celebrated before both authorities. The minimum age for marriage is set at 12 for girls and 14 for boys, but those under 21 must have parental permission.

Both the Constitution and the Civil Code deal extensively with the rights and obligations of marriage. The Constitution pledges the state to protect marriage and the family and guarantees the rights of children, both legitimate and illegitimate, to parental support and guidance. The Civil Code, in addition to setting forth the requirements and limitations of marriage and divorce, contains a detailed set of prescriptions for the regulation of property rights between the spouses.

In general, the husband is invested with a dominant role in matters of the family economy. Except when an agreement to the contrary is entered legally before the marriage, the wife's property becomes part of a conjugal partnership administered by the husband. In most cases a wife is held legally incompetent to contract, engage in business or to appear in court without her husband's consent. The law does, however, make provisions for limiting the power of the husband. It permits the contracting of premarital property settlements, excluding some specific part of the wife's property from the conjugal partnership. This provision is of considerable importance in the case of spouses from wealthy families, and a property settlement is almost invariably entered as a part of upper-class marriages. Further, the law provides that if a wife has engaged openly in a business or profession without objections from her husband, the latter may not later pose such objections.

Civil divorce is permitted by law on many different grounds, including mutual consent, abusive or cruel behavior by either spouse, adultery by either spouse and conviction of either spouse for a serious crime. Decrees of divorce and approval of property settlements arising therefrom must be issued by a provincial judge after several hearings, including a formal effort at reconciliation.

In upper- and middle-class households throughout the country formal marriage, before both the Church and the state, is almost universal, even though some men in both classes maintain mistress relationships in addition to their conjugal ties. Furthermore, although common-law marriage is not unknown among the urban and rural lower classes of the Sierra, a majority in those groups are also legally married. No official statistics were available on the subject in 1965, but sample surveys indicated that common-law marriages, perhaps 10 percent of all conjugal unions in the Sierra, were more common among the *mestizo* lower class, especially in the cities, than among the Indian peasantry.

By contrast, in the coastal lowlands, formal marriage is much less frequent in lower-class households. Estimates of the frequency of common-law marriage in such provinces as Guayas, Los Ríos, Manabí and Esmeraldas range from one-half to two-thirds. Some support for these estimates is evident in the 1961 birth registry for Esmeraldas Province, which indicates a ratio of illegitimate births to legitimate births of more than 2 to 1.

Many social, religious and economic factors are cited in explaining these contrasts. The costs of formalizing a marriage and the dispersion of rural populations (especially on the Coast) far from administrative centers are often given as reasons. Although the fees charged by civil and Church officials are generally modest, the customary wedding *fiesta* can impose a major burden on a poor family, and many well-populated parts of the country are several days' walk from a parish seat. In the rural areas of the Sierra, however, even the most impoverished members of society, among whom formal marriage is the rule, seem able to overcome these hindrances.

The prevalence of formal, stable marriage in the rural Sierra appears to be strongly associated with the generally stable quality of social life. Sierra peasants—and especially the Indians—move about very little. Typically, an individual remains during his entire life within the same community, living with and depending upon a limited range of neighbors and kinsmen. Typically, too, he remains bound to the same agricultural holding, a portion of which may have come to him in marriage. The narrow range and stability of life thus tend strongly to impose continuity of obligation within family bonds and, more specifically, within marriage. Reinforcing this tendency toward stability is the strong influence historically wielded by the Catholic clergy.

The *montuvio* of the coastal lowlands, whether independent farmer or wage laborer, tends to be much more mobile. Coastal communities lack the stability characteristic of those in the Sierra. Given an abundance of land, a man is not so dependent upon specific individuals, and marriage plays virtually no part in regulating the distribution of property. Furthermore, the Church has never exercised great influence over the *montuvios*. Lacking such constraints to stability, many men of the coastal lower class hesitate to commit themselves irrevocably to a lifetime of family responsibility. Hence, conjugal ties tend to be not only unsanctified, but also rather brittle (see ch. 6, Social Structure; ch. 11, Religion).

For much the same reasons the incidence of common-law marriage and conjugal instability is rather high among the urban poor, even in the Sierra. The influence of the clergy is considerably weaker than in the Indian communities; family organization is less tightly knit; and the sense of continuing obligation and trust among kinsmen and in-laws is considerably weaker.

Both the Constitution and the Civil Code assert the principle that illegitimate offspring are entitled to paternal support in the same measure as those born in wedlock. This principle is, however, at variance with prevailing social custom, and claims against deserting common-law husbands are rarely pressed.

In respect to formal marriage, however, public opinion and social custom strongly support legal principle. The divorce rate is extremely low (little more than 1 percent in 1962). A man's economic responsibilities to his legitimate family are seen by all segments of society as permanent and absolute, and dereliction of this duty is accorded the strongest opprobrium. Moreover, the priority accorded paternal and maternal roles over the purely personal bond between the spouses has tended to reinforce the durability even of incompatible partnerships. Yet another force for stability in marriage—especially at the highest social levels—is the traditional importance of in-law ties in regulating wealth, status and political influence. Thus, wide circles of kinsmen of both spouses are likely to feel a personal stake in the stability of their marriage and to exert pressure for reconciliation upon them when they are feuding.

Members of all classes and ethnic groups see married life as properly dominated by the husband. This feeling is especially strong in the more Hispanic segment of the society, whose values historically have placed great emphasis on the contrasting roles of men and women. The strictest fidelity is expected of wives. In the Spanish value tradition adultery by a woman is seen not merely as an offense against her vows but also as the most grievous possible affront to her husband's honor and self-esteem. By contrast, even though the civil law makes it a ground for divorce, a man's adultery is scarcely deemed an offense of itself in the popular view of Spanish-speaking Ecuadorians. A man's extramarital adventuring most typically calls forth a reaction ranging from tacit public acceptance to the actual admiration of his fellows. Such behavior, as a rule, attracts strong reproach only when it causes a husband to neglect his economic duties to his legitimate family or when it is carried on so blatantly as to bring ridicule, gossip and shame upon his wife, since a married woman derives her status from that of her husband (see ch. 12, Social Values).

Although the highland Indian value patterns also stress male dominance, there is considerably less preoccupation with the contrasting role of the sexes. In particular, the tacit acceptance of male adultery is lacking. If infidelity is seen as reprehensible in wives, it is seen as scarcely less so in husbands. In addition, the active role played by Indian women in their household economies is reflected in a generally higher expectation of activity and initiative on the part of wives.

FAMILY AND KINSHIP ORGANIZATION

Family Size and Composition

In 1962 the mean family size was estimated at about 5 members. Urban-rural and regional fluctuations around this mean were rather small. In general, urban families were slightly larger (with a mean of 5.2 members) than rural families (4.9 members), and those on the Coast (about 5.3 members) were slightly larger than those in the Sierra (4.7 members).

The typical household unit in all social segments is the nuclear family—a father and mother living in permanent, though not necessarily formal union, along with their unmarried and minor children. Nevertheless, perhaps one-fourth of all household groups contain residents other than members of the nuclear family. Upper-class families typically honor the strong obligation of mutual aid among kinsmen by offering shelter to impoverished, orphaned or otherwise dependent relatives. As elsewhere in Latin America, therefore, a wealthy family is likely to be constituted as a *familia grande* (great family), consisting of a core family and one or more retainers of varying degrees of blood relationship.

Among less prosperous families, which have restricted living space and resources, this pattern of extended household is less strongly developed. Nevertheless, where it is possible to do so, most families readily extend permanent shelter to relatives in need—especially the orphaned children of close kinsmen. In the case of lower-class families such dependent relatives are often illegitimate children left in the charge of maternal relatives by their mothers who have migrated elsewhere to work. Another variation from the nuclear pattern, common among the urban poor and on the Coast, is the household consisting only of a woman and her illegitimate children, to which a succession of men attach themselves as temporary residents.

Family Roles

Value traditions among the Spanish speakers and the highland Indians alike stress paternal dominance in most aspects of domestic life. This patriarchic view of family life continues to have clear reflection in the civil law which, in addition to investing the husband with control over the family's economic destinies grants him, except in cases of legally declared incompetence or dereliction, the final and deciding word in all matters of child rearing. For Hispanic Ecuadorians these legal provisions express a clear principle that the father is not only the provider for his family but also its ultimate arbiter and spokesman before the outside world.

In the more educated segments of the society, the new ideals of female emancipation have achieved a measure of advocacy. Some women of the middle class, in particular, having asserted their equality by taking paid employment, have begun to express a growing demand for a greater voice in matters affecting their households, but the old values show great persistence under the pressures of social change. Men have been reluctant to surrender their traditional rights of dominance, perhaps at least partly because the merest hint of domination by one's wife can be seriously damaging to one's public image and self-esteem (see ch. 12, Social Values).

Although the dominance of the father is, both in legal theory and in the social ideal, virtually complete, he seldom pays much attention to the day-by-day functioning of the household. As a rule, he leaves routine budgeting to his wife, provided that she maintains the household to his standards within the allowance set by him. In fact, ignorance of petty domestic detail is a matter of masculine pride.

Similarly, the father's actual role in the rearing of children is limited in most Spanish-speaking families. Although fathers are usually open in their expressions of affection toward their children, especially the younger ones, the prevailing social view invests the mother with the primary responsibility for the work and routine decisions entailed in child rearing. A father's most important contributions lie in providing a model of manhood for his sons and in the occasional exertion of a final and dire disciplinary authority in cases of unruliness beyond the mother's control.

The Hispanic social tradition grants men the right of a broad public life, led largely independently of their families. Many men therefore spend much of their leisure time in the company of male friends in bars, clubs, coffeehouses or simply in the street and consider such activities as their sole and personal concern. Those who exercise this freedom of action are usually careful to keep their social diversions separate from those they share with their families. Men can be truly close friends for years without ever exchanging home visits, partly because these men are likely to be admiringly aware of each other's occasional lapses in marital fidelity.

A woman's range of normal activity, which lies chiefly within the home, is largely autonomous. Whether or not she has the assistance of servants and the advice of older female relatives, she is completely responsible for domestic functioning and for the care, deportment and training of her children. She can expect to make most of the necessary decisions without interference and, often, without other than financial support from her husband.

The Spanish social tradition invests the maternal role with great sentimentality. Typically, the feeling toward mothers is one of unreserved affection, little short of piety, in contrast with that toward fathers, which often bears overtones of fear and reserve. The maternal role is popularly seen as having a heroism of its own. In the ideal, the mother finds solace for the domineering mien and occasional infidelities of her husband in the love of her children—a love she rewards richly by her sacrifice on their behalf. Alongside this deeply rooted sentimentality is a well-established notion that the mother bears total and ultimate responsibility for the well-being of her children in case of default by their father. Men living in common-law unions can, and frequently do, abandon their children without incurring great opprobrium, but maternal desertion is looked upon as especially reprehensible (see ch. 12, Social Values).

If her duties leave her the time, a woman is allowed a limited range of social life, chiefly within the kinship circle, although more prosperous women also have memberships in clubs and charitable organizations. Leisure activities for upper-class women, whether with female relatives or friends, are concentrated in a round of home visits punctuated with occasional afternoon teas and card parties.

For most upper- and middle-class families shared social participation and diversion are limited to certain specific activities and events, such as weddings, funerals, christenings and occasional Sunday outings. On weekends the clubs, which during the week cater largely or exclusively to men, provide a locale for family outings. Balls and other periodic club functions also give rise to opportunities for joint socializing by husbands and wives.

These patterns of clearly separated male and female family roles are subject to considerable variance of circumstances in less prosperous Hispanic-oriented families. Where the household depends for sustenance on farming, artisan activities or petty commerce, the wife often works alongside the husband, making a contribution of equal importance to his. For peasant families, too, much of the recreational pattern is tied in with work, with weekly visits to the market town and with religious *fiestas,* all occasions for joint participation.

Although family life in Sierra Indian communities is also invested with a strong tone of paternal dominance, it differs in many ways from the Hispanic pattern. In many communities the deference of wives for their husbands and male kinsmen is expressed in certain visible and stereotyped ways, such as walking behind the latter and eating only after they have been served. Nevertheless, both the exigencies of peasant life and traditional social custom assure women a degree of importance and power. Like their counterparts in the Hispanic-oriented lower classes, Indian wives must make a full contribution to their families' economy. When the family is at all dependent on the cash marketing of produce, it is often the wife's responsibility to do the selling, and her voice in domestic economic matters is likely to be enhanced.

Although the Indian values generally include the notion that men are due the obedience and deference of their wives, they place less stress on the demonstration of masculinity as a necessary part of public image and self-esteem. Consequently, there is much less assertion of independence. Furthermore, observers generally report a strong feeling that a wife's consultative rights in all matters regarding the household deserve full respect.

The Kinship Circle

Given the importance of kinship in the social life, ties with kinsmen beyond the nuclear family are generally strong for persons in all classes and ethnic groups. In the upper class, where wealth traditionally has resided in land and other hereditary assets, kinship bonds across several degrees of relationship and ties with in-laws are especially crucial in the distribution and maintenance of properties. Further, kinship and descent are extremely important in fixing social status, especially in the Sierra. Admission to elite social circles is regulated by principles of distinguished ancestry, and those who have wealth, but no distinguished ancestors, seek to marry their children into aristocratic lines. Political power also flows largely in lines of blood and affinal relationship.

These factors combine to create large and cohesive, though overlapping, kin groups in the upper class. Groups of closely related heirs share a continuing mutual economic interest; social status is asserted and validated through genealogies; and the official influence of kinsmen is sought for personal advantage. Solidarity is expressed in an active and highly ceremonialized social life. Nuclear families spend much time calling upon relatives of varying degree, and weddings, baptisms and funeral masses can call forth the attendance of dozens of kinsmen. The society pages of newspapers are replete with accounts of extended family life, usually ornamented with genealogical detail. Upper-class kinship solidarity has visible expression in the ready assumption of mourning costume, especially by women, for even fairly distant relatives.

At the less prosperous levels of Spanish-speaking society there are fewer bases for broadly extended kinship solidarity. Family fortunes in hereditary assets are either restricted or entirely absent; there is less influence available to those who can claim kinship; and there is little social advantage to be gained by genealogical demonstration. In consequence, groups of cooperating and interacting kinsmen tend to be smaller in the middle than in the upper class and even smaller in the urban lower class and among the Spanish-speaking peasants of the Coast. Nevertheless, the notion that one's kinsmen are the first and best line of defense in adversity is universally accepted, and though lower- and middle-class kinship life is less extended and elaborate than that of the elite, loyalties tend to be strong.

In the more stable rural Sierra, and especially in Indian communities, extended kinship loyalties are broader and more compelling, for the most part, than in the cities and on the Coast. Given the low level of mobility and the strong tendency for marriage partners to be chosen from nearby, large groups of kinsmen are most often concentrated within small areas. Thus, much of community life—solidarity against threat from the outside and communal work, for example—is in fact kinship life as well. Kinship solidarity on these grounds is reinforced, too, by the importance of marriage and inheritance in regulating ownership of scarce lands.

COMPADRAZGO

The importance of kinship in ordering social life is further reflected in the tradition of *compadrazgo* (lit., coparenthood)—a relationship of affection and mutual obligation arising between people as a result of a ritual. An institution common to all of Latin America, *compadrazgo* has generally served as a means of extending one's circle of intimacy and mutual trust through the establishment of bonds amounting to ritual kinship.

The most significant *compadrazgo* in most areas is that established with the baptism of a child. The parents and godparents, who address each other as *compadre* (cofather) and *comadre* (comother), are conceived as bound to each other for life by ties of loyalty and affection approaching those of kinship. The solemnity of the bond is underscored by an absolute prohibition of marriage and sexual relations between those who call each other *compadre* and *comadre*. In religious law the godfather and godmother (called *padrino* and *madrina* by the godchild) bear an important responsibility to the child whose baptism they have sponsored. They are expected to insure the physical welfare the religious training of their godchild (*ahijado*) and, at least theoretically, must agree to adopt the child on death or dereliction of the parents.

In most cases the relationships of baptismal godparents with their *compadres* and *ahijados* fall considerably short of the value ideals. Godchild adoptions, for example, are quite rare. Nevertheless, these ties do bear definite overtones of affection, responsibility and loyalty. Most parents ask only those whom they trust and respect to serve as *padrinos*, and the person asked, whether or not he accepts the request, must respond in a manner indicating that he has been honored. *Compadres* living near each other commonly exchange ceremonial visits, usually bearing token gifts. In rural Sierra communities it is customary for a godchild meeting his *padrino* on the street to ask the latter for his blessing. In some cases, too, godparents enjoy a privileged relationship as advisers to their *compadres*.

Compadrazgo is established at other rituals—most notably marriage and confirmation—as well. In some parts of the rural Sierra, *compadrazgo* of marriage is accorded as much importance as that of baptism. On the other hand, ties rising from confirmation and other ceremonies are transitory and of little importance, serving at most to underscore old friendships between participants.

Marital *padrinos*, of whom a couple may have several, are usually seen as lifelong advisers, responsible for mediating disputes between the spouses. *Padrinos* of matrimony not uncommonly serve as baptismal godparents to the couple's first child.

Cultivation of *compadre* ties with wealthier and more powerful men is a traditional means of defense for poor families. In many areas, Indians seek such bonds with merchants in nearby villages and towns. Workers often look to their employers as potential *compadres*, and political retainers look to their leaders. There is a clear hope that higher status *compadres* will use their influence and wealth to benefit their dependent clients. For their part, businessmen and politicians usually accede readily to invitations to sponsor baptisms and weddings, for poor *compadres* reciprocate small loans and the exertion of political influence by being loyal customers and retainers.

At another level, *compadrazgo* provides a means for cementing preexisting relationships among social equals. In many rural communities ramified bonds of *compadrazgo* serve to reinforce bonds of blood kinship and neighborly mutual aid and cooperation. In the upper class such ritual sponsorships play an important part in establishing and maintaining friendships among unrelated or distantly related kin groups.

CHILDHOOD AND YOUTH

Parenthood is a welcome role among all classes and ethnic groups. In Spanish tradition fatherhood is seen as a demonstration of manliness, and motherhood as virtually the sole means for fulfilling feminine destiny. Although the explicit values of the Indians regarding parenthood have never been described, it is clear that for the majority the birth of a child is the occasion for great rejoicing.

In the Sierra baptism is universal; on the Coast it is estimated that a considerable portion of all children, especially in the more remote rural areas, go unbaptized. For Indians and lower-class *mestizos* of the rural highlands, the sense of religious obligation to baptize infants is strengthened by a common belief that the unbaptized, after death, become malevolent spirits.

A christening is, for most families, an important social event. Godparents are usually chosen with great care, and the ritual is followed by generous festivities. Poor families will frequently delay a baptism, if the infant is in no apparent danger of death, until resources can be accumulated for an appropriately elaborate feast. Baptisms in upper-class families often command considerable space in newspaper society pages.

Although they are subject to many perils, reflected in the high rate of infant mortality, babies of the lower class are generally treated with great affection and solicitude. In most poor families an infant is only one of his mother's concerns, but as a rule his cries call forth an immediate comforting response. Feeding is generally on demand; and nursing mothers are a common sight in all places, public and private. Swaddling is customary among Indians and poorer, more conservative *mestizos*. For periods ranging from 3 to 6 months infants are kept as inert bundles, trussed from feet to shoulders in cloths and belts, carried on their mothers' backs in shawls.

With rare exceptions, babies of peasant and lower-class families enjoy the doting attention of all members of their families. This affectionate and protective attention is withdrawn slowly as the child becomes self-sufficient and capable of simple tasks—usually not long after the third birthday—unless a new baby is born, in which case the loss of attention can be quite sudden and drastic.

Infants in upper- and middle-class households usually enjoy the full time and attention of their mothers and the solicitude of nursemaids (*niñeras*) and other servants. As a child grows old enough to express his whims, these are usually indulged by both parents and servants. Typically, the mother and the *niñera* hover over an ambulatory child, nervously attempting to protect it from falls and other injuries, no matter how minor. This gentle regime is interrupted rather abruptly when the child goes to school and has its first contact with strong discipline at the hands of teachers.

Children in peasant and lower-class families are assigned simple chores when they have barely emerged from the toddler stage. Five-year-old children of both sexes are often seen herding pigs or, on occasion, caring for younger siblings. Play is interspersed with duties throughout the day. Often, children of poor urban families are sent into the street to peddle small items, such as lottery tickets. Gradually, lower-class children begin to learn their future roles. Daughters assume a growing burden of domestic duties and other feminine activity. Sons of rural families begin to accompany their fathers to the fields, lending a hand and learning a farmer's tasks. Many urban lower-class boys spend an increasing amount of time in street trades and doing odd jobs. In the cities and more accessible rural areas, this pattern of work and task learning is interrupted briefly, for a growing number of children, by a few years of primary schooling.

When a family is so impoverished that it cannot support its

offspring, one or more may be turned over to a prosperous household to provide domestic service in return for sustenance and shelter. Often, such children are too young, at first, to do any useful work and are entrusted to the care of other servants until they can be set to simple tasks. Although social custom requires that such children be treated humanely and that they be given schooling, actual treatment often falls short of this standard. When children are entrusted to godparents, they are usually treated with greater kindness.

In the impersonal and unstable life of the urban slums abandonment of children by desperate parents is not unknown, despite the strong opprobrium accorded such behavior. Some abandoned children receive shelter in orphanages, but many lead a hand-to-mouth existence, begging, stealing and sleeping in doorways and under vendors' stalls in the public markets.

Boys of upper- and middle-class families emerge from the solicitous supervision of parents and *niñeras* to a period of considerable freedom. Except for their studies, little in the way of duty is expected of schoolboys, and within limits that broaden with age, they are free to choose their companions and to seek adventure.

By contrast, girls of wealthier and higher-status families remain under the close supervision of their mothers and other female relatives. From the time they reach school age they are discouraged from boisterous play and urged to adopt the graces of a lady. Their playmates are usually subject to close parental scrutiny. As their brothers' world of activity and experience widens, theirs tends to narrow.

For young people of the lower classes adolescence is little more than a brief period marking a smooth transition from childhood to an early adulthood. After learning adult work and social roles and, occasionally, after brief schooling they have acquired the knowledge necessary to farmer, worker or wife.

In many areas adolescence is a period of freedom and adventure for boys and, in lesser degree, for girls. Even from the stable and conservative Sierra, boys of 16 to 18 years often travel to the Coast or other distant places for a period of wage labor. At the same age some girls seek domestic employment in the cities.

Sexual awareness arises early in peasant and urban lower-class children, given their usually crowded living conditions, and is often followed by early experimentation. In early casual liaisons, formed at *fiestas* and in pastures, many young men and women quickly find their way into conjugal unions, either formal or common-law. In 1961 more than one-third of the women and about one-fifth of the men entering marriage were under 20 years of age. Although no detailed census breakdowns were available, local surveys indicate that such marriages are concentrated in the poorer and rural segments of society.

On the Coast, where land is abundant and a man can easily set up a squatter holding or find some sort of work, the establishment of a new peasant family is usually little more than a matter of erecting a hut and sowing some crops. In the crowded agricultural communities of the Sierra many young couples must spend the first few years of marriage with in-laws, until fields and a house plot are acquired. In the urban lower class the establishment of a conjugal union, whether legal or common-law, depends on the ability of the man—and sometimes also the woman—to find employment.

Boys in the upper-and-middle classes enjoy a protracted adolescence of freedom and experimentation. Almost all continue their training through secondary school, and a majority go on to the university. Having little more than their studies to concern them, boys from prosperous families are free, as students, to become actively involved in political matters and to engage in sexual experimentation, chiefly with prostitutes. On terminating his studies a middle- or upper-class young man enters a profession or seeks employment, and at this time can begin to engage in serious courtship leading to marriage.

Social change has brought greater freedom to many girls of the upper- and middle-classes than their mothers enjoyed. Complete secondary training is the rule, and many girls seek a university education. Not uncommonly, young women of prosperous families take paid professional or white-collar work until they are married, and many middle-class women work after marriage. Nevertheless, supervision of adolescent girls and young women is much stricter than that imposed on their brothers. Acquaintances are inspected sharply by mothers and aunts, and fathers and brothers characteristically adopt a jealous and protective attitude, challenging the intentions of even casual male friends. Although dating has become acceptable in more cosmopolitan urban circles, more often than not it is looked upon as a serious and definite step toward engagement, and chaperonage remains quite common.

CHAPTER 8

LIVING CONDITIONS

Living conditions vary markedly by region and by socioeconomic class. There are major differences in diet, clothing, and style and materials of housing between the tropical lowlands and the temperate highlands. The relative isolation of the rural inhabitants, who make up well over half the total population, encourages a dependence on local resources which reinforces these differences. Even in towns and small provincial cities access to goods originating from outside the immediate locale is limited. Varied, relatively cosmopolitan markets are located principally in the two largest cities, Guayaquil and Quito (see ch. 22, Domestic Trade).

Agriculture is the principal means of livelihood in the country; artisanry, manual labor, domestic service and marginal activities in the city. The lower class, about 88 percent of the whole population, lives under very poor conditions. The middle class, probably no more than 10 percent, generally has satisfactory housing, clothing, food supplies and a few conveniences and luxuries. The upper class, not more than 2 percent, lives comfortably and, in the cities, has access to luxuries; it often has impressive living quarters, dresses fashionably and travels abroad. The discrepancy between the classes removes much of the meaning of the average annual per capita income figure, which is the equivalent of $US132.

Health conditions are generally poor. Potable water and sewage disposal systems are generally lacking. For almost two-thirds of all families, living quarters consist of one or two rooms unprotected from disease carriers. Hygiene in personal care and food preparation is not widely practiced. Inadequacies in diet and clothing serve to heighten susceptibility to disease. The incidence of, and death rate from, infectious diseases, especially those affecting the respiratory and gastrointestinal systems is high. The rate of death among infants, in most cases delivered at home without professional supervision and then poorly nourished and clothed, is also high.

Programs and systems for the physical care and material assistance of the population are maintained by the government and, to a lesser extent, by the Church and other private entities. Chief public responsibility for health and welfare rests with the Ministry of Social Welfare. The principal efforts have been directed toward public health and the provision of medical facilities. Considerable assistance has been rendered to national entities by international organizations, especially in the area of disease control.

It is estimated that, within the Ministry, roughly 50 agencies, for the most part autonomous, have some responsibility for public health. Attempts to centralize administration, in order to increase efficiency and reduce costs, have met resistance, principally from the city of Guayaquil, which has been influential in the public health field.

Social assistance has operated on a more modest scale and has been aimed at a variety of specific small groups. The largest of these are the salaried workers who benefit from several social insurance programs. Child welfare is another area which has received attention for some time.

In recent years the government has displayed growing interest in expanding its role in health and welfare. Within the General Plan for the Economic and Social Development of Ecuador (1964–73) are a number of sections devoted to social welfare. Recognition of the inadequacies of existing medical facilities prompted the establishment of the Ten-Year Health Plan, aimed primarily at consolidating administration and resources and extending health services to all parts of the country. Other specific plans deal with housing, rural development and the cooperative movement. For the realization of these plans the continuing assistance, both financial and technical, of international and foreign agencies is necessary.

PATTERNS OF LIVING

Rural

For the great majority of rural residents, who comprise almost 65 percent of the total population, life revolves around small-scale agriculture. The remainder are largely artisans and small tradesmen, many of whom also engage in agriculture on a part-time basis. The population is rather widely dispersed, especially in the lowland regions. Settlements are extremely small, the majority having populations of less than 200. As a result, the economic activity of the rural dweller is characterized by a high level of self-sufficiency.

Extremely small plots of land, farmed under ownership or some form of tenancy, provide practically all the food consumed by the agricultural family. Farming tends to be limited to the cultivation of a few basic crops—corn and potatoes in the Sierra, rice and beans in the lowlands. The domestic animals which are often kept in small numbers occasionally provide additions to the basic diet. On the Coast fishing also supplements the diet.

Dwellings are usually constructed from available materials by the individual, with the help of friends and relatives. Simple in design, the typical dwelling is a one-storied structure of one or two rooms. In the Sierra the walls are most often made of adobe and the roofs of thatch. In most cases the floor is hard-packed earth. A low door provides the only opening. In the towns of the highlands a few houses may be somewhat more spacious and may have flooring and roofing made of manufactured materials, windows and possibly an interior patio. In the lowlands wood and cane stalk are the principal building materials. Walls may be only partially filled in, and elevation of the dwelling on stilts is frequent. In the towns two-storied wooden houses, painted in pastel colors, are fairly common.

Dwellings tend to be sparsely furnished, often with homemade items. In the Sierra cooking is done on the ground or in a rudimentary oven of bricks or hard-packed earth set up in a corner; in the lowlands cooking is done in a similar manner. Ceramic and wooden utensils are used, and on the Coast, some cheap manufactured goods also are used. Furniture is generally limited to a few chairs or benches and a table. In the Sierra the bed consists of skins placed directly on the floor or on a simple, slightly raised structure. Hammocks are frequently used in the lowlands. In addition to housing the family, the dwelling serves as a storage place for produce, seed and farm implements and, in colder areas, sometimes as a shelter for animals.

Clothing, especially in the Sierra, is also commonly made at home. In many Indian communities the cloth itself, usually wool, is produced at home on simple looms. The *mestizos* prefer manufactured yardgoods. Similarly, in the lowlands, clothing may be made at home, but usually from manufactured cotton fabrics. With the exception of the Indians, who maintain distinctive styles of dress, the rural population dresses in the modern European manner (see ch. 5, Ethnic Groups and Languages). Male attire consists of trousers and shirt, made of wool or cotton, depending on the climate, and sometimes a suit or suit jacket; female attire consists of a simple dress or skirt and blouse. In colder areas ponchos and shawls are also worn. In most cases, an individual has no more than two changes of clothing, and the same clothing is normally worn for sleep as well. Both in the Sierra and on the Coast, many people commonly go barefoot. Sandals and, to a lesser extent, shoes are worn by the more affluent.

Maintenance of the household usually occupies all members of the family. If the family derives its main support from artisanry or trade, the men assume the chief responsibility and are assisted by the women and older children, who usually tend the family's plot and animals. In agricultural families farming is primarily a male responsibility, but women sometimes help during the busy seasons. The tending of the animals, food preparation, the making of clothes and child care are accomplished by women and the older children. Weaving, pottery making and the making of farm or household implements are sparetime activities for both men and women. Family members may engage in additional activities which provide a modest cash income. A portion of the small crop, animals and animal products, and handicrafts are often bartered or sold to friends or at the open markets held weekly in most communities. Engaging in part-time or seasonal labor is another common means of producing cash income.

Cash is used to obtain certain necessities, such as salt or matches, which cannot be made at home. It is also used for entertainment in town on market days or at *fiestas*. *Fiestas* are given to celebrate a religious holiday; a special occasion within the family, such as baptism or marriage; or the termination of a project of joint labor, such as housebuilding. Among Indians the *fiesta* is the sole organized diversion; as sponsorship carries prestige, *fiesta* costs are an important cash expenditure. Other Ecuadorians also spend money on such diversions as radios and movies and, in addition, seek home improvement or better clothing. Both groups make cash outlays for land and livestock. In the lowlands, where land is available in greater quantity and mobility is more widespread, extra cash is more apt to be used for luxury items.

The attitudes of rural residents toward their environment and type of existence are difficult to ascertain. Migration, both within and from rural regions, however, may give some general indications. From 1950 to 1960, roughly 400,000 people migrated, mainly from the overcrowded Sierra to the less densely populated Coast or Oriente or from rural areas to the cities, principally Guayaquil. Few Indians migrated from the Sierra because they tend to feel a strong attachment to their land and their community. Migration from country to city has taken place primarily on the Coast. Although social and economic discontent among the rural population has not reached proportions of widespread militancy, observers report an increase in recent years as communications have improved. Focus and channels are still largely lacking, and aspirations are consequently likely to be directed toward modest material increases rather than toward fundamental change.

Urban

Typically, urban dwellers display a wide variety in income, activity and material condition. Differences are apparent from city to city as well, Quito and Guayaquil being the centers where wages are highest and material goods are in greatest quantity. Lower-class workers—domestic servants, petty tradesmen, manual laborers and others—make up the largest segment of city dwellers. Within this group, monthly family income would not be likely to exceed S/1,100 to S/1,200 (in 1965, S/18.5 equaled US$1—see Glossary), and the average income probably does not exceed half that amount. Urban dwellers earning from S/1,500 to S/10,000 monthly, a small group, make up the economic middle class. Most are in the professions, medium-scale commerce or some form of white-collar work. An even smaller group, the economic upper class comprises those with an income greater than S/10,000 monthly. Economic and social categories do not necessarily correspond, as there are those who earn a lower-class wage but consider themselves in the middle class by virtue of such factors as occupation, education or family position. Conversely, persons of great wealth may not be considered members of the social upper class for similar reasons (see ch. 6, Social Structure).

For the urban group as a whole, food is the greatest single expenditure, consuming over 50 percent of income. Some attempts have been made by the government to establish controls on the prices of meat, milk and staples, with little success. Food is normally purchased fresh daily. For the most part, canned or dried foods are imported and too costly for the average buyer.

Accounting for about 15 percent of income, clothing is the next greatest expenditure. Dress has traditionally been important as an indication of status and social class. In style and quantity, the clothing of the urban lower class is similar to that of the rural *mestizo* peasant, although the use of some kind of footwear is more widespread in urban areas. Among the middle and upper classes great emphasis is placed on elegance and good quality, especially in the largest urban centers. Those of modest means will frequently go to considerable sacrifice to dress in the manner they feel their position requires. In style, the orientation is European, though United States fashions are beginning to have appeal. Readymade clothing is available, but most people prefer custom-made garments. In general there is a tendency toward formality. In the Sierra, for instance, informal attire is reserved for sports events, country outings or the home. On the Coast dress is considerably less conservative.

An average of 12 percent of income is devoted to housing, but this figure is somewhat deceptive. Whereas homeowners, about 35 percent of the urban population, have extremely low costs directly or indirectly involving housing, renters, representing 55 percent, often devote a substantial portion of their income to housing. According to a government-sponsored housing census made in 1962, 40 percent of those who rented their dwellings were paying between S/100 and S/300 monthly. A substantial number of these were probably members of the economic lower class and, as such, had earnings of only S/600 to S/700 a month. In Guayaquil, where wages are higher, observers report that rents of S/400 to S/500 a month are not uncommon in the burgeoning slum areas.

Urban housing standards contrast favorably with rural ones. Over three-quarters of the urban dwellings are constructed of permanent, durable materials. In addition, the great majority have electricity and some form of plumbing, either indoor or outdoor. There are, however, housing shortages, particularly for low-income groups. Almost two-thirds of the urban dwellings consist of only one or two rooms and in most cities and large towns are likely to be located in old buildings in downtown areas. Frequently, limited space is used both for dwelling and business. Modest housing facilities are also found to some extent in fringe areas, particularly around Guayaquil. In recent years makeshift dwellings have increased there with the result that the *suburbios*, as the areas containing these dwellings are called, comprise roughly one-third of the city.

Housing designed and built by professionals is usually contracted on an individual basis for private homes. Cost is prohibitive for all but members of higher-income groups as land and building materials are expensive and long-term credit facilities generally lacking.

The remainder of the income is spent on transportation, health and medical services, education, recreation and, in the middle and upper classes, domestic service. Among the more well-to-do, money is also spent for such luxury items as automobiles and televisions and, to some extent, for investments. Income has not commonly been channeled toward savings or insurance.

For much of the urban population economic demands strongly limit leisure time. Among the lower and middle classes, multiple jobholding is frequent. Popular forms of public recreation or entertainment include movies and football matches. In the highlands there is also a short bullfighting season which is enthusiastically supported. Most leisure time is spent in informal or formal social activity involving family, close friends, private social or civic clubs and religious or charitable organizations. With the exception of family occasions, men and women tend to engage in social activity primarily with members of the same sex. Among children leisure time is usually informal and unorganized. Vacations, taken by upper- and middle-class families, are most often spent at a country home owned by them or a relative.

Probably the greatest pressures are felt by the middle class, especially at the lower levels. Among this element the disparity between income, often not far above that of the lower class, and the standard of living desired is considerable. In general, the middle class has sought to adopt the upper-class style of living which requires attractive living quarters, fashionable clothing, private school education for children and luxury goods and property. Lower-class dissatisfaction and aspiration has been relatively modest, except possibly in the Guayaquil area, where greater mobility and economic vitality have prevailed.

HEALTH

As reflected in mortality and disease rates, health conditions are characteristic of those in the developing countries. In 1963 provisional figures indicated birth and death rates of 44.2 and 13.5, respectively, per thousand population. As nonregistration of both births and deaths is fairly common, the actual rates are probably somewhat higher. Life expectancy, not calculated since 1951, was 52 years, an average of extremely disparate urban and rural rates. In 1960, 56.8 percent of all deaths occurred among those under 5 years and 23.6 among those over 50. The infant mortality rate was 104.7 per thousand live births. Infectious and parasitic diseases were the greatest cause of death, accounting for 18.6 of the total deaths in 1960. Although specific figures are unavailable, the incidence of these diseases is known to be high. An additional 41 percent of deaths were caused by diseases common to early infancy and ailments of the respiratory and digestive tracts. About 25 percent of the total deaths occurred from ill-defined and unknown causes.

Sanitation and Hygiene

The immediate environment of most of the people is deficient in terms of sanitation and hygiene. For most families, which average five members, living quarters consist of one or two poorly ventilated rooms. In the rural highlands dwellings are sometimes shared with animals as well. The materials from which many dwellings are constructed—straw, cane and hardpacked earth—provide breeding grounds for insects, rodents and other disease carriers. An estimated 86 percent of the population, moreover, are not adequately served by systems of potable water and sewage disposal. Natural sources, which may be contaminated, are often used simultaneously for drinking water, waste disposal, washing and watering animals.

The effects of these conditions are compounded by the widespread absence of preventive or compensatory measures at the individual level. Much of the population lacks the knowledge and resources to adopt modern health practices. For example, among the highland lower class bathing, laundering and housecleaning are sporadic. In the production and preparation of food little attempt is made to insure against contamination.

In several areas the public authority has attempted to supervise and promote sanitation and hygiene. According to the National Sanitary Code, the importation, manufacture, sale or storage of contaminated or adulterated food is prohibited. The fact that responsibility for enforcement is not clearly assigned has resulted, however, in administrative difficulty and confusion. The General Directorate of Sanitation and Hygiene, which operates on a nationwide scale though located in Guayaquil, and the National Institute of Hygiene are charged with sanitary control of food. Inspection of meat for disease and parasites is entrusted to the municipalities, most of which maintain slaughterhouses. Slaughterhouses do not have refrigeration facilities, but depend instead on rapid distribution. Although pasteurization of milk is not required by law, dairy herds are inspected for disease in some areas, and dairy plants are subject to control. The quality of inspection and control, however, has not been considered adequate. Open markets, where most other kinds of food are sold, also come under the jurisdiction of food inspection agencies, but facilities have not been sufficient to provide broad coverage.

Attempts also are made by the General Directorate of Sanitation and Hygiene and the National Institute of Hygiene to control the manufacture and use of drugs and alcoholic beverages. Illicit use of drugs, not especially widespread, is confined primarily to cocaine, reportedly brought into the country across the Peruvian border. Highland Indians, unlike their counterparts in other Andean countries, are not coca users, as the plant is not grown in Ecuador. They do, however, manufacture a number of beverages which have been prohibited by law for reasons of health. The most harmful is *guarapo*, made from almost any organic matter, which is allowed to ferment. Although inspectors attempt to stop the production and sale of such beverages, the nature and location of manufacture have imposed difficulties.

In an attempt to control epidemics the General Directorate of Sanitation and Hygiene oversees the distribution of medicines and engages in such preventive activities as rat extermination.

140

The National Institute of Hygiene is responsible for the procurement, production and storage of all vaccines.

The General Directorate has also sought to institute certain controls over prostitution, which is not illegal. All prostitutes are required to obtain identity cards and appear for medical examinations every 2 months. In addition, sanitary police have the right to inspect brothels at any time.

The provision of sanitary water supply and sewage disposal facilities was chiefly a function of the Inter-American Cooperative Service of Public Health (Servicio Cooperativo Interamericano de Salud Pública—SCISP) in the past. SCISP was created in 1948, by agreement between the government of Ecuador and the Institute of Inter-American Affairs, which had been active in the country for several years, to administer the Cooperative Health and Sanitation Program. In 1964 the SCISP was dissolved by mutual consent, its functions reportedly to be assumed by the National Institute of Sanitary Works. In 1963 a project was begun with funds from the Inter-American Development Bank (IDB) to construct water mains and sewage systems which would affect 160,000 people. The municipalities, often with technical or financial assistance from the central government, have also been expanding water and sewage facilities. In 1962 the city of Quito began the expansion of the municipal sewer system and the construction of similar facilities in 15 adjacent districts. Two years later, the city of Guayaquil started similar projects. Both cities were assisted financially by the IDB.

Current plans, expressed in the Ten-Year Health Plan, call for the extension of water and sewage facilities to 52 percent of the population by 1973. In urban areas, 90 percent of the population is to be covered; in rural areas, 24 percent. Planners consider population dispersion, inadequate municipal resources and lack of technical personnel for planning, construction and maintenance the chief difficulties to be overcome.

Principal Diseases

The most widespread diseases are those directly or indirectly related to environmental conditions. Of the six major scourges which the World Health Organization (WHO) categories as quarantinable diseases—plague, typhus, smallpox, malaria, yellow fever and cholera—the first four are present in Ecuador.

Plague has been endemic in certain areas of the country. On the rise in Latin American since about 1960, it reached its peak in Ecuador in 1962, when 326 cases were reported. In 1963 the number of cases was 258, or 5.5 per thousand population. The largest number was reported in Chimborazo and Manabí; others occurred in El Oro, Loja and Tungurahua.

Also endemic, typhus has occurred mainly in the highland provinces during the dry season, but also in the coastal province of Manabí. In 1963 the incidence was 5.5 per thousand population. For the same year the incidence of smallpox, which has occurred throughout the country, was only 1.0 per thousand. Cases were reported in Azuay, Cañar, Carchi, Chimborazo and Cotopaxi. Malaria is confined to certain areas of the Coast. In 1963 there were 3,857 reported cases, or 81.6 per thousand population.

Among other prevalent diseases tuberculosis has been considered one of the more serious health problems. Occurring principally on the Coast, where conditions for the breeding of the bacillus are favorable, the disease was reported in over 5,000 cases in 1963 and accounted for over 1,000 deaths. The city of Guayaquil has one of the highest incidence rates in the world.

Diseases and ailments affecting the respiratory system also have a high incidence rate and account for numerous deaths, particularly in the highlands, where temperature variation is great and much of the population is inadequately clothed. Bronchitis, pneumonia, influenza and whooping cough are the most widespread. Diphtheria is also present, though to a lesser extent.

Closely following are diseases affecting the digestive tract, usually transmitted by impure food or water. Gastroenteritis is endemic throughout the country; dysentery, also endemic, is confined chiefly to the coast. Typhoid has also been reported with relative frequency. Over 3,000 cases, or 63.7 per thousand, were reported in 1963. In rural areas few peasants are without some type of intestinal parasite. Other notable diseases include measles, which frequently leads to death as a result of gastrointestinal complications; leprosy, found mainly in the coastal provinces; and tetanus.

A number of programs exist for the control of disease, conducted by various public health entities, usually with the assistance of international agencies. Malaria eradication is the oldest of these programs. In 1948, after studies had been made which showed that roughly 25 percent of all deaths were caused by malaria, an autonomous agency, the National Service for Malaria Eradication (Servicio Nacional de Erradicación de Malaria—SNEM), was created within the Ministry of Social Welfare and Labor to combat the disease. Working with the Institute of Inter-American Affairs and later with SCISP, the SNEM was able to rid the inter-Andean valleys of malaria and make some progress in coastal malarious areas. In 1956 a new campaign was launched with the technical and financial assistance of WHO, the United Nations Children's Fund (UNICEF) and the Agency for International Development (AID). In 1965 transmission of the disease had been eradicated in all coastal cities and in 40 percent of the original rural malarious areas. In an additional 38 percent of rural malarious areas the rate was reduced to 1.9 percent, and in the remaining territory it was reduced from almost 100 percent to 5 percent. Scheduled to terminate in 1969, the malaria eradication program is to be conducted in its remaining years by SNEM, WHO and UNICEF.

The campaign against smallpox was begun in 1958 by the government of Ecuador with the assistance of the Pan American Health Organization (PAHO), the regional organization of WHO, and completed in May 1964. In the 6-year period, 85 percent of the total population was vaccinated, and routine vaccination is to continue in the future.

The high incidence of tuberculosis prompted Ecuador's selection by WHO, in conjunction with the United Nations Educational, Scientific and Cultural Organization (UNESCO), as a site for widescale vaccination with BCG. These organizations worked principally with the Ecuadorian Anti-Tuberculosis League (Liga Ecuatoriana Anti-Tuberculosis—LEA), an autonomous agency. Programs of detection were also instituted. The continuing high incidence of the disease, however, indicated that the program has not had complete success.

Other campaigns have been aimed at tetanus, diphtheria, whooping cough and poliomyelitis under similar joint sponsorship. By late 1964 roughly 50 percent of the children between the ages of 3 months and 6 years had been immunized against these diseases. Control of plague was also initiated as part of an integral health plan for the province of Manabí, conducted by the government, WHO-PAHO and UNICEF. The same administrative arrangements were made for a leprosy campaign which is to last until 1967. Work methods are being developed in a demonstration area composed of localities in the provinces of Manabí, Azuay, Cañar, El Oro, Guayas, Loja, Los Ríos and Pichincha; this area will eventually be extended.

Diet and Nutrition

The bulk of the population is undernourished according to recommended dietary requirements. Among the lower socioeconomic groups, consumption of one full meal at midday is fairly common; the morning meal consists of a hot beverage and perhaps some bread, and the evening meal, of whatever may have been leftover from the midday meal.

For both economic and cultural reasons the average diet is high in starch content and strongly vegetarian. Cereals and potatoes make up about 50 percent; fruits and vegetables, 22.5 percent; meat, fish, eggs, milk and cheese, about 10 percent; and fats and oils, 5 percent. Annual per capita meat consumption is about

4.2 pounds. The average, however, is built on extremes, as some urban dwellers probably eat meat every day, whereas the urban poor consume it much less frequently and rural peasants, only on holidays or special occasions. For the peasant, meat and animal products are luxuries to be sold. Pork, followed by beef, is the most widely consumed and least expensive meat. Among the highland Indian population, guinea pigs are also popular. High priced, chicken is esteemed at all levels of society. Mutton is available in limited quantities. Milk has not been consumed in great quantity, and its use has generally been confined to urban areas. Among the better off, mineral water and soft drinks are the preferred mealtime beverages; among the poorer people, herb teas.

Fruits, vegetables and cereals consumed vary from region to region according to climatic conditions, basically tropical or temperate. Variety in the consumption of these foods is greater in urban areas, where there are better marketing facilities, than in rural areas. In the rural highlands, for instance, onions and cabbages are practically the only vegetables consumed. Similarly, in rural areas of the Coast, fruit consumption is confined virtually to the banana.

The chief deficiencies throughout the country are in animal protein, which provides amino acids, in calcium and in riboflavin. In the Sierra there are also deficiencies in vitamin A and iodine, which have led to a high incidence of goiter. Niacin and thiamine are deficient in the coastal diet. Beriberi, which results from inadequate consumption of thiamin, is common among coastal peasants. Less specific effects of insufficiencies, in quantity as well as quality, include general debilitation and slow physical development among children. Rural children are not normally weaned until the age of 2 or 3 or until the birth of another child. Without dietary supplements during this period they tend to be below average in height and weight later on. Skin lesions and overpigmented spots are also common. Deficiencies in the diet of both mother and child have been considered important factors in the high infant mortality rate.

Programs in the area of food and nutrition have been limited. The greatest activity has been directed at children through school breakfast and lunch programs, which receive the assistance of the Cooperative for American Remittances to Everywhere (CARE) and the Caritas organization of the Roman Catholic Church (see ch. 9, Education). The National Institute of Nutrition, established within the Ministry of Social Welfare and Labor in 1950, with the help of the Kellogg Foundation, has been engaged principally in making studies and surveys. It has also launched a project of iodized salt distribution. In addition, some attempts have been made to introduce programs of dietary education, as the majority of the population is not familiar with food values and basic concepts of nutrition.

Medical Care

Facilities and Personnel

According to the most complete survey available, in 1960 there were 118 hospitals, which had a total of 2.3 hospital beds per thousand population. General hospitals numbered 96; tuberculosis sanatoriums, 17; mental institutions, 3; and leprosy hospitals, 2. No institutions were devoted specifically to the treatment of the handicapped, which was administered in special wards of general institutions. Cancer cases are treated in special wards maintained by the Cancer Society, an autonomous entity.

Of the total number of hospitals in 1960, 85 were public, operating under the sponsorship of a variety of agencies and entities. Most public hospitals are administered by social assistance boards located in each province. Although theoretically responsible to the Ministry of Social Welfare, the boards have functioned with considerable autonomy. Operating funds have come from the Ministry budget and the income of large landed estates in the highlands, administered by the boards. In 1964, however, these estates were assigned to the land reform program. Other sponsors include the Social Security Fund, which runs several hospitals for subscribers; the LEA, which maintains most of the tuberculosis sanatoriums; the Department of Defense; the National Sanitation Service, which maintains two isolation hospitals; and the Welfare Board (Junta de Beneficencia) of Guayaquil, which administers most of the public hospitals in the port city. Private hospitals, called *clínicas* locally, are operated principally by groups of physicians for profit.

Regardless of sponsorship, hospitals generally are small; 75 percent have fewer than 100 beds. The dispensaries, which provide general services or care for specialized groups, such as infants and pregnant women, are sponsored primarily by the government. In 1963 there were 232 dispensaries.

Ambulance service is provided by the Red Cross, autonomous in administration but supported by the government. The Red Cross also maintains a blood bank and renders assistance in disasters.

In 1962 there were 1,620 medical doctors in the country, or 3.5 per thousand population. Although low in absolute terms, the number of doctors is high in relation to that of most other professionals. The high income and social and intellectual prestige of the profession attract many aspirants to the three medical schools, located in Quito, Guayaquil and Cuenca.

In the same year dentists numbered 529, or 1.2 per thousand population. Dental care has not been widely sought by the public in general; as a result, dentists do not enjoy prestige or economic status equal to that of medical doctors. Training in dentistry also is available in Quito, Guayaquil and Cuenca.

The development of a corps of professional nurses has been slow; in 1962 there were only 274 nurses. A program of improvement in nurses' training, with technical assistance from PAHO, has been underway since 1957 in Guayaquil, and interest in the profession is reportedly increasing there. Most nursing care is provided by some 1,500 or more auxiliaries. Technicians in the medical field exist in extremely limited numbers.

Heavily concentrated in urban areas, curative services have been adequate to cover about one-third of the country in terms of population and area. Approximately one-third of all hospitals are located in Quito and Guayaquil alone, and almost two-thirds of the doctors practice in these two cities. Provincial capitals are less well served. At the cantonal seat level there may be a dispensary which may or may not have a physician in permanent attendance. Without sufficient resources or materials, the dispensaries are frequently unable to serve adequately the areas under their jurisdiction. Below this level medical facilities and personnel are generally totally lacking.

The Ten-Year Health Plan provides for considerable expansion of medical facilities. By the end of the 10-year period planners hope to have constructed dispensaries for all cantons; 10 additional dispensaries for the cities of Quito, Guayaquil, Ambato and Cuenca; 5 specialized hospitals in Quito, Guayaquil and Cuenca; and 60 new wings for existing institutions. Medical stations and mobile medical units are to provide services at the parish level. Somewhat ambitious in scope, projected construction has not been accompanied by plans for making the substantial increases in medical personnel which would seem necessary.

According to government planners, the quality of medical care in public institutions has not been high. The physical facilities have not been adequate to meet public demand, and the fulltime staff has been limited since most doctors spend most of their time at their more lucrative private practices. As a result, the number of patients served per hour of professional attention is extremely high, and diagnostic examinations last on the average less than half an hour in hospitals and less than 15 minutes in dispensaries.

Increasingly, general hospitals have become emergency centers devoted to the treatment of terminal cases and accident victims and the performance of major surgery. Other cases are directed to dispensaries, which often lack equipment for effective diag-

146

nosis and treatment. In addition, observers suggest that hospitals and dispensaries, usually staffed by individuals with no specialized preparation, are not well utilized. Insufficient testing facilities delay the production of results and prolong the average length of stay. As most institutions suffer from inadequate financial resources, moreover, the nature of treatment may be determined by cost alone. Services such as recuperation centers, outpatient clinics and social assistance are generally lacking. Assessment of the nature of care in private institutions is not available.

Practices

Practices and attitudes regarding health and the treatment of illness vary considerably among socioeconomic groups. The upper class and some members of the middle class seek professional medical care whenever illness occurs which cannot be treated with the usual popular patent medicines or home remedies. Members of these groups tend to patronize the small, private clinics, expensive by local standards, when hospitalization is required. Highly specialized treatment for unusual or complicated illnesses and ailments may be sought abroad, often in the United States.

The lower class and the lower middle class rely to a much greater extent on home treatment. In urban areas proprietors of pharmacies, where most medicines can be obtained without prescription, serve as consultants and commonly give a variety of injections. In rural areas patent medicines are used, but dependence on home remedies, which may involve folk belief, is much greater.

Although highland Indians often have some vague concepts of the natural causes of the disease, they also attribute illness to supernatural causes. In their view, the evil eye, bad air or witchcraft, for instance, can cause various aches and pains, dizziness, fevers and loss of appetite. Treatment is sought among professional folk curers, who may determine diagnosis from the arrangement of animal entrails or contemplation of smoke or fire as well as from conversation and physical examination. Treatment usually involves a process, such as sucking or spraying with liquid and then cleansing, believed to draw out the sickening substance. Cigarettes, drink, commercial and herbal medicines, invocations and elements of the Catholic religion may also be used in curing. Scientific medical care is sought by highland Indians only when the ailment and its treatment are external or visible in nature, as in the case of broken bones.

Those members of the lower class who enter hospitals usually do so only in cases of grave illness. Childbirth, for example, occurs at home. Roughly 80 percent of the total births take place without professional supervision—an important factor in infant mortality—and presumably most unattended births occur among the lower class. For urban members entrance into overcrowded public hospitals is usually preceded by a waiting period of several days and consequently is avoided. In rural areas examination and care in a hospital or dispensary with inpatient facilities often means a long trip, followed by a wait. Highland Indians are particularly reluctant to visit hospitals as they fear they will die there.

SOCIAL ASSISTANCE AND WELFARE

Traditionally, the close ties of the extended family have provided the chief source of security for individuals in distress. Until recently the only organized programs of welfare were those maintained by the Roman Catholic Church, with some assistance from wealthy citizens, for the needy, sick, orphaned or aged without relatives or friends. Private, nonsectarian efforts and organizations have never been extensively developed. Although still active, constituting the principal private sponsor in the field of welfare and social assistance, the Church has come increasingly to share this role with the state.

Social-mindedness on the part of the government, initially motivated in part by the desire to confine the public role of the Church, became apparent early in the twentieth century. In 1908 large landed estates owned by religious orders were turned over to the state by law, and their income was directed to public welfare. During the next two decades, provincial boards were created to administer the estates and programs of beneficence, principally in the area of health. In 1925 the Ministry of Social Welfare and Assistance was created, and a year later the obligation of the state to attend the mentally and physically ill, the aged, invalids, beggars, the indigent, and women and children was established by law. Administrations in power 10 years later, influenced strongly by socialist thought, increased considerably the programs and social responsibilities of the state. A further expansion came in the late 1950's and early 1960's, within the general current of commitment to social and economic development which has swept the hemisphere.

Social Services

In force in 1965, the Constitution of 1946 declares the state's responsibility to protect the institution of the family, to safeguard motherhood and to protect children, regardless of their origin. The most extensive programs have been developed in

148

child welfare, based on guidelines established in the Code of Minors of 1938.

The Ministry of Social Welfare maintains a variety of institutions for minors. Day nurseries exist for children between the ages of 3 months and 3 years; for working mothers the range is extended to 6 years. There are also homes for children lacking parental support. Most are not true orphans but, rather, have been abandoned or have come from families too poor to maintain them. There is no system of foster home placement or permanent adoption. Both on the Coast and in the Sierra, summer camps have been established, and in 1961 there were 25 establishments serving approximately 3,000 children, a fraction of those requiring attention or care according to Ministry officials. Placement services are provided principally by a corps of trained social workers. Conditions have varied considerably from establishment to establishment, but the majority have been somewhat inhospitable, as a result of limited financial resources and the abilities, attitudes and preparation of the staff.

Facilities for specialized training in social work are limited. Founded in 1945, the oldest institution, the National School of Social Service, graduated 123 students between the date of its establishment and 1961. In general, social work has been a profession of low pay and little prestige. To encourage more personal attention and improve discipline, the administration of many of the establishments has been turned over to religious orders.

The Ministry of Social Welfare maintains five correctional institutions for juvenile delinquents, which in 1961 attended 600 minors. Most of the inmates remain in these institutions for 2 or 3 years and receive some kind of vocational training. Among boys, convictions have usually been for theft; among girls, for theft and prostitution. Juvenile cases are brought before special courts established for minors under the Code of 1938. Before trial, case studies are made by social workers. In Quito, an observation center has been established for this purpose. Minors adjudged delinquent may be returned to their families, placed on probation or sent to one of the correctional institutions.

The juvenile courts also hear paternity cases, which consume most of their time and effort. Paternity cases are usually brought to court to establish legal responsibility for child support. Consensual union is widespread, particularly on the Coast, and often shortlived, with the result that in many homes there is no male parent. In 1964 roughly one-third of all live births were illegitimate; of these 82 percent occurred on the Coast. In Guayas, Esmeraldas and Los Ríos, illegitimate births outnumbered legitimate births. These cases, combined with delinquency, place a heavy burden on the courts. In 1961 there were 15 juvenile courts, located in provincial capitals, and 1 national juvenile court, in Quito (see ch. 7, Family).

More recently, modest programs of family assistance have been established in an attempt to alleviate the unstable conditions underlying most of the child welfare problems. An unemployment or marginal employment are often the cause of family abandonment or abuse of child labor laws, the Social Service Department in the Ministry has sought to improve the economic situation of poor families. A credit cooperative is maintained which assists family heads in establishing a business or trade. A system of centers is also operated in which women are taught useful skills. Department social workers assist and advise in emergency cases involving persons in transit struck by misfortune and families with a parent under hospital care or convalescence. Programs of education in venereal diseases and alcoholism for men are sponsored by the Department. In Quito, family restaurants serve low-priced, balanced meals with food supplied by Caritas.

Some private activity has taken place primarily in the area of child welfare, most of which has been precarious in nature and local in scope. The raising of funds to support institutions and programs and the maintenance of continuing public support and interest have proved difficult. The Church operates a number of homes for children and mother and child care centers throughout the country (see ch. 11, Religion). Civic clubs, such as the Rotarians and Lions, and charitable clubs, supported by socially prominent women, make periodic contributions to needy children. The National Children's Trust (Patronato Nacional del Niño), a permanent organization presided over by the wife of the president of the country, provides food and clothing.

Similar *patronatos* operate on a local scale in some of the larger cities. The Foster Parents Plan, with headquarters in the United States, distributes monetary subsidies to needy families, mainly in the Guayaquil area, accompanied by counseling services provided by local social workers. A variety of programs for young people is offered by the Young Men's Christian Association (YMCA) in Quito. Initially located in a lower class neighborhood, YMCA headquarters were recently moved to a higher income section, and officials reportedly fear the organization may not be so successful in reaching needy young people. According to reports, YMCA facilities are also scheduled to be established in Guayaquil.

Care of the aged is provided in a few homes maintained by the Ministry of Social Welfare or the Catholic Church. In most cases residents are drawn from the elderly of the lower class who have no families to care for them.

Social Insurance

Social security programs, administered by an autonomous agency of the Ministry of Social Welfare, the National Social Security Institute (Instituto Nacional de Previsión), provide old-age, disability, death, sickness and maternity benefits. Established by law in 1935, the social security system in 1962 had roughly 177,500 affiliates, or 12 percent of the economically active population. At that time the system covered commercial, government and industrial workers. Teachers and members of the armed forces participated in separate systems linked to the National Social Security Institute. In 1964 the government substantially extended coverage to include artisans, domestic servants and lawyers. Members of other professions were to be brought into the system on a voluntary basis in 1965. Those remaining outside the social security system included agricultural workers and temporary workers.

Financial support of the Social Security Fund is distributed among affiliates, employers and the government. Affiliates contribute 5 percent of their earnings plus 1 percent for the death grant program; employers contribute 6 percent of the payroll, according to wage classes. The maximum earnings limit for worker eligibility is S/6,000 monthly, a relatively high income. The government covers 40 percent of the pensions paid. In 1962 the Fund's resources were S/5.58 million.

To qualify for old-age pensions, affiliates must be 55 years old and have made contributions for 30 years or meet the alternative age-years of contribution standards of 60 and 25, 65 and 15, 70 and 10, or 45 and 25 and unemployed for 6 months. Pensions are equal to 43.75 percent of average earnings during the 5 highest years, which need not be consecutive, with an increase of 1.25 percent for each year of contributions beyond 5 years. After 40 years of contributions, the pension is equal to 100 percent of earnings. Minimum pensions are S/270 per month, and pensions are adjusted every 3 years in accordance with the cost-of-living index. Pensions for disability are adjusted on the same basis. Those who have lost one-half of their normal working capacity and have made contributions for at least 5 years are eligible.

Widows of affiliates who have made contributions for 5 years receive 30 percent of the insured's pension, in monthly payments equal to a minimum of S/80. Orphans' benefits are equal to 15 percent of the insured's pension or to 30 percent if he is a full orphan, paid until age 18. He is paid to age 21 if he is a student. An orphan is paid indefinitely if an invalid or unmarried daughter. Mothers or invalid fathers of affiliates are entitled to 15 percent of the pension; brothers and sisters under the age of 18, to 10 percent. The death grant covers burial costs.

Sickness benefits are open to those who have made 26 weekly contributions, 8 of which have been made in the 6 months immediately preceding illness. To qualify for maternity benefits, 26 contributions must be made in the preceding 12-month period, a minimum of 4 being paid during the first quarter. General and specialist care, surgery, hospitalization, medicines, laboratory services and dental care are included and are offered at facilities maintained by the Social Security Fund. Until recently sickness benefits included cash payments only to cover costs in cases where Fund facilities were unable to provide services and affiliates were consequently treated in other establishments. In 1964 the government extended benefits, allowing cash subsidy, but no information is available on the nature of payment or amounts. In maternity cases affiliates receive 75 percent of earnings 3 weeks before and 4 weeks after confinement. Neither sickness nor maternity benefits are available to dependents.

The social security system has not functioned with great efficiency. The payment of benefits to affiliates has often been delayed for long periods as a result of administrative breakdowns. To improve this situation, certain changes were instituted in 1964. Until that time, government workers' benefits and private employees' benefits were handled by two separate funds which were unified with the hope that delays would be reduced and greater general efficiency encouraged. An additional difficulty, still unresolved, however, is the inadequacy of the medical facilities devoted to the care of affiliates. Although social security hospitals and dispensaries are generally superior in quality to other publicly supported establishments, they are overburdened. Except in emergency cases, affiliates may lose 2 or 3 days of work while waiting to receive medical attention.

Work injury insurance is available to employed persons in both the private and public sectors. The entire cost is covered by the employer. When disability is permanent, employees receive 40 percent of earnings or a lump sum equal to 3 years' earnings. In cases of partial disability, pensions are scaled proportionately. Full medical care is also provided. In the event of death, pensions in the amount of 40 percent of earnings or lump sums equal to from 1½ to 3 years' earnings are paid to legal heirs. A funeral grant of a maximum of S/300 is also paid. No minimum qualifying period applies to work injury insurance.

Those employed by commercial and industrial enterprises or by the government who earn less than S/6,000 monthly qualify for unemployment insurance. Financial support of the program comes from insured persons, in the amount of 2 percent of earnings, and by employers, in the amount of 1 percent of the payroll. The government contributes only as an employer. To receive benefits, insured persons must have made 24 monthly contributions and been unemployed, for any reason, for 2 months. The benefit consists of a lump sum which varies according to wage class and length of contribution. Scales are fixed annually.

Housing

Housing conditions, principally among the lower classes, have been recognized by public officials as a primary area of social concern. According to the 1962 housing census, 47 percent of the existing dwellings could be defined as houses; the remainder were impermanent, inhospitable structures. The total housing deficit, made up of a combination of the number of new dwellings required and the number of substandard dwellings to be replaced, was estimated at 585,940 units. The Social Security Fund, which makes housing loans to members, has been an important source of home finance to the middle class, which, with upper-income groups, has not had difficulty in obtaining housing.

The problem of obtaining such housing has been very great for the lower class. To meet it, the government has begun to assume an active role in developing low-cost housing, with financial support from foreign loans. In addition, the Ten-Year Housing Plan has been formed as part of the General Plan for the Economic and Social Development of Ecuador. The Housing Plan anticipated the fulfillment of 28.2 percent of the need by 1968.

In 1961 the government created the Housing Bank (Banco de la Vivienda) to provide funds primarily to lower income groups. A $5 million loan was secured from AID by the Bank to promote the establishment of mutualist savings and loans associations. The following year the IDB made a loan of $10.6 million to assist in constructing 6,600 new units and rehabilitating 1,500 units. By July 1965, 170 houses had been built under the aided self-help project, and 1,772 houses had been built through the savings and loan system. Under the IDB loan, 112 units were completed; construction had begun on 2,528; and preparatory work was started on an additional 689 by the end of 1964.

Under the Housing Plan several additional programs were also adopted. During the first 2 years, 7,500 units were to be built under a variety of cooperative, aided self-help and direct construction systems. Rehabilitation or completion of houses in the low-income sections of Guayaquil was also contemplated. No information is available on the progress of these programs.

Community Development

In recent years the idea of stimulating, promoting and assisting local effort to improve living conditions and raise cultural levels through a variety of small projects at the community level has won increasing support which has been manifested in a proliferation of programs. To a great extent, the Andean Mission has been the generator. The Andean Mission was created in 1951 by joint agreement of the International Labor Organization (ILO) and the governments of Ecuador, Peru and Bolivia, with the purpose of improving the way of life of the highland Indian population. In Ecuador, programs were implemented in 1954, first in the province of Chimborazo where conditions were most grave and later in the provinces of Imbabura, Tungurahua, Cañar, Azuay and Loja. Activity and staff, however, have continued to be the most extensive in Chimborazo.

The Andean Mission has sought to train and encourage community leaders through the *cabildo* (community assembly) and various cooperatives and local clubs it has established and through the promotion of community improvement projects, such as roadbuilding and school construction. Specific areas of activity have included agricultural extension, development of artisanry and home industry, education, sanitation, nutrition, health and medical service. To instruct and assist the Indians, two types of teams were developed—one composed of an agronomist, a social worker and a specialist in fundamental education and the other of a medical doctor, a sanitary inspector, a registered nurse and a nurse's aid. Communities were visited once a week by the mixed team and once every 2 weeks by the medical team.

During the first 2 years within the Andean Mission program communities are subject to an intensive campaign, which is eased as new ideas and practices take root. In addition, the Mission established two educational centers—one for the training in artisanry and the other for leadership training. Despite difficulties in coordinating activities with a variety of government agencies and ministries and in overcoming the suspicion and distrust of the Indians and other local residents, the Mission has had considerable success in bringing about change. In 1964 complete administration of the organization was assumed by Ecuador. Early in 1965 work was being conducted in almost 100 communities by about 150 staff members.

A modest effort in rural areas of the Coast has been made by the Inter-American Cooperative Agricultural Service (Servicio Cooperativo Inter-Americano de Agricultura—SCIA), a joint organization of the Ecuadorian Government and AID. In addition to its main function of agriculture extension, SCIA has done work

154

in home demonstration. In 1963 the government of Ecuador began moving toward full assumption of administration of SCIA activities.

As part of the 10-year social and economic plan, a nationwide rural development plan has been formulated. The plan is scheduled to operate simultaneously on three fronts: education for development, improvement of living conditions and increase of production. Specific projects include community organization, the establishment of communal service centers with tools and equipment to improve the physical environment, health and sanitation, nutrition and food education, home improvement, education and a variety of economically oriented activities. Many of these projects will be conducted by existing community, government, intergovernmental, international and private agencies. The Andean Mission is to be broadened to act as executive administrator of the plan.

Initially, the most intensive activity is to take place in the Sierra, where past experience can be used. As specific knowledge of the social and economic conditions in rural coastal areas is lacking, an initial period of study and research is scheduled to precede activity there. It is hoped that all base communities, those with populations of over 200, will be brought into the plan by the end of the 10-year period.

Additional community development programs are operating which have not been exclusively rural in focus. In 1962 civic action programs were launched with funds from the government of Ecuador, AID, Food for Peace and the United States Military Assistance Program. In carrying out requests for local communities the Ecuadorian military has received cooperation from the government and United States agencies. By 1965 civic action had engaged in the construction of access roads, irrigation canals, schools, community centers, community service facilities and houses and in the installation of potable water, sewage and electrical systems in various parts of the country (see ch. 27, The Armed Forces).

Since 1964 a town plan project has been functioning with the assistance of various government agencies and Alliance for Progress funds. Limited aid is given to local community organizations which wish to develop self-help improvement efforts. The first three town plans were formulated jointly by officials of the government, community and AID for Esmeraldas, Guaranda and Pelileo on the basis of needs and resources. The Esmeraldas town plan included the establishment of a refrigeration plant and fishermen's cooperative and construction of access roads and a hospital outpatient clinic. In Guaranda an access road was built; smokeless kitchens and latrines were installed; a reforestation project was launched; a carpenters' cooperative was established; and a leadership training course was given under the town plan. Soil conservation, irrigation, construction of a canning plant, equipment for a hospital and an industrial training center for tailors and weavors, and preparatory work for the installation of a potable water system were features of the Pelileo town plan. Plans for Cayambe, Loja, Quevedo and Chimborazo have been formulated and reportedly are in progress. Groups and organizations outside the town plan program and unable independently to complete projects already initiated also receive assistance. The town plan project is scheduled to continue until the end of fiscal year 1969.

The cooperative movement has been growing rapidly and has been receiving increased official support and assistance. In 1963 it was estimated that there were a total of 850 cooperatives in the country and that 50 cooperative organizations were forming annually. Credit cooperatives are the most numerous; others are devoted to housing, marketing, production and consumption. To make technical and financial assistance available, the Cooperative Bank was organized by the government. Plans also call for complete surveys of the present system, the establishment of 33 model cooperatives and the reform of present laws affecting the cooperative movement.

Peace Corps Volunteers have been involved in almost all types of local projects and activities. Credit cooperatives have probably engaged the greatest number. Although Volunteers are active throughout the country, concentration has been in rural areas. In urban centers the most notable developments have been taking place in Guayaquil, where neighborhood organization in the low-income sections has been gathering momentum. In general, considerable success has been achieved in the establishment of good relationships at the local level. Reportedly, communities are eager to have Peace Corps Volunteers, and view them as a source of prestige. Since early 1962, when the program was initiated, roughly 600 Volunteers have participated, including the present contingent of 291. Small groups from Germany, Belgium, Italy and Canada with similar aims have also operated in the country.

CHAPTER 9

EDUCATION

The educational system is divided into three basic levels: pre-elementary and elementary, secondary and superior. For children aged 6 to 14, roughly the elementary-level age group, education is legally compulsory and free in all institutions, regardless of sponsorship. Public schools are maintained principally by the central government and by municipalities. There are also schools at all levels administered by private interests, largely Roman Catholic. In recent years about 80 percent of enrollment has been in public schools; about 20 percent in private schools.

Despite legal requirements most Ecuadorians have had little or no formal education. A study made in 1962 by a United Nations Educational, Scientific and Cultural Organization (UNESCO) mission revealed that the average length of school attendance among the adult population was approximately 3 years. Facilities have not been adequate, especially in rural areas, where well over half the population resides, to serve the entire elementary school-age population. The extreme poverty of most rural and urban lower-class families, which has frequently required children to begin working at an early age, has also limited or prevented school attendance. In addition, until recently negative attitudes toward formal education were widespread among the large Indian population, centered in the rural Sierra.

In 1962, according to government figures, 70 percent of the elementary school-age children were enrolled. The past rate of retention suggested, however, that almost half would be lost by the end of the second grade. Lack of schooling and marginal education produced an illiteracy rate of 43.7 percent among the population over 10 years of age. Literacy campaigns, designed to combat the effects of educational deficiencies, have caused a 9-percent reduction in the rate since they were begun some 20 years ago.

A secondary diploma or a degree from an institution of higher learning is the mark of educated individuals, who constitute a small minority. There are secondary schools and institutions of higher learning only in the larger urban areas, and these serve primarily the needs and interests of the middle and upper classes. In 1962, 9 percent of those in the secondary-level age group were enrolled, and it was estimated that roughly one-third would graduate. Although similar data on higher education are not available, the general pattern throughout the hemisphere suggests that figures are probably somewhat lower. At the secondary and higher levels, a variety of programs exists, but the emphasis has been on the more academic or intellectual courses of study which prepare for white-collar and professional occupations.

During the last few years the educational system has come increasingly under official examination, largely as a result of the movement toward social reform and economic development which has been apparent in most countries of the hemisphere. A long-range planning system for education was created in 1960, and by 1964 a 10-year plan had been formulated. The basic aims, viewed by planners as essential complements to economic progress, are improvement of the general cultural level of the population and orientation of the educational system toward the manpower needs of a developing nation. Expansion of the school system to incorporate greater percentages of the school-age population, particularly at the elementary level, and of adult education programs is contemplated. To bring about qualitative improvement and to relate education more clearly to the social and economic environment, curricula are to be altered, teaching and supervision improved, and modern equipment and teaching aids supplied.

The investment in study and planning, steadily increasing allotments for education (which comprise the largest single expenditure in the national budget), the continuity in policy and activity during a period of changing administrations, and the progress made in some phases of the plan by 1965 augured well for at least partial realization. In addition, substantial assistance, both financial and technical, has been given by a number of international organizations, by the United States Government and by private groups, mainly for specific projects in accord with present policy. Commitments for further assistance have been made by many of these agencies and groups.

HISTORICAL ANTECEDENTS

The first schools were established in the colonial period by members of the religious orders, who followed soon after the arrival of the conquistadors. They were designed to teach Spanish arts and handicrafts and, at times, the rudiments of reading and writing to small elements of the Indian population.

As civil life took shape, a Spanish upper class emerged that desired the same kind of institutions and culture as those of Spain. Children from this group received their initial education at home from tutors or relatives. Further education was obtained at the seminaries, which were roughly the equivalent of secondary-level schools, and at the universities. No formal, integrated system was developed, however, and the lines between the different types of institutions were blurred. The only admission requirement was "purity of ancestry" (*limpieza de sangre*). As educational institutions were directed and staffed by the religious orders, primarily for the purpose of training new members, studies were oriented toward theology, philosophy and canon law. The first seminaries, known as *colegios,* appeared after the middle of the sixteenth century in the principal population centers. The first university was established in Quito by the Augustinians in 1586. A second was established soon thereafter by the Jesuits and a third at the end of the seventeenth century by the Dominicans, both of them also in Quito.

Toward the end of the colonial period, as liberal ideas began to spread among some educated elements, the concept of general public education began to win some adherents. A few schools run by nonreligious personnel began to appear. Further impetus was given after the War of Independence by Simón Bolívar, who himself had been educated in the ideas of the Enlightenment. As president of the Gran Colombian Republic, of which Ecuador was a part, he was instrumental in introducing public schools. About 20 were established in Ecuador. The chaotic conditions following the demise of Gran Colombia in 1830, however, did not allow much official attention to education. In addition, funds were scarce, and general interest was lacking. As a result, schools continued under religious sponsorship, much as they had in the past.

Significant change did not take place until the era of Gabriel García Moreno, who was in power directly or indirectly from 1860 to 1875 (see ch. 3, Historical Setting). García Moreno had great interest in education and sought the expansion and improvement of facilities, charging foreign religious orders with the mission. The elementary system began to take definite shape as elementary education was declared free and compulsory for all, and the number of schools more than doubled. Universities were founded in the cities of Cuenca, Guayaquil and Loja to supplement the remaining colonial university of Quito. Interest in technical advancement was reflected in the establishment of the National Polytechnic Institute in Quito.

After the death of García Moreno the flurry of activity and interest abated and did not resume until the turn of the century, when the Liberals came into power. The Liberal desire to assure the supremacy of secular authority led, among other things, to concern for the development of public education. Liberal administrations adhered to the concept of free, compulsory and nonsectarian education for elementary school-age children. Missions were contracted during the early decades of the twentieth century from France, Germany and the United States to assist in the establishment of teaching institutions and in the introduction of contemporary methodology and school organization.

In 1930 growing interest led to the calling of the National Congress of Elementary Education and Teacher Training in Quito. Consideration was given to legislation; the problems of rural education, curricula and programs; and the improvement of teachers. The findings were formalized in the Education Law of 1938, still in force, and in later constitutions. The basic philosophy and aims of these documents included the control of all education by the state; free and compulsory elementary education; the elimination of illiteracy; the development of vocational education; and the creation of social services. For the most part these ideas and goals are still advocated.

ADMINISTRATION AND FINANCE

Public Education

The general lines for the administration of public education were set up in 1938 under the Education Law. General authority over all schools rests with the Ministry of Education, except for the universities, which are autonomous, and a few institutions for specialized education maintained by other ministries. Although schools may be national or municipal in local terminology, administration is highly centralized in practice, and municipal schools enjoy little independence.

Direct assistance to the minister and his deputy is provided by the Department of Education (which was created as an advisory body on policy but which has become a kind of court to hear complaints) and the permanent Secretariat for UNESCO and International Affairs. Daily administrative routine is handled by various sections which correspond to the levels of the school system, grouped together under the General Directorate of Education. An attempt toward decentralization was made with the creation of the Subdirectorate of Guayaquil, which has jurisdiction over elementary education in the coastal provinces of Esmeraldas, Manabí, Los Ríos and El Oro and on the Galápagos Islands.

There are several sections within the General Directorate which deal in specialized areas, such as adult education, music education and physical education, or which supervise related activities, such as school construction and social assistance. The school lunch program, which operates with the aid of the Cooperative for American Remittances to Everywhere (CARE); the award of scholarships to students in elementary, secondary and state-run higher-education schools; and the donation of school materials and texts (textbooks are not normally provided by the schools) to needy students are handled by the social assistance section.

Wth the exception of the minister, his deputy and the director general of education, who are political appointees, positions are held by career personnel who enjoy considerable job security. For the most part former teachers without training in administration, members of the staff are not well paid. As a rule there is little delegation or assumption of authority below the highest executive levels.

In each province there is a directorate of education responsible for local supervision and administration, principally of elementary schools. The minister appoints the provincial directors, and political considerations usually play a part in their choice. By law they have executive responsibility, but in fact they serve as administrators of directives from the capital.

Contact between individual schools and the administration is maintained through a system of school inspection. At the elementary level school inspectors are attached to the provincial directorates, and liaison with the Ministry is provided by counterpart inspectors within the Section for Elementary Education. Inspection of secondary schools is carried out directly from the Ministry by inspectors in the sections for the various kinds of secondary schools.

The system operates under a number of handicaps. There are few inspectors. In 1964, 177 elementary school inspectors were charged with the supervision of 17,735 elementary school teachers. No figures were available for the secondary level. The lack of funds to provide transportation or travel expenses makes it difficult for inspectors to visit schools outside the national or provincial capitals.

The municipal, provincial and central governments all contribute to the financing of education. The municipal and provincial governments must allot at least 15 percent to education and culture before their budgets may be passed by the National Board of Planning and Economic Cooperation, which exercises the power of review. In comparison with the expenditures of the central government, however, municipal and provincial contributions are small. In 1962, the last year for which comparative figures are available, the national budget allotted S/377,445,000; the provincial budgets, S/5,120,000; and the municipal budgets, S/51,200,000 (in 1965, approximately S/18.5 equaled US$1—see Glossary). In 1965 the central government's contribution had risen to S/412,-000,000, or 19.9 percent of the total national budget.

Elementary education absorbed roughly half the education budget; secondary education, 27 percent; and higher education, 16 percent, the remainder being distributed to adult education, sports promotion, cultural extension, planning and administration. Salaries, representing more than half the budget, constituted the greatest single expenditure. An unknown additional sum is raised through various modest fees charged by secondary and higher schools and through percentages on certain general taxes. The relatively large investment in education funds is not adequate, however, to do much more than maintain the present facilities. Salaries are low, especially at the elementary level.

Outside assistance, in the form of grants and loans, has provided a substantial supplement to local resources. Between 1960 and 1965, funds amounting to roughly $9.5 million were received, mostly in support of higher education. The principal sources were the United Nations Special Fund which provided $2.3 million; the Agency for International Development (AID), $5.5 million; and the Inter-American Development Bank (IDB), $1.6 million. Other sources included the Ford Foundation, the Rockefeller Foundation and the Fulbright Commission.

Private Education

Private schools operate under no central administration. Those under Roman Catholic sponsorship, which constitute the overwhelming majority, do not function as a parochial system, but are administered for the most part by the various religious orders. The few nonsectarian private schools, located in Guayaquil and Quito, have been established by teachers or groups of professional men and operate independently.

Nevertheless, both the Constitution and the Education Law impose certain norms and restrictions on private schools. All must be authorized by the Ministry of Education and may be closed by it if legal requirements are not met. Private elementary education must be tuition free. At all levels study plans and programs must include the subjects outlined by the Ministry for the public schools. In the area of staff and personnel the law requires that all private school principals and history and geography teachers be Ecuadorian, that Spanish teachers be native speakers and that general qualifications and salaries correspond to those required in the public system. At the same time the law grants certain rights to private education. A functional senator for private education sits in the National Congress and a representative is on the National Council of Education (see ch. 13, Constitution and Government). The services of the social assistance section are extended to private schools.

Relations between private education and the public authority have generally been harmonious. Private schools have tended to conform to legal requirements, and the Ministry has exercised minimal supervision or interference. The public school inspectors, who are supposed to visit private establishments as well, are handicapped by lack of funds.

No limits are imposed by law on the funds or capital equipment with which private schools may operate. The nonsectarian schools above the elementary level generally rely principally on tuition for income and, for the most part, are in precarious economic situations. As new, usually small establishments, they lack the social or academic prestige required to attract the more affluent.

In the Catholic schools above the elementary level matriculation fees and tuition are, at times, high by local standards, but families are willing to make considerable sacrifices to enroll their children. The middle and upper classes hold the public schools in low esteem and seek the more exclusive, conservative atmosphere of the private religious school. In addition, the Catholic schools depend on donations, inheritances and contributions from the central government and municipalities. A conservative estimate placed the state budgetary allotment to private education at nearly S/4.7 million in 1962. Land has also been granted for private school sites. Foreign contributions, in unknown quantity, have provided additional resources, primarily at the higher-education level.

THE SCHOOL SYSTEM

The Lower Levels

Structure and Character

Preelementary school is for children from 3 to 5 years of age. In 1964 approximately 13,500 children were enrolled in 117 schools, located in the larger urban centers. Both morning and afternoon programs are customary, giving preparation in language, vocabulary, games, drawing and dancing.

Elementary education includes six grades in urban schools and four in rural schools. Of the 700,000 children enrolled in 1964, slightly more than half attended urban schools. The school year is 165 days, running from October to July in the Sierra and from April or May to January on the Coast. Among the subjects listed by the Ministry of Education as being taught are Spanish, arithmetic, social studies, natural science, arts and handicrafts and domestic skills. Schools are permitted to select their own textbooks; the only restriction is that books conform with democratic principles. In practice, however, textbooks are not used extensively. After completion of the elementary program a certificate is awarded to students who have obtained a minimum of 60 out of 100 points on final examinations.

The elementary system operates under a great number of difficulties. Rapid population expansion has aggravated the problems of classroom shortages and overcrowding. Pressures have also increased as many elements of the rural population, traditionally indifferent to formal education, have begun to clamor for schools. The average number of students per class is 40 or more. As schools are not equally distributed geographically, however, extremes of 90 students per class on the one hand, or 15, on the other, are not uncommon.

In 1964 the emergency solution of creating parallel classes in existing schools in morning, afternoon and evening sessions was adopted. Some 1,368 new teaching positions were established, and 223 additional temporary teachers were hired to handle the expanded enrollment. Still, most recent estimates place the number of children not in school because of classroom shortages at 300,000. Although close to 800 classrooms have been built since 1962 under a joint project of the Ecuadorian Government and AID, which is to continue until 1967, an additional 11,000 are required to bridge the gap in the next few years.

The existing schools are generally in poor physical condition. As funds assigned for maintenance are inadequate, over half the 17,000 classrooms have been judged no longer usable or in acute need of repair. A substantial number of classrooms are located in rented buildings which were not originally designed for educational purposes and have not been subsequently adapted. School supplies, basic equipment, furniture and teaching aids are frequently lacking, especially in rural areas. Two 4-year projects, which also involve the Ecuadorian Government and AID, were begun in 1964 to produce 2 million textbooks and to equip 100 schools with manual arts training materials.

Although no figures are available on school attendance, absenteeism is reportedly a problem, particularly among children from lower-class families. Some parents, unfamiliar with formal education, at times withdraw their children after several weeks or months in the belief that the rudiments have been acquired. In other cases the need of a child's labor to assist the family economically results in complete withdrawal, absenteeism during extended periods throughout the year or attendance during only part of each day. The introduction of the school lunch program, which reaches more than 40,000 children, has encouraged more regular school attendance.

During the last few years the retention rate, from initial matriculation to completion of the sixth grade has been about 20 percent, which represents a slight improvement over the past. In virtually all cases rural school children are automatically excluded, as the program available to them covers only the first 4 years. In the same period approximately 18 percent were repeating a grade.

Secondary education prepares students for admission to institutions of higher learning, elementary school teaching and certain vocations. Programs, which last for 6 years, are given in three basic types of schools, called *colegios:* the academic *colegio,* the vocational *colegio* and the normal or educational science *colegio.* The school year is the same as at the elementary level. For admission, students must be between the ages of 12 and 16 and have the elementary school certificate (which automatically excludes children who have attended the 4-year schools), a health certificate and any other document required by the individual *colegio.* To enter night schools, which exist in limited numbers in the academic and vocational programs, students must be at least 16 years old. Although there are coeducational schools, separation of the sexes is more common. Secondary education is not free, for students are required to pay fees for matriculation, examination and diploma and any other charges the Ministry of Education may establish. Upon completion of the program, a certificate of successful completion, known as the *bachillerato,* is awarded.

The academic secondary program is divided into two basic courses, modern studies and classical studies. In modern studies all students study the same subjects during the first 5 years and in the final year select a group of subjects for specialization in literature and philosophy, physics and mathematics or chemistry and biology. Premilitary instruction is required for boys; domestic education for girls; and the study of English for all students. The classical course corresponds in its essentials to the modern, but in addition, includes Latin, Greek and general classical studies.

Vocational *colegios* are of three different types—industrial, commercial and agricultural. In addition to the 6-year *bachillerato* program, each offers shorter courses. The industrial *colegios* award the *bachillerato técnico industrial* in mechanics, electricity, radio technology and graphic arts. A 3-year course yields a certificate of "master" (*maestro*) in ironwork, sanitary and electrical installations, carpentry, tailoring and shoemaking; the 4-year program yields a certificate of *maestro industrial* in industrial and automotive mechanics, electricity, telegraphy, graphic arts, cabinetmaking and wood carving. In the commercial *colegios* students receive the *bachillerato* in commercial and administrative sciences after 6 years, a diploma in secretarial and stenographic work or accounting after 5 years, or a diploma which gives the title of office assistant after 3 years. Studies in the agricultural *colegios* include 6-year *bacaillerato* programs in agricultural science or agronomy and 4-year courses which award the title of agricultural practitioner. In addition, artisan schools offer a program of 3 years of classroom study and 1 year of practical work. Students who complete the program are permitted to enter the third year of the regular vocational *colegios*.

Teacher training is given in normal *colegios* for urban elementary teachers and in rural normal *colegios* for rural elementary teachers. Until 1959 the program in the rural normal *colegios* was only 4 years in duration, but upon the recommendation of the Seminar on Planning of Teacher Training, a movement was launched to extend it to 6 years. In 1961 about 50 percent of the rural normal schools had a 6-year program. In the 6-year course the first 4 years of study correspond to the modern studies in the academic *colegios,* and the last 2 are devoted to pedagogy. The urban normal *colegios* usually maintain working relationships with specific elementary schools for student practice teaching. The rural normal *colegios* function as the center of a nucleus of rural elementary schools, making available such facilities as libraries and medical stations and supervising and assisting teachers. Practice teaching is done in a laboratory school, maintained by the *colegio,* which offers the complete 6-year elementary program.

In addition, there are several postelementary schools which offer more specialized types of education. Among these are the Conservatory of Music, which offers 7 years of study; 7-year music schools attached to the state universities in Cuenca, Quito and Guayaquil; the National School of Fine Arts, which has a 6-year program; fine arts schools attached to Central University in Quito and the University of Cuenca; and religious seminaries, which offer 6-year academic programs.

In the 1963–64 school year there was a total secondary enrollment of 94,676. Of these, 59 percent attended academic *colegios;* 33 percent, the vocational *colegios;* and 8 percent, the normal *colegios.* The 412 secondary schools were distributed by type in approximately the same proportions. Academic studies, the traditional form of education at the secondary level, continue to enjoy the greatest prestige. Among families at the upper socioeconomic levels such education is considered a matter of course. Students from the lower strata who wish to continue their education and are able to do so incline toward academic studies, which offer the greatest possibilities for achieving higher status.

Economic considerations, however, often make enrollment in the academic *colegios* impossible. Although the Ministry of Education has a scholarship fund, the number of annual grants is small, and grants awarded by the National Congress do not satisfy the needs. Consequently, enrollments in the other types of *colegios*, which involve minimal costs, are usually constituted by those who cannot attend an academic *colegio*. Though seen as less demanding academically, the normal schools are attractive to many, as they provide training for a professional career. Within the vocational program, about 75 percent of the students take the commercial courses, for white-collar jobs, though often low paying, are considered far more desirable than those which involve manual labor.

Education tends to be highly theoretical, the lecture serving as the principal tool. The use of textbooks is limited, and educational facilities, such as libraries, laboratories and workshops, are frequently lacking. In range and number the required annual load of courses is demanding, especially in the academic program. Elementary level materials are often included as a result of inadequate elementary school preparation and limited coordination and contact between the two levels. The extensive requirements and uniformity of curriculum for all students in each program and the differences between programs tend to make student transfer difficult. For the most part, concentration has been on the classroom experience, with little development of organized extracurricular activities. Relationships between teachers and students tend to be formal and impersonal. Similarly, little contact takes place between teachers and parents, although parents' associations do exist.

The percentage of students who complete secondary programs is low. In 1960 roughly one-third of those who had enrolled 6 years previously graduated. The retention rate in the private schools, which substantially outnumber the public schools at the secondary level, was somewhat higher. Of those who complete a secondary education, the great majority do not go on to higher education. For those who aspire to white-collar positions, finding employment often proves difficult. The schools have not operated placement services nor student counseling programs. A movement in this direction has begun, however, in four modern technical schools, recently completed under a joint project of the Ecuadorian Government and AID and designed to stimulate and improve vocational education.

Teachers

In the 1963–64 school year there were 26,122 teachers, approximately two-thirds at the elementary level and one-third at the secondary level. Distribution between the public and private systems was in approximately the same proportion. The number of men and women teachers is roughly equal, though at the elementary level women outnumber men, and at the secondary level the reverse is true.

In general terms the number of teachers has been adequate to handle enrollments. There are, however, shortages of teachers in particular areas and of trained teachers in all areas. At the elementary level slightly less than one-third had received training for teaching; almost half had had no training; and the rest had had training in other fields. According to UNESCO studies, the existing normal school facilities are sufficient to produce a satisfactory number of teachers. About half the students do not complete the program, however, and of those who do, less than half go into teaching. Some seek better paying positions; others claim that they cannot find teaching posts. The seeming paradox is explained by the fact that few are willing to go to rural schools, and the result is too many applicants for positions in urban schools and too few to meet the needs of the rural areas.

Among secondary school teachers the percentage with specific training is still lower. Training for academic and normal school teachers consists of 4-year courses given at the Higher Teaching Institutes (Institutos Superiores de Pedagogía) in Quito and Guayaquil and at the Schools of Philosophy, Letters and Educational Science at the universities. No specific programs exist for vocational school teachers, who are expected to have the equivalent of the kind of education they are teaching. About 6 percent of all secondary teachers have had specific training in teaching; 30 percent have had a secondary-level education; 4 percent have had less than a secondary education; and the rest presumably have had some kind of higher level education. It has generally not been difficult to find teachers for posts in academic and normal schools. In contrast, with the exception of the commercial program, shortages or inadequacies have been great in the vocational schools.

Some effort has been made to improve the quality of the teaching force, especially at the elementary level, through raising normal school standards and through programs which enable teachers without degrees to obtain them and teachers with degrees to increase their knowledge. UNESCO and UNICEF have been giving technical assistance and financial aid to the normal school at San Pablo del Lago in the province of Pichincha. Recently, AID began a 4-year project to modernize the administration, equipment and curricula and to train faculties at two normal schools—one on the Coast and one in the Sierra.

To plan, coordinate and assist in training programs for teachers in service, the government created the National Institute of Educational Training and Experimentation (Instituto Nacional de Capacitación y Experimentación Pedagógicas—INCEP) in 1962.

In 1963 improvement courses planned and assisted by INCEP and directly administered by the provincial directorates were given to elementary teachers in Esmeraldas, Portoviejo, Guayaquil, Machala, Quito, Latacunga and Loja. During the following year, a 3-year project was drawn up for short courses in such special subjects as manual arts and agriculture, courses for school principals and courses for school inspectors to be given twice each year both on the Coast and in the Sierra. AID will provide technical assistance. In addition, the three normal schools which have been receiving technical assistance have been sponsoring in-service and summer training courses. Improvement programs for secondary school teachers have been limited to summer courses given at the Central University in Quito.

At the elementary level teachers, as well as school principals, are supposed to be appointed by provincial directors but, in fact, are usually appointed directly by the Ministry of Education. Appointments for secondary school positions are also made directly by the Ministry from lists submitted by the personnel of individual schools.

Elementary, vocational and normal school teachers usually work on a full-time basis. For academic secondary teachers, a minimum number of weekly hours is required. As most school budgets do not permit payment beyond the minimum, teachers work at several schools, both private and public, to increase their income. The average weekly load has been estimated at 16 to 20 hours and usually includes a variety of courses in which the teacher may or may not have a specific academic background. As the majority are professionals, teaching is usually combined with other positions. Of all public employees, teachers enjoy the greatest job security.

Salary scales are determined by the Law of Teacher's Pay and Scales, which establishes 10 professional and economic categories, based on educational background, length of service and merit. The minimum monthly salary for the first category is S/800. In the succeeding categories the rate increases by 10 percent per step. During the 1962–63 school year the average annual salary among elementary school teachers was S/13,784, not an adequate wage for those who participate in the money economy. In many families both parents teach in order to obtain an adequate income. At the secondary level the average annual income for teachers in academic, vocational and rural normal schools was S/20,280. Teachers in the urban normal schools earned an average of S/24,480. All teachers are automatically members of the Social Security Fund and the Pension Fund, which provide health insurance, maternity benefits, retirement benefits and death and disability insurance. Members are also entitled to obtain mortgage loans.

A decree issued in April 1964 improved retirement benefits, making them equal to 100 percent of the average of the 5 years' highest salaries after 30 years' service. The retirement age is 55. During the first 5 years of service teacher contributions to the Pension Fund are matched by the government. Subsequently, only 2 percent of the contribution comes from the teachers, and the government pays the difference (see ch. 8, Living Conditions).

Professional association is accomplished through the National Teachers Union (Unión Nacional de Educadores—UNE). The UNE is open to all, but most members are public elementary school teachers, and therefore UNE activity in such areas as economic improvement and defense of teachers before the Ministry has been oriented toward the elementary level. The strength and influence of the organization has depended almost entirely on the government's attitude toward it.

The status of the teacher within the social context varies from level to level and from group to group. Elementary school teachers enjoy considerable prestige among the lower classes, from which they tend to come. In rural areas, moreover, the elementary teacher, as the most educated resident, is a natural leader and is sought out for advice on virtually all matters that affect the community or its individual members. Superior in social and economic standing to the rest, he is also frequently requested to assume the important role of *compadre* (see ch. 7, Family). Among the educated elements of the population in general, however, teaching at the elementary level accords little prestige.

Teachers at the secondary level, by contrast, are held in widespread esteem, but among the different types, something of a hierarchy exists. The highest position is occupied by the teacher in the academic *colegio*. Status tends to derive from middle- or upper-class origins and training in one of the professions, common characteristics of academic teachers, rather than from the occupation as a teacher. In addition, association with the academic life implies intellectual interest and capacity, traits which are generally admired. Normal school teachers, of more modest background and training, occupy a lesser position. For the same reasons the vocational school teacher enjoys the least status of the three.

Higher Education

In 1964 there were 17 institutions of higher education in the country, concentrated in the two largest cities, Quito and Guayaquil. The universities are the principal centers, accounting in that year for approximately 90 percent of the total enrollment of 11,400 at the higher education level. The 5 national universities are the University of Cuenca, the Central University of Ecuador (Quito), the University of Guayaquil, the University of Loja and the University of Manabí (Portoviejo). The 2 private universities are the Catholic University of Ecuador (Quito) and the Catholic University of Santiago de Guayaquil.

Of the universities, the largest and most influential is the Central University in Quito, which dates from the late eighteenth century, followed by the University of Guayaquil, established in 1867. The smaller universities of Cuenca and Loja were founded around the same time as the University of Guayaquil, whereas the rest have appeared during the last 20 years.

Other centers of higher learning include two polytechnic schools in Quito and Guayaquil; two higher schools of education for secondary teacher training, located in the same cities; four schools of social service, also in Guayaquil and Quito; and two military schools run by the Ministry of Defense. With the exception of the National Polytechnic Institute of Quito, which was established in 1870, all are of recent creation.

The universities are governed by a decree-law issued by the government in March 1964, which generally reiterates the main points of previous legislation. The Minister of Education is charged with the duties of approving university statutes and budgets, revoking the authorization of component entities within the universities, when necessary, and generally supervising adherence to the law. The National Technical Council on Higher Education, composed of the minister, top officials from the schools, representative professors, the president of the National Board of Planning and Economic Cooperation and representatives from the principal economic sectors, was created for the purpose of coordinating and improving higher education. The Council is also supposed to determine the distribution of funds, in accordance with the manpower needs set by the National Plan for Manpower; regulate the teaching profession at the higher education level; and formulate a plan to renovate the traditional university structure.

In internal administration and organization the universities are granted autonomy, a principle long cherished throughout Latin America as protection from intervention. In each of the universities structural and administrative lines are similar, patterned on European models. The institutions consist of various colleges, called *facultades,* schools and institutes, brought together in a loose framework. Executive officials are elected by an assembly made up of professors and students representing the *facultades.* The authority of national university officials has depended upon their popularity as they lack an internal enforcement agency and, under the principle of autonomy, cannot turn to outside entities. Private universities, by their nature, have maintained stricter control and discipline at the highest administrative level.

Routine administration is handled by the University Council, composed of the minister of education, the university officials and representatives of the professors and students. Innovations of the decree-law were the requirement that student representatives be selected from among those with the highest academic standing and the restriction on the vote of student representatives in matters concerning university personnel. The University Council is responsible for drawing up the university statutes and budget; approving the internal regulations established by the *facultades,* schools and institutes; creating, modifying or abolishing these entities; hiring and discharging personnel; and authorizing expenditures. The *facultades,* schools and institutes operate on a similar basis, electing their own deans or directors and managing their internal affairs through representative councils. As a result, they enjoy considerable autonomy and are somewhat isolated from each other as well as from the central administration.

The resources of the national universities come from the central government and are guaranteed by law. In addition to the university patrimony, funds are provided in the budget of the Ministry of Education, which, in 1965, amounted to S/69 million. Percentages of general taxes and modest student fees, totaling S/200 to S/500 annually per capita, add to this income. The private universities are supported by fees, donations and a portion of the Ministry of Education's general allotment to higher education. All the universities experience economic pressures and are barely able to support existing programs and facilities. In addition, there is no certainty as to the total funds that will be available each year. Budget allotments are made annually, and other income fluctuates in amount. Estimation based on past revenue has been difficult since central records have not been kept.

The universities are almost exclusively teaching centers. With the exception of the University of Manabí, which offers studies only in mathematics, chemistry, physics, agricultural engineering and veterinary medicine, all the universities have *facultades* of philosophy and letters (in some cases education is a part of these *facultades*) and of law and social science. The smaller Catholic universities and the University of Loja have an additional *facultad,* and the Central University, the University of Guayaquil and the University of Cuenca have an additional five or six, including studies in such areas as medicine, dentistry, engineering, architecture, economics, chemistry and agriculture. Programs vary in length, ranging from 3 years in journalism, for example, to 7

172

years in medicine. Most, however, last 5 years. Degrees conferred also vary considerably, indicating the specific profession, such as engineering or architecture, in which training has been given. The more general degree of *licenciado* is used in less specific fields, such as the social sciences.

As undergraduate programs are so specialized, graduate studies are not extensive. In most cases they consist of the preparation of a thesis, at times in combination with an additional year or two of study or practical experience, and award the degree of doctor. Postgraduate study abroad, particularly in technical fields, is considered desirable and is popular among those who can afford it or obtain scholarships.

Admission to the university is usually handled directly by each *facultad*, school or institute. Students with academic *bachilleratos* who are at least 18 years old and have completed their military obligations are eligible to enter all *facultades*. In some *facultades* completion of a preuniversity summer course or a passing grade on an entrance examination is also required. Those with other types of *bachilleratos* may enter *facultades* which continue their specialization. In addition, modest fees are required in the national universities and fees and tuition in the private universities. These are waived for students who cannot afford to pay. The government also makes available a limited number of scholarships and, at the Central University, provides attractive low-priced dormitory accommodations for several hundred students. The most popular *facultades* are medicine, engineering and law, which together account for almost 60 percent of the enrollment.

The university school year runs 30 weeks, from October to June in the Sierra and from April to January on the Coast. Classes are given 5 days a week, and there are no minimum attendance requirements. As at the secondary level, orientation is toward the theoretical, lecture notes constituting the main—and, in many cases, the sole—channel of information. Examinations are consequently based on the lecture and are not expected to cover textbook information, though textbooks may in theory be required. Laboratory facilities are sometimes outmoded. The university libraries are relatively small and follow less than efficient procedures. Upon graduation students, especially those in technical fields, often are not as well equipped to engage in their professions as those who have received their training abroad.

For both professors and students association with the university is basically a part-time activity. As city institutions with no campus complexes, the universities tend to draw on the local population for their faculties and student bodies. Professors, drawn from the ranks of local professionals, combine university teaching with private practice or other occupations. An average of 4 or 5 hours a week is devoted to teaching. Reportedly, the considerable prestige accorded university professors is the motivating factor. Salaries range from S/600 to S/5,000 monthly. Although the amount is not a living wage at the lower levels, the teaching salary is generous when the number of hours worked is considered and provides a supplement to other income.

Close to half the students are employed, usually as white-collar workers in private or government offices. At the national universities the students are coming increasingly from the middle class and, to some extent, from the lower class. Families from higher socioeconomic levels prefer to have their children educated at the private universities, where discipline is greater, or abroad.

To accommodate the schedules of both professors and students, classes are usually concentrated in the early morning, at noon and late in the afternoon, leaving the universities virtually deserted during the greater part of the day. This system has impeded programs of research and publication. It has also made difficult the maintenance of academic standards.

With widely varying interests and activities and no professional association, the university teaching staff is not particularly cohesive. Collective action occurs only when some infringement has been made on the rights of the university.

Students, on the other hand, feel and express a degree of unity and constitute a noticeable and, at times, influential group. Within the society as a whole their status as university students automatically accords them considerable distinction. Although the student may not be particularly serious about the academic aspects of the university experience, he usually sees himself as a potential member of the directing elite, a view also held by most educated elements. As such, he is ideally bound to take interest and be active in both internal and external issues and events. In addition, these pursuits frequently seem more attractive and essential than academic ones and often offer a means to influence and even exercise power over fellow students.

Within the university informal student grouping occurs at the *facultad* level, for most students identify more readily with the *facultad* than with the university as a whole. Formal association takes place through the Federation of University Students of Ecuador (Federación de Estudiantes Universitarios del Ecuador —FEUE), which has branches in all universities. Either formally, through the FEUE, or informally, students frequently react to what they perceive as injustices or infringements on their privileges in the university with demonstrations or other forms of pressure. Professors who are unpopular because of their professional performance or political attitudes have at times been forced to resign. Unpopular measures by the government or disapproval of government figures have caused strong pronouncements or the call to demonstrate by FEUE leaders. In such cases students are frequently supported by politically active professors, most often from the *facultades* of law and economics.

The military government, in an effort to stop disturbances, has closed the universities several times for short periods since it came to power. At the outset it chose the top officials at the Central University, and some professors resigned.

During the last few years attempts have been made, principally at the Central University, the Catholic University in Quito and the University of Guayaquil, to bring about qualitative and quantitative improvement. Facilities have not kept pace with expanding enrollments, up 128 percent from 1951 to 1961. The retention rate has dropped from about 25 percent to only 18 percent. Substantial financial aid has been received from a variety of foreign private and governmental sources. With the financial support of AID, missions from the University of Pittsburgh, the University of Houston and Saint Louis University have been assisting the Central University, the University of Guayaquil and the Catholic University in Quito, respectively, in improvement programs. The principal areas of activity include the reform of central administration, the institution of basic studies programs for all students before further university work and the strengthening of the *facultades* dealing in disciplines directly related to social and economic development. Plans also call for the promotion of greater stability and a calmer, more exclusively academic atmosphere.

ADULT EDUCATION

Adult education has been devoted principally to reducing illiteracy, which is widespread, even though persons who can do little more than sign their name are considered literate. According to the 1962 census, 43.7 percent of the population over 10 years of age was illiterate, and about 83 percent of the country's illiterates are to be found in rural areas among the large, indigenous population. Similarly, illiteracy is much higher among women, bound by greater cultural conservatism, especially in indigenous communities, than among men.

The first literacy campaigns were begun in 1945 as a result of the Literacy Law passed the previous year. Responsibility was divided between the National Union of Journalists (Unión Nacional de Periodistas—UNP), working in the Sierra and the Oriente, and the Ecuadorian Literacy League (Liga Alfabetizadora Ecuatoriana—LAE), active on the Coast and on the Galápagos Islands, which split the S/500,000 allotted by the national budget each year. By 1960 an estimated 250,000 people had been taught to read and write. The effects, however, were often not lasting as there were no follow-up programs, and the knowledge acquired did not prove especially applicable to the environment in which the new literates lived. Although intentions were excellent, the UNP and LAE did not have the resources, organization and background to handle the problem.

Recognition of these difficulties and inadequacies prompted the government, through the Ministry of Education, to become more actively involved. In 1962 the Department of Adult Education was established within the Ministry with the help of UNESCO. A decree-law was also issued making literacy training compulsory for all those between the ages of 15 and 50 who were unable to read and write. In 1963 campaign plans, administrative organs and materials were formulated. Recognition of past defects has led to an emphasis on integral education, which combines instruction in reading and writing with rudimentary studies equivalent to the elementary school curriculum, modified to the interests and necessities of the environment.

Plans also include centers offering programs in community education, vocational training and more advanced instruction for those who wish to continue formal studies. By 1964 approximately 330 centers were reported in operation, staffed primarily by elementary school teachers, some of whom had received special training in the teaching of illiterate adults. Inspectors had also been assigned to oversee the program.

In comparison, other programs of adult education have been extremely limited. Since 1940 the Central University in Quito has sponsored a modest program of cultural extension and maintains a "Popular University," which offers 3-year courses in secretarial skills, accounting and nursing to adults who did not complete secondary education. Housed in a downtown Quito office building, the "University" is staffed by volunteers from FEUE and the professors. The new vocational high schools established by the joint program of the Ecuadorian Government and AID also offer evening courses to adults. Besieged by applicants, these night schools graduated close to 700 students in 1964.

EDUCATIONAL PLANNING

The 10-year plan, formulated from 1962 to 1964 by the Department of Integral Planning for Education within the Ministry, envisions substantial changes in the educational system. At all points the emphasis is on quantitative expansion, to raise the general cultural level, and reorientation, to adapt human resources to the demands of national social and economic development.

Elementary level education has been an area of particular concentration. Certain specific goals have been set for 1973 which include 100 percent enrollment of all elementary school-age children, the construction of 9,000 additional classrooms, the creation of 7,000 new teachers' positions and 207 new school inspectors' positions, the improvement of the retention rate to 60 percent and a substantial decline in the grade-repeater rate. By legislation the elementary program is to be extended to 6 years in rural schools. The program of social services is to be expanded. Textbook production and distribution, stipulated in the plan, has also been initiated. Reorientation and qualitative improvement at the elementary level is to be brought about through revised curricula and study plans, which have been formulated and are beginning to be implemented on an experimental basis. Emphasis has been placed on the practical; longer periods are to be devoted to skills and crafts, and a correlation is to be made between subjects and the immediate environment. The new plans attempt also to correlate subjects, establish continuity in them from grade to grade and introduce greater student participation.

At the secondary level quantitative goals include the expansion of enrollment by 50,000, which will bring the percentage of the school-age population in school up to 25 percent; the construction of 1,000 classrooms; and the expansion of the teaching staff to about 7,700. The aim for the rentention rate is 70 percent. As specialization is initiated at this level, reorientation has been given particular importance. During the first 3 years the same course of studies is to be given to all students and specialized studies are to be given in the second 3-year cycle. It is hoped that the change will permit students who only complete the first cycle to obtain jobs more easily. By delaying the choice of specialization and providing counseling services, more students may be encouraged to enter vocational fields, where manpower needs are greatest. In addition, the first 3-year cycle can be made available in smaller population centers.

As at the elementary level more emphasis has been placed on practical work for all students and on greater student participation in the classroom. The new system was introduced in six *colegios* in the Sierra in October 1963 and in six on the Coast in April 1964. Two pilot schools are to be added each year until 1967, when an evaluation, followed by general implementation, is scheduled.

At both levels private schools are expected to take part. The quantitative goals set by the central government were formulated on the assumption that private education would continue to handle about 20 percent of the enrollments. Interest has already been shown by some private schools in the new study programs, and a few have requested permission to participate in the pilot projects. A degree of resistance, however, has been the more general rule.

As the universities are autonomous, no plans have been drawn up to include them in overall educational development. The National Technical Council on Higher Education, however, was created to prompt organized appraisal and recommendations for improvement. Education officials would like to see substantial expansion of university enrollments, which would correspond to growth at the lower level, and a similar emphasis on technical careers oriented toward development needs. Scholarships, particularly for study abroad, are to be increased in number and granted principally to students in technical fields.

In adult education the 10-year goal is to reduce illiteracy to 15 percent. From 1964 to 1967 the programs tried experimentally in 1963 will be implemented at the cantonal and parish levels. In the subsequent 5-year period they will be continued at these levels and expanded to villages, hamlets and tribal settlements in the Oriente.

CHAPTER 10

ARTISTIC AND INTELLECTUAL EXPRESSION

The panorama of Ecuadorian cultural history dates back to several thousand years before the birth of Christ. The indigenous period, by far the larger portion, is known only in sparse outline, through archaeological remains and oral accounts. Since the conquest, formal, self-conscious cultural expression, dominated by the Spanish-speaking European-oriented elite, has been cast decidedly in the Western mold. Despite the continuing presence of a large Indian population, aboriginal traditions have been all but lost, surviving in highly fragmented and modified form at the folk level and in popular culture.

As in the case of most other Latin American nations, the cultural foundations of Ecuador were laid by Spain. Reflecting these origins, literature and the arts have been the dominant forms of expression, and in the general area of scholarship, the concentration has been on the humanities. Interest in the sciences has not been totally lacking, but, except for medicine, the scientific disciplines have held little attraction.

The scope of artistic and intellectual life was determined in great part by the elite social concepts and practices derived from Spain. For the most part only a small minority with education and a degree of leisure and affluence have ever been involved or affected. Both direct participation, especially in letters and intellectual activities, and appreciation and support, consequently, have been confined to the same small group. As members of this group have had numerous other interests, activities and responsibilities, this involvement has frequently assumed the character of a secondary pursuit or an avocation.

Such limitations have also been influential in the selection of the particular media to be cultivated within the favored realm of arts and letters. Those of a more individual character, such as poetry or painting, have prospered, whereas those requiring group effort and mass support, such as the performing arts, have not. For many years, moreover, the location of most of the elite in Quito resulted in the concentration of activity in that city.

Pride in past achievement and respect for tradition, therefore, have been strongest there. In the present century the rise of the coastal city of Guayaquil, economically, socially and politically, brought about a geographical broadening of activity.

Within this framework, developments have generally been oriented toward the ebb and flow of European aesthetic and intellectual movements. Modified by the influence of the local environment and the process of transmission, they have not been merely faithful copies. Initially, formal association with Spain led to a direct and unself-conscious emulation. After the association was terminated sources of influence proliferated, and imitation, prompted by the desire to achieve cultural as well as political equality, became more conscious. More recently, the questions of originality and national distinctiveness have assumed importance. The artistic and intellectual manifestations that have emerged in this atmosphere, however, have continued to reflect techniques, devices and attitudes borrowed elsewhere and have been in line with similar currents in most nations of the hemisphere.

THE EVOLUTION OF TRADITION

Indian Ecuador

As archaeological investigation has been limited, knowledge of cultural development before the Spanish conquest is somewhat fragmentary. It appears that throughout the period heterogeneity and regionalism were characteristic; there was little unity of traditions. Knowledge of the indigenous cultures is limited to the crafts, which reached a relatively high level of development among some groups. Of the crafts the most notable were ceramics, stonework and metallurgy. The building and textile arts were generally rudimentary.

The earliest known cultural remains are found on the Coast. The first of the cultures, known to archaeologists as the Valdivia, produced pottery of considerable quality, which is the oldest yet discovered on the Pacific coast of South America. Characteristic features included female fertility figurines and incised geometric decoration based on zigzag and parallel lines. Over a long period of time, Valdivia influences penetrated the interior of the country, and traces of the geometric decorative tradition have been found in the Oriente. In the subsequent coastal culture, designated as Chorrera, painting was added to incision as a decorative technique, and geometric patterns were replaced by spirals. Anthropomorphic forms, both masculine and feminine, were common.

The earliest known archaeological remains in the Sierra are dated at about 100 B. C. For several centuries there was little contact among the various peoples, but around A.D. 1000, a degree of integration took place, apparently as a result of east-west migrations.

The most advanced stage of development was reached on the Coast, principally in the areas of Manabí and Esmeraldas. The only culture to build extensively with stone, the Manabí tradition also included simple statues, plaques and U-shaped seats resting on pedestals representing crouching animal or human figures. In Esmeraldas, stone was used to produce sculptured heads somewhat reminiscent of Mayan and Egyptian styles. Metallurgy, with gold the principal material, was also a characteristic, and probably more notable, activity. Both cultures continued to improve the ceramic tradition, adding new forms and techniques. In the Sierra the region south of Cuenca also became a significant center of metalworking.

By the time of the Inca invasion in the latter part of the fifteenth century there had been a stagnation in the development of the arts and crafts. Little inspiration or change was brought by the Inca conquerors, as their own culture was notable more for its political than its aesthetic achievement. In addition, the Incas were only in the area about 50 years and never were able to attain complete supremacy. The few palaces and monuments they built in the Sierra could not compare with the celebrated constructions raised in Peru.

Elements of the Inca educational system were also introduced, in the form of the *amautas*, court scholars who taught the sons of the nobility and preserved through memory the history of the empire. Music was another means of remembering the past, through songs of heroes, events and gods. It was usually intimately connected with religion and magic as well. Music, however, was not an innovation of the Incas, though perhaps they used it more extensively than had been previously customary. Lack of data prevents the establishment of any chronological development, but it is known that indigenous Ecuadorian groups had long fabricated simple wind and percussion instruments and composed songs using three-, four- and five-tone scales.

The Spanish Colony

The arrival of the Spaniards in 1534 brought a sharp break with the cultural past. With little modification, Hispanic traditions quickly and firmly replaced native ones. Only those elements of local culture which could be easily incorporated or utilized were allowed to continue. The Catholic Church, vigorously supported by the Crown, was the chief civilizing agent. Principally through the numerous religious orders which operated in the area, it oriented, stimulated and otherwise contributed to artistic and intellectual life. As a result the general atmosphere had strong religious overtones, and few cultural manifestations did not bear some connection with the Church, its administrators or its teachings.

The greatest activity and achievement took place in the plastic arts. The need to establish settlements gave great impetus to building and, consequently, to architecture, which in turn generated activity in the other forms of plastic expression.

As the administrative capital, Quito became the center for artistic endeavor and production. The growth of a firm artistic tradition, which reached its greatest heights in the seventeenth century with the coincidence of excellence and productivity in all the arts, made Quito one of the principal art centers in the Spanish colonies. Works of art came to constitute an important export. Almost purely European in derivation, local styles also traveled beyond the confines of the Audiencia of Quito, as Ecuador was then known (see ch. 3, Historical Setting).

Although civil requirements were not neglected, the greater part of local resources, enthusiasm and time was devoted to the ecclesiastical. During the initial 150 years ecclesiastical structures proliferated. Modest parish churches were built, and a cathedral was begun shortly after Quito's elevation to a bishopric in 1545, but the intensive construction was caused mainly by the influx of religious orders. Upon arrival the orders immediately set out to erect handsome complexes of monasteries, convents and churches which took from 25 years to several decades to complete.

The Franciscans were the first, arriving in 1534. In the following year construction began on the monastery and its three associated churches. One of these, the Church of San Francisco, was the most significant monument constructed in the sixteenth century, for it became an archetype throughout South America. Most influential was the facade, which through the influence of Flemish members of the order was designed along the classic, balanced lines of the Italian Renaissance. The Franciscans also built the convent of San Diego and the convent and college of Santa Clara. Following the Franciscans the Dominicans, Augustinians and many other orders expanded the number of churches and convents. Most were Italianate in design or mixed Italian and contemporary Spanish elements.

With the appearance of the Jesuits shortly after the turn of the century, however, these styles began to give way to a new architectural approach. Their church, La Compañía, was modeled on the order's mother church in Rome, which was baroque in style. New elements of agitation and complication transformed the calm, ordered facades of the Renaissance. Classical severity was likewise replaced with elaborate, sensuous embellishment. During the course of the seventeenth century and throughout most of the eighteenth, baroque was the predominant style.

After the completion of the principal monuments architecture ceased to be the foremost of the plastic arts. The construction of new buildings declined in intensity, and much activity involved the renovation or modification of existing structures which required additions, had been destroyed by natural calamities or were no longer in line with prevailing tastes.

As supportive arts, painting, sculpture and handicrafts did not emerge until late in the sixteenth century, when the architectural movement was well underway. Nevertheless, the foundations were laid early. Soon after their arrival the Franciscans established a school in which native talents were channeled into European painting, sculpture, drawing, metalworking and wood carving. In time, Spanish artists began to arrive, establishing workshops that were centers of instruction as well as centers for the production of paintings, sculpture and tapestries destined to beautify churches and convents in the area.

The guild system, imposed in the Spanish Empire by Ferdinand and Isabel, also began to take shape. Under this system artists and artisans in the same craft were brought into professional association; standards of quality and proficiency were supervised; and techniques were imparted and perpetuated through the instruction of apprentices. In this type of creative environment art was rather impersonal and the product of collective effort. With the exception of the painters, most artists and artisans were Indians or *mestizos*.

Of these various arts painting achieved the greatest fame. Stylistically, it combined a variety of European currents which were introduced through exposure to imported works and through the influence of individual artists. The instructors at the early Franciscan school, for instance, were Flemish. A later master, Father Pedro Bedón painted within the Italian mannerist school, having received his own artistic education in Lima, under a disciple of Michelangelo. In addition, there were a number of Spanish master-painters. In theme, painting was almost entirely religious, portraying the prominent figures of Christianity in stylized poses.

Although excellent work was produced in the first half of the seventeenth century, painting achieved its finest expression after 1650 in the persons of Miguel de Santiago and José Javier Goríbar. Comparable only to his European contemporaries, Santiago was a prolific artist who produced works for most of the religious orders in Quito. Santiago was variously inspired by the Spaniards Ribera, Zurbarán, Murillo and Velásquez and by Rembrandt.

Goríbar, Santiago's nephew and disciple according to tradition, was a more forceful painter. Less eclectic, he modeled his art on that of the Italian school. A steady stream of artists followed Santiago and Goríbar, carrying the painting tradition well into the nineteenth century; many were competent, but none could equal the excellence of these two masters.

Sculpture was widely used for decorative purposes. Facades were embellished with sculptural details in stone or stucco, especially after baroque styles became popular. Interiors provided numerous possibilities for decoration, such as columns, pulpits, altars, choir lofts and ceilings. Elaborate carving in wood was common, particularly in the baroque period. After the middle of the seventeenth century, however, most sculptors devoted their principal efforts to a distinctively Spanish genre, the life-sized, free-standing figure. Done in wood, these figures were realistic. Portrayals of Christ on the cross and of the Virgin Mary, were especially numerous. Polychroming was usual, and Quiteño statues were notable for their brilliant finish. To heighten the effect of realism, garments made of cloth hardened with paint and plaster, jewelry, glass eyes, eyelashes and eyebrows were often applied. Of the sculptors, the most admired were Father Carlos, a contemporary of the painters Santiago and Goríbar, and the Indian Manuel Chili, whose nickname was "Caspicara," active in the latter part of the eighteenth century.

The minor arts also reached a high level of development and productivity. Metalworking, in gold and silver, was an important craft, devoted largely to the creation of architectural decoration and ecclesiastical articles. Gilding and silverplating were also commonly used decorative techniques. Of the artisans the goldsmiths and silversmiths were among the most numerous and constituted an elite. In seventeenth-century Quito there were approximately 50 silverworking studios alone. Ceramics was another notable craft. As a ceramic center, Quito was rivaled only by Mexico. A variety of wooden furniture, based on Spanish models, was also produced locally.

In contrast with the arts intellectual life developed slowly and did not involve or directly affect much of the population. Whereas art, as a means of glorification of religion and spiritual uplift of the masses, was readily comprehensible by them, speculative and natural philosophy and theology, the principal areas of intellectual activity, were far beyond the grasp of the majority. Crown policy involved the subordination of culture to religious and political needs; basically, it strove to maintain the traditional authority vested in church and state. The establishment of the Spanish Inquisition reflected this policy. As a result, academic education was considered necessary and desirable for only a small minority, made up principally of churchmen, who were the protagonists and promoters of intellectual activity.

Established by religious orders primarily to prepare new clerics, institutions of learning, particularly the universities, were the intellectual centers. The first university was founded by the Augustinians in 1586; a second was created a few years later by the Jesuits; and a third was established by the Dominicans toward the end of the century. Highly erudite thought and investigation dealt with theology or were theologically oriented, within the general system of scholasticism. For scholasticism there was only one problem—the relationship of faith and reason.

Although scholasticism was dying out in the rest of Europe in the sixteenth century, it continued to be championed in Spain and, consequently, in the colonies. Established doctrines on religion were considered eternal truths, subject to further investigation but not to challenge or change. An unchanging, God-centered universe was the cosmological view. Discussion and debate therefore revolved around method, not theory, and differences were based on the varied approaches of the scholastic authorities to which the orders appealed.

The classroom and the pulpit were important media of expression. Writing was seen principally as a means of preserving didactic treatises or maintaining records. Written by hand and usually in Latin, the earliest learned writings were not intended for wide circulation and were usually kept only in university or monastic collections. The first of these treatises were chronicles, set down in most cases by the priests who arrived on the heels of the conquest. Though none are extant, subsequent writers indicate that, in a mixture of fact and fancy, they described Indian custom and history, local flora and fauna, and the events of the early colony.

Later writing dealt with more abstract philosophical subjects, often obscure and involved. The same complication that became prevalent in art during the baroque period was reflected in the form and content of letters. Gaspar de Villarroel, active in the seventeenth century, is representative and probably the best known writer of his time. An Augustinian priest, Villarroel was variously a professor of theology, a bishop in both Spain and the colonies and royal chaplain. In his numerous writings most of the pertinent topics of the day were covered. One of the most interesting was the relationship between church and state, which in the colonies was intimate, but not always harmonious. In his principal work, *El Gobierno eclesiástico pacífico o los dos cuchillos*, he sought to define the basis of peaceful relations between civil and ecclesiastical authorities. Villarroel also wrote sermons, commentaries on scripture and doctrine and elegies to the Virgin.

Verse was also used, generally with lyric, emotional content. Poets were variously inspired by the secular, usually some event involving the crown, or the religious. The seventeenth-century poet Xacinto de Evia of Guayaquil combined the two in his *Ramillete de varias flores poéticas recogidas y cultivadas en los primeros abriles de sus años*. Epigrams and burlesque pieces were set down alongside mystical, amorous and funereal poetry in this work, one of the few of its kind produced in the colony.

More numerous were the poets who used exclusively religious themes. The strong mystical current that produced some of Spain's greatest poetry in the period was represented in the Audiencia by Catalina de Jesús Herrera, who wrote of her own mystical experiences in verse. Several works, written mostly in the eighteenth century, were also dedicated to the life of Mariana de Jesús, a seventeenth-century Quiteña who was later canonized.

Like the prose writers, the poets gave considerable attention to form. Their undisputed stylistic mentor was the great Spanish poet Luis de Góngora, who developed a poetry of verbal virtuosity, complicated syntax and difficult classical allusion. Although Góngora died in the early seventeenth century, his poetic style, known as *culturanismo*, was emulated by local poets well into the eighteenth century. In time, its effects were apparent also in the public speeches and pronouncements of lay and religious authorities.

The Influence of the Enlightenment

The decidedly Spanish orientation of cultural life began to undergo some modification in the eighteenth century as the range of influences in the colony broadened. France, which had assumed a position of cultural leadership on the European continent, was the chief source. Contacts were both direct, through the infiltration of books and foreign visitors, and indirect, channeled through Spain itself, which had come under French influence with the establishment of the Bourbon monarchy at the turn of the century. On the surface, new styles and aesthetics appeared to challenge or merge with the old. More fundamental, however, was a tendency toward secularization, manifested in a shift of emphasis in interests and concerns and in the emergence of an intelligentsia outside the clergy.

Artistic contributions in general declined in both quantity and quality. Since the needs had been met and religious zeal abated, the construction of great ecclesiastical monuments all but ceased. The building that did take place revolved around civil architecture, principally private houses. Especially toward the end of the eighteenth century and in the beginning of the nineteenth, the well-to-do erected large, two-storied residences, of stone in the

Sierra and of wood on the Coast. Though the central patio plan used was Spanish, the facades, influenced by contemporary French styles, were severely classical, relieved only by imposing entrance-ways. Interiors revealed a new taste for the refinement, grace and light touch of the French rococo, with decoratively painted walls and furnishings that were imported from France or executed in the French style. This type of construction and decoration did not encourage the continuation of the strong tradition of the minor arts. Though less severely affected, painting and sculpture also lost some of their momentum. In these forms of expression themes continued to be religious, but changing taste introduced a lighter palette and style of composition and execution.

On the other hand, there was an upsurge of activity in thought and letters, generated by exposure to new European currents in those areas. An increase in individual book collections made it possible for the owners and their associates to become relatively well versed. The curiosity of visitors from abroad, mainly scientific, about the region was met with a curiosity of equal intensity about European developments among the *criollos* who acted as their hosts. One of the earliest and most influential of these visitors was the Frenchman, La Condamine, who traveled to the colony in 1737 to pursue his interest in the natural sciences. Others followed, among them the German naturalist Alexander Von Humboldt, who spent several years in the area in the early nineteenth century.

Among younger, more restless minds, the tradition of scholarship, erudition and criticism was directed away from theology to secular studies. One of the first, Pedro Vicente Maldonado, who lived during the first half of the eighteenth century, devoted his energies to mathematics, geography and astronomy. Writing in the second half of the century, Father Juan de Velasco produced the first history of the Audiencia. Divided into three volumes—Natural History, Ancient History and Modern History—the work was not a history in the modern sense, for it was filled with fables, legends and imaginative passages. It nevertheless was a rich source on pre-Colombian and colonial events, local flora, fauna and social customs. In addition, it reflected the growing interest in investigation and in greater knowledge of the material world.

Increased information and new discoveries, received firsthand or through reading and discussion, made the continued acceptance of the scholastic method of inquiry and view of man and the universe difficult. In the second half of the century scholasticism came increasingly under attack. Although the universities continued to teach within the scholastic system, they became centers for the consideration of new ideas and philosophical systems through informal discussion and contact among students. The expulsion of the Jesuits, the chief educators and proponents of scholasticism, from the colonies in 1767 by the Spanish Crown was of considerable significance in these developments (see ch. 11, Religion).

Those dissatisfied with scholasticism turned to the philosophical systems devised by late Renaissance thinkers and their heirs, the group known as the Encyclopedists. Although that group was not homogeneous, it did hold in common the belief in the authority of reason in thought and conduct and in nature as a source of knowledge. The independence of science and philosophy from religion in the view of these thinkers came to have a parallel in political thought. The concept of the divine right of kings was disavowed as was the traditional role of the Church in the affairs of the state. In their stead the liberal thinkers subscribed to the sovereignty of the people, secular law and secular states.

Of the supporters of the Enlightenment in the Audiencia, Francisco Eugenio de Santa Cruz y Espejo was the most enthusiastic and renowned. Born in Quito in 1747, Santa Cruz y Espejo studied under both the Dominicans and Jesuits, eventually receiving a medical degree from the University of St. Thomas Aquinas. While practicing his profession he continued his education privately and, like many of his intellectual mentors, wrote critical and didactic pieces on medicine, theology, law and letters. Literary aesthetics were of particular concern to him. Reflecting the precision and rationalism valued by the new age, he became a sharp critic of the twisting obscurities and complexities of style which had appeared in the previous century and continued to enjoy popularity.

In Ecuador, however, Santa Cruz y Espejo is most highly honored and regarded for his political thought and role as an intellectual precursor of the independence movement. Known by local authorities as a critic of the regime through his satires and articles, he was imprisoned in 1787 and sent to the viceregal capital, Bogotá, for trial. There he became friendly with Antonio Nariño, Colombia's chief precursor of independence, with whom he avidly discussed recent events in France. In Bogotá he also established a friendship with an influential young nobleman, the Marquis de Selvalegre, from Quito, who later played an important role in revolutionary events at home.

On his return 4 years later, Santa Cruz y Espejo was named Quito's first public librarian and became the guiding light of the Patriotic Society (Sociedad Patriótica de Amigos del País), established in 1794. Although the Society was founded in accordance with a decree by Charles III, which ordered the establishment of such organizations throughout the colonies for the promotion of letters, art, agriculture and commerce, it became a forum for the discussion of new ideas among the well-to-do *criollo* membership. The periodical *Primicias de la Cultura de Quito,* which provided an early impetus to the independence movement, was directed by Santa Cruz y Espejo and written almost entirely by him. When a conspiracy against the colonial government was suspected in 1795, his support of such issues as freedom for the colonies, the right of self-government and of constitutions and the rule of law made him a natural suspect. Arrested in 1795, Santa Cruz y Espejo died after several months in prison.

The importance of the ideas held by men like Santa Cruz y Espejo in influencing the course of events which led to political independence from Spain in the first quarter of the nineteenth century is difficult to ascertain. Although local socioeconomic factors and political events in Spain were most crucial in determining specific actions, these ideas doubtless provided the ideological context and justification. They also served as a source for the formulation of governing documents and political institutions in the aftermath of military victories (see ch. 3, Historical Setting).

Although most of those who wrote in this era of change adopted a didactic approach to reflect contemporary events and interests, there were also those who sought creative expression. Born in the latter part of the eighteenth century, José Joaquín Olmedo became the poetic voice of the independence movement, achieving fame not only in Ecuador but throughout the continent. Intense admiration for the northern independence leader, Simón Bolívar, whom he met while participating in the local revolutionary government of Guayaquil, inspired his major work, *La Victoria de Junín, canto a Bolívar.* In accordance with the neoclassic aesthetic, which was the literary face of the Enlightenment, Olmedo wrote with the lyric grandeur and measured verse of the classical epics of Greece and Rome. A number of other long poems were produced, also dedicated to significant battles and their heroes. In later life he wrote little, but continued to be prominent in local life as a member of the national Congress.

Polemics and Apprenticeship

During the first epoch of the republic, from 1830 until roughly the end of the century, cultural activity reflected the contrasting currents of political turbulence and social traditionalism that dominated national life. Politics acted as the generating force for most of the best minds and active spirits of the period. Thus Quito, the capital, remained the focal point, though contributions

189

came increasingly from other areas. Within the rather passive, provincial confines of a society which seemed to seek a peaceful way of life through the continuation of familiar patterns, the purely creative spirit was subdued.

Throughout the period letters functioned as the most prominent form of expression, and within the general discipline, political writings were foremost. After independence was achieved questions of political philosophy or ideology, so compelling in the immediate past, were abandoned for issues of a more local and specific nature. Usually, they arose from the conflict between the two political groups, the Liberals and the Conservatives, and their leading personalities, often authoritarian. Among the young intellectuals, university educated and reasonably well-to-do, who took the cause of one side or the other, the formal, didactic prose of the past gave way to polemics of great vitality and passion. In growing numbers newspapers appeared to provide a forum for airing opinions and ideas. Small in size and often dependent upon one individual, these periodicals tended to be short-lived, dying with a particular issue or the lessening of interest on the part of their owners.

The first of these newspapers was *El Quiteño Libre,* written by a group of young intellectuals and former independence fighters, which appeared 3 years after the establishment of the republic. Hotly opposed to the country's first president, General Juan José Flores, who had been born in Venezuela, the group was nationalistic, antimilitary and anti-Colombian (in reaction to Ecuador's association, until 1830, with Gran Colombia). The unexplained deaths of several of the key figures of the group not long after publication began put an end to *El Quiteño Libre.* A succession of newspapers followed, including several run by Gabriel García Moreno, who later became president. In his periodicals, which bore such names as *El Zurriago, El Vengador* and *La Nación,* García Moreno fought the authoritarian General Flores with sharp, bitter prose during the General's last days in power in the 1840's.

Ironically, the greatest writer in the genre and, indeed, one of the greatest nineteenth-century literary figures in Latin America, Juan Montalvo, was the arch enemy of García Moreno, who, once in power, proved no less authoritarian than Flores. Born in 1832, Montalvo did not begin his writing career until 1866, after several years of diplomatic service in Europe. Hoping to prevent the return of the Conservative García Moreno to a second presidential term, Montalvo published *El Cosmopolita,* which was hailed as the voice of the Liberal opposition. The electoral victory of García Moreno forced Montalvo to seek refuge on the Colombian-Ecuadorian border, where he continued to turn out fiery pamphlets.

When García Moreno met death in 1875 at the hands of an assassin, Montalvo is said to have exclaimed, "My pen killed him!"

Returning to Ecuador, Montalvo edited a new periodical, *El Regenerador,* designed to offer guidance during the period of political reconstruction. The emergence of a new political power, General Ignacio de Veintimilla, brought an end to *El Regenerador.* In combat once again, Montalvo wrote *Las Catalinarias,* sharp, brutal episodes illustrating his thesis against Veintimilla, and had them published in Panama, under the sponsorship of a fellow exile and champion of the Liberal cause, Eloy Alfaro. After the overthrow of Veintimilla, though elected to Congress, Montalvo chose to go to Europe to pursue his literary activities. There he produced many works, including his major one, *Los Siete Tratados* (The Seven Treatises), a collection of moral essays on political events. The later style, however, could not equal the brilliant, incisive prose of the earlier days, which was Montalvo's most original and lasting achievement.

The newspapers continued after Montalvo, but the relative calm on the political scene softened the tone and content. Not until the Liberal revolution of the 1890's and the early twentieth century did events and personalities provide material for a return to truly fervent polemics. Manuel Calle, a partisan of the Liberal cause, was most notable among the many writers. Editing newspapers and, in association with the young intellectuals in Guayaquil, preparing for revolution, Calle achieved great prominence and influence with the Liberal success in 1895 (see ch. 3, Historical Setting). In Quito, where close contact could be maintained with the new Liberal government and its principal leaders, Calle became the party's apologist in his column "Charlas." He also wrote several books revolving around his political experiences and the men of his era. Later political writing lost its preeminence in letters as the climate and concerns changed and the range of expressive forms broadened.

In the shadow of journalistic polemics other types of literature began to appear, somewhat cautiously, in the second half of the nineteenth century. As in the past, European movements, only slightly transformed locally, provided the models. Subject matter and aesthetics were largely within the current that had already prevailed for a generation on the continent—romanticism. The sentimentality and love of beauty, nature and the distant past that had come to characterize the romantic movement in Europe suited the taste and inclinations of the conservative local society. Exaltation of the individual, rebelliousness and the simultaneously brooding and tempestuous spirit that had been the stamp of early European romanticism, if expressed locally, were expressed only in the political arena.

Most numerous were the practitioners of an old genre, verse, who turned variously to local scenery, national history, the mysteries of religion and human existence for inspiration, producing poems of careful construction and sonorous vocabulary. The great majority of these compositions were not published and, if circulated at all, were seen only by the poets' friends and associates. Moreover, as writing verse was considered a cultured pastime of the educated, most of the writers were "Sunday poets" who devoted the greater portion of their energies to family enterprises, politics, or other forms of literature and cultural activity. None received widespread or lasting renown.

Increasingly, prose began to offer expressive outlets to those who did not care to deal with politics or academic subjects. The newspapers, which, after the initial years, often contained literary supplements, gave rise to a new form—the short, artistically conceived article on local customs and scenery. Known as *costumbrismo,* this type of writing emphasized sentiment, morality, the picturesque and the light, often humorous, touch. Although for a long time individual writers garnered little fame themselves, the *costumbrista* sketches enjoyed considerable popularity.

Equally reflective of the spirit of the era and more significant for future development was the novel, which had taken shape as a literary form with the romantic movement. The local initiator was Juan León Mera, who wrote during the 1860's and 1870's and who wrote the words to the national anthem. Mera, who centered his activities in his native Ambato, expressed the versatility expected of educated men of the times through the various roles of teacher, newspaper editor, provincial governor and national congressman, as well as writer. He began his writing career with verse in *Melodías indígenas* a romanticized treatment of the Inca and colonial past, and in *La Virgin del Sol,* based on an Inca legend.

Mera's novel, *Cumandá,* also dealt with the Indians, but during a later period, around the time of independence. The choice of a native setting and an Indian girl as protagonist was somewhat revolutionary for the period, but the style, presentation and underlying philosophy were strictly contemporary. Influenced by the French romantics, Mera created idealized, exotic figures and involved them in a complex, melodramatic plot of tragic love, heavily overlaid with sentiment. Poetic descriptions of lush jungle scenery east of the Andes and sketches of local ways in the *costumbrista* style were interspersed. A conservative, both politically and socially, Mera reflected his strong sympathies for the Church, the landowning class and the existing political system throughout his narrative. *Cumandá* was well received at home and abroad, where it was considered one of the major works produced in Latin America.

Among the other traditional activities, only painting attracted many practitioners and private interest among the elite. Throughout most of the century the Salas family served as a nucleus for the arts. Antonio Salas, trained under the apprentice system late in the colonial period, did much to continue the old method of art education through the establishment of his own workshop. There he taught a great number of the relatively rich generation of artists born between 1830 and 1845, among them several of his sons.

After midcentury, although artists continued to establish studies and take on pupils, a more formal, academic training became prevalent. Travel to Europe became fairly common, and among those who studied abroad were Antonio Salas' grandsons. The elder Salas was also active as a promoter of art through his connections with the Escuela Democráticia de Miguel de Santiago (Democratic School of Miguel de Santiago), a society which held the country's first exposition in 1852. Although short-lived, the society staged several additional shows during the 1850's in which prizes were awarded.

In his paintings, Salas mirrored the style and subjects that were to remain fairly uniform during the century. Composition, color and drawing were technically competent, though somewhat dry and uninspired. To the religious themes of the past, portraits and scenes of the independence battles were added. The latter were most often commissioned by the government, which was interested in decorating official monuments with tributes to past glories.

Official attention to cultural activity was not limited to the commissioning of art works. General Flores had attempted to promote music through the establishment of a musical society under the direction of a government-contracted English musician. Other presidents also displayed interest. Well-educated and well-traveled, García Moreno sought to make the capital more cosmopolitan through the creation of a music conservatory and an art school under the direction of foreign teachers and the establishment of a polytechnic institute with the assistance of scientists from abroad. The public buildings constructed during the García Moreno period were also designed by foreigners hired by the President himself. Such stimuli were without exception short-lived, however, and had no great effect on the general provincial atmosphere. In the 1870's and 1880's visitors from abroad noted the placid tempo of existence in Quito, where the only forms of entertainment were social gatherings and religious processions. Observers in Guayaquil during the same period were impressed by the city's commerce but distressed by the absence of institutions of higher learning, museums, book collections and general cultural activity.

The Rebellious Search

The generations of the 1890's and the early twentieth century were bred in an atmosphere of change and uncertainty. With the rise of the Liberal party and of Guayaquil as a principal political and economic force in national life, the old, conservative era seemed to be challenged by the promise of a new era. Greater contact with the world outside the national borders, which itself was in a state of still greater transition, introduced stimulating and somewhat disquieting currents. Until the late 1920's the predominant direction in cultural activity remained undefined. Among individuals and groups it was variously a period of irreverence for tradition, of introspection and disillusionment, of optimistic eagerness and of experimentation.

Intellectual and academic circles experienced some growth as contact and interchange among individuals, formerly the practice only among partisan journalists, began to take place. Likewise, although simultaneous activity in several fields by intellectuals continued to be the rule, a greater seriousness of purpose seemed to prevail. Scholarship in various aspects of the humanities held considerable attraction.

Most representative of this trend was Federico González Suárez, who devoted his early energies almost exclusively to the Church, which led to his election as bishop of Ibarra in 1895 and archbishop of Quito in 1906. González Suárez did most of his writing while occupying these high positions in the Church hierarchy. Attracted to the past, he wished to write a general history of America, of which the history of the Church and of Ecuador were to be chapters. Only four volumes were written, however, covering the pre-Colombian and colonial eras in Ecuador. Based on careful scholarship in the archives of Spain and in local colonial manuscripts and a high level of objectivity, the volumes provoked considerable public controversy. In the last volume the criticism of the colonial ecclesiastics displeased many clergymen and conservatives. In addition, González Suárez wrote on literature in *Estudios literarios*, which were discussions of his personal favorites from the past and present, and on his own philosophic reflections in *Hermosura de la naturaleza y sentimiento estético de ella*.

Among young creative talents the scorn for old styles and approaches acted as a common denominator. In the search for more satisfactory forms of expression, however, there was no

194

such unanimity. In letters attempts at complete originality and innovation existed alongside the quiet, but persistent transformation of tentative developments already present. Initially, the former tended to predominate within the movement known as modernism, which produced a number of notable contributions, and then within a current of postwar eclecticism, which generated considerable activity but nothing of great quality.

Heavily influenced by currents in Europe, particularly in France, the modernists sought beauty without sentimentality; elegance and purity of form; exotic, often pagan images and symbols; and the unusual. They generally believed in the value of art for its own sake and saw themselves as lone individuals of superior taste and refinement engulfed by a world of mediocrity and materialism which could not understand them. In Ecuador, as elsewhere, poetry was the favored form of modernist expression.

Around 1910 three young poets, Arturo Berja, Ernesto Noboa y Caamaño and Angel Medardo Silva, emerged as the movement's principal exponents. All three chose to escape or ignore the political embroilments and social disorders at home, which they found distasteful, and turned instead to the beauties of ancient Greece, the glory of Versailles or the subjective experiences of disillusionment in love and morbid longing for death. Their poetry was published on the literary pages of the newspapers of the day, and only Medardo Silva saw his verses collected in book form during his lifetime. None of the three reached the age of 30.

Gonzalo Zaldumbide brought modernism to prose. Above all a stylist, Zaldumbide did not adopt the escapism or the spiritual disillusionment of the poets. Like many of his contemporaries in other Latin American countries, he was greatly influenced by *Ariel*, written by the Uruguayan José Enrique Rodó. In *Ariel*, Rodó admonished a generation haunted by the suspicion of inferiority before the exuberant technological prowess of the Anglo-Saxon world to recognize the worth and creative force of Latin American ideals and moral spirit. In an early essay, *De Ariel*, written at the turn of the century, Zaldumbide gave forceful expression to this philosophy of optimism.

A trip to Europe led Zaldumbide to a further study of the intellectuals who dominated the age, set down in such critical works as *En Elegio a Henri Barbusse* and *La Evolución de Gabriel D'Annunzio*. After returning to Ecuador, he wrote *Egloga trágica,* a novel which described, in poetic prose the provincial Ecuador of his day. Reflecting the taste and aspirations of many young men, the hero spends several years in Europe, leading a life of aristocratic refinement, but unlike the others, upon returning to his native land, he is captivated by its beauty and becomes involved in its customs and daily life. By developing a plot portraying tragic love, however, the author returns to the modernist preference. During the rest of his long life, Zaldumbide wrote principally on the great literary figures, past and present, of Ecuador and Spanish America.

Less striking at the time, another current, realism, was also developing. Built on the foundation of the *costumbrista* sketches which continued to appear in newspapers, Luis A. Martínez' novel *A la Costa,* which appeared in 1903, was the initiator. Martínez had a genuine desire to present what he saw as the local reality of his day in a simple straightforward manner. To some extent, Martínez' work was autobiographical. Born in the Andean city of Ambato, he participated in the Liberal revolution of 1895 and later took part in the government as a deputy in the national Congress, as minister of education and as political chief of Ambato. The protagonist of *A la Costa,* which begins in the Sierra during the revolutionary period, is a farmer who participates on the Conservative side. When the Liberals come to power, however, he begins to see the necessity for change and for a different sort of life. Consequently, he abandons the Sierra for the Coast, which seems to offer the hope of a better existence. Although at first he finds the new environment full of marvels, he eventually realizes that life is not easy there either. Nevertheless, on the Coast he finds work and love, which had been lacking in the Sierra. Martínez' thesis, which corresponded with the thinking of many of his contemporaries, is clearly presented, and the narrative is rich in descriptions of the people, customs and scenery of the two sharply contrasting regions.

After World War I a growing number of writers joined the circle of the realists, and concentration on the local scene began to replace the orientation toward distant times and places. Similarly, while the emphasis on style and form did not completely disappear, continuing to be inspired by the imported "isms" that proliferated after the war, content was increasingly more compelling. Growing social consciousness, bred by the changing environment and by the influx of new doctrines from abroad, gave a new dimension to the incipient realistic approach. Newspapers and magazines, often short-lived, were filled with articles and selections which gave expression to new ideas, anxieties and expressive ambitions.

Innovation also took place in painting, still the only medium of notable activity within the arts. The National School of Fine Arts, founded in 1904 and still functioning in 1965, was the nucleus. Initially, the school was staffed with local painters, most of whom were in the final years of their careers. As replacements became necessary, the European artists who were hired introduced ideas and techniques new to Ecuador. The principal guiding spirit was the Frenchman Paul Barr, who arrived in 1912. Under Barr a generation of artists abandoned academic styles and imitation of the old masters for impressionism. Coloring was lightened, and form and composition lost some of its former importance. Instead of working exclusively in the studio, young artists began to paint outdoors, and landscape painting became extremely popular.

The use of local scenes as subject matter, combined with the influence of literary supplements and magazines, prompted artists to turn to national subjects. One young artist, Camilo Egas, found inspiration in the Indian, while others depicted scenes from local folklore. A new technique, caricature, lent itself well to depictions of local elements and was particularly exploited by the artists who contributed to *Caricatura*, a review which appeared from 1918 to 1924. Until roughly 1930, however, experimentation and solution were only tentative.

THE CONTEMPORARY PERIOD

Trends and Characteristics

Within the artistic and intellectual community, preoccupation with the immediate environment has been the central theme in the contemporary period. The nationalist movement was launched around 1930 by a generation that felt the collision of a continuing idealism, renovated by social consciousness and leftist political philosophies, with the discouraging social, economic and political developments of the 1920's (see ch. 3, Historical Setting). In the two decades that followed the movement gathered force as the inclinations and attitudes of artists, writers and intellectuals intensified. Events at home were no more encouraging than in the recent past. Furthermore, no distraction was offered by new foreign currents for, abroad, troubled times led to a similar cultural withdrawal. Absorption with local themes, derived mainly from the rural environment, was virtually complete. Productivity was great; activity was widespread; and Quito and Guayaquil served as the principal centers.

Among the many individuals and groups an unprecedented spirit of fraternity prevailed. Similarly, there was a rare homogeneity in direction and stylistic approach. Considered shocking at first, the movement eventually won general acceptance, but with acceptance its vitality, creative momentum and unity were weakened.

The most intensive activity has probably been in letters. Writers of fiction, who have been the most emphatic and persistent proponents of the nationalist theme, have made the novel and short story popular and accepted, and won critical acclaim both at home and abroad.

Several socially conscious young writers made sharp portrayals of national realities by presenting segments of the local environment and population in a documentary fashion. The lower class, as seen through a series of characters drawn as prototypes, was the principal focus. The atmosphere in which the characters operated was invariably negative, although the incidents of their lives followed in quick, grim succession.

Within this framework attention was divided about equally between the contrasting coastal and Andean environments, producing a kind of literary regionalism. On the Coast the revolution was inaugurated with *Los que se van,* a collection of short stories written by Enrique Gil Gilbert, Demetrio Aguilera Malta and Joaquín Gallegos Lara. Through these stories, the authors described the coastal peasants (*montuvios*), their lives and the sensuous physical environment. The presentation and exposition reflected the writers' desire for greater realism, their haste and their inexperience. Rough, choppy, but vigorous, the language incorporated the colloquialisms and profanity typical of the peasant. Incidents involving sex were liberally interjected for the first time in local letters.

Having achieved considerable renown, all three continued their writing careers. Gallegos Lara dealt with the plight of the urban lower class of Guayaquil in his novel *Las Cruces sobre el agua.* After writing a second collection of short stories, Gil Gilbert firmly established his reputation throughout the continent with the novel *Nuestro pan,* a story of rice, the staple in the coastal diet, and of the peasants of the ricefields, trapped by both man and nature. An early member of the Communist Party, Gil Gilbert devoted most of his later energies to politics. Aguilera Malta also continued to write about the peasant, using a central theme of the hypnotic encounter between man and the physical environment in novels like *Don Goyo* and *La Isla virgen.* In later life he spent most of his time outside the country, serving as a diplomat and writing for the stage and screen.

Other writers wrote variously on the city and the country; on the *montuvio,* the Negro and the mulatto; on the contemporary scene; and on the recent past of change and political revolution. They saw the life of the great bulk of the coastal population beset by economic hardship and social oppression. The coastal type emerged as a volatile, often resentful individual.

Among the writers of the Sierra there was greater uniformity, for, almost without exception, they were adherents of *indigenismo.* Appearing at roughly the same time in all the Latin American countries with sizable Indian populations, *indigenismo* was another facet of the nationalist tendency. In a somewhat romantic fashion the Indian was championed as the wellspring of local identity, and elements of his culture were seen as the only truly national (regional or local) manifestations. There was a general, though rather abstract desire to restore to the Indian the dignity of his pre-Colombian past.

Appearing shortly after *Los que se van,* Jorge Icaza's *Huasipungo,* one of the earliest and probably the most celebrated *indigenista* novel in both Ecuador and the hemisphere, became a generic prototype. Essentially, it was the story of the landless Indian peasant, working a small plot of land, the *huasipungo,* on a large Andean estate. The plot, loosely strung together, presented a series of unrelieved misfortunes and tragedies visited on the Indians by the principal figures of Hispanic authority, the landlord, priest and political lieutenant, who were depicted as evil, unscrupulous figures, motivated by greed, lust and the desire for power. The Indian characters, though distinguished by name, were indistinguishable as individuals, all sharing a stoic resignation and a deep-rooted love of the land, the family and the miserable hut that served as a dwelling. Like the coastal writers, Icaza used sex and forceful language, laced with profanity, to underscore the harsh realism and shocking power of the basic content. *Huasipungo,* which was translated into several languages, inspired considerable comment at home and abroad. Icaza went on to write a number of novels in the same vein, dealing with the problems of the Indian or the lower class *mestizo (cholo),* and several plays, but none achieved the fame of *Huasipungo.*

Humberto Salvador has been the most prominent novelist of the region after Icaza. Though a native of Guayaquil, Salvador has spent most of his adult life in Quito, which has been the setting of most of his works. Unlike most of his contemporaries, Salvador has written extensively on the middle class, using a psychological approach. The interior monologue, rather than the narrative, has been his chief instrument of exposition. In Salvador's themes most critics have identified the dual currents of Freudianism and Marxism.

A growing investigative interest was also apparent among non-fiction writers, giving rise to a number of works on various aspects of national life. Sociological writing was inaugurated by Pío Jaramillo Alvarado, who began his career earlier in the century, but has contributed most in recent years. His most famous work, regarded as a classic of its kind, *El Indio ecuatoriano,* was followed by numerous books and articles dealing with national origins and development, culture and politics. A contemporary, Isaac Barrera, wrote extensively on literary history and criticism, areas which previously received only fragmentary coverage, and Oscar Efrén Reyes' *Breve historia general del Ecuador,* which has gone through several editions since its original publication in 1938, is still the best compact history available.

Prose has been the predominant vehicle of literary expression, but some poets, using techniques and styles learned from foreign mentors to voice local themes, have been influenced by the same intellectual and physical environment that touched the prose writers. By nature more subjective than prose, poetry has tended to express a more subtle, less materially rooted literary nationalism. Both Jorge Carrera Andrade and Gonzalo Escudero, who led the movement toward nationalism in poetry, abandoned the escapism and obsession with artistic purity of modernism in search of a more personal and, consequently, national form of expression. Carrera Andrade developed a poetry filled with images drawn from the land and primitive culture. In Escudero's works the power of the Andean environment was revealed in a cosmic quality and epic magnitude. Others were less able to reconcile the new tendencies with the nature of the literary form, producing poetry which was self-consciously social revolutionary, primitivist or *indigenista.*

The literary scene continues to be dominated by those figures who initiated the nationalist trend and have remained active, though many have lost the militancy of earlier days. Most of the younger novelists and short-story writers were reportedly producing softened or modified versions of already proved formulas. The more varied, universalist trends, which have generally taken over in the rest of the continent, have won some adherents. Little activity seems to be taking place in the area of didactic prose. The poets, on the other hand, are said to be increasing in number. In verse the tendency has been to establish a harmonious arrangement of universal themes within the framework of national elements.

The primary artistic medium, painting, has expressed visually the same general themes and subjects found in fictional literature. For the most part the nationalist painters have looked specifically to the Indian-dominated rural Andes for inspiration. Initially, they adopted a style which, combined with the distinctive *indigenista* content, was the pictorial face of continental *indigenismo.* The early works of Osvaldo Guayasamín, the most influential and best known internationally of the nationalist painters, are representative.

Landscape, the focus for the impressionists, receded to the background as the human figure again became all-important. Simplified and somewhat stylized along primitive lines, human forms were depicted in the attitudes and poses of everyday life.

In the statuesque monumentality and dignity of his subjects the artist registered his admiration; in the suffering of their countenances and the meanness of their condition he registered his protest. The pastels of the impressionistic palette gave way to the strong, rich color of the Andean surroundings. In composition an almost design-like quality was achieved through simplification of the pictorial elements and attention to the overall superficial pattern of their placement.

Gradually, Guayasamín and most of his contemporaries evolved different styles to express the *indigenista* attitude. In this process the influence of international currents became apparent. For the most part the *indigenistas* adopted an expressionistic approach, replacing the former angularity, static quality and attitude of social commentary with greater fluidity and subjectivism. Guayasamín has gone somewhat further in the latter part of his career. An element of abstraction and extreme stylization has been introduced through the combination of components in a manner strongly reminiscent of Picasso.

The most important exception to the adoption of *indigenismo*, or the *indigenista* attitude, was Manuel Rendón. Learning his art in France, where he spent the greater part of his early years, Rendón returned to live in Ecuador in 1937. More intellectual and international in his painting than his compatriots, he was the abstractionist among *indigenista* realists. The early works were built around graceful, linear human figures. Rendón then moved toward a more flowing form of expression, incorporating the superimposition of figures, large areas of warm color and organic shapes. Luminous color has been retained in the later paintings, but component areas have been reduced in size, and the angle has replaced the curve. Long an isolated, uncelebrated figure in local art, Rendón gradually achieved considerable stature.

Among the notable painters of the most recent generation, a preference for abstraction or the purely abstract has been apparent. A feeling of unity among these painters, engendered by the desire to channel painting into new, more universal directions, has led to a number of group shows. In style they have demonstrated variety and individuality. Generally in a formative, experimental period, some have adopted a controlled, intellectual approach; others, a dramatic subjectivism of intense emotion; and still others have not yet associated with an identifiable tendency.

A similar, more internationally oriented trend has developed in architecture. Until recently activity in the field was limited, and the nationalist movement had little effect. Increased construction, which began in the late 1940's, provided the initial stimulus. The need to construct a number of large buildings in Quito, prompted by the city's selection as the site of the second Inter-American Conference of the Organization of American States, and the boom in residential construction in both Guayaquil and Quito gave further impetus. Most of the work has been done by a dozen, locally trained young architects. In style, designs featuring an emphasis on the horizontal, the vertical, or the contrast between the two have been predominant. Concrete, stuccoed brick and glass have been the most common materials used; wood and stone have been used for decorative detail. In public or commercial constructions some use has also been made of sculpture and mosaic or bas-relief murals.

The Artistic and Intellectual Community and Environment

Among the middle and upper classes a high value has traditionally been placed on letters, the arts and intellectual pursuits. Interest and activity in these spheres have marked the individual as cultivated, refined and educated and have served as a class determinant. In addition, these areas have been a vehicle for the expression of the versatility considered desirable and, to some extent, necessary in an individual of a certain status. Among writers, for example, the cultivation of several forms simultaneously, such as the novel, the short story or the newspaper article, has been characteristic.

Involvement in several unrelated fields has been equally common, and the gentleman-scholar or poet with separate business interests has been a persistent phenomenon. Even among those more professional in orientation, who come increasingly from the middle class, full-time dedication is not the rule. As members of the articulate and sophisticated minority, most feel compelled to assume responsibility also in such areas as education, government and politics, and many writers, intellectuals and artists have been attracted to political groups on the Left. In addition, multiple activity is usually an economic necessity, for few of the more serious literary practitioners have independent means, and artistic, intellectual and literary endeavors usually do not provide an adequate income. Many who take up creative careers early in life later abandon them for more lucrative careers or retain them only as a secondary interest.

The influence of the artistic and intellectual community has not been commensurate with its prestige. The concentrated and enduring protest and exposition of national social and economic ills ardently put forth by most artists and intellectuals, for example, have had little tangible effect. Extremely small potentially, the audience or market for the product of artistic and intellectual activity is often confined to the individual's friends, family and colleagues.

Active interest in and support of cultural affairs, even among the elite, have been limited by poorly developed formal channels of communication and exposure. Such stimulants as museums and libraries are few in number. Public programs are apt to be poorly attended and, if staged for profit, seldom financially successful. For the artist regular avenues of sale and exposition are restricted to a few galleries and the patronage of wealthy sponsors. The situation of the writer is similar. Publication and distribution are most frequently undertaken at his own initiative and expense. Although editions are small, demand does not usually exhaust the supply (see ch. 16, Public Information).

Attempts to bridge these gaps have been made both by the artists and intellectuals themselves and by the government at various levels. Literary reviews and journals, usually short-lived, have often been financed and edited by writers and intellectuals. Similarly, galleries and shows have come into being through the efforts of artists, usually acting in concert. At times the two groups have collaborated in projects of mutual interest through the Society of Artists and Writers (Sindicato de Artistas y Escritores), founded in the late 1930's.

The most important government-sponsored institution is the Casa de la Cultura, an entity unique in the hemisphere, dedicated to the support, administration and stimulus of cultural life. The Casa was established in the early 1940's, in great part through the efforts of the artistic and intellectual community, led by its undisputed spokesman, the writer Benjamín Carrión. Carrión became the Casa's first president and continued in the office until recently, when his outspoken sympathy for Fidel Castro and his affiliation with Castroist groups alienated many of his colleagues and supporters. Most of the executive and staff positions have been filled by active artists, writers and intellectuals, a practice which has enabled many to concentrate more exclusively on cultural interests.

The formal functions of the Casa and its 12 provincial branches touch on most fields of creative or intellectual activity. In letters the Casa has supplemented local facilities through the publication of 50 books each year, selected by disciplinary boards from among the numerous manuscripts submitted. Distribution is accomplished through outlets maintained by the Casa and through private bookstores on contract. The authors receive a percent of the sale. In the plastic arts, the Casa sponsors group shows and annual salons in which substantial monetary prizes are awarded. In addition, scholarships for training and subsidies for travel abroad are given.

Attempts are also being made to stimulate the performing arts through classes in theater and ballet, the formation of a mixed chorus and the sponsorship of recitals. Administration of the National Library and Museum of Fine Arts, supervision and approval of public commissions in the arts and protection of the national artistic patrimony are also functions of the Casa. Although the accomplishments of the Casa de la Cultura have been notable, in recent years the tempo of activity has slackened primarily as a result of inadequate funds.

The government also aids indirectly in the development of cultural life through its financial support of the universities, in which most of the facilities for formal training are located. On a limited scale these institutions also sponsor student programs. At the local level the larger municipalities have at times organized competitions in arts or letters, sometimes with monetary as well as honorary awards. Such competitions, however, are not usually permanent features.

CHAPTER 11

RELIGION

The overwhelming majority of people consider themselves to be Roman Catholic even though for many the amount or degree of observance is minimal; although estimates vary, the figure is no less than 90 percent. Small but unknown numbers of Indians in the Oriente practice tribal religions, which remain undescribed. There are also an estimated 2,000 Jews, primarily of recent European origin. Protestantism, introduced by missionary groups at the turn of the twentieth century, has made little headway. In 1962 there were reportedly about 4,000 communicants in a total community of 11,500, the smallest Protestant group in relative terms of any country in Latin America. The maintenance of the most powerful radio transmitter in Latin America by an inter-denominational group centered in the United States, however, has been a notable activity of the Protestant movement (see ch. 16, Public Information).

Although the Catholic Church in Ecuador is often cited as one of the strongest and most influential in the hemisphere and although it is strong in the Sierra, it has no such importance on the Coast. To a great extent, the differences stem from the Church's important role in national history. The Church was established soon after the Spanish conquest, which was centered almost exclusively in the highlands, and rapidly became one of the most significant institutions of society and a basic element of culture in that area. Isolated and undeveloped, the rest of the country was attended by missionaries. The fundamental respect and attention paid the Church by the colonial authorities as well as by the general public carried over in great degree to the republican period.

In the later half of the nineteenth century, however, the coastal region experienced rapid economic development and rose to challenge the highlands, the traditional center of power. Coastal elements, imbued with a spirit of liberalism and progress as well as ambition, found in the Church a target in their bitter political feuds with the more traditional highlanders. Thus, intense anticlericalism long colored national politics. Through the influence of the Coast, the Church's legal position was undermined, with the introduction of separation of Church and state and of religious tolerance. Nevertheless, much of the flavor and atmosphere of traditional relationships remained in the Sierra.

Practices and attitudes toward religion tend to be in keeping with the distinctive, local patterns of development of the two regions. Thus, in the highlands outward respect and conformity with obligations are widespread. On the Coast more casual observance is customary, and reportedly less than half of the people have been baptized. Within the general population the highland Indians are a large and notable group. Practicing a form of Catholicism with several features different from that of the rest of the country, they are deeply attached to the Church as represented in their local parishes and priests.

In its view of society the Church has tended to be conservative, perhaps chiefly because both the hierarchy and the clergy are drawn predominantly from the Sierra. In recent years, however, there have been some indications of greater dynamism, liberalism and social consciousness. Administrative organization has been strengthened and updated. Acting in concert, the hierarchy came out strongly in favor of social and material change, including agrarian reform, in May 1963. In addition, a number of prelates, notably the bishops of Riobamba, Guaranda and Ibarra, have been active in developing socially oriented programs and projects for improvement which supplement traditional Church activity in the social sphere.

THE CHURCH IN RETROSPECT

Colonial

At the time of the conquest a strong and militant spirit of religious commitment prevailed in Spain. Through the efforts of Ferdinand and Isabel, religious as well as political consolidation had been brought about with the expulsion of the Moors and the Jews. The Inquisition had been revived and given a distinctly Spanish imprint. Subscribing to the contemporary view of rule by divine right, the monarchs saw themselves as primary secular defenders of the faith. The state and the Church were not seen as entities existing in mutual independence; in an age which held the universe to be God centered and temporal existence to be a brief passage to an eternal world, the civil and religious aspects of life freely intermingled.

Discovery of America brought both the opportunity and the responsibility of extending Christianity and, with it, the institutions and atmosphere in which it had developed in Spain. Monks accompanied the expeditionary party that visited the coast of Ecuador during the initial stages of the conquest of Peru and the forces under Sebastián de Benalcázar, which conquered Quito in 1534 (see ch. 3, Historical Setting). The first mass was said in Quito in August of that year. Within 11 years, the Church and the population in the colony had expanded sufficiently to warrant the establishment of a diocese, with Quito as its seat.

Expansion continued as large numbers of religious personnel traveled to the colony, particularly in the late sixteenth and early seventeenth centuries. The local population also contributed to the ranks of the religious. Growth in personnel was accompanied by a proliferation of churches and monasteries. Quito, the principal center, became known as the city of convents. From one of these came Mariana de Jesús, who was beatified in the nineteenth century and canonized in 1950.

In addition to meeting the spiritual needs of the Spanish population, concentrated in towns and cities, the Church also undertook the conversion of the Indians. In the highlands the Indians were brought together into *encomiendas* and *reducciones*, institutions set up by the Crown to make indoctrination easier and to provide labor. Under the *encomienda* system a group of Indians was placed in the charge of an individual who received a portion of the product of the land in exchange for supervising their moral and civil education. Moral education, which was understood to mean religious conversion, was entrusted to a member of the clergy. *Reducciones* were Indian settlements, under the jurisdiction of civil or, at times, religious authorities, where the same type of dual education was attempted. Missionaries also traveled to the outlying lowlands, establishing settlements among the more primitive tribal Indians. The Jesuits, who worked in the Mainas area, which forms part of present-day Peru, were particularly active until their expulsion by royal order in 1767.

From the outset, Church involvement and participation in colonial life was not confined to the spiritual sphere. As in Spain, relationships with the state were close. By a series of papal decrees issued between 1493 and 1508, the Spanish monarchs obtained a number of rights over the local Church, which together were known as *real patronato* (royal patronage). Devotion and a deep sense of religious responsibility were not at all incompatible with the desire to strengthen royal authority, especially in the New World.

Real patronato entitled the monarchs to perpetual title over tithes from the colonial territories; to taxation of ecclesiastical income; to selection of archbishops, bishops and other offices of high rank; and to presentation of canonicates and ecclesiastical benefices, which were then authorized by the Pope. In addition, royal approval was necessary for the travel of ecclesiastics to and from America, for the foundation of churches, monasteries and other ecclesiastical edifices, and for the circulation of papal pronouncements.

Thus, the Church (excluding certain religious orders) in Ecuador, as in the rest of America, had no direct contact with Rome. In addition, as in Spain the Inquisition was established with little connection with the Italy See; the Indians were not subject to its jurisdiction. In return, the Church received the financial and moral support of the Crown. The wealth it was able to acquire over the years and the natural influence it possessed in a religiously oriented society further enhanced its power.

At the local level conflicts between civil and ecclesiastical authorities were not uncommon. Difficulties usually arose over differences in interpretation of the respective areas of authority. Bishops threatened civil authorities with excommunication while the civil authorities retaliated with threats of warrants and civil punishments. Initially, an important conflict existed, involving the Indian population, which transcended local confines. The Crown and the Church assumed the role of protectors of the Indians, in contrast to local figures who adopted practices and measures which were frequently abusive.

Although ecclesiastical advocates were initially successful in persuading the Crown to legislate in favor of the Indians, fierce reaction among Spanish colonists, who saw their position of wealth and power threatened, eventually forced compromise. Still, for the most part, the Church continued to defend the Indians, where possible, from the abuse of landlords and officials. In response, the Indians developed considerable loyalty and dependence upon the clergy in their immediate environment.

The Church and its representatives also acted as the chief agents for the introduction and development of Spanish culture and social institutions in the colonies. Formal education was established under its sponsorship. A number of secondary schools and three universities were founded by religious orders, primarily for the training of new members. Schools of arts, crafts and basic learning were also established to train the Indians in useful offices. Less formally, the Indians were exposed to new techniques in agriculture, new crops and new livestock. The missionaries were also responsible for spreading the Quechua language, which had been introduced to a limited extent shortly before the conquest by the invading Inca, throughout the highland region (see ch. 5, Ethnic Groups and Languages).

Similarly, artistic and intellectual life developed principally through the efforts of churchmen. Clerics wrote and collected manuscripts in convent and university libraries. They also directed the construction and embellishment of the many temples, which provided the chief inspiration for the production of the art works which made Quito famous (see ch. 10, Artistic and Intellectual Expression). The organizations formed by artisans who labored in these projects were associated with the Church and engaged in religious as well as trade-oriented activities. Care of the sick and needy, in institutions founded for these purposes, was another function assumed by the Church.

Republican

After independence there was little initial change in the role and position of the Church. Strong moral influence over the general public and prominence in the social sphere continued. Similarly, the relationship to the state remained unaltered, a condition that generated considerable friction. Under the Spanish monarchs, who had been sympathetic to the Church, the privileges of *patronato* had been acceptable in principle and, usually, in practice. Assumption of the *patronato* by the republican government, less concerned with Church interests, was not. Heated argument arose between the canonists, who viewed the *patronato* as a privilege conceded to the Spanish kings and their heirs alone, and the regalists, who saw it as inherent in sovereignty and, thus, transferable to the republican state.

To the dismay of local churchmen, the regalists won out, and *patronato* was incorporated in the Constitution of Cúcuta (1824), to which Ecuador subscribed as a member of the Gran Colombian Republic, and the Constitution of 1830, Ecuador's first charter after secession from Gran Colombia. The Vatican, supporting the position of the local Church, did not give its approval to this unilateral assumption of privilege. Clauses specifying Roman Catholicism as the sole religion of the state, contained in both documents, however, won strong Church approval.

After the early flurry of debate and conflict the Church accepted in practice, if not in principle, the constitutional prescriptions, and in 1838 the Vatican extended formal recognition to the Republic of Ecuador. Harmony was disrupted only sporadically when governments attempted to inject a note of religious tolerance or to encourage the secularization of education, which the Church continued to control. Popular opinion in these matters was strongly with the Church. Opposition came principally from a minority group of politically liberal intellectuals who, imbued with the ideas of the French and North American revolutions, desired a complete separation of Church and state.

As Gabriel García Moreno emerged in public affairs in the mid-nineteenth century, the Church-state question gained great force. It became the chief point of conflict and most ardently debated issue for decades between the two political parties, Conservative and Liberal, which began to crystallize at this time. As a senator in the 1850's the conservative García Moreno successfully introduced bills to reinstitute the free establishment of religious orders curtailed by *patronato* and to prohibit the establishment of masonic lodges.

Serving as President of the Republic or as the power behind the presidency from 1861 to 1875, García Moreno adopted measures that reflected his belief in religion as the only truly national tradition and chief instrument of unity. Roman Catholicism was reiterated as the religion of the state; the exercise of all others was prohibited; and adherence to the faith was made a requirement for citizenship. A concordat was signed with the Vatican, which granted the Church a position of greater independence and power than it had enjoyed under the Spanish monarchs.

Intensely interested in education, García Moreno had legislation passed to stimulate the establishment of public schools, which were placed under the direction of religious orders, some of which were contracted abroad. Toward the end of his period of influence the republic was dedicated to the Sacred Heart of Jesus by a Church Council and the National Congress.

Although García Moreno's policies probably did not distress the general public, which was predominantly Roman Catholic and socially conservative, they were strongly opposed by the liberal intellectual elements that were emerging as an effective force. Opponents, whose particular motives were never made clear, brought his rule to an end with assassination. Shortly thereafter, the Archbishop of Quito met a similar fate, when he was poisoned, according to tradition, by wine at the cathedral altar.

For roughly the next 20 years government behavior oscillated, as moderate Conservatives and liberally oriented administrations held power. The Church did not remain aloof from politics; it advised the faithful to elect Conservatives, who could be expected to continue the policies of García Moreno. The Liberals protested vigorously. In 1895 the Liberals launched a revolution, with the religious question as a prime, though not exclusive, motive. Liberal strength was centered in the coastal city of Guayaquil. A port of some consequence during the colonial period, the city had nevertheless been something of an outpost, isolated from Quito and the highlands. Experiencing a relatively recent and dynamic growth in commercial enterprise and population, the city countered the sense of tradition, in which the Church was an important element, of the Sierra, with progressive sentiment.

Under the two principal Liberal leaders, Eloy Alfaro and Leónidas Plaza Gutiérrez, who alternated in the presidency from

1895 to 1916, tensions between Church and state and between pro- and anti-Church factions mounted. The Liberals saw the Church as a reactionary force, impeding progress and state authority. The Church, on the other hand, ably defended by Federico González Suárez, considered Ecuador's greatest churchman, looked upon the Liberals as enemies, bent on destroying national unity and order.

Initially, changes were moderate. The first Liberal constitution, formulated in 1897, continued to recognize Roman Catholicism as the state religion, although liberty of conscience was admitted. The document also prohibited the immigration of additional foreign religious orders and the holding of political office by the clergy. Subsequently, laws and measures became more extreme. *Patronato* was reenacted, giving Congress the right to create new parishes and elect high Church officials, cutting the Church off from direct contact with Rome and making it financially dependent on state-raised revenue.

The Church lost the right to oversee the press and the circulation of books. Priests were forbidden to teach anything but religion, a measure that greatly hampered the educational system, still largely sponsored by religious orders. The Law of Religions, passed in 1904, established freedom of religion and offered state protection to ministers of non-Catholic faiths. It also gave Congress the right to authorize the sale or transfer of Church-owned rural properties, with revenue going to the Church, and prohibited tithing, the collection of first fruits and funeral taxes, all important sources of Church income. Reaction among the conservative element, which included churchmen, most of the highland population and the Conservative Party, was fierce, and tempers ran high.

In 1906 a new constitution was drafted which inclined toward greater moderation. The state assumed a position of greater neutrality. Freedom of conscience was asserted, and no specific religion was mentioned in association with the state. Political office was prohibited to ministers of any faith. The Roman Catholic Church was given control over its own financial affairs and not prevented from entering into free communication with Rome. As the state system of *patronato* had fallen into disuse and was not reiterated in the Constitution, the Church was also able to direct its internal affairs without interference. Although public education was made secular, the Church was not prohibited from maintaining schools.

Despite these modifications conservative elements saw the new constitution, with its lack of specific support of the Church and Roman Catholicism as a threat. President Alfaro's attempt to negate the election of the popular and widely respected González

Suárez to the archbishophric of Quito brought further objections. Although frequently at odds with Liberal governments, González Suárez adopted a course of conciliation which was responsible for lessening tensions. He objected to the passage of civil marriage and divorce laws and the nationalization of Church-owned rural lands, for example, but prohibited clerics under his authority from supporting political parties and engaging in political activity.

After the Archbishop's death in 1917, which had been preceded by the assassination of Eloy Alfaro in 1912 and the passage of Plaza Gutiérrez from the presidency in 1916, the controversy lost the last of its principal figures. Though the issue retained sufficient force occasionally to inspire high emotions and heated outbursts, it no longer figured as a principal source of friction. Church power and influence were somewhat reduced, and the state followed a policy largely of noninterference.

THE CHURCH TODAY

Administration and Organization

Structure

Ecclesiastical divisions of national territory are of two types, diocesan and mission. All the diocesan divisions are located in the developed, relatively heavily populated Coast and Sierra regions. The three archdioceses are Quito, Guayaquil and Cuenca, the latter two having been elevated to that status in 1957. Within the province of the archdiocese of Quito in 1965 were the dioceses of Latacunga (raised in 1963), Riobamba, Ibarra, Guaranda and Ambato. The province of Cuenca includes the diocese of Portoviejo and the independent diocesan jurisdiction of Los Ríos. All these ecclesiastical divisions correspond in geographic extension to the political provinces in which the diocesan seats are located, with the exception of the diocese of Ibarra, which includes the province of Carchi as well as Imbabura.

The entire Oriente region, the Galápagos Islands and the coastal province of Esmeraldas constitute mission territory. There were four apostolic prefectures and five apostolic vicariates in 1965.

The hierarchy presiding over these divisions consisted of three archbishops, seven bishops, two coadjutor bishops, one auxiliary bishop and two bishop prelates. The Archbishop of Quito, Carlos María de la Torre, was also a member of the College of Cardinals. In addition, there was a papal nuncio, the diplomatic representative of the Vatican to the Ecuador Government.

Parishes, the smallest unit and under the authority of the diocese or mission divisions, numbered 535 in 1964. The greatest concentration was in the Sierra, which had over twice as many as there were on the Coast; only 2 percent were in the Oriente. In geographical extension the parishes ranged in size from an average of less than 200 square miles in the Sierra to between 250 and 640 square miles on the Coast and more than 3,000 square miles in the Oriente.

Clergy

In comparison with other Latin American countries, Ecuador has a large number of priests. In 1964 there were 1,243 priests, or 1 per 3,685 inhabitants. Geographical distribution throughout the country, however, was uneven. Although only slightly over half the population lived in the Sierra, almost three-quarters of the priests were located there. In contrast, the Coast, which accounted for 46 percent of the population, had only 22 percent of the total number of priests. Thus, in the Sierra there was an average of 2,475 inhabitants per priest while in the Coast, no circumscription had fewer than 5,000 per priest. The Oriente, which had only 2 percent of the total population and 7 percent of the total number of priests, had a favorable ratio, but the scattered settlement patterns and enormous territorial extension diminished the advantage.

Of the total priests there was roughly equal division between the secular—under the authority of the diocesan bishops—and the regular—members of orders subject to the authority of their superiors. Most of the secular priests were engaged in parish work, so that in all dioceses at least 50 percent were secular. The inadequate number of secular priests, principally on the Coast and in the Oriente has caused many regular priests to engage in parish work. One-third of the regular priests of the country do parish duties. Other pursuits include teaching, general mission work, social action and the maintenance of churches not within the parish system.

In recent years the ranks of the clergy have been expanding at about the same rate as the general population. For the most part new members have been drawn from the local population. During 1954, 15 new priests were ordained, and roughly 170 students were enrolled in seminaries. As a result, recourse to foreign clergy, a widespread practice elsewhere in the hemisphere, has been limited.

In 1960 only 14 percent of the secular priests were foreign. Most were from Spain; others were from Italy and the United States. Over half the regular priests engaged in parish work are foreign, coming principally from Italy and Spain. Most foreigners are active in the Oriente, which is administered completely by religious orders, and on the Coast, especially in Guayaquil and Esmeraldas.

Members of religious orders for men or women are also relatively numerous. The most recent available figures indicate that in 1960 there were 1,167 in male orders and 3,222 in female orders. Growth in membership between 1945 and 1959 was considerable, substantially outpacing the rate of expansion of the total population.

The regular clergy was distributed among 506 houses, 170 for men and 336 for women. Orders and congregations for men numbered 18, and of these, the largest was the Society of San Juan Bosco, followed by the Franciscans, Jesuits and Dominicans. Of the 37 orders and congregations for women, the Sisters of Charity, the Dominicans, the Congregation of Santa Mariana and the Franciscan Missioners had the greatest numbers. Other female orders and congregations were small, having only 2 or 3 houses.

Parish work occupied the greatest number of religious houses for men, followed by teaching and the administration of special churches and missions. Other functions included social action and the formation of new members. There was an absence of male contemplative orders. Over two-thirds of the houses for women were engaged in teaching. The Sisters of Charity, Congregation of Santa Mariana, Franciscan Missioners and Missionaries of María Immaculata have been particularly notable in this field. A significant number were active in social and charitable work. The rest were devoted to contemplation, missions and other activities.

The greatest concentration of the regular clergy is in the Sierra. Similarly, in terms of general population there is also a large number in the Oriente. The religious orders and houses, particularly those for men, also tend to be concentrated disproportionately in large population centers. Although cities with 50,000 inhabitants or more accounted for less than 20 percent of the population, over half the male and female regular clergy was located in these urban centers. In contrast, less than 20 percent resided in settlements of 10,000 inhabitants or less, which account for roughly half of the total population.

RELIGIOUS LIFE AND PRACTICE

Ecuadorians see religion as an intensely personal matter, in which inward belief and the relationship between the individual and the supernatural are far more important than manifest piety and the strict practice of moral precepts. In this spirit there is little inconsistency in the popular characterization of "a great sinner and a great believer." Closely related is a view that good or bad fortune in this world result from the concession or denial

214

of grace by the supernatural, with little relationship to the behavior or immediate circumstances of the individual.

In the practice of religion, therefore, acts of personal supplication—prayers for the good fortune, in general, and for the success of specific ventures—assume relatively more importance than observance of formal ritual. Hence, too, the role of saints as intercessors before Divine Providence dominates act and sentiment. Commonly, people develop attachments, characterized by an affection bordering on possessiveness, to specific saints or to a specific manifestation of the Virgin. The accent on these personalized relationships has generally bred a lack of feeling for the Church as a community of shared purpose.

Within this broad context, patterns of attitude and practice vary. In the Sierra the prevailing atmosphere favors religious commitment and practice. Socially conservative and rather resistant to change, the highland population generally accords positive value to tradition, which counts Roman Catholic practice and the Church among its more important cornerstones. Reflecting past times, when to speak Spanish was to speak *cristiano* and to be *cristiano* was to be Roman Catholic, the people make little or no distinction between religion and local culture. Most individuals automatically consider themselves Catholics, regardless of personal compliance with obligations, and would be offended if their status were to be doubted or challenged.

Those who hold no belief or subscribe to different faiths usually are not apt to be publicly verbal about their convictions. To the majority, such persons seem alien and, to some extent, are viewed with distrust.

Among culturally Hispanic highlanders religious observance is strongest within the upper classes, which have tended to associate the faith with the existing order. It is somewhat less strong among the middle and lower classes.

In all groups women tend to be more strict practitioners than men, and religiousness in women is admired. Looked upon as primary preservers of public morality and good taste, women are also charged with the important function of almost exclusive supervision of the moral and religious training of young children. Until the age of adolescence, while under the close direction of the mother, children of both sexes are expected to be serious practitioners.

The later lack of observance among males is tacitly accepted as the values of masculinity and religiousness tend to conflict (see ch. 12, Social Values).

A religious career for males is not unpopular, however, as indicated by the relatively large number of vocations which come almost exclusively from the Sierra, and young men entering the priesthood or religious orders usually enjoy the pride and respect of family, friends and the general public. The economic stability and opportunity for advancement which the Church offers may be additional inducements to entrance into the clergy.

Within the highlands the Indians form a distinct group. As the missionary priests of the colonial era covered the highlands rather thoroughly, all the Indians are Catholics. Their religious belief and practice differ from that of the Hispanic society, however, for they have retained features from both the pre-Colombian and colonial periods.

In beliefs the Indians seemingly have not developed the extensive syncretism between Catholicism and pre-Colombian religions characteristic of their counterparts elsewhere in the Andes. This apparent difference may, however, be attributable largely to the nature of investigation in the area, which has been highly limited. Most Indians have a rudimentary knowledge of the tenets of the faith, acquired through study of a simple catechism taught by priests, parents or *rezachidores* (literate Indians who teach from pamphlets).

Other beliefs usually exist alongside the rudiments of Catholic doctrine. Rainbows, for example, are invested with supernatural power, being attributed with the origin of sickness. Offerings are given for appeasement. Mountains and lakes are personified as male or female and are believed to house a spirit. Local observers report Indian belief in the wailing of animals as a presage of death and in the veracity of prophesy made from dreams. Amalgamation of Christian and non-Christian belief is evidenced in the burial of the dead fully dressed in the best clothes, with food, money and other objects after last rites have been performed in church cemeteries. Similarly, in some areas widows and widowers are thrown into cold water the day after burial of the deceased spouse to cool their grieved souls and free them from ties with the deceased. The power to cause misfortune attributed to night spirits has been extended to unbaptized souls, who are also believed to wander at night.

Participation in rites and ceremonies of the Catholic Church is widespread and generally regular. Virtually all Indians baptize their children and take the role of godparent very seriously. The same holds true for church marriage, although this may take place after a couple has been living together for some time. Confirmation and first communion are observed with a lesser degree of uniformity. Attendance at mass is fairly regular, according to scattered reports. Since the small Indian communities are often without priests, most Indians must travel to their parish, and nonattendance often results from the necessity of keeping a few individuals in the community to guard livestock and homes. Parish priests usually visit the surrounding communities, which maintain a small chapel, a few times a year on special occasions. Attachment to the local parish is strong, and attempts to create new parishes, which may be closer, are usually met with resistance. The parish priest is a figure of great authority who commands considerable loyalty.

Many Indian communities also have a traditional religious organization, which links the community to the parish and fulfills a number of functions locally. The most complete description comes from the Diocese of Chimborazo, but organization in other highland areas is probably similar. Each year the parish priest names a number of Indian officials who have a variety of duties. The *gobernador*, an Indian who lives in the parish seat, is the first authority among these; he receives gifts from Indians of the surrounding communities in return for the initiation of action on requests for marriage ceremonies, funeral rites and other ecclesiastical services. Each community has one or two *regidores* who see that the residents fulfill their commitments to the church, oversee public morality and provide workers for collective work projects for the town and the church. Officials called *alcaldes* and *alguaciles* assist the *regidores*.

The *prioste*, another Indian official, is associated with an important activity, the *fiesta*. The *fiesta* may be specifically religious, celebrating the day of the community's patron saint, for instance, or may be held on important civic events or family occasions, such as baptism or marriage. In religious *fiestas* all expenses for food and drink for all members of the community are borne, by the *prioste*, who must normally save throughout the year to meet the cost. Considerable prestige is associated with the function, and all adult males are expected to assume the responsibility at some time.

In this group feeling the Indian differs from the Hispanic Ecuadorian. The *prioste* is selected by the parish priest or, in the surrounding Riobamba, by an official called the *apu*, a white man who acts as intermediary between the Indians, the parish priest and the political lieutenant. The religious part of the *fiesta*, a mass preceded by a procession, is celebrated in the evening. Attendance is often very poor. Subsquently, the entire community takes part in drinking, eating and dancing, which may go on for several days. The latter part of the *fiesta*, which is one of the few social functions of the Indian, is probably a continuation of pre-Colombian practice.

The religious climate of the Coast is decidedly different. Although most of the population claims some association with the Church, indifference and laxity are reportedly the rule. In reli-

217

gious practice the pressure of society and Church toward compliance are apparently slight. Less than half the coastal population has been baptized, according to reports, and of all the sacraments, baptism is the one most widely kept. The great number of consensual unions which never result in legalized marriage and the high rate of illegitimate births, in some provinces exceeding the number of legitimate births, also attest to widespread lack of practice.

In the more farflung church organization of the Coast, parishes have more numerous inhabitants per priest, and ecclesiastical services are less readily available than in the Sierra. Significantly, the only mission territory in the more developed part of the country is the coastal province of Esmeraldas. Lack of contact is particularly notable in rural areas, where settlements are widely scattered. According to reports, coastal peasants, unlike their highland counterparts, usually do not regularly travel to the parish seat to attend religious services nor do they maintain chapels.

The absence of attachment to the parish and community religious organization or observances may be caused in part by the common practice among many coastal peasants of moving rather frequently. In most peasant dwellings, however, religious pictures and images indicate the existence of some allegiance to the faith. Belief in supernaturals also extends to the non-Christian, including such powers as the evil eye, which can bring a variety of misfortunes. *Curanderos,* healers who incorporate elements of magic in their treatments, are also found in rural communities of the Coast.

Within this environment the same differences in views toward religion for men and for women held in the highlands prevails. The demand for religiousness among women and outward respect for it among men, however, are doubtlessly not so strong. Men are likely to show slightly reluctance in displaying a degree of disparagement, especially toward those who choose to enter the Church. In contrast with the highlands, the religious career holds little attraction. In 1959, of the 521 diocesan priests in the country, only 12 came from the coastal region. Whereas the highland provinces had from 20 to 40 priests per 100,000 population, those of the Coast had 1 or less.

CHURCH, STATE AND SOCIETY

Current relations between state and Church are based formally on a modus vivendi established with the Vatican in 1937. Under this agreement the Church was required to respect the right of liberty of conscience and refrain from interference in politics and government affairs. Ownership of estates was confirmed, and the right to acquire additional property affirmed. The Church was also granted the right to establish educational institutions of Catholic orientation on the conditions that trained teachers be employed, education laws be observed and official curricula and programs be used. Election of candidates to high church office was returned to the Holy See, although presentation of lists to the government before publication to prevent the selection of politically unsatisfactory individuals was required.

The constitution in force, promulgated in 1946, guarantees the right of liberty of conscience and prohibits discrimination for reasons of ideology or race. In the preamble the phrase "In the name of God" is used, for the first time since the days of Eloy Alfaro and Leónidas Plaza Gutiérrez. Attempts by Liberal congressmen to withdraw this phrase in 1951 met with popular protest and great argument.

Occasionally, actions of the government or the Church provoke anticlerical debate and criticism. In 1951, for example, a pastoral letter written by Cardinal de la Torre, which reminded parents that enrolling children in non-Catholic or mixed schools was prohibited, received strong Liberal protest. Somewhat later, the government turned over the administration of several correctional institutes for children to religious orders, which brought charges of clericalism. Again in 1965, the issue of relations was raised in regard to the question of government economic support of Church-run schools. At that time, General Marcos Gándara, speaking for the government, defined laicism, the official policy, as "neutrality and independence before religious concerns." Throughout the period, the assertion of Church influence over highland voters in rural areas, in favor of conservative groups, has been commonly heard in Liberal quarters.

For the most part conflict is unusual, and the old issues have lost their fervor. Relations are cordial and at times very close. Churchmen are commonly included on government advisory boards and committees set up to represent the panorama of national interests. Similarly, the inauguration of important public works projects, certain official ceremonies and religious functions are attended by both government and ecclesiastical personages of high rank, without comment.

In the social sphere education is the Church's most significant activity. During the 1963–64 school year roughly 20 percent of the schoolchildren were enrolled in Catholic-sponsored institutions. Activity was especially notable at the secondary level, where Church-supported schools and enrollments accounted for 65 percent and 42 percent, respectively, of the totals. The Church also administers elementary schools and two universities, one in Quito, the other in Guayaquil. Although in quality there is considerable variation, the Catholic schools generally enjoy good reputation and are preferred by the middle and upper classes (see ch. 9, Education).

Charity and medical care are also activities of considerable consequence. Religious orders assume much of the responsibility, some 3 houses for men and 74 for women being devoted almost exclusively to these functions. In addition to clinics and dispensaries, institutions for the care of the aged and the orphaned are maintained. The great majority are located in the highlands. Individual priests have also been active in socially oriented campaigns and projects, usually in urban areas. Irregular financial support and frequently short-lived public interest are often obstacles to the development of such enterprises.

In contrast, little activity has taken place in channels of public information. Two daily newspapers are published by dioceses, but neither has nationwide circulation. On January 1, 1965, a new daily of some importance, *El Tiempo*, appeared in Quito; though not specifically Catholic, it is owned in part by two dioceses. Altogether there are 43 Catholic-oriented publications, with a total circulation of 116,800. The Church also maintains a 16-station radio network known as Cadena Católica (see ch. 16, Public Information).

CHAPTER 12

SOCIAL VALUES

Founded in the Spanish conquest and dominated continuously by a white, Spanish-speaking elite, Ecuadorian society functions within guidelines set by values of the Hispanic cultural heritage. The value heritage of the large Indian population has contributed little to the patterning of national life, because the Indians have never participated fully as members of the society. For the Indians, social life within the narrow limits of community and locality is governed by values of their own heritage. For those who are involved even peripherally in the broader, white-dominated society, however, participation must be on terms set by the Hispanic social tradition (see ch. 5, Ethnic Groups and Languages; ch. 6, Social Structure).

Shaped by an embattled people whose identity and unity grew out of centuries-long warfare, the Hispanic social tradition has been extremely durable, surviving with little change in the face of continual upheaval and the onslaught of foreign cultural influences. After more than 400 years since the conquest, Hispanic America remains a highly distinctive cultural unit, and Ecuador, despite its large Indian population, continues clearly to share in that unity. As changing conditions and foreign influences have transformed the bases of the society, many of the traditional values have been reinterpreted, but few have been supplanted or changed beyond recognition.

Probably the most striking aspect of the Hispanic social heritage is a preoccupation with individuality and a strongly held complex of ideas regarding the individual and his place in society. At the heart of this notion of individuality is a conviction that every person is unique and endowed with an inner dignity (*dignidad*) that is both inalienable and worthy of universal respect. The concept of *dignidad* is widely reflected in social life, perhaps most dramatically for foreign observers in a sensitivity to praise, affection, insult and slight that often seems to verge on touchiness.

At another level the preoccupation with individuality gives rise to a strong emphasis on personal qualities and interpersonal trust over more abstract notions of institutional loyalty. Trust and obligation are generally seen as residing much more in specific persons—friends, retainers and kinsmen—than in institutions and other impersonal social entities. As a corollary, there is an overwhelming stress on family and kinship loyalties, and individuals are usually judged and ascribed social status largely on the basis of what is known about their kinship connections.

Another distinctive feature of the social tradition is a tendency to exalt the masculine role in most areas of life and to see that role as embodied in a highly stereotyped ideal of masculinity commonly known as *machismo* (lit., "maleness"—see Glossary). The ideals of *machismo* encompass much more than simple virility; they include such qualities as daring, both physical and intellectual; forcefulness; and a zest for competition. Taken together, these virtues are an important, though by no means the sole, yardstick against which men are measured, and they define a clear image of heroism.

If all individuals are seen as unique and endowed with a personal dignity, they are by no means seen as equal. To be sure, the notion of inner dignity confers ultimate spiritual equality on all people, but in the temporal sphere men and women are esteemed or disparaged as they are measured against the clearly defined prsonality ideals of the value heritage. Furthermore, social inequality, with a rigid stratification of wealth and privilege, is an ingrained and accepted part of the tradition. Although the social structure has always offered limited possibilities for upward movement, both the humble and the well-born have tended to see their positions as the inevitable and proper working of destiny.

Along with the acceptance of social inequality there is a clearly defined concept of the personal qualities and behavior appropriate to those of high status, including personal cultivation, generosity, a zestful enjoyment of leisure and a studied disinterest in materialistic goals and activities. These ideals are expressed in a strong disparagement of manual and routinized work and a preference for activities with at least an aura of professionalism. Such standards are important not only in regulating the behavior of the elite but also for the models they provide for socially ambitious persons of lower-class origins.

Ideally, at least, power and privilege are balanced with clearly defined responsibilities of rank. Relationships between superiors and inferiors—whether employers and employees, leaders and followers, or rulers and subjects—are seen as properly personalized. The inferior must evince deference, but the superior is no less obligated to evince a friendly, personal interest. These notions are crystallized in the distinctive Hispanic tradition of the *patrón* (sponsor or protector), the upper status employer or leader who forms long-term paternalistic ties with his retainers, rewarding deference and loyalty with protection and an active personal interest. If in real life these precepts are often violated, the good employer, ruler or leader is expected to approximate the ideal of the *patrón*.

The ideas and precepts of Sierra Indian social life have not been studied so systematically or extensively as those of the Spanish-speaking Ecuadorians. It is possible to describe the social values for the most part only through inferences drawn from observations of overt behavior. Descriptions of observers indicate a basically uniform value pattern throughout the Sierra.

Archaeological evidence suggest that in pre-Inca times the sedentary peasant peoples of the Ecuadorian Sierra were all similar to each other in way of life, notwithstanding considerable variation in detail. Although the short-lived Inca domination had little specific cultural impact on the various Ecuadorian Sierra peoples, the Spanish rule which followed worked in many ways to impose further uniformity. All of the Indian groups were similarly reduced to a marginal and subservient place in the colonial society. All were converted to Christianity shortly after the conquest, and both the precepts of the religion and the demands of the missioners came to be reflected in the Indian way of life (see ch. 3, Historical Setting; ch. 5, Ethnic Groups and Languages).

Integrated to the national society more as subjects than as participants, and not sharing many of its basic orientations, the Indians have usually seen it as hostile and exploitative. Accordingly, their views of the society reflect chiefly reaction and adaptation. Distrusting the Spanish-speaking whites and *mestizos* (see Glossary), they have typically sought to withdraw from most forms of contact with the powers and institutions of the nation. In most cases this tendency toward withdrawal has been balanced with a stress on intracommunity solidarity.

At the levels of community, family and individuality the values of the Indians appear, by report of observers, to be much more positive in content than and basically in contrast to those of the Hispanic heritage. Probably the sharpest contrast lies in the relative absence, in the Indian view, of stress on the person and self-expression. The premium placed on aggressiveness and forceful expression by the Spanish speakers is diametrically opposed in the Indian view, which emphasizes circumspection and conformity. Similarly, whereas the Hispanic social view stresses purely personal characteristics in the judgment of men, that of the Indians appears to emphasize substantive achievement and social contribution.

THE HISPANIC VIEW

Individuality

As they are verbalized, the traditional Hispanic concepts of individuality and the person sound much like those of English-speaking North Americans. In both traditions there is a great concern with the dignity and integrity of the individual, and in both the right of free self-expression is vigorously espoused. The words comonly used to express these ideas sound very much alike —dignity (*dignidad*) and freedom of expression (*libertad de expresión*), for example. Such cognates and the apparent similarity of the ideas they express tend, however, to mask significant disparities in concept and outlook. The North American view stresses a respect for the individual born of the similarity and kinship of men; that of the Spanish speakers stresses a respect of personal uniqueness. The North American concept of dignity usually refers to human dignity. By contrast, the concept of *dignidad* usually bears overtones of a purely personal dignity (*dignidad personal*).

At least in the ideal the North American concept of common humanity and human dignity leads to an egalitarian credo. The ideal society provides equality of opportunity as a minimal condition for personal fulfillment. In the Hispanic view fulfillment is essentially independent of social status and material opportunity. In such a view there is no contradiction whatever between an overt acceptance of social inequality, on the one hand, and a strong respect for individuality and personal integrity, on the other.

The concept of inner dignity compounds such qualities as integrity, personal honor and self-esteem. All people are deemed to be endowed with such a *dignidad,* and any attack on it is seen as properly evoking a bitter hostility. A failure to recognize a person's worth or a suggestion of personal inadequacy, whether intended or not, can call forth a reaction that would appear to North Americans as excessively violent. Even worse than frontally directed insult is an attitude of indifference or insensitivity or behavior which treats an individual as a nonentity.

This basic notion of respect applies in all relationships between people, regardless of social status. There are many ways in which the social inequality between rich men and poor men and between leaders and followers can be expressed, but etiquette also prescribes ways in which a more general interpersonal respect must be expressed. If an upper-status person is not expected to treat his inferiors in any way suggesting equality, he is expected, at least theoretically, to express a due regard for their personal worth. For example, artisans and other skilled workmen do not expect to be addressed as *señor* (sir or mister) by their higher status patrons, but they can properly expect to be called *maestro* (master), a title specifically accorded those with skills.

In real life these precepts are often violated. Men of high status sometimes behave toward their inferiors not only in a manner calculated to express social distance but also with disdain. Given their power and privilege, they can usually do so with impunity, but not, however, without arousing the resentment of those they disdain. Moreover, such behavior is universally condemned in the abstract. Thus, if the ideals are subject to violation, they are no less important in defining what is appropriate.

Notwithstanding the high value placed on individuality and personal uniqueness, the Hispanic social heritage also prescribes a generally accepted range of role ideals, and, to a considerable extent, an individual's public image is established by the degree to which he approximates those models. There is a sharp sexual differentiation in ideals of personality and social role. Men are viewed as ideally aggressive, competitive and self-expressive. Women are viewed as properly passive, submissive and abnegating. Leadership, adventure and broad-ranging activities have traditionally been reserved to men. Women, especially after marriage, have been expected, in the same traditions, to confine the range of their actions and interests to the household and kin group.

Men: Machos and Caballeros

The highly stereotyped virtues of *machismo*—including aggressiveness, competitiveness, a zest for both physical and mental action, a will to conquer and a clearly demonstrated sexual prowess—are popularly conceived to form an inseparable complex. They embody in a single image a model of manhood and heroism. The qualities of being a *macho* can be expressed in many areas of life. In politics and intellectual debate aggressiveness and daring evoke admiration. With few exceptions assertive, daring and aggressive politicians have attracted a larger popular following than those with obvious ability but less forcefulness. Similarly, in intellectual life the brilliant, self-assertive polemicist, rather than the pedestrian seeker of facts, often has the greater appeal for readers.

At the informal level amatory conquest assumes considerable importance in defining the male personal image. In their clubs, in bars and coffeehouses, and in street gatherings, men spend considerable time in good-humored and admiring gossip about each other's mistresses and casual liaisons. Official disapproval of such behavior by the Catholic Church weighs little against a general tolerance on the part of men and a tacit, resigned acceptance by women (see ch. 7, Family).

Although the dynamism and heroism of the *macho* image are universally admired in the Spanish-speaking society, the opportunities for broad self-expression and public flourish are limited to a few men. Hence, Ecuadorians, especially in the lower class, are capable of laughing at the same virtues, in a folk humor that sometimes presents the grand as merely grandiose and the hero as merely bombastic. If, at one level, the forceful and forthright *macho* is a folk hero, so, at another, is the "sharpy" (*vivo*).

For men with any claim to high social status there is a parallel set of role ideals which are by no means contradictory to the *machismo* image—the values that prescribe the behavior appropriate to the gentleman (*caballero*). Basically, the ideals of the upper-class role include good breeding, intellectual cultivation, generosity and a disdain for purely pecuniary activity. Wealth, far from being an end, is conceived in the ideal as providing a base of comfort and leisure for a gracious life. Similarly, although industriousness is not in itself a virtue, neither is laziness positively valued. In the pursuit of socially acceptable goals, such as prestige and broad public expression, the upper-status man is capable of great energy output.

For many upper-status men the practice of arts, letters or a learned profession serves as an outlet both for the demonstration of personal ability and culture and for the broad self-expression that is so vital to a man's personal image. Indeed, in a country where educational opportunities have been sharply limited, intellectual activity and the professions have traditionally been of considerable importance as a class determinant. Nevertheless, artistic and intellectual activities form only one element in an image of versatility. Ideally, the *caballero* combines aspects both of the man of ideas and the man of action. For many, the latter concept applies specifically to political action. Although historically the Ecuadorian elite has remained somewhat aloof from the arena of electoral politics, at other levels it has exercised the controlling influence. Traditionally, it has been the upper-status writer who has provided the intellectual leadership in political life, and certain areas of governmental function—a prime example is the Ministry of Foreign Relations—have been dominated by members of the upper class.

The dual commitment to ideas and politics is a theme common to the careers of many outstanding Ecuadorians—for example, José María Velasco Ibarra, whose achievements as a social and political essayist have been obscured largely because of his spectacular political activism; Jacinto Jijón y Caamaño, conservative politician, writer and archaeologist; and Julio Tobar Donoso, public man, jurist and essayist.

Given the disapproval of purely materialistic pursuits, entrepreneurial activity has generally commanded little esteem, although many upper-class men find it necessary to take a direct hand in business. There is a widespread preference for a combination of passive investment—"interests" (*intereses*)—and some type of professional practice over full-time involvement in business (*negocio*), even when the latter promises to be more remunerative. Manual work and activities entailing routine and mechanical operations are strongly disparaged.

The ideal of the leisured gentleman, largely unconcerned with the details of making a living, took deepest root in the Sierra, the colonial heartland of Ecuadorian society. It is held somewhat less strongly on the Coast, where society underwent its full development after independence, when the country was drawn into world markets. Whereas the Sierra elite grew up as a landholding aristocracy whose fortunes were founded on large tenant-worked agricultural estates, typically with hired managers, that of the Coast has always been more a mercantile class. Even those coastal families whose fortunes were made in agriculture have operated in a mercantile economy, producing for world markets. This difference in orientation is one of the major components of the regionalist cleavage between Quito and Guayaquil. Nevertheless, if the ideals of the genteel and cultured man of leisure are expressed less strongly on the Coast, they are not absent. Even members of families whose wealth was made in some form of commercial enterprise often seek, where possible, to delegate management of their businesses and take up the genteel and leisurely life of the *caballero*.

As the pressures of economic and social change are felt more strongly, many of these status ideals will undoubtedly undergo some modification. The slow expansion of commerce and industry appears already to have caused some softening in the old prejudices against entrepreneurial and technical activity, even in the conservative society of Quito. Engineering, agronomy and other technical professions have begun to hold greater attraction for upper- and middle-class youth. Moreover, if the aims of the agrarian reform laws are achieved, even partially, the absentee-owned landed estates, worked by a virtually unpaid tenant labor force, will disappear, and with it, one of the chief economic props of the traditional *caballero*. On the other hand, the much stronger prejudice against manual labor, no matter what the skill, as proper only to persons of low status has not diminished greatly. Socially ambitious members of the lower class still regard a white-collar career as the surest route for personal advancement—a perception reflected in a marked and continuing preference for academic, rather than vocational, courses in secondary school curricula.

The broadening of educational opportunities has also had some impact on the old *caballero* ideal, for it has brought about a degree of professionalism in many intellectual fields. In journalism and some academic disciplines full-time commitment has become possible, even, in some cases, for those of modest personal means. Nevertheless, the gentleman-scholars have by no means been completely supplanted by full-time professionals. Moreover, the new trend has not significantly modified the ideal of the man of action and ideas, for the full-time intellectual by vocation is no less a political activist.

Most Ecuadorian men are baptized Catholics, and a majority profess an active faith, especially in the tradition-bound Sierra. Nevertheless, overtly demonstrated piety is not an ideal of the male image at any social level. With a few exceptions (the most illustrious being the nineteenth-century president, Gabriel García Moreno), men have seen religious belief as a largely personal matter, scarcely needing public display. Furthermore, the outward humility and the restrictive sexual morality preached by the Church are at direct variance with cherished virtues of the popularly conceived male image. For the most part, formal religious observance and expressions of fervor are looked upon as appropriate only to women, children and members of the clergy. Indeed, professed piety on the part of a man can lead his fellows to question his manliness.

Women and Maternalism

The traditional ideals of womanhood are, in most ways, antithetical to those of manhood. Men are expected to be assertive and competitive, to raise or defend their own status; women are seen as properly submissive and passive, deriving their status from husband and family connections. In family life the husband properly leads and the wife follows. Although in fact the day-to-day administration of household affairs is entrusted to wives, the values confer the right of final decision on the husband (see ch. 7, Family).

Like other aspects of the value heritage, the old concepts of femininity have felt the pressures of change. In most particulars women have been made the equals of men before law, and economic opportunities previously denied them have been opened. To some extent even the old customs of close supervision over young unmarried women have been relaxed. As a result of these changes, some women have come to reject the traditional female role ideals and so, at least verbally, have some men. Nonethe-

228

less, no new values have emerged to supplant the old ones. If the old image of the sheltered and subordinate woman has begun to fade, many of the ideals defining it continue to exist. The proper focus of female activity, both before and after marriage, is the household and kin circle. Young unmarried women are ideally kept under the close supervision and protection of parents and married kinsmen. The rituals of kinship, on which depend the cohesiveness and broad extension of family kin, and the sentiments of kinship are reinforced by women's observance of such customs as mourning.

Within the household women of all classes exercise many roles. Almost the entire burden of child-rearing is placed on the mother. Whether she does it singlehandedly or with the assistance of servants, a woman is expected to assume complete charge of household operations. The role of mother and wife is deemed, in the prevailing social view, to involve considerable abnegation and self-sacrifice. Children are seen as "belonging" more to the mother than to the father; hence, if it should become necessary, she must be prepared to provide the sole economic support. Desertion of children, reprehensible in men, is seen as heinous in women. In addition to bearing these responsibilities, both immediate and ultimate, a woman is culturally expected to submit to the domination of her husband and to accept his wide-ranging independence of action and even, provided that it is not flaunted in her face, his occasional sexual lapses (see ch. 7, Family).

This image of strong, but retiring, responsibility and protectiveness is associated with a filial affection bordering on piety. Great popular sentiment attaches to all aspects of motherhood and maternity, and mother love is widely celebrated in song and verse.

Part of a woman's responsibility to her household lies in religious observance. If men are popularly excused for all but a cursory attendance to formal religious duty, their wives are expected to display a higher standard of piety. Furthermore, the mother bears virtually the entire burden for the early religious training of the children.

One of the few roles outside the home traditionally ascribed to women is charity. Women of prosperous families expend much of their time and energies organizing charity balls and personally distributing bounty to the poor.

These ideals of femininity, though held by Spanish speakers at all levels of society, can be embodied fully only in upper-class families. A retiring, economically passive wife is a luxury scarcely feasible for most lower-class men. Typically, poorer families, especially in the cities, require the active economic contribution of their female members. Traditionally, for example, many areas of petty trade in urban markets have been dominated by lower-class women. In this setting women develop an aggressiveness and loquacity far from according with the prevailing values.

The Society

Personalism

The Hispanic social heritage places a far greater emphasis on personal trust and loyalty than on institutions and abstract ideologies, and this emphasis is apparent throughout the society. In all aieas of life men feel their greatest security in well-established bonds with specific persons, and they extend their loyalties more readily to persons than to impersonal institutions. Historically, governments have been overthrown on many occasions because the personal attraction and interpersonal loyalties of ambitious political leaders have outweighed more abstract civic sentiments. Similarly, in the past, party loyalties appear to have been determined to a considerable extent by networks of personal association and kin loyalties. In modern days, as the base of suffrage has expanded, the traditional parties, lacking personal bonds with the more humble segment of the electorate, have often been bypassed completely by the direct, if mass, personal appeal of charismatic political figures—most notably José María Velasco Ibarra (see ch. 14, Political Dynamics). Even in economic activity the stress on personal trust over institutions is clearly apparent in the fact that even large-scale enterprises are, for the most part, family held.

History and national events are popularly conceived to be more a result of the acts of men—good and bad, able and stupid—than of impersonal social forces or the application of abstract theories. In the same spirit current political debate often rests heavily on a combination of personal appeal and ad hominem attack.

Ideas and issues are certainly not absent from political discourse. Both in the ideal and, often, in reality political figures achieve and validate their stature at least partly through the vigorous espousal of ideas and ideals. Nonetheless, of necessity, ideas must be subordinated to the appeal of personality and the manipulation of personal loyalties. In addition to the value preference for established personal trust, the generally low educational level of the electorate limits the potential utility of ideological appeals. On the other hand, the espousal of ideas often assumes overtones of political competitiveness, becoming more a campaign weapon than a form of intellectual expression. Typically, therefore, the man of action and ideas reserves his best efforts for publication in books directed at his educational equals

230

and, in addressing the mass of voters, concentrates on the arts of personalist politics.

More general concepts of responsibility are by no means absent from social and political life. Ecuadorians have fought and died for patriotic causes. At least abstractly, moreover, citizens and journalists are more than willing to attack the nepotism and personal favoritism that have been a traditional feature of government. Often, however, this concern is rendered academic, for it conflicts with deeply rooted social values. When a man achieves power and influence, he usually has done so through the active support of friends and kinsmen, and in the prevailing social view failure to reward them can be more reprehensible than a lapse in probity.

Interpersonal Relations

In the society of Hispanic Ecuador the nuances of personal interchange and overt demonstration of affection and regard are extremely important. Reflecting this importance, social life, even at the most informal level, is far more ritualized in quality than in the United States. In consonance with the stress on self-expression, open demonstrations of friendship and regard in words and gesture are obligatory at all encounters between acquaintances. Friends, business associates and even casual acquaintances greet each other unfailingly with handshakes and, in many cases, with an *abrazo* (an embrace with simultaneous and mutual backslapping). In any meeting, however brief, etiquette requires mutual inquiry by acquaintances regarding each other's well-being and that of their kinsmen.

These rituals are not meaningless formalities; they are the means by which respect for *dignidad* is expressed. It is extremely important to avoid treating any acquaintance as a nonentity. On encounters between two groups of people it is mandatory that all members of both groups be introduced, individually, to all other members. Anyone left out of such a round of introductions is likely to be deeply insulted.

Hospitality, as a means of communicating interpersonal esteem, is invested with a considerable measure of forcefulness and ritual. Hosts typically ply their guests with food and drink to capacity, and an empty glass is seen as a potential reflection on the quality of the hospitality. Guests, for their part, are obligated to respond with effusive gratitude and, to the best of their abilities, enthusiastic acceptance. Lapses in this interchange strike a sour note.

Persons who develop easy rapport and spontaneous cordiality in interpersonal relations are described by the adjective *simpático*. There is no exact English equivalent for this adjective; such dic-

231

tionary translations as "nice," "likeable" or "congenial" fail to convey its full sense. A person who is *simpático* combines many attributes, such as empathy, good humor, warmth and a genuine enjoyment of sociality.

Even in business the quality of personal interchange has great importance. The personal sensitivities of bargainers are as much an aspect of negotiations as the material issues. Furthermore, since the best basis of security lies in personal trust, a man will enter a transaction with at least as much interest in the person of the other negotiator as in the firm or group he represents. Consequently, such sessions, especially between strangers, are likely to be protected and interlarded with carefully directed smalltalk, a tangential interchange that strikes the much-desired note of cordiality and provides some basis of mutual judgment.

In the absence of well-defined and intimate relationships—preferably kinship or longstanding friendship—it is difficult to establish a secure basis of trust. For this reason strangers who come together in negotiations most often spend considerable time seeking the possible existence of a mutual kinsman or friend. If such a person can be found, at least a tentative bond of mutual confidence is established, and the way for negotiation is considerably smoothed.

For the most part kinship and friendship can be operative only at roughly the same social level. Often men find it desirable to establish some form of mutual trust across class lines, and most commonly they do so within the context of the traditional *patrón*-retainer tie. As a rule, a *patrón* is an employer, a political leader, a landowner or a merchant. Poor and powerless men seek protection by attaching themselves to such figures as clients and retainers. The *patrón* tie, like friendship, develops over time and, ideally, is characterized by mutual affection, trust and respect. In contrast to friendship, however, it is based on an explicit recognition of status inequality.

The *patrón* maintains and demonstrates a paternalistic interest in his retainers, offering them advice, influence on their behalf and material deference. Spanish-speaking Ecuadorians see the *patrón* tie as the natural and desirable outcome of any sustained contact between persons of different status. Often, *patrones* and their retainers reinforce the bond by the establishment of ritual kinship (*compadrazgo*) through godparenthood (see ch. 7, Family).

Hierarchy and Leadership

At all levels social life is invested with strong overtones of dominance, authority and hierarchy. Even at the most informal levels the competitiveness of the *macho* ideal leads men often to measure each other, and any group is likely to be separated into

232

winners and losers in such competition. The man who emerges as most forceful in even the most informal grouping is likely to assume an attitude of overt dominance. In family life the paternal will is seen, at least ideally, as being supreme; although aspects of paternal authority can be delegated, the father remains the prime arbiter in all matters. At the most formal levels, especially in political life, authoritarian rule has often been accorded a wide popular acceptance. In local politics and community life the strong sense of hierarchy is reflected in a definite feeling that the most prominent persons, although they may occupy no formal positions, often wield more effective power than the duly established local officialdom (see ch. 3, Historical Setting; ch. 14, Political Dynamics).

The traditional ideals of leadership are, in many respects, at variance with the democratic forms on which the state is constitutionally based. A leader, whether established by due process or by force, is looked upon much more as a spokesman and arbiter of policy for his group than as a moderator and executer. Rather than merely represent the will of his followers, he properly interprets it on his own authority, acting with little consultation of his subordinates. The personal qualities of a leader and his continuing ability to command loyalty and deference from his supporters are crucial to group unity. This has been perhaps most graphically demonstrated in modern Ecuadorian life in the dramatic expansions and shrinkages of personalistic election parties and coalitions, notably those of the magnetic Velasco Ibarra.

Two images drawn from the value tradition—the strongman (*caudillo*) and the *patrón*—are prominent in the tone of leadership. In all affairs a man who seeks to speak for, anu to dominate, his fellows must validate his claim by approximating both images in varying proportions.

Allegiance and deference are accorded a man largely because his followers see him as most capable of advancing their interests. In forming this crucial opinion the ideals of the *machismo* image —forcefulness, decisiveness and dramatic activism—play a major part. Historically, the *caudillo*—the strongman with a drive to dominate his fellow man, very often, but not necessarily, a military figure—has enjoyed a clear-cut claim to leadership in these terms.

Not only does the *caudillo*-leader strike a note of confidence in his retainers, he also provides a basis for their self-esteem. As a rule, a socially recognized group derives its character and public image largely from that of its spokesman. Hence, weaker and less effectual members are rewarded for their support and deference by public association with a man who fulfills many of the ideal attributes of manhood. As long as he maintains control of his followers by forceful projection of his personality and by effective action on their behalf, the strong leader can expect devoted and largely unquestioned acceptance of his domination.

Conversely, however, the leader can expect challenges to his position, no matter how well consolidated. The strongman image is established in an intense personality competition, and ambitious challengers are by no means lacking in any group. Indeed, much of the fragility in political parties and other groups, evidenced in the frequent defection of splinters, can be explained by the actions of rival aspirants to leadership who, though unsuccessful in dominating the whole group, nonetheless develop followings of their own. Even in the absence of personal competition the position of a personalist leader is precarious, for followers seldom exhibit great patience with even occasional lapses in effectiveness.

In addition to looking to their leaders for the furtherance of their interests men also seek the deeper satisfaction of mutual trust and esteem with their leaders. Hence, in varying degree, the *caudillo* must also display the personal commitment, the wisdom of guidance and the readiness to lend assistance that are the hallmarks of the *patrón*. This theme is apparent in virtually all areas of social and political life and in groups of all sizes. Even in the ultimate instance—the President of the Republic—there are means of at least symbolically personalizing the bond between leader and followers. During the 1960 election, for example, successful candidate Velasco Ibarra, recognizing the mushrooming growth that had taken place in the electorate, journeyed far and indefatigably to establish face-to-face bonds with the most humble voters.

THE INDIAN VIEW

In sharp contrast with the Hispanic heritage the value patterns of the Sierra Indians place marked stress on the social role over the qualities of individuality. Where specific criteria for ascribing prestige and public esteem can be identified, they appear to emphasize past, substantive achievement over innate personal quality. An individual establishes and maintains stature in the eyes of his fellows by fulfilling the responsibilities and expectations of adulthood. Contribution to the collective welfare— materially, as in community public works projects, and spiritually, as in the sponsorship of religious *fiestas*—provides the quickest route to prestige. Almost everywhere in the Ecuadorian Sierra, the *fiesta* is especially important in establishing measures of personal worth. On the one hand, some *fiesta* role is usually expected of all men, as a minimal condition of adult status. On the other hand, those who exceed minimal expectations enjoy a rapid increase in stature in the eyes of their fellows.

234

Persons commanding specialized skills—for example, in curing —are conceded to have useful talents, but seldom do their skills entitle them to an especially high social status. Similarly, although industry is very much a virtue and wealth is valued highly, a farmer who is more industrious and successful than his fellows cannot expect to enjoy great prestige unless the fruits of his efforts are contributed in some way to the collective welfare.

In a value heritage that stresses the social role over the qualities of individuality, a considerable premium is placed on conformity. Gossip and public ridicule are powerful mechanisms of social control. In the Indian social context the forceful projection of personality and the overt aggressiveness of the Hispanic values are almost inconceivable. One of the most obvious ways in which Indian social life contrasts with that of the whites is in the lack of exuberant public behavior, the *abrazos* and other open demonstrations of esteem that create much of the color and noise in the Hispanic community. Similarly, although oratory is quite important in many areas of Indian community life, eloquence for its own sake is not especially prized. Attention-seeking and obvious attempts to dominate one's fellows by sheer force of personality are, by reports of observers, generally disparaged; those who indulge in such behavior even on a minor scale are subjected to ridicule.

Where there are defined roles of leadership, these reflect the prevailing personality ideals. According to most observer reports, leadership is seen as entailing not domination but mediation and the determination of consensus. Given the emphasis on conformity, consensus is usually achieved with ease, for those who feel themselves to be in a clear minority position will often remain silent.

In family life and at the community level sex roles are clearly differentiated, but the sharply stereotyped sex role ideals of the Hispanic tradition are lacking. Male dominance is clearly the rule, in both domestic and public life, but usually it is tempered by a sentiment that wives have a right to be consulted on significant decisions and that their opinions merit respect. The concept of the *macho* as a social type has scant meaning in Indian terms, and virility does not call forth any measure of public acclaim. Within the division of labor certain kinds of work are considered appropriate only for one or the other sex, but both men and women are deemed capable of equal industry.

The religious *fiestas* that are a major part of the community social and recreational life provide an important outlet for tensions built up from repressions, inhibitions and, not least important, a hard and insecure material lot. Lasting up to several days these affairs are marked by considerable gaiety and by the

consumption of prodigious quantities of alcohol by adult participants. During the earlier stages the quiet, almost sullen mien of
the Indians is replaced by excitement, exuberance and boisterous-
ness. Loud laughter and argument provide much of the over-
tone, and old animosities are expressed in occasional outbreaks of
fist-fighting. Between *fiestas,* however, community life returns
to its settled and sober quality.

Seeing the surrounding social order as exploitative and potentially hostile, the Indians can find security, for the most part, only
in an orderly and exclusivistic community life. Often, not only
Hispanic Ecuadorians, but also Indians from other communities
are seen as potential enemies, and this attitude toward outsiders
is sometimes expressed in physical violence. The need to maintain a degree of solidarity before the outside world tends to reinforce the premium placed on personal conformity.

Some students of Sierra Indian society, and especially the *indigenistas* (see Glossary), have been struck with what they take
to be a tendency toward collectivism, in some cases ascribing it to
a social instinct deeply rooted in the preconquest heritage. On
careful inspection much of this speculation, based largely on patterns of cooperative labor, is exaggerated and misleading.

Certainly most Indian communities display a high level of integration, but the basis for this appears to lie principally in the need
to adapt to a hostile social order, rather than in the maintenance
of specific age-old traditions. In part, too, it can be explained by
a lack of alternatives. An Indian peasant, especially if he owns
land, has few possibilities of mobility out of either his social status
or his community. Consequently, the drive to achieve a measure
of harmony with his neighbors is quite strong. Moreover, the
patterns of communal labor stem, in many cases, not from the will
of the community, but from the demands of the white local officials, who sometimes use public works labor on projects of little
or no benefit to the Indians.

Where it exists, labor cooperation in private tasks—farming
and house-raising, for example—is usually structured by kinship
lines and is reflective more of kin loyalties than of those directed
at the community, at large. Furthermore, where there is a clear
conflict between obligations to kin and those to the whole community, the former are likely to prevail.

SECTION II. POLITICAL

CHAPTER 13

CONSTITUTION AND GOVERNMENT

Ecuador, perhaps even more than most other Hispanic-American nations, has ben plagued by frequently recurring periods of chaos, when little effective government has existed on the national level. During such times a constitutional convention has usually been called, apparently on the assumption that those who participated in drawing up a constitution would seek to bring about a modicum of functioning government under its provisions. This device was resorted to in 1812, 1830, 1835, 1843, 1845, 1850, 1852, 1861, 1869, 1878, 1884, 1897, 1906, 1929, 1945 and 1946.

Counting the Gran Colombia Constitution of 1821, which had been drawn up without Ecuadorian participation, the country has had a new constitution on the average of every 9 years. However, only the 15 charters since 1830 normally are called "Ecuadorian" constitutions. The two previous ones are referred to as the "Quito State" and "Gran Colombia" (or Cúcuta) constitutions, respectively.

A major factor making for continuity in orderly government throughout the country's constitutional history has been the semi-autonomous status of the municipalities, which have continued to function, in varying degrees of effectiveness, whether or not government on a national and provincial level has existed. This status of the municipalities had been recognized in all constitutions except that of 1843, which was in effect for only 2 years.

Contributing to the frequency of new constitutions has been the general view that a constitution can no longer be held in esteem once it has been violated. Politically sophisticated Ecuadorians take the view that it is the purpose of the constitutional and legal systems to serve as ideals and to elevate the political behavior of the nation's citizens. They do not, on the other hand, hold to the notion that their constitutions are immutable statements of principle and procedure, good for all time (see ch. 17, Attitudes and Reactions).

Significantly, however, the frequent rewriting of constitutions has brought about little change of form or even of wording. With the exception of issues relating to the role of the Catholic clergy, there has been no change in basic political philosophy since the birth of the nation.

All 15 constitutions since 1830 have provided for a centralized unitary state under a presidential—rather than parliamentary—system with separate executive, legislative and judicial branches. In all cases there has been a detailed enumeration of rights (usually called guarantees) similar to those in the first 10 amendments of the United States Constitution, called the Bill of Rights. A bicameral legislature, made up of the Senate and Chamber of Deputies, has been the rule. Most constitutions have also provided for a Council of State, at times called Council of Government, composed of representatives of all three branches of government and the armed forces, plus additional members. It has served to act on behalf of Congress when the latter is not in session. In practice, aside from providing coordination between the branches of government, the Council of State has served to legitimize what has often amounted to arbitrary rule by decree on the part of the president (see ch. 3, Historical Setting).

Nevertheless, popular participation in government has broadened gradually over the past 135 years. Although literacy requirements continue to disfranchise a large segment of the population, property requirements were eliminated more than a century ago. Moreover, since about 1945 the government has been making a genuine effort to increase the literacy rate and thereby enfranchise a significant portion of the population. Between the presidential election of 1933 and that of 1956, the number of registered voters increased more than tenfold, while the population increased only by about one-half. To a large extent, this growth reflects an increasing interest on the part of the people in participating in what had traditionally been considered the private preserve of the few wealthy families. The 1948 upsurge of citizen participation in government was accompanied by the beginning of an unprecedented 12-year period of relatively stable constitutional rule and change of regimes by constitutional means (see ch. 14, Political Dynamics).

Before this date the usual means of changing the incumbent president had been by coup. Even during the half century of rule by the radical Liberal Party, between 1895 and 1944, most of the 30 changes in the office of chief executive were accompanied by violence or the threat of it. There were 14 presidents in the decade of the 1930's alone. Under such circumstances the principal energies of the chief executive had to be directed toward staying in power by purchasing sufficient support through favors and promises, while attempting to beat down the ubiquitous plots of potential rivals (see ch. 3, Historical Setting). No stable civil service has yet developed. It has been customary for a new president to reward all of his politically significant supporters with government posts of little or great responsibility or power. The patronage system encompasses all positions of authority within the executive branch and extends downward, even to unpaid but often profitable positions on the local level. Even minor clerks in inconsequential departments have been replaced by members of the victorious party at each change of government. This has had the effect of involving the bulk of the literate population in the nation's politics. While certainly public-spirited men consider it an honor to serve the country, government jobs continue to be intensely sought after by many, more for their accompanying influence and prestige than for the salary, which may amount to less than what is earned by a manual laborer. Although the country's president earns a larger salary than any other bureaucrat or official, even this is less than the amount earned by a well-to-do businessman in Quito (see ch. 17, Attitudes and Reactions; ch. 18, The Economic System).

THE HISTORICAL CONTEXT

Constitutional history, from the 1812 Quito State Charter to the Constitution of 1945, was dominated by one basic issue: the relationship between civil and church authority. This question has provided the principal basis for the enduring dispute between the Conservative and Liberal factions, the one representing primarily the interests of the Sierra and the other representing those of the Coast. In a certain sense too, the issue was rooted in rivalry between the two major cities—Quito, the capital, and Guayaquil, the chief port and center of commerce.

Because this struggle for power intimately affected the interests of only a few families in each of the basic regions, it was imperative that issues of principle be developed to involve a broader segment of the population. No issue could do this better than religion. Nothing has meant so much to the average highlander (*serrano*) as being Catholic, and it was this, he was told, that was being threatened by the Liberal factions, which had their strength on the Coast, where, historically, clerical influence has been minimal.

Except for certain economic issues, clearly reflecting divergence of regional interests, the basic positions taken by the two factions have been distinguishable from each other only on the questions of church and state. Some historians, pointing to the lack of divergence on other issues, have made the accusation that the Liberals depended on militarism and *caudillo* rule more than did their competitors, to obtain and maintain political power on the national level (see ch. 3, Historical Setting).

With the exception of the constitution promulgated by General Flores in 1843 and the liberal instrument of 1878 (which reflected the anti-García Moreno reaction), the nine constitutions in force between those of 1812 and 1884 show the clear imprint of the proclericalism of the Conservatives, who were dominant during most of the period. Conversely, the four Liberal Party constitutions between 1897 and 1945 place strong emphasis on the separation of church and state. The first two—those of 1897 and 1906—were practically dictated by General Eloy Alfaro, one of the three outstanding *caudillos* and the founder of the Liberal Party.

The 1946 Constitution represented a compromise and a synthesis of the conservative and liberal currents. In effect, it seemed to have closed the book on the Catholic versus anticlerical debate. By the time of its promulgation more urgent economic and social issues had come openly into prominence.

The Beginnings of Constitutional Government

From its founding in 1534 until the breakdown of Spanish colonial authority in 1809, Ecuador (then called variously the Gobernación, Audiencia or Presidencia of Quito) was alternately under the jurisdiction of the Viceroyalties of Peru and New Granada. In 1809 a small group representing the most affluent and influential families of Quito proclaimed independence from Spain (which had just been conquered by Napoleon) and formed the sovereign Junta of Quito. In 1810 a newly elected junta declared its independence from Bogotá and, in 1811, called for a constitutional convention representing the "Nation of Quito." On February 15, 1812, the first constitution was promulgated. This charter never acquired anything resembling full effect outside of the city of Quito, partly because of internal dissension, but, more significantly, because Spanish authority was reestablished by November 8 of the same year (see ch. 3, Historical Setting).

The Quito Constitution of 1812 called for a popular and representative "State of Quito" established through indirect elections by its citizens. Although it was not stated directly in the Constitution, it was clearly understood that the term "popular" was meant to include only wealthier and more influential persons. In the next seven constitutions this was to be made explicit by clearly defined property requirements for citizenship. The constitutional convention had been composed, in its majority, of the wealthiest and most conservative colonists, who were apparently far more afraid of democracy than of Spanish rule.

The Constitution stipulated that, although there was to be an executive called President of the State, supreme authority was to be vested in the Chief of State, who was defined as the legitimate King of Spain. The Chief of State was to be the King of Quito without in any way subordinating Quito State to the Spanish State. This might have been based on the precedent of Charles V, who was at the same time monarch of both Spain and Austria. The State of Quito was to be a democratic monarchy.

The Constitution proclaimed that Quito "is and shall be independent" but made provisions for entering into a confederation of all America or of those states of it wanting to confederate (a theme to be repeated in two of the subsequent constitutions). It proclaimed the principle of divine origin of civil authority (meaning that civil authority was wielded in the name of God and was to be exercised and obeyed as such) and called for a harmonious relationship between church and state.

Municipalities, which actually had been in existence for centuries, were legally established, but no specific provision dealt with their functioning. Legislative power was vested in a senate (also called council), and the judiciary was headed by a high court of justice. Parliamentary immunity from arrest was extended to include all of the national government. There were no concise and explicit personal guarantees of individual rights.

With the exception of the purely local Cuenca Constitution and the provisional charter of Guayaquil, both of 1820, Ecuador was not under constitutional rule again until after the 1822 Battle of Pichincha. In the latter year the Ecuadorian nation was first established as such, and it immediately joined Simón Bolívar's Gran Colombia. This affiliation placed Ecuador under the 1821 Cúcuta Constitution, which had been drawn up without Ecuadorian participation. From the viewpoint of Bogotá, Ecuador was the southern "section" of Gran Colombia, and there was no legal provision for it as a nation or even any mention of its individuality.

Bolívar rectified this in 1826 by officially recognizing Ecuador as a nation with "a certain unity and autonomy." Bolívar's resignation, accepted by the 1830 Constitutional Convention of Bogotá, was seized upon by Ecuador as a pretext for secession from Gran Colombia and the establishment of an independent Ecuadorian state. The Venezuelan general, Juan José Flores, who had been left in charge by Bolívar, was named the supreme civil and military authority by a Quito "popular assembly"; he, in turn, convoked a constitutional convention (see ch. 3, Historical Setting).

The Development of Constitutional Principles

Although a new constitution was introduced on the average of once every 9 years, basic constitutional principles have evolved gradually and have usually achieved permanence through appearance in several consecutive charters. The six constitutions between 1830 and 1852 inclusive had many provisions in common. All imposed property or professional requirements for citizenship (distinguished from nationality, which is acquired by birth or derivation from parents). They established higher property requirements for candidates to the legislature and still higher ones for candidates to the presidency. Voting was made indirect, through electors, in both congressional and presidential elections. The presidential term was set at 4 years, except in the personalist 1843 Constitution of General Flores, in which there was an 8-year term.

Another major exception found in the 1843 Constitution lies in its provisions for freedom of conscience, permitting the private practice of religion other than Roman Catholicism. In this it was unique among the first 11 constitutions. All others, before the liberal period beginning in 1897, made Roman Catholicism the religion of the state and established the government's duty to protect it to the exclusion of all others. Also, of the first 6 Ecuadorian constitutions, the 1843 charter is the only one which does not begin with the words "In the name of God" (see ch. 11, Religion).

Beginning with the Constitution of 1845, the independence of the judiciary was reduced. Both the Quito and the Cúcuta instruments, as well as those of 1830, 1835 and 1843, provided for lifetime appointments to the superior and supreme courts, depending only on good conduct. In the subsequent 12 constitutions, justices were appointed for fixed terms (normally for 4 or 6 years), usually by Congress, by the president or by the two in agreement. In practice, it has become customary for local judicial personnel to change with every change of government. Judges of cantonal and provincial courts are appointed for 2-year terms by the superior court having jurisdiction over the province or canton in question.

A bicameral congress, composed of the Senate and Chamber of Deputies has been the rule. Only the 1812 Quito State charter and the constitutions of 1830, 1852 and 1945 provided for a unicameral legislature. Of these constitutions, only that of 1830 remained in effect for more than 1 year.

Whereas nearly all the constitutions prohibited the immediate reelection of the chief executive, in practice nearly all of the historically outstanding presidents managed to violate this provision in spirit if not in letter. Generals Flores and Alfaro and Gabriel García Moreno managed to rule behind the scenes between their terms of office. Nevertheless, there has been a strong and enduring sentiment against long-term monopoly of the presidency. García Moreno was assassinated before his inauguration to a third term. Flores survived his attempt but was overthrown by force of arms. Eloy Alfaro was lynched after the failure of his attempt at a third term. No other president except José María Velasco Ibarra has seriously attempted to assume office more than twice; perhaps significantly, Velasco Ibarra managed to complete only one of his four terms.

Although no constitution has provided for a term of less than 4 years, the government has changed hands on the average of every 2 years, since as of 1965 there had been 67 such changes in 135 years. Probably most of the names of current prominent families have appeared on the list of chief executives at some time since 1830.

General belief, clearly reflected in constitutional law, is that the legislature is both cumbersome and expensive to maintain and should be limited to as few and as brief sessions as possible. Provisions for annual congressional sessions have been included in only about half of the constitutions, and in most cases the sessions were limited to 2 or 3 months. Under five constitutions Congress was to meet once every 2 years, and under the 1843 document only once every 4 years. In such a setting a strong executive branch was indispensable for effective government and has in the popular mind been the ideal.

Nevertheless, a number of recent constitutions (including that of 1946) attempted to limit the president's customary excesses by declaring the legislative branch to be theoretically superior to the executive and the president answerable to Congress in nearly all matters. This may be explained in part by the fact that constitutional conventions (aside from choosing or confirming the president) also fulfill the functions of Congress until the regularly scheduled election takes place.

Voting age has been set variously at 22, 21 or 18. Women obtained the right to vote with the Constitution of 1884. Before then, being married or having been married was considered for men as an alternative to having reached voting age. For example, under the 1830 Constitution, to vote, a man who was literate and could meet the property or income requirements was required to be either married or over 22. Under the 1946 Constitution, suffrage was extended to all men and women over 18 who could read and write. Property or professional prerequisites to voting were done away with in the 1861 Constitution of García Moreno.

Statements providing for freedom of speech and assembly have been included in all constitutions since 1830. Freedom of the press is also mentioned, but only freedom from prior censorship. Under most constitutions, including that of 1946, a writer could be prosecuted for anything appearing in print if it proved offensive, either to another person or to the government, and could be placed in the categories of "malice, calumny, personal insult, immorality or contrary to national interests." The right to petition is, in almost all cases, qualified, by the provision that no one has the right to petition "in the name of the people."

Such basic guarantees as the inviolability of the home and mails are always accompanied by the vague provision "except in cases provided for by the law." Imprisonment for debts has been prohibited in all constitutions since 1830, but most documents have had a provision under which a debtor's rights of citizenship could be suspended. Although the 1946 Constitution does not specifically mention debt, it does state that the right of citizenship can be lost or suspended "in all other cases specified by law."

Punishment of persons other than the guilty one, confiscation of property as such and being forced to testify against oneself or close relatives have been prohibited in all constitutions since 1830. Except for the documents of 1843 and 1946, all constitutions guarantee the right to be tried by local judges. That of 1946 specifically prohibits the confining of coastal political prisoners in the Sierra and vice versa. Forced exile has been prohibited in most constitutions since 1884, including that of 1946. Jurisdictional authority of military officers has been specifically limited in most of the constitutions to military personnel on active duty. This issue is avoided in the 1946 document. The right of habeas corpus has been included since 1929.

The death penalty for both political and common crimes has been eliminated since the 1897 Constitution of Eloy Alfaro (who himself had a large number of political opponents executed). It had been prohibited for political crimes under four of the previous constitutions.

Flogging, torture and other forms of corporal punishment have been prohibited in the seven constitutions since that of 1869. Corporal punishment was specifically authorized in several constitutions before that of 1852.

The 1830 Constitution specifically authorized military, church and commercial tribunals of justice to judge the crimes of members of those professions, in accordance with the Spanish tradition of group privilege (*fuero*). Except for military courts, no mention is made of other tribunals in the following constitutions, except the four liberal documents between 1897 and 1945, which specifically prohibit ecclesiastical courts as a substitute for common ones. Although the 1946 Constitution avoids the issue, church courts still function for members of the clergy, and bishops are still expected to excommunicate persons who bring charges against priests before the secular court system (see ch. 11, Religion).

From the 1845 Constitution to that of 1878, all constitutions stated that no one shall be born a slave, nor could one enter the country without becoming free. Beginning in 1878 and continuing through the Constitution of 1897, it was stated that there were no slaves in Ecuador, nor would there be any.

The 1830 charter, under the title of "Civil Rights and Guarantees," names parish priests as the tutors and protectors of the Indians and charges them with ministering to the needs of this "innocent, abject and miserable class." The 1946 Constitution prohibits depriving Indians of their *huasipungo* (serf-plot; see Glossary), without cause. The constitutions between those of 1830 and 1906 totally ignore the Indian population, and the documents of 1929 and 1945 give the impression that serfdom (*concertaje*) has been legislated out of existence (see ch. 8, Living Conditions).

Although primary schooling has, by constitutional law, been both free and obligatory since 1884, the country has never had half of its school-aged children in school, nor even had the classroom space for more than a small minority. It is doubtful that more than about one-fourth of the population in 1965 had had the opportunity to make full use of what has been an obligatory provision of constitutional law for 81 years (see ch. 9, Education).

For most of postconquest history, the great majority of the people were considered to be less than fully human. As late as 1931, a "liberal" Ecuadorian expert on constitutional law could still write in a basic textbook:

> The Indian mass is, after all, a material element of the nation, like the cosmic forces which enclose its territory; his dull and primitive spirit does not . . . assimilate the fruit of sensibility . . . nothing interests him. We have already said it: he has a soul of stone.

In 1931 between one-half and two-thirds of the population was thought to be in this category. It has never been seriously considered that the personal guarantees stated in the Constitution were intended to be applied to the rural population. The combined categories of peasant (*campesino*) and Indian (*indigena*) made up in 1965 the majority of the inhabitants, but they were not considered to be Ecuadorians in common usage of the term (except in population statistics) (see ch. 12, Social Values; ch. 17, Attitudes and Reactions).

THE 1946 CONSTITUTION

Although the 1946 Constitution was drawn up by a largely conservative constitutional convention, it bears more resemblance to the three liberal charters immediately preceding it than to the conservative proclerical documents of the nineteenth century. It especially resembles the 1906 charter of Eloy Alfaro, which had been in effect, on three separate occasions, for a total of 30 years.

245

Some provisions were also borrowed from the constitutions of 1929 and 1945. In essence, it repeats what has been said in previous constitutions, with some recombining of the elements. Perhaps most significant is its relatively greater realism in eliminating or toning down excessive guarantees and provisions (such as guaranteeing pure drinking water and full employment) of the two constitutions immediately preceding it while containing no provisions that would arouse either conservative or liberal objections.

The 1946 Constitution is the only one in the twentieth century issued "In the name of God," but it does not mention a state religion and provides for complete freedom of conscience. Besides declaring the government to be popular, representative, elective, responsible and alternating (as had every constitution since 1835), it declares the state to be unitary, sovereign, independent and democratic.

Article 6 recognizes Ecuador's cultural affinity and common economic interests with other Hispanic-American states and provides for the possibility of forming associations based on common interests. Three previous constitutions (counting the Quito State charter of 1812) had even stronger statements, providing for a possibility of confederation (see ch. 15, Foreign Relations).

The traditional distinction is maintained between Ecuadorian nationals and citizens. Citizenship consists of the right to vote and to hold public office. Making literacy (combined with having reached 18 years of age) a prerequisite to enfranchisement has, in effect, eliminated most Ecuadorians from participation in the political life of the nation.

Voting is compulsory for men and optional for women, among those able to meet the qualifications, but the provision is seldom, if ever, enforced. Members of the armed forces on active duty are prohibited from voting, as they are charged with maintaining orderly election procedure and guaranteeing honest elections.

A distinction is made between the functions of the military and the police; the former charged with maintaining constitutional order, and the latter with safeguarding internal order and security (see ch. 14, Political Dynamics).

Several constitutions explicitly gave the armed forces the right to refuse to obey orders which were manifestly illegal. Under the 1946 Constitution such a statement does not appear. Article 155 states, in its entirety: "The public forces are not deliberative. Only the authorities giving orders shall be responsible for orders that are manifestly contrary to the constitution and the laws." Also, in contrast to traditional constitutional principle, in case of war, the military commander in a declared zone of operation may be given jurisdiction over civil authorities. Frontier commands also "have civil powers in conformity with the law."

The President of the Republic and most members of Congress have been elected directly by popular vote since the 1861 Constitution of García Moreno. Under the 1946 document, as amended in 1960, each of the 19 provinces elects 2 senators, and the Galápagos Islands elects one for the entire archipelago. However, as no senatorial election has been held since the amendments went into effect, each of the four Oriente provinces is still represented by only one senator. Consequently, when Congress last met in 1962, there was a total of 47 senators, including 35 regional ones. Senators serve for 4-year terms and are elected at the same time as the president.

Since 1929, a portion of Congress has been reserved for "functional representation." Under the current charter there are 12 such senators: 1 each for the armed forces, public education, private education and the press and cultural entities (i.e., scientific and literary associations); 2 each for agriculture, commerce, labor and industry. Of the latter, one in each category represents the Coast and the other the Sierra. These senators are chosen by the institutions they represent and are expected to further the interests of those institutions (see ch. 14, Political Dynamics). They are chosen by electoral colleges especially convoked for the occasion by the professional societies and economic interest groups concerned.

The senator for public education is chosen by 2 delegates each from the five national universities. The senator for private education is selected by 19 delegates representing private educational institutions in each of the provinces. Editors of all the newspapers, together with the heads of all scientific and literary associations which have juridical status, meet in each province to choose delegates for the national electoral college, which then chooses the senator for cultural entities. The two senators for commerce are chosen by delegates representing all of the chambers of commerce in each of the two major regions. Voting is weighted in proportion to the number of Ecuadorian citizens affiliated with each chamber. The two senators each for labor, industry and agriculture are elected in a similar manner by professional associations representing each of these economic interests. Delegates representing both enlisted personnel and officers from the army, navy and air force participate in the election of the senator for the armed forces, usually a military man.

The 1946 Constitution specified that each province should have one national deputy for every 50,000 inhabitants (plus one more if there remained more than 25,000 additional inhabitants).

However, as no national census had yet been taken, an arbitrary formula was agreed upon and remained in effect until the 1960 elections. Between 1960 and 1962 there were 73 members in the Chamber of Deputies.

Each province is entitled to at least 2 deputies; Pichincha and Guayas have 8 and 12, respectively. The Oriente region, which contains less than 2 percent of the population, is represented by 8 deputies, the same number as Pichincha Province, which contains about 10 times as many inhabitants.

Although a legal procedure for amending a constitution under its own terms has always existed, it has seldom been used. A dilemma facing the military government in 1965 was that, whereas it would like to have the Constitution amended rather than call a constitutional assembly, it could not legally do so, since it did not want to convene Congress before leaving office.

The 1946 Constitution specifies that the procedure for amendment follows the same procedure as for the enactment of other laws. The only significant difference is that such an amendatory law remains without effect until it is ratified by an absolute majority of Congress during a regular session following an intervening election of the Chamber of Deputies (normally every 2 years). The amendments of 1960, aside from increasing the number of senators from the Oriente region, are largely devoid of substance and deal with editorial changes.

STRUCTURE OF GOVERNMENT

Since July 1963 the country has been ruled by a four-man board of military government (*junta militar*). Before assuming power through a coup d'etat these men were the chiefs of the navy, army, air force and War College (*Academia de Guerra*). Although the military government decreed that the general provisions of the Constitution of 1946 would continue in effect, it took over supreme executive and legislative responsibilities. No effective checks on its power exist, but its rule has been relatively mild (see ch. 14, Political Dynamics).

The National Congress did not meet for its regularly scheduled annual 2-month sessions between 1963 and 1965 and was not expected to meet again until 1967, but the military government has declared its willingness to return the reins of government to a freely elected civilian president on September 1, 1966, followed within several months by new congressional elections (see ch. 14, Political Dynamics).

Within days of assuming power, the military government suggested the promulgation of a new constitution and charged a committee, made up of Supreme Court justices, with drawing up a basic charter better suited to the needs of the country than the 1946 Constitution. Democratic political parties were also invited to draw up suggested constitutions. Several of these proposals were completed and published, but the government decided that the necessary changes could be effected by amending the 1946 document. In any case, barring any unexpected developments, it seems reasonably certain that either before the return of civilian rule or shortly thereafter the present constitution will be substantially changed or replaced (see ch. 14, Political Dynamics).

The Congress

The 1946 Constitution requires that Congress meet for 60 days annually, beginning on August 10, with the possibility of extending its session for another 30 days. During the remainder of the year the legislative function is to be divided largely between the Council of State and the Legislative Committee. Both are composed of representatives of all three branches of government, and neither has been inclined to exhibit independence from presidential influence.

The Council of State is expected to insure that the president stays within constitutional bounds, to grant or deny him extraordinary powers, to advise him on nearly all matters of importance and to approve or disapprove most of his actions. It has been, in practice, an extended Cabinet including members of the other branches of government and serving principally as a sounding board and a stamp of approval.

The Legislative Committee was established to propose, draft, codify and publish laws, except those of an economic character, which were to be handled by the National Economic Council, whose organization and function were deleted from the Constitution by the amendments of 1960. In practice, most important laws have originated as presidential decrees and have later been approved or ignored by subsequent sessions of Congress.

Theoretically, the functions of Congress closely parallel those of the United States Congress. In practice, Congress has been limited largely to budgetary questions and to exhibitions of eloquence without substance, to which Ecuadorians commonly refer by the pejorative term of *politiquería*. The inability of Congress to cope with national problems and to pass vital legislation has been a prime and perennial cause of government overthrow (see ch. 17, Attitudes and Reactions).

The Judiciary

The court system is, and traditionally has been, a highly centralized one that has local courts subordinate to provincial courts, which are under superior courts. At the top is a 15-man Supreme Court, divided into three nonspecialized chambers which take by lot their turn at trying cases (see ch. 25, Public Order).

With the exception of the introduction of fixed terms with the Constitution of 1845, there has been little, if any, evolution of the judicial system since 1830. Supreme Court and superior court judges are selected and appointed by Congress for 6- and 4-year terms, respectively. Superior court judges, in turn, may freely appoint and remove the judges under them within geographic areas of their own jurisdiction.

Normal proceedings are exceedingly long; individual cases commonly remain in process for 1 or 2 years. There is much emphasis on reducing every aspect of a case to written records and on giving lengthy explanations of the rationale behind each decision. Bribery is routine at lower levels, and political influence is keenly felt at higher levels. There are few, if any, functioning safeguards against abuse of the system at local levels, especially in places distant from the capital (see ch. 25, Public Order).

The Executive Branch

Throughout Ecuador's history the ideal chief executive in the popular view has been a strong-man president who could dominate the Congress and had sufficient power to get things done. Nevertheless, total arbitrariness, without regard to public opinion, has never been tolerated. Presidents who declared themselves dictators or attempted to prolong their term in office beyond what had become traditional limits were without exception immediately overthrown or killed. Even the three most powerful *caudillos,* Juan José Flores, Gabriel García Moreno and Eloy Alfaro, never established dictatorships based on terror, and none remained in office for more than 6 consecutive years (although each dominated the country's politics for a 15-year period). Even the arch-autocrat, García Moreno, did not promulgate his so-called Black Charter (the Constitution of 1869) until after it had been approved by popular referendum (see ch. 3, Historical Setting).

Ecuadorian critics consider that most of their country's rulers lacked the qualities of personality that would have enabled the people to submit willingly and warmly to them. By far the least tolerated presidential characteristic has been weakness combined with arbitrariness. Unless the president could clearly demonstrate that he was worthy to be accepted as a *caudillo,* he was expected to observe the letter and the spirit of the Constitution then in force. If he was strong enough to violate the basic charter with impunity, however, he was usually applauded, if he was careful not to transgress basic sensitivities. Both Flores and Velasco Ibarra's last regimes were terminated at the height of their power by an attempt to levy additional taxes arbitrarily (see ch. 17, Attitudes and Reactions).

Military dictatorship has not been prominent in the country's history. Although on many occasions, the armed forces have assumed power, they have seldom abused it or taken advantage of their position to enhance excessively their own privileges. As a rule they maintained order until a constitutional government could be reestablished. In 1937–38 and since July 1963, the armed forces have been accepted by Ecuador as seeking to bring about badly needed social and economic reforms, without which the constitutional system would be jeopardized.

An example of deference to popular will was demonstrated during the disorders which resulted in Velasco Ibarra's overthrow in November 1961. Congress declared itself in favor of Vice President Carlos Julio Arosemena, whereas the chiefs of the armed forces declared, through leaflets and newspapers, that they favored the President of the Supreme Court as the next chief executive. After about 24 hours, during which the majority of the provincial capitals sent word that they favored Arosemena, and Quito public opinion became unified on the same point, the armed forces agreed to back Arosemena as the man specified under the constitutional clause of presidential succession (see ch. 14, Political Dynamics).

Immediately under the president is the Cabinet, composed of nine ministers—Government, Foreign Relations, Education, Public Works, Industry and Commerce, Defense, Social Welfare, Finance, and Agriculture and Livestock. The Constitution specifies that, in order to be valid, all decrees, decisions and resolutions of the president must be countersigned by the appropriate minister.

Although these men are (and have been under nearly all constitutions) selected and appointed solely by the president, Congress has the right to censure them for personal or official misconduct. The Constitution specifically states that they shall be held responsible for "taking bribes, extortion, misappropriations of public funds, undue compulsion, negligence or delay in the execution of the laws or executive decrees, and for any other serious offense."

Votes of lack of confidence (as are customary under the British parliamentary system and in some other Latin American countries) are specifically prohibited by the Constitution. The principal criteria by which ministers are chosen are family connections and an emphasis on a regional and political balance which reflects the power structure of the country. There usually are an equal number of coastal and Sierra ministers, and certain posts, by tradition, go to specific parties. The foreign minister is usually a Conservative, and the education and social welfare posts usually go to the Socialists (see ch. 14, Political Dynamics).

The attorney general, comptroller general and superintendent of banks are not included in the president's Cabinet and are selected jointly by the president and Congress.

Since September 1963 the Technical Secretariat of Administration has been functioning as a central organ for planning and coordination of all aspects of government administration and is responsible directly to the military government. Its three principal branches are the National Offices of Organization, Personnel and Budget. Its principal tasks are administrative and financial reform; elaboration of a general plan of development; and technical advice for public administration in all aspects and at every level of government.

A principal part of the planned reform has been the establishment of a permanent career civil service. One had previously been set up under the administration of Galo Plaza Lasso (1948–52) but was immediately abolished by his successor, Velasco Ibarra. Beginning in February 1964 the government promulgated a series of decrees dealing with a career civil service. Since then tests have been devised for determining eligibility to various posts, as well as for promotions. Over 5,000 positions have been classified and reduced to 242 categories. Studies have been made to determine the salary level of these categories to make them roughly equivalent to comparable jobs outside the government.

By July 1964 more than 500 public servants and officials had completed, or were taking, extension courses dealing with such topics as personnel supervision and selection, classification of positions, financial legislation, recordkeeping, accounting, and public relations. However, at the end of the same month only 18 officials had attended full-time training courses, and only about 200 persons had been certified as career civil servants. In January 1965 civil servants became beneficiaries of a family subsidy program which had previously existed only for the armed forces and police. The United States Agency for International Development (AID) program has helped the civil service reforms, providing both money and technical advice.

The civil service law guarantees equal opportunities to all applicants on the basis of competence and assures promotions on the basis of merit. It also protects civil servants from arbitrary dismissal for political purposes. Nevertheless, the previous civil service was abolished at one stroke by a popular politician who felt obligated to fulfill his preelection commitments to political supporters. Whether current civil servants can survive a change of administration will depend largely on political factors unconnected to the merits of the present system. In part, it might hinge on whether the transition to civilian government takes place peacefully.

More significant, however, is the central role which patronage and personalism play in the political system. Unless a substitute channel of favors develops, it would appear likely that either the civil service law will not be applied strictly or there will develop significant pressure for eliminating the career civil service entirely (see ch. 14, Political Dynamics).

Another reform introduced by the military government has been the reduction of the large number (estimates range between 400 and 900) of autonomous government agencies, which collect their own funds and establish and execute their own programs, totally independent of what the central government may be doing. Already abolished have been the Guayas Executive Committee of Roads (placed under the Ministry of Public Works), the National Housing Institute and the National Pro-Oriente Junta. Many others have been consolidated, and the process is expected to continue, even though there has been strong and vocal opposition from various interests on the Coast, especially in Guayaquil (see ch. 14, Political Dynamics).

Provincial and Local Government

Provincial governors are freely appointed and removed at the president's discretion and usually change with each change of administration. The governors of provinces, in turn, are free to appoint or remove the key figurehead of rural authority, the political chief of the *cantón*. The *cantones* are in turn subdivided into parishes, which in the countryside are theoretically under the authority of a political lieutenant whose prestige and sphere of influence among the rural population, and especially among the Indians, rarely equals that of the parish priest (see ch. 11, Religion). The political lieutenant is also appointed by the governor of the province, but usually on the advice and with the consent of the political chief directly over him.

In the urban areas, especially the provincial capitals, there exists a relatively strong institution of local government, called the municipality. It is a city council, freely elected by popular vote of all the urban citizens, and is relatively free to handle all purely local matters without outside interference. Although a municipality has the theoretical right to levy local taxes for local public works, it seldom has the necessary coercive power to collect such taxes.

The urban centers which have grown sufficiently to qualify as provincial capitals (whenever a town becomes large enough, a new province is carved out and it becomes a provincial capital) are in the fortunate position of having their municipal council called a provincial council and qualify for funds from the central government on the basis of the number of inhabitants residing in the province. Such funds are seldom expended for the benefit of anyone except the townspeople. If a town has a post office, a jail, a hospital, streetsweepers, public toilets and a sewage system, it is usually (if not always) a provincial capital (see ch. 8, Living Conditions). In nearly all cases such services are paid for entirely out of funds from the central government. If the central government fails to pay municipal employees for 2 or 3 months at a time, the result is usually a province-wide general strike. If a sufficient number of provincial strikes occur simultaneously, the government falls.

There are no city limits. Towns are not thought of as having a separate existence from the area surrounding them. Practically by definition every town is the administrative center of a parish, *cantón* or province. Only provincial capitals have mayors, funds and public services. They are the centers of political power because all persons of influence in the province normally have at least one of their residences there. Quito, the capital, and Guayaquil, the principal port and largest city, are both also the provincial capitals of Pichincha and Guayas, respectively. A town built solely for commerce, industry or any reason other than to be the administrative center of a rural area would probably not survive (see ch. 6, Social Structure).

Any population center that is not an administrative unit of the central government is either a landed estate or a village. On an estate the owner (or in his absence, the administrator) by custom and by economic hegemony is the absolute ruler. If the area is sufficiently removed from Quito, his virtually complete rule over all residents and communities within the estate may well escape any effective check or control by governmental agencies.

A Law of Communities (*ley de comunas*), enacted in 1937, guarantees villages organized under its provisions a considerable measure of autonomy in local matters. This innovation, introduced to spark local initiative, has been spontaneously accepted in very few areas, and the guarantees of autonomy have not been uniformly implemented. Under its provisions a village elects, by universal adult suffrage, a council consisting of president, vice president, secretary, treasurer and four other members. Where such village councils exist, they were usually adopted in response to outside pressures and are relatively ineffectual, as they are totally devoid of coercive power and the sanction of tradition. If a village has a few literates or semiliterates, these will usually be elected, and reelected each year, though sometimes changing titles in the process. Their roles seldom transcend that of messengers and spokesmen for the community in its relations with the political lieutenant or persons appointed by him. In most cases such persons had probably served the same functions informally before the introduction of the community council.

Both Indians and poorer rural *mestizos* are used to obeying orders of persons outside their community and above them in social and economic status and petition them for help and favors. The concept that authority can be vested in one or more of the members of their community by election is alien and incomprehensible to them. Prestige is usually vested in those who are older or better educated, but these factors are seen as constants unaffected by elections (see ch. 5, Ethnic Groups and Languages; ch. 6, Social Structure).

To the average Ecuadorian national, "government" means the political lieutenant and the authorities of the provincial capital. These authorities (aside from the local priest and bishop) are the persons who are appealed to in case of disputes between communities; in case of extreme abuse by a local landowner or his administrator; and in criminal cases dealing with theft, manslaughter and similar incidents. The political lieutenant is empowered to requisition labor for communal work projects, such as road repair or school construction; to levy fines for noncompliance; to issue marriage licenses; to settle minor quarrels; and to supervise the division of inheritances. All matters of a more serious nature, especially disputes with persons of higher status, are brought to the provincial capital for solution (see ch. 6, Social Structure).

CHAPTER 14

POLITICAL DYNAMICS

One of the durable factors in politics is a strong regionalism. The division is deepest between the Sierra and the Coast, but there are also intense rivalries and antagonisms within both regions, often resulting in alignments of two or more cities in both regions against Quito, the mountain capital, or against Guayaquil, the major port and center of commerce.

The cleavage between Coast and Sierra has arisen not only from the competition of interests between two centers of power, Guayaquil and Quito, but also from fundamental differences in traditions and outlook. The issue of Church-state relations, which, more than any other, set the tone of political dispute in the first century of independence, clearly reflected the difference in customs and values between the conservative Sierra and the less tradition-bound Coast (see ch. 3, Historical Setting; ch. 17, Attitudes and Reactions).

Equally important as a political factor is the rigid class structure and strong class consciousness, especially in the Sierra, which separate the elite of landowners and merchants from the impoverished and historically passive masses. This separation has limited effective political voice to a small minority, and government and parties have not concentrated on pressing social problems. Most governments, having failed to appeal to the majority, have been unable to develop broad and continuing support. In some measure the narrowness of support has contributed to the historical pattern of instability, revolt and coup, especially as members of the lower class have become more aware and more active politically.

During most of the present century two parties have been most active in the political arena. The older and larger of these is the Conservative Party, by long tradition representing the Church-oriented Sierra landowners. The newer party, dominant between 1895 and 1944, is the Radical Liberal Party (or, in common usage, simply the Liberal Party). It arose as the representative of the anticlerical coastal merchants, although it has maintained a following in Quito as well.

Until a few decades ago political dispute between the Conservatives and the Liberals rested principally on the Church-state issue. As this once-burning issue has subsided in recent years, the two parties have come to resemble each other closely in avowed principles and programs. Both parties have proved responsive on most issues to the interests of the upper- and middle-class minorities even, as is often the case, at the cost of mass support.

The other parties of recent years have been small, ephemeral or far to the right or left of the ideological mainstream. The Ecuadorian Socialist Party (Partido Socialista Ecuatoriano—PSE), while durable, has never been large enough to make a significant impact. Some of the newer parties are still largely personalist movements, with little life and identity independent of their leaders.

For several reasons the parties have come to have a decreasing relevance to political life, especially as the base of suffrage has expanded to include the burgeoning lower class. By well-rooted social tradition political attachments are usually based far less on ideological commitment than on family connections, personal trust and loyalty, congruence of economic interest and regionalist sentiment. Although these factors have usually coalesced within party structure, very often they have created intraparty factionalisms which, given the unimportance of doctrine and program, are not easily bridged by appeal to common convictions.

This lessening of party importance has been demonstrated in all recent elections, but perhaps most vividly in 1960, when José María Velasco Ibarra, the most effective political figure in recent Ecuadorian history, without the support of a single party, polled the largest number of votes ever given a candidate. Appealing directly and personally to the masses—whom he addressed as "my beloved rabble" (mi querida chusma)—Velasco Ibarra established a bond of trust which no party could have commanded. Further demonstration is provided in the fact that, in the past two decades, only one successful presidential candidate, Camilo Ponce Enríquez, has owed his victory to the support of a single party. Most often, presidential candidates have found it necessary to seek support of ad hoc coalitions, with components of support from several parties and from independents.

When the armed forces replaced the civilian government of Carlos Julio Arosemena Monroy in July 1963, one of the first moves of the new government was to appeal to popular antagonisms toward the parties and the "oligarchy." For more than a year this appeal continued to enjoy clear success, especially as the military government appeared to be seeking solutions to social problems that had been ignored by its predecessor "politician" governments.

Nevertheless, by the end of 1965, opposition to the military government, within the parties and within the population as a whole, had become significant. This resulted from a growing desire to return to civilian rule and also from antagonisms created in certain quarters by the adoption of reform measures.

Perceiving the need for broader support, the parties have begun to reorganize, most of them under younger and more dynamic leaders, and to seek ways to address themselves seriously to questions of greater significance to the broader electorate. At the end of 1965, therefore, many observers saw grounds for the belief that, with return to civilian rule, the parties might play a more active and effective role in government and in the formulation of long-range social and economic policy.

DOMINANT INTEREST AND PRESSURE GROUPS

The Church Hierarchy

Although nearly all of the Church's land was confiscated by the government of Eloy Alfaro at the turn of the century, the Church in the Sierra has by no means lost its preeminent position in social and economic life. Its political strength exists insofar as the parish priest is seen often as the ultimate temporal, as well as spiritual, authority in the more remote villages and small towns of the Sierra. In such areas the people do not draw clear lines of demarcation between what is religious and what is secular nor between influence and authority.

The contrast with the Coast in this regard is pronounced. While the Church enjoys unparalleled power in the highlands, its influence is weak on the Coast. In all of Latin America the Coast of Ecuador is the only major region where the majority of Spanish-speaking inhabitants remain unbaptized (see ch. 11, Religion).

The Coast is the base of the Liberal Party, whose major platform has historically been anticlericalism. Although this party's founder, Eloy Alfaro, claimed that he was working toward the separation of Church and state, he was in fact attempting to make the Church subservient to the state. During his term in office tithes were legally forbidden, the Church was prohibited from owning income-producing property and priests were allowed to have no income other than that paid by the state. Moreover, the government demanded the right to present candidates for the office of bishop, and foreign clergy were not allowed to enter the country.

Many of these restrictions were in reaction to the exceedingly important role played by clergy during the second term of Gabriel García Moreno, which began in 1869. The enforcement of such strict anticlerical policies, however, caused counterreaction on the part not only of the clergy, but of many devout laymen who rose to the defense of the Church and its prerogatives. The Church-state conflict ceased to be a major political issue on the national level by about 1945, but in some areas of the Sierra feelings remain strong.

Politicians of the Liberal Party occasionally still attack the Church with the claim that priests force people to vote for the Conservative Party, but trustworthy reports of overt interference in party politics by the clergy have become rare. On the other hand, the Church hierarchy has taken a stand on some of the major issues. During May 1963 a pastoral letter was read from the pulpit of all the churches urging the faithful to help bring about land reform and a more just system of taxation. It also reminded landowners and businessmen of their obligations to laborers and encouraged a recognition of the human dignity of workers.

The Church has also used its influence in more direct ways. In at least three of the provinces (Bolívar, Chimborazo and Imbabura), the major urban and rural development programs have been initiated and directed by local bishops.

The Armed Forces

In the long-range historical perspective political participation by the military establishment has been increasing. At the turn of the century, when Eloy Alfaro considerably diminished the institutional strength of the Church, the armed forces stepped into the vacuum and began to play an important part in the political process. Most of the military presidents, who constituted about one-third of all chief executives, were in power during the half-century of Liberal Party rule ending in 1944. Whereas the Conservative Party from its beginning leaned on the Church, the Liberal Party was in its turn more closely allied with the armed forces. Consequently, the military establishment contrasts with those in the majority of Latin American countries in that it is more closely identified with liberalism than with conservatism.

The members of the armed forces take pride in their place as custodians of constitutional order, a function with which they are invested by the Constitution, and in the fact that most of the social welfare measures and similar reforms were brought about under military rule. The armed forces, unlike the police, are considered to owe their primary loyalty to the nation and not necessarily to the particular government which happens to be in power.

The military institution has, however, interfered infrequently in the process of governing. When interventions have occurred, they have arisen most often over issues considered basic by the military leadership—relations with Communist countries, for example (when the leaders of the armed forces in March 1962 caused President Arosemena to revise his foreign policy). When the military finally intervened to oust President Arosemena in July 1963, it was only after more than a year of encouragement by various political factions and economic interest groups, all of which were concerned about the chaotic drift in national affairs and outraged by Arosemena's personal conduct.

After assuming power, however, the military government became increasingly confident of its ability to rule better than civilians. Nevertheless, differences arose which caused the expulsion from the four-man governing board of the air force commander, Colonel Guillermo Freile Posso in November 1965.

The Upper Class and Commercial Interests

Members of the upper class seldom participate personally in politics. When they do, it is usually in a diplomatic post in Europe or the United States or as foreign minister. Nevertheless, political affairs often appear to be managed in ways which are advantageous to the "oligarchy," a term which, as popularly used, includes the old Quito upper class, whose fortunes were originally amassed through ownership of land, and the still more wealthy commercial groups in Guayaquil.

In the past the upper class has been considered to enjoy an essentially above-the-law status, regardless of the particular political faction in office at the moment. In 1965 the prevailing attitude among upper class persons reflects their conviction that their position—still greatly privileged—cannot last much longer. The Church, the armed forces and nearly all political parties have declared themselves in favor of basic structural reforms, especially in land tenure and taxation. Many individuals who enjoy wealth and high social status accept in principle the need for such changes without, however, being willing to put into practice measures which would adversely affect their fortunes.

Guayaquil's commercial and financial elite (of which former President Arosemena was a member) is the wealthiest in the country, but it lacks the claims of aristocracy of the Quito upper class. Its members espouse liberal principles, but in most cases they seem even less disposed toward reforms than do their counterparts in Quito. The coastal elite does, however, participate in the political process by financing the campaigns of various parties and factions. It is also well organized, principally through the Guayaquil Chamber of Commerce, and capable of raising the banner of regional autonomy whenever its interests are threatened.

Organized Labor

The labor force is one of the least organized and least unified on the continent. From a political point of view the Communist-dominated Confederation of Ecuadorian Workers (Confederación de Trabajadores Ecuatorianos—CTE) is the most important labor organization. Aside from being by far the largest and most powerful, it has also been politically the most active. Claiming to represent the interests of the working class, it played a major role both in maintaining Velasco Ibarra in the presidency in 1960 and in overthrowing him the following year. It was one of Arosemena's principal supporters until his break with Cuba in 1962.

Theoretically, the CTE is aligned with the Cuban labor movement and possibly receives funds from outside the country, but in late 1965 there was no evidence that it had committed itself in the Moscow-Peking split. In order to keep its predominantly non-Communist following, the CTE has had to maintain a semblance of independence and has usually taken positions that could be made to appear consistent with its self-proclaimed role as defender of the Ecuadorian working class. Nevertheless, it makes no secret of its solidarity with world communism nor of the admiration of its leaders for Fidel Castro.

The CTE's ultimate, long-range goal appears to be the effecting of a Castro-style revolution in Ecuador, but it seems in no great hurry to accomplish this. It gives the impression of following the more cautious Moscow line of "peaceful coexistence" rather than Peking's "guerrilla warfare now" program. This orientation may be because the leadership of the Communist Party of Ecuador (Partido Comunista del Ecuador—PCE), which controls the CTE, is aligned with and dependent on Moscow or because a too radical program could cause it to lose the bulk of its support among the workers. It is also possible that the CTE has been considerably weakened by government restraints and by the fact that its top leaders have been in jail for most of the time that the military government has been in power.

The only other politically significant labor organization has been the Ecuadorian Confederation of Catholic Workers (Confederación Ecuatoriana de Obreros Católicos—CEDOC), which is aligned (although unofficially) with Ponce Enríquez's Social Christian Movement (Movimiento Social Cristiano—MSC), as well as with the International Confederation of Christian Trade Unions (Confederación International de Sindicatos Cristianos—CISC). The CEDOC is about one-third the size of the CTE and is far less active politically. Its importance is more in its potential than in its current political role, which has been relatively conservative. The CEDOC's cooperation with the Church greatly increases its ability to win adherents among the conservative *campesinos* (peasants), who stand to gain the most, politically as well as economically, from unionization (see ch. 21, Labor Relations and Organization).

Provincial Landowners

The provincial landowners form the most reactionary group of all significant political sectors. In contrast to the national elite, their principal residence is usually in the provincial capital. Their strength is much greater in the Sierra than on the Coast. They are especially powerful in provincial and municipal affairs in the South. In Loja Province, which borders on Peru, they form part of a closed social and political network (called *argolla*), composed of the authorities and other powerful persons who reinforce each other in maintaining their power.

The associations of provincial landowners of Cañar and Azuay Provinces condemned the relatively modest agrarian reform law put into effect in July 1964 and announced their determination to prevent its application in their respective areas. Since central government authority is seldom effective that far from Quito, it appears that their opposition may be successful within the foreseeable future.

In the past the *hacendado* (landowner) associations have had strong representation in Congress, both through the regional senators and deputies representing the southern highland provinces and through the functional senators elected by the associations themselves (see ch. 13, Constitution and Government). Since there are few prominent persons in the Sierra whose origin is not from among the major landholding families, there is broad sympathy and support for the *hacendado* viewpoint among those who monopolize most instruments of power.

Students

The Federation of University Students of Ecuador (Federación de Estudiantes Universitarios del Ecuador—FEUE) is important as a political pressure group for two related reasons. It has played a role in every nonconstitutional change of government since 1944, and it has been dominated by Communists or *fidelistas* for most of the past 10 years. The reasons for political extremism among students are numerous. More literate than the bulk of the population, they are more concerned with improvements in the society. In view of the country's past, they see little hope of change through normal constitutional means and tend to be attracted by radical solutions.

Under the Ecuadorian educational system students for generations have had a strong voice in administrative matters within the state universities, and most professors have had to receive student approval to maintain their positions. Alliances between ambitious professors and displeased students have resulted in the unjustified dismissal of competent, but strict professors, and classroom discipline has suffered. Since many students seldom attend classes, they have time for political activity (see ch. 9, Education). Moreover, many of the nation's outstanding Marxists tend to gravitate toward the faculties of law and economics at all of the national universities.

Many students whose parents can afford it are sent abroad or to private universities, principally the Catholic University of Ecuador in Quito. At the state institutions education, including room and board, is free for those who cannot afford to pay. Since students at public institutions of higher education believe that, if the society remains in its traditional mold, avenues of opportunity will continue to be reserved for the sons of the wealthy, they feel that they have little to lose and much to gain by social upheaval (see ch. 9, Education).

POLITICAL PARTIES AND SIMILAR ORGANIZATIONS

Individual parties play a small role in the political process. Even when they unite in common purpose, they usually represent less power together than any one of the major interest and pressure groups. Parties are merely one element in a complicated formula, usually effective only in combination with other factors. The opposition of the parties to continued rule by the armed forces since July 1964 has not alone represented a major threat to the government. On the contrary, the military government has made use of the antagonism of the parties to pose as defenders of "the people" against "the politicians" who, they asserted, were in the "service of special economic interests" (see ch. 17, Attitudes and Reactions).

Since small individual contributions to parties are rare and since each of the parties has a small following, parties have to depend to a considerable extent on the largesse of wealthy individuals or economic interest groups. It is customary for most donors to expect large returns on their investment, and most of them assume the role of *patrón* (see Glossary) toward the dependent party leaders, who are expected to assume a proper subservient attitude. Consequently, many politicians point out that they are members of no political party. Since 1944 only one chief executive, Ponce Enríquez, has been a party man, and even he selected a nonpartisan Cabinet and pledged a nonpartisan administration.

Principles, issues or party platforms have also played a minor role. In late 1965 there were, with few exceptions, only minor differences in the programs of most parties. There is broad agreement among all but a few numerically insignificant right-wing groups that agrarian reform and redistribution of wealth are necessities. All parties are opposed to the 1942 Rio Protocol with Peru by which Ecuador renounced its claim to vast Amazonian territory, but some use the issue to get votes (see ch. 15, Foreign Relations). The same general agreement exists regarding such issues as the incorporation of the Indian into national life, the need for expanding and improving educational facilities and regional development.

The Conservative Party

The Conservative Party (Partido Conservador), the oldest party, has been, at least since 1944, the strongest, largest and best organized of the major parties. Many of the nationwide coalitions since that date have had as their principal objective the withholding of the presidential office from the Conservatives.

The party was founded by Gabriel García Moreno in 1869 and had no effective competition until the consolidation of the Liberal Party in 1895 (see ch. 3, Historical Setting). Its strength and endurance in the Sierra can probably be ascribed to three primary causes. Most of the inhabitants of the Sierra (outside of Quito) have always been, by temperament and tradition, highly conservative in most matters. The part historically has aligned itself closely with Sierra landowners and clergy, representing their interests and taking advantage of their influence and prestige. Finally, since the turn of the century, its avowed principles have professed to serve the ideals of social justice stated in the encyclical *Rerum Novarum* of Pope Leo XIII in 1891.

The Radical Liberal Party

The major party between 1895 and 1944 was the Radical Liberal Party (Partido Liberal Radical). There have been innumerable splits within its ranks since its consolidation in 1895 by Eloy Alfaro, but most of them resulted in short-lived splinter groups, usually representing small factions crystallized around a dominant figure. In 1952 a major split occurred in which each faction nominated its own presidential candidate. After both candidates were badly defeated, the two groups reunited.

Since its founding the Liberal Party has been strongest on the Coast, but in the past decade it has also won a significant following in Quito. Elsewhere in the Sierra the party has made no more inroads than the Conservatives have on the Coast, and the two major parties continue to be strong representatives of regional interests.

To compensate for the Conservatives' alliance with the Sierra clergy and landowners, the Liberals have aligned themselves with the armed forces, the commercial interests and reputedly with the continent-wide masonic movement. Trade and banking interests continue to finance the Liberal Party, but the armed forces have tended to be neutral since 1942. It has been suggested that Ecuador lost the border war with Peru in 1941 partly because much of the army had been kept in the major cities to maintain political stability there and was thus impeded from fighting at the border. The massive public indignation that followed the defeat was directed largely at the Liberal Party and its leader, Carlos Arroyo del Río, who was president at the time.

Since the overthrow of Arroyo del Río by a broadly based revolt in 1944, the Liberal Party has not won a presidential election nor a majority in Congress. It has, however, been regaining strength gradually, and in 1956 the coalition of which it was a part lost the presidential election to a Conservative-backed candidate by only a narrow margin.

Once anticlericalism ceased to be an effective issue (about 1945), the Liberal Party's principles and platform differed little from those of the Conservatives. According to the 1923 party program (which was readopted in 1953), the guiding principles are religious tolerance; the broadening of educational opportunities; the ending of *concertaje* (the archaic agricultural labor system, including the institution of *huasipungo*—see Glossary) ; the spiritual rehabilitation of the Indian; technological improvements in agriculture; and agrarian reform radical enough to eliminate the large, inefficient estates. The Liberal Party also condemns rule by *caudillos* (see Glossary), militarism, imperialism, plutocracy and violence contrary to human dignity. In addition, the party in 1953 explicitly condemned totalitarianism of any kind and "adopted as an integral part of its principles the Declaration of Human Rights, as approved by the United Nations." The Liberal Party also seemed to have borrowed from such papal encyclicals as the *Quadragesimo Anno* of Pope Pius XI and the *Mater et Magistra* of Pope John XXIII in emphasizing the social function of property and the duty of the state to protect the family, even to the point of family subsidies.

In August 1965 the Liberal Party, in a joint statement with the Radical Party of Chile, declared a common front in the fight for liquidating the remnants of feudal systems. The two parties also declared themselves to be representatives of the working class fighting for social and economic democracy and against foreign intervention.

The Left

The PSE is an extremely small group of intellectuals (probably less than one-tenth the size of the Conservative Party) which is

266

influential only through coalitions either with groups on the Left, including the Communists, or, more often, with the Liberal Party. There has recently been talk of collaborating more closely with the MSC, an offshoot from the Conservative Party.

While most of the PSE's members espouse Marxist doctrine, the party is dependent on wealthy groups and individuals for support. It is significant more for its historical role in giving birth to both the PCE (the Moscow faction of Communists) and the pro-Cuban Socialist Revolutionary Party (Partido Socialista Revolucionaria—PSR) and for its part in formulating social welfare legislation than for its current strength or influence. Its major distinction is that it is the only party that is neither regional-based nor personalist in character.

Inspired originally by the Russian Revolution, it was founded in 1925 as a section of the Communist International. By 1928 the founding group of writers, lawyers and professors had become divided over the issue of allegiance to the Soviet Union. After the resulting split the larger faction continued to call itself the PSE, and the minority group (loyal to Moscow) became the PCE. Within the PSE remained two distinct groups of Marxists—one opposed to alliance with Soviet-style Communists because it considered the Communists too radical and the other opposed because it felt that the Soviet model had little relevance to Ecuadorian conditions.

From the mid-1950's the two factions became increasingly estranged until 1962, when the more radical group splintered off to form the PSR, with close ties to Fidel Castro. The remainder of the PSE is largely a group of moderates, some of whom call themselves Socialists or Marxists.

The PSR, by contrast, has become the most violence-prone and revolutionary group in the country. Some observers have attributed their truculence to control by the Chinese faction of the Communist movement, but PSR members themselves emphasize only their solidarity with Cuba's Castro.

Neither the PSR nor the PCE has made a serious attempt within the past decade to gain strength or influence through the electoral process. In March 1963, for example, the PCE officially proclaimed that it would boycott the 1964 elections as it had done in 1962. It has concentrated, rather, on infiltrating and, when possible, dominating organized labor, student organizations and the educational bureaucracy. It has no significant voter appeal and appears to believe that scattered victories at the polls would not give it any significant measure of power. The PCE itself is split between a minority which looks to China for guidance and the majority which appears to be controlled, or at least strongly influenced, by Moscow. Both the PCE and the PSR have been outlawed since July 1963, and their strength within the educational structure has been seriously reduced by arrests of leaders and by other security measures of the government (see ch. 26, Subversion).

Personalist Movements

Although only the Conservatives, Liberals and Socialists are legally recognized as parties—and therefore not required to circulate petitions for signatures before presenting candidates for each election—there are dozens of personalist movements which, by their titles, are indistinguishable from political parties. In nearly any local election several of these movements are involved, most composed principally of the leader, his extended family, his close friends and his employees. In the majority of cases the number of members does not exceed 100. Although many of these groups make a pretense of having a political program, in fact they usually exist only to further the interests of the person leading the movement. Occasionally, several of these groups form a coalition and manage to win municipal or provincial elections.

At the other extreme of the same category are a few quasi-parties, which at times are stronger than the established parties. These major personalist movements are highly fluid, however, and, as a rule, do not have a life and personality separate from that of their leader; the Velasco Ibarra movement, for example, dropped from about 400,000 in 1961 to less than 40,000 in 1962.

Although such groups may have a meaningful party program, adherence of party members is more to the person than to the principles or program involved. Of all personalist movements only the MSC of Ponce Enríquez and the Concentration of Popular Forces (Concentración de Fuerzas Populares—CFP) of Carlos Guevara Moreno (a strongly regionalistic group with strength only in Guayaquil) gave indications in the 1960's of developing into genuine political parties with an existence separate from that of their leaders. *Arosemenistas* and *velasquistas* (followers of ex-presidents Arosemena Monroy and Velasco Ibarra, respectively) showed no promise in this direction. The former had by 1964 dwindled down to relatives and personal friends of long standing. The latter had no hope of continuing as a movement much longer, since Velasco Ibarra was already in his seventies, had no protege and had done nothing to organize his followers.

The MSC is principally a personalist party emphasizing doctrinal principles to gain adherents on a larger scale. However, Ponce's movement has in no way repudiated any of the principles of the Conservative Party. On the contrary, the two groups share an identical base of principles—the papal encyclicals—although there are differences in emphasis. Yet political groups, such as the Liberals and the Socialists who as recently as a decade ago were irrevocably opposed to anything the Conservatives stood for and for whom anti-Conservatism was the principal battle cry, find nothing contradictory in their attempts to form alliances and common fronts with Ponce's movement.

Although recently some foreign journalists have grouped Ponce with such radical social revolutionaries as Eduardo Frei of Chile and Rafael Caldera of Venezuela, there is nothing in his background, speeches or platforms to justify the alleged relationship. His presidential term between 1956 and 1960 was a model of conservatism and stability, and there is nothing to indicate that he has become more liberal. His movement has been expanding rapidly, largely at the expense of the Conservative Party.

ARNE

The Ecuadorian Nationalist Revolutionary Action (Acción Revolucionaria Nacionalista Ecuatoriana—ARNE) is unique among political groups in the country. Although it owes much to the leadership of its three past and present chiefs, it has never been a personalist movement. ARNE originated in 1942 as an expression of outraged nationalism at the loss of territory to Peru. It had its greatest impact upon student groups and continues to have its strongest appeal among youths who are disillusioned with the general state of affairs and want to participate in a program of action.

In its mode of operation and its appeal it is highly reminiscent of the well-known American Revolutionary Popular Alliance (Alianza Popular Revolucionaria Américana—APRA) movement of Victor Raúl Haya de la Torre in Peru as it was a generation earlier. It is in part an indigenist movement, emphasizing the role and contribution of the Indian. Moral regeneration, highly structured organization and strict discipline are emphasized. Arnistas see themselves as the future leaders of the country and put much stress on training and self-improvement.

Unlike most political groups, ARNE does not attempt to expand rapidly and makes no pretense of being a mass movement. On the contrary, the stress is placed on preparing an elite for leadership positions. Its ultimate aim is a corporate state not greatly different from those of Portugal and Spain.

Members of ARNE insist on a radical restructuring of society and are among the country's most outspoken critics of existing injustices and general social conditions. They argue that Ecuador has been degenerating morally, economically and politically and that radical remedies are required. The Arnistas see their overall plan of action as involving four states—doctrinal development (1942–48); obtaining general support and increase of mem-

269

bership (stage reached in the mid-1960's); capturing power (sometime in the indefinite future when the organization is sufficiently large and enjoys popular support); and ultimately the transformation of the country. The means by which they hope to obtain power are not specified, but most Arnistas prefer the ballot box to use of armed force.

Before becoming a full member, aspirants must go through a long period of training and may be rejected at any time. Eventually, they may be invited to undergo 3 months of intensive training, including indoctrination, followed by a rigorous formal examination. Even full members continue to receive training, often in such skills as use of firearms.

Highly nationalistic, Arnistas consider themselves as the country's main defense against international communism. They claim to have neutralized a brief attempt by the Communists to launch a nationwide campaign of terror by effective (if violent) countermeasures. There have been numerous incidents of violence involving young Communist or *fidelista* militants. Nevertheless, on occasion there have also been formal public debates between Arnista and Communist youths.

To some extent, ARNE has copied methods of organization from Ecuadorian Communists and other similar groups operating within the country. There is a strong emphasis on structure and on firm control by the leadership. ARNE has also learned to conduct covert operations and currently claims to have the most effective intelligence network on Communist activities.

Politically, Arnistas tend to collaborate with Conservatives and members of the MSC, whose principles they share. In 1952, however, their strong support for Velasco Ibarra almost caused a major split within the organization, even though the emphasis on nationalism provided common ground between the group and Velasco Ibarra.

Coalitions

Every president elected to office since 1944, with the exception of Velasco Ibarra, has owed his victory to a coalition rather than to a single party. Many coalitions (such as that which backed Galo Plaza Lasso in 1948) are ad hoc groups created to elect and support a specific individual at a specific time, and they usually disappear once the individual is either defeated or leaves office. Most of the innumerable local coalitions formed just before municipal and congressional elections every 2 years are of this type.

A few coalitions have a semipermanent character, emerging from dormancy at each election and representing roughly the same groups and interests each time. Perhaps the most important has been the National Democratic Front (Frente Democrático Nacional—FDN), which invariably has been formed around the nucleus of the Liberal Party, usually along with the PSE. The Liberals have provided the center and the Socialists the principal satellite, but in many cases the numerical strength of these two groups has been surpassed by that of dozens of national and local personalist and ad hoc groups flocking to the coalition. Although the FDN has at times had a majority in Congress and on at least one occasion provided the only substantial political backing for an incumbent president (Arosemena, in April 1962), it has never supported a winning presidential candidate.

More often successful than the moderate FDN has been the conservative Popular Alliance (Alianza Popular—AP), which was responsible for Ponce Enríquez' victory in 1956. It was also victorious in the congressional elections of 1958 and 1962. What distinguishes the AP most clearly from the FDN is its strong orientation toward a single group—the Conservatives. It is usually composed of Conservatives, Arnistas and Social Christians.

An interesting example of a highly unstable coalition has been the Ecuadorian Democratic Alliance (Alianza Democrática Ecuatoriana—ADE). It was first formed in 1944 as a popular front anti-Liberal coalition, which included such diverse elements as Socialists, Conservatives, independents and Communists. Dormant most of the time since 1946, ADE was resurrected by Conservative groups in May 1964 for the purpose of forcing the military government out of office. It had ceased to show any sign of life by mid-1965 and had probably been supplanted by the Constitutionalist Front (Frente Constitucionalista) of rightists, Socialists and Liberals, founded in June 1964.

During February 1965 a new coalition appeared—the Democratic Institutionalist Coalition (Coalición Institucionalista Demócráta—CID). While it was unclear what political groups or parties composed it, it appeared to be a businessmen's pressure group instituted to combat economically harmful measures. It had its strongest support in Guayaquil.

In June 1965 most of the significant parties united in the National Patriotic Committee (Junta Patriótica Nacional—JPN) for the purpose of returning the country to constitutional government. Immediately, it became by far the strongest purely political force in the country, although it was not clear to what extent it depended on such powerful economic interest groups as the Guayaquil Chamber of Commerce and the Sierra landowners. The Liberal and Socialist parties were not members of the committee (probably because it was headed by a leader of the Conservative Party), but they appeared to be supporting it.

RECENT POLITICAL DEVELOPMENTS

Twelve Years of Constitutional Government (1948–60)

Galo Plaza Lasso, elected to the presidency in 1948, was the first president since 1924 to complete his 4-year term. He was also the first twentieth-century president to be elected without the backing of the Liberal Party. Perhaps his greatest asset was that he was supported by no regularly established political organization and capitalized on the people's disdain for the traditional parties, which had acquired the reputation of being instruments of the wealthy minority.

To a considerable extent Galo Plaza was elected by recently enfranchised voters (the electorate had increased from 50,000 to 280,000 during the 15 preceding years) who were not backers of either of the two major parties. They were overwhelmingly members of the lower class. The Church-state issue used by both the Conservatives and Liberals had obviously lost its power to sway the voter. Plaza Lasso launched an expensive political campaign, stressing economic development as his major theme. Both the method and the issue were unprecedented in the nation's political history. The outcome of elections had previously been much more dependent upon family connections, which Galo Plaza also used to good effect, and cliques of local-level *caudillos,* each with his own loyal following.

The nature of Ecuador's politics changed significantly during the 1940's, as did the society itself. The intensifying conflict with Peru had, throughout the 1930's and 1940's, brought about increasing nationalism and a genuine fear of being absorbed by the powerful neighbor to the south. The 1941 border war convinced Ecuadorians that an emphasis should be placed upon technological advance, for which an increase in the rate of literacy would be a prerequisite.

The government therefore made a genuine effort to expand educational opportunities. With an increase in literacy came an increase of eligible voters. Because the political and economic structure of the nation remained in its traditional mold, however, the majority of voters continued to be largely excluded from participation in the economic and social benefits of society. By 1944 the political consciousness of the people at large had increased to the point that a government could be overthrown not only through the political machinations of a small, privileged clique, but also as a result of sharply focused mass discontent.

Velasco Ibarra rode to the presidency in 1944 on the shoulders of popular acclaim, only to illustrate once more the basic shortcomings of the political system. He proved—as he had in 1934— that he could rally the people behind him, but since he was unable to gain the cooperation of the powerful minority, he failed to govern effectively either time and was, in each instance, deposed by a palace coup.

Velasco Ibarra's third chance came during the presidential elections of 1952. Like Galo Plaza before him, he ran against all of the established parties. His radicalism frightened the landowning uppper class, the commercial elite and considerable portions of the middle class, but he succeeded not only in captivating most of those who had been uncommitted to any party but also in diverting the popular following of the Communists and other extreme leftist groups. Many observers believe that Velasco Ibarra is the principal reason for the weakness of the Communists since he appeals to the same element of society, but more effectively.

This time, Velasco Ibarra remained in office for a full 4 years and transferred power peacefully to his constitutional successor in 1956. Some observers give major credit for this to his predecessor, Galo Plaza, whose 4 years were generally acclaimed to have provided the finest example of economic progress and political stability in more than 70 years. By contrast, Velasco Ibarra's tenure was unstable from the start, and when he left office, there was a deficit of almost S/500 million (at that time, about S/15 equaled US $1). It is claimed that popular concern with Ecuador's international image was the principal reason Velasco Ibarra was allowed to complete his term without being ousted by force (see ch. 17, Attitudes and Reactions).

Velasco Ibarra was continually at odds with a majority of Congress while it was in session, and on occasion had difficulty with his own cabinet. While he maintained relatively broad appeal, his followers were totally unorganized, sharing only a personal and usually symbolic bond to the leader. Velasco Ibarra was not able to coordinate their power against the traditional political structures, and no significant reforms were effected. On the contrary, in nearly every way the situation deteriorated. Velasco Ibarra's actions frightened the country's commercial and financial interests, inducing them to send increasing amounts of capital abroad, and also alienated potential foreign investors. For most of his 4 years there was a steadily increasing fear of political violence on a broad scale. While no one seriously doubted his appeal to the masses, many were concerned lest his "beloved rabble" get out of hand to the extent that he could no longer control it.

When Velasco Ibarra peacefully turned the presidency over to conservative Camilo Ponce Enríquez in 1956, there seemed to be general agreement that a period of relative peace and stability was needed. Ponce provided just such a pause. There were no spectacular advances or reforms, but the economic outlook improved greatly. The currency became the strongest it had been in two decades, and foreign investment increased at an unprecedented rate. The prospects of a healthy economy, a relatively stable political situation and a conservative president proved appealing to foreign capital.

Although President Ponce had gone through the gesture of breaking with the Conservatives and forming the MSC, the strength of his support came from the Conservative Party, and until he became president hardly anyone had heard of the Social Christians. In 1956 the movement was composed principally of Ponce and a few friends and relatives. It arose not so much as a splinter of the Conservative Party as a means of obtaining at least the passive support of those who by tradition were implacably opposed to the Conservatives. Many of Ponce's followers called themselves Social Christians without giving up their ties with the Conservative Party, as the two were not really in opposition at that time.

Although in relative terms the period between 1948 and 1960 was more stable than the preceding half-century, it was not uniformly peaceful. During Galo Plaza's term there were at least four antigovernment plots or revolts, and in 1949 there was an attempt on his life. There were also several riots in early 1952, but these had more to do with Velasco Ibarra's candidacy than with Galo Plaza's government or policies.

During Velasco Ibarra's 1952–56 term serious incidents of political violence, such as riots, revolts, street clashes and bomb plots, occurred at an average rate of at least four per year. The most serious incidents, which occurred in 1956, were related to Ponce's candidacy. At least two people were killed and dozens injured in incidents arising in the presidential campaigns and elections. In August 1956 there was a full-scale rebellion in the province of Manabí, on the Coast, in an attempt to prevent Ponce's inauguration.

Ponce's term was exceptionally quiet. The only incidents of political violence occurred during the last year, and almost all were related to the 1960 presidential campaign, in which Velasco Ibarra was again the successful candidate.

The Return of Velasco Ibarra

The candidacy of Velasco Ibarra, announced in January 1960, brought with it recurring political violence which did not subside until his ouster in November 1961. By March 20, 1960, at least seven persons had been killed and dozens injured in clashes between his supporters and opponents. By this time Communist youth groups were well aware that *velasquismo* represented a major threat to their cause by undercutting their support among the slum dwellers and other impoverished groups.

During the 1960 campaign, Galo Plaza ran as the candidate of the FDN, a coalition of liberals and moderate Socialists; reputedly, he represented above all the commercial interests of Guayaquil. The Conservative Party, strong only in the Sierra, but in 1960 the undisputed party of the whole region except for Quito, backed Gonzalo Cordero Crespo.

Both Cordero and Velasco Ibarra ran on a program of vigorous social reform. Although Cordero had been labor and social welfare minister under Ponce, his backing by the Conservative Party made his reformism less believable than that of Velasco Ibarra, who, in this election as in others, seemed to vibrate with the popular clamor.

Being highly sensitive to the mood and feelings of the people, Velasco Ibarra was able to turn the growing nationalism to his own advantage. In general terms he promised social and economic reforms for the benefit of the poor and revived hopes of recovering the territory annexed by Peru in 1942. In the June 4 election, Velasco Ibarra won an unprecedented 373,000 votes, an amount roughly equal to that of all of the other candidates combined. Antonio Parra Velasco, the candidate of the coalition of all the parties of the Left (including the Communists), received a mere 44,000 votes.

Nevertheless, the majority of the nation's political institutions and interest groups viewed Velasco Ibarra as a major threat to their own positions and closed ranks, denying him cooperation. Those leading figures of the various political parties who had accepted posts in the Velasco Ibarra government found themselves estranged from the core of their parties. Lacking institutional support, Velasco Ibarra turned to organized labor as a political base. In return he proclaimed friendship for the Fidel Castro regime, a move which alienated what remained of moderate support. However, since nearly all of the middle class had voted for either Galo Plaza or Cordero, the loss was not great.

How little Velasco Ibarra trusted the military establishment was indicated by his removal of 48 of the top-ranking officers of the armed forces on September 1, 1960, his first day in office. In this performance he was somewhat more moderate than he had been in 1952, when he dismissed 70 officers. Another matter settled the same day was the question of the 1942 Rio Protocol with Peru, which Velasco Ibarra declared void (see ch. 15, Foreign Relations).

By the end of 1960 there had been at least three politically motivated riots in Quito, two of them directed against the United

States (as a guarantor of the Rio Protocol and as an enemy of Castro's Cuba) and the third as a result of the ouster of the pro-Castro Minister of Government. That incident sparked bloody street battles.

It had become clear also that the economic situation had seriously deteriorated. Velasco Ibarra was still attempting to spur industrialization, the construction of public housing and agrarian reforms, but most of his measures went only a little beyond the planning stage.

Throughout 1961 the unrest continued. There were pro-Castro demonstrations and bombings in Guayaquil during February. Reportedly some 3,000 small arms had been smuggled into the country by mid-March for the purpose of arming leftist groups. Chinese Communist agents arrived from Cuba in May and were expelled from the country several days later. By mid-July there was an open split between Velasco Ibarra and his vice president, Carlos Julio Arosemena Monroy.

By midyear Velasco Ibarra had given up his ties with the Left and embarked upon a policy of friendship to the United States. Previously, Fidel Castro had called him one of the best friends of the Cuban revolution, but now the animosity of the Communists and related groups was an additional problem for him. On July 16 a split between Velasco Ibarra and Arosemena was brought out into the open by Velasco Ibarra's news-conference attack on the Vice President. Arosemena had in the meantime demanded closer relations with the Communist countries and had joined forces with Manuel Araujo Hidalgo, the leading *fidelista* of the country, in pressing for agrarian reform and opposition to Velasco Ibarra.

Attempting to help salvage a badly deteriorating economy, in early October Velasco Ibarra issued a decree placing various taxes on 30 consumer items. As a result immediate protest strikes occurred in five of the major cities. On October 16 the government claimed to have quashed a nationwide plot to overthrow the government, led by a retired army colonel and involving legislators of both the Left and the Right. Two days later antigovernment riots broke out in Cuenca and were soon joined by sympathetic students in Guayaquil.

From then until Velasco Ibarra was forced out on November 8, riots, demonstrations, regional general strikes and clashes with police and army were almost a daily occurrence throughout the country. He had, during the previous week, flown to various trouble spots in an attempt to restore order personally, but succeeded only in fanning the riots. The resulting increase in student casualties made the situation worse. By the time he finally took refuge in the Mexican Embassy, at least 35 persons had been killed and probably over 100 wounded.

The "National Disgrace" (November 1961 to July 1963)

Immediately after his overthrow Velasco Ibarra blamed the uprisings principally on the CTE, the FEUE and the Revolutionary Union of Ecuadorian Youth (Unión Revolucionaria de la Juventud Ecuatoriana—URJE), an organized, militant and violence-prone group of followers of Fidel Castro of Cuba. All three groups were as prominent in the victory celebration on the day after Velasco Ibarra's downfall as they had been in the streets 2 days earlier. Leading Arosemena Monroy's victory parade, however, was the PCE. In his inaugural address the new president stressed his intention to establish closer ties with the Soviet bloc and with Cuba. Fidel Castro was overtly jubilant over the situation in Ecuador. On the other hand, some of the most enthusiastic backers of the new president were the commercial and banking groups to which the Arosemena family belongs.

Arosemena appeared to enjoy an overwhelming popularity both in Quito and in Guayaquil, and whatever opposition he might have had a day or two before seemed to have vanished completely. To all appearances, both the Communists and the upper class were convinced that they could depend on Arosemena. The people were considerably relieved that the crisis had passed without the bloodbath that had been predicted. The general mood was one of optimism and gaiety. Even the United States announced, through Senator Hubert Humphrey (who had taken a special 2-day trip to Ecuador), that the new government was moderate and broadly based.

Among the indications of moderation were the appointment of a Cabinet which represented all political tendencies except the far Left and the rejection of demands by the CTE and the FEUE that Alfredo Pérez Guerrero, an outstanding leftist, be appointed vice president. Instead, the Arosemena-dominated Congress elected Colonel Reynaldo Varea Donoso, despite violent opposition from the galleries, which were packed with students and CTE members. Also important were the words of former President Galo Plaza, whom Arosemena had sent to the United States with assurances that the new government was not pro-Communist and with requests for loans under the Alliance for Progress.

By mid-December, however, moderates and Conservatives were beginning to have some serious misgivings. The few well-placed Communists and *fidelistas* in government were making their influence felt. Most notable among them were the Under Secretary of Government, the Under Secretary of Labor, the Director of

Propaganda in the Ministry of Education and the news editor of the national radio network.

On December 16 a mass demonstration by several thousand *campesinos* brought into Quito by the CTE caused considerable alarm in some quarters, as did Arosemena's lengthy meetings with the Cuban Under Secretary for Foreign Affairs during the second half of December.

Two events in Havana spread and intensified anti-Castro feelings in Ecuador by the beginning of 1962; Castro had openly espoused communism, and a group of fleeing Cubans had been shot to death on the grounds of Ecuador's Embassy in Havana. When Arosemena refused to have Ecuador cast its vote for sanctions against Cuba at the Punta del Este conference in January 1962, anti-Communists staged a mass demonstration against the government in Quito. Both the Conservative Party and the MSC broke with Arosemena over the issue.

By March 1962, Arosemena was under considerable pressure from both the Right and the Left to define the position of his government. The President himself was a member of no political party and had no clearly defined political orientation. He had called himself a "pragmatist" and during 1961 had interpreted all of his pragmatism in leftist (and especially pro-Castro) terms. He realized that he owed his position principally to the Communist-dominated CTE and FEUE, but the popular mood was moving away from the Left. To remain in office he realized that he would have to retain the support and cooperation of the armed forces, the business community, the foreign investors and the Church. Arosemena attempted to temporize and to offend no one. One day he would make a speech to please the Communists; the next day he would make one to soothe the armed forces; and on the third day he would plead for more foreign loans and investments.

Rumors about his personal habits caused speculation, gossip and scandal. Often he disappeared for days at a time.

During the latter part of March 1962 the army commander of the Cuenca garrison arranged meetings with various other local commanders to assure himself of their support. Toward the end of the month he sent Arosemena an ultimatum to break with Cuba and to oust prominent leftists from his government within 48 hours or face an overthrow by the armed forces. Arosemena first announced that he had quashed a conspiratorial plot of the officers and then that a national referendum would be held on the issue of breaking diplomatic relations with Cuba. Two days later his entire Cabinet resigned.

On April 2 the FDN (perhaps the most powerful political group at that time) offered to support Arosemena on the condition that he break with Cuba and take five members of the coalition into his Cabinet. The President accepted, canceled his proposed plebiscite and 2 days later broke diplomatic relations with Cuba, Poland and Czechoslovakia. A giant rally in Quito demonstrated public support of the move. The Communists were unable to stage a counterdemonstration. Several similar demonstrations took place in various cities during the next 2 weeks, one even in Guayaquil, the traditional center of leftist strength. Among the causes of the now fierce tide of anticommunism was a public statement by Fidel Castro denouncing Arosemena and calling him a "drunken coward." Ecuadorians were incensed at the insult to their national honor by an outsider.

Paradoxically, the series of incidents actually strengthened Arosemena's position. A month earlier, many observers were convinced that the President was on his way out, having countless enemies and no real support. By mid-May he was firmly in command and even felt strong enough to take reprisals against most of the high-ranking army officers who had put pressure on him 3 weeks earlier. Some were dismissed; others retired; and a few were transferred.

Somehow, the political situation was more stable than it had been at any time in the past 2 years. An ill-prepared attempt by URJE to stage a guerrilla revolt on orders from Cuba only served to rally the bulk of the population behind the government and to discredit *fidelismo* in the country even more thoroughly. By April 10 the last of the guerrillas had been captured, and there had been no strike, demonstration or other show of leftist strength anywhere in the country.

The government was clearly embarked on a course of moderation. Only two major problems remained—the continuing failure to begin introducing badly needed structural reforms (especially land and tax reform) and President Arosemena's personal misconduct.

In August, Congress tried, in secret session, to impeach Arosemena on the charge that he was not fulfilling his duties. By the end of August strikes had erupted all over the country. Most of them were sparked by nonpayment of municipal employees and similar economic grievances. To all appearances they were not politically motivated. There was no bloodshed, nor even any excessive violence. Once the grievances were met, the country remained calm throughout the rest of 1962 except for a brief transportation stoppage in Quito in late December. Late in the year, when Arosemena arrived at the airport to meet President Alessandri of Chile on an official visit to Guayaquil, uncomplimentary pictures of the President were published in *El Universo* of Guayaquil. An attempt to call a special session of Congress failed to get the necessary support.

The domestic political situation remained quiet throughout the first half of 1963. By March, however, rumors of an impending coup were rife. There were a number of harmless bomb explosions in Quito, believed to have been set off by ARNE to provoke the ouster everyone had long been expecting. When the armed forces finally made their move on July 11, there was no organized opposition outside of the Guayaquil CFP and some student groups in Quito. The takeover was executed efficiently, and the members of the military government (Navy Captain Ramón Castro Jijón, Army Colonel Marcos Gándara Enríquez, Army Colonel Luis Cabrera Sevilla and Air Force Lieutenant Colonel Guillermo Freile Posso) were themselves surprised at their own popularity and the general enthusiasm with which the coup was accepted (see ch. 13, Constitution and Government).

Government of the Armed Forces

Military intervention to remove a president who no longer had the ability to maintain order had been fairly frequent in the past. The usual procedure had been to install an overwhelmingly popular candidate or, alternatively, a relative nonentity to whom no major faction or interest group had serious objections. Military government had seldom been resorted to, usually only when there was no other solution in sight or when there was an urgent need for structural reforms. The last such case occurred in 1937 and lasted only 1 year (see ch. 13, Constitution and Government).

The military government stated formally that Arosemena had to be removed because he had hurt the nation's honor by unbecoming personal behavior and because his government lacked the will or ability to introduce long-overdue basic reforms and to forestall a Communist takeover.

Practically the first act of the military government once it was firmly in power was to order a sharp crackdown on all Communist activities. Key Communist Party members, leaders of similar groups (for example, PSR and URJE) and some fellow travelers were arrested. Some were exiled, and a few were released, but most were jailed. This done, the stage of siege, curfew and similar security measures enacted in the coup were withdrawn within less than a week, as they were obviously unnecessary. The public cheered the members of the military government whenever they appeared.

It was understood that the military government would stay for from 6 months to 2 years. When opposition developed, the head of the military government, Captain Ramón Castro Jijón, said on

July 14 that the government would be returned to civilians much sooner than 2 years. The military government was eager to obtain diplomatic recognition and knew that the Kennedy government had already set the precedent of requiring a time limit on the duration of military rule before recognizing a government brought about by nonconstitutional means. Although the major political parties and factions had backed the coup, they also were pressing for a quick return to civilian government. Most of them, nevertheless, agreed to support the military government for a year.

On October 8 the Communists and other far-left groups began their counterattack, involving demonstrations, protest marches, *hacienda* invasions, bomb explosions and student riots in widely dispersed sections of the country. Although these incidents lasted until the end of October and were supported by a propaganda campaign from Havana and Peking, they won little or no public support and were effectively neutralized by the government.

The first serious incident during the new administration occurred on January 29, 1964. University students organized a protest march on the anniversary date of the Rio Protocol, despite a ban on demonstrations. Considerable violence broke out, and there was destruction of foreign-owned property by the marchers. As a result, some 200 students were arrested, and the university was temporarily closed. Although all but about 30 of those arrested were released in less than a week, the incident marked a turning point in the nearly unanimous popularity the government had enjoyed. Various political figures seized upon the occasion to criticize the military government.

Nevertheless, the government continued to enjoy broad popular support throughout its first year. The serious opposition of some segments began after it became clear that the government would complete 12 months in office without having effected any basic transformation (although many minor reforms had been instituted) and without having specified the date for a return to civilian rule. The government explained its relative inaction in the field of reform by the need for thorough planning, and it promulgated an agrarian reform law at the beginning of its second year.

The first 3 months of the second year—July, August and September 1964—saw a flurry of activity. Besides actually implementing agrarian reform on a modest scale, the government also implemented a far-reaching tax reform and began restructuring the unwieldy form of government, including the institution of a competitive civil service. By October reform had proceeded so far that most of the major interest groups had begun to see a threat to their interests. At that point the opposition became more intense. By the end of September, after Captain Castro Jijón had bitterly attacked "economic oligarchies" in his speech of September 26, Guayaquil had become the focal point of opposition to the government.

Specifically at issue was a decree which transferred some tax powers from the Guayas Provincial Council to the central government, an issue that hit at several of the most explosive sensitivities existing in the country. Involved were regional autonomy, the sacredness of tradition embodied in the existing (but archaic) tax structure and the privileged position of the most powerful economic interest group—Guayaquil commerce. By the time the riots and demonstrations were over a former president and about 20 outstanding political figures had been jailed (but almost immediately released) on charges of "subversive activities," and the entire Guayas Provincial Council had been discharged, although the members claimed that they had resigned.

One cause of local opposition throughout the country had been the filling of provincial council posts by appointment. When the 2-year terms of the elected councilmen expired on September 1, the government reappointed most of the same persons to continue in office until elections at an indeterminate time in the future. The opposition stemmed from the fact that on the recommendations of provincial military and civil chiefs, who in most places had supplanted the governors, many councilmen were replaced rather than reappointed at the expiration of their terms. By tradition provincial councils had never been dependent for tenure on the central government.

When Captain Castro Jijón, in his New Year's message, indicated the government's intention to stay in power for an unspecified period of time, the opposition became stronger and more unified. For the first time it became dubious whether the government still had the majority of the people behind it. By January 15 all of the major political parties had protested. On January 19 a signed statement was released by the government specifying that local elections would be held in July 1966 and that presidential elections would be scheduled for sometime in the first half of 1967, followed by congressional elections several months thereafter. Under this plan, Congress would not meet until sometime in 1968, although the government would be out of office by September 1967. The antagonism between the government and the political parties became more intense and was expressed, among other ways, by a vociferous campaign of mutual abuse and recrimination carried on through the mass media.

On January 29 the students in Quito again held their annual "march of silence," commemorating the loss of territory to Peru in 1942. This time the government had given permission for the demonstration, but the march ended in a riot, as it had the previous year. Students hurled rocks and flaming gasoline-filled bottles into the presidential palace, injuring four of the palace guards, who had attempted to defend themselves by firing into the air. At least 14 students and political leaders were arrested. The government prohibited any kind of demonstration after January 31, but on February 4 about 500 high school students had to be dispersed by tear gas.

Throughout the first half of 1965 there was increasing unrest, especially among university students, who went on a series of strikes in an effort to discredit the government. Many Communist agitators were arrested, and considerable quantities of arms and explosives were found by the police, especially in Guayaquil and other towns on the Coast.

Guayaquil again provided a focal point for groups opposed to continued rule by the government during the week of May 10 to May 17, 1965. Specifically at issue was a dispute between the government and the Guayaquil Chamber of Commerce over increased customs duties decreed by the government. The result was a general strike and a series of demonstrations and riots, dispersed by police and army units using tear gas. By May 14 martial law had been declared in the city; the two major newspapers had been closed; paratroopers had been sent from Quito; and many businessmen were under arrest.

The Esmeraldas Chamber of Commerce expressed support for Guayaquil, while that of Portoviejo sided with the government. The artisans of Quito took the role of militant backers of the government by demonstrating against the "communist oligarchs and those who create confusion [in] . . . their attempt to bring down the armed forces government." The conflict ended in a compromise in which both the government and the Guayaquil Chamber of Commerce backed off from their original positions, but most of the concessions were made by the government. After considerable pressure from a coalition of most of the major parties, in addition to that of various economic interest groups, the government announced in June that it would step down 1 year earlier than previously announced. The new date for the installation of a civilian president was to be September 1, 1966. It was announced at the same time that the Constitution of 1946 would be reinstated either with or without the reforms drawn up by the military government, according to the results of a national referendum.

Most political parties were far from satisfied. Only some Conservatives wanted to return to the Constitution of 1946, as they had had the principal role in drawing it up. Nearly all other parties insisted on a constitutional assembly, but the government made clear its opposition to such procedure. The Liberal Party, among others, still insisted that the government leave office before July 11, 1965, as it had originally promised. By the end of June support was growing for the idea of forcing the government out if it did not leave within the original 2-year period.

The JPN, a popular front coalition of most major political parties, whose purpose was to force a return to constitutional government, had gathered considerable strength by June 1965. It took up the challenge of a government member who expressed doubt that the political parties could get 20 persons together to support the position of the parties. The JPN demonstrated in Guayaquil on July 9, even though permission had been denied, bringing 2,000 soldiers and a week of rioting to the port city.

Velasco Ibarra had promised to attend, but later said that he could not come because no airline in Buenos Aires would sell him a ticket. Former President Ponce Enríquez was jailed for encouraging antigovernment demonstrations as were more than 100 other persons. A number of the principal opposition leaders were exiled to Paraguay, and one Quito newspaper, El Tiempo, was shut down for a brief period. The riots which began on July 9 did not end until former President Galo Plaza and the Auxiliary Archbishop of Quito began to mediate between the government and the opposition. By July 16 the government had freed Ponce, agreed to release most other opposition leaders and promised again to give up power by September 1, 1966. By the time the disturbances ended, several persons, including one policeman, had been killed.

On July 29 the Cabinet was replaced by one composed principally of civilians, and on August 3 agreement was reached between the government and the opposition to conduct talks concerning the transfer of power to an elected civilian government. The military government was seeking assurances that the transfer would be accomplished in an atmosphere of tranquility, that social reform begun under military rule would be continued and that security measures taken against subversion would not be relaxed. The opposition leaders, on the other hand, demanded a general amnesty for participants in the July 9–16 disturbances, the return of political exiles, an end to press restrictions, an interim government to supervise the proposed elections and the calling of a constituent assembly to draft a new political charter and later to assume the functions of Congress.

Toward the end of November, when it became clear that talks had made no progress, a new series of disturbances broke out, consisting principally of student demonstrations and a number of harmless bomb explosions for propaganda purposes. There was also opposition in various cities to what was called interference with municipal self-government.

On November 29, Colonel Freile Posso was dismissed from the government by the three other members, discharged from the air force (of which he had been the head) and placed under house arrest. He was charged with using his official position as a means of furthering his personal political ambitions.

The open demonstration of disunity within the armed forces emboldened the opponents of the military regime in their demand for an early return to constitutional government. Support for the opposition was reinforced by increasing economic difficulties both in foreign trade and on the domestic scene. The significant increase in prices of basic commodities and in unemployment since mid-1965 caused a widespread undercurrent of resentment against the government in power.

By mid-December the two principal members of the Cabinet (the Ministers of Government and Foreign Affairs) resigned; university students were again demonstrating against the government; and a new antigovernment coalition of nearly all the major political parties was formed. On December 17 the government officially announced its decision to amend the 1946 Constitution by decree on the first of March, to hold elections for president on June 5, 1966, and to surrender power on September 1, 1966. The announcement stated that the amendments to the Constitution would prohibit the reelection of former presidents, thereby eliminating the three strongest contenders, abolish the office of vice president and reorganize Congress.

On the same date the Conservative Party joined those who had been demanding the calling of a constituent assembly. All the significant political parties except the CFP and ARNE rejected the government's plan. Leaders of four of the more important parties (Conservative, MSC, PSE and CID) accused the governing triumvirate of having established a personal dictatorship. They called openly upon the members of the armed forces to withdraw support from the government. Their manifesto was called a seditious proclamation by a government spokesman, and the signatories were called conspirators, but no formal action was taken against them.

CHAPTER 15

FOREIGN RELATIONS

For more than a century the cornerstone of foreign policy has been defense of territorial integrity, and present policy derives directly from the history of that contact. Indeed, for most of the time before World War II, the systematic and clearly enunciated foreign policies were those relating to territorial questions. Moreover, since 1952, the border dispute with Peru (which other countries of the Western Hemisphere had considered settled by the Rio Protocol of 1942) has not only been given increased emphasis in foreign policy, but has become the most emotionally charged political issue within the country.

Except for economic relations, in which Ecuador is strongly bound to the United States and, to a lesser degree, to Western Europe and Japan, nearly all aspects of foreign policy are implemented through the United Nations and the Organization of American States (OAS). In both organizations, Ecuador usually votes in conformity with its avowed principles:

> The juridical equality of all states disregarding factors of economic or military power; respect for national sovereignty, territorial integrity and freedom from external intervention; the proscription of violence, territorial conquest, or moral coercion in international relations; and the peaceful solution of all international conflicts.

In the United Nations, Ecuador places great emphasis on maintaining the voting unity of the Latin American bloc on all important issues, in order to have a significant voice in world affairs. If the principles of the United Nations Charter, and especially the Declaration of Human Rights, are involved in an issue being voted on, Ecuador can be counted on to support the issue vigorously. It is a strong supporter of disarmament, anticolonialism and aid to developing nations.

DEFENSE OF NATIONAL TERRITORY

The current dispute with Peru has its roots in the colonial past. When the Audiencia of Quito was first established in 1563, it consisted of a 720,000-square-mile subdivision of the Viceroyalty of Peru (Ecuador's present extension is slightly less than 110,000 square miles). It then contained the cities of Pasto, Cali and Popayán, in what are now the departments of Nariño, Cauca and Valle in Colombia; and in Peru all of the department of Túmbez and major portions of Cajamarca, Amazonas and Loreto Departments (then called Jaén and Maynas Provinces). Its coast was twice the present length, extending from Buenaventura in the north to Paita in the south.

In 1739 the Audiencia of Quito was removed from Lima's jurisdiction and included in the newly formed Viceroyalty of New Granada (with its capital at Santa Fe de Bogotá) and in the process was reduced to approximately 400,000 square miles. Within a few years Quito was again transferred to the Viceroyalty of Peru, where it remained until 1739, when it was returned to Bogotá's jurisdiction (see ch. 3, Historical Setting).

The immediate cause of the dispute between Ecuador and Peru was the Royal Decree of 1802, which transferred the province of Maynas (including all or most of Ecuador's Amazonian lowlands) to Lima's jurisdiction. The grounds for the transfer were the complaints of missionaries and others in Maynas concerning the difficulty of communicating with Bogotá and the threats of Portuguese expansion into the territory. Neither Bogotá nor Quito appeared capable of effectively defending the territory against Portuguese incursions. The president of the Audiencia of Quito requested the reincorporation of Maynas in 1814, but apparently without effect.

By the time of Quito's independence from Spain in 1822, the decree of 1802 had been only partially implemented, but Maynas, along with Jaén, had elected to join Peru and was represented in the Peruvian legislature. Whereas Jaén was a heavily populated mountain province and the desire of its inhabitants to belong to Peru could not be seriously disputed, the opposite was true of the sparsely populated jungle province of Maynas. Here the question was one of possession of territory which had never been clearly delineated, since there had been no need for precise borders when it all belonged to Spain, and which contained principally tribal Indians.

Immediately upon being freed from Spain, Quito elected to join Bolívar's Gran Colombian Republic (previously the Viceroyalty of New Granada). Bolívar redrew the boundary between what had been the Presidencia of Santa Fe (Bogotá) and Quito in such a manner that the Southern District (now Ecuador) contained only Quito, Azuay, Guayaquil and the territories directly to the east of those departments, whereas Cauca Department, including

288

the cities of Pasto, Cali and Popayán, was made part of New Granada (the Central District).

In 1828 war erupted between Gran Colombia and Peru, partly over territorial questions. At the Battle of Tarqui in February 1829, Peru was defeated by Gran Colombian forces, and in September of that year the two countries signed the Treaty of Guayaquil, in which it was agreed that the boundaries would correspond to those of the previous Viceroyalties of Peru and New Granada (without, however, specifying the date or whether the settlement was to be de facto or de jure) and that a boundary commission would be named to trace the border and make minor, mutually acceptable changes.

At this time Peru was willing to have the Marañón-Amazon River line established as its northern boundary, as indicated by the Pedemonte-Mosquera Protocol of 1830. However, before any agreement could be ratified and before the boundary commission could begin its work, Gran Colombia disintegrated as a political entity as Venezuela withdrew, followed by Quito in May 1830.

The constituent assembly which met in Riobamba in August 1830 declared that the departments of Azuay (Cuenca), Guayas and Quito would form the separate state of Ecuador and that the territory of the new state would be that of the three departments. No attempt was made to include the now Colombian Department of Cauca nor the Peruvian ones of Jaén and Túmbez, as the inhabitants preferred to remain Colombian and Peruvian, respectively.

Ecuador did, however, attempt to maintain the Marañón-Amazon border with Peru, which the latter rejected. For more than a century after 1830, Ecuador insisted that Peru honor its commitment under the 1829 treaty to establish the boundary commission called for in that treaty. Peru's position was that it did not recognize Ecuador as Gran Colombia's heir in the dispute over Maynas.

The Garcia-Herrera Treaty (1890)

Although perhaps half a dozen attempts had been made at settling the border issue, nothing significant was accomplished until 1887, when both Ecuador and Peru agreed to ask the King of Spain to arbitrate their border problem. As each side feared, however, that the award (which was to be unappealable and absolute) might entirely favor the other party and each felt that its claims were weakly supported in certain areas, another attempt was made to reach a mutual agreement. The result was the García-Herrera Treaty of 1890, which divided the disputed area roughly in half, giving Ecuador an outlet on the Marañón, but not on the Amazon proper. Under this treaty most of the

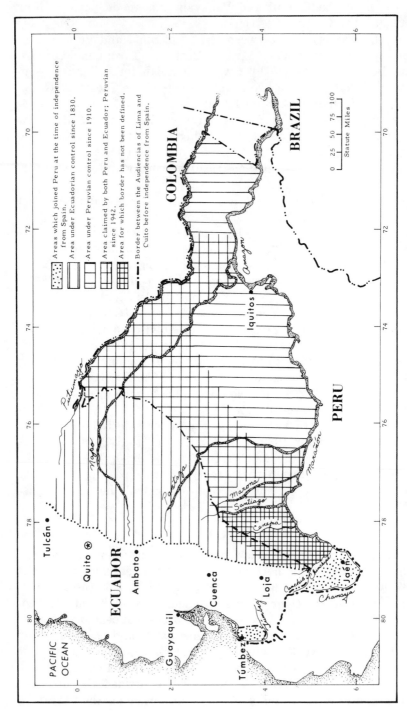

Figure 5. Territory in Dispute Between Ecuador and Peru.

Areas which joined Peru at the time of independence from Spain.

Area under Ecuadorian control since 1830.

Area under Peruvian control since 1910.

Area claimed by both Peru and Ecuador; Peruvian since 1942.

Area for which border has not been defined.

Border between the Audiencias of Lima and Quito before independence from Spain.

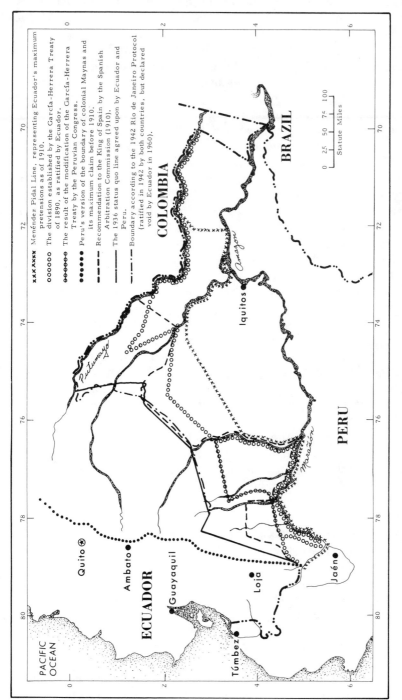

Figure 6. Boundaries Between Peru and Ecuador as Proposed Between 1890 and 1942.

xxxxxx Menéndez Pidal Line, representing Ecuador's maximum pretensions as of 1910.

ooooooo The division established by the García-Herrera Treaty of 1890, as ratified by Ecuador.

ⓄⓄⓄⓄⓄ The result of the modification of the García-Herrera Treaty by the Peruvian Congress.

●●●●● Peru's version of the boundary of colonial Maynas and its maximum claim before 1910.

– – – Recommendation to the King of Spain by the Spanish Arbitration Commission (1910).

——— The 1936 status quo line agreed upon by Ecuador and Peru.

–··–·· Boundary according to the 1942 Río de Janeiro Protocol (ratified in 1942 by both countries, but declared void by Ecuador in 1960).

291

Napo River, as well as all of the Santiago and Morona Rivers and the right bank of the Pastaza, would be within Ecuadorian territory (see figs. 5 and 6).

During the early part of the eighteenth century Peru was too occupied with other problems, especially with boundary controversies with each of its other neighbors, to give much attention to its northeastern frontier, its most remote territory. There were few Peruvian settlers in the disputed area and almost no development of communications facilities. The only significant settlement with a predominately Peruvian population north of the Marañón-Amazon was Iquitos (where, incidentally, Ecuador maintained a consulate until 1905, tacitly recognizing Peruvian control of the area).

However, during the rubber boom of the 1880's, because of the easier access to Peru by river than to Ecuador overland, Peruvian traders and rubber gatherers soon came to outnumber the few Ecuadorian settlers and missionaries in the area. Furthermore, by this time Peru had established regular river communications routes and an effective military presence, reinforced by several heavily armed river launches. Most of the Ecuadorian settlements were economically tied to Iquitos, as they could not effectively be supplied from the Ecuadorian Sierra. From the most distant Ecuadorian settlements communication with Quito and Ambato involved a 2-month journey on foot and by muleback, whereas Iquitos was only a few days away by launch from such important Peruvian towns as Moyobamba and Pucallpa.

Aside from Peru's concern over possibly losing Jaén and Túmbez by arbitration, the only leverage in Ecuador's favor at this time was Peru's temporary weakness arising from its defeat in the war with Chile and the pressures of its remaining territorial disputes with Brazil, Bolivia and Colombia.

The Ecuadorian public was convinced that all of the territory between the Marañón-Amazon and the Putumayo was beyond doubt Ecuadorian and that Peruvian assertions arose as outright aggression, based purely on force and expansionist ambition. Consequently, the García-Herrera Treaty was not popular in Ecuador, as it appeared to be giving Peru one-half of the Ecuadorian Oriente. Nevertheless, Ecuador's Congress was persuaded to ratify the treaty on the basis that postponement of the boundary solution would only work on Peru's favor, as that country's military, economic and numerical advantage was increasing each year.

The Peruvian Congress ratified the treaty only on the condition that the borderline in the southern part of the Oriente be redrawn in such a way that Ecuador would be excluded from the Marañón and give up most of the territory between navigable portions of the Morona and Pastaza Rivers (several thousand square miles). For Ecuador it was a matter of historical right and national pride to be recognized as a riparian power on the Amazon, together with Brazil, Colombia and Peru. Ecuadorians have always considered the discovery of the Amazon by an expedition from Quito the cause of their special historic glory. To be denied recognition as an "Amazonian country" (País Amazónico) was the one thing Ecuadorian national pride could not accept.

Although the Peruvian foreign ministry was fighting a determined battle with its own Congress, insisting that the legislative branch had no right to modify treaties, hostile demonstrations broke out in Quito. After the Peruvian consulate was stoned in October 1893, Peru took countermeasures which resulted in further violence to Peruvian officials in Quito and Guayaquil and to those of Ecuador in Lima. After several months of reprisals and counterreprisals by enraged mobs in both countries, Ecuador severed relations with Peru and declared its army "in campaign."

War was averted by the mediation of Colombia and the Vatican, but in July 1894, Ecuador's Congress nullified its ratification of the García-Herrera Treaty. The boundary problem had arrived at an impasse. The demands of both sides became more extreme, and each insisted that it would never again concede as much as it had under the García-Herrera Treaty. Ecuador then demanded all of the territory between the Marañón-Amazon and the Putumayo, and Peru insisted on its rights to all that Ecuador claimed to be its Oriente.

Arbitration by Spain

After it became obvious that a mutually agreeable solution was impossible, both Peru and Ecuador requested resumption of arbitration by the King of Spain in March 1895. Both parties had agreed in a number of previous treaties that their boundaries should correspond to those between the Audiencias of Lima and Quito. The King of Spain had as his principal task the definition of these colonial boundaries. However, no limits had been placed upon the King, before 1895, concerning the amount or location of territory to be arbitrated. According to the Ecuadorian delegate to the arbitration proceedings, a secret agreement between the Ecuadorian and Peruvian delegates was concluded that year to guarantee Túmbez, Jaén and Iquitos (each of which had a considerable Peruvian population) for Peru and an outlet on the Marañón-Amazon for Ecuador.

Ecuador's case consisted of the assertions that the decree of 1802 only dealt with administrative, ecclesiastical and military jurisdictions, but had no territorial effect. Besides, the victory of Colombian forces over those of Peru at Tarqui in 1829 nullified the effect of the 1802 document and eliminated Peru's rights to territory north of the Marañón-Amazon River, as indicated by the Pedemonte-Mosquera Protocol of 1830. From Ecuador's point of view the only task for the arbiter was to establish a boundary commission and complete the delineation of the border between the Pacific Coast and the Marañón River, as called for in the 1829 treaty, and to confirm Ecuador's right to the territory between the Putumayo River and the Marañón-Amazon.

Peru's case was that, contrary to Ecuadorian assertions, the 1802 decree did specifically refer to territory and land, was implemented and did, in effect, eliminate any Ecuadorian claim to Amazonian lowlands by transferring all such territories to Peru. Furthermore, from Peru's point of view, the 1829 Treaty of Guayaquil was between Peru and Gran Colombia and ceased to have any effect whatever once the latter entity disintegrated. Peru also asserted that Ecuador originated as a nation in May 1830 through the self-determination of the people of the three southern departments of Gran Colombia (Azuay, Guayaquil and Quito), not the jungle province of Maynas, which was already represented in the Peruvian Congress. Peru also emphasized that Ecuador was unable, even in 1895, to supply or defend the Oriente territories it claimed.

The arbitration proceedings lasted for 15 years (1895–1910) and proved extremely expensive for both parties. Allegedly, Peru spent much more than Ecuador—in excess of a million Peruvian soles (at that time about $500,000)—in employing the legal opinions of famous international jurists and prestigious Spanish political figures. Whereas Ecuador was able to prove (through secret Peruvian documents it had obtained) that Peru in the 1820's and 1830's considered the Marañón-Amazon as a satisfactory northern border, nearly all of its other assertions were rejected.

The Spanish arbitrators decided that Gran Colombian treaties were not applicable to Ecuador. Consequently, the 1829 Treaty of Guayaquil had no obligatory force. The commission also decided that the decree of 1802 had been in force at the time of independence and that it did have territorial application. On the other hand, the province of Maynas was declared to be less extensive than claimed by Peru, and its boundaries with Quito's territories were set at the first rapids, falls or other obstructions to navigation on the major rivers. Also, the area west of the Morona River was not included in Maynas Province.

Although Spain said that Ecuador had no legal rights in what had been Maynas, it awarded considerable portions of that territory in equity, as compensation for the loss of Túmbez and Jaén, which had elected to join Peru. Ecuador was also to have right of access to the Amazon proper, although it would not receive territory on its banks. All in all, Ecuador would receive slightly less territory than it would have received under the unmodified García-Herrera Treaty, but considerably more than that treaty had included after the modification by the Peruvian Congress. More important, it would receive well over 100 miles on the northern bank of the Marañón.

Vásquez, attempting to have the decision modified, prepared a memorandum informing the Spanish Government that he could not accept the decision "because it contains fundamental errors." He published the minority opinion of the arbitrators, which was more favorable to Ecuador, and insisted that only it was founded on law. The Spanish press and public opinion turned strongly against Ecuador. Vásquez argued that, since the decision had not been announced by the King, it was not yet binding and that he therefore had a right to attempt to influence the final award.

Ecuadorian President Eloy Alfaro had made it clear that he had been against the arbitration since 1900, as he saw that there was little likelihood of his country winning the contest. His ambassador in the United States let it be known that neither Alfaro nor any other president could make his country abide by such an unfavorable award. In April 1910 the Quito government proposed that each country set its maximum line and then arbitrate the difference. Ecuador indicated that its maximum aspiration was delineated by the Menéndez Pidal Line. Ramón Menéndez Pidal was a Spaniard commissioned by the Spanish Arbitration Commission in 1904 to determine the maximum territories which could be given to Ecuador (that is, those not under firm Peruvian control), should that country win the arbitration. He spent 2 years (1908–10) in the Oriente determining the line (see fig. 6).

President Alfaro was convinced that Ecuador's mistake had been to insist on an award based on claims to legal title. He proposed direct negotiations including Peru and Colombia, conducted under the "moral influence" of several neutral mediating powers to reach a decision based on "justice and mutual advantage" (that is, on the principle of equity rather than on the basis of titles).

When the King of Spain withdrew as arbiter on November 24, 1910, his government expressly blamed Ecuador. On September 2, the Ecuadorian Congress had voted in favor of an absolute rejection of the proposed award and proceeding to make the award might have meant war. In April 1910 mob violence broke out, first in Ecuador and then in Peru. War was narrowly averted by the mediation of Argentina, Brazil and the United States. All three sent strongly worded notes to Quito, accusing the government of an uncooperative attitude.

While Peru indicated willingness to continue diplomatic discussions with Ecuador in an attempt to define the border, it was also advancing its control in the area. Ecuador, in the meantime, did very little to expand into the vast area between the effective national territory of the two countries. Some of the former Ecuadorian missions were turned into small military garrisons or outposts, but these were underarmed, lightly equipped and largely isolated from the rest of the country.

Ecuadorian military garrisons could offer no effective resistance to Peruvian expansion and in some cases even found themselves economically dependent upon the nearby Peruvian settlements. Every few years there were incidents and protest notes to indicate that Peru's expansion did not go unchallenged, but it soon became clear that direct discussions were futile. Peru was not willing to discuss any line that would give it less territory than had been conceded by the Spanish arbiters, and Ecuador insisted on a solution between the proposed award and the 1830 Pedemonte-Mosquera Protocol—the Marañón-Amazon line. Spain's decision could not serve as a starting point for discussions because it was less than the minimum that either of the disputants was willing to settle for.

In 1924 a protocol was signed between Peru and Ecuador providing for continued discussion in Washington, with United States assistance. It was agreed that the President of the United States would act as arbiter, if no accord was reached. In 1933 the two countries acted on the agreement, preparing an identically worded request asking President Roosevelt to act as arbiter. The President agreed in February 1934 to meet with the ministers of both countries as requested, and in July 1936 a protocol was signed in Lima establishing the arbitration proceedings. The same protocol also called for the maintenance of the status quo as indicated by a line which both countries recognized as showing their respective areas of control as of July 1936. (This line was practically identical with that later agreed upon in Rio de Janeiro, in January 1942, as the final and permanent border between the two countries.) The talks ended without positive results in 1938.

The Border and the Rio Protocol

In May 1941 the United States, Argentina and Brazil offered to mediate. Ecuador immediately accepted, but Peru refused. On July 5 large-scale fighting broke out. A Peruvian invasion began July 23 and halted July 31, on a cease-fire order of the three intervening powers. Ecuador had been unable to stop the Peruvian advance. Peru had committed a force of 5,000 to 10,000 troops, whereas Ecuador had between 800 and 1,600. Of the about 500 casualties, counting both killed and wounded, at least two-thirds were Peruvians.

All of El Oro Province (on the Coast) was occupied, as were several thousand square miles of the Oriente beyond the status quo line of 1936. The invaded sector of the Oriente was largely uninhabited.

The military situation remained essentially static between the end of July and September 13, when Lima offered an ultimatum to the mediators. Peru would evacuate El Oro Province only if Ecuador would agree to a final and binding solution to the border problem within 6 months. The settlement procedure was to be conducted under the supervision of the three original mediating powers and Chile, which expressed interest in participating in any conference that would settle the Peru-Ecuador dispute. If Ecuador did not propose an acceptable treaty within the specified half year, Peru was to impose a solution by force.

The Ecuadorian defense minister agreed in principle to the traditional border between the two countries in the west (on the Coast and in the Sierra) and to a line connecting the navigable limits of the major streams in the Oriente, if the mediators would participate in the negotiations.

Brazil's foreign minister took the initiative at a Rio de Janeiro meeting in attempting to induce the disputants to reach agreement. The Ecuadorian delegates, headed by Julio Tobar Donoso, tried to obtain possession of the Santiago River as a minimum fulfillment of Ecuadorian national aims, but the government agreed to settle essentially on Peru's terms. The Protocol of Peace, Friendship and Boundaries between Ecuador and Peru (popularly called the Rio Protocol) was signed on January 29, 1942, and guaranteed by Argentina, Brazil, Chile and the United States. Ecuadorian officials were generally relieved that the results had not been more damaging. Even after the government of President Arroyo del Río was overthrown in 1944, José María Velasco Ibarra, who succeeded, stated Ecuador's acceptance of the 1942 Rio Protocol.

The Ecuadorian Reaction

At the end of World War II it seemed that public emotion on the Peruvian border question had subsided. All indications were that Ecuadorians had resigned themselves to the loss of their national claim in the Amazon basin.

In 1946, however, the United States Air Force, in the process of photo-mapping the area between the Santiago and Zamora Rivers discovered an additional 120-mile-long river system between the other two. The river, the Cenepa, had been known to exist, but it was thought to be short and insignificant. Now it greatly complicated the problem of marking the border between the two countries because, according to the Rio Protocol, the division between the watersheds of the Santiago and the Zamora river systems was to serve as the boundary.

The problem was not only that now there were two such divisions, instead of one, but that the Cenepa River, which flows into the Marañón, revived Ecuador's hopes for territory on the Marañón-Amazon. Between 1947, when the geographic discovery became common knowledge, and 1951, when Ecuadorian cooperation in placing boundary markers stopped, the Amazon issue returned with full vigor. Of special significance was the fact that the area involved was not covered by the 1802 decree, which gave Peru title to most of the rest of the area ceded to Peru by the 1942 Protocol. In fact, the area between the Condor mountain range and the Santiago River (the area left in dispute after discovery of the Cenepa River system) is specifically where Peru's claim was the weakest.

On August 10, 1951, the Ecuadorian president, Galo Plaza Lasso, in his annual message to Congress, stated that Ecuador would not recognize a boundary in the undefined area (about 5,000 square miles) unless his country were given an outlet on the Marañón-Amazon. The next day, the Peruvian president, Manuel Odría, replied that his country would refuse to discuss the issue. Serious border incidents soon broke out, followed by a series of mutual protests. A few months after Velasco Ibarra won the presidency in 1952, through a campaign stressing the border issue, his government declared the Peruvian ambassador persona non grata on a question of protocol, thereby breaking diplomatic relations.

Although incidents continued throughout 1953 and 1954, both sides increased their armaments purchases, there were no signs that either country was actually preparing for war, according to reconnaissance by the guarantor powers.

In 1956 the situation cooled down somewhat, and diplomatic relations were reestablished. During most of the term of President Camilo Ponce Enríquez (1956–60), relations remained calm, if cool. When Velasco Ibarra was reelected in June 1960, the issue flared again. A *velasquista* congress, on August 26, ratified Velasco's statement of the previous week that the Rio Protocol was void. Velasco repeated his declaration on September 1 in his inaugural address, and on September 28, Ecuador's foreign minister, Chiriboga Villagómez, announced Ecuador's nullification of the 1942 Rio Protocol to the General Assembly of the United Nations. Soon thereafter, Ecuador's Supreme Court also declared:

. . . that the absolute nullity of the Rio Protocol is an incontrovertible thesis of scientific and juridical value and a matter which originates a problem of life and death for Ecuadorian nationhood. . . . The hour has arrived to determine whether enlightened international opinion will tolerate triumphs of force, whether Pan-Americanism is only an empty and fantastic dream, or if it is, in reality, a body of principles, flesh of our flesh and blood of our American blood for the reign of justice and morality in the life of nations.

INTERNATIONAL RELATIONS IN RECENT TIMES

Relations with the United States

Between 1910 and January 1942, Ecuador hoped to attain an outlet on the Marañón-Amazon, the benevolent concern of the United States. The disillusionment of the Rio Protocol, which was guaranteed by the United States, together with the three most powerful nations of South America, left a sense of disappointment. The United States' delay in returning World War II military and naval bases at Salinas and on the Galápagos Islands to Ecuadorian control and Ecuador's increasing economic dependence upon the United States were exploited by leftists and nationalists to create strong anti-United States sentiments between 1945 and 1948.

After mid-1948 unfavorable attitudes toward the United States were to some extent balanced, if not largely neutralized, by the election of Galo Plaza Lasso, who was an admirer of the United States, had lived there for many years and had received all of his higher education at United States universities. He had more or less successfully transplanted to Ecuador many modernizing notions in the fields of politics and economic development. His success in obtaining extensive technical and financial aid from the United States was conspicuously reflected in Ecuador's unprecedented prosperity and stability (see ch. 14, Political Dynamics; ch. 18, The Economic System).

Galo Plaza Lasso was succeeded in 1952 by Velasco Ibarra, who exploited the resentment against Peru and the latent reserves about the United States. He criticized the conditions allegedly imposed by United States economic aid and the so-called United States neglect of its obligations to Latin America. The last year of Velasco Ibarra's term (1956) coincided with the beginning of the Soviet Union's economic and diplomatic offensive in Latin America.

During Camilo Ponce Enríquez' term (1956–60) relations with the United States were cordial, even though in 1958 he informed the United States that the Soviet Union was offering economic aid on considerably more advantageous terms than had the United States and that Ecuador would have to consider such offers unless the United States increased its commitment (see ch. 24, Foreign Economic Relations).

Analysts of the political situation in 1960, when Velasco Ibarra was reelected, saw as a contributory factor his link with the temporarily popular appeal of *fidelismo* and his vigorous nationalism. The years 1960 and 1961 coincided with the height of Communist and *fidelista* appeal and influence in Ecuador. Pro-Communist and, especially, pro-Castro slogans, combined with anti-United States propaganda, appeared in major cities. There were numerous anti-United States demonstrations and riots and occasional stonings of the United States Embassy and United States Information Agency centers.

The climax of anti-United States feelings came in December 1960, when the United States and the other three guarantors of the Rio Protocol—Argentina, Brazil and Chile—officially rejected Ecuador's unilateral abrogation of the 1942 document. Velasco Ibarra praised Khrushchev as a great statesman and world leader, and one member of his Cabinet publicly suggested establishing diplomatic relations with Moscow as a reprisal for the United States position (see ch. 14, Political Dynamics). Within half a year, however, the appeal of Castro subsided, Velasco Ibarra moderated his policy, and when United Nations Ambassador Adlai Stevenson arrived on June 19, 1961, he received an enthusiastic public welcome.

As general disillusionment with Castro's Cuban government intensified, the position and prestige of the United States were correspondingly improved. The military government which took the reins from Carlos Julio Arosemena Monroy in mid-1963 followed a moderate course, but after July 1964 the leaders of various political parties gradually forced it to take a more vigorous stand. By March 1965 it opposed the Rio Protocol, and by October 1965 it was again impounding United States fishing boats for violating Ecuador's 200-mile territorial waters (this had last occurred in June 1963, 1 month before Arosemena was ousted) (see ch. 24, Foreign Economic Relations).

The Communist Bloc

By tradition and practically uninterrupted usage, the foreign minister has been a member of the Conservative Party. Foreign policy has nearly always been strongly anti-Communist. The major exception was the period between 1960 and 1961 when the strong popular appeal of Castro's Cuba prevented the government from taking a stand against him. Various minor contacts with nations of the Communist bloc, especially Castro's Cuba, have taken place between 1956 and July 1963; they included an official visit to Moscow by the Vice President and a visit by a member of the Cabinet to Czechoslovakia.

The country's continuing border difficulties with Peru made the United States Government reluctant to increase substantially its shipment of arms to Ecuador. When Adlai Stevenson arrived in Quito in June 1961, he was handed a request for loans and grants amounting to US$174 million and a request that the United States act to prevent the fall of prices of Ecuador's export commodities on the international market.

Ecuador has had no formal diplomatic relations with the Soviet Union or Communist China since the start of the cold war. It has had some commercial contacts with several Eastern European countries, and in late 1965 there were some economic contacts with the Soviet Union, Poland, Czechoslovakia, Hungary, Bulgaria, Romania, Yugoslavia, East Germany and Communist China. On the other hand, there have been no relations whatsoever—political, economic or cultural—with Castro's Cuba since April 1962 (see ch. 14, Political Dynamics; ch. 24, Foreign Economic Relations).

Other External Relations

Except in the economic sphere where there is considerable trade with Western Europe and Japan, little significant contact exists with other nations outside the framework of the OAS and the United Nations. The special arrangements which exist between Ecuador and the other former members of Gran Colombia (Colombia and Venezuela) deal exclusively with economic matters (see ch. 24, Foreign Economic Relations).

Ecuador's voting record and other roles within both the OAS and the United Nations differ in no significant respect from those of other Latin American nations. Within the OAS, Ecuador is a member of the Program and Budget Commission, the Inter-American Conferences Commission and the Juridical-Political Matters Commission. In the United Nations it was voted a member of the Economic and Social Council for the 3-year term ending in December 1966.

THE MINISTRY OF FOREIGN RELATIONS

The conduct of foreign policy has always been the responsibility of the president, but in practice the minister of foreign relations has usually had more freedom of action than other Cabinet members, and foreign ministers have often survived changes of administration. Most presidents have been too occupied with domestic matters to be able to devote much attention to foreign affairs (see ch. 13, Constitution and Government; ch. 14, Political Dynamics).

According to the 1964 Organization Law of the Foreign Service, foreign policy is made (or at least suggested) by the Foreign Relations Joint Council. Among its members in 1965 were a Supreme Court justice, the commanding general of the armed forces, the archbishop of Quito and 10 citizens, as well as representatives of the press, the universities and the Ministry itself. Although this council differs greatly from the Permanent Consultative Commission for Foreign Affairs, which existed for at least two decades, it appears to be somewhat more formalized. Also as a result of the

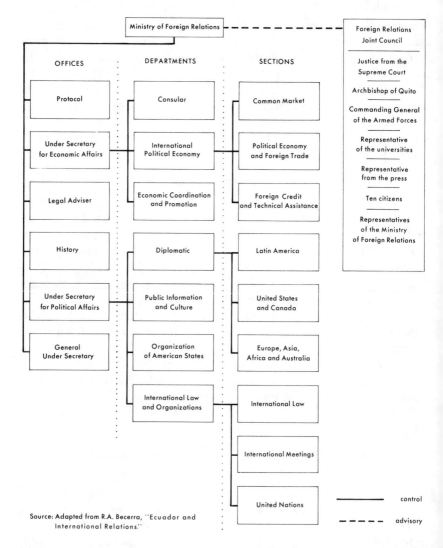

Source: Adapted from R.A. Becerra, "Ecuador and International Relations."

Figure 7. Structure of the Ecuadorian Ministry of Foreign Relations, 1965.

1964 law, the structure of the Ministry of Foreign Relations itself is more formally organized (see fig. 7).

A candidate for a diplomatic career must be Ecuadorian by birth and at least 21 years of age; have a record of good conduct; speak at least one foreign language; and, preferably, possess the title of doctor or lawyer. No detailed educational requirements are specified. In practice, many appointments have been political, and diplomatic careers have been interrupted in recent years by changes of administration. A diplomat may also be retired by his own request or for reasons of age or health.

CHAPTER 16

PUBLIC INFORMATION

Literate Ecuadorians have long been served by a responsible press, relatively free from government interference. This press, dominated by four leading daily newspapers—two in Quito and two in Guayaquil—has had an important role in shaping public opinion.

Despite the influence of newspapers and periodicals on their readers, their impact on the country as a whole has been limited by a poorly developed transport and communications system and by a general illiteracy rate of about 50 percent. In recent years radio, which is entirely privately owned, has become the country's most effective channel of information by carrying news to every stratum of society, even in the remote areas.

In 1964 the daily newspapers had a combined circulation of about 250,000, and 246 radio transmitters reached about 500,000 receiving sets. Periodicals and books have few readers. Television, which began operating in the early 1960's, and the widely attended motion pictures are more sources of entertainment than of information.

Communist agencies have used both the press and radio for propaganda purposes. During the years it was legal, the Communist Party of Ecuador (Partido Comunista del Ecuador— PCE) developed an extensive propaganda apparatus which has continued to function clandestinely or from outside the country since the government outlawed the party in 1963. Its effectiveness has not been great, and it has had little influence in the non-Communist press, despite the leftist bias of some important publishers.

FREEDOM OF EXPRESSION

Article 187 of the 1946 Constitution, covering individual rights. guarantees:

Freedom to express thoughts by word of mouth, in the press or by other means insofar as such expression does not involve malice, calumny, personal insult, immorality or run contrary to the national interest.

The government, however, has frequently exerted mild but firm pressure on the various news media and has at times cited the phrase "contrary to the national interest" to justify its punishment of those expressing dissenting viewpoints. Late in 1953, while José María Velasco Ibarra was president, *El Comercio*, with its affiliate *Ultimas Noticias* and its radio station Radio Quito, was closed down for 44 days for refusing to publish an announcement by the government that it would not tolerate severe newspaper criticism.

During the intervening Ponce administration (1956–60) there was no apparent press censorship, but it was resumed when Velasco Ibarra returned to the presidency in 1960.

There has been much criticism of the military government in the press, but no system of prior censorship has been imposed. In July 1964, *Vistazo*, the leading monthly magazine, criticized the accomplishments of the military government after a year in office and stated that, although most newsmen believed the coup was necessary when it took place, 60 percent of them opposed the government a year later.

As of late 1965 the only instance of prior censorship recorded since the military government took over occurred in August 1963, when the Civil and Military Chief of Esmeraldas Province closed the liberal, stanchly anti-Communist newspaper, *El Clarín*, for a few days and jailed its editor because of a critical article it had printed. Shortly thereafter *El Clarín* published an official communique requiring that all radio stations, news publications and other information media in the province submit all programs or articles scheduled to be published or broadcast to the civil and military chief for approval.

The military government has occasionally taken action against newspapers and radio stations which refused to print or broadcast its views on an issue or which were accused of distorting the government's case. During an antigovernment demonstration in Guayaquil in October 1964, the editors of the city's leading newspapers were arrested, and five radio stations were closed for allegedly refusing to report opinion favorable to the government's point of view.

On July 10, 1965, *El Tiempo* of Quito was closed by the government, which claimed that it had, since its establishment 6 months earlier, persistently maligned the government and fostered a climate favoring subversion and the disruption of public order. Newspapers of all political positions protested this action as being a constitutional violation. The National Union of Journalists (Unión Nacional de Periodistas—UNP) protested that, as long as *El Tiempo* remained closed, freedom of the press could not be considered to exist in the country. The Inter-American Press Society (Sociedad Interamericana de Prensa—SIP), from its headquarters in New York, protested to the government. The closure was lifted on July 19, 1965, to strengthen the climate for national harmony, according to government spokesmen. The SIP, at its annual meeting in October 1965, stated that although there had been some harassment of the press in Ecuador, neither censorship nor restriction on the press existed in that country.

On October 1, 1965, the director of one of the television channels in Quito was arrested and sentenced to from 4 to 30 days in jail by a police court for broadcasting a news bulletin "injurious to the military government," but he was released later on the day of arrest.

According to the Constitution, freedom of expression is bounded by certain standards of public morality. In both Quito and Guayaquil are municipal reviewing boards which bar the showing of films deemed immoral. The boards also publish weekly in the leading newspapers an artistic and morality rating of the major films being shown during the week. In September 1965 the Municipal Council of Guayaquil ordered that the advertising material to be used for a particular picture be submitted for censorship prior to use.

THE PRESS

The press has roots extending far back in national history. In the late eighteenth century, Francisco Eugenio de Santa Cruz y Espejo wrote and published a periodical called *Primicias de la Cultura de Quito* which provided an early impetus to the movement for independence from Spain. During the early decades of the republic most periodicals were short-lived diatribes against the government currently in power. The most famous of these was *El Cosmopolita*, by Juan Montalvo, attacking the dictatorship of Gabriel García Moreno. When Montalvo heard of García Moreno's assassination, he boasted, "My pen killed him!" In 1884 the Guayaquil daily *El Telégrafo* (still a leading voice in the nation) was established as the first periodical in which editorial concerns transcended current political problems (see ch. 10, Artistic and Intellectual Expression).

Newspapers

El Telégrafo was followed 22 years later by the Quito daily *El Comercio;* since then daily newspapers have been established in at least 13 other cities or towns throughout the country. In recent years some 30 different newspapers which could be called dailies have appeared, although some have proved ephemeral and others have lapsed to weekly or irregular publication.

During 1964, 24 daily newspapers in 11 cities or towns were being published more or less regularly, with an estimated combined daily circulation of about 250,000, or 5.8 newspapers for every 100 persons. There were at least 25 weekly newspapers, with circulations ranging from a few hundred to 5,000. The dailies of Quito and Guayaquil produce most of the total circulation and have influence greater than the size of their circulation would seem to indicate. One daily from each of these two cities receives countrywide distribution. Because of their normally restricted coverage, the local newspapers in the smaller cities and towns usually have small circulations—sometimes no more than 1,000—but at election time their circulations often increase considerably.

The four largest dailies, two in Guayaquil and two in Quito, reach about 85 percent of the country's readers. *El Universo* is the largest newspaper in the country and *El Telégrafo* the oldest; both are independent morning newspapers in Guayaquil. The two Quito newspapers, both published by the same firm, are the morning *El Comercio* and the evening *Ultimas Noticias*. In the last 5 years all four newspapers have adopted progressive attitudes and advocated needed reform. None is the organ of a political party.

The general quality of the major dailies is high. Despite occasional problems with the government and the obligation to print official news releases, they are independent of outside control. Although the Quito and Guayaquil newspapers, reflecting a long tradition of regionalism, are committed to their respective local interests, on most issues they present a generous diversity of opinion.

The four major newspapers have patterned their format and manner of presentation on United States models. All carry a good coverage of domestic and international views and are considered to be moderate in outlook and nonsensational in views, treatment and format.

Although the big dailies are strongly nationalistic, the editorial tone is seldom chauvinistic. Editorial policies in general are friendly toward the United States, but on occasion the newspapers may criticize specific United States actions.

El Universo of Guayaquil, founded in 1921 and controlled by the Perez family, has a daily circulation of about 60,000 and a slightly larger Sunday circulation. It is standard in size, uses a 9-column page and varies from a minimum of 20 pages to as many as 50 pages on Sunday. It costs S/0.80 (in 1965, S/18.5 equaled US$1 —see Glossary) for the daily edition and S/1.20 for the Sunday edition and carries advertising on all pages.

Its editorials are liberal in orientation, dealing chiefly with the problems of Guayaquil and the Coast. United Press International (UPI) and Agence France Presse (AFP) supply its international news. It carries full reports of government and international views on the front page and, as a leading coastal newspaper, carries extensive commercial and economic news. Social and sports coverage is also extensive. The last page and one or two inside pages are devoted to the unsensational treatment of accidents and crimes. Occasional articles by United States columnists are printed, but most columns are written by Ecuadorians. The comic strips are almost entirely translations of United States comic strips.

El Telégrafo of Guayaquil, a morning newspaper founded in 1884 and published by the Castillo family, has a daily circulation of more than 25,000 and a Sunday circulation of more than 33,000. It is a standard-sized, 8-column newspaper with from 16 pages daily to as many as 40 on Sunday. The daily edition costs S/0.80, and the Sunday edition, S/1.20 per copy. Advertising appears throughout the newspaper.

The editorials, which reflect the coastal viewpoint often critical of the military government's policies, are center of the road in orientation and moderate in tone. The front page emphasizes national news and items of special importance. Other important items appear on the back page of the first section. International news is furnished by the Associated Press (AP). In addition to extensive coverage of national and international news, there is good coverage of commercial, social and local news. Sports are featured in the first two pages of the second section. Comic strips are all of United States origin, translated into Spanish. Crimes and accidents are covered only on the back page and are nonsensational in treatment.

El Comercio, Quito's leading daily, founded in 1906 and published by the Martilla family, is a morning newspaper with a circulation of about 36,000 on weekdays and slightly higher on Sundays. It is distributed throughout the country, appeals particularly to the middle and upper classes and has an influence far greater than the number of copies distributed would seem to indicate. When it was founded, the liberal government of Leónidas Plaza encouraged it, allowing it to use the government telegraph lines without cost and to import newsprint without customs duties. Since then its editorial policy has been to support the government while reserving the right to attack measures the editors consider detrimental to the country as a whole.

News coverage is ample. For international news El Comercio depends on the UPI and AFP; for national and local news it depends on its own correspondents. It is a standard-sized, 8-column sheet, varying from 24 to 64 pages and selling for S/1 daily and S/1.20 on Sunday. It devotes its front page entirely to major international and national events, with no advertisements. Sports and social news are extensively covered. Local news and news from all parts of the Sierra are also featured. The comic strips are translations of United States comic strips. The last page reports crimes and accidents in a restrained fashion.

Ultimas Noticias, the evening affiliate of *El Comercio,* has a daily circulation of 28,000, almost entirely within the Quito area. It has no Sunday edition. It is only half the size of *El Comercio,* but its content is similar. Its news coverage emphasizes late-breaking followups on items appearing in *El Comercio.*

El Tiempo, a Quito daily, began publication on January 1, 1965, as a morning newspaper. It is a tabloid, restrained and conservative in presentation. A considerable share of the newspaper is owned by two of the Sierra dioceses of the Catholic Church. The principal members of the staff are experienced writers, but new to the field of journalism. *El Tiempo* has often criticized the policies of the military government and has consistently favored a return to constitutional government.

Magazines

The 23 magazines being published regularly in early 1965 had a combined circulation of 77,300. There were 3 religious magazines, with a combined circulation of 35,000; 2 monthly sports magazines (*Estadio* of Guayaquil, with a circulation of 10,000, and *Aucas* of Quito, with a circulation of 2,000) ; 3 general-interest weeklies, with a combined circulation of 6,000; and 15 monthlies, with a combined circulation of 24,300. *Vistazo,* a 100-page illustrated monthly magazine somewhat similar to *Look* in format, has a circulation of 5,000 monthly and is the most widely read of the general-interest magazines. Foreign magazines in the Spanish language, particularly the illustrated ones, are very popular.

Journalists

Journalists have compiled a distinguished record of international awards. In recent years five journalists and newspaper directors have been awarded the Maria Morrs Cabot medal, established by Columbia University in New York for outstanding newspapermen of Latin America. The most recent recipients were Alejandro Carrión, columnist for *El Universo,* and Jorge Fernández, editorial writer for *El Comercio.* Carrión, a widely known poet, author and journalist, has for years written a column under the pen name Juan Sin Cielo. In addition to his work in journalism, Fernández has achieved renown as a novelist.

There are several facilities for the training of journalists. Both the Central University of Quito and the University of Guayaquil have undergraduate schools of journalism. At the advanced level the International Center of Graduate Studies in Journalism for Latin America (Centro Internacional de Estudios Superiores del Periodismo para América Latina—CIESPAL), founded in 1960 under the auspices of the United Nations Educational, Scientific and Cultural Organization (UNESCO), offers an intensive 2-month course. The CIESPAL classes are taught by distinguished journalists from Europe and the Americas, and the program is headed by Jorge Fernández.

Journalists are represented by a professional association, the UNP, established in 1940. The UNP is not affiliated with any national labor organization, but maintains ties with the Inter-American Federation of Working Newspaper Organizations. The UNP, with a membership of about 300, has been entrusted with executing the government's national literacy program.

RADIO

All radio broadcasting stations are privately owned. Most stations are weak in transmitting power and have very limited range, but the most powerful broadcasting station in Latin America—HCJB, the missionary-sponsored Voice of the Andes—is located near Quito. In addition there are several less powerful but important commercial stations, most of which adhere to one of the four major national networks, and a few fairly strong nonaffiliated stations. Many of the stations broadcast for only a few hours a day, but at least six broadcast on a 24-hour basis.

The *World Radio and TV Handbook for 1965* listed 95 shortwave stations broadcasting within the shortwave band, 107 mediumwave stations broadcasting within the standard-broadcast band and an additional 40 shortwave transmitters broadcasting within the standard-broadcast band. These figures represented an increase of more than 40 percent since 1961 in number of radio stations. There were estimated to be more than half a million receivers in 1965.

On July 13, 1965, the director of telecommunications of the Ministry of Public Works declared that the government was seeking to bring greater order into radio broadcasting, which had over 240 transmitters compared to only 64 in Argentina and 78 in Venezuela.

The noncommercial, religious station, Voice of the Andes, often called Vozandes, is owned by the World Radio Missionary Fellowship, which is supported chiefly by various Evangelical Protestant sects in the United States. Vozandes, which broadcasts from 5:30 a.m. to 11 p.m. daily, has seven transmitters located near Quito; the most powerful is a 40-kilowatt station which transmits shortwave broadcasts in nine languages, including Spanish, Russian and Portuguese, to all parts of the world. The locally directed 1-kilowatt station, operating in the standardwave band, broadcasts in both Spanish and Quechua. Vozandes has aided in increasing the local radio reception by producing low-receiving sets in its own shops.

The important independent commercial stations are located in Guayaquil and Quito. In Guayaquil the 5-kilowatt station CRE is very influential in busines circles and carries high-quality news broadcasts. The 5-kilowatt station Ondas del Pacifico, which uses AP newswire services, has a wide lower middle-class appeal. The 5-kilowatt station Cristal has strong lower-class appeal, and the 5-kilowatt El Mundo has a general audience. The 2-kilowatt station La Prensa, owned by the newspaper of that name, carries the UPI newswire service and appeals to an upper-class audience. The 2-kilowatt Ifesa has a broad audience.

In Quito the 5-kilowatt Ecuatoriana is the most powerful station on the standard-broadcast band; it has good news coverage but does not subscribe to a wire service. The ½-kilowatt Cordillera features music almost exclusively. The 2-kilowatt station Tarqui is leftist oriented and aimed at the lower class. Except for Tarqui, which is strongly anti-United States, all networks and stations make extensive to moderate use of material from the United States Information Service (USIS) and the Voice of America.

Each network is made up of a number of loosely affiliated, individually owned and operated stations which enter and leave the network at will. Most of the stations join the network only for news, sports and special events.

The largest of the networks is the Cadena Nacional Ecuatoriana, known as NE, which in 1964 contained 33 stations and had as its key station Emisora Gran Colombia, a 1-kilowatt station in Quito. NE, which emphasizes sports, does not subscribe to an international news service. It has additional stations in Quito as well as stations in Guayaquil, Cuenca, Esmeraldas, Ambato, Riobamba, Azogues, Latacunga, Ibarra, Otavalo, Tulcán, Santo Domingo de los Colorados, Santa Elena, Gualaceo, Salcedo, Machachi, Manta, El Angel, Tarqui and Guaranda. This network provides news services for a number of small newspapers throughout the country.

Cadena Amarillo, Azul y Roja, known as AAR, had, in 1964, 20 member stations with 1-kilowatt key stations called Espejo, in Quito and Guayaquil. This network has many commercials. Although it subscribes to no international wire service, it furnishes good news coverage.

The network Ecuadoradio, known as ECR, in 1964 included 17 stations; its key station, the 3-kilowatt Radio Quito, is owned by *El Comercio*. It emphasizes news, using both UPI and AFP news services and broadcasting 5 minutes of news every hour and a half hour of international and national news in the afternoon. Thet network has at least one member station in Guayaquil, Cuenca, Poroviejo, Bahía de Caráquez, Latacunga and Ibarra.

The fourth major network, named Circuito HCMQ for its call letters, contains 17 members stations; its key station, the 1-kilowatt Atahualpa, is in Quito. It carries a well-balanced program and subscribes to the UPI news service.

The other networks are Cadena Católica, known as CC, with 16 stations; Emisoras CENIT, with 5 stations; and Azul y Blanco, with 4 stations.

Expansion in broadcasting was brought about largely by the importing of comparatively inexpensive receiving sets from Japan and an increase in local production. Since even the cheapest Japanese transistor set costs about S/200, many families must make a considerable financial sacrifice in order to buy one. Many of the sets are battery operated, independent of electric power outlets.

No license is required in order to own a radio receiver. In an attempt to combat the serious interference difficulties resulting from the excessive number of transmitters in Quito and Guayaquil, the government has required that all transmitting stations be moved outside of the city limits and has closed down a number of stations for noncompliance with this regulation.

TELEVISION

Ecuadorian television is in its infancy. The first station was established on a noncommercial basis by Vozandes in Quito. Early in 1964 there were reported to be 4,000 television receiving sets in the Quito area, with an estimated audience of 30,000. Primera Televisora Ecuatoriana set up a commercial television station, Channel 4, in Guayaquil, and in April 1964 the same company established Channel 6 in Quito. These two channels operate from 5:30 p.m. to 11:30 p.m. daily. By mid-1965 there were at least 40,000 television sets in the country, divided about equally between the Quito and Guayaquil areas.

Advertisements in the daily newspapers offer for sale a number of different makes of television receivers, such as National, Philco, RCA, Westinghouse, Admiral and Philips. Although the dealers advertize installment buying, the market for television sets is very restricted, since a high income is necessary even to pay the monthly installments, which range from S/195 to S/463.

FILMS

Motion pictures are an important recreational outlet. Prices range from a maximum of about S/15 for the best seats in the best theaters to S/2 or less for gallery seats in the smaller theaters. Even in the best theaters, gallery seats cost less than S/4. The films shown are almost entirely foreign imports; few if any commercial films are produced within the country. Between 450 and 500 films are imported yearly; most of them are from the United States, but a number come also from Mexico, Argentina and Europe. The newsreels, which are shown along with most feature pictures, are also almost entirely of foreign origin.

In 1963 there were 122 motion picture theaters, with a seating capacity of 91,000 or one seat for every 50 inhabitants. Quito had 14 theaters. Guayaquil had 30, with individual seating capacities of from 400 to 2,050 and a total capacity of 32,000.

During 1963 a total of 6,677,855 paid spectators was reported in Guayas Province, about 7 attendances per capita. In many small towns or villages films are shown each week in stores, schools or other available places. Such showings vary greatly in content and consist of USIS films, travelogues or old United States or Mexican films for which a very small charge is made. The showings in remote areas seem to have popular appeal regardless of their nature.

BOOK PUBLISHING

The volume of publication is small. The most important publisher is the government-subsidized Casa de la Cultura, which publishes about 50 books a year in editions varying from 2,000 to 3,500 copies, mostly in paperback, which are distributed by the Casa and by commercial bookstores. Most often, these small editions are sold out shortly after publication.

During the politically stable year of 1958 only 70 titles were published—40 by the Casa de la Cultura, 5 by Editorial Universitaria, 1 by Universidad Católica and 24 by all other houses. Except for those works published by the Casa de la Cultura, the authors must pay all costs of publication and advertising. For this reason the physical quality of books is not high, and in general the only advertising comes from reviews of the book in the literary columns of the newspapers. Book imports, which are not extensive, come chiefly from the United States (see ch. 10, Artistic and Intellectual Expression).

COMMUNIST PROPAGANDA

Until the government outlawed the PCE in July 1963, the Communist press proliferated. Even after diplomatic relations with Cuba and the Communist bloc were broken in April 1962, the Soviet news agency Tass, the New China News Agency and the Cuban Prensa Latina continued to function in the country until the military government took over. At that time all known Com-

314

munist newspapers and periodicals were closed, including *El Pueblo*, the official weekly newspaper of the PCE, published in Guayaquil; *Revolución*, a weekly published in Quito jointly by PCE and the left-wing Socialists; *Proletarios*, a monthly published in Guayaquil; *Voz Rebelde*, an irregular organ of the hard-line PCE; the extreme left-wing magazine, *Mañana*, published weekly in 2,500 copies in Quito; and the Quito newspaper of the left-wing Socialists, *La Tierra*, which had been distributing 2,000 copies daily.

Since then all of the Communist periodicals have continued to be published clandestinely and irregularly. In addition, new Communist organs have appeared. *Liberación*, a mimeographed theoretical magazine of the hard-line PCE, was started in June 1964; *La Chispa*, a newspaper of the soft-line PCE was established in Guayaquil in November 1964; and *Cuadernos Ideológicos*, another hard-line newspaper appeared. In addition, the PCE has made extensive use of inflammatory leaflets distributed in the streets of Guayaquil.

On the air, Radio Havana, an organ of Prensa Latina, Tass and the New China News Agency, all carry many news and propaganda programs for Latin America which can be clearly heard in Quito.

CHAPTER 17

ATTITUDES AND REACTIONS

Political awareness and a sense of effective participation in national life have been limited largely to members of the upper and middle classes and, more recently, the wage-earning lower class. The peasants, especially in the Sierra, have had little concern with any but local issues; their world consists of their minuscule plots of land, the local authorities who give them orders and the provincial capital (see ch. 6, Social Structure).

Members of the upper class, though aware of the political issues, have tended to remain aloof from most forms of active participation. Many have often been more interested in international events than in those in their own country. The issues of nationalism have held little appeal for them.

The most politically articulate segment of the population consists of the urban lower and middle classes, approximately one-third of the total. These are, in political terms, "the people." They are the people who vote and who can influence governments that are insufficiently responsive to their demands. They have played the major role in six of the eight changes of government during the past 25 years (the replacement of José María Velasco Ibarra by Colonel Carlos Mancheno in 1947 and the 1963 military coup being the exceptions), and it is to them that nearly all political speeches are addressed. It is to the middle class and the urban workers, moreover, that the strong and growing nationalist sentiments are most meaningful (see ch. 14, Political Dynamics).

This pattern has begun to change in recent years, although the evidences of change were only minimally apparent in 1965. The slow spread of literacy to the countryside and an increased level of communication between rural and urban areas have worked to bring the peasants into the national arena, at least marginally. They probably will soon link their hopes and frustrations with the activities of the central government.

Political leaders, churchmen, military men and other influential members of society have become increasingly aware of the potential importance of the rural masses. In the 1960 elections,

317

for example, candidate José María Velasco Ibarra felt constrained to extend his campaigning to a few of the more remote rural communities, a move with few precedents in the country's history. In the same spirit, there has been a growing recognition of the need for fundamental reforms, especially in the agrarian economy, and for the wider extension of educational and social services. In some degree, this concern can be attributed to pressures, at least incipient, from the politically awakening lower class. More importantly, however, it reflects a clear awareness by educated and influential Ecuadorians that a unified and effective nationhood can be achieved only on the basis of an active, informed and reasonably prosperous citizenry.

THE SOCIAL SETTING

Regionalism

Since colonial times Ecuador has been divided by a regionalism perhaps unsurpassed in intensity anywhere in the hemisphere. While the major division is between Sierra and Coast, there are intense rivalries within both of these regions which occasionally result in alignments of two or more cities from both regions against Quito, the mountain capital, or Guayaquil, the major port and center of commerce.

Quito's only rival for power in the Sierra is Cuenca, the major city of the southern highlands. This city is not in a position to entertain serious hopes of displacing Quito, either as the nation's capital or as the major highland city, but it is in a position to make its influence felt in national policy.

As the third largest city, with a history of prominence in national affairs dating back to colonial times, Cuenca has often cast a deciding vote in the frequent deadlocks between the two major cities, and whose power is about evenly matched. When conflicts have been cast in terms of the Conservative-Liberal dispute, Cuenca, as have most other highland cities, has often lined up solidly behind conservative Quito. When, on the other hand, there has been a question of central government interference against regional autonomy, Cuenca has more often supported Guayaquil.

Cuenca's displeasure with the national government has been a factor in many nonconstitutional changes in the office of chief executive. Velasco Ibarra's ouster in 1961 was precipitated partly by riots and a general strike in Cuenca, with which Guayaquil lost no time in declaring its sympathy. Similarly, Julio Carlos Arosemena Monroy's downfall in 1963 was related to the break with Cuba brought about by military pressure initiated by the command of the Cuenca garrison (see ch. 14, Political Dynamics).

318

On the Coast, Guayaquil similarly has no rival for preeminence as the dominant city of the region. People in other coastal towns, especially Esmeraldas, feel that their progress is held back largely because of policies consciously formulated to strengthen Guayaquil's dominance.

Ecuador's regionalism is greater in effect and intensity than that of any other nation in South America at least partly because it was one of the last countries to construct effective communications between major population centers. It was not until the twentieth century that a railroad connected the two major cities, and a road had been constructed only about three decades before the railroad.

Even more important, however, are racial and religious cleavages. Negro admixture is prominent in most people on the Coast, but almost entirely absent in the highlands, where Indian blood and cultural features predominate at the lower-class levels. While religion plays a dominant role in the lives of the Sierra people, it hardly touches the values and practices of those on the Coast (see ch. 5, Ethnic Groups and Languages).

The Sierra had been largely cut off from the rest of the world until the advent of air transportation, which became significant after World War II. Consequently, there developed a strong conservatism and resistance to change. Highlanders justify their disdain for the coastal population in terms of what they see as their own cultural superiority and possession of tradition, contrasted to the propensity to violence they believe prevalent on the Coast.

The coastal people, for their part, feel resentful at the dominance over their local affairs by a central government controlled by "backward" highlanders who are "living in another century" and are seen as exploiting the Coast, which produces nearly all export commodities and most government revenues. In the Sierra the country's glorious past and depth of national culture are emphasized, while on the Coast people want to break with the past and are always searching for new ideas, new fashions and new ways of doing things. Riots, revolutions and rebellions have originated or taken place most frequently on the Coast, perhaps partly because the government has always been located in the Sierra (see ch. 13, Constitution and Government; ch. 14, Political Dynamics).

Personalism, Leadership and Loyalty

At all levels of political functioning the effects of *personalismo* (the tendency to emphasize personal qualities and interpersonal trust over abstract ideas and civic loyalties) are clearly apparent. Followers are more easily rallied around specific men than around ideas and symbols. Thus, any attractive and forceful political leader is potentially the core of a new party or electoral alliance, and parties proliferate, splinter and recombine. Similarly, the strength of *personalismo* in government itself tends to create administrative inefficiency, for it is often difficult to maintain lines of authority, given a general reluctance of those with any power to follow the directives of others, and it is often equally difficult to establish effective cooperation between officials of equal rank (see ch. 12, Social Values; ch. 14, Political Dynamics).

In the arena of small and fragile political parties competition for leadership and power is fierce. The characteristic figure in this competition is the *caudillo* (the domineering, daring strongman—see Glossary), who has to possess outstanding character and personality traits; above all he has to be self-assertive and haughty. He also has to have broad enough recognition as a leader that his followers will not lose status for subjugating themselves to him. When such a leader shows weakness, indecisiveness or a streak of bad luck, he may lose half of his followers practically overnight.

For purposes of partisan politics most personalist leaders will give their group a name and a semblance of a political orientation. The next step is an effort to incorporate the largest possible number of similar groups by attempting to persuade other *caudillos* to subjugate themselves and their followers. Since other leaders are equally jealous of their personal power, no matter how small the group under their sway, such mergers are possible only when proposed by a man of exceptional forcefulness or attractiveness (see ch. 14, Political Dynamics).

In general, men follow only those who possess such unquestioned power or prestige that submission does not entail loss of status. From his own point of view, the follower draws satisfaction in proportion to the power wielded by the *caudillo* whom he follows. When such a leader emerges, his will usually prevails in any process of collective decision-making.

One practical consequence of such attitudes is the 1965 organizational chart of the government. Between 500 and 900 government agencies are "autonomous," partly because subordination of such agencies to one or another government department might make the agency head resign rather than obey orders given by the department in question. The organization chart puts many of the agencies under certain departments for organizational purposes but shows the connection only by dotted lines, explaining that they are under the personal authority of the chief executive and not the minister in question.

The tradition of personalism also affects the range and intensity of cooperation among members of such groups as political parties.

Without some sort of personal bond among members, even the strongest leader could fail to produce and maintain a high level of cohesion and effectiveness. The importance of widespread personal bonds is especially apparent in the case of the Conservative Party, which has been the largest and most durable, chiefly because nearly all its significant members are bound by the sentiments of class and kinship common to Sierra landowning families. The party's great voting strength is maintained also by the fact that most Sierra voters are employed by, or otherwise beholden to, the landowners (see ch. 14, Political Dynamics).

Such a political climate favors leaders who subordinate party programs to the establishment of personal bonds, real or symbolic, with the "man in the street." In general, they assume the role of *patrón* (trusted sponsor or protector—see Glossary) for those who have none.

GOVERNMENT AND NATION

Government, Law and the Constitution

The political powerlessness of the great mass of the people, the importance of personal loyalties and the difficulty of reconciling regionalist interests have had the effect of making efforts to overthrow the government seem a normal part of the political process. Most of the nation's heroes came to power through means other than electoral victory and constitutional processes. Those who used legitimate means have been assigned a minor role in history (see ch. 13, Constitution and Government). Part of the explanation is that past governments, in order to remain in power, had to pay political debts and pacify powerful potential rivals rather than devote themselves to improving the situation of the masses.

Many people have avoided paying taxes to governments which, they have felt, have done little for them. Consequently, taxes have usually been levied not so much on a basis of equity or economic rationale as on a basis of ease of collection; this system has caused almost the entire burden to fall on the very small middle class of merchants and white-collar workers. By 1965, however, an expanding base of political participation and a growing conviction that reforms are necessary justified the hope that a higher level of trust and identification could be established between the government and the people.

Knowledge of and attitudes toward the law differ greatly between the lower class and those of higher status and educational attainment. Among those who have completed more than the 6 years of primary education and especially those who have had some university training, the law and legal systems provide constant and engrossing topics of thought. Traditionally, the legal career has attracted the largest proportion of university students. Statesmen have commonly seen legal systems as both an expression of national aspirations and a tool for reform. At the same time there is a recognition that specific laws will be ignored, broken and selectively enforced as well as a conviction that no law, however well conceived, should be treated as an invariant constraint.

Members of the lower class, lacking the education to understand legal theory, judge the law by its practical effects on them. To them, laws appear to strengthen the advantage of the rich and powerful rather than help *la clase humilde* (the humble class). Moreover, they lack confidence in the persons who interpret and administer such laws (see ch. 14, Political Dynamics).

Nationhood and Nationalism

There is a profound and strongly expressed nationalist sentiment. Attachment to the national (*patria*) is felt by most politically aware Ecuadorians, illiterate and well-educated alike. Patriotism is widely expressed in popular culture as, for example, in love songs that present feminine beauty not only for its own sake but also as an expression of national pride.

There are many laws and public policies, especially in the area of education, to express and support the growth of national sentiment. By law, only Ecuadorian citizens may teach history and geography, and primers in elementary schools must contain a broad range of patriotic materials. In the same spirit martial parades of uniformed schoolchildren are an important part of holiday observances throughout the country.

Nationalism is focused overwhelmingly on the century-old boundary dispute with Peru. Few politicians dare fail to attack the 1942 Rio de Janeiro Protocol in their campaign speeches (see ch. 15, Foreign Relations). The cry "Viva el Ecuador" (Long live Ecuador) is customarily uttered at the end of the day by schoolchildren and soldiers. Radio stations punctuate their programing with the slogan "Ecuador has been, is and shall be an Amazonian country."

Ecuadorians feel strongly that they are at a disadvantage in the world markets; that at best they are overdependent on the industrialized nations, especially the United States; and that, more often than not, they are exploited by those nations. In recent years these attitudes have been expressed increasingly in drives to develop some measure of industrial self-sufficiency through the adoption of tariff barriers and tax concessions for the protection of national manufacturing enterprises (see ch. 20, Industry).

Nationalism is associated with a broad array of sensitivities, most of them centered upon questions of sovereignty. In pronouncements before international bodies and in political writings there is a continuing stress on the juridical equality of all nations. A slight to this equality, especially by a larger country, gives rise to strong resentments.

One of the most important sensitivities is any suggestion of foreign interference in domestic affairs. For a time the Alliance for Progress was widely attacked on this basis. Fidel Castro lost much of his appeal because of several actions that were considered to be either an affront to Ecuador's national dignity or interference in the country's internal affairs (see ch. 14, Political Dynamics).

Ecuadorians are aroused by any comment which could be interpreted as slighting any aspect of national power, especially the size, effectiveness or appearance of their armed forces. The symbolic association between a military uniform and national honor is very strong (see ch. 27, The Armed Forces).

In evaluating prominent figures of the immediate postindependence period, there is a tendency to stress the contributions of men born within what is now Ecuadorian territory over those of men born in what are now Colombia and Venezuela. Thus, for example, the first President of Ecuador, General Juan José Flores, born in Venezuela, is usually given less prominence in history books than his successor, Vicente Rocafuerte, whose impact on early national history was less significant but who was born in Ecuador.

Even though nationalism is an important factor in historical interpretation, it has been overshadowed, on occasion, by regionalist sentiment. The two men who had probably the greatest influence on the economic and political development of the country, Gabriel García Moreno and Eloy Alfaro, have never been unanimously accorded places as truly national figures. Persons from the Coast, anticlericals and Liberals, often criticize García Moreno, and Sierra inhabitants, especially Conservatives, adopt a similar attitude toward Alfaro.

OTHER PEOPLES AND COUNTRIES

The average urban Ecuadorian lumps most North Americans together with other English speakers as Anglo-Saxons, but considers those of German, Latin or other non-English ancestry in the light of their origins, even if remote. Anglo-Americans are thought to be highly capable in organization and technology, practical, friendly, generous and essentially democratic in spirit. They are also considered naive in dealing with Latin Americans, arrogant, materialistic and uninterested in Latin America.

Ecuadorians find Latins in general and Spanish speakers in particular to be proud, disdainful of work, stubborn, willful, courageous and emotional. Latin peoples are thought to lack "seriousness," persistence, reliability, a sense of teamwork and an aptitude for technical and scientific work. They are also seen as easygoing, dedicated to causes, sophisticated, socially graceful and fond of strong family ties.

Germans are thought to possess admirable, but not necessarily likeable, traits. They are thought to be hard working, highly disciplined, austere, efficient, scientifically and technologically the most capable and probably the most intelligent. They are also thought philosophical and romantic, studious, dedicated, strong, healthy, courageous and noble.

Nazi propaganda before and during World War II created a rather strong anti-Semitism. Jews are generally thought to be successful in business, shrewd, dishonest, frugal and avaricious, as well as of superior intelligence. As a means of distinguishing non-Jewish Germans from the significant German-Jewish minority residing in Quito, the former are referred to as *alemanes propios* (real Germans).

Arabs, also called *turcos* (Turks), are seen as typified by the large number of Lebanese and Syrian merchants in Guayaquil and other coastal cities. The stereotype of Arabs is similar to that of the Jews but somewhat less emphatic in both positive and negative aspects.

Among South Americans, Ecuadorians are most favorably disposed toward Colombians, Chileans and Brazilians. Ecuador has had the most commercial ties and a history of largely harmonious past relationships with Colombia. Chile has played a significant role in helping with Ecuador's military training, and together with Colombia, is looked upon as a strong potential ally against Peru. Brazil actively sought Ecuador's friendship for some time. Although Brazilians in Ecuador are both liked and respected, there remains some resentment against Brazil for its leading role in bringing about the Rio Protocol (see ch. 15, Foreign Relations).

Although attitudes toward the United States vary from class to class, the most clearly defined and significant aspect is resentment. Ecuadorians admire United States' achievements and emulate its fashion and living standards, but resent their own weak position in trading with the United States. They believe that the United States should guarantee a minimum price for Ecuador's products. While reasoning in such economic terms is typical only of educated Ecuadorians, many of these notions have been communicated to members of the lower class, principally by Communist and other leftist propaganda. Except in times of political upheaval, however, such attitudes toward the United States are seldom extended to individual United States citizens, who are usually well liked.

There has been a steady emigration of Ecuadorians to the

United States. Even many radical leftist student leaders would not turn down an opportunity to study in the United States. In one anti-United States riot such students expressed resentment at the difficulty of obtaining a scholarship to the United States.

The Alliance for Progress was in 1965 receiving a positive response from many middle- and lower-class Ecuadorians, perhaps because it has been identified with John F. Kennedy—considered practically a national hero in Ecuador—and because the "oligarchy" and wealthier members of the middle class are opposed to it.

Fidelismo, the ideological commitment to all of Fidel Castro's policies and statements, was very strong in Ecuador during 1960 and 1961. By 1965, however, the enthusiasm had paled largely because of the awareness that Cuba had become a Soviet satellite and because other aspects of the Cuban revolution were found repulsive (see ch. 14, Political Dynamics).

SYMBOLS OF THE NATION

The national flag in its present form was adopted in 1900. Together with the flags of Colombia and Venezuela, it is derived from that used by the early independence leader General Francisco de Miranda in 1806. Similar to the flags of the other two states of Gran Colombia, the basic design consists of three horizontal stripes of gold, blue and red (from top to bottom); the gold field is twice the width of the others.

In its basic form the flag has been in continuous use since its reintroduction by García Moreno in 1860. The modification of 1900, which applies only to official flags used by the national government, consisted of the addition of the coat of arms in the center of the flag, superimposed on all three fields. Municipal flags omit the coat of arms and substitute a circle of white stars at the center of the blue field equal in number to the number of provinces composing the republic (19 in 1965). Merchant ships and other nongovernment users are not permitted to include the coat of arms. Consequently, their flag is a simple tricolor identical to the national flag of Colombia.

The coat of arms, designed in 1900, consists of an oval shield containing a symbolic representation of Mount Chimborazo and the Guayas River, with a steamship in the foreground. The upper part of the shield contains the sun in the center of a golden arc representing a portion of the zodiac and containing symbols representing the months of March, April and June. The shield is flanked by four flags and has an open-winged condor above and a Roman fasces below. Protruding from the upper portion of the flag is a sheaf of laurel on one side and one of palms on the other.

The national anthem ("Himno Nacional") was composed in

1865 by Juan León Mera, a well-known Ecuadorian writer and poet, and was put to music by Antonio Neumane, a Corsican who was then residing in Guayaquil. It was last modified in 1948, when it was officially adopted by Congress. The anthem begins with the chorus:

Hail Fatherland, a thousand times!
Oh, Fatherland, glory to you!
Your breast overflows with joy and peace, and your radiant face delights us more than the sun.

There is no broad agreement as to the number of national holidays in Ecuador. Certain legal holidays are celebrated only regionally or by members of certain political parties. Others, usually religious celebrations, have always been observed nationwide as legal holidays but have never been accorded official recognition.

Principal among civic holidays recognized in legislation are: August 10, First Shout of Independence, in 1809 (the principal civic holiday of the Sierra); October 9, Independence of Guayaquil in 1820 (principal holiday on the Coast); November 3, Independence of Cuenca in 1821 (not considered important elsewhere); May 24, Battle of Pichincha of 1822 (less important on the Coast than in the Sierra); and July 24, Birth of Simón Bolívar, in 1783 (largely ignored). Other important national holidays are: May 1, Labor Day; October 12, Day of the Race (Columbus Day); and December 6, Founding of Quito, in 1563. Religious or semireligious holidays celebrated actively throughout the Sierra, and at least passively observed elsewhere are: January 6, Day of the Magi; two weeks preceding Lent, Carnival (celebrated by dousing each passer-by with water); the week preceding Easter, Holy Week; November 1, All Saints Day; November 2, Day of the Dead; November 21, Festival in Honor of the Virgin of Quinche; December 25, Christmas Day; and December 28-January 6, Innocents (equivalent of April Fool's Day elsewhere).

SECTION III.   ECONOMIC

CHAPTER 18

THE ECONOMIC SYSTEM

In 1965 the economy was based primarily on agriculture. Industrial capacity was limited, and mining, so important in the
other Andean countries, contributed little to the national income.
With respect to the rest of the world, the country was an exporter
of a narrow range of primary agricultural products and an importer of manufactured goods and capital. Basically, the economy was one of free enterprise.

The lofty Andean mountain range divides the country into
major regions that differ substantially in climate, topography and
natural resources. Agricultural resources are especially varied.
The Sierra is suitable for temperate zone crops and provides grazing land for livestock. The Coast can produce a wide range of
tropical crops and has extensive stands of virgin forest. Offshore
fishing grounds are among the richest in the world. The oilfields
in the Coast region constituted the most valuable mineral resource
known to be exploitable during the early 1960's, but because of
incomplete exploration, the full extent of the country's mineral
wealth was undetermined. Hydroelectric power potential, although little developed, was substantial, especially in the Sierra.
Relatively inaccessible, the Oriente region, with its tropical forests, was very thinly populated, and its economic potential was
unknown (see ch: 2, Physical Environment).

A distinctly regional pattern of economic development remained
evident during the early 1960's despite increasing interregional
communications and a general trend toward a more integrated
economy. The Sierra, which covers about one-quarter of the
country's territory, contained over half the total population, including most of the Indians. In terms of usable rural land this
region could be considered overpopulated compared with the rest
of the country. Land distribution was unequal, embracing extremes of both very large and very small landholdings. A large

body of landless tenants was a source of cheap labor. Farming methods were generally inefficient, and productivity was low by modern standards. Agriculture and industry in this region produced almost wholly for domestic consumption.

The Coast covers an area roughly equal to that of the Sierra; in the early 1960's the population was smaller, but the region was receiving a gradual flow of migrants from the Sierra in response to a shortage of labor and other economic opportunities. Guayaquil, which had more than half a million inhabitants, was the country's largest city, main commercial center and principal seaport. Many of the rural areas were sparsely populated and little developed. Sizable reserves of cultivable land belonged to the state, and there was little of the traditionalism that pervaded the agrarian structure of the Sierra.

The country does not suffer from any critical lack of natural resources, but their exploitation, despite recent advances, was hampered during the early 1960's by low capital accumulation, technology and productivity. Much of the population lived either at the margin of a subsistence economy or was engaged in producing primary agricultural commodities. The low real income of the great bulk of the people and the low overall purchasing power of the economy resulted in a restrictive domestic market, not conducive to balanced output growth. There was lack of an adequate supporting social base, such as housing, communications, health and educational facilities, upon which to build a stronger economy.

Committed to the Alliance for Progress, the administration in power in 1965 was attempting to accelerate the advances toward a higher general level of living achieved by the country since the early 1950's. The economy, as measured by the gross national product at current prices, had been growing at a sustained, if unspectacular, rate of between 4 and 5 percent per year. For 1964 the gross national product was estimated at S/18.58 billion (in 1965, S/18.5 equaled US$1—see Glossary). National income, or total net earnings in the production of goods and services, amounted to S/15.77 billion for 1964. More than one-third of this sum was derived from the agriculture, forestry and fisheries sector, which traditionally made the largest contribution to national income. The next largest contribution came from manufacturing, including handicrafts, which earned about one-sixth of the total (see table 6).

From time to time in the past the country's administrations sponsored legislation or special projects intended to expand and strengthen individual aspects of the economy, but the beginning of a coordinated approach aimed at comprehensive development dates only from the mid-1950's. The National Planning and Economic Coordination Board (Junta Nacional de Planificación y Co-

Activity	1963	[2]1964
Agriculture, forestry and fisheries	5,202	5,540
Mines and quarries	320	374
Manufacturing	2,409	2,690
Construction	526	642
Public utilities	181	221
Transportation and communications	609	654
Wholesale and retail trade	1,745	1,864
Banking and insurance	428	526
Real estate	931	978
Public administration and defense	914	965
Services	1,252	1,319
Total national income	14,517	15,773
Per capital national income	3,090	3,230

[1]The official selling rate for 1963–64 was S/18.18 equaled US$1; see Glossary.
[2]Provisional.

Source: Adapted from Banco Central del Ecuador, *Memoria del Gerente General: Correspondiente al Ejercicio de 1964.*

ordinación Económica) was established in 1954 to serve as the government's central advisory agency for policy and planning in economic matters. The Board acted as a clearinghouse for economic surveys and studies, prepared special plans and coordinated foreign aid at the planning level. In 1960 it produced an overall 2-year economic development plan for 1961–62. Because of lack of full government support, the plan was not very successful.

By subscribing to the 1961 Charter of Punta del Este, Ecuador joined the United States and 18 other Western Hemisphere countries in the Alliance for Progress. The Charter is a broad multilateral agreement to take steps to accelerate economic and social development in the subscribing nations. The action is to proceed on the basis of mutual assistance and individual self-help. The social goals are stressed. The Charter and associated resolutions established a general program, overall objectives of a more detailed nature and an institutional structure for promoting, coordinating and carrying out the various tasks of development. The program envisages a total investment target over a period of 10 years of $20 billion, at least half of which is to be furnished by the United States. Participants receiving aid agreed, among other things, to formulate and follow comprehensive development plans which would include measures aimed at social betterment and the strengthening of democratic institutions.

Most development projects in Ecuador since adoption of the

Charter of Punta del Este have been within the framework of the Alliance for Progress. The reform-minded regime that came to power in 1963 espoused economic and social policies in keeping with the principles defined in the Charter. In 1964 the government adopted the 10-year General Plan for the Economic and Social Development of Ecuador (1964–73).

The Plan covers all segments of the economy and is based on the general principle that the private sector is primarily responsible for developing production activities, such as agriculture, industry and mining, whereas the public sector will concentrate on infrastructure and remove institutional obstacles. Direct investment by government in productive enterprises is to be limited to strategic or crucial projects.

Under the Plan the general objective is to sustain a yearly growth rate in the gross national product of 3.3 percent per capita over the 10-year period. This would be brought about by gross investment totaling S/45 billion, which is about 2½ times the investment accomplished during the preceding 10 years. About 57 percent of the total would represent private financing. The Plan anticipates that the equivalent of about $600 million would have to come from external sources. Manufacturing, including handicrafts, was estimated to require the largest single share of total investment—about 19 percent (see table 7).

Table 7. Planned Allocation of Total Investment According to the 10-Year Development Plan of Ecuador, 1964–73
(in millions of sucres)*

Activity	Value	Percent
Agriculture, forestry and fisheries	6,905	15.2
Mining and petroleum	631	1.4
Manufacturing	8,780	19.3
Power, water supply and sanitation	4,708	10.3
Transport, storage and communications	7,000	15.4
Buildings	8,015	17.6
Construction and miscellaneous	9,519	20.8
Total	45,558	100.0

*In 1965, S/18.5 equaled US$1—see Glossary.

Source: Adapted from Ecuador, Junta Nacional de Planificación y Coordinación Económica, *Resumen del Plan General de Desarrollo Económico y Social del Ecuador, 1963.*

Late 1965 projections indicated that the rate of growth of the gross national product for 1965 and possibly for 1966 would fall somewhat below the 4.8 percent rate for 1964. However, substantial progress in industrial expansion, housing construction and work on the transportation system was reported. The consultative group formed by the Inter-American Development Bank (IDB) to assist Ecuador with external financing had been very successful in arranging for long-term credits, but there was a sizable backlog of undisbursed loans resulting from bottlenecks in the development mechanism. That the bottlenecks were being broken and the economy's capacity to make use of external financial resources was growing was indicated by the fact that disbursements of external loans rose from the equivalent of $12 million in 1964 to $20 million in 1965.

Agriculture provided almost all of the country's exports during the early 1960's. The amounts earned from export crops determined both domestic purchasing power and the country's capacity to import the goods it needed. These earnings thus had great influence on the course of development of all sectors of the economy. Except for a remarkable boom in the production of bananas for export, agricultural production after the mid-1950's lagged behind the overall economy in rate of annual growth. Export earnings were dangerously dependent on uncertain prices in the world market for a very few commodities. Production for domestic consumption was scarcely keeping pace with population growth. To overcome these disadvantages the General Plan for the Economic and Social Development of Ecuador aimed at diversifying production for export and strengthening the domestic food consumption sector.

Because of the magnitude of the banana trade, the country had virtually a one-crop economy during the early 1960's. Bananas were by far the most important cash crop and, with coffee and cacao, brought in well over three-fourths of all export earnings. Other commodities ordinarily exportable but of less value were rice, sugar, pineapples and citrus fruit.

The Plan stresses attainment of self-sufficiency in food production and has a goal of raising the rather low caloric level of the average diet at the same time. During the early 1960's the country was raising enough fruits, vegetables and livestock for its own use and produced sufficient foodgrains, except wheat and oats. Production of dairy products and edible oils failed to satisfy domestic demand, and supplementary imports were necessary. The catch from the country's rich fishing grounds was increasing substantially, but an inadequate distribution system and market prevented full use of this source of food and diverted the greater part into export channels (see ch. 8, Living Conditions; ch. 19, Agriculture).

Industrial crops were not of much importance during the early 1960's. Production of pyrethrum for both domestic use and export was expanding, and in 1965 Ecuador was the third largest producer in the world, surpassed only by Kenya and Tanzania. With the exception of pyrethrum, the export commodities were all products of the Coast (see ch. 24, Foreign Economic Relations). Some short-staple cotton was planted to supply the domestic textile industry. Small-scale development of rubber plantations, still in the early stages, was intended eventually to provide a domestic source of raw material for a number of factories making rubber products. Endowed with extensive forests, the country produced enough lumber for its own use and exploited a number of forest products for export. It was the world's leading producer of balsa wood and tagua palm (source of vegetable ivory) and exported a number of other forest products, such as kapok and chinchona bark, on a minor scale. Straw from the toquilla, or jipijapa, palm was the basis for the Panama hat industry (see ch. 20, Industry).

The government was committed to reforming the country's agrarian structure and institutions. Agrarian reform was a prominent feature of the 10-year Plan, but the program was only beginning to have effect in 1965. Its object embraced both economic and social betterment. The process involved breaking up the very large or unproductive estates by expropriation and redistributing the land to landless country people in family-sized farms or to cooperatives. Very small holdings were to be consolidated into plots of economically viable size. Compensation for expropriation was provided for in the form of government bonds.

The reform also included measures to protect the interests and enhance the status of farm laborers and tenants. Closely related to land redistribution was a colonization scheme which opened up additional new farm acreage by grants of unimproved public land and gave legal title and other assistance to squatters already occupying holdings in various parts of the country (see ch. 19, Agriculture).

Industrial development has been a major economic aim in the country since World War II. The administration that took office in 1963 showed great interest in industrial expansion and strengthened the existing programs of benefits and incentives designed to attract new enterprises and general industrial investment. Since the policy in 1965 was to look upon industrialization in the manufacturing and extractive sectors as primarily a matter for private enterprise, the role of government was to establish and maintain a favorable investment climate that would attract foreign as well as domestic capital. Direct industrial operations by the state were largely confined to public utilities and transportation facilities (see ch. 20, Industry).

In 1965 the government's principal agency for promoting industrial growth was the Development Center (Centro de Desarrollo—CENDES), which made feasibility studies, pinpointed specific investment needs and opportunities and furnished technical aid to private enterprises. The industrial development laws were instruments for influencing the structure and direction of industrial expansion by conferring tax and other benefits on enterprises that were of special importance under the 10-year Plan. Import policy was designed to stimulate industry through customs duty concessions or exonerations and through protection against foreign competition (see ch. 24, Foreign Economic Relations).

The manufacturing establishment during the early 1960's consisted almost wholly of light industries producing staple consumer goods. Plants ranged from factories well-equipped according to modern standards to very small handicraft and artisan establishments or home workshops that disposed of little fixed capital. Handicraft enterprises provided a livelihood for the great bulk of the manufacturing labor force, although at a generally low level of income, since the productivity of artisans was far less than that of factory workers. To increase output and raise income levels, the government was encouraging handicraft shops to convert to modern factory methods by offering financial inducements under the 1965 Law for the Development of Artisan and Small Industry.

During the early 1960's food processing was the leading manufacturing activity, but plants were also producing a considerable variety of other consumer goods, such as textiles, wearing apparel, leather, plastic and rubber fabrications, drugs, fertilizers and wood and metal products. Production was becoming more diversified, and among the new enterprises being established in 1965 were plants to make paper products, a bus body assembly plant and a household appliance factory. Practically all the manufactures were for domestic consumption.

Manufacturing plants tended to cluster around the country's two main population and marketing centers—Guayaquil and Quito. Because of manpower implications and the urban problems caused by these industrial concentrations, a policy to encourage decentralization of new enterprises was adopted. This policy, with the assistance of improved transportation facilities, was resulting in a more balanced spread of manufacturing through the country and a somewhat wider marketing pattern.

Petroleum from the Santa Elena Peninsula oilfields was the only domestic mineral product of much importance during the early 1960's. The crude oil was refined in the country, and output was nearly sufficient to meet the needs of the economy. Increasing domestic consumption and continuing depletion of reserves made it important to discover new fields and bring them into production. Otherwise, there would be mounting expenditures of foreign exchange for essential petroleum products. In 1965 several foreign-owned companies were engaged in exploration in the Oriente region. The heavy foreign exchange expenditures required to provide the producer goods and capital equipment needed for development underlined the importance of determining and exploiting all domestic sources of raw materials and power for basic industries.

In terms of numbers there was no lack of human resources to support industrial development. In fact, one of the important problems confronting the economy was to provide enough new job openings for the growing population. Many skilled craftsmen were engaged in handicraft work, such as weaving Panama hats, but workers trained in modern manufacturing skills and technology were in short supply. There was also a shortage of managerial skills, and productivity sometimes suffered because of failure to take advantage of new techniques. Because of a lack of reliable statistics, the number of workers belonging to unions cannot be given with any accuracy. In 1965, however, organized labor represented only a small fraction of the labor force, and the labor movement as a whole was not very effective (see ch. 4, Population and Labor Force; ch. 21, Labor Relations and Organization).

An inadequate highway network retarded the country's development for many years and was still a major structural weakness in the economy during the early 1960's. Difficulty of travel within the country prevented the growth of an integrated national economy and brought into being a pattern of regional economic activity that made for a restricted national market. The economy was denied much benefit from the possibilities for domestic trade offered by the complementary nature of the natural resources of the Sierra and the Coast. A great part of the rural population lived virtually isolated in their local areas, and many were outside the cash economy for most practical purposes.

The need for a better transportation network led to a drive for improvements after World War II. During the early 1960's construction of new roads and improvement of the existing system comprised one of the government's principal public works programs. Emphasis was on trunk roads that would give access to undeveloped areas and on additional highway links between the Sierra and the Coast.

The important role assigned the road program is indicated by the fact that one-fourth of all government development investment was earmarked for highways in the 10-year Plan. Some 750 miles of road were under construction in late 1965. Much of the work in progress or planned for the near future had been financed by the International Bank for Reconstruction and Development (IBRD) or by other foreign sources (see ch. 24, Foreign Economic Relations).

To obtain external financing for economic and social development projects was a major objective of the country's foreign economic policy in 1965. The country was assisted by the IDB, which acted as Ecuador's fiscal agent for development financing. The IDB was advised by the specially organized Consultative Group on External Financing for Ecuador, made up of representatives from 18 of the more developed countries and from 11 multilateral financial institutions. Its functions were to assess funding and technical aid requirements and find sources of credit for approved projects. Nearly all official loans, other than those from the United States, came from multilateral sources, such as the IBRD, in which Ecuador held membership. The United States, in addition to extending credit indirectly through subscriptions to the multilateral institutions, furnished bilateral financing, on either a loan or grant basis, through the Agency for International Development (AID) and the Export-Import Bank of Washington.

The country's import policy, long concerned primarily with producing government revenue, was substantially changed in 1962 in an effort to stimulate industrial and agricultural development. A new customs tariff retained revenue features, but import incentives and protective functions were added. Duties on imports of capital and producer goods of special importance to the economy were reduced or eliminated, and rates were raised on foreign-made products that might compete with local goods. Nontariff controls were also applied for protective purposes and to conserve foreign exchange for essential development expenditures abroad. Import controls included licensing and other documentation, exchange controls, prior deposits and some prohibitions (see ch. 24, Foreign Economic Relations).

The country was basically committed to a policy of multilateral trade and payments in the early 1960's, but it also espoused special arrangements for regional economic integration and trade through the Latin American Free Trade Association (LAFTA). The members of the association (Ecuador, Argentina, Brazil, Chile, Colombia, Mexico, Paraguay, Peru and Uruguay) were joined in a basic agreement to progressively eliminate artificial barriers to trade among themselves, to work for a common consumer market and to stimulate regional development on a coordinated basis. There was no common external tariff. Ecuador was granted special tariff-cutting exemptions and preferential trade treatment by the other LAFTA countries.

The country enjoyed consistently favorable merchandise trade balances from 1950 to 1964, when there was a small deficit. Roughly half of both the import and the export trade was with the United States. During the early 1960's a number of other countries were increasing their share of trade at the expense of the United States. Trade with the other LAFTA countries, however, amounted to less than one-tenth the value of Ecuador's total trade (see ch. 24, Foreign Economic Relations).

In contrast to the favorable balances on merchandise trade the country generally incurred large deficits for services, including heavy profit remittances to foreign investors, which resulted in the balance of payments current account ordinarily showing a deficit. The country was able to offset this condition by attracting an inflow of capital from foreign private and official sources. The economy was suffering some loss of foreign exchange reserves in 1964 and 1965, but there was nothing to indicate whether this would become a long-term trend.

The combined annual expenditures of central and local government increased substantially between 1950 and 1965, both in absolute terms and in comparison to the increase in gross national product. By the early 1960's government expenditure represented about one-fourth of the gross national product. Consequently, government decisions regarding allocations of expenditures greatly influenced patterns of economic activity. The gross expenditure provided a significant stimulus to the economy as a whole. This, together with sizable inflows of foreign investment funds, caused inflationary pressures. Well-calculated monetary policy, however, succeeded in maintaining a sound national currency, and in 1965 there was no serious problem of inflation.

Between 1960 and 1965 all of the central government's annual operations budgets showed deficits, resulting partly from administrative deficiencies, many of which were imposed by outmoded legal requirements. Furthermore, the highly decentralized collection and disbursement of public funds made for inefficiency and uneconomical use of funds. Of more importance, however, was the fact that the revenue system was weak and structurally ill suited to provide the resources the government needed to meet the increasing requirements of economic and social betterment. Recognition of these conditions led to studies which were the basis of a number of fiscal reforms put into effect in 1964 and 1965. The reforms included administrative measures and changes in the tax system aimed at consolidating various kinds of taxes, simplifying the process of collection, achieving greater tax equity and increasing the tax revenue. How successful these reforms would be was not apparent in 1965 (see ch. 23, Fiscal and Monetary System).

CHAPTER 19

AGRICULTURE

Agriculture has been the lifeblood of Ecuador since pre-Inca days. The Spanish conquerors found an agricultural Indian people concentrated in the intermont plateaus and valleys of the Sierra. Present-day society continues to be fundamentally rural and agricultural; production has expanded from the Sierra to the Coast and, to some extent, to the Oriente. The continuing significance of agriculture is illustrated by the fact that the major part of the national income and employment stems directly or indirectly from it.

Agriculture, livestock raising, forestry and fishing provided a livelihood for 56.5 percent of the economically active population in 1962, generated 37.3 percent of the gross domestic product and accounted for 93 percent of the value of all exports. Indirectly, agriculture makes an additional contribution to the national product and to employment in such manufacturing branches as processing of food and beverages, which account for 55 percent of the value of manufactured products and employ a large segment of the industrial labor force.

As a result of historic geographic, climatic and ethnic differences, the Sierra and the Coast, which are the major producing areas, have developed distinctive patterns of crops, land tenure and labor practice.

Indians have long lived in relatively dense populations in the Sierra, where the Spanish conquerors also settled. The high altitude encouraged the cultivation of temperate climate crops and fruits. Indian and white farmers alike produce food crops for domestic consumption, but on plots of ground that exhibit great contrasts in size and location. The major part of the most productive and accessible land is concentrated in *haciendas* (large estates) in the hands of a few *hacendados* (landowners), many of whom are absentee.

Cultivation on the Sierra *hacienda* is directed by an overseer, usually a *mestizo*. Labor is provided by native Indians under a serf-like system by which the *huasipunguero* (laborer—see Glossary), is granted the use of a small plot of land called a *huasipungo*, and certain privileges, such as water, firewood and pasturage, in return for virtually unremunerated labor on the estate. In contrast to the *hacendado*, the Indian landowner farms a plot which has been reduced in size through generations of inheritance division until it is too small to support a family comfortably and which, moreover, contains the least productive land and is most unfavorably situated. The Indian farmer sells his small surplus in the local market, but essentially lives outside the money economy.

Methods of cultivation in the Sierra do not differ significantly between large and small landholdings and in many instances have not greatly advanced beyond those in use at the time of the conquest. The small Indian farmer cultivated all of his land, which has become unproductive through centuries of use, whereas the estate owner left a considerable part of his land unused. In neither instance have modern methods been adopted to any marked degree.

Geography and population size have been important factors in the failure to develop a market economy and progressive methods of cultivation in the Sierra. The rugged character of the Andean terrain has contributed to the growth of self-sufficient communities, cut off from the rest of the highlands and from the outside land and not exposed to new and changing ways of life and production. Isolation has limited the marketing area and perpetuated subsistence agriculture. Furthermore, the abundance of cheap labor, which stems from a high rate of population increase, has discouraged modernization on the large estates.

In spite of the hardness of his life, the Sierra Indian is deeply attached to the land, whether it be his own or the plot assigned to him by an estate owner. Lack of contact with outside influences has further served to intensify his loyalty to long-established methods of cultivation and ways of life.

On the Coast, population centers and agricultural production developed much later than in the Sierra. Epidemics of malaria and other tropical diseases delayed development until better sanitation and health measures made the area safe for settlement. Around 1930, Guayaquil was declared a safe port, and development has been rapid since then (see ch. 8, Living Conditions). Tropical crops flourish on the coast, and proximity to ocean transportation has channeled coastal agriculture toward production for export trade and a market-oriented economy.

Both large and small landholdings exist in the coastal region, and contrasts in tenure are much less sharp than in the Sierra, given the lower density of population and the availability of new land which can be cleared and brought into production when roads are constructed. New units which have been carved out of virgin land tend to be of medium size. Large estates are devoted to commercial agriculture, and even the owner of the *minifundio* (small landholding—see Glossary) produces for the market.

Agricultural labor is in greater demand on the Coast than in the Sierra, where it is in excess supply. Workers, who may be either resident or temporary, are paid in cash, enjoy an independence unknown to their counterparts in the Sierra and are not fettered by devotion to a particular area or piece of land.

The Oriente, which in the past has been cut off from both the Coast and the Sierra by mountains and by lack of roads, is only beginning to open to settlement and agriculture. Little can be said about the patterns that may develop there in the future.

During most of the period between 1950 and 1963, agricultural production lagged behind the national economy in rate of annual increase. Although there has been a sharp rise since 1955, the increase has been accounted for almost entirely by the banana boom, and domestic production has not been sufficient to outpace population growth significantly. Most people suffer from dietary deficiencies, the elimination of which is a basic goal of the agricultural development plan. Food imports, principally wheat, edible oils and dairy products, are relatively small, but as a percentage of the total they increased from 1.8 percent in 1957 to 7.3 percent in 1962.

The unprogressive state of the agricultural sector is commonly ascribed to a highly adverse pattern of land and labor use, technical backwardness and lack of investment in agriculture. A lack of roads, storage and distribution facilities, illiteracy and cultural dissimilarities also present obstacles to progress (see ch. 9, Education; ch. 22, Domestic Trade).

In 1961 it was estimated that only 27 percent of total fixed investment had been channeled to agriculture. Per capita investment of S/11,800 (in 1961 about S/20.20 equaled US$1—see Glossary) was the lowest of all economic sectors, in contrast to S/18,000 in industry and S/53,000 in all other sectors. Investments are larger in export installations, resulting in an output per worker about triple that generated in domestic crop farming. Despite the relative advantage, the productivity of export crops lags behind that of nearby countries.

In spite of the many and obvious handicaps to efficient and adequite production, there are also dynamic elements. In contrast to many other countries, where arable land constitutes a small part of the total surface and where additional usable land is almost nonexistent, large expanses of potentially productive land on the Coast and in the Oriente are state owned and can be brought into use. Although relatively little new good land can be brought into production in the Sierra and much of the land has been worn by constant cropping and lack of care, more land on existing *haciendas* can be farmed, and studies have indicated that yields can be greatly increased through irrigation, the use of fertilizers and fungicides, and better seeds and plant strains.

Acceleration of highway construction is increasing the feasibility of opening up new lands, and the elimination of landholding inequities and unjust labor practices is a goal of the Agrarian Reform and Colonization Law, passed in July 1964. In 1965 the strongest emphasis in actual implementation was placed on colonization, but elimination of exploitative labor practices reportedly had also begun.

In the General Plan for the Economic and Social Development of Ecuador, agriculture is accorded a dominant place. An average annual growth of output of 7 percent and an increased yield per unit of land of almost 50 percent are envisioned for the 1964–73 decade. To achieve this goal, total expenditures of S/3.1 billion by the public sector and S/4.4 billion by the private sector are projected. Supporting projects in roadbuilding, irrigation, technical assistance and education are also programed (see ch. 18, The Economic System).

Past plans have been limited in effectiveness by the magnitude of the need, a lack of integrated planning, inadequate resources and discontinuities in government policies. If the proposed integrated 10-year plan can be carried to a successful conclusion, a dynamic agriculture which could contribute to higher levels of national prosperity may be the result. However, achievement of the overall goal is heavily dependent upon the success of many sectoral goals, such as those projected for infrastructure, education and domestic savings. Success will also require a degree of cooperation among the diverse elements of society and a continuity and consistency of governmental policy difficult to achieve.

LAND USE

Since topography, comprised of steep mountain ranges and almost impenetrable tropical jungles, has presented a formidable obstacle to accurate analysis of land area and use, figures—which are conflicting at best—must be considered approximate and should be taken only to indicate ranges of magnitude. To overcome the lack of basic knowledge, the Military Geographic Institute, with the cooperation of the Inter-American Geodetic Service and the United States Air Force, is conducting a complete survey of land area and resources.

The government conducted an agricultural census in 1962, and the National Board of Economic Planning and Cooperation has undertaken the classification of actual and potential land use, as well as classification by size of landholding and land tenure. As of mid-1965, such studies were either still in progress or only partial results had been established, and until their completion information concerning land use and land tenure must be based upon data developed in the Agricultural Census of 1954 with appropriate recognition of the general direction of change since that time.

In 1954 it was estimated that approximately 5.1 million acres were cultivated, 3 million acres were in natural pasture, and 2.8 million acres in forests and underbrush in the two major agricultural regions, Sierra and Coast.

In the Sierra, according to the Agricultural Census of 1954, there were 2.1 million acres planted to crops, 2.3 million acres of natural pastureland, and 1.1 million acres in forest and underbrush in 1954. Since that time the proportion of croplands to pastures has increased.

In the intermont basins land use, which is determined largely by altitude, rainfall and soil composition, covers a wide variety of domestic crops, ranging from potatoes and barley in the higher and colder areas through wheat, corn and vegetables at a lower and warmer level to sugarcane and cotton in the valleys.

Among the more productive areas are the southern part of the basin of Quito and the basin of Cuenca, where the soil is better than in most and rainfall is plentiful. The southernmost basins of Oña, Loja and Zaruma, which lie along streams, are also fertile and support a variety of crops. Among the less fertile areas are those around Latacunga, Ambato and Riobamba which are handicapped by dry and porous soil.

The high grasslands, known as *páramos,* are used for grazing as well as for cold-weather crops. In particular, the southern highlands support large herds of cattle. Such forest cover as exists is necessary for the protection of soil and water.

On the Coast the census estimated that there were 3 million acres under crop cultivation; 740,000 acres in natural pastures, and 1.7 million acres in forest and underbrush. Since 1954 the establishment of new banana plantations has increased the land under cultivation by clearing areas of government-owned virgin forests, particularly in the province of Esmeraldas.

Land is fertile, with the exception of the desert area of the Santa Elena Peninsula, and, in contrast to the Sierra, is devoted to export and commercial crops, such as bananas, cacao, coffee, rice, sugarcane and cotton. The alluvial fans of the Guayas River basin are particularly productive (see ch. 2, Physical Environment).

LAND TENURE

Patterns of land tenure exhibit great contrasts, which are not only regional but also intraregional. Statistics compiled for the promulgation of the General Plan for the Economic and Social Development of Ecuador, presented in 1963 to the Inter-American Committee of the Alliance for Progress (known as CIAP—see Glossary), indicate a very uneven distribution of land and a high concentration in the hands of a few proprietors. According to those figures, there were about 250,000 agricultural holdings of less than 12 acres, constituting 73 percent of all farms but accounting for only 7 percent of the land in use. At the other extreme, there were approximately 1,300 holdings of 1,200 acres and over, constituting about 0.4 percent of all farms, but covering 45 percent of the land (see table 8).

Table 8. Distribution of Land in Ecuador, 1963

Size (in acres)	Number of holdings	Percent of total holdings	Area*	Percent of total area
Less than 12.4	251,686	73.1	1,068	7.2
12.4–49.2	57,650	16.7	1,398	9.4
49.2–247.0	27,742	8.1	2,813	19.0
247.0–1,235.0	5,787	1.7	2,856	19.3
More than 1,235.0	1,369	0.4	6,686	45.1

*In thousands of acres.

Source: Adapted from Alianza para el Progreso, Comité de los Nueve, *Evaluación del Plan General de Desarrollo Económico y Social del Ecuador, table 1–5, p. 52.*

In the Sierra in 1954 approximately 235,000 *campesinos* (peasants), mostly Indians, cultivated landholdings which were smaller than 25 acres each. These small farms, which comprised 90 percent of all agricultural units and 16 percent of the lands reported to be in agricultural use, accounted for more than 45 percent of the land actually under cultivation. At the other extreme, 389 large estates, each containing 2,500 or more acres, which comprised less than one-tenth of 1 percent of farm units by number, owned 41 percent of the reported agricultural lands, but accounted for only 10 percent of the cultivated area. Much of the land on the large *haciendas* lies completely idle. In the intermediate group, 7 percent of landholdings were in the range from 25 to 125 acres, whereas only 1 percent were in the group from 125 to 250 acres (see table 9). In addition, it is estimated that about 2 percent of the total Sierra lands under cultivation are communally held, chiefly by Indian villages.

Table 9. Size, Number and Area of Agricultural Properties in the Sierran and Coastal Regions of Ecuador, 1954

Size of properties (in acres)	Number of Properties	Percent of total	Area contained*	Percent of total area contained	Area cultivated*	Percent of total area cultivated
SIERRA						
Less than 24.7	234,569	90.3	1,226.0	16.4	961.6	46.0
24.7–123.5	18,292	7.0	894.0	12.0	396.0	18.9
123.5–247.0	3,594	1.4	540.0	7.3	157.0	7.5
247.0–1,235.0	2,368	0.9	1,163.6	15.6	281.0	13.4
1,235.0–2,470.0	330	} 0.4	563.9	7.7	97.6	4.7
More than 2,470.0	389		3,072.0	41.0	199.0	9.5
Total Sierra	259,542	100.0	7,459.5	100.0	2,092.2	100.0
COAST						
Less than 24.7	53,340	63.0	512.0	7.0	416.0	13.7
24.7–123.5	22,523	26.6	1,293.8	17.6	784.7	25.8
123.5–247.0	4,733	5.6	811.0	11.0	384.0	12.6
247.0–1,235.0	3,419	4.0	1,692.0	23.0	685.7	22.6
1,235.0–2,470.0	334	} 0.8	583.9	7.9	205.8	6.8
More than 2,470.0	316		2,465.0	33.5	563.0	18.5
Total Coast	84,665	100.0	7,357.7	100.0	3,039.2	100.0

*In thousands of acres.

Source: Adapted from U.S. Department of Commerce, *Investment in Ecuador*, 1954, p. 34.

A number of factors have entered into the perpetuation of the *hacienda* system as a way of life. The importance of stockraising in some areas, leading to the accumulation of large acreages in pasture, and the ready availability of cheap labor have encouraged the development of large estates. Furthermore, the possession of an *hacienda* confers social distinction upon the owner. On the other hand, the limited land remaining, the growth of population and the attachment of the Indian to the Sierra have resulted in a proliferation of fragmented holdings.

Campesinos who cultivate for family use land to which they do not hold title are mostly *huasipungueros,* who give labor service to the estate owner for the privilege of tilling the land, water rights, pasturage and use of access roads. Legally, the *huasipunguero* is to be paid a minimum wage for his labor, but this convention has seldom been observed. There are also sharecroppers who hold small parcels of land from large landowners. The sharecropper provides his own seeds and tools and pays for the use of the land with a portion of the crop raised. Relatively few *campesinos* in the Sierra rent land for a fixed payment.

On the Coast, according to the Agricultural Census of 1954, slightly more than 53,000 small farmers, mostly of mixed race, cultivated landholdings of less than 25 acres. These small farms constituted 63 percent of all agricultural landholdings on the Coast, 7 percent of the land area used for agriculture and approximately 14 percent of the land actually under cultivation. Plots of medium size were more prevalent on the Coast than in the Sierra. Slightly more than 25 percent of all exploitations fell in the 25- to 125-acre range and accounted for 25 percent of the land actually under cultivation. Since 1954 the rapid growth of banana cultivation has increased the number of farms ranging between 25 and 250 acres.

Among those who cultivate land belonging to another person commercial production has encouraged tenancy for fixed rent. Although sharecropping exists, it occupies a minor position, and the *huasipungo* system does not exist on the Coast.

PATTERNS OF CULTIVATION

Although patterns of cultivation vary from archaic to modern, there is no well-defined line of demarcation between geographic areas, export and domestic agriculture, size of landholding or different crops. Both modern methods and ancient practices may be found within each category.

In the main, farmers in the Sierra have tended to resist change, and there is relatively little difference between methods used on the large *hacienda* and on the small farm. Crop production, which is varied on both large estate and subsistence plot, is carried on by primitive methods which have scarcely changed in centuries. In some places the ox-drawn Mediterranean plow introduced by the early Spaniards is used. On steep hillsides sometimes a digging stick suffices for cultivation, but the most universally employed instrument used by the Indian *campesino* is an *azadón*, a hoe with a large blade and a sturdy ax-like handle. On the *hacienda* the resident *mestizo* overseer, who is rarely trained in agronomy, favors traditional methods of cultivation, and the abundant labor militates against mechanization. The *campesino* has neither the knowledge nor the financial resources to adopt new techniques, and mechanization would be out of the question on steep and small hillside plots.

The need for positive conservation practices in the Sierra is critical. Mountain streams have cut deep gorges in the loose and porous volcanic soil and created a serious problem of erosion which has been exacerbated by the age-old practice of destroying ground cover to increase the cultivated area. Rainfall is deficient, and irrigation is inadequate.

Fertility of the soil has been further diminished by constant cropping, failure to rotate crops and the inability to permit a field to lie fallow. Traditionally, animal fertilizer has been the only type used, and even this, according to qualified observers, has been inefficiently used.

In spite of the overall unsatisfactory agricultural practices, there are exceptions within the Sierra. There are a few large estates devoted to the efficient production of a single crop where fertilizers and insecticides are used; fertility is renewed by planting legumes; and machinery is used for cultivation and harvesting. Even some smaller landholders have adopted better methods through the assistance of agricultural extension agents. Yields of crops grown in the Sierra are low, but their increase since 1950 bears witness to an upward trend in techniques, inadequate though it may be.

On the Coast, with the exception of small garden plots where food for the owner or for permanent workers is grown, all land is devoted to the production of commercial crops, mainly for export. On the majority of small or medium-sized farms and even on some large plantations, production has been diverse rather than specialized. New medium-sized exploitations tend to be monocultural, concentrating on banana cultivation.

Whereas scarcity of additional land for the small farmer has led to overcropping and exhausted soil in the Sierra, abundance has led to prodigal use and neglect of land on the Coast. New exploitations which have been hacked out of government-owned coastal forests by the traditional slash-and-burn method were initially productive, but the soil of tropical forests is highly unstable, and fertility is easily lost through rain leaching. In an assessment of land quality one agronomist estimated that there is practically no virgin land in the country which does not require fertilizer to maintain natural productive capacity. Fertility is further threatened by lack of drainage of the flood plains of the Guayas River basin, which has resulted in increased salinization of the land.

Although the use of fertilizer has been more prevalent on the Coast than in the Sierra, it has been limited to a certain extent to the larger enterprises. Since the small supply of guano has been exhausted it has been necessary to import ingredients for inorganic fertilizer, and the cost burden to small producers has thereby been increased. The use of fungicides and insecticides to combat diseases which have beset two of the main export crops, bananas and cacao, has increased as research has developed effective treatments. Although modern agricultural techniques are used on some large holdings, such as sugar plantations, most operations—preparing the ground, planting and harvesting—are carried on by hand, sometimes in a completely primitive fashion.

Throughout the Sierra and Coast, labor on small holdings tends to be furnished by the owner or renter and his family. It has been estimated that on at least half of the farms between 10 and 250 acres all labor is provided by members of the family; those exploitations above 250 acres use some type of nonfamily labor, either on a permanent or temporary basis. The need for seasonal agricultural labor on the Coast is filled by landless farmhands, who are paid in cash.

On the *hacienda* in the Sierra, labor is provided by the resident *huasipungueros,* and the seasonal needs of the *campesinos* are supplied largely through mutual assistance.

Mechanization is not widespread. The Food and Agriculture Organization (FAO) reported in 1960 that only 1,550 tractors and 134 harvestor-thresher combines were in use. Man, frequently unaided by animals, still provides an overwhelming source of energy in the country. It has been calculated that no more than 0.1 percent of all farm units are completely mechanized in operations. Although animals provided traction for more than 50 percent of all farms in 1954, there were 140,000 which were operated without benefit of any source of traction, either animal or mechanical. This lack was not confined solely to small farms; it was found that about 60 percent of all farms comprising more than 500 acres used neither animals nor machinery for planting, cultivating and harvesting.

CROP PRODUCTION

Principal Crops of the Sierra

Upland Grains

Temperate climate cereal grains—barley, maize and wheat—are the most important crops of the Sierra and cover about two-thirds of the acreage devoted to annual food crops (see table 10). Barley and maize, which thrive in the temperate climate of the Sierra, have long been staple articles of diet for the population of the area, particularly the Indians.

Table 10. Principal Crops of the Sierran and Coastal Regions of Ecuador, 1963

Crop	Area planted (in thousands of acres)	Production (in thousands of tons)
SIERRA		
Barley	296.4	84.0
Maize	543.4	164.0
Wheat	172.9	70.0
Sugarcane	80.3	1,787.5
Potatoes	148.2	240.0
Legumes	259.4	48.5
Pyrethrum	7.2	1.3
COAST		
Bananas	370.5	2,175.0
Cacao	494.0	40.0
Coffee	321.1	42.9
Sugarcane	49.4	1,740.0
Rice	271.7	154.0
Cotton	45.7	8.5
Rubber	12.4	0.3

Source: Adapted from Ecuador, Junta Nacional de Planificación y Coordinación Económica, *Resumen del Plan General de Desarrollo Económico y Social del Ecuador*, Cuadro II-12, p. 87.

Introduced to the Sierra at the time of the Spanish conquest, barley proved to be highly adaptable to the rigorous climate of the highlands. It is cultivated on all types of farms, both large and small, along with other crops. It is of particular importance in the provinces of Cotopaxi, Tungurahua and Chimborazo. In Chimborazo it is of such importance to the native population that it is said to be a "way of life."

About 40 percent of the crop is produced on farms under 12 acres, but it is also cultivated on the large *haciendas*. Yields are relatively low, but reach a more satisfactory level in the provinces of Carchi, Pichincha and Bolívar, where better methods of cultivation are used.

Although there has been a trend away from using barley as a cereal, there has been a considerable increase in industrial demand by a growing brewing industry, and total demand is expected to rise sharply. The area planted was about 296,000 acres in 1963, when 84,000 tons were produced. A study of potential has led to the conclusion that by 1973, with the use of improved seed strains and cultivation methods, production could be almost doubled and anticipated demand could be met, with no increase in the area under crops.

As a basic source of food, maize even antedates barley, since it was cultivated by the highland Indians before the conquest. It is considered possible that it was the cultivation of maize which transformed the nomad tribes into a settled agricultural people and permitted the growth of an Andean civilization.

In 1963 it was estimated that approximately 543,000 acres were planted to maize, of which 494,000 acres were for human consumption and the rest for livestock feed. Small farms accounted for at least 70 percent of the area devoted to maize, and most of their produce was for human consumption. The major part of the maize grown for feed was produced on large or medium-sized livestock *haciendas*.

The main producing areas are the provinces of Bolívar, Tungurahua, Pichincha and Azuay, where 8 to 10 months are required to bring a crop to maturity. On all but the most important livestock farms, methods of cultivation are primitive, and yields are low. A small amount of land (about 50,000 acres) on the Coast is planted with maize, mostly for livestock feed. There, better seeds and mechanized methods have increased yields.

Although an increase in total production through improved technology is envisaged for the future, the area cultivated is expected to decline between 1963 and 1973. The projected decline for the Sierra is about one-third of the area cultivated in 1963. Area devoted to human consumption in 1973 is expected to be less than one-half that of 1963. On the Coast the area is expected to increase somewhat, entirely for livestock feed.

Wheat, which has assumed increasing importance as a cereal grain because of the growth of population and a greater acceptance of wheat flour as a dietary staple, is cultivated in all provinces of the Sierra, from Chimborazo to the Colombian border. The province of Pichincha is the most important producer, followed by Chimborazo and Carchi. For the most part, production is carried on by *mestizo* farmers on medium to large (but not on the largest) farms, which use better than average cultivation

348

practices. Some attention is given to the use of fertilizer, and at least 80 percent of the crop is threshed by machine.

Production more than tripled between 1945 and the peak year of 1961, rising from 25,000 tons in 1945 to 78,000 in 1961. Yields increased by about 140 percent in the same period, although they are still considered somewhat low in comparison with those of large wheat-growing countries.

Wheat production has been encouraged by the government through a guaranteed price to producers and by the establishment of an experimental station at Izobamba, where research in the development of disease-resistant strains has been undertaken with the technical and financial help of the Rockefeller Foundation.

Despite noteworthy improvements, production falls short of requirements by 50,000 tons per year. To meet this deficit, an increase in area planted, from almost 173,000 acres in 1963 to 333,000 acres in 1973, is planned. The projected expansion is expected to be accomplished by the diversion of a portion of the land now planted to maize, barley and potatoes and by the incorporation of some lands used as natural pasture in the provinces of Imbabura, Bolívar and Loja. Although the agricultural development plan projects a decrease in total area devoted to raising maize and potatoes, no decrease is planned for barley, but acreage is expected to expand in the cold, higher grasslands known as *subpáramos*.

Sugarcane

Sugarcane is grown both in the Sierra and on the Coast. However, the circumstances of culture and use of the cane differ between the two regions.

In the Sierra thousands of *campesinos* grow sugarcane on small landholdings, which generally range from 12 to 25 acres. For the most part, the cane grown is used for the production of *panela* (raw sugar-cake) and *aguardiente* (a raw distilled liquor made of sugarcane extract) both of which are processed and consumed in the Sierra.

A long-cycle cane which requires 18 months to mature is grown. Methods, traditionally rudimentary, result in low yields. No irrigation or fertilizer is used; crop rotation for the renewal of soil is not practiced; and mechanization is impractical on small farms.

Because of the installation of a large sugar refinery in Imbabura and one in Loja, there is a new demand for cane for refined sugar and an increase in total demand in the Sierra. It has been estimated that the cultivation of sugarcane could be increased in the province of Imbabura with an improvement in irrigation.

Approximately 80,000 acres of sugarcane were under cultivation in 1963. Although a modest increase in acreage is projected

349

for 1973, total production is expected to rise principally through the improvement in methods of cultivation.

Potatoes and Other Vegetables

Potatoes are the most important vegetable crop. Although there are a few exploitations devoted to potatoes, for the most part, they are grown in conjunction with other crops on farms of all sizes, from great estates to subsistence plots. The provinces of Cotopaxi, Chimborazo, Pichincha and Tungurahua are the main areas of production.

Potatoes, which grow easily in the high, cool areas of the Sierra, have profited by research in better seed strains and methods of cultivation which has been undertaken through the collaboration of agricultural experimental stations and the Rockefeller Foundation. With improved seeds and the use of fertilizer, yields increased from 3,200 pounds per acre in 1953 to 7,500 pounds in 1963. The area harvested more than doubled between 1953 and 1963, when it stood at approximately 148,200 acres. With continuing improvement of cultivation practices, it is expected that total production may be almost doubled by 1973, while the area under cultivation may be reduced by one-third. If marketing and storage facilities are improved, it is considered possible that potatoes might develop into an export potential.

Many varieties of beans, peas and lentils are grown, both as foodstuffs and as forage. Among the other important foodstuffs are sweet potatoes, yucca and peanuts.

Fruits

Many temperate-climate fruits, such as pears, peaches, plums and avocados, are produced. Although the climate is conducive to the growth of fruits, production has been limited by poor care and lack of irrigation. As a crop, fruit is generally produced in conjunction with other crops on landholdings of all sizes. There are, however, a few large *haciendas* in the inter-Andean basins devoted to the production of fruit under irrigation. It has been estimated that with better care and the extension of irrigation production could be increased significantly with no increase in acreage.

Pyrethrum

The cultivation of pyrethrum, a small daisylike flower which thrives at high altitudes and which is an ingredient of insecticides, became important during World War II, when supplies from Africa were hard to obtain. Subsequently, use of pyrethrum declined in favor of synthetic products, but its lack of harmful qualities has again increased its use. Most of the crop is exported.

Ecuador is now the largest producer of pyrethrum in the Western Hemisphere and the third largest in the world, exceeded only by Kenya and Tanzania. The main producing provinces are Tungurahua, Pichincha, Chimborazo and Carchi.

The bulk of the pyrethrum crop is produced on holdings of large export companies backed by foreign investment, but small farmers also produce under contract to exporters. Pyrethrum is a perennial which blooms within 6 to 12 months after planting and continues to bloom twice each year. Much of the cultivation and harvesting on both large and small holdings is done by Indian women.

Principal Crops of the Coast

Bananas

Since 1957 bananas have been the most valuable export crop. Although banana cultivation has spread to the lower western slopes of the Sierra provinces to a certain extent, the coastal provinces are the main producing area. Guayas has been outstanding for banana production.

Although bananas have long been produced for domestic consumption and were originally grown near riverbanks on the lower coast, since 1948 they have enjoyed a most remarkable growth in production and in importance to the economy. Before then the Central American countries had been the principal suppliers of bananas for the world market, but a series of misfortunes—the appearance of two plant diseases, sigatoka and so-called Panama disease, and the ravages of hurricanes—greatly reduced production in that area.

A combination of circumstances made Ecuador the logical successor as the most important banana producer. The humid, tropical climate of the coastal area fostered growth of the plants, and an abundance of idle government-owned land made possible the expansion of production. Furthermore, the use of virgin land where no treatment of soil or plants was needed reduced the cost of operation from that of the disease-ridden Central American plantations and increased the profitability of production.

Because of the later appearance of the Panama disease in the north, where commercial production began, cultivation has shifted inland closer to the Sierra, where water is more plentiful.

The area planted in bananas increased tenfold in a period of 6 years, from about 37,000 acres in 1948 to about 370,000 acres in 1954, an area which has since remained fairly stable.

The bulk of the banana crop is produced by individual holders of small parcels of land. It has been estimated that 87 percent of all exploitations do not exceed 250 acres. Wasteful practices in cultivating, harvesting and marketing have been used. Until recently, little attempt was made to develop a strain with greater resistance to disease, and it has not been the general practice to use fertilizer. Control of disease has improved with the development of fungicides. Poor handling methods and the lack of good roads are responsible for excessive damage in marketing, and it was estimated that only about half of the banana production was marketed in 1963.

The growth of banana cultivation has been nurtured by progressive, forward-looking policies on the part of the government, the large growers and the exporters. Government-held lands on the Coast have been sold to individuals on liberal credit terms and working capital provided by the government's Development Credit System and by exporting firms. In 1955 a government decree created the National Banana Growers' Association of Ecuador (Asociacion Nacional de Bananeros del Ecuador—ANBE) to fight diseases and plagues which threaten banana culture. Since its initiation the function of ANBE has expanded to cover all problems which confront the industry. Funds for operations are derived from taxes paid by exporters on each stem exported.

The national development plan projects a 3.5-percent growth in the real value of banana exports between 1964 and 1973. This projected increase is based upon improved methods of cultivation and marketing rather than on increased area under production.

Cacao

In the latter part of the nineteenth century and first part of the twentieth century, the economy was built upon cacao, which flourished under the climatic conditions of the Coast and was of high importance in the world market because of its excellent quality. Huge cacao plantations near riverbanks in Guayas and Los Ríos made fortunes for their owners, who frequently lived in Paris, leaving the care of the plantation to a resident manager.

The peak of cacao production was reached in 1914, when 47,200 tons were exported. Within a few years cacao plantings were attacked by two plant diseases, monilial pod rot and witches broom, which reduced within 10 years the annual crop to one-third of its maximum in 1914. At the same time the sharp drop in world prices for cacao discouraged efforts to look for methods to control blight, and many owners abandoned their plantations.

After World War II the rise in cacao prices gave impetus to a renewal of the industry. With the assistance of the government, which made available new disease-resistant strains of plantings, established the Cacao Renovation Enterprise (Empresa Renovadora del Cacao) and increased available credit, cacao has again

352

achieved a place of major agricultural importance, but under different conditions of cultivation.

Although there are a few large plantations, owned by exporters, cacao exploitations tend to range from medium to small in size. Many of the former large enterprises have been broken up and sold in parcels of approximately 25 acres. In other instances holdings have been held intact, but cacao cultivation is carried on by many individuals who work small areas of the land by hand with little attention paid to pruning and spraying. Larger exploitations, which employ modern techniques of cultivation and disease control, account for a significant part of the crop. New plantings have been established in irrigated areas in the Bahía de Caráquez and Machala regions.

The agricultural development plan does not project an increase in area under cultivation between 1963 and 1973, but expects to double production by improved methods.

Coffee

Coffee, which is grown largely for export trade, since Ecuador consumes little domestically, has consistently placed as one of the three most valuable commercial crops since 1950, when it ranked first. The coastal provinces of Manabí, Guayas and El Oro are the principal producing areas, although some is produced in the province of Loja in the Sierra.

For the most part, coffee is grown on small landholdings which range from 3 to 8 acres in size. It has been estimated that about 90 percent of the crop is produced by farmers who annually grow no more than 25 bags (of 100 pounds each).

Bananas and plantains are frequently planted for the protection of the young coffee seedlings. Care of the trees has remained elementary, with little use of fertilizer, and harvesting methods have been careless, to the detriment of the trees.

Encouraged by rising coffee prices and the consequent increasing importance to export earnings, the government in 1949 established the Ecuadorian Coffee Institute (Instituto Ecuatoriano del Café—INECAFE) to promote and improve cultivation. The INECAFE has performed notable research in plant strains and has been influential in encouraging better marketing methods. Most of the crop is now depulped and washed before marketing, which increases its value.

Although yield per acre is much lower than in Colombia and Mexico, research indicates that more careful methods of cultivation and fertilization can increase productivity. Based upon this assumption, the national plan for agricultural development projects an increase, between 1963 and 1973, of 60 percent in production but no increase in area cultivated.

Sugarcane

In 1963 it was estimated that slightly less than 50,000 acres were planted to sugarcane on the Coast, almost entirely in the province of Guayas. Sugarcane grown on the Coast is destined for the production of refined sugar for the domestic market and, increasingly, for the export trade.

Circumstances of production differ greatly from those in the Sierra. On the Coast, cane is grown on large plantations by owners of sugar mills who have adopted the use of fertilizer and machinery for planting and harvesting. The largest sugar mills have holdings of over 12,000 acres, not all of which are under cultivation. Smaller mills have holdings of 2,500 to 7,000 acres; holdings of individual growers range from 200 to 600 acres. Owners of large plantations have experimented with new varieties of cane, and unit yields in Ecuador exceed those of Brazil, Colombia, the United States and Mexico. Only a slight expansion of area cultivated is proposed for the decade between 1963 and 1973, but more than a 50-percent increase in production is projected.

Rice

Rice is a basic article of diet on the Coast, just as are barley and maize in the Sierra. Cultivation has become increasingly important because of the growing substitution of rice for barley and maize in urban centers in the Sierra and because of its potential as an export commodity.

All rice is produced in the provinces of Guayas and Los Ríos on the flood plains of the Guayas River basin. Most of the crop, known as the winter crop, is planted in December and January and harvested in May and June after the waters recede. A small crop is planted in early summer, after the seasonal rains, and harvested in September and October.

At least 70 percent of the area is cultivated by day laborers who rent not more than 2 to 4 acres from a large landowner, grow rice for their own use, and sell their small surplus as an extra source of income. The renter who pays for the land with a fixed amount of rice provides all his own materials and is always in debt.

The most primitive cultivation methods are used, to the detriment of the crop yield and of the soil as well. All operations are performed by hand. Frequently, the ground is not even plowed, and no use is made of fertilizer or crop rotation. The grower depends almost entirely on natural rainfall, and no effort to conserve natural moisture is made. After the crop is harvested the grain is threshed by beating it on the ground. The grower retains what he needs for his own use, and the surplus is sold to the government at a fixed price (see ch. 22, Domestic Trade). The yield on miniscule plantings is very low, but a study made by the Central Bank indicated that on holdings of 170 acres or more the yield is at least one-third higher.

Because of the vital importance of rice as a domestic food, a significant increase in acreage is planned, particularly in the vicinity of Babahoyo. An increase in average yield is projected through the use of better seeds, fertilizer, irrigation, some mechanization and better credit facilities.

Cotton

Cotton has been a low-productivity, low-income crop. It is produced on thousands of small holdings by rudimentary methods, and low prices are paid for the local short-staple variety, which is prone to insect damage. Cotton is produced in the coastal provinces of Manabí, Guayas and Los Ríos, and in the Sierra province of Imbabura.

The size of the crop, which has varied from a low of 3,700 metric tons in 1952 to a peak of 11,820 tons in 1957, has been declining since 1959. The area cultivated declined by more than 50 percent between 1949 and 1963, when it stood at about 46,000 acres.

Because of the importance of cotton as an industrial raw material, it is considered highly desirable to achieve domestic self-sufficiency, and efforts have been made by the government to encourage production. Imports are limited, and the textile industry is obligated to purchase the native crop at fixed prices. Small cottongrowers, however, make little, if any, profit because of the exhorbitant price they must pay for credit, and the disadvantage of marketing through middlemen (see ch. 22, Domestic Trade).

The National Cotton Commission was created by decree in 1955 to promote improvement and expansion in cotton production. At the farm maintained by the Commission near Bahía de Caráquez, experiments have been conducted with improved strains, which show higher yield. Some technical assistance is provided for growers. The area under cultivation is expected to increase in the future, but better credit sources and better marketing mechanisms are essential to real improvement in cotton production.

Rubber

The cultivation of rubber as an agricultural crop is in its initial stage. In 1963 rubber plantings covered approximately 12,000 acres, mainly in the area near Tenguel and San Lorenzo.

Because of the increasing consumption of raw rubber by Ecuador and adjoining Latin American countries which are in the process of industrializing, attention is being given to the cultivation of rubber as an import substitute and a potential export.

The agricultural experimental station at Pichilingue has conducted research in varieties of rubber best suited to natural conditions and zones for cultivation. Areas in the neighborhood of Santo Domingo de los Colorados, Quinindé, San Lorenzo and Tenguel have been selected as the most appropriate zones, and an expansion up to 700,000 acres is projected for 1973. For the future the Oriente may hold possibilities for profitable rubber culture, but lack of infrastructure is an inhibiting factor in the immediate future.

The establishment of rubber plantations is time consuming and costly, and the fulfillment of desired goals will be dependent in part on the availability of investment funds, construction on the necessary infrastructure and technical research. Priority will be given to supplying the needs of the new rubber industry of Cuenca.

Fruits

Tropical fruits, such as citrus fruits, pineapples, melons, guavas, mangoes and some distinctly native varieties, are grown on the Coast. Oranges and pineapples are considered to have export potential.

LIVESTOCK RAISING

Livestock raising, on a broadly varied scale, is widespread throughout the country. At one extreme of magnitude is the *campesino* who raises guinea pigs and, perhaps, a few other animals to contribute to a meager sustenance and income. Such activity is always secondary to the main business of cropping. At the other extreme are the large *haciendas*, where livestock raising is a major commercial enterprise.

Cattle raising, about 60 percent of which is in the Sierra, is almost entirely confined to the large *haciendas*. Urbanization, improved standards of sanitation for milk production and a growing emphasis on the protein content of the diet have encouraged the establishment of large dairy and beef farms near cities, both in the Sierra and on the Coast (see ch. 8, Health and Welfare). Enterprises devoted exclusively to cattle raising account, however, for only a part of the total production. In addition, most of the large Sierra *haciendas* devoted principally to crop production also maintain herds of commercial size.

Sheep raising is carried on almost exclusively by Sierra Indians, in flocks ranging from a few to perhaps 50 head. *Huasipungueros* and other dependent peasants are usually granted grazing privileges for their flocks on *hacienda* lands as part of the recompense for their labor.

Hogs are raised principally by small farmers, who market them for cash income. Chickens are raised in small numbers by peasant wives throughout the country for sale in nearby markets. Near the cities a few large-scale commerical chicken-raising enterprises have been established in recent years.

The varieties of livestock that now provide food for a growing population and the major source of traction for cropping were introduced by the Spanish conquerors. Livestock native to the area—llamas and guinea pigs—are still raised, but their importance has declined greatly.

The provinces of Pichincha, Loja and Azuay are the chief cattle-raising areas in the Sierra; sheep raising is concentrated in Cotopaxi, Chimborazo and Pichincha. Hogs are raised throughout the region, but the principal centers are Loja, Pichincha, Bolívar and Chimborazo. The raising of poultry is also widespread, but concentrated mainly in the provinces of Loja, Azuay, Bolívar and Pichincha.

On the Coast the provinces of Manabí and Guayas are important producers of cattle. In hogs and poultry the province of Manabí significantly leads all others, both in the Sierra and on the Coast. Guayas is also a major producer of hogs and poultry.

In the Sierra there has been some crossbreeding of traditional Spanish strains of cattle (commonly called *criollo*) with other strains, particularly with the Holstein Friesian, which have been found to be prone to tuberculosis. In 1961 the native variety still made up 61 percent of herds in the highlands. Although small amounts of alfalfa and grain are used, cattle are mostly turned out to natural pasture for fodder. Little care has been given to the improvement of strains or to the care of individual herds. Slaughtering is not carried out on a scientific basis for maintaining well-balanced herds, and the yield of beef per carcass has been low. In spite of the generally underdeveloped state of cattle raising, there has been an increased interest in scientific breeding and maintenance of herds, and a number of wealthy landowners have turned their estates into stock farms where purebred cattle of the highest type are maintained.

On the Coast the *criollo* cattle have been crossbred with the Zebu, and there are also some herds of purebred Brown Swiss. Natural pasturage in the Coast is limited, and storage facilities for feed are insufficient. Bananas and plantains have been used to supplement the short supply of food.

The consumption of livestock and livestock products was estimated in 1963 to comprise the following: beef, 39,900 tons; pork,

357

16,464 tons; lamb, 3,641 tons; poultry, 2,682 tons; eggs, 12,360 tons; and milk, 444,301 tons. The growth and productivity of the livestock sector holds high priority as a future goal.

FOREST PRODUCTS

The exact extent of land in forests and brush is not known. Various estimates have been made, but they can be considered only as approximations; a more accurate picture may be expected when a survey of resources is completed.

The total area forested has been estimated at 84 million acres, the major part of which lies in the Oriente. Extensive areas of the coastal lowlands are forested, as are the eastern and western Andean slopes, where trees provide indispensable protection for soil and water resources. The densely populated Sierra basins were long ago cleared of virgin forests to provide more space for pasture and agriculture and to provide the wood used for fuel and construction material. Eucalyptus trees, brought from Australia in the 1860's, now supply the Sierra with fuel and construction material.

The forests of the Oriente are largely unexploited because of isolation, whereas the coastal forests, wherever accessible, furnish most of the lumber for domestic use and for export. A study of potential forest use has reported that, nationwide, 74 million acres could be made available if technical studies of forests were made and access roads were constructed.

The Coast produces a wide variety of trees that fill domestic needs. There are abundant softwoods for construction purposes and similar uses. Domestic resources also furnish potential raw material for the pulp and paper industry. A number of varieties of hardwoods of value and beauty, suitable for the making of furniture and fine cabinetwork, are found, particularly in the provinces of Esmeraldas and Manabí. Exploitation of forests is conducted largely by small-scale enterprises in areas accessible to rivers, roads or railroads. As a rule, logging, processing and distribution are carried on by different operators. Sawmill operators seldom engage in timbering themselves, but typically depend on indepedent contractors and middlemen for supply.

Forest products with commercial value aside from construction and furniture making are balsa wood, used in insulation and for many other purposes; rubber; cinchona bark, from which quinine is extracted; mangrove bark, used in tanning leather; tagua nuts (vegetable ivory nuts); kapok, which comes from the ceiba tree; palm oil; and toquilla, straw which is used in the making of Panama hats. Balsa wood valued at S/29.2 million and tagua nuts worth S/4.3 million were exported in 1961, together with smaller amounts of kapok and Panama hats. A small amount of lumber, including plywood, was also exported.

FISHING

The Pacific waters along the coast and as far west as the Galápagos Islands have abundant and varied fish resources. Among countless other varieties, the catch includes mackerel, sailfish, skipjack, snapper, sea bass, shad, broad sole, Peruvian hammerhead, spiny lobster, shrimp, tuna and various mollusks. Small fish, such as sardines, herring and anchovies, also exist. Many kinds of fish add variety and protein to the diet of families living near the sea, but tuna, shrimp and lobster are of greatest commercial importance. The principal fishing ports are Guayaquil, Manta, Santa Rosa, Puerto López, Jaramijó and Esmeraldas.

Fishing is carried on by a few large commercial enterprises and by a host of small family enterprises for whom fishing is a full-time occupation. It was estimated that there were 10,000 small fishermen plying the waters along the coast and off the Galápagos Islands in 1961. Such small, autonomous enterprises accounted for more than 70 percent of the tonnage caught and a like share of the value. In addition, countless individuals take advantage of the supply of seafood for family use. Small fishing enterprises supply the domestic market; the commercial fisheries are oriented toward export markets.

Since 1956 the fishing industry has developed significantly in all phases. Despite its abundance, fish was little consumed domestically in the past. Lack of refrigeration and transportation confined the use of fish to the coastal areas near fishing ports, but improvement in freezing and preserving capacity has made possible more widespread and increased domestic consumption and a growing export volume. Between 1957 and 1961 the total catch more than doubled, rising from 26,447 to 59,922 metric tons. In the same period domestic consumption of fish products rose from 24,728 to 46,951 metric tons, and exports more than quadrupled, rising from 2,411 to 9,748 metric tons.

The dynamic element has been the growing importance of tuna, which is marketed in fresh, frozen and canned forms. Whereas small fishermen account for part of the frozen tuna, large commercial enterprises are solely responsible for the production of canned tuna, which increased eightfold between 1957 and 1961, from approximately 33,000 to 266,000 cases. Domestic consumption multiplied tenfold, rising more than production destined for export.

Shrimp, which are found in the Gulf of Guayaquil and off the coast of Esmeraldas, are exported in frozen blocks. Spiny lobsters are also exported. In 1961 the total export value of all seafood products was $5.4 million.

Development of fisheries is in the hands of the National Institute of Fishing (Instituto Nacional de Pesca), assisted by agents of the FAO. The Institute operates a refrigerated warehouse and buys fish from fishermen for resale to wholesalers. Marketing is chiefly in Guayaquil and Quito, the latter reached by both airplane and truck. The Institute is studying the possibility of extending markets by establishing a chain of refrigerated warehouses in various areas.

Ecuador claims territorial jurisdiction over coastal waters for a distance of 200 miles, but permits vessels of foreign fishing companies to exploit its waters upon payment of registration and license fees. After 1 year vessels desiring to continue fishing the waters must transfer to national registration. Commercial enterprises, part of which are United States owned, enjoy government concessions concerning duties and taxes, but they are also obligated to establish freezing and processing operations within the country (see ch. 24, Foreign Economic Relations).

IMPROVEMENT PROGRAMS

There has long been recognition of the need to improve the use and distribution of land and to increase agricultural productivity. In the past this need has been expressed by a series of abortive efforts toward agrarian reform and by fragmented programs of assistance which, though excellent in themselves, were not coordinated and were inadequate, considering the magnitude of the problem.

In 1936 the government, which possessed vast areas of unexploited public lands on the Coast and in the Oriente, passed the Public Lands and Colonization Law, which made possible the sale, on reasonable terms, of state-owned lands for approved purposes. To insure the productive use of land and to discourage mere speculative holding, a condition of purchase was the cultivation of one-fourth of the land within a period of 5 years; otherwise, the land would revert to the state, and the payments would be regarded as rent. The size of parcels of land was about 125 acres, although under some circumstances they could be as large as 500 acres.

Since the available land consists of tropical forests, use depends on construction of penetration roads. The growth in profitability of banana cultivation has encouraged roadbuilding and new settlement in the coastal area, but the extreme isolation from markets of the Oriente has been a deterrent to exploitation of land east of the Andes.

In addition to building roads, the government from time to time has undertaken other services of assistance to agriculture and to agrarian communities. As early as 1928 the government set up channels to provide credit for agriculture, but the credit supply was inadequate, costly and mostly unavailable to small producers. As part of his extensive and frequently unrealized plans for development of the country, President Velasco Ibarra, during his 1944–47 term, founded the National Irrigation Agency (Caja Nacional de Riego) to take responsibility for larger scale irrigation works.

In 1952 the government entered into a pact with the United States for the organization of extension services operating through the cooperation of the Inter-American Cooperative Agricultural Service (Servicio Cooperativo Inter-Americano de Agricultura—SCIA) and the Ministry of Development. Another international cooperative program, designed to meet the social and economic problems of the Sierra Indian peasantry, was the Andean Program, sponsored by the International Labor Organization, various agencies of the United Nations and the government. In this multiplicity of projects, there was, until recently, no comprehensive plan to draw together all the facets of agricultural development and to attack the core problems—inequity in distribution of land and archaic and unjust labor practices.

Steps Toward Land Reform

The first concrete step toward land reform was taken when the National Planning and Economic Coordination Board (Junta Nacional de Planificación y Coordinación Económica), created on May 29, 1954, by emergency decree of President Velasco Ibarra, presented a preliminary plan for an agrarian law. The function of the Board was purely advisory, and the recommendation was not acted upon. The next step was taken by the new president, Camilo Ponce Enríquez, who, in 1957, established the National Colonization Institute (Instituto Nacional de Colonización), which was charged with surveying possible land for settlement and establishing families on the land. Before the end of his term in office, President Ponce Enríquez issued a decree authorizing the government to break up and sell large government-owned estates which it had been renting to private operators.

After 1957 pressure for agrarian reform accelerated, and the concept of the problem broadened to include the low level of living of agricultural workers. Congress created a commission to prepare an agrarian reform proposal. The preliminary draft, presented to Congress in September 1961, just before the coup that unseated President Velasco Ibarra, met with opposition from the various political factions, and efforts to amend the bill were unsuccessful.

An avowed goal of the military government which assumed

control on July 11, 1963, was the completion and passage of a comprehensive agrarian reform law in keeping with the principles defined in the Charter of Punta del Este in 1961 and with the goals of national economic and social development (see ch. 18, The Economic System). Efforts to hammer out an acceptable law were carried forward with the help of such organizations as the National Planning and Economic Coordination Board, the Ecuadorian Commission of the Alliance for Progress, the Liberal Party and the Congressional Commission. In order to insure a reasonable consensus, a special commission to study the last draft was appointed from representatives of government, agriculture and the universities. Suggestions were also taken from specialists from the United States Agency for International Development (AID), the Inter-American Development Bank (IDB) and FAO. On July 11, 1964, 1 year after the junta took control, the final draft was issued, and on July 23, the Agrarian Reform and Colonization Decree (No. 1480) became effective.

Agrarian Reform and Colonization Law

The Agrarian Reform and Colonization Law is comprehensive and covers in detail the basis for, and regulation of, landholding; the abolition of such undesirable forms of land tenure as the *huasipungo;* agriculture wages; inventory and registration of land; legalization of land titles; colonization; and the provision of credit, educational and technical services, and social welfare. The law further provides the framework for making decisions concerning legal questions and establishes an autonomous agency for administration—the Ecuadorian Institute of Agrarian Reform and Colonization (Instituto Ecuatoriano de Reforma Agraria y Colonización—IERAC), with headquarters in Quito—to supersede the National Institute of Colonization. The management and administration of IERAC are entrusted to the Board of Directors, the Executive Committee and the executive director. The IERAC consists of a Department of Agrarian Reform, Department of Colonization and such other departments or divisions as may be deemed necessary.

The Board of Directors is made up of nine members—the ministers of Development, Social Welfare, and Defense; the technical director of the National Planning and Economic Coordination Board; the general manager of the National Development Bank; two representatives of farmers, directly elected by the respective Chambers of Agriculture of the First Zone, representing the Sierra and the Oriente, and the Second Zone, representing the Coast and the Galápagos Islands; and two farmworkers, one representing the Coast and the other representing the Sierra and Oriente. The Board of Directors appoints and removes the execu-

362

tive director and the directors of the Departments of Agrarian Reform and Colonization and in general functions as a policy-making body and board of review. The Board is specifically charged with the preparation of rules and regulations for applying the law and with approval of the annual budget of the IERAC.

Active preparation of programs and execution of those which are approved are delegated to the Executive Committee, composed of the executive director and directors of the Departments of Agrarian Reform and Colonization, who are professional, full-time employees. The executive director is responsible for the organization, staffing and performance of the IERAC; he legally represents the Institute and is responsible for the exercise of its functions according to law. He has financial authority and responsibilities and has the duty of granting property deeds awarded under the law.

In addition to the main function of initiating and directing all programs for distribution or redistribution of land, the IERAC forms and maintains the inventory and National Registry of Lands, for the purpose of determining location, size and forms of landholding and of barren lands suited for colonization. The National Registry of Lands also serves as a frame of reference for tax purposes.

The capital of the IERAC consists of the assets of the former National Colonization Institute, land transferred to it by the state or acquired under the Agrarian Reform Law, land previously administered by welfare agencies and state bonds up to a total of S/50 million, redeemable in 20 years and bearing 8-percent annual interest.

The Agrarian Reform and Colonization Law provides that arable land which has not been used for 3 years or which is used inefficiently may be expropriated and, as part of the patrimony of IERAC ownership, may be transferred to small- and medium-scale farmers or cooperatives for personal and efficient cultivation. Land which is efficiently cultivated may also be expropriated if it is deemed necessary to eliminate population pressure. Lands suitable for farming which have been unexploited for 10 years also revert to the state.

The maximum allowable single landholding in the Coast is about 6,200 acres of arable land, plus 2,470 acres of grassland; in the Sierra, the maximum is almost 2,000 acres of arable land, plus 2,470 acres of pastureland. Farms efficiently exploited and used for supplying raw materials for their own industrial plants, such as sugar plantations, are exempt from the maximum-size limitation, as are productive livestock-farming enterprises. Minimum standards also are considered. The ideal grant of land is the family-sized farm, which had not been defined in 1965, although preliminary studies leaned toward a definition of 62 to 74 acres. Until such standards are set no grant less than 12 acres may be made. Another aspect covered in the agrarian program is the consolidation of minuscule plots into larger, more efficient plots.

Compensation for expropriation is to be effected by three classes of agrarian reform bonds issued by the national government—Class A bonds, with 15-year maturity and 16-percent annual interest; Class B bonds, with 20-year maturity and 5-percent annual interest, with a 5-year period of grace; and Class C bonds, with 30-year maturity and 4-percent annual interest, with a 10-year period of grace, during which only interest payments are met. Agrarian reform bonds are exempt from income taxes and serve to guarantee livestock farming and industrial loans granted by the Development Credit System Banks.

Of equal importance with redistribution of land are the provisions covering labor arrangements between landowner and worker. The Agrarian Reform and Colonization Law removes the legal basis of servitude by outlawing *huasipungo*. It further provides that a *huasipunguero* who has rendered services on rural property for 10 years will be considered as having made contributions equivalent to the price of his tenant plot, which is therefore to become his property. Shorter periods of service apply proportionately to the purchase price of land.

One year from the time the law became effective was set as the date for the termination of the *huasipungo* system, and the liquidation had reportedly begun in mid-1965. The magnitude of the task is indicated by the fact that the number of exploitations operated by *huasipungueros* is estimated at almost 20,000. Public ceremonies have been held in the provinces of Chimborazo and Pichincha at which *huasipungueros* received title as owners of land. Other labor payment arrangements are dealt with in the law, and money is made the only legal form of payment for services.

As a second phase of the goal of bringing idle land into productive use and raising the level of living, the Agrarian Reform and Colonization Law delegates to IERAC the responsibility for supervising spontaneous colonization and preparing plans for colonization in the future. In preparing these plans, the IERAC is directed in accordance with the Ten-Year Development Plan to establish a priority system for opening new colonization zones and to determine a policy for guidance of such projects.

Colonization

The existence of large areas of potentially productive public land, plus a permissive governmental policy, led to the growth of a number of spontaneous settlements, many of them ill chosen in location and lacking roads and the fundamental technical, economic and social services to make them successful. In some instances, members of such settlements, called *colonos,* held title to the land they occupied, whereas in others they were squatters. Information presented in the General Plan for the Economic and Social Development of Ecuador in 1963 estimated that about 12,000 units in the Sierra were exploited by *colonos* and that more than half were exploited without legal title. Although the situation in the Coast is less acute, the legalization of land titles is a pressing need, since farmers without legal title are unable to obtain credit to expand production.

The creation in 1957 of the National Colonization Institute signaled the initiation of a positive approach to colonization, with careful planning, selection of location and preparation for settlement to avoid the uneconomic use of land and labor. However, a lack of continuity in policies and a lack of financial and technical resources have impaired its effectiveness.

In 1958 an experimental pilot plan for the colonization of Santo Domingo de los Colorados was undertaken. Only a small number of colonists were involved, and all planning and preparation were government controlled. The plan was abandoned in 1962 as being too costly and too paternalistic.

The following year, a loan of $2.6 million was granted to the National Colonization Institute by the Social Progress Trust Fund, which is part of the Alliance for Progress mechanism, created by the United States and administered by the IDB. The purpose of the loan was to assist a larger spontaneous colonization in the same area, where 1,600 low-income rural families had managed to bring about 64,000 acres into production, but were facing economic and social problems. The loan was used to provide access roads, housing and working material for the colonists; government funds were allotted to schools and to legal, medical and technical assistance, and construction services.

As part of the General Plan for the Economic and Social Development of Ecuador, the General Program of Colonization, covering the 20 years between 1964 and 1983, has been developed. The overall objectives of the plan comprise the provision of assistance to selected colonies already existing; the establishment, after careful study, of centers of colonization on new land; and the legalization of land titles. The government does not propose to distribute land free, but it does take responsibility for providing essential services. In 1965, 16 zones where colonization had been started and 12 zones considered for opening new colonies had been selected for assistance during the two decades. It is anticipated that the completed national program of colonization will benefit 92,320 families settled on nearly 6.7 million acres, of which

4.7 million acres will be land newly opened. Total investment in the program for the first 10 years is expected to reach S/1.3 billion. Investment in construction and land by the public sector is estimated at S/455.2 million, and the cost of operation, at S/35.7 million.

Priorities in the execution of projects have been established for 5-year periods. The presently settled zones of Santo Domingo-Quinindé-Chone-Quevedo and the Coast are allotted first place for continued assistance, and it is estimated that the area will support 10,000 new colonists in addition to the 5,000 already established there. To encourage migration to the Oriente, two settlements—at Valle del Upano and in the area of Valladolid-Zumba-Yacuambi-Zamora—have been chosen for assistance in the first 5 years, and plans for the period also include a new settlement at Valle del Nangaritza.

Irrigation Programs

Sizable areas of land, both in the Sierra and on the Coast, are under irrigation, mostly through ditches dug by individual farmers. Organized irrigation, planned with regional benefits in view, began when the National Irrigation Agency (Caja Nacional de Riego) was established in 1944. Based on findings of studies undertaken, a comprehensive program of irrigation was proposed, but because of a lack of funds, the National Irrigation Agency was able to execute only a part of the initial plan. At the end of 1962, works with an irrigation potential of 54,000 acres were functioning in Pichincha, Chimborazo, Guayas, Cañar and El Oro. This potential was actually being used to irrigate only 29,000 acres.

The National Irrigation Agency plans and executes the major works, and it is acknowledged that this has been well carried out, but the constructioon of distribution canals is the responsibility of landowners, who are limited in means and who are not organized in groups capable of financing distribution and carrying out integrated schemes for water use.

As part of the Ten-Year Development Plan, a program of irrigation, including six projects in the Sierra and four on the Coast, has been formulated. It is estimated that, at the completion of the program, water will be brought to an additional 284,000 acres of land, after a total investment of S/370.1 million, of which the public sector is expected to provide S/182.1 million. These projections, however, can be only tentative, since their achievement rests on the ability to organize farmers to exploit such works for productive purposes. Realistically, it is predicted that the actual achievement will probably fall short of the goal. During 1964, work was continued on the four irrigation projects already under construction, in Chimborazo, Pichincha, Guayas and Cañar, and it is expected these works will be completed before undertaking other major programs.

To realize maximum potential benefits, it has been suggested that government responsibility should include the distribution system as well as the intake works and main canals and that the National Irrigation Agency should be reorganized to embrace three levels—central, regional and district. It has also been suggested that cooperatives of farmers be formed to make efficient use of the water supply. The National Irrigation Agency functions under the Ministry of Agriculture and Livestock, which, since its creation on November 20, 1964, coordinates the work of a number of quasi-independent agencies in the field of agriculture.

Exploration of water resources has been late in starting. Among the studies in progress in 1965 was a study of the water resources of Manabí, where extreme drought has recently caused damage, and a study by a mission of the Organization of American States (OAS) of the resources of the Guayas Basin, where floods cause frequent loss of crops and damage to property and roads.

Agricultural Credit

The principal sources of agricultural credit are the National Development Bank (Banco Nacional de Fomento) System, reorganized from the former Development Credit System in late 1964; the commercial banks; and the Central Bank of Ecuador (Banco Central del Ecuador). A small operation, the Agricultural Credit Fund (Caja de Crédito Agrícola), a semiofficial institution organized and operating under special legislation, furnishes a modest amount of financial assistance to agriculture, particularly for storage facilities. Credit is also provided by exporters and other private sources, usually at a much higher rate of interest (see ch. 23, Fiscal and Monetary System).

The Development Credit System, a government lending agency founded in 1944, was authorized to make short-, medium- and long-term loans to agriculture and industry. In practice almost 80 percent of its loans have been short term, and the major part, about three-fourths, has gone to agriculture. In mid-1965 little information was available on the activities of the recently organized development banks, which are expected to be the main source of credit for agriculture and artisan industry in the future.

Total bank loans destined for agriculture increased from S/442 million in 1959 to S/632 million in 1964, an average annual increase of 7 percent. The growth in working capital during the period came from the commercial and central banking system; loans from the Development Credit System remained relatively steady. The Central Bank, in particular, has become increasingly important as a source of funds. The commercial banking system has made increasing amounts of funds available to agriculture, but they account for less than 4 percent of the total loan portfolio and do not constitute a source of supply for small farmers, who need to make long-range improvements to increase productivity.

Interest rates charged by the development banks (and, earlier, by the Development Credit System) are 8 percent, whereas commercial banks charge 9 percent; both rates are set by the Monetary Board. In 1963 agricultural activities were supported by loans of S/202 million from the Development Credit System; S/99 million from commercial banks; and S/104 million in direct credit from the Central Bank.

Additional measures have been taken to increase the supply of credit. Effective late in 1964, the Superintendency of Banks established a policy requiring private banks to extend credit to the agricultural sector in the amount of 15 percent of demand and time deposits. The IERAC was directed to set apart not less than one-tenth of regular income to finance a subsidy credit system for the beneficiaries of programs of agrarian reform and colonization. As a further measure, a Cooperative Bank has been established with funds supplied by the AID, the government of Ecuador and the local Federation of Cooperatives for the purpose of lending to farmer, consumer and artisan cooperatives.

Although forward steps have been taken to improve the supply of funds for agriculture and livestock, success in meeting the demands of a developing agricultural sector will depend heavily upon adapting the type of credit to the needs of the prospective project. The prevalence of short-term credit in the past, which has favored large-scale commercial growers, has discouraged long-range productive investment in improvements and equipment by medium- or small-scale farmers and has led to an overwhelming number of loan renewals and defaults and a decline in new funds available.

Agricultural Education, Research and Extension

Agricultural education is carried on at several different levels, from universities to elementary schools. At the highest level, four of the country's seven universities—the Central University in Quito, the University of Guayaquil, the University of Loja and the University of Manabí—have schools of agronomy, agricultural engineering and veterinary medicine. Of the four, Central University and the University of Guayaquil have by far the largest enrollments.

In the last few years, Central University and the University of

Guayaquil have received assistance from several sources. The United States has furnished help in the form of technical assistance provided by the University of Idaho, the Texas Agricultural and Mechanical College and the University of Pittsburgh. In 1962 the Special Fund of the United Nations allocated $1.2 million to assist in improving the facilities of agronomy and veterinary medicine at Central University. At the same time a loan of $2 million from the proceeds of the sale of surplus food from the United States and a grant from the Rockefeller Foundation made possible the completion and equipment of a building for the School of Agronomy and Veterinary Medicine at the Central University. The four universities, which are autonomous, had a total agricultural faculty of 130 in 1960.

At the intermediate level are two types of institutions offering education in agriculture and livestock raising—vocational schools, until recently under the direction of the Ministry of Development, and technical high schools, under the direction of the Ministry of Education. At the lower level there are two centers of agricultural training—one at Otavalo and one at Chunchi—which at last report were directed by the Ministry of Development.

Instruction in practical agriculture and care of livestock has recently been extended to elementary schools. The Agrarian Reform and Colonization Act provides that the Ministry of Education incorporate livestock and farming instruction in all rural elementary and high schools. To further this program, part of a loan from the Social Progress Trust Fund, made in January 1963, is being used for the establishment of small demonstration and training plots in the elementary schools of the Sierra.

In spite of the obvious effort to provide agricultural education of diverse character, a recent review of the present program by specialists in the field pointed up a number of weaknesses in the system, and in some instances made suggestions for improvement. At the university level one of the main problems is the lack of a full-time teaching staff, as a majority of faculty members, because of the low salary level, must combine teaching with other professional activities.

Since enrollment in the schools of agriculture at the Universities of Loja and Manabí is low, it was suggested that activity be centralized in the University of Guayaquil and the Central University at Quito as a means of raising salaries and upgrading the quality of instruction. It was also suggested that more field work and greater contact with practical problems were needed. At lower levels the study criticized the division of direction of schools as an obstacle to an integrated program and underscored the need for more centers of practical training, particularly for Indian communities in the Sierra. Recent changes should meet some of these criticisms. In March 1964 a law regulating higher education established the minister of education as the principal authority in the field of higher education, thus establishing a basis for integrated programs. Further, recent plans for rural development incorporate the establishment of more centers for practical training.

The greatest obstacle to progress lies in the limited interest evinced in the fields of agronomy and veterinary medicine by students at the higher educational levels. During 1962 and 1963 only 752 students out of a total of almost 11,000 were enrolled in university schools of agronomy and veterinary sciences. Interest in agricultural technical training has been equally low; the four technical high schools graduated only 223 students between 1954 and 1960.

Until recently there was no official organization charged with preparing and executing an integrated comprehensive program of agricultural and livestock research. In 1952, by agreement with the government, SCIA assumed management of the experimental station at Pichilingue on the Coast, where, in addition to research covering a wide range of tropical crops, improved varieties of corn and cacao have been developed and methods of banana and cacao blight control have been established. Improved seed, corn and cacao plants distributed by the station have contributed significantly to the agricultural economy. The Pichilingue station has also made its facilities available to students and faculty members of schools of agronomy for working out experiments on improved strains.

A limited amount of research for specific crops—cotton, wheat, bananas and coffee—has been done by commodity associations, such as the National Cotton Commission; the National Wheat Commission; the Franco-Ecuadorian Institute for Agronomic Research, which is interested in banana culture; and the Ecuadorian Coffee Institute. The Rockefeller Foundation has collaborated in research which has raised unit yields of wheat and potatoes. Central University has also performed limited research in plant and animal pathology.

In 1959 the National Institute for Agricultural and Livestock Research (Instituto Nacional de Investigación Agropecuaria—INIAP) was established as an autonomous agency to organize and carry out a nationwide program of applied research. The Institute did not begin operating until September 1962, when it established the Central Experiment Station at Santa Catalina, near Quito, where research is concentrated on temperate climate crops. At the same time, a substation at Portoviejo, on the Coast, was established for research on cotton, corn and oil crops for the area.

In 1963 the experimental station at Pichilingue was transferred from the direction of SCIA to INIAP, and a new substation was established at Santo Domingo for research on crops of the area, including African palm.

Each experiment station and substation has a director who reports to the director of INIAP in Quito. The general research policy is determined by the director and by the Board of Directors, which consists of the minister of agriculture, the president of the National Development Bank, the technical director of the Planning Board, a representative of IERAC, a representative of the Rockefeller Foundation and the director of INIAP.

In 1965 the staff of INIAP consisted of 60 members with professional degrees, 21 student assistants and 70 support members. The budget for capital and operating expenditures was S/24 million in 1965. It was anticipated that the projected expansion of functions will require staff increases far beyond the number of technically trained personnel currently being graduated by the schools of agronomy.

The practical application of research and education, improved farming techniques, better seeds and plant strains, and better land use are traditionally brought to rural communities through agricultural extension services. Extension services are provided by a diverse group of organizations, characterized by dedication but also by lack of unification. Although some services were provided by the Technical Division of Agriculture and provincial agronomists in the 1940's, it is generally conceded that the inauguration, in 1954, of the National Extension Service (Servicio Nacional de Extensión) by SCIA marked the initiation of an extension service according to the modern concept.

In addition to the National Extension Service, a number of other organizations carry on extension work of a specialized character. The FAO participates in extension activities, but limits its work to the province of Imbabura. The Andean Mission, sponsored by the International Labor Office in Geneva, which administers the Andean Program, incorporates agricultural advice and assistance in its work. The Center for Economic Reconversion of Azuay, Cañar and Morona has initiated its own service, and numerous exporters and commodity associations furnish technical advice to growers of specialized crops.

In 1963 the agreement with SCIA was terminated and the government assumed responsibility for the National Extension Service, which suffered a temporary decline in efficiency and a greatly reduced budget. It is estimated that at that time there were 34 agents, 51 assistant agents and 15 home economists, under the direction of 12 regional supervisors. Approximately 80 4–F Clubs (the counterpart of 4–H Clubs in the United States), with an aggregate membership of 1,722, and 41 home economics clubs, with 1,753 members, had been organized for rural youth.

Observers consider that the agricultural extension services are carried on by a staff of sincere and able, although sometimes inadequately trained, workers. The effectiveness of the program has been limited, however, by lack of funds, inadequate transportation for field workers and a lack of job security for agents.

CHAPTER 20

INDUSTRY

Industry has grown slowly and makes a relatively small contribution to the economy. In 1962 the total industrial contribution to the gross domestic product was 23 percent, distributed as follows: mining, 2.4 percent; manufacturing, 15.4 percent; construction, 3.8 percent; and electricity, water, gas and sanitary services, 1.4 percent. Since 1955, when industry accounted for 21.6 percent of the gross domestic product, relative participation has increased only 1.4 percent.

According to census figures, employment in the principal industrial branches declined from 22.1 percent of the labor force in 1950 to 17.7 percent in 1962 (see ch. 4, Population and Labor Force). In 1960 the value of fixed industrial capital (plant and equipment) was S/6.23 billion (in 1965, S/18.5 equaled US$1—see Glossary), approximately one-fifth of the total value of permanent structures, tools and machinery in the country.

Except for mining and petroleum extraction, which have been developed largely by foreign capital, investment in industry has been essentially domestic. Manufacturing enterprises have attracted some foreign capital, and there is a growing trend toward ventures with mixed foreign and domestic capital.

Mining and petroleum extraction have not played a dynamic role in industrial growth. There has been no development of essential industrial minerals, such as iron and copper. Coal, which is known to exist, is unexploited. Exploration of mineral resources is more difficult and, hence, more costly in Ecuador than in neighboring Andean countries. Throughout most of the Sierra, thick volcanic deposits cover rock strata which might be mineral bearing, and in many parts of the country heavy forests mask possible mineral outcroppings and add to inaccessibility. There is speculation that the rich Andean mineral deposits may end at the northern border of Peru, but only extensive exploration will determine whether this is so. Since exploration is difficult and costly, mining firms have made greater investment in areas where profit on capital invested is greater. Results of petroleum explorations, except on the Santa Elena Peninsula, the chief oil-producing area, have been inconclusive and relatively unprofitable.

Of all the industrial activities, manufacturing makes the most important contribution to the gross domestic product (15.4 percent in 1962), employs the largest segment of the labor force (14.1 percent) and holds the greatest share of fixed capital (11.4 percent). Manufactured products are concentrated in staple consumer goods, such as food, beverages, textiles, clothing, leather and wood products, and factories have tended to cluster around the largest and oldest population centers, Quito and Guayaquil. As a result of an improvement in transportation, smaller industrial centers are developing in the provinces of Azuay, Cañar, Manabí, Tungurahua, Imbabura and Chimborazo, and new industries are adding to diversification.

The growth of manufacturing has been limited by the small size of markets, the lack of domestically produced industrial raw materials, an inadequate supply of energy and the lack of trained managerial and labor forces. Manufacturing productivity is kept low by the existence of large numbers of artisan and handicraft establishments which do not use modern techniques.

The development of domestic industry has been encouraged by tariff protection and by tax incentives to existing or new industries which are considered essential or desirable. The main objective of industrial development laws passed in 1957, 1962 and 1964 is diversification of output for the purpose of increasing exports, substituting domestic products for imports and making greater use of, or developing, national raw materials. To obtain benefits under these laws, a firm's eligibility must be decided by a group representing the central government and various financial, industrial and planning institutions.

In 1965 the procedures for classifying industries and establishing procedures were substantially simplified. Among the specific industries decided to be of special interest in 1965 were those providing nitrogenous chemical fertilizers, glass containers, structural steel, iodized refined salt, sulfuric acid, agricultural machinery and appliances, caustic soda, handtools, kraft paper, cellulose, ceramic bathroom fixtures and dinnerware, and mechanical and electronic precision implements. Incentives have been moderately successful in broadening the structure of manufacturing.

PLANNING AND DEVELOPMENT

Planning for economic development was initiated by the government shortly after World War II. During his presidency, which began in 1948, Galo Plaza Lasso was responsible for the preparation of a general inventory of national problems, resources

374

and existing facilities and for the introduction of technical experts to study and recommend solutions which, unfortunately, were not acted upon before administrations changed.

Comprehensive planning was institutionalized through the establishment of the National Planning and Economic Coordination Board (Junta Nacional de Planificación y Coordinación Económica) in 1954, under President José María Velasco Ibarra. Since that time the government has assumed increasing responsibility for setting national goals and formulating and coordinating sectoral plans to meet the needs of the Ten-Year Development Plan (1964–73) prepared in accordance with the Alliance for Progress (see ch. 18, The Economic System).

Responsibility for industrial development rests with the National Board of Planning and Economic Coordination, which is an agency of the presidency, the minister of industry and commerce and the Development Center (Centro de Desarrollo—CENDES). In addition to programing overall and sectoral development objectives, the National Planning and Economic Coordination Board is also responsible for the interpretation and technical administration of the industrial development laws and for the setting of priorities for tax benefits.

CENDES, created in 1962 as an outgrowth of an Agency for International Development (AID) program, is an autonomous agency charged with the preparation of industrial feasibility studies to locate investment opportunities for private capital, with the active promotion of industry and with the provision of technical assistance to private industry. Administrative decisions and final authority for the activities of CENDES rest with the minister of industry and commerce.

Other agencies have been established for development planning in special fields, such as the National Electrification Institute. Long-term credit for development of private industry is provided by the newly enlarged Securities Commission—National Financial Corporation (see ch. 23, Fiscal and Monetary System).

The government participates in the actual operation of industry to a very limited degree. The established policies generally limit the role of government to the provision of infrastructural facilities and to the encouragement and channeling of industrial development by private enterprise.

MINING

Mining has not played a dynamic role in the economic development of the country. Hampered by the virtual inaccessibility of the regions in which minerals are thought to exist, explorations have been incomplete and reports inconclusive. Furthermore, the

375

difficulties encountered in extraction have inhibited exploitation of some minerals known to exist, although in undetermined quantity and quality.

All minerals and fossil substances found within the earth are legally the property of the nation and considered as part of the national patrimony, although concessions may be granted for private explorations. Mining activities are governed by the General Mining Law, the Law on Gold Washings and the Petroleum Law, all promulgated in 1937.

Under conditions established in the basic laws the state may grant the usufruct of mines by concession to individuals and to civil or commercial companies, either domestic or foreign. Provisions cover the size of grants for exploration and exploitation and the period for which such grants will be in force, usually 30 or 40 years with the option of renewal. Schedules of license fees, taxes and royalties are also set forth specifically in each law. Royalties and fees vary according to the type of mining. For lode and placer mining the royalties are approximately 6 percent of the gross value of the monthly output of the mine. For petroleum extraction royalties vary from 5 to 11 percent of net production.

The government fixes both the price paid to producers for petroleum products for domestic use and the retail sale price for petroleum products used domestically. According to the Petroleum Law, the difference between the two prices is to be used for road construction.

Mineral Resources

Gold, silver, copper and lead are found together in lodes in El Oro Province. Gold is also found in alluvial deposits throughout the country, particularly in areas near the Colombian border, and silver deposits have long been known to exist in Azuay Province. In addition, iron deposits have been found in Guayas and Manabí Provinces. Manganese is known to exist in El Oro; copper, in Pichincha and Cotopaxi; magnesium, in Chimborazo; and platinum, in Esmeraldas and the Oriente.

Among the nonmetallic minerals known to exist are kaolin, mined in Cuenca, and sulfur, which is obtained from two small mines in Carchi. Limestone and gypsum are quarried in many places, mainly in small operations which supply neighborhood needs. Salt deposits are found on the shore in Guayas and in the Galápagos Islands.

Coalbeds are known to exist in Loja, Azuay, and Cañar. The largest known deposit, which is thought to have reserves approaching 38 million metric tons, is found at Biblián in Cañar. Conflicting opinions have been advanced concerning the quality of coal and the feasibility of exploitation. According to a survey made in 1960, the quality of coal is poor, high in sulfur and ash content, unsuited for domestic use and of limited industrial use. However, in 1962 a French mining engineer stated that in his opinion the coal deposits at Biblián are easily workable, amount to 50 million tons of hard coal of good quality and are low in sulfur and ash content and high in caloric content.

Metals

Gold, silver, copper and lead are produced commercially from lode mines in the Portovelo district of El Oro, which is in the more accessible southern part of the country. Gold is by far the most valuable metal; small amounts of silver, copper and lead are obtained as byproducts of gold refining.

The Spanish conquerors discovered the gold lodes of Portovelo in 1549, and the mines have been in operation almost without interruption since then. The first sizable exploitation was initiated by British capital in 1880, when the Great Zaruma Gold Mining Company was granted a concession which it operated until the firm became bankrupt in 1896.

After the failure of the British enterprise the South American Development Company, owned by United States capital, assumed the concession and carried on mining operations at Portovelo for more than 50 years. Plagued by high taxes, low-grade ore and operational difficulties, the company suspended operations in 1950, 10 years before the termination of the grant, and sold the mining installations and equipment to the government at a nominal price.

To provide work for the miners and exploit the remaining ore, the government sponsored a new company, owned jointly by the municipality of Zaruma, the miners who remained and a private business group. Known as the Compañía Industrial Minera Asociada (CIMA), the firm has continued to operate the Portovelo mine and is the sole producer of metals.

Production of metals from the ancient mines of Portovelo has been declining for some time. In 1963 the production of 21,000 troy ounces of gold was slightly less than one-fourth the 1950 output. The quantity of silver and copper produced also declined between 1950 and 1963; only the quantity of lead produced remained fairly stable.

According to incomplete records, between 1951 and 1957 the mines at Portovelo produced gold, silver, copper and lead valued at S/69 million from a total of 387,170 metric tons of ore. In 1958 it was estimated that reserves of the mines owned by CIMA were 49,028 metric tons of ore having 0.423 troy ounces of gold per metric ton. In spite of the adverse forecast, the average annual production of gold since 1958 has been more than 18,000 troy ounces, and the exportation of metals continues to provide a small, but welcome, source of foreign exchange.

For a short period the Macuchi copper deposit in Cotopaxi was exploited by the Cotopaxi Exploration Company, a subsidiary of American Metal Company of New York. In 1937 the firm was granted a concession and, after 3 years of preparatory work which included building 70 miles of road, began production on a commercial scale. Mining continued during World War II, when the demand for copper was strong and prices high, but was discontinued soon after the war.

Petroleum

Exploitable quantities of petroleum, the most valuable of all mineral resources in Ecuador, are found on the Santa Elena Peninsula. According to tradition, petroleum was known in the sixteenth century, and it is reported that ships of the Spanish Armada were caulked with tar from the Santa Elena Peninsula. In 1917 a Canadian firm, the International Petroleum Company (a subsidiary of Standard Oil of New Jersey), and two British firms, Anglo-Ecuadorian Oilfields, Ltd., and McKay Harmsworth Oil Exploration, began exploration on the Santa Elena Peninsula with the expectation of commercial production.

The International Petroleum Company conducted exploration in the coastal area for a number of years with considerable financial investment and indifferent success. In 1947, after drilling 20 wells at an investment of $20 million, International Petroleum gave up its concession, but maintained an importing agency in Guayaquil.

Anglo-Ecuadorian Oilfields, Ltd., has conducted exploration and exploitation activities since its arrival in 1917. Activities of Anglo-Ecuadorian have largely been centered in the Ancón oilfield, discovered in 1923 and the most profitable field as yet discovered.

McKay Harmsworth, which operated in the Tigres oilfield on the Santa Elena Peninsula, was taken over by another firm, the Ecuadorian Oilfields, and the concession has changed ownership a number of times. In 1951, Ecuadorian Oilfields yielded its concession to the Manabí Exploration Company, a firm owned by United States capital. The Manabí Exploration Company operated the concession until 1958, when another United States firm, Tennessee del Ecuador, acquired all assets of Manabí. Since that time, Ecuadorian capital has become associated with Tennessee, and in 1964 it was reported that the firm had become the Empresa Petrolera Ecuatoriana, C.A.

The search for petroleum in the Oriente was begun in 1937 by the Shell Company of Ecuador (a subsidiary of the Royal Dutch

Shell Company). In 1948, Shell was joined in the search by Standard Oil of New Jersey. In 1950 the concessions were abandoned after an investment of more than $40 million, most of which was provided by Shell Company of Ecuador.

The petroleum industry has been developed by private capital. Foreign capital has been the main source of development, but private Ecuadorian capital now participates to a greater extent than formerly.

In 1963 there were five companies in operation: Anglo-Ecuadorian Oilfields, Tennessee del Ecuador, Petropolis Oil Company, Caroline Oil Company and Otto Carbón Avellán. Anglo-Ecuadorian is now owned by joint British and United States capital; Tennessee del Ecuador (later Empresa Petrolera Ecuatoriana), by mixed United States and Ecuadorian capital; and Otto Carbón Avellán, by Ecuadorian private capital. Petropolis Oil Company and Caroline Oil Company are subsidiaries of Anglo-Ecuadorian.

Anglo-Ecuadorian Oilfields, which is by far the largest producer, accounted for almost 87 percent of crude petroleum produced in 1963; in combination with the two subsidiary companies, the firm produced 92 percent of total output. Tennessee del Ecuador accounted for 6.7 percent of output; and Otto Carbón Avellán, for 1.3 percent.

The number of wells in production has been declining. Between 1955 and 1963, wells in production declined more than 20 percent, from 1,457 in 1955 to 1,135 in 1963. Anglo-Ecuadorian Oilfields operated 857 wells (75 percent of the total), and Tennessee del Ecuador operated 171 wells; together, they operated 90 percent of all wells (see table 11).

The three refineries in operation in 1963 had a total refining capacity of 21,500 barrels daily. The largest of the three, the refinery of Anglo-Ecuadorianat La Libertad, had a topping capacity of 11,300 barrels daily and a thermal cracking unit with a capacity of 6,000 barrels daily. Because of the rapid growth of demand, Anglo-Ecuadorian increased its daily capacity by 3,500 barrels in 1964. The other two refineries are those owned by the Cautivo Empresa Ecuatoriana, with a topping capacity of 2,500 barrels daily, and by Santiago Petroleum Company at Tigres oilfield, with a topping capacity of 1,500 barrels daily.

National production includes most types of refined products. All producing companies are equipped with pipelines for delivering crude petroleum from the oilfield to the refinery. Anglo-Ecuadorian maintains highway tank trucks for transportation of products, maintains storage plants in the principal cities and operates retail gasoline stations. Empresa Petrolera Ecuatoriana also has developed a system for marketing its products (see ch. 22, Domestic Trade).

379

Table 11. Daily Production of Crude Petroleum in Ecuador, by Company, 1963

Company	Average daily production[1]	Wells in production	Average daily production per well[1]
Anglo-Ecuadorian Oilfields	5,830	857	6.8
Tennessee del Ecuador[2]	460	171	2.7
Petropolis Oil Company	90	21	4.3
Caroline Oil Company	280	75	3.7
Otto Carbón Avellán	90	11	8.2
Total	6,750	1,135	5.9

[1] In barrels.
[2] Name changed to Empresa Petrolera Ecuatoriana in 1964.

Source: Adapted from Alianza para el Progreso, Comité de los Nueve, *Evaluación del Plan General de Desarrollo Económico y Social del Ecuador*, p. 305.

The petroleum industry has remained more or less static since the early 1950's. Employment in mining and petroleum extraction declined from 5,000 in 1950 to 3,000 in 1962, when it constituted a negligible 0.2 percent of the labor force. Petroleum extraction employs the largest numbers, and the major producer accounts for 50 percent of the total employment. Labor employed in oil production has tended toward leftist affiliation, but recently agreements between producers and workers have been reached amicably (see ch. 21, Labor Relations and Organization).

Production of crude petroleum, which reached a peak of 148 million gallons in 1955, fell to 101 million gallons in 1963, almost 20 percent less than production 10 years earlier (see table 12). Production of all derivatives has increased. Production of commercial gasoline, which doubled between 1953 and 1963, increased from 37 million gallons in 1959 to 63 million gallons in 1960, but declined in the following years. Other derivatives have increased at a similar or greater rate, particularly diesel oil, which first entered commercial production in 1955.

Meanwhile, because of an improvement in roads and a modest growth in industrialization, national consumption of petroleum products has outstripped production. Although information concerning consumption of petroleum derivatives in 1962 and 1963 was not available in 1965, a comparison of available production and consumption figures indicates that a deficit in production, met by importation, has frequently occurred since 1953.

Because of the inadequacy of domestic refining facilities in the

Table 12. *Production and Consumption of Petroleum and Petroleum Derivatives in Ecuador, 1953-56 and 1956-61*

(in thousands of gallons)

Year	Crude petroleum* Production	Gasoline Production	Gasoline Consumption	Kerosene Production	Kerosene Consumption	Diesel oil Production	Diesel oil Consumption	Residual fuel oil Production	Residual fuel oil Consumption
1953	124,601	24,708	31,574	6,948	6,199	408	12,369	25,062	31,672
1954	132,150	27,412	41,312	7,750	6,995	437	14,434	30,132	32,924
1955	148,284	27,880	46,800	8,250	7,846	11,110	16,934	32,526	36,452
1956	143,652	28,676	51,288	9,029	8,666	15,006	18,061	31,561	37,460
1959	115,869	36,975	62,136	10,669	10,726	26,912	24,810	28,797	40,045
1960	115,762	63,117	67,518	12,622	12,779	29,028	29,277	52,031	46,942
1961	122,904	51,234	70,331	13,357	13,265	31,432	29,946	64,836	46,795

*Data on consumption not available.

Source: Adapted from Banco Central del Ecuador, *Boletín*, August-October 1964, p. 157; U.S. Department of Commerce, *Investment in Ecuador*, p. 60; and Ecuador, Ministerio de Formento, *Informe a la Nación*, I, 1962, p. 109.

past, crude petroleum was exported, and refined products were imported to supply the domestic market. Expansion of refining capacity by both major producing companies has diminished the need for exportation of crude oil, which declined from 194,000 metric tons in 1955 to 37,000 metric tons in 1959; during 1960 and 1961, none was exported. Nevertheless, increased domestic refining capacity has not diminished importation of petroleum and petroleum products, which doubled in volume between 1955 and 1963. The relative importance of petroleum products in value of total imports has risen from 2.7 percent in 1960 to 4.8 percent in 1963.

The lagging state of the industry is a cause of concern. In 1959 thermoelectric generation of power used 60,000 metric tons of petroleum, about 15 percent of the total domestic oil consumption. Accelerating industrial growth, which creates new demands on electric power generation, could require vast new sources of petroleum, unless hydroelectric potentials are rapidly developed.

All the petroleum produced at present comes from wells on the Santa Elena Peninsula, where reserves apparently are being depleted. The average production of the Anglo-Ecuadorian wells was 6.8 barrels per day in 1963, and production of the Tennessee del Ecuador wells was only 2.7 barrels per day. The average well depth more than doubled between 1952 and 1962, and production is said to decline rapidly after the initial flow.

Petroleum companies have been notably disinterested in greater activity in the coastal oilfields. In 1960, California Ecuador Petroleum Company abandoned a concession of more than 5 million acres in Guayas, El Oro, Manabí and Esmeraldas Provinces, and in 1961, Tennessee del Ecuador abandoned a concession of almost 900,000 acres in Guayas, Manabí, and Los Ríos. Drilling activity diminished from 75 wells in 1960 to 22 in 1962.

The reluctance of private capital to increase investment in the area is influenced not only by the poor results from past exploration but also by low profits. Prices to producers for petroleum products sold domestically are fixed by the government, based on rates which have not been changed since 1946. Since the domestic market absorbs nearly all production, low prices discourage expansion.

Recent concessions granted for exploration and exploitation in the Oriente may hold some promise as new sources of oil. Norsul Oil and Mining, Ltd., a Canadian company, was granted an 11-million-acre concession in the Oriente, which it plans to develop in cooperation with Union Texas Petroleum Company (a subsidiary of Allied Chemical Corporation); in addition, the Union Texas Petroleum Company and Gulf Oil Corporation were awarded approximately 3.5 million acres in the Oriente near the Colombian border. Successful exploration in adjacent Colombian territory has aroused hope that the field may extend into Ecuador.

POWER

The electric power supply is inadequate for current needs and presents an obstacle to economic growth. To remedy the disadvantageous situation, the government, assisted by various international organizations, has made studies of the power system and has prepared a national plan for electrification.

Power is generated both by thermal units using petroleum derivatives and by hydroelectric units. Despite the scarcity of domestic petroleum derivatives and the apparent abundance of hydraulic resources, thermal units account for 60 percent of total installed capacity. On the coast approximately 97 percent of installed capacity is thermal. Hydroelectric plants provide 80 percent of power potential in the Sierra. Most hydroelectric installations are small. Among the larger ones are the stations at Cumbaya and Guangopolo, which serve Quito, and at Cuenca and Riobamba.

Between 1955 and 1962, installed capacity, including the capacity of privately owned units not providing public service, increased from 66,000 kilowatts to 160,000 kilowatts, and total power generated increased from 241 million kilowatt-hours to 471 million kilowatt-hours. According to calculations of the National Planning and Economic Coordination Board, total power generation increased by an annual cumulative rate of 10 percent, and generation per capita increased at the rate of 7 percent. In spite of the significant increase in power installation, according to a study of electrification in Latin America made by the United Nations in 1961, energy consumed per capita ranked near the bottom among South American countries; only Bolivia and Paraguay consumed less. In 1963 there were 105 kilowatt-hours available per capita, and only 36 percent of the population was supplied with electric power.

All of the principal cities and most smaller towns are served by electricity, but electric power is not available in rural areas. Public power is produced by numerous autonomous municipal plans. The largest power company in operation is the privately owned Empresa Eléctrica del Ecuador (a subsidiary of the American and Foreign Power Company, Inc.), which services Guayaquil and Riobamba. Guayaquil has an installed capacity of 43,475 kilowatts, and in 1962 the peak load was 34,855 kilowatts. The second largest company is the Empresa Eléctrica de Quito, which is owned jointly by the city and the Social Security System of

Ecuador and furnishes power for Quito and its vicinity. Total capacity for Quito in 1964 was 40,000 kilowatts, and the peak load was estimated at 30,000 kilowatts.

Although installed capacity is distributed almost evenly between the Sierra (49 percent) and the Coast (51 percent), distribution within the regions is highly uneven. Taken together, the two largest cities, Quito and Guayaquil, absorb 60 percent of the electricity generated but contain less than 19 percent of the population.

There are a few other plants of modest size, such as Miraflores at Cuenca, Alao near Riobamba and Illuchi at Latacunga, which serve more than one community, but most plants are very small, having a capacity of 100 to 600 kilowatts and providing for the minimum needs of the community.

Investment in power generation has been comparatively small. In 1960 the value of electric power installations was S/380 million, which accounted for only 1 percent of the total fixed capital in Ecuador.

Of the total power consumed in 1962, 47 percent was destined for residences and commercial enterprises, 27 percent for industry, and 8 percent for public lighting. Although most of the existing industries are not large consumers of electric power, the supply available is inadequate to meet industrial needs, and many firms have found it necessary to install private generating units, which provide about 17 percent of total electric power. To ease the present power deficit, some 18,000 kilowatts of generating capacity are being provided by ships moored among the coast and furnished by the United States Government.

Based on a survey of existing conditions, the National Planning and Economic Coordination Board in 1955 reported that the development of electric power had been hampered by the preponderance of minuscule plants, by the lack of national or regional networks and by the absence of a coordinating authority. The report further pointed out the disadvantages arising from a lack of knowledge of production costs and of an appropriate base for rate schedules. The National Plan of Electrification presented with the report has been revised to meet the goals of the Ten-Year Development Plan.

As a step toward implementing the national plan, the Basic Law of Electrification promulgated in 1961 created the office of Director General of Hydraulic Resources and Electrification, which functions under the Ministry of Industry and Commerce. The law also established the Ecuadorian Institute of Electrification (Instituto Ecuatoriano de Electrificación (INECEL), which is charged with preparing feasibility plans for expansion and overseeing the execution of plans, channeling investment and making studies of production costs and rate schedules. INECEL exercises no direct regulatory power but submits advisory opinions to the minister of industry and commerce, who is the final authority on rate changes.

The National Plan of Electrification envisions the formation of nationally connected regional networks and conversion, wherever possible, to hydroelectric units. Specific goals are the immediate addition of 360,000 kilowatts of capacity and the development of 16 regional networks which can be connected nationally.

To assess the hydroelectric potential, resource studies assisted by a grant from the United Nations Special Fund are now in progress. Priority is given to a study of the potential of the Jubones River as a basis for a hydroelectric installation in Guayas and of the Cola San Pablo site on the Paute River as a source of hydroelectric power.

Loans totaling more than $12 million have been made by the International Bank for Reconstruction and Development (IBRD), the AID and the Export-Import Bank of Washington for improvement of existing facilities. The full magnitude of international loans necessary to achieve planning goals cannot be determined until completion of studies of the hydroelectric potential.

CONSTRUCTION

The construction industry enjoyed a period of consistent growth between 1950 and 1960. In the first half of the decade construction increased at an annual rate of 8 percent and contributed 2.8 percent to the value of the gross domestic product. In the second half of the decade activity accelerated to an annual growth rate of 10.6 percent. Between 1960 and 1962 there was a downturn in activity, with a mean annual increase of less than 1 percent annually. In 1963 contribution to the domestic product had fallen to 3.6 percent. Employment in construction activities increased from 27,000 in 1950 to 48,000 in 1962 and from 2.2 percent of the labor force in 1950 to 3.2 percent in 1962.

A sharp expansion of construction began in 1952, when Velasco Ibarra embarked on an uninhibited program of public works which his predecessor, Plazo Lasso, had avoided as putting too great a strain on the stability of the currency. A comprehensive blueprint for highway development was evolved and construction initiated. Among other projects undertaken was the building of 400 new schools distributed widely over the country.

Although the new administration in 1956, under President Camilo Ponce Enríquez, claimed that existing plans for public construction were unworkable, the highway plan was revised, and with the assistance of loans from the IBRD and the Export-Import Bank, construction of roads and necessary bridges continued (see ch. 22, Domestic Trade).

The building of the new port of Guayaquil, a project of great significance to foreign and domestic trade, added considerably to the value of construction. Work on the port, which was started in 1959, was completed in January 1963, at a total cost of $16 million, of which $13 million was provided by a loan from the IBRD.

Activities of the private sector reinforced the mild building boom during the 1950's. Because of the growth of population and migration to the cities, construction of residential and commercial buildings increased markedly. Although building was concentrated largely in Quito and Guayaquil, there was some activity in most of the other cities as well.

The decline in construction after 1960 has been attributed to retrenchment in public investment after the short monetary crisis of 1961. The austerity program caused widespread domestic dissatisfaction, and pressure to accelerate the execution of public works programs was brought to bear on the central government through strikes and petitions in early 1963.

The present outlook is for rising construction activities during the next 10 years. Among the concrete projects for the near future are the building of a bridge over the Guayas River; the further expansion of the new port of Guayaquil, which proved inadequate in less than a year after its construction; and the improvement of other ports. The completion of the 5-year national highway program has been assured by the conclusion in 1964 of an agreement between the central government and a consortium of international lending agencies for a loan of $39 million for construction of roads.

Further stimulation of the construction industry may be expected from residential building and from increased electrical and irrigation installations. In 1961 a new institution, the Housing Bank (Banco de la Vivienda), was created to facilitate financing of housing projects, and feasibility studies are now in progress for a national electrification program and a national irrigation program (see ch. 23, Fiscal and Monetary System).

MANUFACTURING

In 1962 manufacturing was the principal producing sector after agriculture. Its contribution of 15.4 percent of the gross domestic product, less than half that of agriculture (37.3 percent), has grown very slowly—by less than 1 percent between 1955 and 1962. The total value of manufacturing production was about S/2.83 billion, and manufacturing enterprises employed 14.1 percent of the labor force. The principal manufacturing branches by value of products include food and beverages, textiles, chemicals and fabricated metals (see table 13).

For tax purposes manufacturing establishments are classified according to size of investment, value of output and number of workers employed. Establishments employing no more than six people and producing no more than S/15,000 in sales per month are classified as artisan industries and receive tax benefits not accorded to larger establishments.

Food and Beverages

The production of foodstuffs has been expanding steadily as a result of population growth, an increase in per capita income and a policy of protection of domestic industry. Although domestic production does not supply all demands, food imports have been decreasing and in 1963 amounted to S/140 million in contrast to S/161 million in 1955.

Table 13. Major Manufactured Products of Ecuador, 1961 and 1962

Industrial branch	1961		1962	
	Amount*	Percent	Amount*	Percent
Food	1,081,893	42	1,231,603	44
Beverages	276,792	11	305,982	11
Tobacco	29,569	1	31,837	1
Textiles	358,490	14	382,360	14
Printing and publishing	76,691	3	86,543	3
Chemicals	167,170	6	180,154	6
Petroleum derivatives	271,922	10	268,357	9
Nonmetallic mineral products	124,383	5	111,790	4
Other	206,681	8	226,985	8
Total	2,593,591	100	2,825,611	100

*In thousands of sucres; for value of the sucre, see Glossary.

Source: Adapted from Banco Central del Ecuador, *Memoria del Gerente General: Correspondiente al Ejercicio de 1963*, p. 136.

No large, integrated meatpacking plant exists. Slaughtering is done locally, either by farmers or by municipal plants under poor conditions. In most instances meats are distributed and consumed within 24 hours because of the lack of preservation and storage facilities. Refrigeration plants are, however, slowly increasing in number and are found in Quito, Guayaquil, Cuenca and a few other larger cities, such as Riobamba and Ambato. Most cured meats are produced in small shops or on farms, although sausage is produced commercially in plants in Quito, Guayaquil, Cuenca and Ambato.

The canning and food-preserving industry is small. The chief products are fish—mainly tunafish—tomato products, some fruit and a small amount of meat. Canned tunafish is by far the most important product. The largest firm, the United States-owned Industria Ecuatoriana Productora de Alimentos, C.A. (INEPAC), has a canning plant in Manta, with a capacity of 100 tons of tunafish daily. Four plants in Guayaquil and two in Manta also can sardines.

Although tropical and temperate climate fruits and vegetables are plentiful, only a few firms can them. There are two firms in Guayaquil, one in Quito and a new firm in Cayambe, which also can meat products. A recent addition to the field of preserved foods is dehydrated bananas, which, it is hoped, will find a growing acceptance as a baby food.

Except for Guayaquil, the dairy industry is essentially limited to the Sierra. Three plants in Guayaquil and two in Quito supply pasteurized milk, butter and cream. In Quito, where there is a municipal ordinance forbidding the sale of raw milk, pasteurizing capacity has recently been increased to satisfy consumer demand. Cuenca and Latacunga are also supplied with pasteurized milk, but in the rest of the country raw milk is consumed. Cheese is produced in many places in the Sierra, mainly on dairy farms, but there has been a growing tendency toward market expansion, and San Gabriel, Latacunga, Ibarra and Cayambe have cheese factories. Two plants in Cayambe also process powdered milk.

Cane sugar production, which was 52,000 metric tons in 1950, is expected to reach a little more than 180,000 metric tons in 1965. Eight mills on the Coast and, since the end of 1964, one in the Sierra, supply refined sugar for domestic consumption and support a growing export trade. To meet domestic demand and to take advantage of the allotted export quota, the industry is expanding.

Production has long been dominated by two plants, Ingenio Valdez and Ingenio San Carlos, near Guayaquil. Both plants, which are modern and well equipped and rank among the largest and most progressive in the country, have increased their capacity. In 1965 their combined output is expected to be 168,000 metric tons. Smaller coastal mills are modernizing equipment and increasing output potential.

The Tababuela mill, the first large-scale sugar refinery in the Sierra, is owned by the Social Security System. It began production on a trial basis in November 1964. The mill, which is located near Ibarra in Imbabura Province, was built at a cost of

S/92.5 million and has a grinding capacity of 750 metric tons per day. It is faced with a shortage of raw materials, and it is estimated that the 1,500 acres under cane cultivation nearby will supply the mill for a grinding season of only 3 months per year.

Sugar is exported to Chile, and Ecuador was allotted an export quota of 51,121 short tons by the United States in 1965. Molasses is also produced, and there is a small candy industry which has been under study for expansion.

Since 1943, when the first processing company, Industrias Ales, C.A., was organized, production of edible oils and vegtable shortening has grown rapidly. In 1963 there were eight producing firms, located in Guayaquil and Manta, and output reached about 2 million quarts of edible oil and 7,367 metric tons of vegetable shortening. Potential capacity has been increased by the establishment of Cultivo y Extracción de Oleaginosas, S.A., at Guayaquil. The industry, which processes oilseeds, soybeans, cotton seeds, palm seeds, sesame seeds and peanuts, has been limited by inability to obtain sufficient raw materials in the domestic market and has been forced to import vegetable oils and oilseeds. Under a grant from the Inter-American Development Bank (IDB) studies are being conducted on the feasibility of growing the African palm on a large scale to eliminate the deficit in raw materials.

Rice milling, which is an important industry on the Coast, is concentrated in Guayas, Los Ríos and Manabí. There are about 50 public mills, which handle about 95 percent of the crop, and innumerable smaller private mills. One of the largest mills, Piladora Modelo, owned and operated by the National Development Bank (Banco Nacional de Fomento), exports rice and processes and sells it in the domestic market (see ch. 19, Agriculture).

About 20 mills in the Sierra and 3 on the Coast produce wheat flour. Milling in the Sierra is concentrated in Quito, Ambato, Riobamba and Cuenca; a few other mills serve neighborhood markets. All mills on the Coast are located in Guayaquil. The largest mill in the country, Harinas del Ecuador, C.A., which was established in Guayaquil in 1952, is said to have an annual capacity of 55,000 tons, more than half the combined capacity of the 20 larger mills in the Sierra, which is estimated at 90,000 tons.

There is considerable conflict of interest between millers on the Coast and those in the Sierra. Efforts of the government to provide encouragement for wheat growing in the Sierra by protection from foreign competition have met with disfavor on the Coast, where no wheat is grown and millers use imported wheat. Since the price of flour is set by government, a tax on wheat imports, which raises the cost of production, creates an adverse profit situation for coastal millers.

Increased production of wheat flour has made possible the expansion of the baking industry. Practically all of the larger cities have commercial bakeries which produce bread and cakes. The principal beverages produced are beer, wines, liqueurs, carbonated drinks and mineral waters. Coca-Cola, Pepsi-Cola and Orange Crush are produced under franchise from parent companies in the United States.

Two large breweries, Compañía de Cervezas Nacionales in Guayaquil and Cervecería y Maltería La Victoria in Quito, are the only producers of beer. The output of both plants was 63 million bottles in 1963, a decline from 68 million bottles in 1960. Until the mid-1950's beer was made with imported malt. In 1955, Cervezas Nacionales constructed a malting plant near Quito, and 2 years later Cervecería y Maltería La Victoria built a malting plant at Latacunga. Both plants process domestically grown barley, and capacity has increased to the point that the national product provided 98 percent of all malt used in brewing.

Wine is not widely consumed, and relatively little is produced. The manufacture and sale of all beverages of high alcoholic content is controlled by the central government.

Tobacco Products

Two firms, El Progreso and Intaca, manufacture tobacco products. El Progreso, which accounts for 90 percent of total production, operates one plant in Guayaquil and another in Sangolquí, near Quito. Intaca operates one plant in Quito.

Cigarettes constitute the main product; the output of cigars and pipe tobacco is small. In 1962 the total output of cigarettes was 45 million packages, in contrast to 60 million packages in 1950.

Foreign-made cigarettes are preferred to domestic brands, which, in the main, are made from darker native-grown tobacco. Both foreign-made cigarettes and bulk tobacco are imported, and imported cigarettes make up about one-third of known consumption. Since importation is government controlled and there is a 50 percent ad valorem tax on imported cigarettes, a considerable contraband trade flourishes (see ch. 24, Foreign Economic Relations).

Textiles and Wearing Apparel

The textile industry, which ranks next to foodstuffs in value of production and in labor employed, is centered in the Sierra, where it originated as an outgrowth of home weaving. Cotton constitutes the major part of textile production, and silk, synthetics and woolen fabrics are also produced. Production methods range from large, modernized factories, such as Fábrica La Internacional in Quito and Industria Algodonera Imbabura in Atuntaqui, through small plants with antiquated machinery to cottage weaving.

Products include knitwear as well as woven goods, and several firms in Quito produce nylon hose. Total output for 1961 was estimated at 32.8 million yards of cotton fabrics, 4.6 million yards of silk and synthetic fabrics and 437,000 yards of woolen materials. Traditionally, domestic cottons have been considered inferior in quality to imports, but there has been considerable effort since 1950 to upgrade quality and increase the variety offered. Woolen textiles are of high quality and enjoy wide acceptance. Woolens woven by the Otavalo Indians, in particular, are highly prized (see ch. 5, Ethnic Groups and Languages).

Domestic raw materials are not adequate in quantity nor considered to be of the best quality. In 1961 only 52 percent of the cotton used by the textile industry was of domestic origin. All silk and synthetic fibers are imported, since they are not produced locally, and the supply of wool is augmented by imports. Increased use of domestic raw materials has high priority for import substitution, and agricultural research organizations are giving attention to improved productivity and quality of domestic cotton and wool (see ch. 19, Agriculture).

Wearing apparel has been mainly the product of individual artisans or small artisan workshops employing not more than five workers. Factory-made clothing has only recently begun to compete with handmade products in some fields. The main products are men's shirts, suits, pajamas, underclothing, bathrobes, children's clothing, work clothes, rainwear, felt hats and shoes.

Although most clothing factories are small, recently there have been new establishments large enough to command a significant part of the market. In the field of men's suits, Lanafit, a Guayaquil firm established in 1961, expanded the value of its production from S/1.7 million in the first year of operation to S/5 million in 1963, and by 1965 served 10 percent of a market which had previously been served by thousands of custom tailors. In the field of footwear, four new factories in Guayaquil, which produce low-priced plastic and canvas top shoes, have a combined annual capacity of over 1 million pairs, more than 50 percent of the entire annual consumption of shoes.

The best-known article of apparel is a hat woven of toquilla straw and known as a Panama hat, although it originated in Ecuador. Panama hats are produced by artisans, mainly in Manabí, Azuay and Cañar, and are known universally for their excellence. Production has been declining since 1950 (see ch. 24, Foreign Economic Relations).

Printing and Publishing

Newspapers and periodicals are the most important branches of the printing industry, measured by volume of capital invested and number of workers employed. Although books are also published, a need has been expressed for more firms publishing the works of native authors, a need that will be only slowly filled, given the restricted nature of the markets. Job printing is largely an artisan industry.

Chemicals

Chemical products, destined mainly for consumer use, include pharmaceuticals, soap and detergents, cosmetics, matches, plastic articles, bottled gas, insecticides, paint and varnish, and fertilizers. The chemical industry has attracted some foreign capital, particularly in the fields of pharmaceuticals, paint, insecticides and fertilizers. With a few exceptions, installations are small (see ch. 24, Foreign Economic Relations).

The largest manufacturer of pharmaceuticals is Laboratorios Industriales Farmaceuticas Ecuatorianas (LIFE), which was established in Quito in 1940. LIFE operates a well-equipped plant with laboratory facilities and employs well over 500 people. Many products, including vitamins, vaccines, medicines, disinfectants and products for veterinary use, are manufactured. No antibiotics are manufactured. LIFE carries on a thriving export trade with Latin American countries and supplies a large share of the domestic market. In 1964 a United States-based firm, Dow Chemical International, purchased a controlling interest in the company.

Production of insecticides based on pyrethrum, a daisy-like flower grown in the Sierra, is a rapidly expanding branch of the chemical industry and has attracted foreign capital. To supply the rising domestic and export demand, a new processing plant has been constructed, and increased acreage has been planted (see ch. 24, Foreign Economic Relations).

Production of fertilizer has been inadequate to meet domestic demand, most of which has been met by importation of fertilizers or of basic ingredients. In 1946 a small plant was established by the Ministry of Development at La Libertad on the Santa Elena Peninsula to produce fertilizer through crushing guano and oyster shells. Since the supply of basic materials is depleted, the plant has ceased operation. In 1961 a small plant was established in Quito by the Ministry of Development to produce organic fertilizer through processing garbage. A similar installation at Cuenca completes the sources of domestically produced fertilizer.

Four mixing plants also exist. Fertilizantes Ecuatorianas S.A.

(FERTISA), in which Chemoleum Corporation of the United States has an interest, built a mixing plant near Guayaquil at a cost of S/9,250,000. The plant entered production in 1964, and FERTISA is planning to install both a sulfuric acid and an ammonium sulfate plant to supply basic raw materials.

Production of industrial chemicals is in an early stage. Caustic soda will be made by a salt-producing firm at a plant under construction on the Santa Elena Peninsula. A plant in Guayaquil produces explosives, and a few other industrial chemicals are produced by a plant in Quito.

Matches, which were formerly a government monopoly, are manufactured in Quito by a cooperative organization using the former government facilities. Competition from contraband matches reduces the size and profitability of the venture.

Nonmetallic Mineral Products

Cement production increased from 58,000 metric tons in 1950 to 219,000 metric tons in 1961. Two plants are responsible for the supply of cement, and a third plant has been constructed but was not in production in mid-1965. Cemento Nacional Rocafuerte, which was established by private capital in Guayaquil in 1935, remained the only domestic source of supply until 1956, when Cemento Chimborazo was established near Riobamba to supply the Sierra market. Cemento Chimborazo was established through investment of the Development Bank, the municipality of Riobamba, the Social Security Fund, and a German firm which supplied the machinery. In 1955 construction was started on a third plant, Industrias Guapán, at Guapán in Cañar. Capital has been provided by the Social Security Fund and the Pension Fund. The plant is completed, but in mid-1965 production had not begun, for lack of sufficient electric power.

Increased demand for cement, which was engendered by the building boom, was accompanied by additions to plant capacity by Cemento Nacional, as well as by construction of Cemento Chimborazo. The present potential capacity of the two plants is estimated to be 310,000 tons per year, which is considered adequate to meet foreseeable demands of increased construction activity.

Structural clay products, including refractory brick, building brick and tile, are produced by small factories for neighborhood demand.

Wood Products

Requirements for wood products are largely filled by local industry from native woods. Furniture making is almost entirely carried on by craftsmen in small workshops, although a small amount is factory made in Quito and Guayaquil. Commercial establishments in Guayaquil and Quito also provide factory-made doors, window frames, flooring and plywood. Recently, parquet flooring has been added to the output.

Rubber Goods

The most important addition to the rubber industry is the establishment of a tire-producing plant at Cuenca by the Ecuadorian Rubber Company, a joint venture of the General Tire and Rubber Company of the United States and national capital. The plant began operation in 1963 with an annual output capacity of 40,000 tires and the expectation of expansion to 100,000. A plantation to produce natural rubber for tires has been established about 40 miles from Guayaquil.

In Ambato, Fábrica Venus, the largest plant in the country, produces tennis shoes, rubber boots, garden hoses and automobile accessories. Five other plants in Ambato manufacture rubber goods, and four plants in Quito produce rubber balls, toys and footwear. Plants in Guayaquil manufacture tennis shoes and rubber heels, and there are tire-retreading shops in Quito and Guayaquil.

Leather Goods

Leather is produced by some 20 tanneries, more than 50 percent of which are located in Ambato. The combined annual output of the 4 largest tanneries (in order of size)—Tenería ENIC in Quito, La Iberia in Guayaquil, La Renaciente in Cuenca and Curtiduría Salazar in Ambato—is estimated at 2.3 million square feet. The leather is soft, easily scratched and often has holes from tick bites.

The manufacture of leather goods is largely an artisan or handicraft industry. Shoes, belts, pocketbooks and other accessories are made mostly by hand in small workshops, which also serve as retail sales outlets. Factories producing leather shoes are located in Guayaquil, Quito and Riobamba.

Paper and Paper Products

Ecuador is not self-sufficient in the production of paper. There is no integrated pulp and paper mill using wood. The only existing paper mill, which is located at Latacunga, produces brown kraft paper from cellulose from banana stalks. All types of paper, including board for boxes, are imported.

Bags, cartons and boxes are produced by a number of firms, mostly on the Coast. Industrial development and new techniques of marketing are responsible for the expansion of packaging facilities. In response to a change in banana marketing, two coastal firms, owned jointly by Ecuadorian and United States capital, have expanded their capacity to make boxes for banana exports.

The development of an integrated pulp and paper industry using domestic raw materials held high priority in planning for industrial growth and import substitution in 1965. Studies were being made of forest resources, and the establishment of a mill near Guayaquil to produce paper from wood pulp was projected. Although no paper is produced from bagasse (fiber from sugarcane), the possibility is under consideration.

Metals Fabrication

Fabricated metal products traditionally have included aluminum cooking utensils, metal office furniture, bicycles, nails, screws, nuts and bolts. Recently, production has been expanded to include plumbing fixtures, agricultural handtools, automobile parts, galvanized pipe and structural iron rods. One of the most recent additions is Acerías Nacionales Ecuatorianas, owned by national and Chilean capital. At the new plant, established near Guayaquil, the firm manufactures structural steel products with raw materials from the Huachipato steel mill in Chile.

ARTISAN INDUSTRY

Artisans constitute the bulk of the manufacturing labor force. According to a census sponsored by the National Planning and Economic Coordination Board, in 1962 approximately 227,000 persons, or 89 percent of the total manufacturing labor force of 257,000, were classified as artisans. Factory industry employed slightly less than 30,000 persons.

Because of the small amount of capital invested in machinery and tools, the artisan industry is characterized by low productivity and a low level of worker income. Of the total of S/4 billion invested in fixed capital in manufacturing, only S/155 million is invested in the tools and equipment of artisan workshops and home industries, and it is estimated that the productivity of factory labor is 10 times that of the artisan working with only handtools.

Approximately 53,000 dressmakers, tailors, shoemakers, cabinetmakers and carpenters working full time in urban areas produce 95 percent of all clothing and shoes and at least 86 percent of all furniture and other wood products. In addition, individual workers, or shops employing no more than six persons, produce construction materials, engage in printing and bookbinding, weave fine fabrics and fine straw hats, and work with precious metals. In rural areas articles produced at home by part-time workers supplement the family income.

Concern for the welfare of this large group of workers was evidenced by the Decree Law for the Protection of Artisans of 1953. Provisions were made for health, welfare and education facilities, and tax relief was granted to entrepreneurs who met the qualifications outlined as to number of workers, amount of sales and capital involved. The measures of the law, which were not always fully observed, served to perpetuate small industry rather than encourage growth, as many workers preferred to limit their activities rather than become involved in the tax intricacies that would accompany a higher industrial status.

As an encouragement to greater manufacturing production and higher income levels, the Law for the Development of Artisan and Small Industry was decreed by the government on January 15, 1965. The objective of the new law is to encourage the transition from artisan workshops to small factories by raising the limit of fixed capital, by granting relief from numerous provincial and municipal taxes and by giving concessions on reinvested capital and on the importation of machinery, tools and raw materials. A further objective is the encouragement of production of goods for export by the forgiveness of export taxes (see ch. 23, Fiscal and Monetary System).

The law established the Committee on the Growth of Artisan and Small Industry, and a division for small industry has been established by CENDES. Recognition has also been given to the desirability of increasing production and opening markets for handicrafts (see ch. 22, Domestic Trade).

CHAPTER 21

LABOR RELATIONS AND ORGANIZATION

The Ecuadorian environment has not been especially favorable to the development of organized labor. The nature of the national economy, preponderantly agricultural with little development of modern industry, and a deeply rooted social and political conservatism have been major impediments. Other factors have been a nationwide low rate of literacy and the cultural isolation of the Indians, who form a large segment of the population.

Organized labor is a small force. The total number of organized workers can be only roughly estimated. As no agencies exist for the collection of labor statistics, there are no official figures. Union records, when they are kept, are not always dependable, particularly about the size of membership. In 1965 there were probably no more than 100,000 organized workers, a very small minority of an economically active population of about 1.5 million. Union members have been drawn principally from the ranks of manual laborers, white-collar workers and artisans, employed in industry, government and commerce. Although a few unions have been established in recent years among peasants and coastal plantation workers, the agricultural sector remains virtually unorganized. Geographically, labor unions are highly concentrated in Guayaquil and Quito.

On the whole, the movement has suffered from internal weaknesses. Limited economic resources, low educational levels and lack of experience in cooperative action among most union members have discouraged the formation of a healthy, vigorous base. Confederations and other large labor bodies do not truly represent the consolidation of grassroot movements, but rather represent the effort of a few individuals, usually drawn from intellectual circles rather than from the working class, who have acted in concert with outside groups. Personal rivalries and ideological differences among these individuals have divided labor organizations and the movement as a whole.

In 1965 there were three nationwide organizations: the dominant Communist-controlled Confederation of Ecuadorian Workers

(Confederación de Trabajadores Ecuatorianos—CTE); the far smaller Ecuadorian Confederation of Catholic Workers (Confederación Ecuatoriana de Obreros Católicos—CEDOC); and the Ecuadorian Confederation of free Labor Organizations (Confederación Ecuatoriana de Organizaciones Sindicales Libres—CEOSL). Little independent action has been taken by these groups to strengthen and expand the movement. That which has taken place seems to have been inspired largely by international entities and labor organizations, which in recent years have demonstrated growing interest in, and influence on, local labor.

Other factors have also limited labor's general effectiveness and influence. Employers, for example, who tend individually to occupy positions of greater economic, social and political importance than do their employees collectively, have generally demonstrated conservative, if not hostile, attitudes toward labor unionism. As the majority of the unions have neither the power nor the skill to counteract employer resistance, they have not usually been able to obtain gains independently. In many cases, therefore, rather than work through the standard channels of collective bargaining and other direct dealings with employers, labor tended to look to broader political sectors to achieve its ends.

As in most Latin American countries, the government plays an important role in labor affairs. The government's involvement comes through its role as the largest single employer in the country; through legislative programs, chiefly the Labor Code of 1938; and through executive fiat, expressed in decrees or, less formally, in direct action. Legislation, for example, affects the organization of each union, which must receive recognition by the national executive before obtaining legal status. To an even greater extent, the law governs labor relations, outlining procedures and introducing government participation. Executive action can bring increased benefits or the curtailment of activity by unions and their leaders.

The labor movement's relative weakness before government power has placed it in a position of dependence. For the most part, labor has not been able to win constant and unequivocal official support either through economic pressure or through the more common Latin technique of political activity. The main body of the labor movement, brought together in the CTE, has maintained formal ties with a political party, the Communist Party of Ecuador (Partido Comunista del Ecuador—PCE), but the Communists have never been able to win power through election or even to collaborate in government through coalition. In the opposition, they have seldom gained influence sufficient to command real consideration. Other labor organizations, though politically oriented, have not been politically active. The non-Communist parties likewise have demonstrated little interest in cultivating labor groups outside the CTE, probably because of their limited strength.

Recent governments have been mildly favorable to labor, in part through conviction but, probably, in greater part in response to popular unrest. Since the military government came to power in July 1963, no clear policy toward labor has been apparent. The approach to labor matters has been pragmatic, following the government's general objective of establishing order and stability. Favorable action toward labor has usually been in the form of legislation to increase benefits or to create new ones. Unfavorable actions have been in the form of temporary restrictions on basic union activities. As a result, organized labor under the military government has been unusually quiet and apathetic.

ORIGINS AND DEVELOPMENT

Firmly rooted in the European tradition, guilds and societies were the first form of associations among the Ecuadorian laboring class. Comprised generally of artisans, these organizations afforded small financial benefits in case of illness or death, professional fraternity and a social outlet to their members. In addition, the activities of guilds and societies often had religious overtones.

As the nineteenth century came to a close, changing circumstances brought new problems and new possibilities for the laborer. A prosperous economy had developed on the coast, giving rise to small factories and a corresponding concentration of workers. As a result of greater economic growth and commercial activity, workers experienced some exposure to the ideas and agents of European labor unionism, chiefly anarchist and syndicalists in orientation. At the same time a political revolution took place which brought the Liberals to power and offered a promise of general progress (see ch. 3, Historical Setting).

In response, a few workers' organizations were established which retained many of the aspects of the older societies and guilds, but which were generally less passive and aloof. The greatest and most energetic activity took place in Guayaquil, the seat of the first regional labor organization, the Guayas Labor Confederation (Confederación Obrera del Guayas), established in 1905. New influences were not confined to Guayaquil, however, for some time later, Quito also became a focus of labor development with the establishment of the Artistic and Industrial Society of Pichincha (Sociedad Artística e Industrial de Pichincha). These organizations took on a new activity, the publication of newspapers.

Though shortlived and small, the publications manifested nascent class-consciousness and economic concern, at least on the part of the leaders.

Discontent, encouraged by working situations and relationships differing from those of the past, found a channel for expression in the new organizations. At an early state this discontent became crystallized in specific goals. In 1909 a labor congress was held in Guayaquil which drew up a list of demands. Attempts were also made to enforce demands through strikes, the first of which was staged by the railroad workers of Durán in 1908. Others followed, particularly after the general economic crisis precipitated by the fall of the cacao market (see ch. 3, Historical Setting).

Partly as a result of these manifestations, legislation was passed in 1916 to regulate the working day and to offer some protection for the worker against abuse by employers. Although additional laws were enacted during the next few years, dissatisfaction did not abate. Strikes continued to take place, culminating in the Guayaquil uprising of 1922, which resulted in the death of many labor leaders. The new administration which came to power in 1925, largely on the wave of social and political discontent, gave some support to labor through the creation of a labor ministry and the enactment of a number of labor laws.

At roughly the same time new political groups, which were to play a significant role in subsequent labor development, were forming. Unlike the traditional political parties the Socialists and soon thereafter the Communists, formed from a Socialist splinter group, were concerned with the working class and sought to develop and gain control of the labor movement (see ch. 14, Political Dynamics). Initially, weakness, inexperience and factionalism within both labor and political circles presented the establishment of clear-cut alignments.

This division was reflected in early attempts to establish connections with international labor organizations. In the mid-1920's elements of the Ecuadorian labor movement attended conferences of the Pan American Federation of Labor, dominated by the United States American Federation of Labor (AFL) and by Mexican Labor unionists, and finally affiliated with that body in 1928. Simultaneously, other elements, probably more political than labor unionist, represented the country in the Latin American Labor Confederation (Confederación Sindical Latino-Americana—CSLA), a Communist organization established in 1929.

By the late 1930's the Communists and Socialists had begun to cooperate, and the prospects for increased labor development seemed favorable. In 1937 centrals were established in Guayas and Pichincha, the two key provinces. The following year government sympathy toward labor, based primarily on the influence of Socialists in the administration, resulted in the enactment of a liberal labor code (see ch. 4, Population and Labor Force). With government approval, national workers' conventions were held in Guayaquil and Ambato in 1937 and 1938 to establish a nationwide labor central. These attempts proved unsuccessful and resulted in the immediate breaking away of the nonleftist minority, which, with encouragement from conservative Church elements, formed its own central, the CEDOC. At the same time representatives of the Communist-Socialist majority took part in an important regional event, the founding of the first genuine inter-American labor organization, the Confederation of Latin American Workers (Confederación de Trabajadores de América Latina —CTAL), which brought together all the principal labor groups of the hemisphere.

During the next few years efforts continued to bring the main body of the labor movement, under Communist-Socialist influence, into a national central. A visit in 1943 by the CTAL secretary general, the Marxist Vicente Lombardo Toledano, who was campaigning for the consolidation of national labor movements, inspired the call for a national congress in Quito. The National Committee for Unification was formed, but, before further steps could be taken, an unsympathetic government broke up the congress and jailed many of its leaders. On release of the leaders the Committee collaborated with the political Ecuadorian Democratic Alliance (Alianza Democrática Ecutoriana), which was working to overthrow the Arroyo del Río government, an endeavor which was successfully completed in May 1944 (see ch. 3, Historical Setting).

Among the promises of the new government, under José María Velasco Ibarra, was the official support and encouragement of the labor movement. Almost immediately a government-sponsored labor congress was held in Quito. Dominated by the Communists, the congress established the CTE. Pedro Antonio Saad Niyam, the leader of the Communist Party, was elected president of the new organization. Affiliation was established immediately with the CTAL, by this time clearly Communist, and in 1945 with the World Federation of Trade Unions (WFTU), which initially included both Comunist and non-Communist elements.

In subsequent years the CTE dominated the labor movement, creating almost a mystique through a largely vocal but militant defense of the worker. For the most part, political aims were the principal concern of the CTE leadership, and little real progress was achieved in the economic sphere. In the late 1950's and early 1960's the CTE seemed to be losing some of its dominance, as new groups, including a national central, were forming.

ORGANIZATION AND OPERATIONS

The right to form unions is recognized in Article 185 of the 1946 Constitution, still in force in 1965. Legal recognition is extended to those unions which bring together workers in related or different activities, as long as they belong to associations in their respective branches, and to the local, provincial, regional or national federations and confederations which they may form. The right to juridical representation is granted upon approval by the Ministry of Labor of union statutes, which must indicate the type and location of the organization and its rules and regulations. That these requirements are not strictly enforced in practice is reflected by incomplete government records. The total number of labor organizations is therefore unknown.

Lower Levels

The *sindicato*, roughly translatable as "union local," is the smallest unit of labor organization. The term encompasses a variety of groups, some of which are not commonly considered labor unions in the United States. Some *sindicatos* are organized by establishment and others encompass all workers in the same occupation in a town or city. As a rule, separate organizations exist for manual laborers and white-collar workers. Among the latter, unionization is fairly widespread. In addition, there are a great number of *sindicatos* composed of artisans. As artisans tend to work alone or with a limited number of assistants, the artisan *sindicatos* are actually associations of self-employed persons or associations which combine employers and employees. A few peasant *sindicatos*, made up of independent and tenant farmers as well as farmworkers, also exist. The mixed nature of these *sindicatos* or the lack of clear-cut employer-employee relationships necessarily precludes most of the activity normally pursued by labor unions.

The *sindicatos*, especially those outside the principal urban centers, are usually small and weak. The majority come into being as a result of temporary crises or the efforts of outside organizers and, at times, of the employers themselves, who establish company unions. Often, therefore, the concepts of continuity and firm group commitment are lacking. Leaders tend to be inexperienced, and the members, frequently indifferent. Funds are limited as dues are extremely low, often amounting to no more than S/1 or S/2 monthly per capita (in 1965, S/18.5 equaled US$1—see Glossary). Low wage levels make even this small contribution a sacrifice for many workers (see ch. 4, Population and Labor Force). Moreover, nonpayment does not bring expulsion or exclusion from the benefits union action may obtain. For these reasons, dues collection is difficult. Though legal, the checkoff system is practiced only when requested by the union.

Most *sindicatos* are not able to establish permanent headquarters and use instead company buildings or temporary facilities for meetings. Services to the membership are also generally lacking. To act during moments of crisis, *sindicatos* must usually seek support or technical aid from the larger organizations to which they belong.

Federations are organized on a provincial or occupational basis. In most of the provinces there is at least one provincial federation composed of *sindicatos* of various types. Artisan *sindicatos* provide the backbone of these federations in the less urbanized provinces. With the exception of the Federation of Chauffeurs, none of the occupational federations are truly national in scope. On the contrary, the concentration of skilled workers around Quito and Guayaquil has given the occupational federations a regional, or, in some instances, even a municipal character. In both types of federations, membership is small, the largest amounting to only several thousand.

In modified form, the federations generally face the same problems of finance and leadership as the *sindicatos*. In the case of leadership, however, the federations are frequently beset with the additional difficulty of in-fighting or struggles between federation and confederation executives, which arise chiefly from personal ambition or political differences. Under these circumstances, federations of some importance have at times assumed an almost autonomous position within the confederation to which they formally belong and thereby produce an obvious weakening effect. A few of the federations, generally occupational, have demonstrated considerable efficiency and effectiveness, however, The Portworkers of Guayaquil, for instance, have obtained good collective contracts and have been able to establish their own headquarters and a high school for workers' children.

Most labor organizations are affiliated to one of the three national confederations. There are a number, however, which are independent, among them provincial federations in Pichincha, Imbabura, Cotopaxi and Carchi; the National Teachers Union (Unión Nacional de Educadores—UNE); the National Union of Journalists (Unión Nacional de Periodistas—UNP) and a number of small local unions, located principally in Guayaquil and Quito.

National Confederations

Of the three national confederations the CTE is the most influential and representative. Early in 1965 its estimated membership was 60,000. Among the CTE's more important affiliates are provincial federations in Pichincha, Guayas and Tungurahua

(Federación de Trabajadores de Pichincha, Federación de Trabajadores del Guayas and Federación de Trabajadores de Tungurahua—FTP, FTG and FTT, respectively) ; the National Federation of Petroleum Workers (Federación Nacional de Trabajadores del Petróleo—FNTP) ; the Federation of Municipal Workers (Federación de Trabajadores Municipales—FTM) and the National Union of Electrical Workers of Ecuador (Sindicato Nacional de Trabajadores Electricistas del Ecuador—SNTEE).

The two most powerful occupational groups are the large National Textile Federation (Federación Nacional Textil—FNT), one of the oldest labor organizations in the country, and the National Federation of Chauffeurs of Ecuador (Federación Nacional de Choferes del Ecuador—FNCE). Composed of employers, employees and owner-operators, the FNCE is fairly well organized and occupies an obvious strategic position in the national economy. Other affiliates include the printers, the brewery workers, the shoe workers and federations in most of the provinces.

Direction of CTE affairs and policy is handled by the national convention, held every 2 years; the National Executive Council, which meets annually; and the Central Executive Committee, the most important of the three. Since the CTE's founding in 1944, positions of leadership have been held by Communists and Socialists, active in party affairs. Leaders like Communist Pedro Saad and Revolutionary Socialist José Telmo Hidalgo Díaz have also assumed overt political roles as labor senators from the Coast and the Sierra (see ch. 14, Political Dynamics). Even when the Communists have been in the minority on CTE administrative organs, they have exerted the greater influence.

As a whole, however, the CTE is not a monolithic Communist structure, nor is it monolithic in any sense. Among the top leaders, agreement has been neither constant nor complete. Tendencies toward dissension have been aggravated, moreover, by recent division based on the international Chinese-Soviet split (see ch. 14, Political Dynamics). In addition, some affiliates, including the important FNCE are led by non-Communists and have more non-Communists than Communist-dominated local unions within their ranks.

Differences have been reflected in inaction at the top or in less than full cooperation with confederation directives among affiliates. Calls for general strikes, for example, have frequently been ignored by a substantial percentage of the member unions. Basic loyalties to the CTE, however, have remained intact. To its members, as well as to many outsiders, the CTE is the traditional militant defender of the workers and the only true labor central. Although the organization has not always been able to produce results, it has consistently offered unequivocal support, both moral and technical, to members in conflict with other elements of society. These attitudes, along with the widespread feeling of the need for labor union unity, have been actively encouraged by CTE leaders. Disassociation from the CTE has consequently been the exception and has involved groups of limited strength and influence. In 1960, for example, some dissident artisan and white-collar groups withdrew to form the Confederation of Trade Unions of the Ecuadorian Coast (Confederación Regional de Organizaciones Clasistas del Litoral Ecuatoriano—CROCLE). The following year a similar process took place in the province of Pichincha.

The Catholic-oriented CEDOC has an estimated membership of 20,000. The confederation's chief support comes from craft unions affiliated through provincial federations. The most important affiliate, however, is the Ecuadorian Federation of Fruit-loaders (Federación Ecuatoriana de Trabajadores de Embarques de Frutas y Anexos—FETEF), which is one of the strongest occupational federations in the country. The FETEF was organized in the spring of 1964 around the Guayaquil Fruitloaders Union, which at that time was reported to have 8,000 members. Among local federations the FETEF is unique, operating as the sole labor contracting agency in fruitloading and, thus, controlling the market. Salaries are paid through the FETEF rather than directly by the companies. This feature, combined with the relatively high wages which the federation has been able to obtain for its members, has placed it in a good economic position. Consequently, the CEDOC's principal financial backing comes from the FETEF.

Although the CEDOC has been in existence longer than the CTE, it has never had notable success among the general body of workers, probably because of its conservatism. Some political opponents of the confederation allege that it was established at the instigation of conservative elements in the Sierra more for promoting religious faith among the workers than for furthering economic and social gains.

During most of its existence, the CEDOC has been dominated by the forceful and dedicated personality of Isabel Robalino, a well-to-do lawyer from Quito. Miss Robalino's formal association with CEDOC has not been as an elected official, but as legal adviser. For many years, her law office served as CEDOC headquarters.

In recent years the organization has shown signs of becoming more active and progressive. Young elements adhering to the liberal philosophy of the Christian Democratic movement, which is gaining force throughout the continent, are rising to positions of leadership. A corps of labor lawyers has been developed to provide member unions with assistance when difficulties with the government or employers arise. To improve the level and capabilities of local leaders, the CEDOC has established two permanent schools, which train roughly 500 persons a year in union affairs. A limited number of organizers has also been active, chiefly among the highland Indians.

The third confederation, the CEOSL, was founded in the spring of 1962 with the avowed purpose of providing workers with an alternative to the two extremes represented by existing centrals. In early 1965 the organization had an estimated membership of from 10,000 to 15,000, distributed, according to incomplete information, among 30 affiliates. Initially, the CEOSL's most important affiliates were the CROCLE and the Workers Confederation of Guayaquil (Confederación Obrera de Guayaquil—COG), which became the regional federation for the province of Guayas. Late in 1962, however, both affiliates were expelled as a result of differences with CEOSL leaders and irregularities in union management.

A new regional federation, the Free Workers Federation of Guayas (Federación, de Trabajadores Libres del Guayas—FETLIG) was created early in 1963. Other CEOSL affiliates include provincial federations in Azuay, Loja and Manabí, the Ecuadorian Railroad Union (Sindicato Ferroviario Ecuatoriano), the Association of Municipal Mechanics of Guayaquil (Asociación de Mecánicos Municipales de Guayaquil) and the Portworkers Union of Guayaquil (Sindicato de Portuarios de Guayaquil), initially an affiliate of FETLIG. As the portworkers have been a relatively well paid, skilled group and their union has been well run, they were the strongest single element in FETLIG and in CEOSL.

Conflicts, largely personal in character, between the leaders of FETLIG and the Portworkers Union brought about the Portworkers Union's disaffiliation from FETLIG. Although the union retained its affiliation to the CEOSL, it has not actively participated. An informal, fraternal association is maintained with the CEOSL by the National Federation of Telecommunications Workers of Ecuador (Federación Nacional de Trabajadores de Telecomunicaciones del Ecuador—FENETEL).

Relations among the confederations are not especially friendly. Strongly felt by at least some of the leaders, ideological differences are a factor. Perhaps more important, however, is competition for influence. Although none of the confederations has been dynamic or agressive, all are interested in expanding their memberships and have made some efforts in this direction. Each of the confederations appears to have had separate conflicts with both of its competitors. Temporary, shifting alliances have not developed.

Of the three, the CEDOC has probably felt the pressures most intensely. Its direct confrontation with the CTE is recent and has centered around the organization of Sierra *campesinos* (peasants), CEDOC's principal organizational activity. Although Communist effort in this field began at about the time of the CTE founding, a firm structure was never established. Unions, organized for immediate political objectives, disappeared with the departure of the organizer, and the Ecuadorian Indian Federation (Federación de Indios Ecuatorianos), which brought them together, was a paper organization. Agitators continue to operate among the *campesinos* and, according to CEDOC officials, constitute the principal problem confronting the program they launched several years ago.

On a limited scale, the CEDOC has attempted to win support and encourage organization by providing *campesinos* with defense against the abuse of large landowners and with literacy courses. These activities, combined with the CEDOC's Catholic orientation, which appeals to the conservative *campesino*, have brought modest successes. Plans call for the formation of a *campesino* federation. Problems with the CEOSL have been slightly different in nature. The CEDOC claims that the CEOSL was established partially at its expense, through raids on affiliates.

Although there is probably some validity to the CEDOC's claims against the CEOSL, the CEOSL's more serious efforts at expansion have involved groups under CTE influence. A number of groups that helped establish the CEOSL were composed of small, dissident minorities which had broken away from the CTE. More recently, attempts have been made to encourage the disaffiliation of several CTE affiliates in the province of Pichincha, including the important FNCE, the graphics' workers and the textile workers. Under non-Communist leadership these affiliates have expressed increasing discontent with the CTE. By early 1965, however, they still seemed highly reluctant to take decisive action, reportedly on the grounds that political conditions necessitated the maintenance of labor unity.

No conflicts of any importance have been apparent between the two confederations in the campaign for influence over new or previously independent groups of workers. The only area in which the CEOSL seems to have an active interest is among white-collar employees. At present, the CEOSL is hoping to bring revitalized white-collar employee associations in several provinces into a national federation which would become an affiliate.

Little current information is available on the nature of CTE activities and aims. At a June 1962 Communist Party congress, however, a report on the CTE stated that agents had infiltrated both the CEOSL and the CEDOC. The report called for increased emphasis on the organization of agricultural labor and recommended more intensive infiltration into the teachers' and journalists' organizations as well as into doctor's, lawyers' and engineers' professional associations. A consensus does not exist on the effects increased competition has had on the CTE. Whereas some observers claim that the confederation is waging a quiet battle to maintain its present strength, others assert that it faces no real threats. The inroads that have been made on CTE groups have been small. Rivals readily admit, moreover, the difficulty in winning over CTE affiliates. At the CTE has been relatively quiet since the military government came to power, indications of reactions to CEOSL and CEDOC activity cannot be ascertained from the tone or volume of CTE pronouncements.

In spite of differences and antagonisms, there has been some interest in modifying existing conditions. By circumstance rather than by inclination, the CEDOC has occupied the pivotal position. Sometime in 1964, informal proposals were made to the CEDOC by the CTE for the establishment of an understanding, the exact nature of which remained unknown in 1965. The CEDOC was unreceptive. Several conversations reportedly had taken place between CEOSL's and CEDOC's top officials, but without the participation of Isabel Robalino, whose attitude toward the CEOSL is strongly negative, they were unproductive.

All of the confederations maintain ties with international entities and labor organizations, which to a varying degree have been active or influential in local affairs. The CTE is the only national labor central in the hemisphere outside Cuba which is affiliated to the Communist WFTU. Until the WFTU's regional organization, the CTAL, was dissolved by its president, Vicente Lombardo Toledano, early in 1964, the CTE was also a member of that body. Since that time the CTE has been represented in the unsuccessful efforts to establish a new, "popular front" regional organization, to be called the Sole Central of Latin American Workers (Central Unico de Trabajadores de América Latina —CUTAL).

The CTE overtures to the CEDOC have perhaps been in line with this hemispheric policy. Another policy, anti-Americanism, has been evident in CTE criticism of the Inter-American Regional Organization of Workers (Organización Regional Interamericano de Trabajadores—ORIT), strongly influenced by the labor education programs of the American Federation of Labor-Congress of Industrial Organizations (AFL-CIO), and the United States

408

Agency for International Development (AID) labor education programs. Little is known of the direct activity of external Communist groups in CTE affairs. Some people believe, however, that funds were coming, until recently, from the Soviet Union and Cuba.

CEDOC affiliations are with the International Confederation of Christian Trade Unions (Confederación Internacional de Sindicatos Cristianos—CISC) and its regional organization, the Latin American Confederation of Christian Trade Unionists (Confederación Latinoamericana de Sindicalistas Cristianos—CLASC). Although the CLASC has become well known for its anti-Americanism, the CEDOC does not share this attitude, at least in hemispheric terms. Likewise, the CEDOC has not adopted the CLASC's principle of political action before economic activity. On the contrary, the CEDOC has increasingly sought means for economic improvement of its membership, though with little success.

Association with the CLASC, however, has probably exerted some pressure for liberalization. A number of CEDOC union members have attended the CLASC's Higher Institute for Labor Studies in Santiago, Chile. In addition, CEDOC personnel have been traveling to CLASC meetings and conferences and thus coming into contact with less conservative elements of the Christian labor union movement. The contribution of funds, which, at least in part, made possible the construction of a new, five-story confederation headquarters in downtown Quito, has had some influence. In labor circles many persons believe that the CEDOC has been helped by the West German Bishop's Fund and the German Social Democratic movement.

The CEOSL is an affiliate of the International Confederation of Free Trade Unions (ICFTU) and of its regional organization, ORIT. In fact, the CEOSL came into being largely through the efforts of representatives of ORIT, which had long been interested in establishing an effective non-Communist labor movement in the country. Intensive activity in this direction began roughly 2 years before the actual formation of the CEOSL in May 1962. The COG, though weak, was used as one of the principal building blocks. The organization had been established in the early 1950's with the assistance of an ORIT organizer and had subsequently affiliated with ORIT. Another was the CROCLE, founded in 1961, also with the aid of ORIT personnel. Other groups, for the most part small, were persuaded to join these two until the number was considered sufficient to establish a national confederation. With CEOSL's affiliation to ORIT, the COG's affiliation to that body became moot.

After its founding the CEOSL continued to receive technical

assistance from ORIT personnel. Recently, however, relationships between CEOSL leaders and the local ORIT representatives reportedly have undergone serious deterioration. In addition, the CEOSL initially received substantial financial support from ORIT. Subsidies were later reduced when ORIT became dissatisfied with the performance of CEOSL leaders and finally terminated in accordance with a general financial policy adopted by ORIT in 1964.

Without firm support from ORIT, the CEOSL's difficulties are likely to increase. Funds raised from the contributions of affiliates are highly limited, the result of the natural local tendency toward reluctance in dues payment, combined with a lack of enthusiasm for the organization. Established somewhat artificially from the top, the organization has lacked strong leaders of experience and dedication.

The CEOSL has also been aided by the American Institute for Free Labor Development, an organization supported by the AFL-CIO, AID and private United States business interests. In 1959 the International Cooperation Administration (ICA), the predecessor of AID, had begun programs of labor education, which were formalized in 1962 with the creation of a labor school. Two years later the school was taken over jointly by the CEOSL and the American Institute for Free Labor Development and named the Ecuadorian National Institute of Labor Education. During the first 5 months, 500 individuals were trained at the permanent center in Quito and in regional seminars conducted by Institute personnel. In addition to union officials and members from CEOSL affiliates, individuals associated with the CEDOC have received training. At the permanent center in Quito, students receive scholarships for maintenance during the period away from their jobs.

In addition, several local federations are affiliates of the International Trade Secretariats (ITS), associative, occupational bodies which work closely with the ICFTU but are not a part of it. The federations include FENETEL, an affiliate of the Postal, Telegraph and Telephone International (PTTI); the Ecuadorian Railroad Union and Ecuadorian Portworkers Union, both affiliates of the International Transport Workers Federation; the Confederation of Electrical Workers, an affiliate of the Public Service International; the National Union of Journalists, an affiliate of the Inter-American Federation of Working Newspaperman's Organization; and the Guayas Provincial Federation of White Collar Workers, an affiliate of the International Federation of Commercial, Clerical and Technical Employees (IFCCTE).

Representatives of the secretariats have often been active in securing the affiliation of these groups and in strengthening them both professionally and organizationally. Largely through the efforts of the representative of the IFCCTE, the Guayas Provincial Federation of White Collar Workers was revitalized in 1963. Attempts are currently underway similarly to stimulate associations of white-collar workers throughout the country to a nationwide federation. The establishment of FENETEL in 1958 owed a great deal to the PTTI representative who, with an Ecuadorian telecommunications worker, organized provincial associations over a period of months, and then to the congress which produced the national federation.

LABOR RELATIONS

Labor relations are in a rudimentary stage of development. Among both employers and unions there is little confidence in mutual dealings. Employers have favored the maintenance of traditional relationships, personal and paternalistic in nature. Attempts to effect change through the introduction of labor union practices—and, at times, the very organization of unions—are frequently seen as acts of disloyalty and inspire reactions of suspicion and dislike.

Employers fear loss of absolute control of concessions and the creation of disturbances in normal routine and work situations. To some extent, the latter concern is not unjustified. In a few instances, extreme leftist organizers have infiltrated business establishments and have paid more attention to agitation than to worker organization. Employers, however, have tended to apply the extreme leftist label indiscriminately to all labor unionists, either tactically or through conviction. In addition, employers often find dealing with worker representatives as equals in a business-like manner alien and uncomfortable. Whereas some have come to accept modifications, albeit grudgingly, others have sought to continue their control, behind the camouflage of empty formalities. Still others have been sufficiently negative in their attitudes to attempt the active prevention of worker organization. Techniques have included blacklisting and forcible expulsion of union representatives from the premises.

Union reactions to the hostility or indifference of employers have ranged from passive submission to outspoken belligerence. In confrontation, their position has seldom been one of aggressive professionalism. Whether seen as the traditional *patrón* or as a more contemporary antagonist, the employer is accepted as superior in power and influence. With reduced numbers and little or no economic independence, the unions feel unable to compel employers to give satisfaction or, at times, consideration to demands, grievances and issues.

In this atmosphere, neither employers nor unions have developed facilities, skills and procedures for effective interaction. Few firms, for example, have industrial relations departments, and the unions do not maintain committees. Consequently, dealings have taken place in a haphazard, often unsatisfactory, fashion or, at best, within the formalized mechanisms established by a third party, government, principally in the Labor Code of 1938. When serious difficulties arise, the tendency is to look to government as an arbiter or defender of rights and privileges. As a result, government participation or intervention in labor relations is a constant possibility which influences the thinking and behavior of both employers and unions. Since the unions are the weaker of the two forces, they have been particularly affected by government activity and policy.

Collective Conflicts

The phase of labor relations which has generally been most notable and in which government has been most active is disputes. Most often, disputes have arisen over work-related issues, mainly wage increases, the expansion of fringe benefits and the reinstatement or dismissal of personnel. First, a statement of specific demands is filed with the labor inspector, the local representative of the Ministry of Social Welfare, who is required to forward the information to the employers within 24 hours. The employer has 3 days in which to reply. If the demands are accepted, a record is made and signed by both sides.

If acceptance of demands is partial or the demands are rejected, the matter is turned over to a conciliation and arbitration tribunal, composed of two members designated by the employer, two members by the employees and the labor inspector, who acts as chairman. The tribunal selects the time and place for the hearing, which takes place within 3 days after the date the case was submitted.

If the tribunal's recommendations are accepted, a record is made and signed by the two sides. When agreement cannot be reached, the tribunal is allowed a period of 4 days, extendible up to 4 months, for further inquiries. Upon the completion of inquiries, an award must be made within 3 days. If no appeal is made within 2 days, the award becomes operative. Appeals are submitted to the director general of labor, within the Ministry of Social Welfare, who acts as a court of second instance. Decisions must be made within 3 days.

The Labor Code also included a number of provisions on another aspect of disputes, strikes. Considered a worker's right, the strike was nevertheless subject to certain legal proscriptions. If a majority of workers in an establishment agreed, a strike could be legally called only when the machinery for peaceful settlement failed through noncompliance with regulations on the part of either the employer or the tribunal. During a strike the police were responsible for preserving order and protecting the rights of both sides. Employers were forbidden to hire substitute workers or to discharge workers taking part in the strike for at least 1 year after its termination. Wages were also to be paid to striking workers. Direct agreement, conciliation, arbitration or executive decree were the means by which a strike could be ended.

These guarantees and procedures did not apply to illegal strikes, which included those called before attempts at peaceful settlement, those in which the majority of workers engage in violence and property damage and those involving government employees. The enforcement of provisions was not always rigorous or uniform. On the one hand, workers did not always benefit from protective devices, and on the other, illegal strikers often were allowed to operate unrestricted.

In the past, disputes were usually settled smoothly with government participation, and consequently strikes were not numerous. Beginning early in the 1960's, however, conditions changed. Late in the last administration of José María Velasco Ibarra, the incidence of strikes increased as popular discontent grew, fanned by the CTE, which was ill-disposed toward the President. The partial success of a general strike staged in the fall of 1961 encouraged CTE leaders to bring pressure on private citizens of influence and on members of congress to join the movement to oust Velasco Ibarra.

Attributing considerable importance to organized labor's role in the ouster, Velasco Ibarra's successor, Carlos Julio Arosemena Monroy, adopted a more lenient labor policy initially, which produced a temporary reduction in conflicts. The disorder which came to characterize the administration, however, brought renewed labor unrest and an increase in strikes, many of them illegal. A great number took place among workers employed by government and semiautonomous government agencies, caused by serious delays in the payment of wages. Organized workers also took part in the municipal and provincial demonstrations. staged against the national government to protest the failure to provide funds for local benefit. Violence and damage of property were not uncommon. In an extreme case, an American-owned plantation, Tenguel, was taken over by its workers, influenced by Communist agitators. Government assistance was limited to securing the release of plantation managers, who had been forcibly detained by workers. Attempts were made by the CTE to take advantage of the widespread discontent by calling general strikes, but were unsuccessful.

To the military government which came to power in July 1963, the imposition of order has been a foremost concern. Initially, a number of labor leaders, mostly from the CTE, were arrested. Although a decree was passed to prohibit mass layoffs, it became generally easier for employers to discharge workers, given the government's negative attitude toward extreme leftists. Most importantly, however, the right to strike was suspended. Although statistics on disputes registered are not available, the number is no doubt limited. Without the declaration of a strike as a potential weapon, unions feel more powerless than ever before regarding demands on employers. Moreover, during the first 2 years of the military government, labor leaders complained of difficulties in establishing contact with the Ministry of Social Welfare, despite the fact that the minister was an avowed leftist.

As a result, little has taken place to disturb the labor scene. Some difficulties, which were quickly settled or ignored, did occur among the banana workers of Guayaquil, the port workers, the government bank workers in Guayaquil and the railroad workers on the southern line. In addition, there were demonstrations in Guayaquil in the fall of 1964, which were part of the city's successful protest of government attempts to centralize local semiautonomous agencies. The desire to pacify the workers reportedly encouraged the government to facilitate the holding of labor conferences, which, as public meetings, have fallen under the restrictions covering the right of assembly (see ch. 14, Political Dynamics).

Collective Contracts

Like most other phases of labor activity, collective bargaining is regulated by legislation. According to the Labor Code, any firm with 15 or more associated employees is required to negotiate a collective contract if the association so requests. If various associations exist, the one with the largest membership represents all workers. Only associations that have been legally recognized are entitled to negotiate contracts. All contracts must be written and signed before appropriate representatives of the Ministry of Social Welfare. In addition, the Labor Code outlines the areas subject to control.

Although legal recognition of the collective contract has existed since 1938, collective bargaining has not been widely practiced. Most unions, including many of long standing with large memberships, have never negotiated a collective contract. During the last few years greater interest and activity have been apparent, attributable, according to some observers, to the training in business aspects of labor unionism made available to union officials by AID and other outside groups. The number of collective contracts in force rose from 5 to 62 between 1959 and 1964. The majority covered skilled and semiskilled workers in the Guayaquil area.

Frequently, however, contracts have only reiterated provisions of the Labor Code and have represented few real gains for the workers. In many cases, moreover, they have not been the product of legitimate collective bargaining. At times, contracts have been drawn up exclusively by employers and submitted to the unions for signature without any negotiation. Employers, unions or both have also tended to rely on lawyers unfamiliar with work practices and situations. All discussion has been carried on by the legal representatives, without direct participation by employers or unions. As union lawyers have often been militant leftists, agreement has not always been easy. Before the military government came to power, demands were frequently exaggerated.

If the demands were rejected, the matter could then be taken to the Ministry, which was likely to be more generous than the employer. Among government workers and employees of semiautonomous agencies the presentation of proposals has been customary. Those accepted, combined with those emanating from the employer, have constituted work regulations.

Several contracts worthy of note were signed recently. Among them is the agreement between Anglo-Ecuadorian Oilfields, Ltd., and its 1,500 oilworkers. Although hostilities characterized past negotiations, the agreement was reached pacifically by union and management representatives without the intervention of lawyers. With this contract, the Anglo-Ecuadorian oilworkers were the first in the country to obtain the 40-hour week. Of perhaps greater importance, the contract also provided for monthly meetings between employers and workers, a feature that has been absent from industrial relations. Other gains include a graduated scale of allotments for dependents, the establishment of a commissary, the doubling of retirement bonuses and free housing with complete utilities.

The dockworkers in Guayaquil also obtained a good contract. Wage increases, which raised daily earnings to roughly S/80, made the dockworkers' salaries the highest for laborers in the city. Fringe benefits included life insurance policies of S/120,000 (the legal requirement is S/19,000), employer contributions to the workers' vacation fund and annual cash bonuses equal to 1 month's salary for every year of service.

Of special significance is the agreement between employers and workers of Los Alamos Plantation in the province of Guayas, which represents the first collective contract signed in the agricultural sector. Workers were guaranteed 2 years' job security, family allowances and the maintenance of a commissary by the employers. The contract also provided for economic aid to the union.

CHAPTER 22

DOMESTIC TRADE

Trade, both domestic and foreign, in 1962 (the latest year for which complete figures were available in 1965) generated about 12 percent of the gross national product; services (exclusive of government) generated about 9 percent; and transportation, about 4 percent. Taken together, the three sectors engaged almost one-fourth of the economically active population. Between 1950 and 1962 the relative contributions of trade, services and transportation to the gross national product remained essentially constant, indicating rates of growth about equal to that of the whole economy. Similarly, the proportions of labor engaged in the three sectors did not vary markedly during the period.

In volume and organization domestic trade reflects the profound disparities that exist between the modern, urban segment of the economy and the relatively less developed rural segment. Consumer markets in Guayaquil and Quito—and, in lesser degree, the larger provincial centers—are characterized by a relative abundance of goods and services, well-capitalized enterprises and generally adequate storage and handling facilities. By contrast, both wholesale and retail trade in rural areas and smaller towns can best be described as rudimentary, in terms of the quantity and quality of goods available, the size and organization of enterprises and the adequacy of storage and handling facilities. Most trade flows through small general stores which have a limited stock; through weekly fairs which attract wholesale foodstuffs buyers from the cities; through peasants seeking to sell small surpluses of farm produce and, in some areas, handicrafts; and through small-scale peddlers of manufactured goods.

Several interrelated factors combine to produce these contrasts. A disproportionate share of the total purchasing power is concentrated in the large cities. Estimates based on the 1962 census and on surveys made by the National Planning and Economic Coordination Board suggest that per capita income in the largest cities is somewhat more than twice that in rural areas. Moreover, most rural dwellers are subsistence farmers who appear in the markets only infrequently, whether as buyers or as sellers. The tradition of self-sufficiency in production and consumption is especially strong among the Sierra Indians, who constitute a sizable segment of the rural population. In addition, there are large and densely settled rural zones that have never been reached by roads capable of bearing wheeled traffic.

Contrasts in the volume and organization of trade are also apparent among the various productive sectors. In general, imported and factory-produced goods are traded through channels marked by high capitalization and adequate warehousing and handling facilities. On the other hand, unprocessed foodstuffs and goods produced in the artisan industries are sold in a marketing system characterized by low capitalization, generally poor storage handling facilities, a multiplicity of middlemen and poor coordination. Spoilage and other forms of transit loss during the trading of foodstuffs seriously reduce profits to producers and aggravate periodic shortages in urban markets (see ch. 19, Agriculture).

In recent years, Ecuador has made considerable progress in integrating its geographically diverse territory through the construction of transport facilities. Until the early twentieth century the trip between Guayaquil and Quito could only be made on animal back and required about 2 weeks. In 1908 a narrow-gauge railroad was opened between the two cities, but for many years thereafter there was no other fast high-capacity link between the Coast and the Sierra, and in large part people and goods continued to be moved on pack trails and natural waterways. Since the 1920's, and especially since the late 1940's, an increasing investment in facilities—principally highways—has done much to correct the deficit. By 1965 highways or railroads connected all of the more populous areas of the Coast and the Sierra and provided routes of penetration to the rain forests of the Oriente. Considerable public investment was also being budgeted for the construction of feeder and farm-to-market routes in areas of new settlement. This growing terrestrial network has been supplemented increasingly by air transport (see ch. 2, Physical Environment).

In addition to investment in transport the prime requisite for interregional trade, the government has devoted considerable attention to improving market conditions and facilities, especially for domestic agricultural produce. A significant portion of the S/7.5 billion (in 1965, S/18.5 equaled US $1—see Glossary) programed for investment in agriculture under the 10-year General Plan for the Economic and Social Development of Ecuador was earmarked for the construction of modern storage facilities, market buildings and slaughterhouses. In addition, the Plan calls for the establishment of uniform grading standards, the traditional lack of which has been a prime factor in the inefficiency and poor coordination of the marketing system and for the establishment of producers' cooperatives to afford small farmers a more advantageous position in the national market.

TRADE

Regulation and Organization

The conduct of trade is regulated by the Commercial Code, enacted early in the present century and much modified by legislative amendment and executive decrees, and by a large body of law that has never been codified. The 1946 Constitution guarantees freedom of commerce, but establishes the bases of government intervention in cases of public necessity. Such intervention has most commonly taken the form of price controls on foodstuffs and other articles of prime necessity, both by the national government and by the municipalities, which, by long tradition, have held the principal regulatory authority over consumer markets. In addition, the maintenance of state monopolies in the production and sale of such commodities as tobacco, alcoholic beverages, salt and matches, as a revenue measure, has been a constant practice since colonial days.

In the last 15 years there has been a tendency toward the relaxation of government controls on commerce. The central government's price-fixing authority, widely used during and immediately after World War II, has been applied in recent years only to a few basic commodities, such as rice, wheat flour, lard, petroleum products and textiles. Such price controls are closely coordinated with government imports of foodstuffs to fill deficits in national production and with government subsidies in certain lines of agricultural and industrial production. Moreover, the diminishing effectiveness of public monopolies as a means of raising revenues has led to a trend toward their abandonment, and by the early 1960's the manufacture and sale of tobacco products and matches had passed to the private sector.

The forms of business organization recognized by law include the sole proprietorship (*comerciante particular*), the general partnership (*compañía en nombre colectiva*), the limited partnership (*compañía en comandita*) and the corporation (*compañía anónima* or *sociedad anónima*). For any large undertaking the corporation has been the preferred form of organization.

The sole proprietorship may be established simply by obtaining the necessary licenses and permits. All transactions and acts are made in the name of the proprietor and are his sole and unlimited responsibility.

A general partnership is formed by legal contract of two or more persons who engage in commerce under a firm name (*razón social*). The firm name may include only the names of the partners or of certain partners followed by "and Company" (y Compañía). In such business organizations all partners share a joint and unlimited responsibility.

Limited partnerships, which can be based either on a simple pooling of capital or on the issue of stock, consist of one or more active partners and one or more silent partners (*comanditarios*). The firm name for such a company must contain the name of at least one active partner and may not contain the name of any silent partner. Active partners have exclusive rights of management and bear joint and unlimited responsibility, whereas silent partners are responsible only to the amount of their capital share.

By law the business name of a corporation does not contain the name of any stockholder or manager; rather, it must incorporate a description of the purposes for which the corporation was established. Corporate capital must be divided into shares or coupons of equal value. A corporation may be formed by two or more persons and may be managed either by stockholders or by non-stockholders. Participants in a corporation are liable only to the extent of their capital share.

In addition to the foregoing forms of business organization, which are presumed to be permanent, the Commercial Code authorizes the establishment of temporary companies (*compañías accidentales*) for specific joint ventures. Typically, such associations are formed between established merchants and investors who are not merchants.

Foreigners may form companies of any sort or participate with citizens in established companies. The law requires that foreign-based firms retain within the country a person with full power of attorney, duly certified by an Ecuadorian consul. Furthermore, the 1946 Constitution provides that any contract made by a foreigner with the Ecuadorian Government or with any Ecuadorian citizen must always contain a renunciation, tacit or explicit, of all claims to diplomatic intervention.

In accordance with the Commercial Code and subsequent legislation all merchants and firms with a capital of more than S/1,000 must be enrolled in the Mercantile Register, recording their principal business, the names of jointly and unlimitedly responsible partners, instruments of establishment or incorporation and other relevant information. Such registers are maintained by the clerks of the ordinary civil courts and are filed with cantonal property records.

The interests of the business community are represented by chambers of commerce in Quito, Guayaquil and a few other cities.

Although many manufacturing, as well as mercantile, firms are included in the chambers of commerce, analogous trade associations have been formed in many other sectors of activity—manufacturing and agriculture, for example. In addition to seeking to influence government action and public opinion on matters affecting business, the trade chambers publish business periodicals and maintain contact with their counterparts in other countries.

Structure and Practices

Wholesale

The wholesale distribution of manufactured and imported goods is effected by specialized agencies, most of them centralized in Guayaquil and Quito, although many have branches in other important population centers. Such firms range in size from single proprietorships handling a small flow of goods to sizable corporations. The fact that wholesaling enterprises tend to be smaller than similar concerns in most other countries reflects the limited availability of capital and a deeply rooted tradition of family-based business organization.

Regardless of size, most wholesaling firms possess or have access to adequate warehousing and handling facilities and are prepared to undertake all phases of procurement, processing and shipping. Thus, the number of middlemen between manufacturer and consumer is held at a minimum. Stable inventories and goods flows can be maintained, and prices are set by competitive conditions in domestic and foreign markets.

Since most manufactured goods sold in the country are imported, the great majority of wholesaling firms, whether or not they also handle domestic goods, are also import agencies. Typically, such firms handle goods in many different lines and represent several manufacturers. Not infrequently the items offered by a wholesale house will vary from time to time, and the variety at any given moment can include articles as diverse as auto batteries, agricultural chemicals, plumbing fixtures, soaps and toiletries. In recent years, however, larger concerns have tended increasingly to specialize in fewer and more closely related lines of merchandise, although many continue to represent several manufacturers.

Other channels for the distribution of imports and manufactures include a few well-known United States and European manufacturers which have established distributing subsidiaries in the country. In 1965 such firms included International Business Machines, Sherwin Williams Paint and Nestlé. In addition, some domestic manufacturers sell directly to retailers or distribute through exclusive dealerships.

Except for export crops, such as bananas and cacao, which are traded principally by large, well-capitalized concerns, wholesaling of domestic agricultural produce is carried on by a multitude of small-scale middlemen at dispersed locations. At all levels, from farm to big city market, operations are hampered by the low capital base of the dealers, often no more than S/2,000—and that, not infrequently, borrowed at interest rates ranging up to 20 percent per month. The trader who buys from the farmer seldom has the resources to do more than ship the produce to a nearby population center, there to resell it to another dealer, who, in his turn, will transport it to the city for resale in the wholesale market.

There is a serious shortage of storage and handling facilities for all domestically produced foodstuffs. Spoilage and transit losses, chiefly the result of poor warehousing, have been estimated at as much as 20 to 25 percent on such staples as barley, corn, potatoes and beans. Warehousing for grains and other important food crops is chiefly in poorly ventilated, often vermin-infested rooms of buildings near public marketplaces or, on occasion, in a corner of the trader's one-room residence. Given the lack of bins, such storage usually requires sacking and thus adds to the costs of distribution.

In Quito, Guayaquil, Latacunga and a few other market centers there are modern grain elevators for the storage of wheat. More than half the total capacity of such installations is located in Guayaquil, however, at a considerable distance from areas of domestic production. For initial storage, therefore, Sierra wheat producers and dealers typically must depend on warehouse storage.

Facilities for the processing and marketing of meat are also grossly inadequate. Even Quito and Guayaquil lack efficient, sanitary facilities for slaughtering, storage and selling. Refrigeration, either in storage or in transit, is virtually nonexistent. In most markets slaughtering takes place on poorly drained concrete floors, and in many it takes place on the bare ground. Sanitary controls and standards, insofar as they exist, are imposed and enforced by the municipalities, which lack the resources either to construct the proper facilities or to provide effective supervision.

The principal flow of foodstuffs is to the municipal markets of Quito, Guayaquil and the larger provincial centers. All these cities have one or more permanent market buildings with facilities for both wholesalers and retailers. Recently, as a result of the continued expansion of the road network, towns at the termini and important crossroads—for example, Puyo and Santo Domingo de los Colorados—have become active trade centers for produce, being convenient places for the exchange of commodities from the climatically diverse lowland and highland regions.

Crops and livestock move toward these major collection points in many different channels. *Haciendas* and other large-scale producing units, especially those located close to primary markets, often sell directly to wholesalers, contracting their own transportation. For most small-scale peasants, however, located at some distance from centers of demand and producing only minuscule surpluses, direct selling is made unfeasible by the cost of transportation, which is high in relation to the profits realized on small sales. Often, subsistence peasants sell their surpluses at the weekly fair in the nearest parish or canton center. Small-scale middlemen travel from fair to fair, buying produce in small lots for resale in the city. Truckers returning to the cities with empty vehicles also canvas farms and fairs along the route, buying small lots for resale at their destinations.

Another important collection point for peasant surpluses is the village store, whose proprietor, in addition to retailing a rudimentary stock of cash goods, accumulates small amounts of local produce to the extent of his modest storage capacity for periodic resale. Often, such village merchants extend loans and retail credit against repayment at harvesttime. Payment may be in cash or kind. If it is in kind the storekeeper invariably calculates a cash equivalent far below the prevailing market prices.

Wholesaling of meat and livestock follows similar patterns. Whereas large stockraisers usually find it profitable to sell directly at the slaughterhouse, smaller operators generally sell to middlemen. A common practice in the marketing of cattle, resulting partly from the lack of refrigerated storage and partly from the restricted cash base of most farmers, is the long-term purchase option. In this system a middleman or a final wholesaler pays a stockraiser in advance for an agreed number of head, but leaves the animals in the latter's custody, withdrawing from the lot whenever the market is favorable. The stockraiser remains responsible for the care and feeding of the animals until they are withdrawn, and the dealer is under obligation to withdraw the entire lot within a stated period, usually 1 year.

Other factors combine with the poor capitalization and inadequate physical facilities to reduce the efficiency of the marketing system. Except for brewer's barley and for wheat, there are no quality standards. Without a uniform and generally accepted grading system, prices can be set on produce only after physical inspection by the buyer. Hence, buying lots tend to be small, even in the Quito and Guayaquil markets. Weights and measures are not standardized. Most commonly, foodstuffs are bought and sold in Spanish pounds (1.0143 pounds) and quintales (100 Spanish pounds), but small lots are also offered in a bewildering variety of volume measures, such as sacks and 5-gallon tins. There is also some regional variation in the definition of traditional weight units. For example, the quintal is reported to vary regionally between 95 pounds and 105 pounds.

The results of these deficiencies are apparent at several different levels. Prices are subject to broad disparities from region to region, and given the limited storage capacity, they reflect a sharp seasonal cycle of glut and storage. The numerous resalers and the frequent transshipments between farmer and consumer work to the disadvantage of both. An economic mission studying problems of agricultural marketing during the early 1960's found that on such dietary staples as barley and potatoes, the average total markup between producer's price and consumer's cost in the Quito market was about 150 percent. Of this, profits to the retailer and to an average of three wholesaling middlemen came to about 135 percent, and transportation—with an average of two transshipments—accounted for the remaining 15 percent.

Prices paid to farmers are subject to severe inelasticities. A drop in prices at points of final demand will usually be passed on to the farmer in the form of lower price, rather than be absorbed in cuts in middlemen's profits. The village storekeeper, the trucker and the itinerant buyer enjoy considerable advantage in price setting over the peasant who, by reason of transport costs and unfamiliarity with urban markets, can sell to no one else. Often, too, this leverage is reinforced by enduring creditor-debtor relationships. In slightly less degree small-scale merchants are at a similar disadvantage with respect to the large urban wholesalers, who are often their primary source of working capital and who have at least a limited capacity to stockpile nonperishables against rises in price.

Until the early 1960's little systematic effort was made by the government or other agencies to remedy the deficiencies in agricultural màrketing. In 1955 the Central Bank of Ecuador and the National Development Bank formed a corporation called General Constructions and Warehouses (Edificaciones y Almacenes Generales—EDIALGE) for the installation of grain elevators in the Sierra. Those it built, however, failed to serve wheat growers adequately, largely because its units were installed at locations inconvenient to many wheat growers and, at the same time, too close to the major flour mills of Quito, which have their own storage facilities. In 1963 an economic study mission recommended the redistribution of EDIALGE's stock to a combination of flour millers and wheat growers' cooperatives. Most other programs were small-scale and uncoordinated attempts to establish farmers' cooperatives.

With the formulation of the 10-year General Plan for the Economic and Social Development of Ecuador, more concentrated attention was turned to the problems of food distribution. A mission of the Rome-based firm ITALCONSULT, which surveyed agrarian problems under contract with the Organization of American States (OAS) and the Ecuadorian Government, undertook a specific study of the marketing system and made a series of detailed recommendations, most of which have been incorporated into the Ten-Year Development Plan.

Programs for improving marketing conditions and methods have, of necessity, been planned on a broad base, including price support policies; the extension of low-cost credit to producers; the construction of storage and handling facilities; the establishment of hygienic and quality standards for meat and produce; and the construction of farm-to-market and feeder roads. Further, the program calls for the establishment of producers' cooperatives among small farmers as an integral part of agrarian reform and colonization projects.

Retail

Traditionally, retail trade has flowed through large collective markets and fairs; through small, family-owned general stores; and through a multitude of peddlers and itinerant merchants. Whatever the channel of trade, retail enterprises have tended to be small and, in most cases, little specialized in their goods offerings. Retailing practice has generally been based on a system of low turnovers and high markups; more often than not, prices have been set by haggling at the moment of purchase. Until recently few merchants have offered any form of retail credit—the principal exceptions being loans made to peasants against future crops and 30-day courtesy accounts to wealthy customers. Moreover, there was little systematic use of advertising.

The scope and volume of retail trading have also been limited by the importance of the artisan industry in the satisfaction of basic consumer wants. Much of the clothing sold is made by tailors under individual contract with clients, with the result that one of the staple bases of retail trade is relatively less important in Ecuador than in many other countries. As ready-to-wear clothing has come into wider use, the scale of retail enterprise has grown.

The municipally owned public markets found in all major population centers bring together foodstuffs wholesalers and retailers and the retailers of manufacturered and artisan-produced goods.

Such installations are typically large, unpartitioned buildings in which merchants rent stalls. Stalls selling roughly the same kinds of merchandise are grouped together. In the streets for a radius of perhaps two blocks around the marketplace, peddlers sell small quantities of the same kinds of goods, usually from makeshift stands, and peasant women squat at the curb offering minuscule lots of produce.

Most provincial and cantonal seats and some parish centers hold weekly or semiweekly fairs, by custom deriving from well back in both the Spanish and the Indian tradition. These congregations of buyers and sellers are essentially a magnified version of the daily activity in the marketplace; large and small vendors operate from portable stands set up, as a rule, in a central plaza and radiating into the surrounding streets.

In Quito, Guayaquil and a few other cities peddlers daily ply the busier streets, selling small quantities of cigarettes, candy and such items as pocket combs and pens, all lumped colloquially under the term *"mercachifle"* (trifle).

In the parish centers and crossroads hamlets scattered throughout the countryside virtually the only retail outlet is a general store (*bodega*), often operated merely as a part-time venture subsidiary to farming or produce wholesaling. These establishments sell small amounts of local produce (especially during preharvest periods of shortage), a limited stock of canned goods and other processed foodstuffs, salt, soft drinks, beer, sugarcane alcohol, cigarettes, matches, kerosene and a few hardware items, such as flashlights, batteries and handtools. In many villages the *bodega* is the sole meeting place, serving as both town hall and social club.

The growth of a more prosperous and sophisticated consumer market in Quito, Guayaquil and, in lesser degree, a few other cities has brought about a considerable modernization in retailing techniques. In Guayaquil and Quito small supermarkets and department stores have been established, selling processed foodstuffs, appliances and other hard goods, and ready-to-wear clothing. These establishments maintain inventories heavily weighted in imports and other expensive goods and do not achieve the sales volumes of similar operations in other countries. Consequently, they offer no reduction in prices, as compared with the more traditional channels. Their primary attraction lies in the immediate availability, the superior quality and the sanitary control of their merchandise.

There has been a growing and more systematic use of advertising, especially in the Quito and Guayaquil markets, and in both major cities there are several advertising agencies. The principal media are newspapers, radio, television and motion picture shorts.

Consumer credit, chiefly for appliances and other expensive durables, has been introduced on a modest scale.

TRANSPORT

At the beginning of the twentieth century the transport pattern both reflected and reinforced the historic division of the country into self-contained and antagonistic regional units—the Coast and the Sierra (the Oriente was virtually unpopulated). The Coastal population, oriented toward the sea and foreign markets, was concentrated near ports and along navigable waterways. Transport routes on the Coast, whether waterborne or terrestrial, were laid out with the primary purpose of moving export crops from areas of production to the ports. Almost no attempt had been made to penetrate and settle the forests of the inner coastal plain and the Andean piedmont. Thus, the Coast and Sierra were divided in the literal, spatial sense by a band of unpopulated territory.

In the more heavily populated Sierra the transport routes were concentrated along the inter-Andean corridor, which, though traversed by ridges, permitted the easy flow of pack-animal traffic. In effect, the Sierra formed a fairly unified and self-sufficient trading community.

Interregional movement was confined to a few crude pack trails, which permitted only a slow and small capacity haulage. Given the limited number of alternative routes and the restricted nature of the trade, most traffic was funneled between various points in the Sierra and the main port, Guayaquil; the small residue flowed to Esmeraldas and other minor ports.

Completion of the Guayaquil-Quito railroad in 1908 provided an effective interregional link for the first time in history. Nevertheless, the divergence in economic patterns was so great that only a limited interregional trade developed principally in import goods from Guayaquil to Quito. The railroad's effect in facilitating trade and shipping within regions was at least as important as its function as an interregional carrier. A rough indication of this restricted movement is offered in the fact that the average length of freight haul has been consistently somewhat less than half the route mileage between Guayaquil and Quito.

Construction of highways began on a small scale in the 1920's and continued slowly and sporadically until after World War II. Between 1945 and 1960 a greatly expanded effort created the outlines of a network covering almost all populated areas in the country. Consisting of two principal north-south trunks, one in the Sierra and one on the Coast, with a smaller coastal trunk and several interconnections, this system has opened vast areas of

427

virgin land to new settlement. Furthermore, it has relieved the historic funnel effect, providing direct and rapid links between several points in the highlands and several widely dispersed points on the Coast. It has also opened access to the Oriente. By making possible a broader pattern of agricultural settlement and by giving access to as yet untapped natural resources, it appears likely that the expanding road system will provide an important base for a truly integrated domestic trade (see fig. 8).

Railroads

In 1965 the principal elements in the 727-mile (track mileage), chiefly meter-gauge railroad system were a truckline running from Durán, opposite Guayaquil, through Simbambe, Riobamba, Ambato and Latacunga to Quito (with a southward spur from Simbambe to Cuenca); and a line running north from Quito to Ibarra and thence northwestward, along a recently completed route, to the port of San Lorenzo. The other elements were three short, isolated lines, one in Manabí Province and two in El Oro Province. All these lines were owned and operated by the national government.

Until the 1950's the railroads moved the overwhelming bulk of passengers and freight, but since then the highway system has posed a growing competition. In addition to offering greater speed and lower shipping costs truck transport provides the convenience of door-to-door delivery and the flexibility of alternative routes and thus reduces the number of necessary transshipments.

The effects of highways competition were felt earliest and most severely on a railroad that connected Guayaquil with Salinas. By 1953 so much traffic had been shunted to the parallel highway that abandonment was unavoidable. For similar reasons traffic on the short lines in Manabí and El Oro had reached uneconomically low levels by 1965, and their abandonment was being contemplated. Although competition was being felt by the Guayaquil-Quito-Simbambe-Cuenca system in 1965, it was not as severe. Only the Quito-San Lorenzo section was totally free of competitive stress, and this advantage was severely vitiated by the low volume of traffic moving toward the northern port.

In 1965, rolling stock and permanent installations were largely obsolete and in varying states of disrepair. Except for a few recently purchased diesel cars most equipment in operation was well over 30 years old. Rights-of-way were in poor repair, and in some sections the rails were too small to support heavy locomotives and carloads. These problems have been seriously compounded by the difficult nature of the terrain. The climb into the Andes is over extremely steep gradients, combined with very sharp curves. There are numerous points at which landslides and

The Ten-Year Plan projects an extensive program of highway construction and improvement, with the basic aims of interconnecting all cantons with more than 5,000 inhabitants; enhancing connections to seaports; and more closely integrating the diverse regions into a single national economy. The Plan calls for the completion of additional interconnections between trunk roads, including a link between Santo Domingo and the Chone-Guayaquil route; another between Santo Domingo and Babahoyo. Also projected are improvements in the Durán-Guayaquil ferry, long a notorious bottleneck, and, by 1970, construction of a bridge between the two cities. The Plan further calls for the accelerated construction of penetration roads into the Oriente and for a nationwide program of farm-to-market roads. There are extensive plans for the rehabilitation and improvement of the Pan American Highway and other main routes, and provision has been made for the systematic study of maintenance problems and for the development of a more effective maintenance service.

Air Transport

Since the 1920's, when the first scheduled commercial air service was established, airlines have held a secure, if limited segment of the transport market. Given the small distances between most population centers in the Sierra and the steadily improving terrestrial network, only a relatively few routes are heavily traveled. The largest volume of domestic passenger and cargo traffic moves between Quito and Guayaquil, on which route air travel time is about 1 hour, as compared with 12 to 14 hours by land. Routes between Quito and Esmeraldas, between both Quito and Guayaquil and between Cuenca and Loja also provide an attractive time-saving over alternative land routes.

The one area in which the airlines are virtually without competition is the Oriente. There are many small, dispersed population centers that would be almost completely isolated from the rest of the country were it not for the services of the various small airlines flying the eastern routes.

The first scheduled airline in the country was established by a German company, the Ecuadorian Air Transport Company (Sociedad Ecuatoriana de Transport Aéreos—SEDTA). During World War II this company was confiscated, and its routes turned over to Pan-American Grace Airways (PANAGRA), which for many years provided the most extensive domestic service, sharing the Guayaquil-Quito route only with the Colombian company Avianca. After World War II the domestic airline Ecuadorian Airways (Aerovías Ecuatorianas—AREA) was established; somewhat later the Ecuadorian Aviation Company (Companía Ecuatoriana de Aviación—CEA) began both domestic and international operations. By the early 1960's most domestic air traffic was being carried by AREA, CEA and several smaller companies, including Eastern Air Transport (Transportes Aéreos Orientales—TAO), specializing in service to the small airstrips in the eastern lowlands. In addition to CEA, Panagra, Braniff and Avianca, international air carriers of several South American and European nations call either at Quito or at Guayaquil.

The largest Ecuadorian-flag carriers, AREA and CEA, were operating between them two C–47's, two DC–4's and two DC–6's in late 1964. Other local carriers were using a broad variety of craft, including single-engine Cessnas and Pipers, C-46 and C-47's. By 1965 all foreign carriers calling at Ecuadorian airports were operating at least a portion of their service with jets.

Mariscal Sucre Airport, at Quito, and Simón Bolívar Airport, at Guayaquil, both of which have undergone large-scale reconstruction in the past few years, are equipped to handle any kind of civil aircraft. Landing facilities at other airports in the country range from simple cleared strips to unpaved, but graded runways.

The Ten-Year Plan includes a number of important programs for the improvement of civil air traffic, chiefly in the reconstruction of airports. One of the major programs calls for the further improvement of facilities—including approach guidance systems, runways and fire-fighting equipment—at Mariscal Sucre and Simón Bolívar. In addition, the Plan calls for the pavement and extension of runways at 12 existing airports and the completion of new airports at Santo Domingo de los Colorados and at Quevedo.

Water Transport

Most of Ecuador's foreign trade moves on maritime shipping, and historically coastal and inland water routes have been crucial components of domestic transport. Until the development of the road network the navigable rivers—especially the Guayas-Babahoyo-Daule system—were the principal passageways for people and goods on the coastal plain. Moreover, most of the pack trails descending from the Sierra converged on the heads of light-draft navigation, thereby tying the rivers into the interregional system. Although competition from the highways has made serious inroads on domestic waterborne traffic, boats continue to ply the traditional routes, calling at towns and agricultural centers not yet reached by wheeled vehicles.

Of the seaports registering regular maritime trade only Guayaquil had facilities for large volumes of traffic in 1965. Loading and discharge by lighter was required at all other ports, although piers and other facilities were either projected or under construction at Puerto Bolívar, Manta, Bahía de Caráquez, Esmeraldas and San Lorenzo. Combining the advantages of superior facilities, ac-

432

cess to navigable rivers and proximity to major production zones, Guayaquil has consistently handled the overwhelming bulk of foreign trade—on the order of two-thirds of all exports and nine-tenths of all imports (see ch. 24, Foreign Economic Relations).

Until recently goods coming into Guayaquil had to be transshipped about 35 miles downstream, because heavy silting barred most oceangoing vessels from the Guayas River. In 1958 the Guayaquil Port Authority, with financing by the International Bank for Reconstruction and Development (IBRD), began construction of a new port facility, located on the Estero Salado, an estuary whose head lies about 6 miles southwest of the city and which is not subject to silting. The new port, completed in 1962, is connected to the city by a good paved road and to the Guayas River by a mile-long canal.

Since the spread of banana cultivation and the settlement of large, dispersed areas on the coastal plain, several other ports—most notably Puerto Bolívar, Manta and Esmeraldas—have begun to show greater activity, underscoring the need for new facilities. The Ten-Year Plan includes several projects designed to accelerate the completion of construction programs underway in 1965.

Ecuador's principal maritime carrier is the *Flota Mercante Grancolombiana*, which it owns jointly with Colombia. When *Grancolombiana* was established in 1947 by the governments of Ecuador, Colombia and Venezuela, Ecuador contributed 10 percent of the original investment, and the other two countries contributed 45 percent each. In 1953, Venezuela withdrew, and Ecuador increased its stock share to 20 percent.

CHAPTER 23

FISCAL AND MONETARY SYSTEM

PUBLIC FINANCE

In 1963 the consolidated income of the public sector (including the central government, the municipal councils, the provincial councils and the autonomous entities) was estimated at slightly more than S/4.2 billion (in 1965, S/18.5 equaled US$1—see Glossary) and accounted for almost 29 percent of the national income, a relatively high proportion. Public investment in the same year represented 5 percent of the gross national product.

Public spending, for roads, schools, irrigation systems, hospitals and other facilities, for wages and salaries, and for transfer payments, has a vital impact upon national well-being and upon social and economic development. The increased importance of the public sector is evidenced by the fact that total expenditures between 1956 and 1963 increased approximately 8.7 percent annually, while the mean annual increase in the gross national product was about 6 percent in current terms.

The collection and disbursement of public funds are highly decentralized, and funds traditionally have been allocated in a manner which discriminates against the central government. In 1963 the central government received 33 percent of the public income; autonomous agencies, 50 percent; municipal councils, 15 percent; and provincial councils, 2 percent. In addition to revenue sources not under control of the central government, municipal, provincial and autonomous entities receive income by subsidies from the funds of the central government.

Collection of revenue is effected at all levels of the civil administration, as well as through customs, the postal system, the public monopolies and the banks. At the lower levels of government some taxes are collected through the auction to private citizens of the collection privilege.

Between 1956 and 1963 the consolidated public account showed a budgetary surplus, of varying size, in 1957, 1958, 1959 and 1963. During the rest of the period there was a deficit which increased sharply in 1960, 1961 and 1962. Within the public sector the central government developed a deficit in its operations budget each year between 1956 and 1965, whereas the autonomous agencies finished each year with unspent balances that were not transferable to fill the gap in income for administration of the central government.

Deficits of the central government, attributable in part to an overestimation of income in planning, have been met by the issuance of short-term obligations to suppliers, by medium-term bond issues (which have been absorbed largely by public institutions), by loans from the Central Bank and, on occasion, by external loans.

The Constitution outlines a conservative and rather inflexible fiscal policy and provides that no pro forma budget may be presented to Congress in which expenditures and revenues are not balanced and that no budget may be issued that does not contain a provision for the payment of the national debt. A further restriction, which, if met, would tend to keep income and expenditures in balance, is the stipulation that administrative expenditures of a permanent character may not be met by loans. In addition to a conservative budget policy outlined for the central government, the Constitution, by providing that no revenue indicated for a special purpose may be applied to the general expenditures of the state, has precluded the use of cash balances of autonomous entities to compensate for the deficits that have consistently developed in the administrative funds of the central government.

Legal and Administrative Bases

The Constitution of 1946, together with a body of legislative acts and executive decrees, is the basis for the conduct of fiscal affairs. Among the constitutional duties assigned to the President of the Republic are the care of the national property and the supervision of the collection, administration, expenditure and accounting of the national revenues. The power to levy or abolish taxes, assessments or other public revenues is vested in Congress, which is also empowered to oversee contracts for loans and bonds pledging the public credit and to determine the manner of dealing with the public debt. Additional fiscal responsibilities of Congress are the determination of the characteristics of the national currency and the enactment of the national budget. To supervise the national accounts, the Constitution created the office of the Comptroller General of the Nation, who is appointed by Congress every 4 years from a list of three names submitted by the president.

The Ministry of Finance, which was known as the Ministry of

the Treasury and Public Credit until changed by a decree of the military government in November 1963, is the arm of the central government chiefly responsible for the administration and execution of fiscal affairs. The Ministry, which is the seat of the governmental revenue collection agency, is also charged with the administration of the public debt, both internal and external; the custody of treasury funds; and the performance of other essential fiscal services.

The Central Bank of Ecuador, which became an organ of the state (although owned in part by the private banks) through the Monetary Law of 1948, also is an important instrument for the execution of fiscal policy. The Central Bank is a major source of government credit and has the exclusive right to issue coins and notes. In addition to these functions the bank is a repository of funds of the central government and of autonomous agencies, is a disbursing agent of government funds and conducts transactions in foreign exchange.

The Constitution provides a degree of autonomy for provinces and municipalities and asserts that the law shall fix the specific taxes and revenues in such a way as to guarantee their economic independence. The right to the receipts from taxes on urban property is vested inalienably in the municipalities.

In addition to constitutional provisions and major laws and decrees the collection and distribution of public revenues has been determined by a vast number of uncoordinated acts passed over a long period of time. These acts provide for a proportional division of taxes and other revenues among government ministries, provincial and municipal entities, state enterprises and autonomous and semiautonomous agencies, for purposes that range from local public works projects to national defense and to working capital for national development banks. An official estimate indicated that 800 different assessments were in existence in 1963. At the local level taxes, fees and assessments are levied through municipal ordinances on sources that overlap those used by the central government.

As a result of studies begun during the late 1950's and continued through the first half of the 1960's, institutional changes have been initiated to bring greater order out of the confusion of revenue laws and collection agencies, to reduce the cost of collection, to discourage tax evasion, to define the fiscal rights and responsibilities of various levels of government and to further the goal of economic development through a higher degree of centralization of resource use and planning in the central government. In 1961, as a step in this direction, the Department of Coordination and Control and the Department of Financing and Fiscal Advisory Services were established within the Ministry of the

Treasury and Public Credit to improve tax administration and to advise on fiscal policies related to government income.

The military government also has made institutional changes with the objective of increasing administrative efficiency. In addition to reorganizing the Ministry of the Treasury and Public Credit into the Ministry of Finance with enlarged powers and responsibilities, a new department, the Technical Secretariat of Administration, was created by decree in 1963 to coordinate and implement new administrative and fiscal procedures at the executive level.

The National Budget

The Constitution of 1946 established the procedure for the preparation and enactment of the annual General Budget Law (Ley de Presupuesto General del Estado). The fiscal year coincides with the calendar year, and the liquidation period of the budget has been set for January 31 of the following year.

The Constitution requires that the chief executive submit to Congress within 3 days after it convenes in ordinary session on August 10 of each year a pro forma budget accompanied by a message explaining the general financial position of the government. Congress is required to enact a budget by October 9. If Congress does not issue the executive budget at this time and does not approve one by the end of the regular legislative session on October 31, the draft budget as originally presented becomes effective for the following year.

Constitutionally, preparation of the pro forma general budget is the function of the Technical Budgetary Commission, consisting of the minister responsible for state finances; the minister responsible for the national economy or his representative; one legislator chosen by Congress in joint session and two alternates chosen from members of the legislative budgetary committee; and one representative of the National Economic Council. The minister responsible for state finances is designated as presiding officer and the director of the budget as secretary of the Technical Budgetary Commission. In the preparation of the preliminary draft the Commission is enjoined to consult provincial authorities, bodies and legislatures concerning the needs of the respective provinces.

On presentation of the budget to Congress by the executive, the Constitution requires that it be referred for study to the Internal Budget Committee, consisting of one representative, either senator or deputy, for each province. Final approval of the budget rests with Congress, and the Technical Budgetary Commission is charged by the Constitution with carrying out the resolutions of Congress respecting the budget.

Until 1963 the operation, but not the preparation, of the national budget was carried on by the National Budget Office, which was located in the Ministry of the Treasury and headed by the National Budget Director. Since then the budgetary process, as outlined by the Constitution of 1946, has been modified through a series of executive decrees which remained unratified at the end of 1965 because of the recess of Congress since the military government assumed authority. In the process of reorganization the National Budget Office was relocated as a department of the Technical Secretariat of Administration and was made responsible for the preparation of the pro forma budget by estimating the probable expenditure necessary and income available to meet routine operating expenses and carry out the annual goals and programs set by the General Plan for the Economic and Social Development of Ecuador (1964–73). Estimates are reached through consultation with the various ministries and agencies and through information provided by the Office of the Comptroller General and the Ministry of Finance. To assure uniformity of program information presented, written instructions have been issued and a manual has been prepared for the use of agencies and departments participating in the central government budget.

In the recess of Congress the draft budget is presented for approval of the policy of expenditures and fiscal management to a new organization, the Finance Committee, consisting of representatives of the Ministry of Finance, the Central Bank and the National Budget Office. Upon approval by the Finance Committee the draft is referred for final approval to the executive authority, which in 1964 and 1965 issued the budget by decree.

The consolidated budget of the central government consists of an operations budget and a capital budget with an annexed budget for state enterprises (which has included state monopolies since 1952) and a series of special accounts. The operations budget, which covers the routine expenditures of the central government for goods and services and the service of the public debt, is financed by tax revenues, income from the national patrimony, such as mining and petroleum concessions and royalties, and other sources. The capital budget covers real investment in new schools, roads, ports, bridges and other constructions, as well as investment in the capital of financial institutions. It is financed by tax income—particularly from export, import, sales and consumption taxes—and also through internal and external loans. Only revenues distributed to the operations and capital budgets are subject to effective control by the central government.

The annexed budget for state enterprises comprises expenditures and income of the National Postal Service, the Automatic Telephone Company of Quito, the Automatic Telephone Company of Guayaquil, the Radio, Telegraph and Telephone Company of Ecuador, the Office of Supplies, the Office of Civil Aviation, and state monopolies. In addition to fees for services rendered, state enterprises are also supported by participation in tax income and by internal and external loans.

Under the classification of "special accounts" are included a vast number of revenue commitments from specific tax sources earmarked for a great variety of purposes and agencies, both local and nationwide in scope.

Since earmarked revenues are for the most part effectively removed from the budgetary control of the central government, the existence of special accounts has contributed an element of rigidity to public finance which has been considered an obstacle in planning for social and economic development. To strengthen the capacity of the central government to direct programs and expenditures toward established development goals, the following autonomous agencies were added to the general budget by decrees issued at the end of 1963: the National Irrigation Agency, the National Service of Meteorology and Hydrology, the National Institute of Agricultural and Livestock Investigations, the National Banana Administration, the Ecuadorian Institute of Agrarian Reform and Colonization, the National Fishing Institute, the Center of Industrial Development and the Ecuadorian Institute of Electrification. These agencies, which formerly collected income and carried out plans independently, began to receive stated annual income related to planned programs instead of proportional participation in the yield of designated taxes and fees. Efforts to incorporate additional autonomous agencies in the general budget have met with resistance in some instances.

Structure of Expenditures

In current prices the combined expenditures of the central government, state enterprises and special accounts almost tripled in the decade from 1956 to 1965, rising from S/1.5 billion in 1956 to a preliminary estimate of S/4.1 billion in 1965. Although total expenditures have increased in every year of the decade except 1962, they have risen sharply since 1958. Provisional figures for 1964, released late in 1965, which indicate an increase in expenditures of almost 30 percent over 1963 (from S/2.4 billion in 1963 to S/3.1 billion in 1964), are not comparable with expenditures of previous years, since major structural changes were made by the addition of a number of autonomous agencies in 1964.

Investment by the central government, which accounts for a minor part of the general budget of the state, has not shown a clear trend since 1956, but has fluctuated from a low of 11 percent of government spending in 1958 to a high of 39 percent in 1960. Since then investment has claimed about 25 percent annually. A great part of public investment is not undertaken by the central government, but by municipal and provincial councils and by other autonomous entities which are outside budgetary control.

Since 1956 the Ministries of Defense, Education, and Public Works have consistently received a high proportion of public revenues. The proportion assigned for defense, which was 21 percent in 1956, decreased to 13 percent of total revenue in 1963, the last year in which the budget structure compares essentially with former budgets. The proportion devoted to education and social security remained relatively steady, at around 14 percent annually until 1962, when their combined share rose to approximately 17 percent, an increase which was maintained in 1963. Expenditure on public works, which is an unstable element in fiscal activity, varying from year to year according to administration policies and the state of works in process, has ranged from a high of 21 percent of total revenue in 1961 to a low of 10 percent in 1958.

Although the proportion devoted to capital contributions and subsidies to autonomous entities has fluctuated widely from year to year, these items have at all times represented sizable amounts. In 1963 the combined expenditures of S/21 million claimed 20 percent of the revenue of the consolidated budget. The cost of the public debt, which includes interest and amortization of both internal and external debt, has shown a clear upward trend, rising from 6.8 percent in 1956 to 15.5 percent in 1963. Considering planned economic development, it may be expected to maintain its relative importance and perhaps increase (see table 14).

The general budget announced for 1965 forecast expenditures and income of S/4.1 billion, an increase of about one-third over the budget for the previous year. Of the total, S/2.9 billion was assigned to the operations budget; S/1.2 billion, to the capital budget; and S/0.9 billion, to the state enterprises budget. Early in 1965, however, it became apparent that because of conditions in world commodity markets, particularly Ecuador's declining position in the banana market, it would be impossible to implement the budget at the proposed level, and revisions of revenue and expenditure estimates were undertaken with the assistance of international financial advisers (see ch. 24, Foreign Economic Relations).

Structure of Revenues

The major source of current revenue for the total public sector has been taxes, which provided slightly more than 70 percent of

Table 14. Estimated Consolidated Expenditures of the Ecuadorian Central Government, by Function or Agency, 1963

	Amount (in thousands of sucres*)	Percent of total
Legislative branch	4,859	0.2
Judicial branch	22,307	1.0
Presidency	6,403	0.3
Ministry of Government	89,163	3.8
Ministry of Foreign Relations	39,969	1.7
Ministry of Education	332,600	14.2
Ministry of Defense	307,218	13.0
Ministry of Public Works	263,139	11.3
Ministry of Social Welfare	68,582	2.9
Ministry of Commerce and Banking	10,003	0.4
Ministry of Development	68,425	2.9
Ministry of Finance	66,050	2.8
Other state agencies	22,807	1.0
International quotas	40,571	1.7
Contingencies	12,776	0.5
State monopolies	74,503	3.2
Capital contributions to autonomous agencies	46,438	2.0
Grants to autonomous agencies	439,237	18.8
State pensions	55,812	2.4
Public debt service	372,801	15.9
Total	2,343,663	100.0

*In 1963 the official selling rate was S/18.18 per US$1 (see Glossary).

Source: Adapted from Banco Central del Ecuador, *Memoria del Gerente General: Correspondiente al Ejercicio de 1963*, table 95.

the annual total between 1956 and 1963. Revenue derived from the provision of public services, the sale and rental of land and buildings, transactions in foreign exchange, and other sources makes up the remainder. Between 1956 and 1963 the average annual participation of the central government in current revenue receipts was slightly less than 36 percent, while the autonomous agencies received an average of almost 48 percent of the total. Of the remainder, which was divided between provincial and municipal governments, provincial councils received less than 2 percent. Since 1963, in order to channel funds to those projects having priority for economic and social development, steps have been initiated to restructure the distribution of public income to increase the proportion over which the central government has control. Although reorganization has had a certain measure of success, change has been strongly opposed in some areas, particularly on the Coast.

Current revenue of the central government has been derived almost entirely from taxes (usually amounting to about 90 percent). Other income has been derived from consular fees, postal charges, charges for telephone and telegraph services, and revenue from government-owned property, state enterprises and monopolies. Income from state enterprises cannot be measured accurately because of a lack of records and a lack of uniformity in accounting practices. Recent surveys, however, indicate that government enterprises, except for the Quito and Guayaquil telephone companies, have operated at a deficit. The contribution of monopolies has been declining, and arrangements have been undertaken to transfer some monopoly operations to the private sector.

Although there have been some changes in the sources of tax revenue of the public sector since 1956, they have not been large. Indirect taxes, which provided around 60 percent of tax revenue annually between 1956 and 1960, have evidenced a slight downward trend and accounted for approximately 56 percent from 1961 to 1963. Of the indirect taxes import duties and consumption taxes, together, have accounted for about 50 percent of all tax revenue. The revenue from import duties, which is highly responsive to current economic conditions, experienced a sharp drop in 1962 as a result of a short monetary crisis and an equally swift rise in 1963 because of the stockpiling of inventory in anticipation of a change in customs duties. Revenue from taxes on consumer goods, which has provided about 20 percent of the total, declined to 17 percent in 1961, a decline that has been ascribed to inefficient tax collection methods.

The increasing contribution of direct taxes reflects a measure of economic growth and preliminary steps toward reorganization of tax administration at the central government level. Taxes on income, which are the principal component of direct taxes and which provided approximately 25 percent of the total from 1956 to 1960, increased slightly in productivity to 28 percent in 1962; a reduced contribution in 1963 was accredited to the complexity of implementing a change in income tax structure. Export taxes have shown a rising trend from 1956, when their share of the total was 7 percent, to 10 percent in 1963.

Extraordinary income, including external and internal loans and balances from previous years, has provided an annual average of 20 percent of revenue, but ranged from 5 percent to 33 percent of the total. The contribution of extraordinary income has been above 20 percent in every year since 1960 (see fig. 9).

Taxation

For a long time there has been a recognition of the need to revise and modernize the tax system, which has been characterized

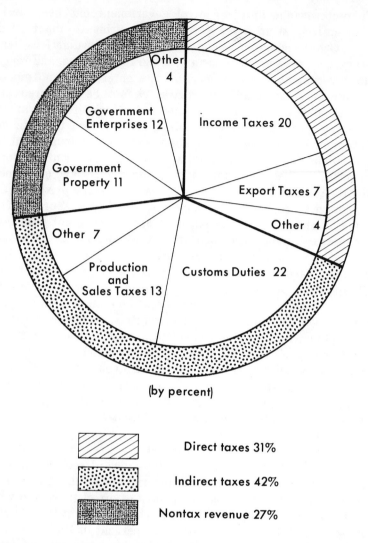

(by percent)

Direct taxes 31%

Indirect taxes 42%

Nontax revenue 27%

Total current revenue : S/3,682 million*

*In 1963 the official selling rate was S/18.18 per US$1
(see Glossary).

Source: Adapted from Banco Central del Ecuador,
Memoria del Gerente General: Correspondiente al
Ejercicio de 1964.

Figure 9. Percentage Distribution of Ecuadorian Government Estimated
Current Revenue, 1963.

as unproductive and difficult to administer because of its complexity and because of a proliferation of taxes, many at the municipal level, on the production, sale and export of commodities. Studies of tax reform undertaken by the National Board of Planning and Economic Coordination soon after its creation in 1954, and later intensified by the work of the Department of Coordination and Control and the Department of Financing and Fiscal Advisory Services of the Ministry of Finance, have been supplemented by studies of a joint mission from the Inter-American Development Bank (IDB) and the Organization of American States (OAS).

The goals of tax reform have been twofold. The first objective has been a revision of existing laws to increase equitability, to simplify provisions of the separate laws and to broaden the tax base by reaching new revenue sources and spreading the tax burden over a larger proportion of the population. A second objective has been an administrative reorganization to simplify the process of making tax returns and improve the collection system to discourage tax evasion and smuggling, make collection methods more uniform and provide a greater proportion of the revenue potential to the public treasury.

As a result of studies undertaken, a number of reform measures were promulgated in 1964. In addition to the revision of the income tax law, some export and excise taxes were revised and consolidated; stamp taxes were codified; and the sales tax was revised.

The abolition in 1964 of almost 800 municipal taxes affecting agriculture was a significant step toward simplification, which was carried further in early 1965 by a decree that eliminated an additional 400 taxes. The decree also defined the following as sources of municipal income: urban and rural property, the purchase and sale of real estate, public events, the sale and registry of documents, and licenses.

Income Taxes

Until 1962 income taxes were assessed under provisions of the law passed in 1946 and its subsequent revisions. In 1962 income tax reform was initiated by the passage of a new law which, because of administrative problems, was not fully implemented and which has been superseded by a law issued in February 1964 and revised in June of the same year. The motive for reform was to simplify and produce greater compliance with the income tax system.

Under the provision of the law in force until 1962 taxes were levied on three categories of income: income from labor, income from labor associated with capital, and income from pure capital. Under the category of labor, which for purposes of revenue calculated tax was further broken down into income from dependent labor and professional services, taxes were levied on all types of wages, salaries, fees, commissions, pensions and annuities. Income from industrial and commercial ventures, including banking and construction, was taxed under the classification of labor associated with capital; income from pure capital covered interest of all types, dividends and undistributed profits.

The amount of taxes due was determined according to a complicated system. All categories except income from pure capital enjoyed a general deduction of S/6,000 for each taxpayer, with additional deductions according to family size. After deductions the basic tax was determined by schedules which differed in rates and degree of progressivity for each class of income. On top of the basic tax a number of additional taxes, which also varied according to income source, were imposed. Since each type of income was taxed at a different rate and required a different return the total liability of an individual who enjoyed more than one type of income was determined by adding the results of the application of the appropriate sets of rates. The process was further complicated by the necessity of making more than one tax return.

Although the 1964 law retains some of the features of the previous one, substantial changes have been made to simplify procedures, improve collectability and increase the equity of the tax burden. The most significant feature of the new law is the adoption of a single schedule for all persons, regardless of source of income, with rates varying from 10 percent on incomes of less than S/10,000 to 42 percent on incomes of S/1 million or more. The general deduction for each taxpayer has been increased from S/6,000 to S/10,000. Family deductions have been increased to S/2,000 for each of the first four dependent children and S/3,000 for each successive dependent child. Thus, deductions for a family consisting of a husband, a dependent wife and four dependent children total S/28,000. Although there has been only a minor decrease in general effective rates, greater progressivity has been attained by making the greatest reductions in effective rates to large families with low incomes.

Further innovations were designed to broaden the tax base by establishing methods for the estimation of tax liabilities of professionals and farmers when tax returns were not made. Although it is recognized that the estimation of income does not guarantee the receipt of revenue by the government, it is a step forward in closing the avenues to tax evasion. As a further measure for tightening enforcement, presentation of personal income tax receipts has been required for the conduct of a number of activities. A total of about 25,000 additional taxpayers were added to the list during 1964.

Import duties, a major source of revenue, have also been used to direct economic growth through the imposition of varying rates upon different classes of goods. The lowest rates are imposed on capital goods and essential raw materials; the highest rates are imposed on luxury goods and imported articles competing with those produced domestically. Most import items are subject to duties both by weight and ad valorem. Ad valorem duties are assessed on value at the port of export (FOB), which excludes maritime freight charges, insurance, consular fees and commission. A new tariff based on cost plus insurance and freight (CIF), announced for May 1, 1965, was not implemented because of the resistance of coastal commercial interests to higher duties.

Numerous ad valorem taxes have been levied for revenue purposes by different levels of government on all the major exports. The unification of export taxes at the national level has been part of the program of tax reform (see ch. 24, Foreign Economic Relations).

A source of substantial revenue as well as a source of administrative confusion and of hardship for low-income families has been the imposition of production and sales taxes by various governmental jurisdictions, particularly municipal, on many articles of common consumption. In accord with the goals of simplification and greater equity, innumerable taxes on the production of sugar, beer and liquors have been consolidated, and 14 separate taxes on salt have been abolished. The base of the sales tax has been expanded, and previous heterogeneous taxes have been replaced by a single national sales tax amounting to 3.5 percent on merchandise and 10 percent on certain luxury services.

Stamp taxes, which were recently codified, are imposed on all types of documents, such as contracts, securities, licenses, registrations, passports, consular invoices, wills and other transactions. In spite of their profusion, stamp taxes have not provided a major source of income.

Other sources of revenue are taxes on gifts and inheritances and on capital, which includes capital invested in urban and rural property and in enterprises. For the purpose of encouraging economic development, capital invested in desirable industry enjoys certain concessions under the Law for Industrial Development (see ch. 20, Industry).

The Public Debt

At the end of 1963 the total internal debt (direct and indirect) stood at approximately S/2.9 billion, and the external debt of the central government (excluding supplier's credits) and other public entities at $103 million. Converting to national currency at the 1963 free market exchange rate (S/19.6 equaled US$1), the total public debt, both internal and external, stood at S/4.8 billion, of which 60 percent represented internal debt. Between 1956 and 1963 the total internal debt increased from S/635 million to S/219 billion, or about 350 percent in current terms, while the external debt slightly more than doubled, rising from $49 million in 1956 to $103 million in 1963. The internal debt consists of direct debt contracted by the central government and indirect debts, many guaranteed by the central government, which are contracted by municipalities and other public entities. In 1963, of the S/2.9 million internal debt, the central government was directly obligated for S/1.8 million.

Debt of the central government consists largely of the floating debt—unpaid balances for goods and services; short-term debt, which, in general, consists of advances against tax collections made by the Central Bank; and long-term debt. From time to time floating and short-term debt is consolidated into longer term obligations with the Central Bank.

Over the years bond issues have been placed by the central government for all types of public works, including highway bonds issued in 1954, repayable in dollars and known as "dollar bonds." In addition to public works projects, bonds have been issued for the benefit of the University of Guayaquil, for the postal system and for other undertakings, at interest rates ranging from 4 percent on bonds of the amortization fund to 10 percent on bonds for the port of Manta. Most importantly, bonds were issued in 1960, 1961 and 1962 to finance the deficit of the general budget. In 1964 planned government expenditures were based on new borrowing, both external and internal. Early in 1964 a S/200 million central government bond issue was brought out, redeemable at par on demand and paying 8 percent interest. The bonds were backed by 30 percent of the proceeds from sales, and the Central Bank served as fiduciary agent. Following the successful disposition of this issue, two issues, one for S/100 million and one for S/50 million, were brought out on similar terms later in the year. The Central Bank invested 50 percent of the deposits of the public agencies in this bond issue.

Although an increasing effort has been made to attract investment by the private sector, the lack of an established stock market and a long-time preference for other types of investment have been deterring factors, and in 1963 slightly more than 86 percent of the internal debt was held by the public agencies, such as the Central Bank, the Social Security System and the National Securities Commission (as of 1964 changed to Securities Commission-National Financial Corporation).

The external debt consists largely of obligations to foreign countries and international financial institutions for loans for the development of the economic infrastructure and support of the budget. Given the need for capital to finance economic and social development, it is anticipated that external loans will continue to be important for some time (see ch. 24, Foreign Economic Relations).

BANKING AND CREDIT

The credit needs of the country are served by the Central Bank, 15 commercial banks, 2 mortgage banks, a development bank for the provision of agricultural credit, a housing bank and a recently organized cooperative bank. Other institutions which mobilize savings and provide credit are the Social Security Fund, the Pension Fund, the Securities Commission-National Financial Corporation, 8 mutual home savings and loan associations and a small group of insurance companies. There is no stock exchange.

The Monetary Board makes policy decisions concerning financial and banking affairs. Supervision of the banking system is under the direction of the Superintendency of Banks, an autonomous agency which examines all banks at least once a year.

Because of the inadequate supply of capital, credit is expensive, and long-term funds for development purposes are difficult to obtain. Most loans are made on a short-term basis for commercial purposes. Because of the lack of a market, the government frequently has had to resort to the Central Bank for funds, a practice which has had mildly inflationary results. Although in the past there has been no great need for a stock exchange because of the small size of the industrial sectors and the fact that most enterprises have been family held, the promise of more rapid industrial development emphasizes the need for growth capital and for a broader base of ownership.

Although for some time efforts have been made to improve the credit system, the pace of change has been accelerated since 1960 by the reorganization of existing institutions and the establishment of new ones. The development banking system has been reorganized to provide more adequate credit, and new banks have been created for special purposes. Changes also have been made in laws governing corporations, with the expectation of increasing ownership and developing a market for industrial securities. These innovations were so recent that their results were not apparent in late 1965, but at least a start had been made in broadening the credit base.

Monetary Board

The Monetary Board, which is a policymaking body at the highest level, is specifically charged with the regulation of the banking and credit system in accord with the Monetary Law of 1948 and any subsequent law or modifications. This duty involves the formulation of rules and controls, among which are the determination of legal interest rates and the reserve ratio that must be maintained by private banks. The Monetary Board is composed of eight representatives from the national government, private banks and the chambers of agriculture, industry and commerce; a ninth member is elected by the other members. To preserve continuity of experience, terms of office vary in length for different groups. Among the duties of the Monetary Board is the appointment of the general manager of the Central Bank, who is responsible to the Board.

Central Bank

The Central Bank (Banco Central del Ecuador) was established by the Monetary Law of 1948 as the successor to an earlier private bank which had performed similar functions. The termination of the charter was set for 1977 and the authorized capital at S/20 million, divided into shares of S/100. The Central Bank is owned jointly by the central government and private banks. Shares are divided into two series: Series A shares may be acquired only by banking institutions operating within the country, and Series B shares may be acquired only by the central government. Banking shares, which may be acquired by a bank up to the amount of 5 percent of its capital and reserves, may be traded among banks. Government shares are not transferable. At the end of 1963 combined capital and reserves reached S/52.3 million, and earnings of S/2.5 million were reported. Offices are located in Quito, Guayaquil, Cuenca, Manta, Bahía de Caráquez, Jipijapa, Esmeraldas, Loja, Ambato, Tulcán and Machala.

The Central Bank, which is subject to the jurisdiction of the Monetary Board, performs the usual functions—both domestic and international—of a central bank. At the domestic level, in addition to the issuance of legal tender, coins and notes, the Bank provides services to the private banking system, the central government, government-related agencies and the public. For the private banking system the Central Bank is empowered to carry on all normal credit operations, such as the discount, rediscount, purchase and sale of bills of exchange, bank acceptances and other credit instruments. The Bank is also the holder of the required reserves, which in 1963 were specified as 25 percent of total sight deposits and 15 percent of time deposits of private banks. The reserves are used as a fund for check clearance, which is operated by the Central Bank.

The Central Bank holds deposits of and provides credit for the central government and acts as fiscal agent for the government and the autonomous agencies. In addition, it is empowered to accept deposits from and grant credit to the public. By provisions of the charter it is also authorized to carry on operations to reduce or increase the money in circulation, in accord with the policies of the Monetary Board, by the issuance and sale or purchase of so-called "certificates of participation" and "stabilization bonds." The effectiveness of this operation, which is performed by central banks in many countries, has been limited by the lack of a private market for official securities.

In the international field the Central Bank represents the government in transactions with foreign central banks, with the International Monetary Fund (IMF) and with other international financial institutions. In pursuance of international economic relations and the conduct of trade, it accepts deposits in foreign currency, maintains convertibility according to IMF standards, buys and sells foreign exchange, and issues import and export permits (see ch. 24, Foreign Economic Relations).

Although it is empowered by law to make loans up to 270 days and, under some special circumstances, up to 1 year, the largest volume of credit is extended for 180 days, and only a small amount for a longer term.

Private banks have been conservative in the use of the rediscount privilege with the Central Bank. Of the internal credit conceded in 1963, S/733 million, or more than 50 percent of the S/1.4 billion total, was granted to the government and official entities. Credit granted to the central government rose sharply in 1960, when a sizable budgetary deficit developed.

Interest rates, which are fixed by the Monetary Board, favor the central government over other sectors of the economy. The Central Bank charges 2 percent interest for official government loans, 3 percent rediscount for government development banks, 5 percent for rediscounts to other banks and for export futures and 10 percent for commercial loans.

Private Banking System

The private banking system comprises 15 commercial banks, 2 of which are of foreign ownership; 2 mortgage banks; and a bank for special agricultural credit. Although all of the banks except 1 have their main headquarters in Quito or Guayaquil, a reasonable distribution of banking facilities has been achieved through the establishment of branches and offices by most of the major banks. It has been estimated that the 3 largest banks, 2 of which originate on the Coast and 1 in the Sierra, account for more than 70 percent of total private banking assets. Among their many functions, commercial banks may accept deposits on a demand or time basis, make commercial loans with or without collateral for periods up to 1 year and mortgage loans for periods not exceeding 5 years; purchase, hold or sell obligations of the central government, municipalities and officially backed institutions; and purchase, hold or sell mortgage bonds issued by their own mortgage departments. Five of the commercial banks are also mortgage and savings banks and, as such, are subject to the requirements of mortgage and savings as well as of commercial banks. Other commercial banks operate mortgage departments and savings departments.

Banks that make mortgage loans issue, on their own guaranty, debenture bonds bearing 10 percent interest, which are sold to the public. This type of mortgage bond, which has been one of the most popular forms of investment, has tended to channel available funds into construction and has been a formidable competitor for funds that might otherwise have provided a larger market for government securities or for industrial financing.

Although commercial banks are permitted to make loans for up to 1 year and for commercial, industrial or agricultural purposes, they have tended to concentrate their rather scarce resources overwhelmingly in the provision of commercial credit for not more than 180 days, which constituted almost 90 percent of credit outstanding at the end of 1963. On December 31, 1963, total capital and reserves of the private banking system were S/364 million, and total resources stood at S/3.5 billion.

Other Credit Sources

The government-owned National Development Bank System was instituted in 1944 as the Development Credit System to provide medium- and long-term credit for agriculture and industry. Working capital for the system, which at the time of organization consisted of a National Development Bank located in Quito and 15 provincial banks, was derived from participation in specifically assigned tax revenue and from Central Bank credit. The Development banks were organized to provide long-term capital, but because of the scarcity of funds and the burden of overdue and defaulted loans, this goal has not been reached. In late 1964 the system was reorganized to provide greater centralization of resources and policymaking, with the hope of providing a more effective source of agricultural credit (see ch. 19, Agriculture).

As another source of specialized credit, the Housing Bank, was founded in 1961 to accumulate and disburse funds to construct and improve low-cost housing. Of the original capital of S/90

452

million, 60 percent was contributed by the Social Security Fund and 40 percent by the Pension Fund. Since its establishment the Housing Bank has been granted a loan from the Social Progress Trust Fund of the Alliance for Progress and from the Agency for International Development (AID).

The Social Security Fund and the government employees' Pension Fund are two of the most important sources of investment capital. Not only have they provided a source of capital for the Housing Bank, but they also hold mortgage securities of commercial banks, invest in industrial enterprises and make direct loans to official institutions and municipalities. The Social Security Fund and the Pension Fund have been important outlets for government bonds, although in some instances government bonds have been held in lieu of the annual contributions due from government.

An additional financing agency of the government has been the National Securities Commission which was organized in 1947 under another name and reorganized in 1955. The purpose of the Commission was the creation of a market for government securities and for mortgage securities issued by agricultural and industrial interests and the establishment of a securities exchange. Originally, the capital of the Commission was derived from earmarked revenues and from Central Bank earnings. Although this source of income was withdrawn in 1959, capital and reserves of the Commission in 1961 totaled S/305.8 million, a sum which was invested in bonds issued by the central government. In late 1964 a further modification was made, and the organization became the National Finance Corporation. The new organization, which is financed partly by the IDB, expected to develop into an industrial bank capable of granting long-term credit and making equity investments. In October 1965 the Corporation agreed to underwrite an issue of mortgage bonds for La International, S.A., the largest textile mill in Ecuador. This was the first mortgage bond issue to be made directly by an industrial enterprise.

CURRENCY AND MONEY SUPPLY

The monetary unit is the sucre, which is divided into 100 centavos. The sucre has a par value of 0.0592447 grams of fine gold, which may be changed if necessary because of the obligations assumed as a member of the IMF. The currency consists of coins and banknotes issued by the Central Bank. Coins are made of nickel, in values of 5, 10, and 20 centavos, and banknotes are in denominations of S/5, S/10, S/20, S/50, S/100, S/500 and S/1,000.

A multiple-exchange rate system is in effect, consisting of an official rate for certain transactions and a free rate. The currency has shown remarkable stability over a long period of time.

In 1950 the official selling rate was fixed at S/15 to $1, a rate that was maintained until 1961, when a monetary crisis brought about a reevaluation to S/18 per United States dollar. In the free market the sucre depreciated sharply at the time of the monetary crisis—from S/17.5 in 1960 to S/22.65 in 1962. Thereafter, it regained some strength and stood at about S/18.5 in relation to the dollar at the end of 1964.

Between 1958 and 1963 money in circulation increased about 64 percent—from S/1,397,462,000 in 1958 to S/2,251,448,000 in 1963. Between December 31, 1962, and December 31, 1963, the money supply increased by 12.5 percent.

The cost of living, which has exhibited only modest annual increases since 1950, has been increasing at a more rapid pace since 1960, when inflationary pressures increased because of rising budgetary deficits which were met in part by a rise in credit from the Central Bank.

CHAPTER 24

FOREIGN ECONOMIC RELATIONS

The economy is heavily dependent on the export of primary agricultural products. Between 1960 and 1964 the value of exports averaged about 15 percent of the gross national product, and of this, more than half was generated by bananas. In the early twentieth century cacao was by far the leading export, followed by coffee and rice. Bananas assumed the dominant place during the early 1950's, supported by cacao and coffee, and there has since been little diversity in the composition of exports.

Overdependence on a single agricultural commodity has left the economy vulnerable to price fluctuations on the world market, to increased competition from other producing areas and to natural phenomena. The government, fully aware of this precarious situation, has striven in recent years to achieve a greater diversity of exports by encouraging production growth in such commodities as fish and pyrethrum (a flower whose extract is widely used as an insecticide). Further, there have been attempts to encourage the development of processing industries within the country, as world prices on processed agricultural products are usually more stable than those on raw materials.

Since before World War II both imports and exports have grown, and the balance of trade was consistently favorable until 1964, when there was a deficit. Traditionally, the composition of imports has been weighted heavily toward consumer goods, in response to demands beyond the range and capacity of national industry. In recent years, however, the government has attempted to foster the growth of import substitution industries and, by application of selective tariff and exchange control policies, to channel more of the importing capacity toward capital goods.

A deficit in international payments has been frequent since 1950. Between 1957 and 1964, some improvement was apparent, and the balance of payments accounts showed a fluctuation between deficits and surpluses.

Although foreign investment, from both public and private sources, has played a relatively important part in the economy, in absolute terms it has been small. The various growth targets established in the 10-year General Plan for the Economic and Social Development of Ecuador (1964–73) require an influx of foreign capital far greater than has been available in the past. In part, this requirement is being met by increases in economic aid under the Alliance for Progress, and the government has also sought, through various means, to improve the climate for private investment (see ch. 18, The Economic System).

FOREIGN TRADE

Foreign trade increased greatly in volume and value after World War II in keeping with expanded world trade and higher postwar prices. The increased demand for Ecuador's agricultural products has been a reflection of both the expansion of world population and the increasing per capita income in the more highly industrialized countries.

Exports doubled in value between 1950 and 1963, rising from $74 million in 1950 to $148.9 million in 1963. Although the long-run trend of the total value of exports has been upward, it has proceeded at an uneven pace. There have been several export recessions, notably in 1953, 1955, 1961, 1964 and, according to preliminary figures, 1965. The most severe decline was in 1961, when there was a shortfall of $19.6 million.

Imports also increased in value between 1950 and 1963 but at a faster pace than exports, moving from $41.3 million in 1950 to $110.5 million in 1963. As a measure of the terms of trade, whereas exports doubled in value between 1950 and 1963, the tonnage shipped quadrupled, rising from 322,000 metric tons in 1950 to 1.3 million metric tons in 1963. During the same period imports, consisting largely of manufactured articles, almost tripled in value, but did not even double in quantity. In spite of the disparate price trend, a favorable balance of trade was maintained during the period. The first excess of imports over exports occurred in 1964. Although the exact extent was not available in late 1965, estimates indicated a recurrence of the trade deficit in that year.

Imports have consisted largely of consumer goods in the past, but the demands of planned economic development and industrial growth will probably shift the balance to capital goods and raw material.

Composition of Trade

Exports

In 1964 agricultural products accounted for 91.3 percent of the value of all exports; fish products, 4.3 percent; manufactured products, 1.3 percent; minerals, 0.4 percent; and miscellaneous products, the remaining 2.7 percent. In the agricultural category, 82 percent of all value was concentrated in three products—bananas, coffee and cacao—and bananas alone accounted for 57 percent of the foreign exchange earned by exports (see table 15).

The fundamental structure of export trade, consisting almost entirely of raw materials, has not changed since the Spanish conquest, but over a period of time the relative importance of products has fluctuated, and new products have been added to the list. In the early part of the twentieth century cacao held the leading place among exports, which was later assumed by rice and Panama hats when the cacao industry met with adverse conditions. After World War II, when rice became unprofitable as an export because of the reentry into the market of low-cost rice from the Far East, the world demand for bananas expanded and this commodity quickly reached a leading position in providing the necessary foreign exchange to support growing imports.

Table 15. *Exports of Ecuador, by Economic Group, 1960–64*
(in millions of U.S. dollars)

	1960	1961	1962	1963	1964*
Agricultural products	141.6	120.6	136.1	137.9	135.0
Bananas	90.0	81.0	88.0	85.2	84.2
Coffee	21.9	14.3	21.0	18.3	21.7
Cacao	21.4	15.6	15.9	19.8	15.5
Rice	3.7	2.8	0.7	3.7	1.1
Sugar	0.9	2.6	6.0	5.6	6.7
Other	3.7	4.3	4.5	5.3	5.8
Mineral earth	0.6	0.5	0.7	0.7	0.6
Fish products	3.6	5.4	5.4	6.3	6.3
Manufactured products	2.1	2.0	1.9	2.2	1.9
Pharmaceuticals	1.0	1.5	1.4	1.8	1.1
Straw hats	1.1	0.5	0.5	0.4	0.8
Miscellaneous	1.1	0.9	1.1	1.8	4.0
Total	149.0	129.4	145.2	148.9	147.8

*Preliminary figures.

Source: Adapted from Banco Central del Ecuador, *Memoria del Gerente General: Correspondiente al Ejercicio de 1964*, p. 128.

Ecuador emerged as a major supplier of bananas in the late 1940's and early 1950's, after the Central American production declined as a result of the sigatoka leaf disease, Panama disease and hurricane damage. Because of its ample supply of virgin land with uninfected soil, which encouraged low-cost production,

Ecuador was able to fill the gap left by the Central American countries. The tonnage of banana shipments almost quadrupled between 1945 and 1947, rising from 17,800 metric tons to 68,900 metric tons. By 1951 bananas had become the most valuable export and the mainstay of the economy, and since 1953 Ecuador has been the largest exporter of bananas in the world. Banana shipments, which have earned more than twice the foreign exchange earned by the other two major products, coffee and cacao, combined, reached 1.4 million metric tons with a value of $84.2 million in 1964.

Global banana production has recently grown more rapidly than has demand, and growing supplies on the world market have caused a decrease in prices, a factor which was responsible for the decline of earnings from a high of $90 million in 1960 to $84.2 million in 1964. Ecuador also faces increasing competition for world markets as a result of improved cultivation and marketing practices in other countries and as a result of expanded cultivation in countries more readily accessible to importing countries with respect to transportation.

After the Central American plantations were destroyed in the early 1950's the large fruitgrowing enterprises of the area initiated research for a variety of banana more resistant to disease and wind than the Gros Michel, which was the variety originally produced in the area and which is still marketed by Ecuador. The Gros Michel excels in flavor and appearance and withstands transportation fairly well; it is, however, particularly susceptible to Panama disease, which now infects some of the Ecuadorian plantings and for which an effective and inexpensive cure has not been perfected. The Central American producers have recently developed new, disease-resistant varieties of higher yield than the Gros Michel and have also developed more efficient and economical techniques for handling and shipping, most notably by discontinuing the wasteful practice of exporting individual perfect stems and, instead, shipping hands of bananas in boxes and crates. The innovation of shipment by box has been adopted by Asian growers also and is accepted by most importing countries.

Along with reestablishing production and adopting better shipping methods the Central American countries have carried on aggressive marketing techniques which have cut into the demand for Ecuadorian bananas in the United States, where purchases declined from 24.3 million stems in 1960 to 20.8 million in 1963. Coincidental with this drop, a sharp increase in demand in the Japanese market more than compensated for any other decline; exports to Japan rose from 1.1 million stems in 1962 to 7.4 million in 1963.

The Japanese market did not maintain the 1963 level, however, because of the recovery of production in Taiwan, which had been the customary source of supply, and Ecuadorian exports to Japan decreased by 2 million stems in 1964. There is, however, some expectation of retaining a share, although perhaps a declining one, of the Japanese market for the next few years. The longrun prospect is less hopeful, since a consortium of Japanese trading companies is reported to be developing large-scale production of bananas in areas with favorable transportation-to-market possibilities. Tariff barriers and preferred suppliers add to competition in other places. Banana sales have been further handicapped by the withdrawal of the United Fruit Company, which is not expected to return to the market in the near future. Although final 1965 figures were not available in late 1965, it was generally conceded that banana earnings continued their downward trend.

Because foreign exchange from banana exports plays a vital part in the success of the economic and social development plan in the near future, steps have been taken to improve the competitive position of the country, and others are under consideration. Producers are beginning to adopt the new practice of shipping in boxes. No steps have been taken, however, to replace plantings with more disease-resistant and productive varieties, although the possibility has been considered. A rapid transformation is impeded by the structure of the industry, which is largely composed of small producers who do not have adequate machinery for cooperative activity (see ch. 19, Agriculture).

At the governmental level also, measures have been taken to aid the industry. Minimum export prices have been set, and export taxes modified. To reduce freight and handling costs, harbor facilities at banana ports were being improved, and in July 1965 an agreement was reached with Israel for the organization of a fleet to carry bananas.

With the object of studying the world industry, a meeting of banana exporting and importing countries, called by the Food and Agriculture Organization (FAO), was held in Guayaquil in October 1964. At this meeting a committee was appointed to consider the basic problems of banana cultivation and trade with the expectation of later forming an international organization for the industry.

Coffee played a vital role in stemming the export crisis of 1965 by absorbing a large part of the shortfall in banana earnings. Although final figures were not available in late 1965, preliminary information indicated that the value of coffee exports in the first half of 1965 more than doubled the value for the same period in the previous year and that the quota for the year would be exceeded. Among the factors contributing to the success of coffee were favorable weather conditions, the harvesting of additional plants which were just beginning to bear and a reported decrease in illegal border trade, which had formerly limited the supply available for export quotas.

Among the marginal exports were rice, castor beans, pyrethrum flowers and extract, balsa wood, fruit, tagua nuts, kapok, refined sugar, processed fish, a few manufactured articles and a few other products.

Because of increased domestic demand and refining facilities, crude petroleum is no longer exported (see ch. 20, Industry). Rice is exported only when the harvest is good and world prices are high; and tagua nuts, which have played only a minor role among exports, have declined in value since 1950. Hats made of toquilla straw (known as "Panama hats"), which constituted a dependable source of foreign exchange in the 1930's and early 1940's, have declined from a peak export value of $6 million in 1946 to $800,000 in 1964. The fall in export value of these hats, which are known throughout the world for their quality, can be attributed to increased competition from cheaper hats and to changing styles. Studies have been made of the possibility of increasing trade by redesigning the hats, but by the end of 1965 no significant changes had been made.

The rising value of shipments of processed fish and refined sugar has introduced dynamic elements into the structure of exports. After the Cuban missile crisis sugar shipments increased more than sevenfold in value, from $900,000 in 1960 to $6.7 million in 1964, and fish products increased from $3.6 million to $6.3 million during the same period (see ch. 20, Industry). Pyrethrum flowers, insecticides based on pyrethrum and castor beans have also exhibited a rising trend as exports. Increased domestic use of insecticides, however, may limit the expansion of pyrethrum as an export earner (see ch. 19, Agriculture).

Imports

Imports, of both consumer and producer goods, have been predominantly oriented toward machinery and transport equipment, various manufactured articles and chemical products. These groups, together valued at $87.4 million, represented about 80 percent of total import value in 1963, the latest year for which complete revised figures were available in late 1965. Food products, which rank fourth, were valued at $7.8 million in the same year (see table 16).

Machinery and transport equipment—since World War II the most important import group—almost tripled in value between 1950 and 1963, rising from $12.8 million to $34.4 million. Despite increasing industrialization and an expanding road network, the relative share of total imports remained essentially stable.

Table 16. Imports of Ecuador, by Economic Group, 1960–63
(in millions of U.S. dollars)

	1960	1961	1962	1963
Food products	7.0	6.9	7.1	7.8
Beverages and tobacco	2.5	2.4	2.6	3.1
Inedible raw materials (excluding combustibles)	2.4	2.7	2.0	2.7
Combustibles and lubricants	2.8	4.2	7.4	5.3
Oils and fats	3.5	3.5	4.7	3.9
Chemical products	13.1	12.3	13.2	13.6
Manufactured products	29.8	26.8	24.3	31.6
Machinery and transport equipment	34.5	36.0	29.7	34.4
Miscellaneous	6.6	6.0	5.2	8.1
Total	102.2	100.8	96.2	110.5

Source: Adapted from Banco Central del Ecuador, *Memoria del Gerente General: Correspondiente al Ejercicio de 1963*, p. 156.

Manufactured articles, covering a wide array of intermediate and consumer goods based on rubber, paper, wood, textiles, leather, glass and metals, ranked second and accounted for an annual average of 27 percent between 1960 and 1963. In absolute terms, value rose from around $15.1 million in 1950 to $31.6 million in 1963. Within the classification, imports of leather, leather products and clothing increased only slightly during the 14-year period. Imports of glass, ceramics and nonmetallic minerals decreased rather sharply after 1959, partly because of an increase in domestic supply and partly because of government protective tariff measures. Manufactures of glass and clay, based on raw materials found near Cuenca, have been placed on the industry priority list. The value of imported metals and metal products has increased more than tenfold since 1950 because of an expansion of light industry and increased household use.

Imports of chemicals and pharmaceuticals, which averaged 12.7 percent of the total value of imports between 1960 and 1963, followed the general import expansion. Import substitution of industrial chemicals also has high priority on the list of desired industrial expansions.

Imported foods, which averaged 7 percent of the total between 1960 and 1963, claimed a significantly increasing share of foreign exchange after 1957, when their participation was only 1.8 percent. Although food products accounted for only a small part of the total, their increasing importance was considered undesirable and disturbing in a fundamentally agricultural country, where increased production of grains and dairy products is a basic goal of the Ten-Year Development Plan. Since year-to-year fluctuations in the quantity of food imported depend to a certain extent on weather conditions, natural disasters could create a need for food imports even after domestic production is increased.

Direction of Trade

Just before World War II trade was almost evenly divided between the Western Hemisphere and the rest of the world; the Western Hemisphere provided a market for 57 percent of exports and supplied about 42 percent of imports. As a result of the industrial expansion and rising income level after the war, mainly in the United States the pattern of trade distribution became heavily channeled toward the Western Hemisphere, which in the peak year of 1951 accounted for $80.4 million, or 75 percent of total trade, valued at $107.1 million, and for 80 percent of export value. After 1951 this dominance in Ecuador's trade was reduced by the economic resurgence of postwar Europe and the opening of markets in other areas of the world. In 1964 the Western Hemisphere provided 58 percent of the total import value of $147.9 million and a market for 60 percent of the exports, valued at $147.8 million.

Between 1951 and 1964 trade with Western Europe and Great Britain increased in both absolute and relative value. As industry was rebuilt in Europe in the 1950's, imports supplied to Ecuador increased from 20 percent of the total in 1951 to 33 percent in 1964; because of rising personal income, Europe absorbed a slightly larger share of Ecuadorian agricultural exports, increasing from 28 percent in 1951 to 30 percent in 1964. Trade with the rest of the world is not large, but it constitutes a healthy diversity of markets and sources of supplies (see table 17).

The United States

In 1964 the United States purchased 51 percent of the exports of Ecuador and supplied 46 percent of the goods imported. Be-

[1]Columns may not add to totals given because of rounding.
[2]Preliminary figures.
[3]Argentina, Brazil, Chile, Colombia, Ecuador, Mexico, Paraguay, Peru and Uruguay.
[4]Belgium, France, Italy, Luxembourg, The Netherlands and West Germany.
[5]Austria, Denmark, Norway, Portugal, Sweden, Switzerland and the United Kingdom.

Source: Adapted from Banco Central del Ecuador, *Memoria del Gerente General: Correspondiente al Ejercicio de 1964*, pp. 127, 130.

Table 17. Direction of Ecuador's Trade, in Percent, 1960–64[1]

	1960	1961	1962	1963	[2]1964
EXPORTS					
Latin America	9	10	6	6	9
Latin American Free Trade Association[3]	5	8	5	6	8
Rest of Latin America	4	2	1	.....	1
European Economic Community[4]	23	25	23	22	29
West Germany	10	13	12	11	16
Belgium	4	4	5	4	5
France	3	3	2	2	2
Italy	3	3	2	2	2
The Netherlands	3	3	3	3	4
European Free Trade Association[5]	2	3	3	2	1
United States	64	60	65	56	51
Japan	1	1	2	11	7
Other countries	1	1	1	1	3
Total	100	100	100	100	100
IMPORTS					
Latin America	4	4	4	12	12
Latin American Free Trade Association[3]	3	4	4	4	4
Rest of Latin America	1	.....	.....	8	8
European Economic Community[4]	25	25	24	21	24
West Germany	14	13	12	11	12
Belgium	4	4	4	4	6
France	2	3	2	2	1
Italy	2	2	3	2	2
The Netherlands	3	3	3	2	3
European Free Trade Association[5]	13	14	13	13	9
United States	48	45	46	39	46
Japan	3	4	4	5	4
Other countries	7	8	9	9	5
Total	100	100	100	100	100

See footnotes on page 462.

tween 1960 and 1964 the relative importance of the United States as a market and a source of supply declined, although not in the same proportion. In spite of the recent downward trend the United States has been the most important single trading partner since before World War II. After the war trade with the United States soared. As a market for Ecuador's exports, the peak year was 1962, when United States purchases accounted for 65 percent of the total export value. Its importance as a supplier of imports has diminished greatly since 1952, however, from 65 percent of the total import value to 46 percent in 1964.

The United States is the principal market for bananas, cacao and coffee. In 1963, 50 percent of the banana stems shipped, 45 percent of the cacao tonnage and 60 percent of the coffee tonnage, as well as sugar valued at $6 million, were destined for the United States. In addition, the United States market absorbs about 95 percent of all canned tunafish exported. Among other products entering the market are frozen fish, shrimp and a small, but important amount of straw hats and handcrafted articles.

The United States provides a diverse array of products in all categories: food for immediate consumption, raw materials for industry, manufactured articles both for personal consumption and for industry, transportation equipment and heavy machinery.

Among food products the United States provides a significant share of all cereal needs; almost all of the dehydrated milk; and the major part of prepared food products. In the category of machinery and transportation equipment the United States is the foremost source of passenger cars, buses, tractors and locomotives and provides a considerable share of heavy machinery for agriculture, woodworking, papermaking, printing and textiles. Chemicals, including both industrial chemicals and those for consumers' use, pharmaceuticals and medicines are important among imports from the United States.

Western Europe and Great Britain

Although trade with Western Europe has not recovered the relatively high position held before World War II, Western Europe and Great Britain comprise the second most important trading area and are of special importance as a source of imports. Western Europe and Great Britain furnished a market for 24 percent of Ecuadorian exports and supplied 34 percent of its imports in 1963. Trade with West Germany, the second most valuable single trading partner, in 1963 accounted for 11 percent of both exports and imports.

West Germany is the third most important market for bananas, after the United States and Japan, and the third most important for cacao, followed by the Netherlands. Spain, France, the

Netherlands and Italy import sizable amounts of coffee; the Netherlands and Belgium together account for about 80 percent of the exchange earnings of castor beans. Great Britain recently has imported sugar.

Western European countries and Great Britain supply products for both consumers and industry. West Germany is the major European supplier of passenger cars, motors, textile machinery and articles manufactured of metal, such as handtools, typewriters, other office machines and bicycles. Great Britain, Italy, the Netherlands and Sweden also supply office equipment. Chemical compounds and pharmaceuticals are supplied by West Germany, Belgium, Italy and the Netherlands. Great Britain also provides passenger cars; tractors; heavy machinery, including agricultural, earthmoving and textile machinery; and a wide variety of manufactured articles.

Belgium is the major supplier of iron and steel plate and tubes. Spain supplies handtools; the Netherlands and Denmark, dairy products; and West Germany and Austria, grains. The balance of trade with Western Europe and Great Britain is generally unfavorable.

Latin America

Trade with the countries of Latin America has generally exhibited a favorable balance since the late 1930's. Although exports to the area have increased in absolute terms, the share of total exports has declined from 19 percent in 1951 to 9 percent in 1964 as world markets for the agricultural products of Ecuador have expanded. Imports, which had been relatively small since 1951, increased sharply from 4 percent of the total value in 1962 to 12 percent in both 1963 and 1964. This increase is partly attributed to a rising volume of petroleum imported from Venezuela.

As trading partners, Colombia, Peru and Chile are the most important. Products traded are diverse and vary in importance from year to year. Colombia provides an important market for cacao; Venezuela supplies crude petroleum; and British Guiana, where sugar is a major industry, is an important source of heavy duty paper and paper cartons manufactured from bagasse.

Other Countries

Export trade with Japan has increased since 1960 from 1 percent of the total value to 7 percent in 1964; imports increased by 1 percent. A very small amount of trade is carried on with Asia, Africa, the countries of Oceania and Soviet Europe.

Illegal Trade

Contraband border traffic with Colombia and Peru, which is considerable, has domestic repercussions through the loss of revenue by the central government through evasion of export taxes and import duties. Although the full extent of illegal trade cannot be measured accurately, a study made by the National Planning and Economic Coordination Board estimated that contraband valued at some S/81 million (in 1965, approximately S/18.5 equaled US$1—see Glossary) entered Ecuador from Colombia in 1962, and illegal exportations to Colombia were valued at about S/18.2 million in the same year.

The main articles illegally transported to Colombia are agricultural products, which bear varying but generally sizable export taxes; basic products declared not exportable because of scarcity; and products on which there is a domestic price ceiling.

Cacao shipments to Colombia, which is a significant market, are underreported. It is thought that as much as 15 percent of actual shipments enter Colombia without having export taxes paid. Sugar illegally enters the Colombian market, where higher prices are paid, and at times when barley was not exportable because of domestic scarcity, it has been reported that considerable amounts were siphoned into the more profitable Colombian market to supply the brewing industry across the border.

Illicit imports from Colombia are largely made up of manufactured products on which import duties have been assessed for the protection or direction of domestic industry. Among the many articles which illegally enter commercial channels are cigarettes, matches, textiles, light bulbs and instant coffee.

The devaluation of the Colombian peso, which has increased the buying power of the sucre in the Colombian market, has encouraged contraband trade from Colombia to Ecuador.

Less is known about contraband trade with Peru, but it is believed to be sizable. It is widely reported that, because of domestic price ceilings on meat, cattle are driven down the mountains to Peru, where they bring a higher price. Cigarettes, matches and blankets are among the articles illegally entering the Ecuadorian market from Peru.

Measures have been undertaken to limit contraband trade. Adjustments have been made in tariff schedules, and others are under consideration. Surveillance of bus passengers at identification points for possible contraband has increased in efficiency and intensity. Furthermore, there has been a general increase in vigilance for possible illegal trade in port cities. Although it is conceded that increasing alertness and the tightening of controls have brought improvement, the lack of sufficient well-trained supervisory personnel handicaps the efforts to stamp out illicit operations.

Trade Agreements

In 1965 there was no treaty explicitly governing trading relations between Ecuador and the United States. A trade agreement signed in 1938 was terminated in 1956 by the United States. There is, however, an agreement governing economic and technical cooperation signed by the two countries in 1951 and amended in April 1962 in furtherance of the aims of the Alliance for Progress (see ch. 18, The Economic System).

In 1962 bilateral agreements were in force with West Germany, Belgium, France, Italy, Norway and El Salvador. Most of the agreements are treaties of friendship, commerce and navigation and provide for the most-favored-nation treatment with specific exceptions. Duty concessions on specific items are incorporated in some treaties as are agreements on the method and time of settling accounts between the two nations. Settlement in dollars is provided for. Many of the treaties were signed between the late 1880's and 1900, but they have been revised from time to time. An agreement covering the treatment of commercial representatives and their samples, signed by Great Britain and Ecuador in 1929, remained in force in 1962.

Ecuador became a member of the Latin American Free Trade Association (LAFTA) by executive decree on October 20, 1961. The purpose of LAFTA is to form, through the mutual lowering of tariffs, a Latin American Common Market similar to the European Common Market. Other member countries in 1965 were Argentina, Brazil, Colombia, Chile, Mexico, Paraguay, Peru and Uruguay.

In accord with the principle of the Treaty of Montevideo forming LAFTA, which was signed February 18, 1960, Ecuador has been given permission for a period of 5 to 8 years to enact protectionist measures against certain imports that compete with newly established industries. The provisions of the General Agreement on Tariffs and Trade (GATT) do not apply to Ecuador.

BALANCE OF PAYMENTS

Since 1950 the balance of international payments has registered a deficit almost as frequently as it has registered a surplus. Although the commercial balance has been favorable since before World War II, the inflow of foreign exchange earnings from exports, foreign private investments and transfers has not covered with consistency and comfort the outflow of exchange for imported goods and services. In most years the margin in either direction has been narrow.

Among the factors responsible for the frequently adverse financial situation are the fluctuations in the prices of exports, which are primary agricultural products, the lack of highly profitable natural resources to attract massive inflows of foreign capital, rising expenditures connected with transportation of increasing imports, larger remittances of profits and interest on foreign private investment and amortization and interest payments on the external public debt.

In 1952, when exports experienced a decisive leap upward, profit and interest remittances increased to $13.7 million from $6.9 million in the previous year. Since that time remittances on direct private investment, which have largely been channeled to the banana firms, have increased but at a much slower pace. In 1959 they reached the high point of $23.3 million, but they dropped back to $17 million in 1964. Meanwhile, expenditures for freight, insurance and commissions attendant upon import shipments almost tripled, rising from $11.2 million in 1952 to $33.2 million in 1964.

Rising remittances and freight and insurance costs negated the positive trade balances in every year except 1950 and 1952, and the deficit on current account balance, which ranged from a low of $1.9 million in 1950 to $55.4 million in 1964, entailed a drainage of foreign currency. Estimates for 1965 fix the deficit on current account for that year at $75 million.

Small official loans from the United States and international agencies have augmented the modest inflow of private long-term capital destined for investment in private enterprise which provide an annually recurring source of foreign exchange to help cover the payments for imported goods and services. Official loan commitments have increased since the initiation of the Alliance for Progress, but relatively minimal sums have been used.

During 1957, 1958 and 1959, Ecuador enjoyed a modest surplus in international payments. Because of a significant increase in the value of exports, not matched by a corresponding increase in the value of imports, the balance on current account achieved the smallest deficit recorded since 1953, sinking to $49 million in 1959. At the same time net capital inflows were large enough to cover the deficit, and the supply of gold and foreign exchange resources increased.

This satisfactory situation was of short duration. Since 1960 both political and economic uncertainties have had repercussions on international trade and payments. A sharp fall in the unit price of exports, accompanied by an equally sharp increase in the unit price of imports in 1960, resulted in a narrowing of the favorable trade balance and a rise in the deficit on current account. The uncertainties of the period were responsible for an acceleration in the outflow of capital, and the combination of pressures produced a deficit in international payments in 1960 and 1961 and a currency devaluation in 1961. Export recovery induced by devaluation of the sucre, coupled with import restraint, made possible in 1962 the return to a surplus on balance of payments, which was improved in 1963, when returning confidence in the economic climate brought an inflow of short-term capital.

Accumulation of inventory in anticipation of changes in import tariffs in 1964 was responsible for an unfavorable trade balance for the first time. However, the inflow of capital funds, particularly $38 million in short-term funds, mostly suppliers' credit, made it possible to end the year with international payments in balance.

The imbalance between the supply of foreign exchange and the demand for payment for goods and services has been met by grants from the United States Government, drawings on the International Monetary Fund (IMF) and the depletion of gold and foreign exchange reserves. Since the prospect in 1965 was for only a mild rise in the value of exports in the near future, it seemed likely that the capacity to import required by the goals of the Ten-Year Development Plan would have to be supported by increasing commitments and disbursements of long-term low-interest loans from official foreign sources or by further depletion of gold and foreign exchange reserves which could not safely be maintained indefinitely.

In June 1965 the Consultative Group on External Financing was convened in Washington by the Inter-American Development Bank (IDB) in its capacity as the financial agent of Ecuador. The Group, which consisted of 19 nations and 11 agencies, expressed interest in assisting with the financing of 40 projects included in the 10-year plan.

FOREIGN INVESTMENT

Because of the scarcity of readily recoverable minerals, foreign capital has not been attracted to the development of resources to the same extent as in other Andean republics, where extractive activities have been more profitable. Shortly before 1900 investment capital from the United States undertook the operation of the gold mine at Portovelo on a commercial basis, and about 1917, British capital was instrumental in opening up the petroleum fields of the Santa Elena Peninsula. Because of dwindling gold reserves the United States-owned South American Development Company withdrew in the early 1950's, and operation of the mine was taken over by domestic interests. Petroleum extraction and refining continue to be carried on by Anglo-Ecuadorian Oilfields, Ltd., which now combines British and United States funds. Agriculture also attracted a modest amount of foreign investment in the mid-1930's, when the United Fruit Company established a banana-growing plantation at Tenguel.

Table 18. Foreign Investment in Ecuador, by Economic Sector, 1959–63
(in millions of U.S. dollars)

	1959	1960	1961	1962	1963
Commerce	9.1	9.8	10.0	10.5	16.8
Industry	15.2	18.8	16.7	15.8	25.7
Agriculture	5.3	5.8	5.3	4.3	1.2
Finance and insurance	1.4	2.2	2.1	8.3	10.5
Petroleum and derivatives	19.7	21.7	27.1	29.1	21.3
Construction	3.8	4.6	6.9	6.4	2.1
Public service	8.1	7.7	10.7	7.8	8.2
Total	62.6	70.6	78.8	82.2	85.8

Source: Adapted from Central Bank of Ecuador, Department of Economic Investigations, official foreign trade statistics.

Between 1959 and 1963 foreign capital increased by slightly more than one-third, from $62.6 million to $85.8 million. Every economic sector except construction and agriculture benefited, although in widely varying amounts (see table 18). The significant drop of $3 million in agricultural capital between 1962 and 1963 was largely the result of the withdrawal of the United Fruit Company from banana production and the sale of the firm's agricultural holdings to domestic investors, mainly former employees. Although the expansion of pyrethrum cultivation attracted new funds from abroad, the increase did not counterbalance disinvestment by the United Fruit Company.

Manufacturing has received the most significant flow of foreign capital in recent years. Spurred by tax and tariff incentives offered to both foreign and domestic investors to speed industrialization in accord with goals for economic development, foreign investment in manufacturing increased by almost 70 percent between 1959 and 1963, and preliminary information indicated that the flow was continuing, although perhaps at a less rapid pace. Chemicals and pharmaceuticals, rubber products and paper and paper products, which are represented by new fertilizer and pharmaceutical facilities, a new paperbox plant and a tire factory, have attracted the major part of new foreign capital since 1958.

Investment in commercial establishments, such as export-import agencies, distributorships and maintenance centers, has increased, and foreign investment for the support of the Housing

Bank and other financial institutions has flowed into Ecuador since 1961. New investment which has been made in petroleum facilities has largely been offset by the abandonment of wells and explorations during the same period. Expansion of the public service facilities of the Empresa Eléctrica del Ecuador, which is owned by the American and Foreign Power Company and which supplies power in the Guayaquil area, has been at a standstill because of pending rate decisions. Foreign capital is represented by direct branches, wholly owned subsidiaries, distributing agencies and joint ventures of domestic and foreign capital which are growing in importance.

Foreign investment is encouraged by amendment of the limitation on the amount of foreign exchange which may be purchased at the official rate and by liberalization of the restrictions on remittance of profits and repatriation of capital. Foreign investors may now remit interest and dividends up to 7 percent annually on registered capital in addition to 15 percent for capital amortization. The previous limit of 15 percent had included all remittances.

Detailed information concerning investment by country of origin has not been made public since 1958, at which time participation by the United States accounted for 65 percent of the total and Great Britain's share was 30 percent (see table 19). Investment by Japan has become more important since then, and capital flows from West Germany, Colombia and Chile have increased.

Late in 1965 the Atlantic Development Group for Latin America (ADELA), organized in 1964 by 54 private companies in the United States, Canada, Europe and Japan, announced that it proposed to invest some $2 million equity capital in five ventures in Ecuador: a development finance company, a slaughterhouse, a refrigerator plant, a plant for rolling steel bars and the expansion of an existing fertilizer plant.

FOREIGN ECONOMIC AID

Since World War II foreign aid programs for cooperation in economic and social development have been undertaken by international organizations and by the United States. Between 1961 and 1964 loans totaling $118.4 million were approved, and $30.7 million were disbursed. Loans were made covering programs in agriculture, manufacturing, transportation, power, housing, education, water supply and sewerage. Voluntary agencies also participated in both countrywide and community projects.

International Organizations

International organizations have provided economic aid through grants and loans, research, surveys and technical assistance of

Table 19. Foreign Investment in Ecuador, by Country of Origin, 1958

Country of origin	Amount (in millions of U.S. dollars)
United States	42.3
Great Britain	19.5
Venezuela	1.1
Switzerland	1.0
Spain	0.6
Panama	0.4
Colombia	0.3
West Germany	0.3
Chile	0.3
Sweden	0.2
Netherlands	0.2
Total	66.2

Source: Adapted from U.S. Department of Commerce, Bureau of Foreign Commerce, *Basic Data on the Economy of Ecuador* (Pt. 1, No. 60-50), 1960, p. 11.

broad scope. Much of the assistance provided by the United Nations, which is carried on as Special Fund projects through the FAO and the World Meteorological Organization (WMO), is directed toward increased knowledge and more productive use of natural resources.

Among the projects which have been undertaken are the establishment of the National Fishery Institute, for the purpose of studying both the immediate and the long-range prospects of the fishing industry; the expansion of meteorological services; the study of water and forest resources; the improvement of agricultural and veterinary educational facilities; and assistance for recolonization. The length of time involved in such programs varies from 2 to 5 years, and the projected total cost is $10.7 million, of which around $3 million will be contributed by the government.

Other programs aimed at the improvement of health, eradication of disease, training of technical personnel and development of better rural living are carried on by the Pan American Health Organization (PAHO), which is the regional arm of the World Health Organization (WHO). Projects are carried on by PAHO alone and also in cooperation with other United Nations agencies. Administration of the most comprehensive program covering social, educational, economic and health improvement of rural life—carried on by the Andean Mission with resources and personnel supplied by the FAO, the International Labor Organization (ILO), the United Nations Educational, Scientific and Cultural Organization (UNESCO) and United Nations Children's Fund (UNICEF) —was expanded and integrated into the structure of the Ecuadorian Government in 1964.

The International Bank for Reconstruction and Development (IBRD) had made total loan commitments of $45 million by the end of 1963 and, in 1964, committed an additional $9 million. Loans from the IBRD have been made for the development of highways, ports and electric power and for technical assistance. The first loan, which was made in 1954, enabled Guayas Province to construct 370 miles of all-weather road. Subsequent highway loans have been instrumental in liking the Coast and the Sierra, and a loan made in late 1964 was for the purpose of assisting in the completion of the national highway system. Funds for the completion of the national highway system have also been pledged by IDB, the International Development Association (IDA) and the Agency for International Development (AID). Of the $21 million pledged in 1964 for highway development, only $500,000 had been disbursed as of mid-1965. In addition to loans for development of facilities and resources, the IBRD has made available an adviser on the revision of fiscal and monetary laws and administration and has financed the foreign exchange costs of a comprehensive study of transportation (see ch. 22, Domestic Trade).

The IDB made loan commitments of $16.8 million between 1961 and 1964. These loans, from the ordinary capital of the IDB and from the Fund for Special Operations, were made for the promotion of wool production and African palm cultivation, for agricultural and industrial development, for technical assistance and for road construction. Although funds were available, only $3.8 million had been disbursed in early 1965, because of the length of time involved in project preparation.

In addition to loans from its own funds the IDB, which serves as financial agent of the Government of Ecuador for purposes of the Ten-Year Development Plan, administers the Social Progress Trust Fund which was established by the United States as part of the Alliance for Progress. From this fund assistance has been made available for housing programs, water supply and sewerage systems, farm settlement and improved educational facilities for the University of Guayaquil and the Central University of Quito. Of the total of $24.8 million available, $4 million had been disbursed by the end of 1964.

In addition to development loans provided by international organizations, at the invitation of the government research and technical assistance concerning taxation and government administration and economic development have been provided by the Tripartite Mission, composed of representatives of the Organization of American States (OAS), the Economic Commission for Latin America (ECLA) and the IDB.

The United States

From 1950 to 1960 a small amount of loans and grants from the United States was made available for assistance. With the initiation of the Alliance for Progress, programs under the administration of AID have accelerated and have been undertaken in furtherance of the aims of the Alliance and of the goals of the Ten-Year-Development Plan. Between 1961 and 1964 loans and grants of $50 million were approved, and $21.9 million were disbursed.

Projects approved have covered assistance in housing; industrial credit, administered by the Securities Commission-National Financial Corporation; and aerial photogrammetric mapping. In addition, funds have been made available to the Ecuadorian Institute of Electrification (Instituto Ecuatoriano de Electrifación— INECEL) for study of the feasibility of a national power grid, and technical assistance has been provided for improved tax collection. The largest loans between 1961 and 1964 consisted of the $13.3 million participation in the highway loan consortium, a budgetary support loan of $8 million approved in 1961 and a budgetary support loan of $7 million approved in 1962.

The Export-Import Bank of Washington has also provided long-term loans since immediately after World War II. Since 1961 commitments of $9.8 million have been made in support of INECEL, agriculture, airport construction and the construction of the Valdes sugarmill.

Loans of local currency, made under the appropriate title of Public Law 480, have been approved for telephone communications systems and paperbox manufacturing. Under Title III of Public Law 480 commodities are used in school lunch programs benefiting 500,000 children.

In addition to assistance through grants and loans, AID is participating in "Town Plan" projects, by which local and international resources are coordinated for community development on a self-help basis. Town Plans have been organized for Esmeraldas, Guaranda and Ambato and are being developed for Loja and Cayambe.

The Peace Corps and many private organizations, large and small, are also active. The National Institute For Agricultural and Livestock Research (Instituto Nacional de Investigación Agropecuaria—INIAP), which has been outstanding in its field, has received both financial and technical assistance from the Rockefeller Foundation.

The organization of project CARE is reported to be particularly efficient. Through CARE food, tools and small machinery are distributed. The costs of administering the program, except those of distribution, are paid for by the government. Ecuador is also a participant in the programs of the Pan American Development Foundation, in which United States citizens and communities join with communities in Latin America to provide materials which can be used for development projects. High school students in Grand Island, Nebraska, sent $150 to the rural school at El Valle in Azuay; parents of the children matched the gift and bought kitchen equipment for the preparation of hot lunches. Among other similar instances, Guaranda, capital of Bolívar Province, received 11 boxes of tools through the Pan American Development Foundation.

Through the People to People Program, which was developed to improve intercultural communication, Quito is the sister city of Louisville, Kentucky; Guaranda, of Johnson City, Tennessee; and Ambato, of Winchester, Virginia.

THE ROLE OF GOVERNMENT

The government has played a minor role in the direct conduct of foreign trade, a role limited essentially to the export of petroleum received as a royalty from concessionaries in the past. Because of the increased domestic demand for petroleum products, this is no longer practiced. Government participation in the value of imports is increasing but only to the extent necessary to fulfill the goal of public investment determined in the Ten-Year Development Plan.

The traditional import policy, whereby tariffs were fixed with the express purpose of providing governmental revenue, has been largely superseded by the image of import policy as a tool for implementation for the goals of national development and the achievement of higher levels of national well-being. The Ecuadorian Customs Tariff of 1962, which after several revisions is still directed toward revenue collection, has as a basic purpose the encouragement of industry and agriculture and the preservation of scarce foreign exchange for essential products. Stimulation of industry is also supported by the provisions of the Industrial Development Law which was published in 1962 and replaced in 1964 by a more effective law having the same goals. For the encouragement of industry low rates are assessed on raw materials used by domestic producers; capital goods are exonerated from most import duties; and tariff duties protect domestic industry. Import policy also encourages agriculture by concessions made for agricultural machinery and equipment. Since importation of luxury goods is restricted or made prohibitive, the loss of foreign exchange through this channel is minimized.

Imports are also subject to controls other than tariff. An import license, obtained by the importer from the Department of Exchange of the Central Bank of Ecuador, must be accompanied by the deposit with the Central Bank of a specified amount of the value of the goods being imported. The license gives the importer the right to receive foreign exchange at the official selling rate; and the prior deposits are returned at the time the Central Bank remits exchange for the import payment. The importer also is required to pay a consular fee at the time the license is obtained, and the documents which are sent to the shipper must be presented at the consulate at point of shipment.

Certain other controls are imposed for the maintenance of quality and sanitary standards. Sanitary or inspection certificates issued in the country of export are required for shipment of yeast, lard, wheat flour, preserved foodstuffs, live plants, seeds, alcoholic beverages and certain articles of clothing. Also commodities used for planting such as seed potatoes, seed rice and fruit require authorization from the Stock Breeding and Veterinary Authority. Each animal shipped must be accompanied by a health certificate.

Control is maintained over the importation of explosives, weapons and small munitions for sporting purposes and of aircraft and aircraft parts. Military weapons may be imported only by the government.

Export licenses, issued by the Exchange Department of the Central Bank, are required for all articles except such minor items as tourist purchases. All exchange earnings from exports must be surrendered to the Central Bank at the official buying rate.

There are two rates of exchange, official and free. The Central Bank, which is the administering agency for foreign exchange, maintains an official buying and an official selling rate. Almost all transactions are carried on through the official market, except dividend remittances or registered capital transactions and other remittances such as student expenses, which are made at the free market rate.

SECTION IV. NATIONAL SECURITY

CHAPTER 25

PUBLIC ORDER

Problems of crime and public disorder are strongly conditioned by economic underdevelopment and by the ethnically fragmented, highly stratified social structure. The highest rates of serious crime occur in the urban slums, especially in those of Guayaquil and Quito, where there are large concentrations of rootless and unemployed people. To some degree, also, the same pattern is found in the growing towns of the coastal lowlands, which have experienced a swell of migration from the rural Sierra with the opening of new access roads.

The Indians, constituting a large segment of the population, do not figure prominently in official police statistics. Separated from the mainstream of national life by cultural differences and social traditions, they seek, where possible, to avoid contact with the police and other agencies of the central government. Hence, offenses and disputes occurring within Indian communities are most often settled internally and never brought to official attention. Moreover, physical and social segregation limits the frequency of offenses committed by Indians beyond the bounds of of their communities.

Civil disorder, politically motivated, is a longstanding problem, although perhaps of less magnitude than in many other Latin American countries. Strikes tinged with violence and street riots have often contributed to the overthrow of governments. In mid-1965 a continuing pattern of violence in Guayaquil, directed at the military government, kept the country at a high pitch of tension.

For the most part, active participation in public violence is limited to a few segments of the population—most notably the university students and the urban poor. In Quito and Guayaquil clashes between students and the police have been frequent. Strikes and demonstrations by urban workers have on occasion degenerated into overt violence.

The Indians have remained largely impervious to the influences of political agitators and have contributed relatively little to the pattern of civil upheaval. In a few isolated instances *huasipungueros* (see glossary) have risen against their landlords, usually as a result of serious and accumulated abuse or in an attempt to take over *hacienda* lands. To all appearances, however, these incidents have been uncoordinated and local in scope (see ch. 26, Subversion).

A more widespread problem of civil violence on the part of the Indians arose during the 1962 census. Ever suspicious of the white-dominated national governments, Indian peasants in widely scattered locations throughout the Sierra attacked census takers and murdered them.

Law enforcement is entrusted chiefly to the National Civil Police (Policía Civil Nacional—PCN), which has both uniformed elements and plainclothes investigative forces, controlled by the central government. There is also a small customs police, and in the Province of Guayas, traffic control is entrusted to a special local force controlled by the provincial council. The police forces are both inadequately manned and insufficiently trained. Large areas of the country are almost wholly without police protection for lack of manpower, and although training has improved substantially in recent years, much remains to be done before the police forces can be judged fully adequate in their methods as measured against modern standards. Corruption and abuse of power have also been reported.

The court system, regarded by most observers as fair and competent, is also seriously understaffed. Consequently, clearance of dockets is notoriously slow. The prison system, consisting of a central penitentiary in Quito, local jails and a penal colony on the Galápagos Islands, lacks the facilities to play a constructive role in the rehabilitation of convicts. Prisons and jails are extremely overcrowded and exercise little more than a custodial function. Conditions make it impossible to segregate young first offenders from hardened criminals.

CRIME AND PUBLIC DISORDER

Crime Rates

A report issued by the Supreme Court for 1958 listed the number of penal cases initiated in each province during that year (see table 20). More recent countrywide statistics on crime rates are not available. Figures gathered in Guayaquil, though not wholly representative for the entire nation, are nonetheless informative.

Table 20. Criminal Cases Initiated in Ecuadorian Courts, by Province, 1958

Province*	Number of cases initiated	Rate per 1,000 persons
Cañar	476	4.02
El Oro	461	3.94
Tungurahua	840	3.73
Esmeraldas	355	3.68
Guayas	2,368	3.18
Azuay	963	3.14
Loja	898	3.14
Imbabura	475	3.03
Pichincha	1,341	2.86
Los Ríos	429	2.15
Manabí	1,131	2.06
Bolívar	270	1.96
Chimborazo	476	1.77
Carchi	159	1.69
Cotopaxi	287	1.45
Total	10,929	2.70

*The provinces of the Oriente do not constitute separate court jurisdiction; consequently, their case statistics are included in those of the Sierra jurisdiction to which they are attached.

Source: Adapted from Ecuador, *Informe Corte Supreme de Justicias de 1959.*

In Guayas Province in 1963, 7 individual provincial courts were devoted exclusively to the trial of criminal cases. Before these courts there were 16,249 cases (about 16 per 1,000 population) pending at the start of the year. During the year, 3,499 trials were initiated, and 2,941 judgments (18 percent of the cases pending in January) were rendered. The nature of the serious crimes can be gathered from statistics of the Guayaquil prison. Of the 536 persons convicted in 1963, 272 were accused of robbery; 81, of homicide; 31, of property damage; 29, of larceny; 33, of assault; 16, of cattle rustling; 4, of narcotics violations; 30, of sexual óffenses; 21, of kidnaping; and the remainder, 19, of unspecified offenses. Of the total convicted, 74 were less than 21 years old, and only 30 were women.

The newspapers abound in reports of murders and physical violence of all sorts. Particularly lurid was an account appearing in January 1964 of the arrest and confession of an outlaw in Manabí Province who had been hired over a period of time to kill 18 persons, apparently by political opponents of the victims. A long-prevalent criminal practice has been the kidnaping of children for forced labor on remote *haciendas.*

In the Superior Court of Guayaquil there were 1,657 criminal cases pending for review at the start of 1963; 1,577 trials were initiated during the year; and 1,167 cases were adjudicated. Thus, at the end of the year 2,067 cases were pending.

Public Disorder

Contrasting with the high rate of common crime, the incidence of large-scale public disorder has been low in recent years. During the 1960–61 term of José María Velasco Ibarra the country was kept in constant turmoil, and unrest continued under Julio Carlos Arosemena Monroy. Since the 1963 coup, when each province was placed under military direction, there has been little unrest outside of the metropolitan areas. The Minister of Government reported in December 1964 that peace and quiet reigned in the provinces. There have, however, been several riots in Guayaquil in protest against the military junta.

Examples of concentrated violence in recent years have been rare outside of the universities. The most serious rural incident occurred on February 5, 1961, when 2,000 Indians, asking for the redress of grievances, rioted on the Columbe *hacienda* in Chimborazo Province and were put down by the police. In March 1962, 200 unemployed banana workers seized a banana plantation near Tenguel belonging to a subsidiary of the United Fruit Company in protest against the failure of the government to expropriate and distribute the land. They were driven off by the police with few injuries and little property damage, but the demonstration moved the government to purchase the 248,000 acres for distribution. In January 1963 a group of persons from Cañar Province invaded the eastern slopes of Guayas Province and destroyed several small hamlets before being turned back by local police. This was only a renewal of a longstanding controversy over the delineation of the boundary between the two provinces.

On August 3, 1964, a police detachment was sent from Quito to Cayambe, where 160 Indians, said to be led by Communist agitators, had seized a large estate. The violent demonstrations of late 1964 in Guayaquil, which lasted for 4 days, involved a large number of people protesting against a law of the junta centralizing in Quito the control of tax collection. In May 1965, after the Chamber of Commerce of Guayaquil declared a city-wide strike of commercial establishments against the junta's imposition of higher customs duties of luxury-type imports, martial law was declared to preserve order.

More typical in recent years have been organized demonstrations by university students. Such incidents of violence were fostered by the Federation of University Students of Ecuador (Federación de Estudiantes Universitarios del Ecuador—FEUE), a leftist-oriented organization. In Guayaquil, in June 1959, 23 persons were killed and 150 wounded in student riots protesting the strong action earlier taken by government forces against rioters in Portoviejo in Manabí Province. The students, using pistols and Molotov cocktails, successfully battled the police for 5 hours until the army moved in. The next day, they fought, burned and looted until martial law was declared in the entire country. On the other hand, later in the year, when Vice President Nixon spoke to the university students, he was listened to, though not with enthusiasm. This was in marked contrast to the treatment he had earlier received in Lima and later received in Caracas.

Most students were ardent supporters of Velasco Ibarra when he took office in September 1960, but just a year later, alienated by his unpredictable policies, they were in the forefront in demonstrations demanding his ouster. When President Velasco Ibarra ordered the police and armed forces to suppress the demonstrators and several of them were killed, the students demanded his immediate removal.

Although it supported Arosemena in his initially strong pro-Castro orientation, the FEUE, on March 2, 1962, led a march on the Presidential Palace, demanding that less money be spent for military installations and more for the universities. During this manifestation some soldiers were manhandled by the mob. When Arosemena was forced to break relations with Cuba, students demonstrated violently in many parts of the country and had to be dislodged from the University of Guayaquil by forceful police action.

When the leaders of the military government deposed Arosemena on July 11, 1963, they arrested a number of leftists, including some students, and forbade meetings without prior governmental approval. In January 1964, when students disregarded the warnings against planned demonstrations, the police quelled riots in Guayaquil and arrested the FEUE president, as well as the president of the student organization of the law school. Later, in Quito, when their demonstrations were opposed by the police using tear gas, the students counterattacked with pistols and Molotov cocktails. As a result, over 30 students were arrested, and the Central University at Quito was closed for 2 months.

On March 30, 1964, the government issued the New Law of Higher Education which reduced the autonomy of the universities and ordered the FEUE disbanded. Acts of protest against this measure continued into mid-1965 with no sign of abatement. These included strikes and the planting of low-powered bombs. Arrests of students were also continual. In January 1965 the

Central University was again closed for a few days, and 20 students were expelled for participating in demonstrations, during one of which they manhandled the rector of the university.

THE POLICE FORCES

Law enforcement and the preservation of public order are primarily the responsibility of the PCN, which functions under the Ministry of Government. The Customs Police, a small and specialized force, is controlled by the Ministry of Finance. The only other law enforcement agency organized under national law is the Guayas Traffic Police, which is responsible to the Provincial Council of Guayas.

National Civil Police

The PCN is headed by a commander of police, who is directly responsible to the minister of government. It is composed of four operational divisions—one for urban police, one for rural police, one for traffic police and one for the detective force, commonly called Investigative Police.

Under the central headquarters there are several district commands, each of which includes a number of provincial units. In each provincial headquarters, there are divisions, corresponding to the four divisions at the national level, that oversee, administer and supply various police posts and detachments in that province.

The commander of the PCN is assisted by a technical staff and is advised by the Superior Council, made up of his deputy commander and the six senior police officers serving in the Quito area. In addition to its advisory role, the Superior Council functions as the selection board for the promotion of police officers. The police officers' school and the police training school are responsible to the commander.

The police force, being a civil institution, does not enjoy the special legal exemptions (*fueros*) accorded the armed forces, but there are special courts set up to handle offenses committed by onduty personnel. The judicial system includes a Supreme Court and several superior courts of justice of the PCN, each made up of two police officers, one officer from the armed forces and two judges from the Supreme Court or the local superior court (see ch. 27, The Armed Forces.)

Through the years there has been built up a complete system of police schools. The Police Officers Training School in Quito, often referred to as the Police Academy, offers a 3-year course leading to a commission as a police officer. The course combines academic subjects with an increasing emphasis, in recent years, on practical work in investigative and other technical police methods.

An officers' school gives both a basic and an advanced inservice training course. For enlisted policemen, there is the School for Perfection and Specialization, a basic training school for urban police in Quito and one for rural police in Babahoyo. In addition, there is a training school for new recruits. During February 1965 there were 621 policemen taking training courses and 1,544 undergoing recruit training.

Since the advent in 1959 of the United States Public Safety Advisory Group, under the Agency for International Development (AID), training equipment and curricula have been greatly updated. By mid-1965 over 150 police officers had completed the training course at the Inter-American Police Academy at Washington, D.C., and the employment of many graduates of this program in the police school system has significantly improved the training. To aid in the training of isolated detachments, there is a mobile instructional team. As the training has progressed, the morale has steadily increased, and the public image of the police has improved.

The Urban Police

The urban police function in the larger towns and cities. In both Quito and Guayaquil the mobile, radio-equipped jeep patrol system is being successfully augmented as rapidly as equipment and trained personnel can be brought together. Their weapons and transportation facilities have been vastly improved.

Crime is particularly heavy in Guayaquil, and immunity from arrest has been indicated to be the chief cause. Patrolling there is still inadequate. Experts have estimated that a minimum of 3,000 urban police are needed in Guayaquil to do a reasonable job, whereas on January 1, 1965, only 700 were assigned there. In an attempt to alleviate the great dearth of police in the poorer suburbs the PCN recently called into active service the local police reserves. During 4 days of violent antigovernment riots in Guayaquil during the fall of 1964, the police, by using tear-gas bombs, were able to maintain control without firing on the crowds, even though 14 policemen and 4 civilians were injured.

The Rural Police

The rural police generally are recruited from the area in which they serve. They are scattered in small detachments throughout the inhabited parts of the country. The local police chief functions as the judge in minor cases. Their ranks have been strengthened by the training of selected men in the rural police school at Babahoyo. In many places the rural police appear to enjoy considerable public trust as defenders of justice and, for this reason, appear to be quite effective. For example in the Puyo-Tena area of the Oriente, the crime rate is very low, and the police relations with the community are described as close and good.

The Traffic Police

The traffic division functions on all the streets and highways except in Guayas Province, which has its own autonomous traffic police. The duty of the division is to enforce traffic rules, check on licenses and investigate accidents. The fact that the accident rate is very high seems to be the result of poor roads and rather aggressive driver attitudes rather than of the inadequacies of the traffic police.

The Investigative Police

The investigative police, officially designated the Office of Criminal Investigation (Oficina de Investigación Criminal—OIC), was a separate unit called the Division of Security, Investigation and Identification before a new organic police law, passed in 1964, placed it under the PCN. It is charged with the investigation of all major criminal cases, regardless of the agency of arrest. In this division, which also operates as a secret police, important posts have often been filled by political appointees.

Despite the attainment of greater professionalism under the junta, the OIC still lacks sufficient technical means for solving crimes, and it has been accused of brutality and of dropping serious cases when unable to solve them in a short time. The OIC, which is the primary intelligence-gathering arm of the police, has become increasingly aware of the Communist threat, has improved its collection capabilities and has established liaison and exchange of information with other intelligence agencies of the government. This cooperation had long been lacking, but during the visit of President de Gaulle in 1964 coordination between the army and the police proved to be very effective.

Effectiveness

There has been intense rivalry between the army and the police through the years, and at times the army has succeeded in making the policeman an object of public scorn. Several presidents have attempted to decrease the political power of the army by building up the police as a loyal counterweight, especially through the distribution of patronage. Consequently, almost every change of administration has caused wholesale changes in the police forces. Nevertheless, the police, as a force, have seldom engaged actively in politics, and, unlike the military, they are regarded as apolitical. Traditional animosity between the army and the police has dissipated to a considerable extent. However, police effectiveness continues to suffer severely because promotions are not based wholly on professional attainments. Moreover, an excessive number of ranking positions are in supply and administration and are bestowed on politically appointed civilians.

The morale of the police improved substantially in January 1965, when the pay and subsistence rates were increased—10 percent for senior officers, 15 percent for junior officers and 20 percent for all others. This increase raised the junior patrolman grade salary from S/800 a month to S/1,000 per month (in 1965, S/18.5 equaled US$1—see Glossary). The government also provided family allowances for the police equal to that of the armed forces. Some improvement is being made in housing for police families, but it continues to be inadequate in many places—particularly in Guayaquil. A definite increase in morale and efficiency has been brought about by the appreciable amounts of equipment, such as vehicles, radios and weapons, being received under the United States AID program. Effective training programs are increasing the confidence of the police and improving their image before the public, and greater professionalism is improving police cooperation with other law enforcement and intelligence agencies. If progress continues at the present rate, it has been estimated that by 1972 the police will be capable of maintaining law and order under normal conditions without aid from the military and other agencies.

Customs Police

The Customs Police was long considered to be the most corrupt of all the police organizations; very few smugglers were apprehended, and little contraband ever reached government warehouses. Under the military government it has improved considerably. By the new decree laws the Customs Police are allowed to carry weapons, to arrest suspects, to search premises and to seize contraband. Two Customs Police schools have started courses— one in Quito and one in Guayaquil. Although as recently as July 1964 the citizens of Ibarra denounced the corruption of the Customs Police there and requested that army troops be brought in to guarantee the rights of the people, records indicate that enforcement has improved greatly. For example, in Salinas, during March 1964 the customs collections were 17 times as much as during the same month in the preceding year.

The Guayas Traffic Police

The Traffic Police of Guayas is organized by national law as an autonomous force. It consists of a small traffic control force which legally has no authority in any other police matters. It is a selected force made up almost entirely of men who gained a reputation for discipline while performing their army service. In 1964 the commandant of the force reported that 70 percent of his men were from Guayaquil; 20 percent, from elsewhere on the Coast; and 10 percent, from the Sierra. All new recruits to the force are given a special instructional course. The force is trimly uniformed, is housed in a new barracks with all modern conveniences and receives better pay than the PCN. Judged from newspaper accounts, some ill feeling appears to exist between the national and the Guayas police. Incidents of violation of the authority of the Guayas police have been ascribed both to the PCN and to the Customs Police.

THE ADMINISTRATION OF JUSTICE

A competent observer has described the judicial system as able and fair. For the most part the judges have been well versed in law, nonpolitical and just in their decisions. This is remarkable because they do not enjoy long tenure, and even the Supreme Court justices are reappointed every 6 years. They receive an annual salary, plus a fee for each case initiated and a larger fee for each case completed during the year. The serious criticism of the courts, which often appears in the national press, centers on their administrative procedures and the lack of speed in handling cases.

The Court System

The court system, in order of precedence, comprises a Supreme Court, superior courts, provincial courts and cantonal courts. Criminal cases are not heard in the cantonal courts, although such courts can conduct preliminary hearings and make recommendations. The court of first instance in criminal cases, except those involving government officials, is the provincial criminal court, which functions independently from the ordinary provincial courts and which is directly responsible to the appropriate superior court (see ch. 13, Constitution and Government).

The Supreme Court is divided into three chambers, each presided over by five judges, and generally functions as three separate courts which can sit simultaneously. There is no specialization; criminal and civil cases are apportioned among the chambers on the basis of chance and workload. For treason and other serious offenses, such as malfeasance in high office, the court sits as a whole. The 15 judges and the prosecutors (*fiscales*) attached to the court are elected by the Congress in joint session for 6-year terms and are eligible for reelection. A candidate must be Ecuadorian by birth, at least 40 years old and have practiced as an attorney or been a provincial or superior court judge for at least 12 years.

The country is divided into nine judicial districts, in each of which a superior court sits permanently. Such courts are located in Quito, Guayaquil, Cuenca, Ambato, Ibarra, Loja, Riobamba, Portoviejo and Machala. Each court consists of from one to three chambers, depending on the population of the district, and each chamber is presided over by three judges. In Guayaquil, where there are three chambers, one is devoted exclusively to criminal cases. The judges and prosecutors are elected to 4-year terms by the Congress and may be reelected. Candidates must be Ecuadorians by birth, at least 35 years of age and have practiced as attorneys or judges for at least 8 years. Each superior court, in addition to its judicial duties, is responsible for the inspection of the penal system within its district.

Each province, except in the Oriente, has at least one provincial criminal court, which sits in the provincial capital, and as many other criminal courts as distances and populations require. Cases originating in the Oriente are heard in the nearest provincial criminal court in the Sierra. The provincial criminal judges, who are appointed by the appropriate superior court for a 3-year term, can try the less serious criminal cases which, according to the Penal Code, can be punished by prison sentences not to exceed 3 years. The provincial criminal courts are independent of the provincial civil courts.

For the more serious criminal cases in each locality where a provincial court sits, a special five-member tribunal is established called the *tribunal del crimen*. The tribunal is presided over by the judge of the provincial criminal court. The second member is the judge's alternate (*suplente*). The other three are taken from a local panel which the superior court names for each provincial court annually. Each panel consists of three principals and three substitutes; members must be lawyers, if available, but otherwise may be prominent citizens without legal training. Conviction or acquittal is determined by majority vote of the tribunal.

Although not viewed as part of the judicial system, political lieutenants (*tenientes políticos*)—who, as a general rule, have no judicial training—handle all minor cases, including many misdemeanors, in the rural parishes where they function simultaneously as judges and prosecutors. To most Sierra Indians, the political lieutenant has been "the government."

Criminal Procedures

After arresting a suspect, except for minor offenses which can be tried by the local police officer, the police must turn the suspect over to a competent judge, usually the judge of the local cantonal court, who conducts an investigation to determine if there are sufficient grounds for trial. According to law, this investigator must forward in writing his findings to the judge of the provincial court within 15 days.

If the recommendation is for trial, power over the accused passes to the judge of the Provincial Criminal Court. The accused is entitled to legal counsel, either one selected and paid by him or one furnished from a panel of lawyers formed annually to serve as public defenders. Usually the proceedings are based on transcriptions of statements made by each side through the *fiscal* or the defender rather than on oral testimony in the courtroom. Although under certain circumstances the accused can be authorized to confront witnesses, this is seldom done.

For serious crimes, which can be punished by sentences of more than 3 years in prison, the accused can demand, through his counsel, trial by a *tribunal del crimen*. In this case the trial proceeds as a court trial presented before the five-man tribunal. The prosecution presents its case, followed by the defense. Witnesses are subject to cross-examination. The accused cannot be forced to take the stand, but he is entitled to take the stand in his own defense should he so desire. To a large extent this testimony is based on material presented at the preliminary investigation, but new testimony, if pertinent, may be introduced by either side. After the final argument by the prosecution and by the defense, the judge may sum up the case before closing the court to permit the tribunal to discuss the case and to vote in secret on the verdict. Guilt or innocence is determined by majority vote.

A written record of all trials including the reasons for rulings and findings is submitted to the appropriate superior court for approval before the verdict and sentence become final. Appeals based on legal grounds may be made to the superior court.

Penalties

The Penal Code provides a maximum sentence of 16 years of confinement at hard labor in a penitentiary for serious crimes committed with particular viciousness. Capital punishment is forbidden by the Constitution. Under the Military Penal Code confinement for life can be given for high treason. Since there are not infrequent cases of civilians involved in riots being tried in military courts, they can also be tried by military courts for treason, and such a penalty can be imposed on civilians as well as on military persons. However, there is no record of anyone ever having received such a sentence.

Lesser penalties for ordinary crimes include confinement under maximum security conditions with hard labor for 4 to 10 years; confinement for 3 to 6 years, with forced labor in workgangs or in agricultural colonies; and prison sentences of from 8 days to 5 years. In addition to imprisonment, the courts can also impose deprivation of civil and political rights, probation, deprivation of the right to exercise a profession, and permanent restrictions from holding public office. Fines may accompany other sentences. For misdemeanors jail terms of not exceeding 6 days or fines up to 50 sucres may be imposed. All sentences carry the requirement to pay civil damages to the injured party. Exile is prohibited by the Constitution, but a person jailed for political reasons may demand exile instead of prison.

The Penal Code specifies the penalty range for specific crimes so that the court may determine the exact penalty according to the circumstances in the crime under consideration. Those convicted of murder and arson can be given confinement of up to 16 years; for robbery, the penalty is from 1 to 5 years in jail; for abortion, 3 to 6 years; for adultery, 6 months to 2 years; for assault, 15 days to 3 months; for perjury, 3 to 6 years; for issuing a check backed by no funds, 3 months to 2 years; and for attempting a coup d'etat, 4 to 8 years.

CHAPTER 26

SUBVERSION

In the pattern of politics in the past, legal governments were often overthrown by arms, but usually to redistribute power within a small civil-military elite. Actively supported, as a rule, by only a small sector of the population, such revolts and coups d'etat seldom embodied any challenge to the traditional social and political order; they fell far short of revolution, both in aims and in execution.

In recent decades, however, there have appeared genuine and potentially effective forces of subversion on the extreme Left, in the form of a Communist Party, illegal since 1963, broadly infiltrated in the arenas of politics and labor, and numerous pressure groups and ad hoc fronts. These groups have found ample grounds for subversive activity in the strong, if historically mute, popular discontent with social and economic conditions, and in the strident, but often frustrated, nationalist sentiment. The rise of Fidel Castro as an indigenous Latin American revolutionary, overthrowing the long-established social, economic and political status quo and challenging the feared and resented power of the United States has provided a strong ideological impetus to the Ecuadorian Left. Moreover, general material assistance from the Communist government of Cuba made possible an increased program of subversion until it was stemmed by the rupture of diplomatic ties with that country in 1962.

Although the rightist Ecuadorian Nationalist Revolutionary Action (Acción Revolucionaria Nacionalista Ecuatoriana—ARNE) has at times used violence as a political weapon, particularly during the presidential campaign of 1952, the aim of this organization is to force constitutional change by legal means. In general, there is no identifiable subversive threat from the Right.

The pressures of recent social change have added further to the potential for subversion and violent revolution. There is clear evidence that the poorer segments of the population, especially the urban working class, are growing more insistent and articulate in their demands for a more equitable share of the national wealth. In a lesser degree the same tendencies are apparent among the *mestizo* and mulatto wage laborers in commercial agriculture. The Indian peasants of the Sierra, traditionally the least privileged, yet most submissive segment of the population, have as yet shown little susceptibility to leftist agitation. Nevertheless, a few incidents of violence in recent years—the 1960 uprising on Columbe *hacienda* in Chimborazo, for example—suggest that this submissiveness may be diminishing (see ch. 14, Political Dynamics; ch. 17, Attitudes and Reactions; ch. 25, Public Order).

The orderly development of democratic government may depend on fundamental reform, supported by an accelerated economic development. The Communists and their allies on the extreme Left until recently were almost alone in calling for such reforms and, therefore, won the support of many students and intellectuals traditionally in the vanguard of reformist and nationalist movements.

Despite the positive action and efforts of the government to counter Communist activities, the threat of subversion remains among the middle and lower classes, as well as among the university students and professors, where there is sympathy for Castro's Cuba and strong anti-Americanism. Only if the government is to bring about real social reforms will dissatisfaction lessen among the many underprivileged.

If an effective leader would arise to shake the Indians from their traditional fatalism, he might provoke revolution, but such a possibility appeared remote in 1965. The government's curb on expression of criticism might eventually drive some of the non-Communist opposition onto a subversive course. The hard-core Communists, who have been able to consolidate and to build up socialist support during their many years of legality, might capitalize on such an eventuality. The danger of a Communist takeover did not, however, appear imminent in 1965.

BACKGROUND

The Communist Party of Ecuador (Partido Comunista del Ecuador—PCE), the central agency of leftist subversion, grew out of several small Marxist groups founded during the 1920's. In the mid-1920's there appeared a biweekly newspaper, *La Antorcha*, which was socialist and pro-Soviet Union. One of its founders, Luis Napoleón Dillon, became a member of the government after a group of radical young army officers engineered the overthrow of the previous government on July 9, 1925. A number of persons involved in the coup d'etat formed, on May 16, 1926, the Ecuadorian Socialist Party, which succeeded in electing a congressman from Guayaquil in 1928 and one from Quito in

1929. A rival socialist group, called the Friends of Lenin and headed by Ricardo Paredes, the editor of *La Antorcha*, was formed at about the same time. Paredes attended the Sixth Congress of the Communist International in Moscow in 1928 as a representative of both groups and was able to have the Ecuadorian Socialist Party admitted as a fraternal member of the Comintern. The groups combined to become the PCE in 1931.

In 1933 a new Ecuadorian Socialist Party was established by dissenters who were branded at the time as betrayers by the Communists. The two parties have since maintained friendly and often close relations in opposing the government. The smaller but better disciplined PCE has been able to manipulate for its own purposes many members of the Socialist Party, particularly in gaining control of the labor union movement.

The Confederation of Ecuadorian Workers (Confederación de Trabajadores Ecuatorianos—CTE) was founded in 1944, with the Communist leader Antonio Pedro Saad Niyam as its first secretary general, and soon thereafter joined the Communist-controlled World Federation of Trade Unions (WFTU). Although in 1946 the Socialists elected seven members to the CTE Executive Committee compared to four Communists, the CTE continued to follow the Communist line with strong anti-United States overtones. The Ecuadorian Indian Federation (Federación de Indios Ecuatorianos) was also organized in 1944, through the efforts of Paredes, under complete Communist control.

The Ecuadorian Democratic Alliance (Alianza Democrática Ecuatoriana—ADE), formed in 1944 to overthrow President Carlos Arroyo del Río, was heavily supported by both the Socialists and the Communists. After Arroyo del Río's overthrow, the government which lasted briefly until rule was assumed by exiled politician José María Velasco Ibarra included the Communist Gustavo Becerra. In that year the Communists won 15 out of 89 seats in the National Assembly, and a Communist was made the minister of education under Velasco Ibarra. Later, the leftists turned against Velasco Ibarra when he failed to give strong support to social legislation acceptable to them, choosing instead to support legislation urged by close, self-seeking friends. In March 1946, Velasco Ibarra outlawed the PCE and jailed many of its leaders.

During the 1948-52 term of the moderate Galo Plaza Lasso complete freedom of speech and of the press was allowed, and the Communist Party was again legalized. During this time the left-wing parties flourished, the Socialists electing 15 congressmen and the Communists, 3. In the 1952 election the representation in Congress was reduced to 8 Socialists and 1 Communist.

Although Velasco Ibarra received considerable leftist support in the elections of 1952, during his period in office (1952-56), which was marked by political chaos, he took strong steps against the university students and against organized labor, the centers of Communist strength. In December 1952 he exiled, allegedly for planning a coup against him, one of his chief supporters, Carlos Guevara Moreno, a former member of a pro-Communist group and the leader of the most powerful political party in Guayaquil, the Concentration of Popular Forces (Concentración de Fuerzas Populares—CFP).

Velasco Ibara's successor in 1956, the conservative Camilo Ponce Enríquez, was able to restore order by wise, if unspectacular, improvements, particularly in finance. Although he was continually criticized by the Left—as represented, for example, by the Communist Pedro Saad, who had been elected to the Senate—for his lack of rapid progress in social reform and was harassed by three major strikes on the Coast called by the pro-Communist labor unions, he was able to complete his 4-year term.

In September 1960, Velasco Ibarra returned to the presidency for the fourth time with the massive vote of the people, including that of many of the Communists. The Communist-dominated CTE at first backed him because of his pro-Castro foreign policy, but when he dismissed Manuel Araujo Hidalgo, his pro-Castro minister of government, it turned against him. Later, the CTE leaders were able to rally all labor unions, including even the Catholic labor unions, to a general strike on October 4, 1961, in protest against his methods. Although the strike was only partially effective, the strikers and supporting students were put down so severely by Velasco Ibarra, using government forces, that he lost all popular support, and a subsequent military coup installed Vice President Carlos Julio Arosemena Monroy in his place.

Arosemena was an admirer of Fidel Castro and a personal friend of Pedro Saad. While in Moscow, he had praised the Soviet system and, soon after taking office, incorporated into his government several adherents of the extreme Left. The Ecuadorian delegate to a labor congress in Moscow carried special greetings from the new president. The Cuban Embassy furnished funds to send a number of the members of the Communist-dominated youth organization, the Revolutionary Union of Ecuadorian Youth (Unión Revolucionaria de la Juventud Ecuatoriana—URJE), to Cuba for guerrilla training.

As late as March 26, 1962, Arosemena denied that any Communist threat existed to the country. On April 3, 1962, however, the armed forces finally forced him to break relations with Cuba. This break was strongly criticized in some intellectual and political circles, including the provincial council of Guayas, and led to violent demonstrations by the Communist-dominated front organization, the Revolutionary People's Movement (Movimiento Popular Revolucionario—MPR), which was composed of the Communist Party, the URJE, the left wing of the Socialist Party and the Federation of University Students of Ecuador (Federación de Estudiantes Universitarios del Ecuador—FEUE) (see ch. 14, Political Dynamics).

After the break with Cuba a number of pro-Castro advocates established a guerrilla group of about 250 persons, many of them teenagers, in the coastal foothills near Santo Domingo de los Colorados. The army arrested about 40 of the leaders, some of whom were Cuban trained, including Jorge Rivandeira, head of the URJE. Elsewhere in the country a number of terrorist attacks made chiefly against right-wing figures were imputed to the Communists. This continuing lawlessness and the President's frequent appearances in public after what seemed excessive drinking were reasons generally given for the seizure of power by the Junta Militar de Gobierno, composed of 4 (later 3) senior military officers (se ch. 14, Political Dynamics).

One of the first acts of that government after it ousted the President on July 11, 1963, was to outlaw the PCE and to take into custody about 200 party members, including Pedro Saad. The pro-Castro municipal council of Guayaquil was replaced by an appointed council under supervision of the local military commander, and a number of government employees suspected of having Communist sympathies were arbitrarily removed from their jobs. In the universities a number of leftist professors were discharged. In addition, the Rector of the University of Loja was relieved, the Rector of the University of Guayaquil resigned and, at the Central University in Quito, the Faculty of Philosophy and Letters, a center of Communist agitation, was temporarily closed. Some observers considered that, by making the party illegal for the first time in many years, there had been severe disruption of the Communist movement.

COMMUNISTS AND THE EXTREME LEFT

Although the PCE claimed 11,000 members in early 1963, most estimates place the total hard-core membership at between 2,000 and 3,000. Most of its numerical strength lies in the labor movement, in which the Communists are a major force. Party leaders are also active in student and youth organizations (see ch. 21, Labor Relations and Organization).

The PCE's claim for sole advocacy of revolutionary social reform has not been seriously challenged by any rival group, such as the non-Communist movement in Peru, the American Popular Revolutionary Alliance (Alianza Popular Revolucionaria Américana—APRA), which held a monopoly over the radical sectors for several decades. Rather, the Communists have been able to manipulate to their advantage a broad, docile following in the ranks of the Ecuadorian Socialist Party and thus to exert an influence far in excess of their numbers (see ch. 14, Political Dynamics).

The PCE has often fostered the formation of front organizations of multifactional membership to further immediate political objectives and at times has operated through and has been the dominant element of these popular fronts. This happened, for example, in early 1962, when the MPR was formed to oppose a break with Cuba.

The PCE functioned openly until it was outlawed in July 1963. It published journals and tracts and conducted other normal political business in a manner similar to that employed by other parties. After the rise of Fidel Castro, however, its activities turned more toward frank subversion. Many party members were sent to Cuba for training in guerrilla methods, and the organization of clandestine groups was financed with funds supplied by the Cuban Embassy. The closing of that embassy in April 1962 cut off the free flow of funds for subversive activity and severely curtailed travel to Cuba.

At the seventh national congress of the PCE, held just before the break with Cuba, the secretary general of the party, Pedro Saad, boasted of the great political gains the party had achieved. The central theme of that congress was the "national liberation revolution."

Since the party was outlawed the Communists continued to manipulate the CTE by exercising control over its executive committee. In addition, a few hundred members of the Communist Youth of Ecuador (Juventud Comunista Ecuatoriana—JCE) completely dominated the vociferous pro-Castro URJE. In the FEUE, although the majority of the students are not Communist sympathizers, a well-organized clique was able to capture the governing groups on the various campuses, where they enjoyed the help and allegiance of many influential faculty members.

The basic unit of the PCE is the cell of a few persons, formed in a factory, office or other establishment. Local committees coordinate the work of the individual cells in the areas. In more populous areas, zonal committees are formed to coordinate the work of the local committees. In each province there is a provincial committee which elects members to the Central Committee, the supreme body in the country, which operates under a permanent secretariat. A national party congress meets every 2 years on call by the Central Committee.

Party members in nonparty organizations, such as mass fronts, labor unions and peasant associations, are required to act as informal splinter groups to promote party aims in these organizations. The strength of the movement lies in such infiltration, reinforced by strict party discipline; according to PCE statute, "party decisions must be unconditionally carried out."

Since the overthrow of the Arosemena government the Communists and their various allies on the extreme Left have found ample opportunity to create or add to political turmoil generated by popular opposition to the military government. In May 1965, for example, leftist student groups formed an enthusiastic and violent contingent in a general strike called by the Chamber of Commerce of Guayaquil to protest recently imposed increases in import tariffs. Similarly, in both Guayaquil and Quito the URJE was a vociferous element in broad-based antigovernment demonstrations. Participation in actions against the government by the extreme Left has been combined consistently with pro-Castro and anti-United States propaganda campaigns. The Communists see their contribution to the antigovernment effort as merely a part of their broader program of subversion; a Central Committee letter of June 23, 1965, directed members, wherever possible, to use for their own ends the discontent of all vested interests in the country.

GOVERNMENT REACTION

An important step was taken against the Communists in April 1962, when the Arosemena government, under pressure from the military commanders, severed all diplomatic ties with the Soviet bloc, breaking relations with Cuba, Poland and Czechoslovakia. In the fall of the same year the government took action against several attempts by local Communists to build up their strength, both armed and political. The police discovered and confiscated several caches of arms, explosives and Communist literature. A Cuban bomb expert was arrested, and $25,000 to have been used for propaganda was confiscated from the Communist leader Manuel Roura on his return from the Soviet Union and Communist China.

On assuming control in 1963, the new government outlawed the PCE and arrested many of its members. In April 1964 it seized a large amount of Communist propaganda in Guayaquil, and later in the year it tried to weaken the Communist voice in student opinion by outlawing the FEUE.

CHAPTER 27

THE ARMED FORCES

Largely because of its long-term dispute with Peru, the country has maintained a large military establishment relative to its resources and to the requirements of internal security. Since independence the involvement of military officers in politics has been almost continuous.

Of the battles since independence, starting with Tarqui, where in 1829 General Antonio José de Sucre defeated a larger Peruvian force, only a few involved attacks across the borders, and most of the attacks were closely connected with internal politics. Some 46 chief executives have been brought to power by military coups. Many presidents have filled certain command positions with political supporters and eliminated officers with dissident views.

The armed forces consist of the army, the navy and the air force. In addition, the National Civil Police (Policía Civil Nacional—PCN) can be integrated to the armed forces in case of national emergency. The president is the Commander in Chief of the Armed Forces. Above the commanding officers of the three services is an Armed Forces General Staff, responsible to the minister of defense, who is directly responsible to the president.

Military men have often taken power with the conviction that they could provide better government than those they have displaced. The army has long considered itself the protector of democratic institutions and of the rights of the people. Military men have not been the best administrators, but social advances, such as the abolition of slavery, have been accomplished during their tenure.

The army has generally enjoyed the moderate esteem of the people, who have long considered it one of the principal institutions of power, along with the oligarchy, the Church and the political parties. Most politically aware people, even those who feel that military men have done a poor job as heads of government, are agreed as to the honesty of purpose of the military in national affairs. In late 1965 continued public support for the existing military government attested to this basic respect.

On several occasions the armed forces have been called upon to maintain internal security. Considerable bloodshed has resulted, and the public image of the armed forces has been diminished. The consequent reluctance to enforce internal security has at times impeded strong governmental action against dissidents.

MILITARY HISTORY

When the Spanish conquistadors arrived in Peru, Quito was the northern limit of the Inca Empire. The area had been conquered at a late stage, and it was still held in subjugation by Inca troops from Peru. The warlike Cañari tribe of the southern Sierra, many of whose members had been slaughtered by the Inca, had become a willing ally of the Spaniards. After the death of the Inca Atahualpa at the hands of the conquerors, the Spaniards, with the aid of the Cañari, defeated and captured his chief lieutenant, Rumiñahui, and thereafter were able to rule the area with little further need for military force. A few outposts were maintained, but the military in the Quito area was essentially a ceremonial force, and the center of military strength of the Viceroyalty of Peru was in faraway Lima (see ch. 3, Historical Setting).

The weakness of the local military forces was demonstrated by their inability to prevent the many piratical raids made throughout the eighteenth century against Guayaquil and other coastal points. It was also evident in 1765, when the people of Quito, protesting customs duties, easily overcame the military garrison there.

The country points with pride to one of the first revolutionary uprisings made in Spanish America. In 1809 the citizens of Quito set up a junta to rule in behalf of Ferdinand VII, who had been deposed in Spain by Napoleon. This junta, supported by most of the leading citizens and by the city's military garrison was at first successful. The viceroys of both New Granada (Colombia) and Peru sent forces against the patriots, however, and by the end of 1812 the entire movement had been crushed.

In 1820 the country again tried to revolt against the Spanish authorities. Encouraged by Simón Bolívar's successes in the north and José de San Martin's successes in the south, a new junta was set up in Quito, backed by the troops quartered there. In reply to requests for aid sent to both Colombia and Peru, Bolívar, in February 1821, sent General José de Mires with a shipment of arms to help in training an Ecuadorian division. He was followed in May 1821 by General Antonio José de Sucre with a force of 700 Colombians and Venezuelans.

After defeating, in August 1821, a royalist force sent to recapture Guayaquil, Sucre moved his forces to the Sierra. The following month, after one of his detachments, under Colonel Luis Urdaneta, was defeated with heavy losses, he sent an urgent request to Peru for reinforcements. General San Martín dispatched a Peruvian division of 1,400 men, under command of Colonel Andrés Santa Cruz, which, by forced marches, joined Sucre at Saraguro in February 1822. The combined force then marched on Quito, where Sucre was able to outmaneuver and defeat Melchor Aymerich, the royalist general, in the Battle of Pichincha which took place on May 24, 1822. This engagement was decisive, for when Aymerich learned that his northern force, which had tried to stop Bolívar's southward march from Colombia, had already been severely mauled at Bomboná, he surrendered all of the Audiencia of Quito to Sucre.

A young officer, Abdón Calderón, still honored as the nation's greatest military hero and in whose honor its oldest decoration is named, was born in Cuenca, the son of a Spanish officer. He fought with great distinction in all of Sucre's battles for the liberation of Ecuador, including that of Pichincha, where he was killed.

In accordance with the grand design of Bolívar, Ecuador was made part of Gran Colombia along with Colombia and Venezuela. It served as the concentration point for Bolívar's campaigns in Peru and furnished him much monetary support, but few men. An aversion developed to the so-called foreign troops that were concentrated in the country, and Bolívar's popularity began to wane. When Gran Colombia disintegrated, Ecuador in 1830 became an independent nation, and its leaders selected one of Bolívar's generals, the Venezuelan Juan José Flores to be the first president (see ch. 3, Historical Setting).

Flores, a brave military leader, was not a capable administrator and was able to rule only by using strong-arm methods against his opponents, including those in the army. By the end of his 15 years of direct rule or influence only 3 of the 15 general officers in the army were Ecuadorians. Most units were commanded by his fellow Venezuelans, and in the privileged cavalry regiments both officers and noncommissioned officers were from Venezuela. His oppressions were so great that eventually a popular uprising overcame the army in a series of bloody riots in 1845, and Flores went into exile in Europe.

For the next 15 years the dominant figure was General José María Urbina, who was a former supporter of Flores but who had abandoned him when his fall seemed imminent. Urbina, who ruled sometimes directly and sometimes indirectly, is honored for freeing the Negro slaves. Many of these freedmen were recruited into the army and became his chief source of military power. During this time civil wars were frequent, as were border skirmishes with Colombia and Peru. One would-be military dictator, General Guillermo Franco, staged a barracks revolt in Guayaquil and sought, unsuccessfully, to keep himself in power by ceding that city to Peru.

The leader of the efforts to end the power of General Urbina had long been a civilian, Gabriel García Moreno. Although, as a young student, García Moreno had been an implacable critic of General Flores, he encouraged Flores to return home and lead the rebels in the fight against the government forces. Flores' soldierly abilities again were evident, when joining with Garcia Moreno, he was able to defeat the forces loyal to the government, thus in September 1860, García Moreno was launched on his 15-year career of absolute, though for a time indirect, rule.

As an extreme conservative who believed in civilian rule, he took immediate steps to eliminate militarism in the government. Doing away with all elements in the army still loyal to General Urbina, he built the army into an effective professional force and used it as a source of his own power. His rule, however, was civilian in character, supported but not dominated by the army. When he was assassinated on August 6, 1875, a new struggle for power broke out.

Backed by the former *caudillo* General Urbina, the commander of the Guayaquil garrison, General Ignacio de Veintimilla, revolted and was able to defeat the forces which had remained loyal to the elected successor president and assumed national rule with the title of Captain General. Strongly supported by friends, whom he rewarded with high office, and by the army, which he had caused to be well paid and well equipped, he remained in office until 1883, when he was ousted by a combined military and civilian group with strong liberal tendencies, headed by a businessman-turned-guerrilla, General Eloy Alfaro.

This group was in turn defeated, and there followed a so-called progressive period of 12 years of civilian rule in which there was intense strife among the contending political parties, the Liberals and the Conservatives. In 1895 the Liberals refused to recognize the elected Conservative government. At the request of Liberal leaders, Eloy Alfaro was recalled to organize a revolutionary army which after several months of fighting defeated the government forces.

There followed a long period of rule by military dictators belonging to the Liberal Party. Eloy Alfaro, who was president from 1895 to 1901, attempted many liberal reforms and sought to eliminate all of the proclerical laws of García Moreno as well as all persons sympathetic to the Conservative Party. The army, which had always been conservative, was deeply indoctrinated with the liberal doctrines of the day. In 1900 it was able to defeat at Tulcán a proconservative attack launched from Colombia. From 1901 to 1905, the military commander of earlier years, General Leónidas Plaza Gutiérrez, ruled as president and, like his predecessor, built up his own faction in the army. Rivalry developed between the two leaders, and when a protege of Plaza was elected to succeed him to the presidency, Alfaro staged a coup and easily overcame the troops remaining loyal to the elected president.

Alfaro ruled increasingly as an absolute military dictator, employing strong-arm methods against his political opponents. In 1907, using a cavalry squadron, he put down a student demonstration with considerable loss of life. He also ordered the public execution of eight soldiers accused of conspiracy against his regime.

In 1911, after Alfaro's duly elected successor died soon after taking office, General Pedro J. Montero staged a coup d'etat in favor of Alfaro, who immediately returned from residence in Panama to lead the fight against the constitutional forces headed by ex-President Plaza, then Minister of War and Alfaro's former close friend. This revolt developed into a bloody regional fight between Quito and Guayaquil. The government forces supported by Quito triumphed, and most of the rebel leaders, including Eloy Alfaro, were captured at Yaguachi. Later, Alfaro was murdered by a mob in the streets of Quito.

Soon thereafter General Plaza returned to power, supported by civilian politicians of liberal leaning and by the army, carefully reconstituted with leaders strongly supporting the government. His term in office from 1912 to 1916 was strongly affected by World War I, which caused serious financial problems with the country.

Guayaquil banking interests were able to exploit these problems and thus dominate a series of presidents and the government, which they then manipulated for their own enrichment. In order to keep the armed forces quiescent they offered the senior military officers many financial plums. Because of the many abuses brought about by the Guayaquil bankers, many elements in the country, led by a league of young military officers, conspired to oust them. In July 1925 the military garrisons in many parts of the country rose against the government. A small military force took the President, the leading bankers and General Plaza into custody.

A seven-man body, including only one military officer, took over the government but ruled for only 6 months. It was followed by a completely civilian six-man group, which after 3 months was displaced by Isidro Ayora. Although he was installed "by designation of the army," one of his first acts was to eliminate the various military clubs or groups which had been in virtual control of the government. In retaliation, a military force captured Ayora and was threatening to shoot him when it was learned that the leader of the military revolt, General Francisco Gómez de la Torre, had in turn been captured by presidential adherents. Ayora triumphed, and the military leaders of the revolt were exiled to the Galápagos Islands.

Plagued by the depression of 1930, Ayora was finally deposed by a bloody military coup in August 1931, which placed Colonel Luís Larrea Alba in power. He soon resigned, however, because of a cleavage in the army resulting in a battle in October 1931, which inflicted considerable loss of life to the pro-Larrea Carchi Battalion.

The 1932 presidential elections resulted in major upheavals. A liberal civilian group in Tulcán seized the local military garrison by assault. A group supporting the candidacy of Commander Ildefonso Mendoza Vera seized control of the navy. The army was split into warring factions. Civil war reigned, and more than 1,000 persons were killed in frenzied and pointless street battles. Later, in May 1933, three army battalions revolted in Riobamba and Ambato, but after 4 days of heavy fighting the revolt failed for lack of effective leadership. When elections were finally held, on December 15, 1933, José María Velasco Ibarra, a Central University professor, was elected president by a large plurality.

Unfortunately for the country, the arrival of Velasco Ibarra on the political scene for the first of his four presidential terms brought no tranquility. Almost immediately he was at odds with the Congress when he refused its request to provide military units to guard its sessions, as provided for in the Constitution. In 1935, when Velasco Ibarra attempted to promulgate a decree giving himself dictatorial powers, the army battalion charged with its enforcement revolted; a small military group placed him in a military prison, and he was later exiled.

Conditions were chaotic for the next 3 years, during which the army was an active participant in political affairs. Immediately after Velasco Ibarra's fall, the Minister of Government assumed power, as provided for in the Constitution, but when he was threatened with civil war by his own leftist supporters, he asked the military to take over. When Federico Paéz, the Minister of Public Works, was then named by the military to be president, he promptly ordered the retirement of most of the senior officers opposing him and repaid his military backers with vastly accelerated promotions to colonel and general officer ranks. In spite of this move, during his short rule he was forced to put down three military revolts by leftist elements in the army.

On November 28, 1936, in the last and most serious of the uprisings against Páez, the soldiers in some army units revolted in favor of leftist retired Colonel Larrea Alba, overcame their officers and turned the artillery on Quito. This revolt, which was joined by many of the people, was severely put down by a cavalry battalion under the direction of the Minister of Defense, General Alberto Enríquez. In October 1937, Paéz resigned in favor of General Enríquez, who ruled for a short time with a military cabinet, until elections could be held. In 1939 a Liberal, Carlos Arroyo del Río, was elected president and attempted to build up the national police as a counterbalance to the army.

In July 1941, as a result of skirmishes between border guards, Peru invaded Ecuador. The small and ill-equipped forces defending the Ecuadorian border fought bravely near Zarumilla in El Oro Province against the much larger and better-equipped invaders, but the Ecuadorian forces received as reinforcements only a few volunteer units and were speedily defeated. The President was blamed for the defeat and for the major territorial loss to Peru suffered as a result of the Rio de Janeiro Protocol, even though there was little he could have done to prevent it (see ch. 3, Historical Setting). On May 28, 1944, the army garrison in Guayaquil, led chiefly by captains and lieutenants, revolted, seizing strategic areas and arming their civilian friends. Although a few army units remained loyal, the chief support for the President came from the police, who were no match for the opposing army forces, and he was deposed.

After a short rule by a junta, Velasco Ibarra was recalled from exile to the presidency with popular acclaim. As unpredictable as ever, he ruled dictatorially for 3 years of near anarchy. On August 23, 1947, the Minister of Defense, Colonel Carlos Mancheno, with a few other army officers, put the President into a guardhouse and assumed control of the government. Velasco Ibarra supporters in the army responded by staging an uprising against Mancheno in Guayaquil and several other parts of the country. Leaders of such a revolt in Riobamba, after overcoming government tanks, captured Quito, with air support, and placed the deposed Vice President Suárez Veintimilla in the presidency pending a final selection by the Congress. The president designated by Congress, Carlos Julio Arosemena, a well-known Guayaquil banker, had to put down a military revolt in the short period before constitutional elections were held in June 1948.

In the election, held without army intervention, a moderate, Galo Plaza Lasso, was elected over both the Conservative candidate and the government-backed candidate of the Liberal Party. Plaza, who allowed a large degree of freedom of political discussion, was still able to serve out his full term (1948–52). During this time the army intervened twice in support of constitutional government—first, in 1949, when the young officers of an armored battalion in Quito ordered seized a group of retired officers who attempted to attack the battalion barracks and again, in 1951, when the first army unit jailed the ringleaders of a mob which had taken the Quito municipal palace, claiming army support.

RECENT MILITARY INVOLVEMENT IN POLITICS

During the presidential campaign of 1952, Velasco Ibarra had much support in the armed forces. A few of the younger officers belonging to the Ecuadorian National Revolutionary Action (Acción Revolucionaria Nacionalista Ecuatoriana—ARNE), an extreme right-wing group of younger people, supported him. Nevertheless, he immediately ordered more than 50 top-ranking army officers into retirement and sent to remote posts other officers known to have opposed his candidacy.

When Velasco Ibarra returned to office in 1960, the senior officers in all three services supported his government, but plotting against him soon spread to the armed forces. In April 1961 he ordered the arrest for conspiracy of former Commander of the Army Colonel Luis Piñeiros Pastor, whom he had retired when he became president. At the same time he ordered into retirement Colonel Aníbal Duarte, Commander of the I Military Zone. The Minister of Defense, Patricio Lasso Carrión, resigned when General Enrique Calle Solano, Chief of the Armed Forces General Staff, was replaced by General Víctor Aulestia Mier. General Calle, together with the Sub-Secretary of Defense, Colonel Gonzalo Coba Cabezas, and the Commander of the Navy, Admiral Ramón Albán, were sent to the United States for duty.

Soon most of the army officers favored the removal of the President. One group urged only his resignation; another, apparently supported by the high command, sought to declare the Chief Justice of the Supreme Court as interim president until elections could be held; and a third group favored the replacement of the President by Vice President Julio Carlos Arosemena Monroy.

In November 1961, a general strike in protest against the actions of the President was called by the Communist-led Confederation of Ecuadorian Workers (Confederación de Trabajadores Ecuatorianos—CTE) and joined by most worker groups. Velasco Ibarra invoked the aid of the army and the police. A protest march in Guayaquil by high school boys was answered by gunfire, and several students were killed. When Vice President Arosemena condemned the excessive use of force, he and a number of his followers were jailed.

An army engineer unit in Quito revolted in support of Arosemena, but it was forced to give up when a tank battalion counterattacked in support of the high command. At the last minute, General Víctor Suárez, the Commanding General of the Air Force, threw his support to Arosemena, bringing the air force with him. Skirmishes between army units resulted in a number of deaths and ceased only when air force planes aided the pro-Arosemena forces and carried the day.

Many people, including most of the military who had supported or accepted Arosemena, distrusted his leftist orientation. When he was vice president, despite President Velasco Ibarra's objections, he had visited Moscow and had returned with high praise for the Communist system, speaking out against the United States. He was also a vociferous supporter of Fidel Castro.

When Arosemena assumed the presidency, he recalled Colonel Aratta Maciás to active duty as Chief of the Armed Forces General Staff and Colonel Arregui Viteri as Commander of the Army. Soon thereafter he also replaced the air force and navy commanders.

On March 29, 1962, Colonel Aurelio Naranjo, the commander in Cuenca, sent a demand to the government that it break diplomatic relations with Cuba within 72 hours. Even though the Commander of the Army censured Colonel Naranjo for his actions, he and the other chiefs of services advocated an immediate break with Cuba. President Arosemena discharged a few of his leftist appointees and, on April 2, 1962, broke relations with Cuba. Shortly thereafter, he replaced the Commander of the Army, Colonel Arregui, with Colonel Luis Cabrera Sevilla and the Air Force Commander with Lieutenant Colonel Guillermo Freile Posso.

In early 1963 the Functional Senator for the Armed Forces, Colonel Marcos Gándara Enríquez, began planning the removal of the President by military intervention. On July 10, 1963, immediately after a banquet at which Arosemena made offensive remarks about the United States in the presence of the United States Ambassador, the three service commanders and other military figures met to consider the action to be taken. The next day a four-man military group deposed President Arosemena.

The group was composed of Colonel Gándara and the chiefs of each of the three services. Each service chief had been appointed by President Arosemena. The army chief, Colonel Cabrera, was appointed after the break with Cuba because he was considered to be nonpolitical. The air force chief, Lieutenant Colonel Freile, was appointed at the same time because he was pro-Arosemena. The navy chief, Captain Ramón Castro Jijón, a personal friend of Arosemena, had been appointed soon after Arosemena took office and had survived the break with Cuba, in which he had supported the other service chiefs. The only member who had been anti-Arosemena before the coup was Colonel Gándara, who had been invited to join only at the last minute upon the insistence of the officers of the War College.

The motives underlying the actions of these men were complex. All were upset to a certain extent by the lack of dignity displayed by the President and the harm he did to the national image. All were apprehensive about Communists in the government and gave this, particularly in retrospect, as a motive for the coup. There is evidence to indicate that they acted more out of concern for the well-being of the military establishment as an institution than for any other reason.

POSITION IN THE GOVERNMENT AND SOCIETY

Legal Bases

The mission of the armed forces is delineated by the current (1946) Constitution, as is the separation between their duties and those of the PCN. Article 153 reads:

> For the defense of the Republic and the maintenance of constitutional order, there shall be a military armed force organized in accordance with the law. For the protection of internal order and security and social services, there shall be a civil police force which is governed by special laws.

Article 92, which states the powers and duties of the President, lists the first to be: "To maintain internal order and to watch over the external security of the Republic." It also authorizes him "to direct the public forces, as their chief when the defense and the public service of the nation so require." In case of war, the President of the Republic may delegate his authority as Chief of the Armed Forces to the commander of the mobilized forces.

The Congress is directly concerned with the armed forces, and, as expressed in the Constitution, its most important duties toward national defense are:

> To fix, annually, the maximum of the armed forces which must remain in service in time of peace. . . . To declare war and settle the peace, having regard for the recommendation of the President of the Republic.

Moreover, it states that "national defense and public education shall receive preferential attention in the budget." In time of war, however, the voice of Congress is displaced by the emergency powers of the president.

Several provisions of the Constitution have attempted to minimize the political involvement of the armed forces. Article 155 states: "The public forces are not deliberative. The authorities giving orders shall be solely responsible for orders which are manifestly contrary to the Constitution and the laws." Other provisions deny the armed forces and the police the right to vote while on active duty. No military man may be elected to a political position in any province where he has exercised command within 6 months of the time of the election. The Constitution provides that a functional representative of the armed forces sit as a member of the Senate.

Several interlocking provisions attempt to protect the professional status of the officer corps by regulating promotions to field grade and above. Promotion lists must be proposed by the executive branch and, for promotion to the rank of major or above, must be approved by the Council of State, which comprises representatives from the three branches of government. Promotions to colonel or general officer rank must be approved by the Congress in a secret ballot.

The new government has governed extraconstitutionally since it seized power on July 11, 1963. No Congress has been convened, and legislative functions as provided in the Constitution, as well as those of the president, have all been performed by the four-man collective leadership. The Law of National Security, decreed on December 15, 1964, codifies the mission and means of the armed forces for both internal and external security as had been already promulgated in the Constitution.

This codification charges the executive, be it the president or the four-man group, with complete responsibility for national security. The chief executive is provided with two organizations to advise him and to implement his directives—the National Security Council and the General Staff of the Armed Forces, respectively.

The National Security Council, which must be convoked at least every 4 months, consists of the Executive of the Republic as its ex-officio president; the presiding officer of the Congress; the Chief Justice of the Supreme Court; all of the ministers; and the Chief of the General Staff of the Armed Forces. Its permanent secretariat, composed of both military personnel and civilians, is headed by a secretary general selected by the president from the senior officers on active duty. The secretary general directs the General Intelligence Service (Dirección General de Informaciónes), which supplies the necessary information on which to base plans for national security and which coordinates the work of all the government intelligence agencies.

The minister of national defense is responsible to the executive power for matters affecting external security. His principal assistant is the Chief of the Armed Forces General Staff, who directs his staff, the highest military organization charged with analysis, planning and technical direction in military matters.

Under the Constitution the minister of government, aided by the ministers of public education and of social welfare and labor, has the primary responsibility in internal security matters. The law directs that he support the armed forces by making conditions in۔ the country conducive to harmony and order and by cooperating with the General Staff of the Armed Forces in any joint operations. The General Staff of the Armed Forces is responsible for formulating and operating the overall plan for the joint use of the military forces and the civil police in assuring internal as well as external security.

The General.Staff of the Armed Forces is charged with planning, organizing, preparing and operating any combined operations of the armed forces. The details are worked out through close coordination among the staffs of the services involved. The General Staff also plans for the coordinated use of all communications media, industrial facilities and strategic materials in case of a national emergency.

Civic Action

For a number of years the army, particularly the engineers charged with building roads, has been engaged in civic action. To aid in expanding civic action, the United States set up an auxiliary program in 1961.

The purpose of the program as carried out by the armed forces is twofold: to improve the public image of the military and to accomplish work projects beneficial to the economic development of the country. The many useful projects in progress and already completed testify to the fulfillment of the second objective; accomplishment of the other objective is more difficult to assess.

The civic action program has become extensive. On October 31, 1964, after 2 years of operation, the United States had spent $350,000 and had allocated an additional $225,000 for new and uncompleted projects. This amount gives little indication of the extent of the program, however, because the Ecuadorian army and people provide almost all of the manpower used, and many of the smaller civic action projects were conducted without United States funds. The projects varied greatly in aims and magnitude. They included the construction of roads, airfields, schools, dispensaries, water conduits, irrigation canals and sports fields; the digging of wells and drainage ditches; and the installation of electric powerlines and sawmills. In addition to a number of completed projects, both large and small, 164 were in progress in October 1964, and plans for a number of others had been approved.

Mostly, engineering troops of the army participate in the civic action program. The men so involved receive on-the-job training which not only increases the technical proficiency of their units but also prepares them for civilian jobs when they complete their military service. Proponents of the program point out that better civilian-military rapport clearly furthers the internal security role of the armed forces. Nevertheless, the program suffers considerable criticism from military officers on the grounds that it takes the men away from their primary military training duties and that manual labor demeans the armed forces.

In addition to the effectiveness of the military men involved, success depends often on the willingness of local assistance, which varies greatly from area to area and from project to project. In some places there is a strong tradition of community labor (*minga*), which facilitates the work; in other places enthusiastic support from local officials or priests assures widespread help. The immediate and readily apparent usefulness of a particular project, such as a well, usually ensures local support. On the other hand, long-range projects—for example, extensive irrigation canals—have suffered from a shortage of volunteer labor and, therefore, from the necessity of using more soldiers to do the manual labor.

Attitude of the People

As an institution the armed forces usually have enjoyed a moderate degree of popular acceptance and esteem. Attitudes toward the military result from a complex of factors and influences which are not uniform throughout the country or at all social and economic levels.

Traditionally, the armed forces, like the Church and the government bureaucracy, recruit more of their career personnel from the Sierra than from the Coast and thus enjoy a greater rapport with the people of the Sierra. Perhaps indicative of the respect for the army in the Sierra was a newspaper item from Ibarra in July 1964, which, in denouncing the Customs Police, urged that an army battalion "with its high morale and discipline" be sent to guarantee the rights of the citizens.

The prestige of the military is low among members of the upper class. Few officers originate in the elite. Political and business leaders are aware of the potential of the military establishment for influencing or even drastically changing the course of political events. Most of them, therefore, seek to maintain ties with military leaders which they may find of value in times of crisis.

The most favorable attitude toward the military is held by the middle class, from which nearly all officers are drawn. Few Indians are conscripted for military service (see ch. 6, Social

Structure). Almost without exception, army and navy officers graduate from one of the service academies, and most of them are from provincial towns. While middle-class people look upon the military establishment as a heavy consumer of their taxes, they also see it as a channel for upward movement, socially and economically. Most noncommissioned officers are drawn from this group.

Most army, air force and naval officers come from the Sierra, but geographical origin does not appear to be a significant determinant of political orientation. The army, by far the largest service and better prepared to intervene in internal political disputes, has the greatest political power, which, however, is diluted by the many diverse factions as compared to the more unified political position taken by the smaller air force. The air force was instrumental in forcing the resignation of Arosemena as president in 1961. Colonel Freile's strength in the governing group rested largely on support from the air force.

The prestige of the navy and air force, which have few conscripts and provide better uniforms for enlisted men, has been higher than that of the army. Nevertheless, even the army conscripts themselves contribute positively to the popular image. The average conscript realizes that army service gives him considerable advantages. Ambitious conscripts have a good chance to become regular noncommissioned officers in one of the three services; between 5 and 10 percent do so each year.

THE MILITARY ESTABLISHMENT AND THE NATIONAL ECONOMY

Budget

The cost of maintaining the defense establishment is relatively high. Military expenditures amounted to 18.9 percent of the total 1963 budget, or 1.7 percent of the gross national product. These percentages are well above those spent by Colombia, but the percentage of the gross national product spent is well below that used by Peru, the feared neighbor. The cost per man in all three countries is comparable (see ch. 18, The Economic System).

MISSION AND TOP CONTROL

Mission

The mission of the armed forces, according to the Constitution, is to defend the republic and to maintain the constitutional order. The PCN is charged with the preservation of internal order, and only when it requires additional help does the armed forces become operational in internal security matters. The Law of Na-

512

tional Security of December 1964 does not change the essence of the mission as stated in the Constitution; it is merely more explicit as to methods and details.

Top Control

Constitutionally, the president is the Commander in Chief of the Armed Forces. His immediate subordinate in military matters is the minister of defense, who for the past 30 years of civilian presidents, has been a civilian rather than a member of one of the uniformed services. The sub-secretary, on the other hand, has always been a military officer. Under the current military government the minister of defense has been an army officer. Directly under and responsible to him is the chief of the Armed Forces General Staff, to whom the commanders of the three services are to report. In practice, however, the service commanders often appeal directly to the minister of defense on important matters. The PCN, which in peacetime is under the minister of government, in time of national emergency automatically comes under the commander of the army.

For advice in defense matters the president can call on the National Defense Council. Habitually, the commanders of the respective services have been the actual commanders in military matters. Despite not infrequent deviations from the chain of command, ordinarily commands proceed from the president (or chief executive) through the minister of defense to the chief of the Armed Forces General Staff, thence to the particular service concerned.

Quasi-Military

The PCN, which is charged with maintaining law and order, is a police force and cannot be considered to be a paramilitary unit, although it is organized along semimilitary lines. It functions under the minister of government through the commandant general of the PCN.

If the police need more force to meet a particular situation, the army, upon request from the local police, assumes the responsibility, and the commander of the local army troops involved directs the entire operation. In case of a national emergency the PCN automatically comes under command of the commanding general of the army, and the local army commanders assume command of the appropriate police forces.

FOREIGN INFLUENCE

The traditional enmity with Peru has had a strong influence on the armed forces of Ecuador, and open hostilities have flared on several occasions. Ecuador considers that Peru despoiled it of much of its territory and continues to view Peru as a serious threat to its sovereignty. Thus faced by a larger and more powerful neighbor, it has tried to maintain armed forces in excess of economic advisability.

As early as 1900, Chile, which had defeated Peru in the War of the Pacific and which had an army trained on Prussian lines, furnished a military mission to the Ecuadorian army. This mission trained the army in German methods, and the cadets of the Military Academy still parade in goosestep. A number of officers have been trained in Chilean military schools, and, as recently as 1962, a Chilean mission did much of the instruction at the War College.

In 1922 an Italian military mission set up a system of training schools for the army in the fields of aviation, cavalry, infantry, artillery and engineering and helped run them until the early 1930's. These schools have since been expanded, but little or no Italian influence has remained.

The United States military first became significant immediately after Pearl Harbor when Ecuador declared war on Japan and granted the United States base rights in the Galápagos Islands, primarily for the defense of the Panama Canal against possible Japanese attack. An airbase was constructed and occupied until the end of the war, when it was turned over to Ecuador. In 1944 a United States military mission was assigned, and limited amounts of surplus United States military equipment began to be received under the lend-lease and, later, the interim aid programs.

In 1954 a military aid program agreement concluded between the two governments resulted in the assignment of United States Army, Navy and Air Force missions and led to the acquisition, through purchase and grant, of significant amounts of United States military materiel. The result has been a gradual but important improvement in the organization, training and equipment of the military forces, which has caused the virtual elimination of all foreign military influence other than that of the United States. United States influence almost certainly will continue to grow as more personnel receive training in the United States and the Canal Zone.

COMPOSITION

The armed forces in 1965 were composed of an army of about 10,000 men, a small navy and a small air force. In addition, the PCN can be transferred to the authority of the Ministry of Defense in case of national emergency (see ch. 25, Public Order). The armed forces consist of a professional officer corps, a corps of career noncommissioned officers, some volunteers and, particularly in the army, a large number of 1-year conscripts.

MANPOWER PROCUREMENT

Officers

Line officers from both the army and the navy are almost invariably graduates of their respective service academies, where academic standards are high and attrition is accordingly heavy. Air force officers are often graduates of the army's Military Academy (Colegio Militar), the Naval Academy (Escuela Naval) or one of the universities who then attend the flying school for officer candidates. In addition, men under 23 years of age who have received their high school diplomas may also enter the flying school.

Noncommissioned Officers

The noncommissioned officer corps in all three services is professional. In the navy and air force almost all of the enlisted men are also regulars. Most regular enlisted men in all three services are selected from the conscripts and volunteers. A large percentage of those who become career soldiers are from the Sierra.

Enlisted Men

According to Article 154 of the Constitution:

> All Ecuadorians and foreigners domiciled in the country are obliged to cooperate in the national defense in the form and manner determined by law. Moreover the law shall establish the system of compulsory military service.

An amended 1933 law, currently in force, provides for the compulsory training for 1 year for all men upon reaching their twentieth birthday. Notices of dates of induction appear periodically in the local newspapers, informing the members of a particular class when and where they are to report for examination, usually to the army division nearest their homes. In addition, the Law of National Security of December 1964 specifies that in case of national emergency all men between the ages of 15 and 60 who have not been inducted into the armed forces must present themselves for duties in support of internal civil operations of the republic.

The law grants exemptions from the draft for a number of reasons. Exempted are only sons, persons enrolled in higher educational institutions and those who are the major economic support of their families. The annual manpower requirement is always well below the total number of the year class physically fit and otherwise available for call. Accordingly, the names of men to be conscripted are determined by a lottery system.

Selective service boards are established in each provincial capital. All men belonging to the 20-year-old class, except those living outside of the country, must report at a specified time and place to take a physical examination given by military doctors. Each selective service board is given annually a quota by the commander of the military zone in which the particular province is located. Lists giving the names of those selected for induction are posted in public places in mid-January of each year. Instructions as to where and when the local selectees will report for induction are posted and also appear in the local newspapers. As a rule the vast majority of the conscripts are inducted into the army. Ordinarily the reporting date for all conscripts is the same, but from time to time the army has inducted one-fourth of its draft in the summer, and in 1964 the navy conscripts had a March reporting date. Most conscripts are from the lower or lower middle class. Few Indians are conscripted.

Officer-Enlisted Man Relationship

A close rapport frequently exists on a professional level among certain career personnel, in spite of the wide educational gap between officers and men of lower ranks. The same men often serve together for a number of years. Socially, however, there is almost no mingling between officers and enlisted men and their families. The conscripts, who do not differ materially in social origins from the career noncommissioned personnel, are regarded as essential working members of the organization. Although the discipline enforced by the noncommissioned officers is strict, the conscripts are not looked down upon by them.

The role of the *patrón* (see Glossary) is quite important. Younger officers often attach themselves to a highly regarded senior officer, as do the enlisted men to an outstanding junior officer. Such attachments occasionally result in the formation of functional groups which move almost en masse with each transfer of their *patrónes*.

TRAINING

Each service has its own system of training schools. The army administers the War College, an advanced school offering joint training. Since 1963 both the air force and the navy have established war colleges of their own. The army and navy each has its own school for preparing cadets to become commissioned officers. Both maintain high educational standards, and the attrition rate is high. The air force, which does not have its own cadet school, conducts a pilot training course open to military academy, university and high school graduates.

Army

In the army all of the schools except the paratroop school are located in the Quito area and are centrally supervised by the Director General of Army Schools, who is directly responsible to the Commanding General of the Army. Courses for both officers and enlisted men are offered at the various branch schools. Often, officer instructors must teach courses at several different schools. The paratroop school is run at Salinas on the coast. The basic training of conscripts is carried out within the units. The dependence of units upon short-term conscripts for the greater part of their manpower and the need to train them within the units seldom enables a unit to proceed beyond the basic training stage.

Navy

The naval school system consists of the Naval Academy, the Naval War College, the Naval Specialist School and the Recruit Training Center. The graduates of the Navy Academy are usually assigned at once to sea duty. Much advanced officer schooling has been performed in the United States.

Air Force

A course for training pilots is conducted at Salinas. An officer's school was established to give technical training to officers and the Air Academy to give technical training to airmen, but much of the technical training for both officers and airmen is accomplished either in the United States or in the Canal Zone.

Indoctrination

Until the Communist Party was outlawed in July 1963, one of its chief propaganda targets was the enlisted men. All services have instituted anti-Communist indoctrination.

RANK, PAY AND PROMOTIONS

Rank

Titles of officer and noncommissioned officer rank and their responsibilities correspond closely to those in the respective United States service. The 1-year conscripts, found chiefly in the army, are given almost no responsibilities (see table 21).

Table 21. Ranks in the Ecuadorian Armed Forces

Title	Approximate United States equivalent	
	Army	Air Force
ARMY AND AIR FORCE		
General de Ejército[1]	Major General	Major General
General de División[2]	Brigadier General	Brigadier General
Coronel	Colonel	Colonel
Teniente Coronel	Lieutenant Colonel	Lieutenant Colonel
Mayor	Major	Major
Capitán	Captain	Captain
Teniente	First Lieutenant	First Lieutenant
Subteniente	Second Lieutenant	Second Lieutenant
Suboficial Primero	Master Sergeant	Master Sergeant
Suboficial Segundo	Technical Sergeant	Technical Sergeant
Sargento Primero	Staff Sergeant	Staff Sergeant
Sargento Segundo	Sergeant	Airman 1st Class
Cabo Primero	Corporal	Airman 2d Class
Cabo Segundo	Private 1st Class	Airman 3d Class
Soldado Voluntario	Private	Airman
Soldado Conscripto	Recruit	Recruit

NAVY	Navy
Vicealmirante	Rear Admiral
Contralmirante	—do—
Capitán de Navío	Captain
Capitán de Fragata	Commander
Capitán de Corbeta	Lieutenant Commander
Teniente de Fragata[3]	Lieutenant
Alférez de Navío[3]	Lieutenant Junior Grade
Alférez de Fragata[3]	Ensign
Suboficial Primero	Chief Petty Officer
Suboficial Segundo	—do—
Sargento Primero	Petty Officer 1st Class
Sargento Segundo	Petty Officer 2d Class
Cabo Primero	Petty Officer 3d Class
Cabo Segundo	Seaman
Marinero Grumete	Seaman Apprentice
Marienero Conscripto	Seaman Recruit

[1]General del Aire in the Air Force.
[2]General in the Air Force.
[3]In the Navy, coequal with the three lower officer grades are the Oficiales de Mar of 1st, 2d and 3d Class; these are specialists, such as engineers, with officer rank, who have risen from the ranks and who cannot be promoted above Oficial de Mar 1st Class.

Pay

Except for those on hazardous duty, the pay for the three services is uniform. The income for career personnel consists of base pay and allowances for living quarters, rations, family and longevity. Under certain conditions additional special allowances are paid. Deductions imposed on the pay of career personnel for retirement, hospitalization and funeral expenses amount to 19 percent of the total pay.

The base pay of career personnel varies from S/4,500 (in 1965, S/18.5 equaled US$1—see Glossary) for general officers to S/500 for privates. Considering allowances and deductions, the take-home pay is commensurate with that received in comparable civilian jobs. On the other hand, the pay of the conscript is very low, amounting to only S/100 per month with few, if any, augmentations. Conscripts receive free food and lodging, which is doubtless better than that received at home.

Upon retirement, officers with a minimum of 10 years' service and enlisted men with a minimum of 15 years' service receive a lump sum as severance pay, and all personnel with a minimum of 15 years' service receive monthly retirement pay. Such funds have been built up as a forced savings from the monthly pay deductions. The lump sum for enlisted men is about S/50,000 and for officers S/152,000. Monthly retirement pay is based on length of service and amounts to 50 percent of base pay for the minimum of 15 years of service; 75 percent, for 25 years; and 100 percent for 30 years.

Promotion

Newly installed presidents have often replaced senior officers with men personally loyal to them, which has been bad on the morale of junior officers. The government sought to impose a degree of stability by decreeing, on April 10, 1964, the Military Personnel Law.

This law, which applies equally to the officers of the three services, gives the requirements for progressive promotion through the various ranks. Such requisites include a time in grade, completion of a particular training course and a period of duty with troops. For promotion to the grade of major or equivalent a tour of duty in one of the more remote stations must have been performed. Promotions to the rank of colonel and above are made upon recommendation of a promotion board, which is required to interview each aspirant. Time in grade for promotion to the next higher grade is 3 years for second lieutenants, 4 years for first lieutenants, 5 years for captains, 5 years for majors, 4 years for lieutenant colonels and 4 years for colonels. The law provides for voluntary retirement, for forced annual retirements of the "less suited" and for mandatory retirement at age 60. The regulations of the individual services continue to govern the promotion of enlisted men.

The law also established in detail rules governing the assignment of personnel to the status of *disponibilidad* (in practical effect, "unassigned"), a preretirement step. An officer can be placed in *disponibilidad* upon reaching the statutory retirement age of 60; for ill health; for being placed on the annual "less-suited" list; as a result of court action; or if there is no suitable command position for the officer. This last provision was specifically made to apply only to the one or two eligible senior officers who are not selected as service commanders.

UNIFORMS

Except in ceremonial units the enlisted men wear United States-type uniforms. The army officers wear uniforms of five different classifications: fatigues, which are similar to the United States Army field uniform; barracks and daily wear, both of which are lapel-type light grey dress uniforms; and the full dress and ceremonial parade uniforms, which have high-collared blouses, are greyish purple and are worn with black trousers or with black breeches and boots, respectively, and an ornate clasp belt in the national colors, yellow, blue and red.

Insignia of rank, worn on shoulder boards (except on fatigues), consist of stars: one silver star for second lieutenant, two silver stars for first lieutenant, three silver stars for captain, one gold star for major, two gold stars for lieutenant colonel and three gold stars for colonel. General officer rank is indicated by one or two stars on a shoulder board carrying the national crest. Branch insignia are similar to those worn by the United States Army, except for the General Staff crest.

AWARDS AND DECORATIONS

Military decorations are worn with great pride. The highest military award is the War Cross, which was created in 1950 to reward officers and men who had distinguished themselves in the 1941 campaign against Peru. The award itself carries no monetary stipend, but families of recipients who died in action receive the active duty pay the recipient would have earned. Preference in the awarding of scholarships is also given to children of recipients. The ribbon is red.

The oldest and second highest award is the Order of Abdón Calderón, named after a national hero who was killed at the Battle of Pichincha on May 24, 1822. This medal is awarded to officers, (national and foreign) in three classes—1st class (gold), 2d class (silver) and 3d class (bronze)—for outstandingly meritorious service to the country or for bravery in action. It carries no monetary award. The medal is worn on dress occasions, and the yellow, blue and red ribbon is worn on the service uniform.

The Medal for Military Service, established in 1921, is awarded to officers for length of service. It is awarded in three classes: 1st class, for 30 years' service, which carries a stipend of 3 months' base pay; 2d class, for 25 years' service, with a stipend of 2 months' pay; and 3d class, for 15 years' service, with a stipend of 1 month's pay. Preference is given to sons of recipients in entering the service academies and in obtaining scholarships abroad. The ribbon has two blue stripes with a white stripe between them.

Enlisted men are awarded no medals except the War Cross, which they wear directly below its ribbon. They are, however, awarded button-like insignia which are worn over the left pocket of the uniform in order from left to right as received. These awards, which carry no stipend, are made for length of faithful service. For 10 years the award is a yellow enameled button; for 15 years, a yellow enameled button with a blue inner circle; and for 20 years, a yellow enameled button with an inner circle of red surrounded by a blue band. An additional award made to enlisted men is the Decoration for Professional Merit, which consists of a black ribbon decorated with the branch insigne of the recipient.

MILITARY JUSTICE

Personnel on active duty who are charged with any crime are tried by military courts according to the military penal code and the code of procedures for military trials. The procedures are similar to those of civil courts. For minor offenses hearings by unit commanders are comparable to those conducted by political lieutenants. For the less serious crimes trial is held before an officer trained in military law. For the more serious crimes the military court procedures are similar to those of criminal tribunals in civil courts. A unique feature requires that any trial of an officer must be before a general court-martial (see ch. 25, Public Order).

When an offense is alleged, the investigation is made by a previously appointed investigating officer (*juez instructor*). In time of peace it must be completed within 24 hours and referred to the judge advocate (*fiscal*) of the Military Zone. In the less serious cases the Zone Commander can award punishment based on recommendation of his judge advocate. For the more serious offenses, which can be punished by confinement in a penitentiary, the report of the investigating officer must be referred to a special court-martial for a hearing and the accused must be furnished a defense counsel.

Procedures in both special and general courts-martial are the same. The senior officer is designated as the president of the court and each has a law member (*auditor de guerra*). Although the basis of the trial rests on the evidence introduced and reduced to writing during the preliminary investigation, both sides may introduce pertinent new evidence and have the right to cross-examine witnesses. The accused may testify in his own behalf, but cannot be required to testify. After the opposing arguments have been completed, the court is closed and a secret ballot of its members is taken to determine guilt or innocence. An absolute majority is required for conviction. The verdict and sentence are announced in open court, but are subject to review by the Court of Military Justice review board before they become final.

Penalties are comparable to those prescribed for civil courts. For example, the maximum penalty is 16 years in the penitentiary for serious offenses such as murder. An important exception to this rule of limitation is made in the case of the military offense of high treason, which can be punished by life imprisonment. For the many derelictions which apply only to the military service, penalties are also prescribed by the code. Examples are 3 months to 2 years in the guardhouse for insubordination, and 3 months to 1 year for absence without leave in peacetime, and up to 5 years in wartime.

BIBLIOGRAPHIES

Section I. Social

RECOMMENDED FURTHER READING

Among the sources consulted in the preparation of this section, the following are recommended as additional reading on the basis of quality and general availability.

Adams, Richard N., et al. *Social Change in Latin America Today*. New York: Harper, 1960.

Bennett, Wendell C. *Ancient Arts of the Andes*. New York: Museum of Modern Art, 1954.

James, Preston Everett. *Latin American*. (3d ed.) New York: Odyssey Press, 1959.

Kubler, George, and Martin, Seria. *Art and Architecture in Spain and Portugal and Their American Dominions 1500–1800*. Baltimore: Penguin Books, 1959.

Linke, Lilo. *Ecuador: Country of Contrasts*. (3d ed.) (Issued under the auspices of the Royal Institute of International Affairs.) London: Oxford University Press, 1960.

Maier, Joseph, and Weatherhead, Richard W. (eds.). *Politics of Change in Latin America*. New York: Praeger, 1964.

Miller, E. V. "Agricultural Ecuador," *Geographical Review*, No. 183, 1959, 183–207.

Parsons, Elsie Clews. *Peguche: A Study of Andean Indians*. Chicago: University of Chicago Press, 1945.

Steward, Julian H. (ed.). *Handbook of the South American Indians*, II, III. Washington: GPO, 1948.

Terán, Francisco. *Geografía del Ecuador*. (2d ed.) Quito: Imprenta del Ministerio del Educación, 1952.

U.S. Department of Agriculture. *Agricultural Geography of Latin America*. Washington: GPO, 1958.

U.S. Department of Labor. Bureau of Labor Statistics. *Labor Developments Abroad*. Washington: 1965.

Uzcátegui, Emilio. "Ecuador's Novel and Novelists," *Américas*, XVI, May 1964, 29–34.

523

OTHER SOURCES USED

Alianza para el Progreso. Comité de los Nueve. "Evaluación del Plan de Desarrollo Económico y Social del Ecuador." Washington: August 1964 (mimeo.).

Alonso, Isidoro, et al. *La Iglesia en Venezuela y Ecuador.* (Estudios Socio-Religiosos Latinoamericanos, Series 3.) Friburg: Oficina Internacional de Investigaciones Sociales de Feres, 1962.

American Geographic Society. *Focus: Ecuador,* IX, February 6, 1959.

Angulo Iñiguez, Diego. *Historia del arte hispanoamericano.* 2 vols. N.pl.: Salvat Editores, 1950.

Anuario pontificio per l'anno 1964. Cittá del Vaticano: Tipografia Poliglotta Vaticana, 1964.

Arias, Augusto. *Panorama de la literatura ecuatoriana.* (4th ed.) Quito: Editorial Lasalle, 1961.

Banco Central del Ecuador. *Memoria del gerente general: correspondiente al ejercicio d 1963.* Quito: Imprenta del Banco Central, 1964.

Banco Interamericano de Desarrollo. Fondo Fiduciario de Progreso Social. *Tercer informe anual: 1963.* Washington: BID, 1964.

Barrera, Isaac J. "Panorama de la Literatura Ecuatoriana," *Mundo Hispano* (Madrid) (Número especial dedicado al Ecuador), 1955, 43, 44, 52.

Bialek, Robert W. *Catholic Politics in Ecuador.* New York: Vantage Press, 1963.

Butland, Gilbert J. *Latin America: A Regional Geography.* London: Longmans, Green, 1961.

Carillo, N. Alfredo. *La Trayectoria del pensamiento filosófico en Latinoamérica.* Quito: Editorial Casa de la Cultura Ecuatoriana, 1959.

Clenetson, Beryl. "Mestizo-Indian Relations in Capilla Loma." (Harvard, Cornell, Columbia Universities Summer Project: 1961) (mimeo.).

Collier, John, Jr., and Buitrón, Aníbal. *The Awakening Valley.* Chicago: University of Chicago Press, 1949.

Cordero Espinosa, Jacinto. "Poesía y Crítica," *Revista del Núcleo del Zuay,* VIII, December 1957, 115–182.

Costales Samaniego, Alfredo. *Tungurahua.* Quito: Talleres Gráficos Nacionales, 1961.

Coxill, H. Wakelin, and Srubb, Kenneth (eds.). *World Christian Handbook—1962.* London: World Dominion Press, 1962.

D'Antonio, William V., and Pikes, Frederick B. (eds.). *Religion, Revolution and Reform.* Washington: Praeger, 1964.

Debuyst, Federico. *La Población en América Latina.* Brussels: Centro de Investigaciones Socio-Religiosas, 1961.

Dutra de Fonseca, Guillermo, and Gelderen, Alfredo M. Van. "La Contribución de la Iniciativa Privada a la Educación en América Latina." N.pl.: Organización de Estados Americanos, January 1963 (mimeo.).

Ebaugh, Cameron D. *Education in Ecuador.* (Federal Security Agency, Office of Education, Bulletin 1947, No. 2). Washington: 1947.

Ecuador. Instituto Nacional de la Vivienda. "Plan Nacional de la Vivienda 1963-70." Quito: 1962 (mimeo.).

Ecuador. Junta Militar de Gobierno. *Mensaje de año nuevo al pueblo ecuatoriano.* Quito: Secretaría General de Gobierno, 1965.

————. *Paz creadora y trabajo fecundo: Mensaje a la nación ecuatoriana, julio de 1963-julio de 1964.* Quito: Talleres Gráficos Nacionales, 1964.

Ecuador. Junta Nacional de Planificación y Coordinación Económica. *Plan general de desarrollo económico y social: Otros servicios y actividades, IV.* Quito: n.d.

————. *Plan general de desarrollo económico y social: Programa nacional de agua potable y alcantarillado.* Quito: n.d.

————. División de Estadística y Censos. *Anuario de estadísticas hospitalarias—1964.* Quito: 1965.

————. *Anuario de estadísticas vitales—1964.* Quito: 1965.

————. *Características de la población y vivienda del Ecuador.* Quito: 1964.

Ecuador. Laws, Statutes, etc. *The Labour Law of the Republic 1938.* Quito: 1955

Pan American Union. *Constitution of the Republic of Ecuador 1946.* Washington: PAU, 1961.

Ecuador. Ministerio de Educación. "Reunión Técnica sobre la Integración de los Planes Sectoriales de Educación en los Planes Generales de Desarrollo Económico y Social." N.pl.: January 1965 (mimeo.).

————. Departamento de Planeamiento Integral. *Informe nacional del Ecuador sobre educación y adistramiento para el examen anual del progreso económico y social de los países latinoamericanos.* (III Reunión Interamericana de Ministros de Educación.) Quito: 1963.

————. *Plan ecuatoriano de educación.* Quito: Talleres Gráficos de Educación, 1964.

Ecuador. Ministerio de Previsión Social y Trabajo. *Informe a la nación 1960–1961.* Quito: Editorial "Fray Jodoco Ricke," n.d.

———. Dirección General de Servicio Social. "Informe." Quito: November 1964 (mimeo.).

Ecuador. Servicio Nacional de Salud. "Plan Decenal de Salud Pública para el Ecuador; Resumen General." Quito: 1964 (mimeo.).

Ferdon, Edwin N., Jr. *Studies in Ecuadorian Geography.* Santa Fe: University of New Mexico Press, 1950.

Fulling, Kay Painter. *The Cradle of American Art: Ecuador, Its Contemporary Artists.* New York: North River Press, 1948.

Garcés Larrea, Cristóbal. "El Arte y la Literatura Ecuatorianos," *Atenéo Ecuatoriano,* III, October 1953, 141–145.

Giner de los Ríos, Francisco. "Historia y Novela del Ecuador," *Cuadernos Americanos* (Mexico), XXXIX, May-June 1948, 286–292.

Guerrero, Jorge. "El Arte Ecuatoriano de la Colonia," *Revista de América* (Bogotá), X, June 1947, 331–344.

Houtart, François, and Pin, Emile. *The Church and the Latin American Revolution.* New York: Sheed and Ward, 1965.

Hurel Cepeda, Jorge. *Estudio biológico sobre el campesino ecuatoriano.* Quito: Editorial Casa de la Cultura Ecuatoriana, 1958.

Inter-American Development Bank. Social Progress Trust Fund. *Fourth Annual Report: 1964.* Washington: 1965.

Jaramillo Alvarado, Pío. *El Indio ecuatoriano.* Quito: Editorial Casa de la Cultura Ecuatoriana, 1954.

Jaramillo Pérez, César. *Historia del Ecuador.* Quito: Editorial la Salle, 1959.

Jurra, John. "The Historic Tribes of Ecuador." In John H. Steward (ed.), *Handbook of the South American Indians,* II. (Smithsonian Institution, Bureau of American Ethnology, Bulletin 143.) Washington: GPO, 1946.

Lannoy, Juan Luis. *Niveles de vida en América Latina.* Geneva: Feres, 1963.

Larrea, Juan Ignacio. *La Iglesia y el estado en el Ecuador.* Sevilla: Escuela de Estudios Hispanoamericanos, 1954.

Linke, Lilo. "Building for a Conference and After," *Américas,* II, October 1959, 9–14.

Llerena, José Alfredo, and Chaves, Alfredo. *La Pintura ecuatoriana del siglo XX.* Quito: Imprenta de la Universidad, n.d.

Mecham, John Lloyd. *Church and State in Latin America.* Chapel Hill: University of North Carolina Press, 1934.

Mena Villamar, Claudio. "Pintura Joven Ecuatoriana," *El Comercio* (Quito), October 26, 1958.

Mencías, Jorge. *Riobamba (Ecuador).* (Estudios Sociologicos Latinoamericanos, Series 16.) Friburg: Oficina Internacional de Investigaciones Sociales de Feres, 1962.

Moreno Galvan, José María. "Pasado y Presente del Arte Ecuatoriano," *Mundo Hispano* (Madrid) (Número especial dedicado al Ecuador), 1955.

Muller, Richard. *The History of the Conquest of Quito.* Santa Domingo: Virgilio Montalvo, 1929.

Navarro, José Gabriel. *Artes plásticas ecuatorianas.* Mexico: Fondo de Cultura Económica, 1945.

Orellana, J. Gonzalo. *Resumen histórico del Ecuador 1830–1930,* II. Quito: Editorial "Fray Jodoco Ricke," 1948.

Organización Iberoamericana de Seguridad Social. Monografías Nacionales. *Los Seguros sociales en el Ecuador.* Madrid: OISS, 1960.

Pan American Health Organization. *Health Conditions in the Americas 1961–1962.* (Scientific Publications No. 104.) Washington: PAHO, August 1964.

————. *Report of the Director of the Pan American Sanitary Bureau. Regional Office of the World Health Organization 1964.* (Official Document No. 63.) Washington: PAHO, August, 1965.

Pan American Union. *The Pan-American System.* Washington: 1965.

————. *Programas para adultos y su integración con los planes nacionales de desarrollo económico y social en el Ecuador, el Perú y Venezuela.* Washington: PAU, 1965.

————. Departamento de Asuntos Educativos. *Carreras Universitarias,* II. Washington: PAU, 1962.

Pan American Union. División de Filosofía y Letras. Departmento de Asuntos Culturales. *Diccionario de la literatura latinoamericana: Ecuador.* Washington: PAU, 1962.

Paredes, Diógenes. "Panorama de las Artes Plásticas Ecuatorianas," *Anales* (Universidad Central del Ecuador), LXXXVI, March 1957, 125–130.

Pareja Diezcanseco, Alfredo. "De la Literatura Ecuatoriana Contemporánea," *Revista Nacional de Cultura* (Caracas), XVI, May-June 1956, 52–78.

————. "El Ensayo en la Literature Ecuatoriana Actual," *Cuadernos Americanos* (Mexico), XVI, July-August 1957, 233–246.

————. *Historia del Ecuador.* (2d ed.) 2 vols. Quito: Editorial Casa de la Cultura Ecuatoriana, 1958.

Pattee, Richard. *El Catolicism contemporáneo en Hispanoamerica.* Buenos Aires. Editorial Fedes, 1951.

Peñaherrera de Costales, Piedad, and Costales Samaniego, Alfredo. *Coangue ó historia cultural y social de los negros del Chota y Salinas.* ("Llacta," No. 7.) Quito: Instituto Ecuatoriano de Antropología y Geografía, 1959.

———. *Los Salacas.* ("Llacta," No. 8.) Quito: Instituto. Ecuatoriano de Antropología y Geografía, 1959.

Reyes, Oscar Efreno. *Breve historia general del Ecuador.* (3d ed.) Quito: Talleres Gráficos Nacionales, 1949.

Ribadeneira M., Edmundo. *La moderna novela ecuatoriana.* Quito: Editorial Casa de la Cultura Ecuatoriana, n.d.

Robinson Perez, Lillian. "Forgotten Treasure in Esmeraldas Province, Ecuador," *Américas,* II, May 1959, 14–18.

Rycroft, William Stanley, and Clemmer, Myrtle M. *A Factual Study of Latin America.* New York: Commission on Ecumenical Missions and Relations of the United Presbyterian Church in the USA, 1963.

Salgado, Luís H. *Música vernácula ecuatoriana.* Quito: Editorial Casa de la Cultura Ecuatoriana, 1952.

Saunders, John Van Dyke. *The People of Ecuador: A Demographic Analysis.* Gainesville: University of Florida Press, 1961.

———. *La Población del Ecuador: Un análisis del censo de 1950.* Quito: Editorial Casa de la Cultura Ecuatoriana, 1959.

Schwartz, Kessel. "Some Aspects of the Contemporary Novel of Ecuador," *Hispania,* XXXVIII, September 1955, 294–301.

Silverman, Martin G. "Community, State and Church: A Study in the Village of San Francisco, Chimborazo Province, Ecuador." (Report prepared for the Columbia-Cornell-Harvard Summer Field Studies Program.) N.pl.: n.pub., 1960 (mimeo.).

Taylor, Paul S. "Ecuador: A Case Study of Relationships Between Community Development and Agrarian Reform." Quito: 1960 (mimeo.).

Technical Assistance Information Clearing House: *Health and Medical Projects Abroad of U.S. Voluntary and Non-Profit Organizations.* New York: 1962.

Torres Caicedo, Reinaldo. *Los Estratos socioeconómicos del Ecuador.* Quito: Junta Nacional de Planificación y Coordinación Económica, 1960.

Toscano, Humberto (ed.). *El Ecuador visto por los extranjeros.* Editorial J. M. Cajica, Jr., 1960.

United Nations Educational, Scientific and Cultural Organization. "Educación y Economía en Ecuador." N.pl.: July 1962 (mimeo.).

U.S. Congress. 88th, 1st Session. House of Representatives. *Special Study Mission to Latin America: Peru, Ecuador Colombia, Panama, Costa Rica.* Washington: GPO, 1963.

U.S. Department of Health, Education and Welfare. Division of International Studies and Services. *Educational Data: Ecuador.* (Information on Education around the World Series. No. 64.) February 1963.

U.S. Department of Health, Education and Welfare. Social Security Administration. Division of Research and Statistics. *Social Security Programs Throughout the World, 1964.* Washington: GPO, 1964.

U.S. Department of Labor. Bureau of Labor Statistics. *Labor Digest,* No. 39, 1964.

U.S. United States Operations Mission/Ecuador. "Country Plan for Hospital and Health Center Coordination and Construction in Ecuador." N.pl.: January 1960 (mimeo.).

Universidad Central del Ecuador. Instituto de Estudios Administrativos Oficina Nacional de Personal de la Secretaría Técnica de la Administración. *Salarios en el Ecuador; agosto-septiembre 1963.* Quito: 1963.

Uzcátegui, Maruja. "Apuntes para una Historia de la Protección y de los Servicios Sociales en el Ecuador," *Filosofía, Letras y Educación* (Universidad Central del Ecuador), April-June 1952, 111–140.

Vargas, José María. *El Arte ecuatoriano.* Puebla: Editorial J. M. Cajica, Jr., 1960.

Von Hagen, Victor Wolfgang. *Ecuador and the Galápagos Islands.* Norman: University of Oklahoma Press, 1949.

Wolf, Theodor. *Geografía geología del Ecuador.* Leipzig: Tipografía de F. A. Brockhaus, 1892.

World Health Organization. *Second Report on World Health Situation 1957–60.* (Official Records, No. 122.) Geneva: WHO, January 1963.

(Various issues of the following newspapers and periodicals were also used in the preparation of this section: *New York Times,* from January 1956 through December 1965; *El Comercio* [Quito], from November 1961 through December 1965; *El Telégrafo* [Guayaquil], from May 1963 through December 1965; and *Washington Post, Evening Star* and *Sunday Star* [Washington], from January through December 1965.)

Section II. Political

RECOMMENDED FURTHER READING

Among the sources consulted in the preparation of this section, the following are recommended as additional reading on the basis of quality and general availability.

Alexander, Robert J. *Communism in Latin America.* New Brunswick: Rutgers University Press, 1957.

"Atlantic Report on Ecuador," *Atlantic*, CCXVI, November 1965, 12–22.

Bemelmans, Ludwig. *The Donkey Inside.* New York: Dutton, 1964.

Blanksten, George I. *Ecuador: Constitutions and Caudillos.* New York: Russell and Russell, 1964.

——. "Ecuador: The Politics of Instability." Chapter 13 in Martin C. Needler (ed.), *Political Systems of Latin America.* New York: Van Nostrand, 1964.

Bowen, J. David. "Ecuador on a Tightrope," *Reporter*, XXVI, March 29, 1962, 30–33.

Casa de la Cultura Ecuatoriana. *El Ecuador exhibe ante el mundo la justicia de su cauca.* Quito: Editorial Casa de la Cultura Ecuatoriana, 1960.

Ecuador. Laws, Statutes, etc.

Pan American Union. *Constitution of the Republic of Ecuador 1946.* Washington: PAU, 1961.

Editor and Publisher International Yearbook 1965. (XLV ed.) New York: Editor and Publisher Company, 1965.

Herring, Hubert. *A History of Latin America from the Beginning to the Present.* New York: Knopf, 1960.

Houtart, François, and Pin, Emile. *The Church and the Latin American Revolution.* New York: Sheed and Ward, 1965.

Ireland, Gordon. *Boundaries, Possessions and Conflicts in South America.* Cambridge: Harvard University Press, 1938.

Johnson, John J. *The Military and Society in Latin America.* Stanford: Stanford University Press, 1964.

——. (ed.). *Continuity and Change in Latin America.* Stanford: Stanford University Press, 1964.

Linke, Lilo. "Ecuador's Politics: President Velasco's Fourth Exile," *The World Today* (London), XVIII, February 1962, 57–69.

MacDonald, Austin F. *Latin American Politics and Government.* New York: Crowell, 1954.

Maier, Joseph, and Weatherhead, Richard W. (eds.). *Politics of Change in Latin America.* New York: Praeger, 1964.

Mander, John. "Mexico City to Buenos Aires," *Encounter*, XXV, September 1965, 5–14.

Merrill, John Calhoun; Bryan, Carter R.; and Alisky, Marvin. *The Foreign Press.* Baton Rouge: Louisiana State University Press, 1964.

Munro, Dana Gardner. *The Latin American Republics: A History.* (3d ed.) New York: Appleton-Century-Crofts, 1960.

Needler, Martin C. *Anatomy of a Coup d'Etat: Ecuador 1963.* (Special Article Series No. 1.) Washington: Institute for the Comparative Study of Political Systems, 1964.

_____. *Latin American Politics in Perspective.* New York: Van Nostrand, 1963.

Nehemkis, Peter. *Latin American Myth and Reality.* New York: Knopf, 1964.

Pitt-Rivers, Julian. "Who Are the Indians," *Encounter,* XXV, September 1965, 41–49.

Poppino, Rollie E. *International Communism in Latin America (1917–1963).* London: Free Press of Glencoe, 1964.

Szulc, Tad. *The Winds of Revolution.* New York: Praeger, 1963.

Williams, Mary W.; Bartlett, Ruhl J.; and Miller, Russel E. *The People and Politics of Latin America.* New York: Ginn, 1958.

Zook, David H. Jr. *Zarumilla-Marañón: The Ecuador-Peru Dispute.* New York: Bookman Associates, 1964.

OTHER SOURCES USED

Barrera, Isaac J. *La Prensa en el Ecuador.* Quito: Editorial Casa de la Cultura Ecuatoriana, 1955.

Bialek, Robert W. *Catholic Politics in Ecuador.* New York: Vantage Press, 1963.

Borja y Borja, Ramiro. *Las Constituciones del Ecuador.* Madrid: Ediciones Cultura Hispánica, 1951.

Bustamente-Muñoz, Antonio. *Lista de los instrumentos internacionales concluidos por el Ecuador.* Quito: Editorial Casa de la Cultura Ecuatoriana, 1960.

"Civil Resentment of Junta is Growing," *The Vision Letter* (New York, May 25, 1965.

Council on Foreign Relations, Inc. *Political Handbook and Atlas of the World 1964.* New York: Harper and Row, 1964.

Davis, Harold. *Government and Politics in Latin America.* New York: Ronald Press, 1958.

Dubois, Jules. *Operation America: The Communist Conspiracy in Latin America.* New York: Walker, 1963.

Ecuador. Junta Militar del Gobierno. *Paz creadora y trabajo fecundo: Mensaje a la nación ecuatoriana, julio de 1963-julio de 1964.* Quito: Talleres Gráficos Nacionales, 1964.

Ecuador. Laws, Statutes, etc. Corte Suprema de Justicia. *Constitución política de la República del Ecuador.* Quito: Talleres Gráficos Nacionales, 1964.

Acción Revolucionaria Nacionalista Ecuatoriana. *Proyecto de constitución para la República del Ecuador.* Quito: Talleres Gráficos Nacionales, 1964.

Elliott, J. H. "The Spanish Heritage," *Encounter,* XXV, September 1965, 34–40.

Espinosa-Polit, Aurelio. *Reseña histórica del himno nacional ecuatoriano.* Quito: Talleres Gráficos Nacionales, 1948.

García-Velasco, Rafael. *El Problema territorial ecuatoriano.* Quito: Editorial Casa de la Cultura Ecuatoriana, 1965.

————. *Ley suprema de la controversia limítrofe.* Quito: Industrias Gráficas "CYMA," 1961.

Jácome Moscoso, Rodrigo. *Derecho constitucional ecuatoriano.* Quito: Imprenta de la Universidad Central, 1931.

"June Elections in Ecuador," *America,* CII, February 20, 1960, 600.

Linke, Lilo, and Albornoz, Miguel. *El Comercio de Quito y la Misión Andina del Ecuador.* Quito: Editorial la Unión, 1962.

Lovato, Juan Isaac; Vázquez-Carrizosa, Alfredo; Rodrigo-Guerrero, Ignacio; and Fernández, Gustavo Ariosa. *Hacia una nueva conciencia americana.* Quito: Industrias Gráficas "CYMA," 1961.

Marin, Rufino. *Ecuador, la grán mutilada.* Quito: Editorial Universitaria, 1959.

Mora-Bowen, Alfonso. *La Educación cívica.* Quito: Editorial Santo Domingo, n.d.

"Morning After," *Newsweek,* LXII, July 29, 1963, 49.

O'Hara, Hazel. "The Voice of the Andes," *Américas,* XIII, September 1961, 27–30.

Operation and Policy Research, Inc. Institute for the Comparative Study of Political Systems. *Methods of Electing National Executives and National Legislatures in Latin American Countries.* (Special Memorandum No. 21.) Washington: COPS, n.d.

Peru. Ministerio de Guerra. *Estudio de la cuestion de limites entre el Perú y el Ecuador.* Lima: 1961.

"Pressure is Growing for Junta to Get Out," *The Vision Letter* (New York), July 14, 1965.

"Progress After a Coup," *Time,* LXXXI, March 8, 1963, 29, 30.

Reyes, Oscar Efreno. *Breve historia general del Ecuador.* (3d ed.) Quito: Talleres Gráficos Nacionales, 1949.

Roberts, Edwin A., Jr. (ed.). *Latin American Newsbook.* Washington: National Observer, 1964.

Rubio-Vasquez, Nicolás. *El Himno nacional ecuatoriano y su autor Don Juan Leon Mera.* Quito: n.pub., 1964.

Shepherd, William R. *Historical Atlas.* New York: Barnes and Noble, 1956.

"Tipple Topple," *Newsweek,* LXI, January 14, 1963, 40.

United Nations Educational, Scientific and Cultural Organization. *World Communications.* New York: UNESCO Publication Center, 1964.

U.S. Department of Defense. Military Assistance Institute.

Country Study: South America. Washington: American Institute for Research, 1962.

U.S. United States Information Agency. *Fact Book for Latin America, 1962.* Washington: 1963.

"U.S. and Ecuador Reaffirm Traditional Friendship" (Text of Joint Communique between President Kennedy and President Carlos Julio Arosemena), *State Department Bulletin*, XLVII, August 13, 1962, 251–253.

University of Guayaquil. Instituto de Investigaciones Económicas. "Guayaquil Económico." Guayaquil: 1964 (mimeo.).

"Upheaval in Ecuador," *New Republic*, CXLV, November 20, 1961, 64, 65.

Urbanski, Edmund Stephen. "Ecuador's Socio-Political Mosaic," *Current History*, XLVI, January 1964, 18–25.

"Violence in Three Stages," *Time*, LXXIII, June 15, 1959, 41.

Whitaker, Arthur P. *The United States and South America.* Cambridge: Harvard University Press, 1948.

Wolfe, N. W. "Images of the U.S. in the Latin American Press," *Journalism Quarterly*, XLI, Winter 1964, 79–86.

World Radio-TV Handbook, 1965. Hellerup: World Radio-Television Handbook Company, 1965.

Yepes, Jesus M. *La Controversia fronteriza.* Quito: Editorial Casa de la Cultura Ecuatoriana, 1960.

(Various issues of the following newspapers and periodicals were also used in the preparation of this section: *New York Times*, from January 1956 through December 1965; *El Comercio* [Quito], from November 1961 through December 1965; *El Telégrafo* [Guayaquil], from May 1963 through December 1965; and *Washington Post, Evening Star and Sunday Star* [Washington], from January through December 1965.)

Section III. Economic

RECOMMENDED FURTHER READING

Among the sources consulted in the preparation of this section, the following are recommended as additional reading on the basis of quality and general availability.

Ecuador. Laws, Statutes, etc.
Pan American Union. *A Statement of the Laws of Ecuador in Matters Affecting Business.* Washington: 1955.

_____. *Supplement: A Statement of the Laws of Ecuador in Matters Affecting Business*, No. 2. Washington: 1961.

James, Preston Everett. *Latin America.* (3d ed.) New York: Odyssey Press, 1959.

Linke, Lilo. *Ecuador: Country of Contrasts.* (3d ed.) (Issued under the auspices of the Royal Institute of International Affairs.) London: Oxford University Press, 1960.

May, Stacy, and Plaza, Galo. *The United Fruit Company in Latin America.* Washington: National Planning Association, 1958.

Organization of American States. *Economic Survey of Latin America, Pt. I.* Baltimore: Johns Hopkins University Press, 1962.

Poblete Troncoso, Moisés, and Burnett, Ben G. *The Rise of the Latin American Labor Movement.* New York: Bookman Associates, 1960.

U.S. Department of Labor. Bureau of International Labor Affairs. Bureau of Labor Statistics. *Labor Law and Practice in Ecuador.* (BLS Report No. 242.) Washington: GPO, 1963.

OTHER SOURCES USED

Alexander, Robert J. *Communism in Latin America.* New Brunswick: Rutgers University Press, 1957.

Alianza para el Progreso. "Report on the Prospects for Ecuadorian Exports," by Remy Freire. Washington: May 24, 1965 (mimeo.).

———. Comité de los Nueve. "Evaluación del Plan de Desarrollo Económico y Social del Ecuador." Washington: August 1964 (mimeo.).

Alianza para el Progreso. Comité Interamericano de la Alianza para el Progreso. "La Política de Desarrollo del Ecuador y las Necesidades de Cooperación Externa." Washington: May 28, 1965 (mimeo.).

Arthur D. Little, Inc. "Screening of Industrial Projects for Feasibility Studies." (A report to Centro de Desarrollo.) Quito: January 1965 (mimeo.).

"Atlantic Report on Ecuador," *Atlantic,* CCXVI, November 1965, 12–22.

Banco Central del Ecuador. *Boletín.* January-May 1964; June-July 1964; August, September and October 1964; January-March 1965.

———. *Comercio Exterior Ecuatoriano* (Nos. 196–201, January-June 1964.) Quito: Imprenta del Banco Central, n.d.

———. *Información estadística.* Quito: 1965.

———. *Memoria del gerente general: correspondiente al ejercicio de 1960.* Quito: Imprenta del Banco Central, 1961.

———. *Memoria del gerente general: correspondiente al ejercicio de 1961.* Quito: Imprenta del Banco Central, 1962.

————. *Memoria del gerente general: correspondiente al ejercicio de 1962.* Quito: Imprenta del Banco Central, 1963.

————. *Memoria del gerente general: correspondiente al ejercicio de 1963.* Quito: Imprenta del Banco Central, 1964.

————. *Memoria del gerente general: correspondiente al ejercicio de 1964.* Quito: Imprenta del Banco Central, 1965.

Beitzel, George B.; Koster, Wesley R.; Hull, Raymond R.; and Ogden, Robert P. "Report on Development Possibilities for Chemical Fertilizers and Basic Chemicals in Ecuador." (Survey and Report sponsored by the International Cooperation Administration in conjunction with the Ecuadorian National Planning Board.) Quito: 1960 (mimeo.).

Butland, Gilbert J. *Latin America: A Regional Geography.* London: Longmans, Green, 1961.

Cámara de Comercio de Quito. *Directorio comercial de Quito, 1964.* Quito: 1964.

Casagrande, Joseph B.; Thompson, Stephen I.; and Young, Philip D. "Colonization as a Research Frontier: The Ecuadorian Case." In Robert A. Manners, *Process and Pattern in Culture: Essays in Honor of Julian Steward.* Chicago: Aldine, 1964.

Chase Manhattan Bank. *Latin American Business Highlights* (Third Quarter), XV, No. 3, 1965.

Checchi and Company. *Expanding Private Investment for Ecuador's Economic Growth: A Report and Recommendations.* Prepared for the Government of Ecuador and the International Cooperation Administration.). Washington: 1961.

Comité Interamericano de Desarrollo Agrícola. *Inventorio de la información básica para la programación del desarrollo agrícola en la América Latina.* Washington: CIDA (published for Pan American Union), n.d.

Dwinn, Alfred D. "Ecuador's New Mineral Development Plan," *Engineering and Mining Journal,* October 1964.

The Economist Intelligence Unit, Ltd. *Quarterly Economic Review: Annual Supplement—Peru, Bolivia, Ecuador* (London), 1963–65.

Ecuador. *Directoria industrial por empresas y por productos elaborados.* (Publicado por la Officina Ecuatoriana para la Asociación Latinoamericana de Libre Comercio.) N.pl.: 1963.

————. Development Center. *Businessmen Look at Ecuador.* Quito: Impreso en Editorial Colon, October 1963.

Ecuador. Instituto Nacional de Investigaciones Agropecuarias. *Informe 1963,* I. Quito: n.d.

Ecuador. Junta Militar de Gobierno. *Mensaje de año nuevo al pueblo ecuatoriano.* Quito: Secretaría General del Gobierno, 1965.

————. *Paz creadora y trabajo fecundo: Mensaje a la nación*

ecuatoriana, julio de 1963-julio de 1964. Quito: Talleres Gráficos Nacionales, 1964.

Ecuador. Junta Nacional de Planificación y Coordinación Económica. "Elementos para la programación agropecuaria del Ecuador." Quito: Organización de los Estados Americanos, 1963 (mimeo.).

――――. Normas para la elaboración de presupuestos municipales. Quito: Estructura Presupuestaria, 1961.

――――. "Plan Carchi." Quito: Diagnostico y Programas Sectoriales, 1962.

――――. Plan nacional de electrificación. Quito: 1956.

――――. "Resumen del Plan General de Desarrollo Económica y Social del Ecuador." Quito: 1963 (mimeo.).

Ecuador. Laws, Statutes, etc.
"The Labour Law of the Republic of Ecuador (1938 with Concordance)." (Trans., R. J. Baker.) N.pl.: 1955 (mimeo.).

Law of Agrarian Reform and Colonization. (Supreme Decree. No. 1480.) Quito: 1964.

Ley de fomento de la artesania y la pequeña industria. (Descreta el 15 de Enero de 1965.) Quito: Editora SECICA, 1965.

Ley de fomento industrial. (Decree of December 29, 1964.) Quito: Editora SECICA, 1964.

Ley de la comisión de valores corporación financiera nacional. (Registro Official No. 316; Decreto Supremo No. 1726.) Quito: Talleres Gráficos Nacionales, 1964.

Comisión Tecnica del Presupuesto. Registro Oficial. Proyecto de ley de presupuesto general del estado para el ejercicio financiero de 1962. Quito: Talleres Gráficos Nacionales, 1962.

Organo del Gobierno del Ecuador. Administración de la Junta Militar de Gobierno. Proyecto de ley de presupuesto general del estado para el ejercicio financiero de 1965, II. Quito: Talleres Gráficos Nacionales, 1965.

U.S. Department of Commerce. Industrial Development Law of Ecuador. (Overseas Business Reports, No. 62-17.) Washington: GPO, 1962.

Ecuador. Ministerio de Fomento. Informe a la nación: Dirección general de minas y hidro car buros, I. N.pl.: 1962.

――――. Dirección Nacional del Banano. Revista ecuatoriana del banano I. N.pl.: 1964.

Ecuador. Ministerio de Relaciones Exteriores. Recapitulación de los instrumentos internacionales celebrados por el Ecuador en materia económica y comercial, by Olemedo Monteverdi Paz. N.pl: 1962.

Inter-American Development Bank. *Activities, 1961–1963.* Washington: IADB, 1964.

―――. *Institutional Reforms and Social Development Trends in Latin America.* Washington: 1963.

―――. Social Progress Trust Fund. *First Annual Report: 1961.* Washington: 1962.

―――. *Second Annual Report: 1962.* Washington: 1963.

―――. *Third Annual Report: 1963.* Washington: 1964.

―――. *Fourth Annual Report: 1964.* Washington: 1965.

International Bank for Reconstruction and Development. *The World Bank Group in the Americas.* Washington: IBRD, June 1963.

International Bank for Reconstruction and Development and International Development Association. *Annual Report, 1964–1965.* Washington: 1965.

International Monetary Fund. *Direction of Trade Annual 1958–62.* Washington: IMF, 1964.

Italconsult. *Elementos para la programación agropecuaria del Ecuador,* VIII. (Report prepared under contract to the Organization of American States and the Government of Ecuador.) Rome: N.pub., 1963.

Minerals Yearbook 1962. (Prepared by U.S. Department of the Interior.) Washington: GPO, 1962.

Naciones Unidas. *Estudios sobre la electricidad en América Latina.* I, II. México, D. F.: 1962.

Pan American Health Organization. *Annual Report of the Director.* Washington: PAHO, July 1964.

Pan American Union. *Ecuador.* (American Republics Series.) Washington: 1964 (reprint).

―――. *Petroleum.* Washington: 1964.

―――. "Taxation in Ecuador." N.pl: 1965 (mimeo.).

―――. Instituto Interamericano de Estadística. *América en cifras, 1963, III: Situación económica, agricultural ganaderia, silvicultura, gaza y penca.* Washington: 1964.

Parsons, Elsie Clews. *Peguche: A Study of Andean Indians.* Chicago: University of Chicago Press, 1945.

Price, Waterhouse and Co. *Doing Business in Ecuador.* New York: 1960.

Production Yearbook, XV. Rome: Food and Agriculture Organization, 1961.

Stanford Research Institute. "The Artisan Community in Ecuador's Modernizing Economy." (Prepared for La Junta Nacional de Planificación y Coordinación.) Menlo Park: November 1963 (mimeo.).

Surveys and Research Corporation. "Economic and Managerial

Appraisal of Ecuador's Government Enterprises." Washington: December 1, 1963 (mimeo.).

―――. "Toward Expansion and Diversification of Ecuador's Exports." Washington: 1963 (mimeo.).

United Nations. Economic Commission for Latin America. "Productivity of the Agricultural Sector in Ecuador," *Bulletin,* VI, No. 2, October, 1961.

U.S. Agency for International Development. *Operations Report, FY 1964.* Washington: 1964.

―――. "Review of Budgets, Government of Ecuador, Fiscal Years 1963-1964." (Prepared by Booz-Allen Hamilton International, Inc.) N.pl.: 1963 (mimeo.).

―――. Point IV Mission to Ecuador. "Objectives and Activities of the Intalconsult Mission to Ecuador." Quito: December 1963 (mimeo.).

U.S. Agency for International Development. Statistics and Reports Division. *AID Economic Data Book for Latin America, Ecuador.* Washington: 1964.

U.S. Department of Agriculture. "A Review of Agricultural Research in Ecuador," by A. J. Loustalot. Washington: 1965 (mimeo.).

U.S. Department of Commerce. *Basic Data on the Economy of Ecuador.* (World Trade Information Service, Economic Reports, Pt. 1, No. 60-50.). Washington: GPO, 1960.

―――. *Basic Data on the Economy of Ecuador.* (Overseas Business Reports, OBR No. 64-74.) Washington: GPO, 1964.

―――. *Economic Developments in Ecuador 1957.* (World Trade Information Service, Economic Reports, Pt. 1, No. 58-24.) Washington: GPO, 1958.

―――. *Economic Review of Ecuador, 1950.* (Foreign Service Reports Series, No. 26.) Washington: 1951.

―――. *Foreign Trade Regulations of Ecuador.* (Overseas Business Reports, OBR No. 64-28.) Washington: GPO, 1964.

―――. *Industrial Encouragement Law of Ecuador.* (World Trade Information Service, Economic Reports, Pt. 1, No. 58-10.) Washington: GPO, 1958.

―――. Bureau of Foreign and Domestic Commerce. *Economic Review of Ecuador, 1949.* (International Reference Service, VII, No. 72.) Washington: GPO, 1950.

―――. *Ecuador-Economic Conditions in 1944.* (International Reference Service, II, No. 49.) Washington: GPO, 1945.

U.S. Department of Commerce. Bureau of Foreign Commerce, *Investment in Ecuador.* Washington: GPO, 1958.

U.S. Department of Commerce. Bureau of International Business, Operations. Trade Missions Division. *Seven Americans in Ecuador.* Washington: 1961.

U.S. Department of Commerce. Office of International Trade. *Economic Conditions in Ecuador, 1945.* (International Reference Service, III, No. 52.) Washington: GPO, 1946.

————. "Economic Review of Ecuador, 1946." (International Reference Service, VI, Supplement No. 11.) Washington: 1949. (mimeo.).

————. *Economic Review of Ecuador, 1947.* (International Reference Service, V, No. 74.) Washington: GPO, 1948.

————. *Economic Situation in Ecuador, 1946.* (International Reference Service, IV, No. 52.) Washington: GPO, 1947.

U.S. Department of Labor. Bureau of International Labor Affairs. Bureau of Labor Statistics. *Directory of Labor Organizations Western Hemisphere,* II. Washington: GPO, 1964.

U.S. International Cooperation Administration. *Ecuador's Participation in the Alliance for Progress.* N.pl: 1961.

University of Guayaquil. Instituto de Investigaciones Económicas. "Guayaquil Económico." Guayaquil: 1964 (mimeo.).

World Aviation Directory, 1963-64. Washington: American Aviation Publications, 1965.

(Various issues of the following newspapers and periodicals were also used in the preparation of this section: *New York Times,* from January 1956 through December 1965; *El Comercio/* Quito/, from November 1961 through December 1965; *El Telégrafo/*Guayaquil, from May 1963 through December 1965; *Boletin/*Ecuador Embassy in Washington/, from July 19 through November 8, 1965; *Economic Summary: Ecuador* [United States Embassy in Quito], from August 2, 1962, through February 19, 1965; and *Washington Post, Evening Star* and *Sunday Star* [Washington], from January through December 1965.)

Section IV. National Security

RECOMMENDED FURTHER READING

Among the sources consulted in the preparation of this section, the following are recommended as additional reading on the basis of quality and general availability.

Alexander, Robert J. *Communism in Latin America.* New Brunswick: Rutgers University Press, 1957.

Blanksten, George I. *Ecuador: Constitutions and Caudillos.* New York: Russell and Russell, 1964.

Ecuador. Laws, Statutes, etc.

Pan American Union. *Constitution of the Republic of Ecuador, 1946.* Washington: PAU, 1961.

Franklin, Albert B. *Ecuador: Portrait of a People.* New York: Doubleday Doran, 1943.

Herring, Hubert. *A History of Latin America from the Beginning to the Present.* New York: Knopf, 1960.

Linke, Lilo. *Ecuador: Country of Contrasts.* (3d ed.) (Issued under the auspices of the Royal Institute of International Affairs.) London: Oxford University Press, 1960.

Munro, Dana Gardner. *The Latin American Republics: A History.* (3d ed.) New York: Appleton-Century-Crofts, 1960.

Needler, Martin C. *Anatomy of a Coup d'Etat: Ecuador 1963.* (Special Article Series No. 1.) Washington: Institute for the Comparative Study of Political Systems, 1964.

Plaza, Galo. *Problems of Democracy in Latin America.* Chapel Hill: University of North Carolina Press, 1957.

Poppino, Rollie E. *International Communism in Latin America (1917–1963).* London: Free Press of Glencoe, 1964.

Stokes, William S. *Latin American Politics.* New York: Crowell, 1959.

Wilgus, Alva Curtis (ed.). *Colonial Hispanic America.* New York: Russell and Russell, 1963.

OTHER SOURCES USED

Borja y Borja, Romiro. *Las Constituciones del Ecuador.* Madrid: Ediciones Cultura Hispánica, 1951.

Borrero Vega. *Estudio del Codigo Procesal Penal.* Cuenca: 1952.

Chiriboga N., Angel Isaac. *Campañas de la Libertad, II.* Quito: Talleres Graficos Estado Mayor General, 1948.

Claggett, Helen L. *The Administration of Justice in Latin America.* New York: Oceana Publications, 1952.

Donovan, John. *Red Machete.* New York: Bobbs-Merrill, 1962.

Dubois, Jules. *Operation America: The Communist Conspiracy in Latin America.* New York: Walker, 1963.

Ecuador. *Informes: Corte Suprema de Justicias de 1959.* Quito: Talleres Gráficos Nacionales, 1960.

———. *Manual de Gobierno.* Quito: Talleres Gráficos Nacionales, 1962.

———. *Recopilación de Leyes.* Quito: Talleres Gráficos Nacionales, 1951.

———. Laws, Statutes, etc.
Constitution y leyes de la republica. Quito: Talleres Gráficos Nacionales, 1960.

Johnson, John J. *The Military and Society in Latin America.* Stanford: Stanford University Press, 1964.

————. *The Role of Military in Underdeveloped Countries.*
Princeton: Princeton University Press, 1961.

Lieuwen, Edwin. *Generals vs. Presidents.* New York: Praeger,
1964.

Linke, Lilo. "Ecuador's Politics: President Velasco's Fourth
Exile," *The World Today* (London), XVIII, February 1962,
57-69.

Mitre, Bartolomé. *Historia de San Martín.* Buenos Aires: n.
pub., 1943.

Prescott, William H. *The Conquest of Peru.* (New American
Library, Ancient Civilizations.) New York: Mentor, 1962.

Reyes, Oscar Efreno. *Breve historia general del Ecuador.* (3d
ed.) Quito: Talleres Gráficos Nacionales, 1949.

Roucek, Joseph Slobey. "Ecuador in Geopolitics," *Contemporary
Review* (London), CCV, February 1964, 74–82.

Schmitt, Kart M., and Burks, David D. *Evolution or Chaos.*
New York: Praeger, 1963.

U.S. Congress. 88th, 1st Session. Senate. Committee on the
Judiciary. *Documentation of the Communist Pentration in
Latin America.* Washington: GPO, 1964.

Urbanski, Edmund Stephen. "The Development of Andean
America," *Current History,* XCII, February 1962, 96-105.

————. "Ecuador's Socio-Political Mosaic," *Current History,*
XLVI, January 1964, 18-25.

(Various issues of the following newspapers and periodicals
were also used in the preparation of this section: *New York
Times,* from January 1956 through December 1965; *El Comercio*
[Quito], from November 1961 through December 1965; *El Tele-
grafo* [Guayaquil], from May 1963 through December 1965; and
Washington Post, Evening Star and *Sunday Star* [Washington],
from January through December 1965.)

GLOSSARY

abrazo—An embrace with simultaneous and mutual backslapping.

AFL-CIO—American Federation of Labor-Congress of Industrial Organizations.

AFP—Agence France Press (French Press Agency).

ahijado—Godchild. *See compadre.*

AID—United States Agency for International Development.

anejos—Lit., annexes; small hamlets.

AP—Alianza Popular (Popular Alliance), a conservative coalition normally composed of Conservatives, Arnistas and members of the Social Christian Movement (Movimiento Social Cristiano—MSC).

AP—Associated Press.

ARNE—Acción Revolucionaria Nacionalista Ecuatoriana (Ecuadorian Nationalist Revolutionary Action), a highly disciplined and tightly organized group of militants with widespread appeal among youth of non-Marxist political orientation.

Arnista—Member of ARNE.

audiencia—Administrative and judicial body and, by extension, territorial division of the Spanish colonial system. (See ch. 3, Historical Setting.)

bachillerato—Diploma from a secondary school.

BCG—Bacillus Calmette-Guérin, a vaccine used to immunize against tuberculosis.

caballero—Gentleman.

cabildo—Spanish and colonial municipal council of government, often elected by local citizens; now, community assembly.

camino real—Highway.

campesino—A rural dweller who earns his livelihood through manual labor in an agricultural or pastoral endeavor.

cantón—A territorial subdivision roughly equivalent to a county. *See jefe político.*

CARE—Cooperative for American Remittances to Everywhere.

Caritas—The distributing agency for Catholic relief services.

caudillo—Forceful leader or strongman. He rules or controls principally by force of personality without necessarily having recourse to rules, laws or other institutional means of control; he often demands total personal loyalty, above legal or moral considerations, from those he leads.

CEDOC—Confederación Ecuatoriana de Obreros Católicos (Ecuadorian Confederation of Catholic Workers), one of the three nationwide labor organizations. *See* CEOSL and CTE.

CENDES—Centro de Desarrollo (Development Center).

CEOSL—Confederación Ecuatoriana de Organizaciones Sindicales Libres (Ecuadorian Confederation of Free Labor Organizations), one of the three nationwide labor organizations. *See* CEDOC and CTE. CEOSL is affiliated with the Inter-American Regional Organization of Workers (Organización Regional Interamericano de Trabajadores—ORIT).

CFP—Concentración de Fuerzas Populares (Concentration of Popular Forces), the personalist political party of Carlos Guevara Moreno, a politician with strength principally in Guayaquil.

chagra—Mestizo peasant of the Sierra. (*See* ch. 6, Social Structure.)

cholo—A Spanish-speaking person of Indian or mixed Indian-Spanish racial and cultural background. It is a familiar form of the word *"mestizo."*

CIAP—Comité Interamericano de la Alianza para el Progreso (Inter-American Committee of the Alliance for Progress), a committee of nine members responsible for coordinating and implementing goals of the Alliance for Progress.

CID—Coalición Institucionalista Demócrata (Democratic Institutionalist Coalition).

CIESPAL—Centro Internacional de Estudios Superiores del Periodismo para América Latina (International Center of Graduate Studies in Journalism for Latin America), an educational institute responsible for training journalists, established in 1960 under the auspices of UNESCO.

CLASC—Confederación Latinoamericana de Sindicalistas Cristianos (Latin American Confederation of Christian Trade Unionists), the regional organization of the International Confederation of Christian Trade Unions (Confederación Internacional de Sindicatos Cristianos—CISC).

Coast—Regional division embracing all of the coastal area and including the important commercial center of Guayaquil.

COG—Confederación Obrera de Guayaquil (Workers Confederation of Guayaquil).

colegio—Secondary school.

compadrazgo—Lit., coparenthood; applied to the ceremonial kinship relationships between parents and godparents. (*See* ch. 7, Family.)

compadre—Lit., cofather; the reciprocal term of address used between parents and godparents. The feminine form is *comadre*. Godparents are called *padrino* (m.) and *madrina* (f.) by their godchildren.

concertaje (also called *huasipungaje*)—A traditional system whereby entailed tenant farmers (*huasipungueros*) are required (as of 1965, no longer by law) to perform 4 to 6 days' labor per week for the landowner, either for pay at about half the free-labor rate or for the use of a small subsistence plot (*huasipungo*) and at least one other privilege, such as gather firewood or pasturing animals on the landowner's estate.

criollo—In colonial times, applied to Ecuadorian-born persons of Spanish descent. In present day, used to describe the Hispanic-derived component of the national culture. (The term is also applied to a breed of cattle in South America.)

CROCLE—Confederación Regional de Organizaciones Clasistas del Litoral Ecuatoriano (Confederation of Trade Unions of the Ecuadorian Coast).

CTAL—Confederación de Trabajadores de América Latina (Confederation of Latin American Workers).

CTE—Confederación de Trabajadores Ecuatorianos (Confederation of Ecuadorian Workers), controlled by the Communist Party of Ecuador (Partido Comunista del Ecuador—PCE). CTE is one of the three nationwide labor organizations. *See* CEDOC and CEOSL.

dignidad—Inner dignity, the characteristic of individuality, found in every person, which is inalienable and worthy of universal respect.

encomienda—Fiduciary grant of tribute collection rights over groups of Indians, conferred by Spanish Crown on individual colonists, who undertook, in return, to maintain order and propagate Christianity among their charges.

facultad—A college within a university.

FAO—Food and Agriculture Organization, a Specialized Agency of the United Nations.

FDN—Frente Democrático Nacional (National Democratic Front), a semipermanent coalition of political moderates usually formed around the Liberal Party at each national election.

FENETEL—Federación Nacional de Trabajadores de Telecomunicaciones del Ecuador (National Federation of Telecommunications Workers of Ecuador).

FETEF—Federación Ecuatoriana de Trabajadores de Embarbaques de Frutas y Anexos (Ecuadorian Federation of Fruit-loaders).

FEUE—Federación de Estudiantes Universitarios del Ecuador (Federation of University Students of Ecuador).

fidelismo—Revolutionary doctrine based on Fidel Castro's speeches.

fidelista—A follower of Fidel Castro of Cuba; also adjective form of *fidelismo*.

fiesta—Feast. It may be a religious celebration held on holy days or honoring the community patron saint; or it may be held to celebrate important civic or family events, such as Independence, baptism or marriage.

FNCE—Federación Nacional de Choferes del Ecuador (National Federation of Chauffeurs of Ecuador).

fuero—Exemptions from ordinary legal processes granted to special groups, such as members of the armed forces, the clergy or commercial groups.

hacendado—Landowner.

hacienda—Rural estate or ranch, which is a largely self-sufficient economic and social organization wherein the work is done by entailed tenant laborers or sharecroppers; also, the form of production which provides a major portion of agricultural products brought to market.

huasipungaje—See *concertaje*.

huasipungo—See *concertaje*.

huasipunguero—See *concertaje*.

IBRD—International Bank for Reconstruction and Development (World Bank), a Specialized Agency of the United Nations.

ICFTU—International Confederation of Free Trade Unions.

IDB—Inter-American Development Bank, an inter-American financial institution comprising 19 Latin American countries and the United States, established in 1959 to make loans for projects contributing to economic growth in Latin American member countries. The IDB officially began operations on October 1, 1960.

IERAC—Instituto Ecuatoriano de Reforma Agraria y Colonización, (Ecuadorian Institute of Agrarian Reform and Colonization), an official agency charged with the responsibility for land reform and resettlement.

ILO—International Labor Organization, a Specialized Agency of the United Nations.

IMF—International Monetary Fund, a Specialized Agency of the United Nations.

indígena—Indian (more polite than the term *"indie"*).

indigenismo—A philosophy, reflected in social and political thought and in artistic and literary technique, calling for the integration of Indian traditions to a new national cultural synthesis.

indigenista—Exponent of *indigenismo*.

546

INIAP—Instituto Nacional de Investigación Agropecuaria (National Institute for Agricultural and Livestock Research).

jefe político—Political chief; a political appointee who is the principal authority of a *cantón*. The *teniente político* (political lieutenant) is his representative at the parish level, and the *gobernador* (governor) is his immediate superior at the provincial level.

JPN—Junta Patriótica Nacional (National Patriotic Committee).

LEA—Liga Ecuatoriana Anti-Tuberculosis (Ecuadorian Anti-Tuberculosis League).

licenciado—A general university degree or a person holding such a degree.

machismo—Lit., maleness. It is applied to a complex of values regarding masculinity and the ideal male personality; from *macho*, the man who seems the epitome of such qualities.

mestizaje—The process of forming a *mestizo* population; miscegenation between Indian and white population elements.

mestizo—Most broadly, a person of mixed Spanish-Indian ancestry. More restrictively, it is applied to persons, irrespective of racial background, who share in the national culture and speak Spanish but whose way of life is notably influenced by Indian traditions.

montuvio—Mestizo peasant of the Coast. (See ch. 6, Social Structure.)

MPR—Movimiento Popular Revolucionario (Revolutionary People's Movement).

MSC—Movimiento Social Cristiano (Social Christian Movement), an offshoot of the Conservative Party, consisting principally of the personalist following of Camilo Ponce Enríquez.

mulatto—A person of mixed white and Negro blood.

niñera—Nursemaid.

nudo—Lit., an elevation that extends laterally from a mountain or range of mountains; a mountain knot.

OAS—Organization of American States.

Oriente—The region east of the eastern range of the Andes; the Amazonian part of Ecuador, including the eastern foothills of the Andes.

ORIT—Organización Regional Interamericano de Trabajadores (Inter-American Regional Organization of Workers), affiliated with the ICFTU.

padrino—See *compadre*.

PAHO—Pan American Health Organization, a regional organization of WHO.

páramos—High grasslands.

patrón—Protector, benefactor or sponsor; traditionally, an employer or social superior who forms long-term paternalistic ties with someone of lower status, rewarding deference and loyalty with protection and an active personal interest.

patronato or *real patronato*—Royal patronage conceded to the Spanish monarchs by the Vatican which gave them a number of rights over the local Church.

PCE—Partido Comunista del Ecuador (Communist Party of Ecuador).

PCN—Policía Civil Nacional (National Civil Police).

personalismo—A complex of values stressing personal status and interpersonal trust over ideology and institutions.

PSE—Partido Socialista Ecuatoriano (Ecuadorian Socialist Party), founded in 1925 as a section of the Communist International.

PSR—Partido Socialista Revolucionaria (Socialist Revolutionary Party).

PTTI—Postal, Telegraph and Telephone International.

Quechua—Language spoken by the Inca and, in modern times, by the largest segment of the Indian population; sometimes used as an ethnic label for Quechua-speaking Indians. (See ch. 5, Ethnic Groups and Languages.)

reducciones—Planned towns in which Spanish colonial authorities resettled the Indian population to facilitate missionization and political control.

Rio Protocol—The Protocol of Peace, Friendship and Boundaries between Ecuador and Peru, signed on January 29, 1942, which terminated the border war between those countries and defined their mutual borders. The Protocol was unilaterally abrogated by Ecuador in 1960.

SCIA—Servicio Cooperativo Inter-Americano de Agricultura (Inter-American Agricultural Cooperative Service).

Sierra—Regional division embracing the Andean Highlands; includes the capital city of Quito.

sindicato—The smallest unit of labor organization.

SIP—Sociedad Interamericana de Prensa (Inter-American Press Society).

sucre $(S/)$—The monetary unit, defined at 49.3706 milligrams of fine gold and containing 100 centavos. On July 14, 1961, an official devaluation changed the value from S/15 per US$1 to S/18 per US$1. There is an official rate and a fluctuating free market rate. As of December 31, 1964, the official buying rate was S/17.82 and the selling rate S/18.18. The fluctuating free market rate was S/18.5, the rate used in this book.

teniente político—*See jefe político.*

UNE—Unión Nacional de Educadores (National Teachers Union).

UNESCO—United Nations Educational, Scientific and Cultural Organization, a Specialized Agency of the United Nations.

UNICEF—United Nation's Children's Fund, a Specialized Agency of the United Nations.

UNP—Unión Nacional de Periodistas (National Union of Journalists).

UPI—United Press International.

URJE—Unión Revolucionaria de la Juventud Ecuatoriana (Revolutionary Union of Ecuadorian Youth), a pro-Castro organization of militant youths.

USIA—United States Information Agency; USIS (United States Information Service) is the overseas element.

velasquismo—Personalist movement centering around José María Velasco Ibarra. The followers of the movement are called *velasquistas*.

WFTU—World Federation of Trade Unions.

WHO—World Health Organization, a Specialized Agency of the United Nations.

INDEX

El Comercio: 306, 307, 308, 309, 310, 312
El Oro region: and agriculture, 353; description, 376, 377, 382, 428, 430, 505; and irrigation, 366
El Telégrafo: 307–308, 309
El Universo: 308, 310
electric power: 138, 155, 327, 373, 383–385
elite: 106–109; in agriculture, 108; and armed forces, 511; and artistic expression, 202, 203; clothing, 137; living conditions, 133; and political interests, 261, 317; and religion, 215; in Sierra, 257; and social values, 227
employers: and labor movement, 398, 411–415
employment: 373, 385
encomiendas: 37, 76; and the church, 207
entertainment: 138–139
Equatorial Current: 17–18
Esmeraldas: description, 15, 20, 28, 121, 212, 319, 358, 359; history, 181; and population, 62–64, 87, 113
Espejo, Eugenio de Santa Cruz y Espejo: 188–189
Europe: and trade with, 462, 464–465
expenditures, government: 336, 435, 440–441, 442 (table 14)
Export-Import Bank: 335, 385, 386, 474
exports: 332, 337, 396, 456, 457 (table 15), 458–460, 468; crops, 331, 339, 341, 351, 422, 455
executive branch: 250–253

Federation of University Students of Ecuador (Federación de Estudiantes Universitarios del Ecuador—FEUE): communist-controlled, 278, 496; and Ibarra, 277; outlawed, 497; and student movement, 174–176; and violence, 480–482, 495
fertilizer: 346, ·349, 392
fiestas: 83, 87, 89, 97, 113, 121, 131, 136, 217, 234–236
films: 313–314
fishing industry: 65–67, 327, 331, 359–360, 455, 460
Flores, Juan José, General: 193; and Constitution, 45–46, 240, 242; as

Flores—Continued
president, 43–44, 250–251, 323, 501–502
Food and Agriculture Organization—FAO: 346, 360, 362, 371, 459, 472
food industry: 333, 387–390
foreign aid: 385–386, 471–476
foreign exchange: 334, 467 *ff.*, 471, 473, 475, 476
foreign investment: 336, 455–456, 469, 470 (table 18), 471, 472 (table 19): and petroleum industry, 373, 379
foreign relations: (*see also* country entries): 287–301, 302 (fig. 7), 303
foreign trade: 335, 456–462, 463 (table 17), 464–467, 475
forests: 12, 13, 14, 327; and products, 332, 358–359
franchise: *see* suffrage
Freile Posso, Guillermo: 261, 280, 285, 507
fruits: 350, 356, 388

Galápagos Islands: description, 11, 17, 19, 22, 359, 376, 478; and history, 299, 504, 514
Gándara Enríquez, Marcos, Colonel: 9, 280, 507
García-Herrera Treaty: 289–293, 295
García Moreno, Gabriel: 323, 325; assassination, 191, 307; Church-state relations, 48, 209–210, 228; and Conservative Party, 6, 49, 265; and Constitution, 242, 243, 247; as president, 47, 159, 190, 250, 502
General Agreement on Tariffs and Trade (GATT): 467
Gonzalo Pizarro: 89, 90
Government: 237–255; attitude toward, 321–322
grains: 347–349
Gran Colombia: economic relations with, 301; and education, 159; history, 4, 22, 23, 42–44, 288, 289, 294
Great Britain: 462, 464–465, 469
gross domestic product: 337, 373, 374, 385, 386
gross national product: 328, 329 (table 6), 330, 336, 417, 455
Guayaquil: 2, 4, 5; and boundary dispute, 294; description, 12, 18, 63,

International—Continued
electric power, 385; and road program, 334–335, 386
International Confederation of Free Trade Unions (ICFTU): 409, 410
International Development Association (IDA): 473
International Federation of Commercial, Clerical and Technical Employees (IFCCTE): 410, 411
International Labor Organization (ILO): and Andean Mission, 82, 96, 371, 472; and living conditions, 154
International Monetary Fund (IMF): and Central Bank, 451; member of, 453; and trade, 469
international organizations: aid programs, 471–474
International Trade Secretariats (ITS): 410
irrigation: 14, 15, 81, 155, 361; and programs, 98, 366–367

Japan: economic relations with, 287, 301; trade with, 458–459, 465
Jews: 205, 324
Jívaro tribe: 93–95, 101
journalism: 310–311
judicial branch: (see also courts): 242, 249–250

kinship: 119; and family, 124, 127–128; and Indians, 236; and social values, 232

labor force: 64 (table 3), 65–66 (table 4), 67–68; in agriculture, 66–68, 338, 339, 346; on Coast, 339; in industry, 373–374, 395; in Sierra, 338; and working classes, 106, 111
labor organizations: (see also Confederation of Ecuadorian Workers; Federation of University Students of Ecuador; sindicatos): 262–263, 334, 397–411; Confederation of Latin American Workers (Confederación de Trabajadores de América Latina— CTAL), 401, 408; Ecuadorian Confederation of Catholic Workers (Confederación Ecuatoriana de Obreros Católicos—CEDOC),

labor—Continued
262, 263, 398, 401, 405–409; Ecuadorian Confederation of Free Labor Organizations (Confederación Ecuatoriana de Organizaciones Sindicales Libres—CEOSL), 398, 406–410; Ecuadorian Democratic Alliance (Alianza Democrática Ecutoriana), 401; Inter-American Press Society (Sociedad Interamericana de Prensa—SIP), 306–307; Inter-American Regional Organization of Workers (Organización Regional Interamericano de Trabajadores— ORIT), 408; International Confederation of Christian Trade Unions (Confederación Internacional de Sindicatos Cristianos— CISC), 262, 409; Latin American Confederation of Christian Trade Unionists (Confederación Latinoamericana de Sindicalistas Cristianos—CLASC), 409; Latin American Labor Confederation (Confederación Sindical Latino-Americana—CSLA), 400; National Federation of Telecommunications Workers of Ecuador (Federación Nacional de Trabajadores de Telecommunicaciones del Ecuador—FENETEL), 410, 411; National Teachers Union (Unión Nacional de Educadores —UNE), 170, 403; National Union of Journalists (Unión Nacional de Periodistas—UNP), 96, 175–176, 306, 311, 403
labor relations: (see also labor force, labor organizations): 411–416; and collective bargaining, 398, 414–416; disputes, 412–414; and government, 68–70, 398, 401, 412, 414, 415; and legislation, 400, 414
land: (see also agrarian reform, colonization): redistribution, 322, 327, 360, 364; tenure, 342 (table 8), 343 (table 9), 344; and use, 340–341
landownership: 80; and political power, 263, 265; prestige, 81; and Sierra elite, 104
Latin America: 9; and foreign policy, 287; and trade with, 335, 336, 465, 467

United States Information Service: 312

universities: 170–175, 473, 495; and agricultural education, 368–369; autonomous, 160, 178; history, 159; journalism, 310–311; and teachers, 169

university students; and communism, 492, 494; and rioting, 477, 480–482

Urbina, José Maria: 46–49, 501

Varea Donoso, Reynaldo, 277

vegetation: fig. 3, 12–17

Veintimilla, Ignacio de, General: 49–50, 502, 505

Velasco Ibarra, Jose Maria: 8, 15, 55–58, 226–230; and armed forces, 275, 506; border dispute, 297, 298; censorship, 306; and communism, 493, 494; and improvement plans, 361, 375, 385; and labor movement, 401, 413; overthrown, 317, 318; and political parties, 258, 268, 270, 284; as president, 243, 250–252, 272–277, 504, 505; and student rioting, 481; and U.S., 299, 300

Vistazo: 306, 310

vocational education: 68, 165–166

Voice of America: 312

wages: 60, 68–69, 70 (table 5), 413; in cities, 137, 138; and per capita income, 417

water transport: 432

welfare programs, 148–151

Western Europe: economic relations, 287, 301

whites: 115; and ethnic groups, 73–74; and mestizos, 113; in population, 59

wholesale trade: 421–425

women: family role, 125–126; and social values, 225, 228–230; and suffrage, 243

World Federation of Trade Unions (WFTU): 401, 408–410, 493

World Health Organization (WHO): 141, 142, 143, 472

World Meteorological Organization WMO: and natural resources: 472

Yumbos tribe: 90–93, 101

Zamora River: 297, 298

PUBLISHED AREA HANDBOOKS

550-65	Afghanistan
550-98	Albania
550-44	Algeria
550-59	Angola
550-73	Argentina
550-20	Brazil
550-61	Burma
550-83	Burundi
550-50	Cambodia
550-96	Ceylon
550-26	Colombia
550-60	Communist China
550-91	Congo (Brazzaville)
550-67	Congo (Kinshasa)
550-90	Costa Rica
550-152	Cuba
550-22	Cyprus
550-54	Dominican Republic
550-52	Ecuador
550-150	El Salvador
550-28	Ethiopia
550-29	Germany
550-153	Ghana
550-87	Greece
550-78	Guatemala
550-82	Guyana
550-151	Honduras
550-21	India
550-154	Indian Ocean Territories
550-39	Indonesia
550-68	Iran
550-31	Iraq
550-25	Israel
550-30	Japan
550-34	Jordan
550-56	Kenya
550-81	Korea, North
550-41	Korea, Republic of
550-58	Laos
550-24	Lebanon
550-38	Liberia
550-85	Libya
550-45	Malaysia
550-76	Mongolia
550-49	Morocco
550-64	Mozambique
550-88	Nicaragua
550-94	Oceania
550-48	Pakistan
550-156	Paraguay
550-92	Peripheral States of the Arabian Peninsula
550-42	Peru
550-72	Philippines, Republic of
550-84	Rwanda
550-51	Saudi Arabia
550-70	Senegal
550-86	Somalia
550-93	South Africa, Republic of
550-95	Soviet Union
550-27	Sudan
550-47	Syria
550-62	Tanzania
550-53	Thailand
550-89	Tunisia
550-80	Turkey
550-74	Uganda
550-43	United Arab Republic
550-97	Uruguay
550-71	Venezuela
550-57	Vietnam, North
550-55	Vietnam, South
550-75	Zambia